W9-ABI-323

PERSONALITY FACTORS IN OBJECTIVE TEST DEVICES:

A Critical Integration of a Quarter of a Century's Research

JOHN D. HUNDLEBY
KURT PAWLIK
RAYMOND B. CATTELL

ROBERT R. KNAPP, *Publisher*
San Diego, California 92107

FIRST EDITION
LIBRARY OF CONGRESS CATALOG CARD
NUMBER 65-15384
MANUFACTURED IN THE UNITED STATES OF
AMERICA

Contents

CHAPTER 1

THE KEY POSITION OF SOURCE TRAITS IN PERSONALITY RESEARCH

1. THE HISTORICAL INHERITANCES OF PERSONALITY RESEARCH

In few sciences have scientifically disreputable methods and concepts hung on so long as in psychology. This is partly due to every man (and woman) considering himself (or herself) a psychologist, so that more disciplined and abstract ideas have difficulty in disembarrassing themselves of the chrysalis of popular prejudices and connotations. But advance has also suffered from "experimental" having been conceived in the Pavlov-Wundt tradition as a "brass instrument" imitation of the traditional manipulative bivariate experiment of the physical sciences, whereas, in fact, the need was acute for multivariate experimental methods appropriate to the complex patterns and multivariate determinations with which behavioral science abounds. Our approach has aimed to give the proper strategic role to multivariate in relation to older bivariate methods, but in this we have been in a minority among personality theorists.

Personality theory, after nearly a century of alleged scientific psychology, is in fact only now beginning to show real shape as a truly scientific set of propositions. It has difficulty in disentangling itself on the one hand from an orgy of irresponsible, untestable theorizing, largely, but not entirely, the stock in trade of clinicians. On the other, it has to escape from the more academic threat of the compulsive pedant of reflexological learning theory who is ready, with his atomistic gadget, to explain what he has never examined, namely, the real structure of personality, with its complex, wholistic patterns and multiply determined relationships. The rank, weedy theories of verbal, literary and clinical psychology exhibit every possible error of scientific conceptualization stigmatized by Francis Bacon and many a keen thinker since. The brass instrument reflexologies with equal impotence continue to go through the motions of science, but the inadequacy of their method to a complex, wholistic phenomenon brings us no more scientific nourishment than the hungry diner gets from handling soup with a fork.

2. THE RECENT BIRTH OF QUANTITATIVE EXPERIMENTAL PERSONALITY THEORY

Recognizing and insisting that a new and genuine growth of personality theory must ultimately grow out of measured and experimental observation, Cattell, around 1930 called for use of a number of new and powerful multi-variate methods, and suggested that existing verbal elaborations were best thrown to the philosophers or even the journalists. This view was unpopular for many reasons. Its call to "hold our fire" in the battle of theories until the emerging quantitative evidence should suggest new outlines threatened to create technological unemployment among theorists! What was worse, it required both the clinical theorists and the non-statistical brass instrument experimenters to learn the new, complex and imaginative techniques of multivariate experiment, such as R- and P-technique factor analysis, type-pattern analysis, configural prediction and broader explicit conceptions of the sampling of people, stimulus-response situations in a culture, and occasions in time in the life of the individual. The growth of a nucleus of personality researchers proficient in these newer scientific methods has necessarily been slow, and yet another lag is now occurring in the adequate stocking of university teaching departments with such men. The gap between graduate student training to realize the concepts involved, on the one hand, and the enormous actual opportunities in terms of contributing to psychology, on the other, is likely to remain painful for another decade.

Fortunately, the devoted labors of the small groups, in three or four laboratories across the world, who have struck this vein of rich ore, and developed the necessary techniques, has resulted during these twenty to thirty years in very considerable advances. In so much accomplishment by so few there has necessarily been some lack of refinement of the product and a wholesale neglect of the need to communicate to others what they are doing. Complaints are heard that the results are scattered in scores of research articles which need integration and explanation for those unfamiliar with the techniques and the terms for the new concepts. There is no question that a real communication problem exists, but in so far as those who complain are psychologists, not laymen, it might be suggested that the blame lies with their own failure to read, learn and acquire the techniques through which alone communication is possible at a professional level in a new field.

The present book is one of five through which workers in this area have attempted a coordinated communication, on the consensus that a degree of ripeness has been reached in twenty-five years which justifies a pause for formulation of theory, as of this stage. The first summary of both facts and theoretical concepts has already been published in Cattell's <u>Personality and Motivation Structure and Measurement</u> (29). The second, by Cattell and Warburton, is entitled <u>Objective Personality and Motivation Tests: A Theoretical Introduction and Practical Compendium</u> (71). It sets out that actual psychological content of the tests, and the principles of objective personality design, which have long been requested in connection with the condensed articles and constitutes an indispensable source of basic data for the present summary. The third companion volume, Personality Theory from Multivariate Experiment (57) is primarily the work of Damarin. It expands upon the most recent research in the present survey, but communicates to the undergraduate student, showing how many of the existing theories he knows about, and the special psychological interests which he possesses, are given precision and enrichment by these newer researches and concepts in personality structure and development. The fourth volume, Cattell's Essentials of Personality Theory (41), not yet published, is a purely formal treatment, abstracted from the content presented in the other volumes, of the conceptual framework of personality theory developed from these researches.

The position of the present contribution in this totality is that it is intended as the definitive survey over the twenty-five years of research now completed on personality structure with an objective, behavioral measurement basis. It asks what is the status of quantitative, correlational evidence on the number and nature of personality dimensions, functional unities or source traits. It covers all substantial studies and examines their sampling of people, their statistical techniques, their choice of variables and the extent of agreement of their results. From the firm ground reached it proceeds to a brief theoretical interpretation of the factors and to the design of a standard Objective Test Battery for psychologists interested in any way in the research relationship of personality dimensions to other concepts and criteria.

It is for the reader to judge now whether the original arguments for this approach have in fact been amply justified and whether psychology is at last possessed of a firm set of source trait concepts, and of operational batteries to measure them with determinate reliability and validity.

3. THE ROLE OF GENERAL PERSONALITY SOURCE TRAITS IN PERSONALITY MEASUREMENT

To state that personality theory is possible only on a basis of meaningful measurement is not to state that what is offered here is the sum total of necessary personality measurement. General personality dimensions comprise only one section of what personality theory has to measure, so it is important that we give a brief section clearly to define the relation of the present measurement advances to what we conceive as the total realm of personality measurement.

As will be seen from Cattell and Warburton's Compendium of the sixteen or seventeen hundred distinct variables arising from objective, miniature-situational tests which represent the theoretical "personality sphere," some of the measures involve manifestations of abilities, while others are dynamic or interest measures. Nevertheless we wish to distinguish from general personality traits specific ability traits on the one hand and specific interest traits on the other. The line is certainly not one between general personality traits as temperament traits and traits which are cognitive or dynamic. For out of the structuring of our objective tests there arises clearly, in the cognitive field, a general intelligence trait -- Spearman's "g" or Thurstone's second-order general ability factor. And, among dynamic concepts, we feel we can interpret certain of our factors as general dynamic integration or ego strength, general inhibition, and, perhaps super ego strength. In any description of the total personality, general intelligence, though cognitive, has its place. Similarly, though the variables are not chosen (in our general personality as distinct from dynamic researches) to represent a lot of specific interest strengths as such, e.g., interest in a political party, in a particular sport, etc., yet broad, formal, structural dynamic traits, such as ego strength, inhibition, and assertion, fall under what we call general personality traits. The area of individual difference phenomena which we cover would thus need to be supplemented only by specific abilities, aptitudes and achievements, on the one hand, and specific interests and qualities of interest on the other.

A second major point to be made is that these researches deal only with common traits, not unique traits, as defined elsewhere (21a). A misunderstanding on this issue is one of the principal roots specifically of the clinician's difficulty in focussing what these trait researches hold for him. His criticism is that he is not so much interested in how intelligent, or schizoid, or dominant or ego-strong the given patient is, but in how the dominance, for example, expresses itself in various areas, or in what memories and experiences the ego weakness resides. With some clinicians the issue is further clouded, incidentally, by a confounding of the processes of diagnosis and therapy and a wishful belief that one can achieve therapy without first understanding, i.e., diagnosing, the patient, but let us consider this is not involved.

Now, there is no doubt whatever that the clinician's diagnosis needs to include the unique trait attachments and individual history of the patient. The levels of such common traits as anxiety or regression (U.I. 24 and U.I. 23, Chapter 7 below) are only to be manipulated by attention to particular dynamic conflicts and relearnings (and drug therapy). But it is important to know--and to know more accurately than by a consulting room conversational estimate--what the individual's levels on these common traits are. They need to be known initially in summing up the patient's problem, e.g., to know his intelligence is inadequate for college or his ego strength for a marital difficulty that others might easily surmount. And they need to be repeatedly measured in the process of therapy to guide its steps intelligently, e.g., by watching anxiety changes in response to situational and therapeutic threats.

The common trait measures are to the psychotherapist what measures of blood pressure, basal metabolic rate, corticosteroid excretion or temperature are to the medical physician. High blood pressure may arise from several different causes in several different individuals, but the maturer science of medicine has no doubts that it needs to measure common traits in understanding individual organisms.

The multivariate experimentalist knows of ways of determining the unique trait structures, e.g., the unique sources and expressions of anxiety in a particular person, by ways more objective than those used by most clinicians. But these ways, which center chiefly in P-technique analysis (170, 107, 99, 58, 47, 35) are not part of the present monograph, which is explicitly concerned only with common traits, by R-technique. The uniqueness of the total individual is, of course, duly respected as a unique quantitative combination of scores on common traits. But this is different from investigating the unique form of a particular cognitive skill or dynamic interest trait in a given individual, in the way which fully fits the clinician's interest in the particularity of attachments, etc. In short, we have no wish to magnify the relative importance of either the common trait (R-technique) or unique trait (P-technique) concepts, but only to insist that in either pure theory or in the applied clinical, educational or industrial fields, each be given its appropriate role. The very significant increases in the effectiveness of prediction of school achievement from measures of personality common traits (46) and of the certainty of diagnoses by measures of the common traits of anxiety, ego strength, regression, etc. (68), show the importance of this common trait role.

A third direction in which the aims of this monograph need to be distinguished from the totality of personality measured is in the differentiation of traits from states. The theory of this has been dealt with elsewhere (29, 35). Its illustration is at present clearest in the clinical work on the distinction of anxiety, stress, and elation-depression, as states, from anxiety, ego strength, etc., as characterological traits (68). Incremental R-technique and P-technique yield respectively common and unique state patterns (64). Although R-technique (individual difference study) itself is commonly regarded as dealing with traits the fact is that any individual's score at a given moment is a combination of trait and state influences. The variance we analyze in R-technique is the sum of inter and intra individual i.e., over time, differences. The only way to escape from major contamination by the latter is to measure each person several times and use his average score in the R-technique analysis. No research institution, still less any individual researcher, has yet had resources for so vast an undertaking, and it must therefore be frankly admitted that some shaping of traits by state variation is included in our picture. However, since it is part of our conception of a trait that its form is to be determined both by its individual difference variation and its developmental or functional change relations, the separation of this modicum of functional change variation is not vital at the present stage.

4. METHODOLOGY OF COMMON TRAIT RESEARCH

The aim of common trait research is therefore to discover the number and nature of the functionally unitary source traits--defined by simple structure in R-technique factorizations--over a representative, stratified sample of total behavior, as defined by the personality sphere concept. The location of such source traits and the ensuing construction of batteries for them creates a turning point in personality research, in such diverse branches as developmental, genetic, physiological and clinical psychology. For whereas with experiments which rested on subjective, arbitrary and uncertain measures--as, for example, when extroversion or anxiety meant a hundred different things to a hundred different psychologists--no architectonic growth in psychological generalizations and laws could possibly be made, now both theoretical development and applied technical accuracy, e.g., in clinical and personnel work, can proceed on firm conceptually determinate steps. All kinds of relational studies then become more worthwhile.

If this view of the possibilities of the current revolution is substantially true, examination of the full basis of the claims to determinateness of the common trait patterns and measurements deserves the intensive technical consideration it is here accorded. Previous surveys of intermediate stages of progress in this area were made by Cattell (18) in 1946, Eysenck (84) in 1947, French in 1953 (95), and by Cattell (29) in 1957. Except for the last named, who began to apply statistical checks as to the similarity of patterns across several researches set out in detail side by side (25), and similar objective criteria, none has previously used such developed techniques of evaluation as we now introduce, nor has any survey been so comprehensive and exhaustive as that now to be described. In view of this dearth of method it is not surprising that, prior to Cattell's 1957 survey, which extracted from the collated researches a series of concepts (almost all of which have stood up to our present more searching statistics), the factors described by previous sporadic studies factoring personality data have not had much effect on psychological concepts. There are probably more ways in which a factor analytic experiment can go wrong than there are for almost any other psychological experiment. In the next chapter it will be appropriate to examine these possibilities under such headings as choice of variables, control of conditions, proof of completion of factor extraction, statistical testing of goodness of simple structure, etc., but here it suffices to mention them. Certainly it must be admitted that some factor analyses "rotated for meaning," i.e., to the experimenter's prior ideas of meaning, or "to a criterion," i.e., confusing a factor with a type, have merely added to conceptual confusion. At worst, the acceptance in the literature of factor analyses, without critical regard for technical quality or nature of operations, the use of push button orthogonal rotations by computers, and the absence of statistical checks, has resulted in no more distortion of theory than through the older invention of polysyllabically naming concepts from an armchair, but it may have deceived more people.

Although this monograph on common traits by objective behavioral measures can be made a reasonably self-contained statement as far as technical procedures are concerned, the wider understanding of its implications requires some knowledge of personality and research strategy. In the limited space we have decided to present this, we can only indicate the reading sources for this background, and briefly sketch the setting in which this specialized presentation is made. Cattell's Personality: A Systematic, Theoretical and Factual Study (1950), sets out the general theoretical position, which is cognate with that of such psychologists as Thurstone (in abilities), Eysenck (90), Guilford (100a) and Sir Cyril Burt (13). Within this general theoretical position, the more specific hypotheses are set out in Cattell's Personality and Motivation Structure and Measurement (1957). At this stage of emergence of findings some considerable differences become apparent both as to vital technical, methodological procedures and to specific psychological hypotheses, from the positions of Guilford (100) and of Eysenck (90). For example, unlike Guilford, Cattell abandons orthogonal factors and uses an interactional (and sometimes hierarchical) model of oblique factors, and, unlike Eysenck, he explores far beyond two or three factors and presents evidence for interactions of at least twenty. The whole picture of first and second-order personality structures becomes more complex and comprehensive in nature than that which has emerged from the comparatively few parallel studies made by the London School.

The present work, however, is confined to only one section within Personality and Motivation Structure and Measurement, namely that concerned with personality structure as found within general personality variables (excluding the specific area of motivational measures as stated above). Furthermore, as will now be stated for the first time, it restricts itself to one specific mode of behavioral observation--that concerned with objective behavioral measures. Though this, in our evaluation, is the most important for general research and practice, it yet remains only one of three media of observation. Indeed, in popular interest the objective test (T-data) realm has been running a poor third to the interest in ratings ("life record," in situ, or L-data) and in questionnaires (Q-data). This is the wrong order as far as the basic researcher and user of experimental methods is concerned! Elsewhere (21a) we have more fully described the properties and distinctions of T-data relative to L-data (commonly but unfortunately obtained by observers' ratings) and Q-data (questionnaire, introspective, self-evaluative, consulting room response). By objective test, or T-data, we have not merely objectively scorable (that is conspective, i.e., perfectly conspect reliable (71) data, as in questionnaires or most selective answer tests) but, additionally, objective in the sense that the person is not evaluating himself but is acting without knowing on what aspect of his behavior he is in fact being scored (sic (32)). Our present analysis, then, is wholly concerned with structure in the realm of T-data, with only incidental references to relations to Q- or L-data. In the total strategy of research in our laboratory the L- and Q-media have primarily been used as avenues to test design in the T-data medium, i.e., as means to clarifying hypotheses better to guide the design and creation of T-data measures.

A final methodological implication which must be stressed is the degree to which and the manner in which the factor analytic methods here employed are related to and epitomize all possible approaches. The fundamental tenet of any factor analytic approach is really identical with that of all experimental evidence, namely, that psychological unities can be recognized only by proof that the elements of behavior cohere in a single pattern. For example, if one is to speak of a concept of "general inhibition" as Pavlov did with insufficient evidence, and as we do in our pattern U.I. 17--we hope with sufficient evidence--then it must be possible to demonstrate that a wide variety of inhibitory responses vary together in strength as we go from one individual to another.

The factor analytic method differs from the covariational inferences of general scientific observation only in the intensity and extensity, and the formality, with which it applies these methods of general science, long laid down by J. S. Mill in his account of "concomitant variation." Those accustomed to believe that factor analysis does this only in one special kind of concomitant variation, namely, in variation from person to person ("individual differences"), have not kept up with its development. In the notion of the covariation chart (71) we see not only R-technique (individual difference factoring) but also P-technique and Incremental R-techniques, which study covariation over time and changing stimulus. Thus as already mentioned from another angle above, the functional unity of a trait must in the last resort be witnessed not only by the elements of the behavior pattern consistently varying together from person to person, but also from occasion to occasion in the same person.

Since the great bulk of studies are still R-technique in design, however, the present work can only employ the most systematic checks across R-technique studies, though regard is given in final conclusions also to P-technique.

5. SUMMARY OF SCOPE AND PRESENTATION

In summary, this work is aimed:

(1) To give an up-to-date, comprehensive, and technically advanced evaluation of the number and nature of common personality dimensions discoverable in adults and children of our culture.

(2) To do so through the medium of objective tests (T-data) only.

(3) Primarily to define the patterns, not to interpret them in any exhaustive psychological sense.

(4) To concentrate on the evidence on structure, leaving to another book the laboratory particulars of the tests used.

(5) To cover systematically all major earlier researches in the area but also to discuss explicitly the theory of checking and to introduce more exact methods of factor identification and critical evaluation of matching.

(6) On the practical side to proceed to the definition of actual batteries of tests for measuring the factors.

In regard to these objectives it should be understood that there is no implication that these 21 factors are the sum total of common personality dimensions. They are "the twenty-one factors established to the year 1964," and though a comprehensiveness of approach described in the next chapter makes it probable that they are the most substantial and important factors, describing a major part of the personality sphere, yet there is, we hope, every likelihood of further factors being added in time.

In terms of advice to various readers we would suggest that the researcher in the field go systematically through, possibly omitting Chapter 11 concerned only with the practical description of a battery. The general student of personality, on the other hand, may wish to skip the systematic and detailed evidential support arranged in Chapters 4, 5, and 6. The clinical psychologist, or anyone primarily interested only in the meaning and practical measurement of the factors, may wish to jump directly from here to Chapters 7 and 8 on factor interpretation, and thence to Chapter 11 on the O-A test battery. Researchers in the developmental field may find some very provocative facts and ideas in a comparison of the adult and child results (Chapters 4, 5, 6, 7, and 8) and the contrasts of the batteries suggested for adults and children, respectively, in Chapter 11.

The researches here described owe their largest fraction of support to the Graduate College Fund of the University of Illinois and to the National Institutes of Mental Health, NIMH, Washington, but the writers wish to express their gratitude also to a considerable list of cooperative individuals and agencies, whose mention must remain in our bibliographies.

The present work was completed while the authors were at the Laboratory of Personality Assessment and Group Behavior at the University of Illinois.

CHAPTER 2

DESIGN OF A RESEARCH CAMPAIGN TO DISCOVER SOURCE TRAITS

1. DISCOVERY OR HYPOTHESIS TESTING?

What happens in the actual historical process of research and what graduate students are taught in designing their theses are two very different things. And not in the sense that the former is reality's unfortunate caricature of the ideal procedure taught in the latter! Whether creativity be in science or music or the plastic arts, there is, as Bernard Shaw pointed out, a vital difference between those who do and those who teach others what to do. The current horror in pedantry is the dictate that every thesis must have no less and no more than one hypothesis!

Science, of course, proceeds by the hypothetico-deductive method, but when this is most effective it is often least formal, and the hypotheses may best be, in the area we are investigating, "that some structure exists." Although Columbus had to dress up some "content" to satisfy the pedants, by saying that he expected to land in China, one suspects that, like Galileo, he murmured an important "aside" to himself. Much that he did suggests that his real hypothesis was that if he sailed westward a couple of thousand miles he would find a new land. Americans may perhaps be forgiven for thinking he found something more important than China.

So in the search for personality structure one may either start with an elaborate hypothesis as to what will be found or with the more general discoverer's hypothesis that if one starts with an efficient method and model, as yet unknown relations and structures will reveal themselves. It so happens that among scientific methods factor analysis is peculiarly adapted to the role of exploring new domains, for, regardless of the hypotheses one enters with, it gives a highly structured, patterned answer, virtually creating concepts requiring interpretation by the experimenter. Of course, there is no lack of hypotheses about personality structure. Everyone has some, and everyone means five billion persons. In the main, however, we avoided new wine in old bottles, and set out with the policy that hypotheses about personality structure should not be the almost formless battered relics of literary, clinical and armchair theorizing, but should arise from relations appearing in the experimental data itself. For why should one invest experimental man-hours and expense on only vaguely statable, non-operational hypotheses when exact evidence of relations based on quantitative data is available?

This betokens no prejudice against, say, clinical hypotheses as such. Indeed, to the chagrin of some brass instrument experimenters who have expressed emotional rejection of all things clinical, we have confirmed and accepted some important clinical concepts (e.g., that of an ego and super ego structure), as far as a less exactly, operationally stated hypotheses can be confirmed by a concept having a precise statement of its terms.

But the spirit of the research planning undertaken thirty years ago in this area by Cattell was definitely one which put the main emphasis on discovery and only a secondary emphasis on checking existing hypotheses. Existing hypotheses were incorporated out of respect for the historical continuity of scholarship. But even so some selection had to be made, for hypotheses, as indicated, have always been a dime-a-dozen in this area. The hypotheses so chosen arose in a few instances from clinical experience (not necessarily clinical theory) and also from an attempt to check any experimental concept that had shown some indication of appearing as a unitary factor. In 1930 such emerging concepts were represented in Spearman's fluency factor; the Dutch work on perseveration-rigidity; McDougall's expression of Jung's extraversion as capacity to dissociate; the notion of differential susceptibility to what are now called adaptation - level effects; the physiological evidence on sympathetic and parasympathetic types; the experimental evidence for "dynamic momentum," and so on. A survey of such emerging factors and of the evidence for them, together with certain new ones from our own work was made in 1944-46 by Cattell (18) in a book which laid the foundations for the comprehensive work to follow.

However, the main emphasis has been on representative design, and the discovery of normal personality structure by investigating relations in as broad an array of behavior as possible. The acceptance of this challenge to represent a stratified sample of the total behavior by which personality expresses itself in our culture committed the investigators to an enormous undertaking of invention. Precise and practicable objective test situations had to be invented for an almost inconceivable range of behavior. It was a labor of love, in that the investigators enjoyed the imaginative enterprise of expressing hundreds of personal clinical hypotheses in operational form. As the Cattell and Warburton Compendium shows, over the course of thirty years some three hundred objective tests have been created, each as different from the others as it is from, say, the Rorschach or others of the two or three tests to which clinicians have continued to confine themselves.

The extent to which this objective test construction (the principles of development of which have been described elsewhere (71)), has already succeeded in spanning most dimensions of personality remains to be determined by continued research. Regardless of its final breadth of cover it is probably at least as important in its psychological contribution as the twenty or so concepts finally emerging in personality structure. For any research can establish relations only among the variables which enter it. And it seems almost certain that but for this prolific and inspired creation of objectively manipulable experimental test situations the best factor analyses in the world would have been able only to reveal and determine some half dozen factors--as existed before this work began--instead of the twenty or more we are to see.

2. THE STRATEGY OF CHOICE OF VARIABLES

The intention of the strategic plan set out in the 1930's and again in 1946 (18) to integrate both with what had gone before and what could be more widely undertaken in the future has been easier to conceive than to accomplish. As far as the preceding years were concerned the difficulty lay in the fact that extremely few researchers had chosen their variables or methods with any wider plan than that of publishing a particular research. Over perhaps four-fifths of the work done in factor analysis then, and perhaps a half of that done since, there hangs a destiny of futility, due to lack of observation of general scientific needs. In the period which we have to survey later, a goodly number of researches, such as those of Burt, Coan, Cattell, Connor, Damarin, Eysenck, Gruen, Knapp, Saunders, and a few others have taken care to include variables relevant to hypotheses and to mutual overlapping. They have moved in the same civility of science. But a greater number still remain in private worlds, or have so ill chosen a set of variables that no sound conclusion can be drawn, and these we have reluctantly had to set aside.

A sufficient overlap of common variables, especially in the sense of the marker variables we shall shortly define, is a first necessity in a series of researches strategically arranged to cover the personality sphere. But, granted this necessity, there are still two distinct concepts or philosophies of choice of variables possible in achieving integration, and which we may call the "global span" and the "consecutive patch" designs. The relative usefulness of these two opposing philosophies in terms of integrating factor analytic studies has been discussed elsewhere (29). In one, the aim has been to get a very large number of variables into a single factor analysis with the express purpose of getting the dimensionality of the greater part of the personality sphere at one and the same time. In the other, a philosophy of creeping forward in pedestrian fashion upon the ultimate objective has been followed. That is to say, one maps out one small area, working with a comparatively small matrix of variables, then moves on to another area, with again few variables, and so on, until the whole area is covered. This is analogous to the mapping of a geographical area by pasting together a large number of aerial photographs of small areas. Unfortunately, for the effectiveness of this procedure factor analytically, the analogy fails because the psychologist does not know beforehand that the variables which he chooses will, in fact, cover only a small number of factors. Furthermore, it fails because the technical conditions are such that one cannot easily fit together a large number of small factor analyses. The issue is too statistically complex to be discussed here, but it is the "global span" principle that has guided the procedures which have been followed in our central, integrating researches. Large matrices and large samples of variables have been maintained though at the explicit expense of reducing the reliability of individual variables. It reduces the reliability of individual variables for the simple, practical reason that subjects cannot be held long enough to be tested on about 110 variables at a time without any one of those variables having to be a relatively short test. However, if a test has moderate reliability, and then shows good factor loading, it can subsequently be lengthened, and given increased reliability, as the research passes from the exploratory phase to the confirmatory phase. This approach is justified further by the fact that one expects relatively few of each batch of newly invented tests to be valid for the desired factor measurement.

Just as the first condition for good research strategy is that each research should cover a considerable area, and in a representative fashion, in order that good overlap may exist among the various researches, so the second condition, stated in the idea of overlap above, is that variables which prove to be good measures of certain factors should be preserved as "marker variables" in further studies. By a "marker" we mean a variable which is among the top three or four in loading on a given factor and which has little loading in any other factor. It should have acceptable reliability, and, for its continued use, retain this higher loading in any second or later study. As will be seen when we come closely to examine the matching process, there is no substitute for good markers when it comes to reliably identifying factors.

Thus the general design includes a basic principle of sampling variables followed by a principle for including markers which has to be tactically worked out in regard to a pattern of separate experiments. Cattell and his co-workers, Coan, Gruen, Saunders, Warburton, Damarin, Rosenthal, and others in the 20 years of work we are now surveying, have followed, indeed, an explicit plan of starting with a deliberately wide sampling of variables from behavior judged qualitatively to be as diverse as possible. From the first exploratory factor analysis, the factors which emerge are carefully studied and hypotheses formed about their essential psychological nature. For example, a newly appearing factor which was first indexed, simply as a pattern, by the number U.I. 24, seemed psychologically to have the quality of anxiety. Accordingly this hypothesis was set up, and further measures which might be expected, theoretically, to be measures of anxiety, were created and included in the next factorization. Thus, the second factorization, which is commonly still only an exploratory factorization, is based on experiment which takes the high loading variables from the first study (perhaps a half of those variables) and adds to them a number of new performances, specifically designed to test hypotheses about the nature of these factors. Typically, rather more of these specially created, hypothesis-directed variables will have substantial loadings than occurred among the first "representative" set of variables.

3. FACTOR COVERAGE AND FACTOR DEFINITION

The global span principle of choosing variables implies that one will expect to work also with a large number of factors. The pros and cons of doing so need to be briefly discussed, as well as the ways in which research designs need to be adjusted in relation to the emerging factors.

As the second and third global span researches proceeded, in the 1940's, still appreciably tied to variables making historical continuity with less comprehensively planned researches, a certain phenomenon appeared. It was noticeable that certain of the factors were relatively poorly represented by 2 or 3 variables, whereas as many as 20 different kinds of behavior were found to load some other factor. For example, in Cattell's first studies in the personality area, some thirty to forty markers for previous factors found in ability and temperament testing were deliberately included to ensure the above mentioned historical continuity as well as to demonstrate whether any new dimensions found were really new, or were simply old dimensions in new dress. On thus entering the new field, it was found that Spearman's G persisted powerfully among personality tests. As it happened, this factor could be readily recognized and set aside before the personality factors were examined, causing no confusion, but it carried with it quite a large number of variables. Similarly, the general factor of fluency which had been encountered by Spearman and Thurstone was found again, though this time it appeared to load many personality variables more strongly than the original cognitive fluency measures, showing that it was not really just an ability factor, but a personality factor which had originally been observed in an outcropping among ability variables and perhaps mistaken for a pure ability. At any rate, it was evident that in relation to the ultimate aim of spanning the personality realm these two older factors had been perhaps too strongly represented, whereas the new factors which came up over the horizon, were first evidenced and located by only two or three variables.

Accordingly, we shall make explicit a third important principle in research (after (1) representation of personality sphere, and (2) the "marking" of former factors in order that they may not be mistaken for new ones), by stating that one should continually "move out to occupy new areas" always quickly building in stronger representation of factors which are first located only by two or three variables and cutting to a minimum of good markers for older factors. Actually, this practice is demanded by two requirements, first the need to move out into new areas, and second the need to have reliable matching; for it is not possible to match reliably a factor across a couple of researches if it only loads 2 or 3 variables in each. For factors may match on 2 or 3 variables yet cease to match when one takes a wider set of variables into consideration, so that without this latter procedure they may falsely be concluded to be the same factor (see discussion page 306ff in (23)).

As pointed out above, it was in this reaching out into newly emerging traits (testing newly suggested hypotheses) that the greater part of the creativity of this work has resided. Among statisticians, particularly, the importance of this aspect of factor analytic work is completely underestimated. Indeed, it would be no exaggeration to say that the experimental and factor analytic aspects of this kind of research, although they are perhaps only carried out with proper refinement in about half of the published researches, are nevertheless only the merest beginnings of sound progress in this area. It is, or should be, possible to take this statistical craftsmanship for granted, as one might take for granted the fact that the researcher has the proper qualifications. What leads to worthwhile discovery and theoretical advance in this scientific area is, first, the sense of strategy which goes beyond technical experimental and statistical competence, and, secondly, the capacity to invent and design new tests according to theoretical principles sensitively devised from the exploratory factor analyses. Although the psychological world has a fair number of test gadgets, there has been a great tendency to concentrate on one or two of them, such as the Rorschach, and the TAT. A grotesque amount of research time has been wasted on repetitive studies on 2 or 3 particular gadgets of this kind, while the whole ocean of possible test behavior has lain all unseen before the clinical and experimental psychologists so engaged.

The factor analytic studies from 1930 to about 1946 surveyed earlier (18) typically employed from about 50 to 80 diverse tests, half of them almost as traditional as the Rorschach, TAT, etc. With the appearance, however, of the wider factorizations and new patterns, around 1950, the new patterns quickly suggested hypothetical interpretations which led to carefully directed new test creation on a considerable scale. Simultaneously with this there was actually much test invention from theoretical discussions on the new factors that were appearing at that time through coordinated research in the L-data (mainly behavior rating) and Q-data fields. The nature of the concepts contributing to test design in this way have been discussed elsewhere. As this invention continued, it became necessary to establish careful indexing and filing systems to insure that ideas were not unconsciously repeated, and by 1955 a first compendium of these tests was published, somewhat on a shoestring, under the title of the O-A Battery, or Objective-Analytic Personality Factor Battery (27), which contained some 50 different tests and permitted the measurement of some 150 variables.

Since this publication of the first O-A Battery, which has sufficed to make available the necessary markers for researchers everywhere (to check structure more than to claim high validity for the factors in individual difference measurement), a more ambitious survey has been made by Cattell and Warburton (71). The Cattell and Warburton Compendium, in fact, covers no fewer than about 400 different tests (both group and individually administered) and 1749 different behavioral variables (Master Index 1 - 1749). For each test the theory, the adaptation of the particular test construction, the administration conditions, and scoring are described. Frequently a new conception could only be put into reality first in the design of an individual test, since the experimenters did not possess the ingenuity to move immediately towards a group test situation that could embody the required principle. Consequently a certain trend of test evolution goes on, in which some tests move from individual tests to group tests, as their practicality in the latter situation is demonstrated. An analysis of the possible combinations of basic principles that can be used in such objective personality tests, together with a discussion of the more artistic and intuitive procedures, is given in a chapter in the Compendium referred to (71). For example, one approach which was found quite useful was to pick out from the sample tested the individuals who were at the two extremes on a particular factor and then to study their behavior in the hope of coming upon other behavior which differentiated them from one another and could be caught in some test design.

Those who wish to study not only the creative process of test development in relation to emerging factor meaning, but also the broader concepts of reliability, homogeneity, hardihood (70a) and other parameters of test properties which arise in this area are recommended to read Chapters 5 and 6 (The Basic Variable Parameters of Test Construction; The Meaning of Consistency, Homogeneity and Validity in Personality Tests) in the work to which we have just referred (71).

4. POLICIES AND STANDARDS IN THE STATISTICAL PROCEDURE

Most of this chapter on the research campaign has so far been devoted to general psychological considerations in strategy and to the question of choice of variables. It is appropriate to spend so much time on what is only the first procedure from the standpoint of factor analysis per se, because the whole success or failure hinges initially on an appropriate general sampling of variables and the specific inclusion of marker variables. However, there are many other aspects of a factor analytic research which can go wrong, and concerning which quite clear policies and statistical procedures are vital. At this point, too, we must draw a distinction between qualities of a single factor analytic research and those more complex desiderata of a whole campaign or strategy of factor analytic research within an area. This distinction is all too frequently forgotten by pure mathematical statisticians, who make very exacting requirements regarding a single correlation matrix and its factorization, but who are very lax and frequently pointless in their requirements insofar as they effect the integration of research across different experiments and data matrices. The difference between the standpoint of a scientist, whether he is a psychologist or any other scientist, on the one hand, and those of the pure mathematical statistician are very real, and disregard for them has long obscured the real issues in this field. To take only one instance, the mathematical statistician has always argued for principal components, using communalities of unity, and for orthogonal rotations, both of these requirements having certain obsession-satisfying symmetry about them, but being quite misleading in their results in a scientific context. But there are several other differences which will become apparent.

This section does not have space to dot all the "i's" and cross all the "t's" of the basic arguments we have in mind, and the reader must be referred elsewhere (162, 23, 104) for the substantiation of some arguments. However, we can briefly run over the main standards and policies that have been followed throughout these factor analytic researches, by analyzing the process of factor analysis into the following steps.

(1) Choices of populations and samples of populations, in relation to one another.

(2) The indices for obtaining the correlation matrices.

(3) The procedures in deciding communalities and in agreeing on the number of factors.

(4) The processes of rotation to maximum simple structure.

(5) The matching of research results in general from one research to another.

In regard to the first, the population and samples from a population, our aim has been to achieve both a check on two samples from the same population, and also to check agreement from one population to another. For, by our general psychological position, we would definitely hypothesize that the source traits with which we are dealing are those which should appear both in normal and abnormal populations, for they are an essential part of personality. They should also appear, though with some continuous modification, over the age range from childhood to the adult level. Because of the greater ease of work and reliability of procedures, it seemed good strategy to begin with the definition of the factors at the adult level, and then to work downwards, by carefully chosen stages, to the youngest child level. The notion of carefully chosen stages is important, because the meaning of a test may change so radically if one jumps from an adult to an infant level, that it is essential to "feel one's way" by using a test which is only modified slightly over an age gap of perhaps four or five years, and, after checking that the factor structure is still recognizable, to take the next step over another four or five years, perhaps with appropriate change of emphasis in markers in the process of cross identification.

Accordingly, the design has been to fix the factor structure in adults, and then to move down in three stages, first to the 11 and 12 year old level; then to the 6 and 8 year old level; and finally to the 4 and 5 year old level. The results of such a carefully chosen series of researches will be explained in Chapters 4, 5, 6, 7, and 8 which follow.

It is also part of our psychological hypothesis that though normals and abnormals may stand at different levels on different personality factors, the essential structure will be the same, and that the same will be true of very different groups within a normal population, such as the general population average on the one hand, and students. For convenience, the first factorings were done on young adult students, but later Air Force subjects, less selected for intelligence and academic interest, were used, over a wider age range. A group of mental hospital patients was also taken soon after that, with results that showed that essentially the same factors do indeed exist. Thus these different groups were deliberately taken to show that population changes may produce changes in selection on a factor, but do not eliminate the basic structure. We did not deliberately seek populations which would exaggerate factors simply in order to see those factors more clearly, because such exaggeration of one factor always results in reduction of others, but we did take different populations with the object of demonstrating that the factor structure would survive the changes of population.

As regards the correlational procedures, our second aspect of procedure above, the great majority of studies have used the Pearson product-moment correlations, with occasional instances of bi-serial correlation. The scaling procedures accompanying this process, have, whenever possible, included the normalization of the raw scores, since it has been pointed out by Thurstone, and verified by our own experience, that a cleaner simple structure arises when this is done. In the personality field, as distinct from the ability field, a goodly number of variables may have the properties of difference and ratio scores, or even complex algebraic functions of actual measurements made on the response. There are certain dangers in this usage, as frequently pointed out by mathematical statisticians, but they are very small compared with the danger of losing important aspects of personality, which would ensue if one kept all variables to a very simple score form. The only real danger is that certain variables might be simple algebraically or experimentally dependent functions of the same raw measures and the implications of this be not understood by the researcher. A special study of Pawlik and Cattell (140a) has been made of the effect of these algebraic dependencies, and shows that when experimenters are sophisticated as to the dependencies they are introducing, the effects can be clearly singled out from any true psychological effects in the resulting factorization. In any case, the basic matrix factorizations reported in this monograph did not in most instances have more than pairs of experimentally dependent variables, at most.

In the earlier studies, the choice of communalities was made by Burt's method (13a), and the decision as to the number of factors to extract was made by Tucker's method (160). With the large matrices which have prevailed throughout this field, a relatively poor estimate of the communalities would have mattered very little, but in fact we have reason to believe that the estimates were very good. The chief workers in this field have had experience with Burt's method, which as Wrigley has more recently shown by empirical data (170a), proved to be the best among those cited as available in Cattell's 1952 Factor Analysis. In the most recent studies, however, the researchers have had the benefit of interative convergence of communalities by successive factor analyses on the computer. The convergence depends, of course, upon the decision as to the number of factors to be extracted.

In the early days of these researches, in the late 1930's and early 1940's, our decision to extract a number of factors which was, in fact, perhaps four times as great as that done by such workers as Eysenck, Wherry, and others in the field, met with considerable criticism. These decisions were based, however, upon very careful examination of the actual matrices, and also upon theoretical consideration from both psychology and from mathematical statistics, which have been proved correct in the fulness of time. As Cattell has pointed out in a recent article (33), the number of factors in actual psychological data is usually at least as large as the number of variables, though owing to the indeterminateness, e.g., of convergence of communalities if one takes more than n/2 factors, it is always desirable to keep below this limit. Part of the reason for the early practice of considering it conservative to stop at very few factors was the erroneous notion that the error variance came out only in the later factors, where in fact it is distributed equally through whatever number of factors one takes out. Indeed, to take out too few factors is far from being conservative. It is reckless, because the missing parts of rotated factors, which would have been presented by later extracted centroid factors, can never be rotated into position no matter how well one rotates a study which has extracted too few factors. There is real distortion there. The danger of over-extraction, on the other hand, is that one may then split a factor, using the same hyperplane essentially for two different factors. The first half of the studies here rested their main decision on the number of factors upon the Tucker criterion, which has been found to work out well empirically, but later on we used also the Guttman criterion (102), and most recently the Sokal criterion (153), which, on empirical evidence, we now believe to be the best. Generally, however, a decision was made on a compromise between two methods of decision, which usually did not disagree by more than one or two factors, and, after deciding on this number, we usually took out one extra factor. Our familiarity with the rotational procedure has usually enabled us to rotate error into this final "garbage factor" and to avoid splitting a real factor through any over-extraction, because we are aware of the signs which indicate such a splitting is occurring, namely, the existence of a high over-lap in the variables in the two hyperplanes, and the arising of a high correlation between the two factors.

5. THE VITAL CHARACTERISTICS OF ROTATION IN RELATION TO RESEARCH DESIGN

In connection with this discussion of the number of factors, critics have sometimes argued that it would be better so to design the choice of variables that only one or two major factors at a time are under experiment. This can, of course, be done, but we have already indicated one serious objection to it above, in the fact that recognition of the main factor space is better gained through the "global span" method of choice of variables than through the "patchwork" approach to covering the same area. However, there are two other serious objections to operating with a choice of variables which gives too small a number of factors, namely, (1) that the proper rotation of a factor by the simple structure criterion requires that there shall be enough variables in the hyperplane of any factor to leave very little doubt as to its position. This condition is best achieved when a factor is only one among quite a number of factors, and is unobtainable when there are only one or two other factors to form hyperplane stuff for the single factor. (2) The determination of the angles among factors, for the purpose of a second order factor analysis, is very incomplete unless the factor stands in the maximally developed factor space. So far we have said nothing about second-order factors, but they are an essential part of the picture of personality structure in objective tests. There turns out to be yet another advantage in an appreciable number of factors, which is evident, however, only at the matching stage which we discuss in the next chapter. It hinges on the fact that one may not match factor X in one series with factor Y in another, unless both series are long enough to demonstrate that some other factor in the second series is not actually a better match for X. If short series only exist, the best possible match is often not the real match.

Providing communalities not unities are used, it is a matter of comparative indifference whether one uses the centroid or the principle axes method of extraction, except for certain niceties of the latter. The latter pulls out the variance a little faster, but by the time one gets to what is considered the complete extraction of factors, there is little to choose between the methods in terms of their accuracy of restoring the original correlation matrix. Since computers are programmed for larger matrices by centroids than by principal axes, and since centroids are more economical of machine time, most of the studies here have used the former.

The heart of a factor analytic research is, of course, the fourth aspect mentioned above, namely the rotation process, for by this it can be either correct, or utterly wrong in a variety of different ways. It has been a prime object of policy, and one of extreme importance, in our work that the rotation for simple structure should be blind, i.e., made without the operator being aware of what variables are in or out of the hyperplane. The operator just seeks the maximum simple structure, defines the maximum total number of zeroes (apart from error) in the totality of hyperplanes in the study. The reason for this insistence is that we are in the area of exploration and discovery, as stated at the beginning of this chapter. Where one is operating in areas which have already been structured there may be some advantage in rotating to a pre-arranged position. As our studies progressed, and especially in the last study of all, we have used also a different approach at the same time, namely that of stating a hypothesis, from previous studies, about what the factor structure would be, and, after writing this out in a matrix, have used the Procrustes program (113) to see with what significance the series of hypotheses could be confirmed.

A blind rotation to simple structure can be sought either by analytical programs, such as Quartimax, Varimax, Oblimax, Maxplane, etc., or by hand rotation. It is a complete fallacy to believe that the automatic analytical rotation programs will bring a study completely to the best possible simple structure. Many of them are erroneous in their mathematical principles, maximizing the wrong function, i.e., some function other than the total number of variables in the hyperplanes. Others, like Quartimax and Varimax, are under the highly artificial restriction of orthogonality. Maxplane, though correct in principle, does not work too well unless certain adjustments are made. Accordingly, although analytical programs, principally the Oblimax program, have been used in the last five years of these researches, the blind rotation to maximum simple structure has always been carried out after the analytical program has gone as far as it can. The real test of goodness of simple structure is a statistical test, like Bargmann's (6) of the extent to which simple structure has actually been obtained, the road taken toward that simple structure being generally unimportant. Actually, that road in the early days of research, from 1930 to 1950, was a very long and weary one, since all the plots had to be done by hand and we commonly made as many as 5 to 15 total shifts, i.e., overall shifts on all factors, before a simple structure considered satisfactory was attained. The check on this being obtained was that the plots of the hyperplane counts in a total study, expressed as a percentage, would climb in a series of rotations to a plateau and remain unimprovable. We usually find this unimprovable level to have from 60 to 75 per cent of variables in the hyperplane, and we have noticed that the majority of studies published over that 20 years in other laboratories did not reach anywhere near this figure of 60 to 75 per cent. In fact, the researchers had generally collapsed of exhaustion before they reached the end of this road. This is easily understandable, but it is questionable whether the results should be published until the experimenter can demonstrate, even if it takes 12 months of rotation as is not unusual, that a position of maximum possible simple structure has been attained. Over the last 8 years, the workers in our own laboratory have more fortunately enjoyed the transfer of a hand rotation process to the rotoplot program on a computer, which has been described elsewhere (54). This program projects all possible plots as pictures on a screen, and the rotation, though judged and guided by the human mind is carried out automatically by the machine. As a matter of interest, it may be mentioned that it has been our practice to make many shifts on any one factor against several other factors in each overall rotation, adopting a certain experimental rule that the sum total of such shifts must not exceed a certain amount. We believe that in this way we have achieved maximum convergence to the ultimate simple structure, which has generally been reached by about 10 overall shifts after the analytical program has gone as far as it can. It will be noted that the percentage in the hyperplane count is quite high in most of these published researches, and that the statistical significances are generally adequate.

After the rotations have been carried out, the results were expressed, in most of the earlier researches, simply in the V_{rs} matrix, i.e., the reference vector structure matrix. In later studies, where we began also to aim at second order factors, we usually also calculated the correlations among the factors, C_f, from the correlations among the reference vectors, C_r, and then worked out the D Matrix by which the reference vector structure could be transformed into the factor pattern matrix V_{fp}. If one's purpose is only interpretation of the factors, not their use to get factor estimates, etc., it makes good sense to leave the factors in the V_{rs} system, for the considerable additional labor in going to V_{fp} is not justified in terms of the increased reliability of interpretation. However, in the finer aspects of factor matching and interpretation discussed in the next chapter it will be evident that the relative variance contribution becomes important and also the difference between correlations and loadings (as brought out in Cattell's recent paper (39)). Consequently, later researches have been brought to V_{fp} and even V_{df} expressions.

6. HISTORICAL SUMMARY OF REALIZATION OF DESIGN

Even by the second of the independent experiments, independently rotated, it became clear that there is considerable stability of pattern of the personality factors in objective tests. Later studies confirmed this, as well as the fact that at least a dozen factors have to be taken into account. Indeed, as we moved away from the simpler kinds of tests certain new factors appeared which pointed to a total nearer to twenty than ten factors.

The comprehensive plan had called for carrying markers from study to study, but as the frontier expanded the difficulties of maintaining these lines of communication across the whole distance increased. One reason for this was that some higher markers appeared in new tests, more ideal for tying research n + 1 with n, yet research n + 1 still needed to be checked against the research one. Another crowding of the original markers occurred when the P-technique factors equivalent to R-technique factors appeared, and suggested additional salients to be tested. Yet another threat to organization of effective interaction in a total program arises from the very enthusiasm of new research associates who perceive that an old marker variable can be made, by certain changes, to load higher on the factor it marks, and who proceed to improve it (and destroy its identity as a marker)!

Some of these more human details of an actual research history have real importance for understanding results and planning future researches. In the present case, by constantly keeping the major goals in mind, and by the exercise of some team discipline compatible with full creativity, it was possible in the end simultaneously to hold the rivets firm while building on new extensions. The only serious difficulty the laboratory finally faced was from certain instances where clerical or research assistants turned two or three out of five hundred scales around, in re-scaling, to fit their personality concepts of what is a psychologically good or high score! An uncertainty still remains on two of these, but if scoring and scaling error is kept down to 1% a laboratory is fortunate.

Continuity of purpose, and reliability of cross reference require much effort within a laboratory, but, in this field in this era, they have been practically impossible of achievement between laboratories. The sheer labor of transmitting detailed test materials and instructions from large studies, has frequently stood in the way of our obtaining from other laboratories certain markers we have wished to experiment upon that would have enabled a cross matching to be made. In our turn, we have had considerable difficulty in finding extra time to prepare additional detailed files of test copies and instructions and to transmit them to those who have requested them. Through the initially voluntary services of the Institute for Personality and Ability Testing, however, many of a long list of objective personality tests have been made available to researchers when larger commercial test companies were unwilling to undertake the burden of this help to science.

Throughout these researches one of the greatest difficulties has been that of retaining subjects for the 10 to 15 hours that are normally necessary to cover about 100 different tests. There has been a fair amount of criticism by theorists which we believe to be misguided, of the low reliability and the low loadings which the majority of tests have shown in these factors. Simply in terms of reaching a certain goal with a given expenditure of research man hours, and in spite of external difficulties of the kind described above, the short test approach has succeeded and justified itself. Hence the intelligent strategist and the academic pedant became separated, for this practice admittedly does not look ideal to those accustomed to high reliabilities and loadings in the traditional well beaten tract of ability testing, but it pays off in a proper sequence of scouting and consolidation. The objectors want science without discovery, or are temperamentally of the kind who would not have consented to go aboard the Mayflower until it was fitted with baths and cocktail lounges. The actual work on lengthening and increasing the item validity, of such tests as contain items, is taking place only now after the factors have been checked sufficiently to highlight which measures justify concentration on lengthening and standardization.

Over much of this twenty-five years of research, we were frequently urged by those on the sidelines to "demonstrate the reality of your factors by showing their predictive power against external criteria." Nothing but confusion could have arisen, however, from getting clinical, occupational and educational relations to only half-defined and weakly measured factors. Moreover, it is partly an illusion that criteria are always criteria. They are sometimes, in rating, merely stereotypes and prejudices. Though such advertising of the factors would have brought far more attention and research reinforcements (of a kind) we felt it better to concentrate on proving and proving again the number and nature of the factors themselves. Rather than "go off at halfcock" we wished our aim to be kept steady, and any announcement of the factor meanings and measurements to be made only when a high degree of certainty was reached.

We were, of course, as keen as anyone to see the ultimate factors tried against outside criteria. Indeed, it cannot be too strongly stressed that we do not regard the factors as an end in themselves--except in so far as any scientific knowledge is an end in itself--but rather as concepts to be used in applied predictions and diagnoses and in manipulative experiment. (Much manipulative experiment is pointlessly vague unless it begins with factors.) It was not until about 1955, however (except for a few experiments by Brogden against educational criteria, Eysenck against clinical syndromes and Sells against military pilot proficiency) that we felt ready to look for these criterion relations. And then the change of research emphasis began more in a spirit of aiding the interpretation of the factors than in any assertion of their immediate applied value.

However, the few but technically adequate researches of Damarin, Knapp, Pawlik, Connor and others over as short an interval as the last three years show that the factors do indeed have powerful predictive value in "real life" situations. In fact, in a recent survey at the APA Annual Meeting, it was pointed out that the percentage of successful criterion predictions is emphatically higher than for other personality measurement approaches, arguing well for what will happen when application really gets started. An earnest of this outcome with more systematic application is now just available in the book by Cattell and Scheier, The Meaning and Measurement of Neuroticism and Anxiety, in which neurotics are shown to differ at the $P < .01$ level on no fewer than six of the present factors. Nevertheless, the proper division of labor in this area is for the basic research teams with their highly specialized experimental and statistical craftsmanship to spend their time only on the complex technical work of factor discovery and definition, and for clinical and manipulative experimental psychologists to turn to these external criterion explorations. The former are all too few to spend their time on less technically complex work. The latter, if properly provided with factor batteries, can by training and interest do a much better job in the applied fields.

Accordingly, the aim of the present monograph has been primarily to assemble factor analytic evidence on the number and nature of the personality dimensions which exist, as patterns in objective behavioral measurements. The interpretation of these patterns is undertaken as a distinct, separable step, and, as far as life record criteria has to enter into these interpretations it has only just begun. Nevertheless, as far as interpretations of twenty-one dimensions -- each on a par with such a common factor as intelligence -- can be condensed into two chapters, Chapters 7 and 8 do this. An increasing number of articles specially devoted to the meaning of one factor or another, is now evident in the journals (139, 40, 64a, 149) expanding on what is given here, and also in such books as those of Cattell (29) and Damarin (51).

The actual plan of exposition in the rest of this book is comparatively straightforward. After a chapter given to the crucial question of matching across researches (Chapter 3) the first three chapters on research and method give way to five chapters on content. Chapters 4 and 5 list, and give detailed information (kind and size of population sample, the number of variables, the nature of the statistical operations, etc.), on the researches at both adult and child levels. Due to the dearth of cross-matchable studies, those reported have their core mainly in the planned interacting researches of our laboratory. The following chapter considers evidence for the matching of factors across different studies. Chapters 7 and 8 are devoted to summarizing and interpreting the evidence associated with each factor. A discussion of the evidence presented in Chapters 4 through 8 as this relates to broad issues in psychological measurement and personality theory appear in the following chapter (Chapter 9).

Since researchers in many areas of personality study, e.g., developmental, clinical diagnostic and therapeutic evaluation, genetics, will now want to use these realistic and meaningful dimensions, which have certainly come to stay, regardless of further directions of interpretation, the next step is a practical one. In Chapter 10 the reasons are given for choosing particular standard batteries of sub-tests, for each factor, respectively for adults and children. A battery of measures for more than one factor are presented in Chapter 11. The actual batteries which result are discussed somewhat more fully in Warburton's Compendium, but especially in the IPAT O-A Battery Handbook, which gives detailed administration and scoring instructions and practical information on time required, reclassifying for longer and shorter tests, etc. But the research justification for the basic construction of these batteries is given in these two chapters.

A brief summary, to remind the researcher and student of the main concepts gained and their evidential background is given in the concluding Chapter 12.

CHAPTER 3

THE METHODOLOGY OF MATCHING AND INTERPRETING SOURCE TRAIT FACTORS

1. WHAT ARE WE MATCHING?

"Factor" is a loose term which always needs more definition if communication is to be clear. Do we mean a rotated or an unrotated factor? Do we mean the factor structure values or the factor pattern values? Do we mean an actual pattern in a particular matrix from a particular sample or some inferred pattern in a population?

Obviously in the present context -- the context of the science of personality -- we are not talking about a mathematical factor from a particular matrix and sample, but about a source trait as a meaningful influence on behavior. Such an influence will express itself differently in different experimental conditions and samples, but with orderly transformations of a kind which permit us to infer that one and the same influence is at work behind the various numerical values obtained. Ideally, therefore, we have either to possess techniques to indicate how the same pattern may get transformed in various situations, or we must hold everything constant when making the comparisons. As we shall see, these technical requirements are not at present fully achieved, but with an intelligent estimation of the sources of modification it is already possible to decide with a good degree of certainty whether a source trait in one research is the same as in another.

Our general position over source traits is that they are single sources of variance either within the person, as in a constitutional trait pattern, or within society (or, at least, the environment) as in what Cattell has called "an environmental mold trait." In either case a pattern of common variance is produced within a set of observed variables, which pattern will alter with particular selection effects in samples, with the changing magnitudes of variance existing in other factors, with age and sex of subjects, etc. These patterns are therefore not themselves precisely what we wish to match. They are only the <u>signs</u> of the influences to be identified from study to study. When the influences are identical, the proof thereof may sometimes even require that the patterns <u>not</u> be identical, and so on.

2. THE PROPERTIES BY WHICH FACTORS ARE MATCHED AND IDENTIFIED

From the early days of the present interlocking researches we have given attention to raising the conclusions on factor matching and replication to a higher level of objectivity and exactness. In the first place one must get away from the idea that it is only a matter of finding agreement of two reference vector correlation columns. Some six properties of the solutions to be compared have been listed by Cattell (39) as relevant to the decisions to be made, and each of these is subject also to consideration of the transformations to be expected through sampling, etc., as described above. They are:

1. The Dimension-Variable Profile Agreement. The term "dimension" rather than "factor" is used here, for sometimes one is dealing with reference vectors and sometimes with primary factors. There are indeed twelve possible dimension-variable systems (39) in terms of which the agreement of two columns of figures could be evaluated.

2. The Correlations of the Factor with Other Factors, examined as a matrix, for its degree of agreement with that of the factor with which the given factor is being matched.

3. The "Size" of the Factor. Agreement of two factors in this way may be assessed through squaring the factor structure column values, expressing the contribution of the factor to the variance of a sufficiently large and defined sample of variables. Matching factors are expected to be of approximately equal relative "size".

4. Agreement in Terms of Circumstantial Relations and Mathematical Modification Under Influences. Elsewhere (39) the idea of circumstantial validity has been defined as the agreement between a measure A and a criterion B, not in direct correlation, but in their statistical and mathematical relation to a host of circumstantial variables. This notion can be extended to include similar modification under "influences" such as sampling selection. It is expanded upon in Section 6 below.

5. Proof of Identity by Elimination. If a sufficiently large number of factors is included in both studies the probability of a match of X in one with Y in the other is increased by the fact that all other factors in the first study have already been matched with all others in the second. This argument must be connected with the discussion of goodness of over-all match, in Section 8 below.

6. Behavior of the Factor in Manipulative and General Experiment. This last is not cognate with the others for it moves from the mathematico-statistical to the experimental-manipulative field. Here we are saying that factor A is the same as factor B, regardless of how it is measured, if it behaves the same way in a scientific field, e.g., if it changes just the same with age, responds similarly to applied experimental influences, distributes itself similarly demographically, and so on. In the main two types of experimental design can be listed for obtaining such experimental evidence on factor matching. In one type of experimental design, the factors are used as dependent variables

and their behavior, under controlled variation of a set of independent variables, is recorded. In the second type of experimental design the factors serve as independent variables and the relationship between a set of dependent variables and these factors is explored.

An example for the first mentioned design is the conditioned response design, used by Cattell and Scheier in this laboratory (64). By testing the same subjects twice or more on the same set of marker variables for a set of factors, the changes in mean factor score between the different testing occasions can be related to either controlled or natural differences between the two or more testing occasions (e.g., testing subjects in a state of fatigue and in a non-tired state, testing subjects before and after physiological or psychological stress, etc.). If the same experiment is also performed for a second set of factors, indirect evidence of the described kind becomes available for identifying factors between the two studies. Besides this condition response design, as a matter of fact, a large number of other experimental designs (e.g., different analysis-of-variance type designs) can be used for this purpose.

In the second type of experiment, for instance, a group of subjects is tested on a test battery for factors $f_{.A}$; after the testing sub-groups of subjects with extreme factor scores are selected. All groups are exposed to the same experimental procedure, e.g., a test of stress endurance; significant differences between the groups in the latter tests can be understood as being caused by the particular factor under investigation, assuming that other possible inter-group differences have been controlled. If the same experiment is also performed using a test battery for factors $f_{.B}$, a comparison between the two sets of factors in terms of the results of such an experiment might provide some basis for identifying factors between the two researches.

The experimental methods for factor matching do not make it necessary that the two factor analytic studies under comparison have a large number of, or even any, marker variables in common. However, successful application of these methods for the purpose of factor matching needs already some insight into the meaning of the factors under comparison if the experimental approach to factor matching shall not become a trial and error procedure.

The "experimental" approach is not discussed at more length here because, at the present stage of research, we must mainly dismiss it as a practical step and concentrate on the other methods, with which the succeeding sections of this chapter will therefore be largely occupied.

3. REFINEMENT OF CONCEPTS IN THE MATCHING FIELD

It will be noted in relation to the above six modes of comparison that some require that the factors to be matched be couched in the same variables (Matching by properties 1 and 3) whereas others can be used even if the same variables do not exist for the factors (Matching by properties 2, 4, 5, 6). Keeping this distinction in mind will help in subsequent mathematico-statistical discussions, as well as in giving proper perspective in weighting independent sources of evidence.

Parenthetically, it is also important to keep in mind the difference between the aims (1) of determining the goodness of match between two experiments each rotated independently to a unique position by some criterion (e.g., simple structure, confactor rotation, etc.) which has been maximally achieved, and (2) of simply taking two studies and rotating them to maximal possible agreement, regardless of the properties of the solution by independent standards in each.

Proposals for achieving the latter aim of maximal agreement of two studies have been formulated by Ahmavaara (1), Cattell and Hurley (113), Kaiser (117), and Tucker (164). The Hurley-Cattell formulae have been programmed for computers and used in several researches over the past eight years. The first aim, however, which is our topic here, is quite different and a set back to the scientific aims of testing factor replication across various researches has occurred through writers confusing these two aims. For example, because of overlap in some formulae the Cattell confactor (proportional profiles) principle of rotation, aimed at finding a unique, meaningful solution with special properties from a scientific standpoint in each of two researches, has been confused with Tucker's "maximum congruence" method (163), the aim of which is solely to get maximum agreement of two studies.

Here we are concerned with all the techniques that have to do with evaluating the statistical likelihood that two factors in two experiments could be considered due to the same source trait, when the solutions in the two researches have been independently arrived at, though by application of the same general scientific standards -- in this case the standards of simple structure. Obviously this is completely different from the aim of producing maximum congruence, as in the Cattell-Hurley Procrustes program (113) and the Tucker 'maximum congruence' formulae (164).

In general, the principle faithfully followed through all the researches here has been: (1) to seek maximum simple structure (maximum hyperplane count in the $\pm.10$ range over the whole factor matrix), as evidenced by a plateau on the "history of the hyperplane" plot (23, 54): (2) to examine, in the more recent studies, the statistical significance of the solution reached, by Bargmann's criterion (6); (3) to test the goodness of match with other studies by one or more criteria.

As Cattell has argued elsewhere (23) the structures in which simple structure should be sought are not the reference vector pattern, V_{rp}, or factor structure, V_{fs}, but the reference vector structure, V_{rs}, or the factor pattern V_{fp}. A further refinement proposed by Cattell (39) is to seek the factor matching in what he has called the dissociated factor matrix, V_{df}, but so far we have not applied this recent notion in present practice. However, the concepts set out in that article (39) on matching and interpretation are highly relevant to the defense of the interpretations adopted in Chapters 7 and 8 here.

4. ACTUAL MATCHING PROCEDURES: EXAMINATION OF TERMS AND PRINCIPLES

In so far as the greatest weight is thrown in this work on matching by the dimension-variable profiles, we shall now concentrate on the theory thereof.

First, we must draw the main division between use of (1) non-parametric approaches, as in the early work (21) of Cattell and the subsequent Cattell-Baggaley "s" index ("salient variable similarity index" (42)), and (2) parametric devices which take actual numerical loading values as such into account. The advantage of the latter is that one does not "lose information" -- a standard objection to non-parametric treatment. The advantage of the former is that "in" and "out" of the hyperplane is a fundamental, meaningful distinction. Moreover, changes in magnitude of another factor, or selection on a variable, or change in reliability of a variable, may change considerably the loading of factor F on variable v -- without, however, shifting it from a non-hyperplane to a hyperplane (or zero) loading.

In the most general case the situation one faces when trying to match factors between different studies might be formally represented in table 3.1.

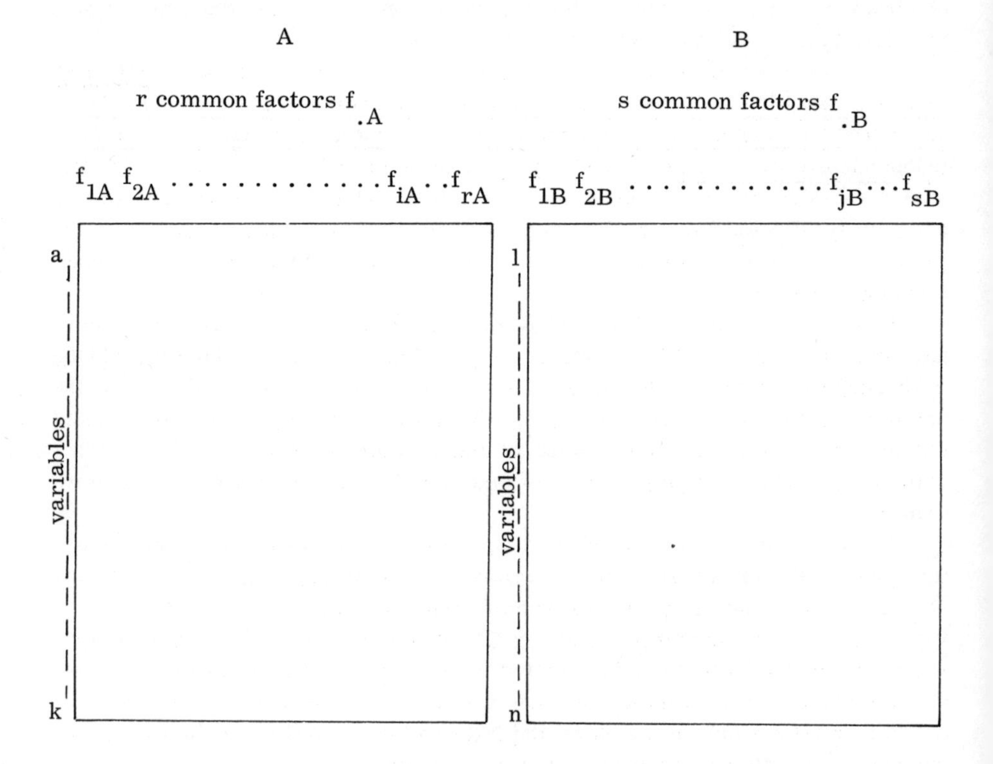

TABLE 3.1

A and B are the two factor matrices after rotation to simple structure which constitute the results of two factor analytic studies. In study A the k variables a to k have been analyzed, in study B the variables 1 to n. The number of variables used in both studies need not be the same. The factors that have been found in the study A are labelled f_{1A}, f_{2A}, up to f_{rA}; the factors found in study B are labelled f_{1B}, f_{2B}, up to f_{sB}. Also, the number of factors found in both studies, r and s, respectively, need not be the same.

A and B usually represent two different populations of subjects. The problem of factor matching can now be stated as follows: Is there any relationship between the set of factors $f_{.A}$ and the set of factors $f_{.B}$, and if so, which is the best match in set $f_{.B}$ for each of the factors in set $f_{.A}$, and vice-versa?

There are three different cases in which this problem of factor matching will arise:

Case 1: A and B are different populations of subjects and also the two sets of variables a to k and 1 to n are different (i.e., the two studies A and B have no variables in common). No statistical solution exists for this matching problem. Only experimental procedures like the ones listed above might provide some help for cross-identifying the two sets of factors between the studies.

Case 2: The two sets of variables a to k and 1 to n are different but the same population of subjects has been used in both studies A and B. In this case Tucker's inter-battery method of factor analysis (163) will allow for identification of factors between the two studies.

Case 3: In the most frequent case, A and B are two different samples of subjects but the two sets of variables a to k and 1 to n show some overlap (i.e., the two factor analytic studies have a series of variables in common). It is in the main this third case of the matching problem with which our present discussion is concerned.

Given case 3, the two factor matrices can be reduced to the n variables common to both studies. In Table 3.2 these two reduced factor matrices A and B are represented. The two factor matrices now contain the same number of n rows

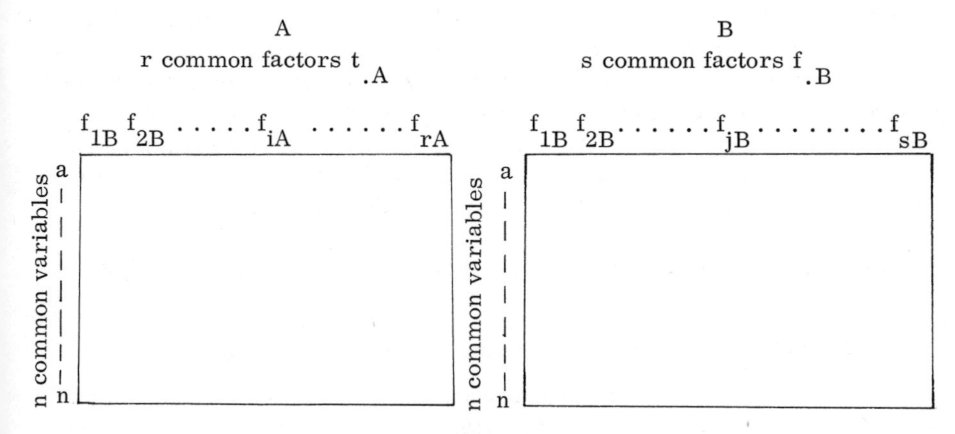

TABLE 3.2

and the rows have been thus re-ordered in the two matrices that any row describes the same variable in both studies. It is this type of factor matrix reduced to the variables common to both studies that is the starting point for the direct statistical methods of factor matching. The aim of these methods is to finally arrive at a matrix C, the structure of which is shown in Table 3.3.

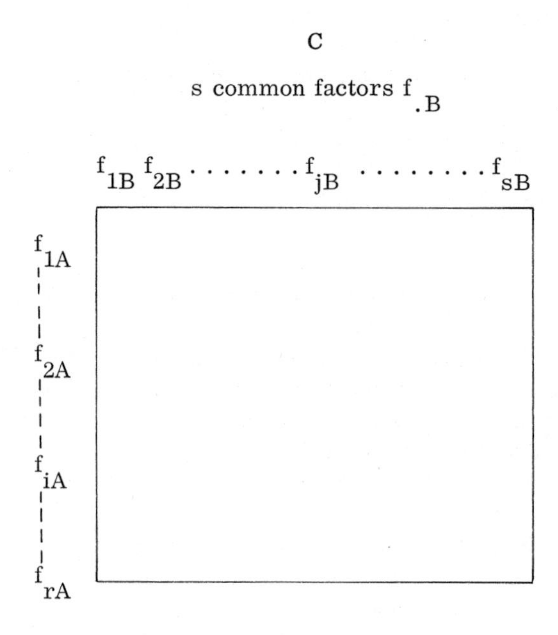

TABLE 3.3

The matrix C, which is r x s in size, contains as rows the factors f_{iA} of study A and its columns are the factors f_{jB} of study B. The kind of elements in matrix C differs with different matching procedures; in general, the elements of matrix C should be some index number, or coefficient, that indicates the degree of similarity, relationship, or correlation between each of the factors of study A and each of the factors of study B. The various direct statistical methods of factor matching differ with regard to the type of index number or coefficient used in this matrix C and with regard to the rationale underlying the derivation of such index or coefficient. Six more or less different methods of this kind have been used which are briefly described below.

5. METHODS RESTING ENTIRELY ON DIMENSION-VARIABLE PROFILE INFORMATION

(1) Marker Count, Average Difference in Size of Marker Loadings

The methods of factor matching described here are very easy to apply. They do not, however, include statistical tests of significance for matches derived. Given two factor matrices A and B[1] quite often one of the two matrices can be regarded as some kind of "criterion matrix"; this might be the matrix from the larger and/or more reliable of the two studies or it might be a factor matrix the elements of which are loadings already averaged across several studies. Let us assume that matrix A is either such a criterion matrix or the factor matrix from which the experimenter arbitrarily decides to start.

If the matrices have been rotated to simple structure each of the n variables will load only some of the r factors of matrix A. A variable loading a factor statistically significant or -- in case no such test of significance has been used -- with a value outside the ±.10 hyperplane shall be defined as a marker variable for that particular factor. Each factor f_{iA} is thus defined by a series of such marker variables. Since the matrices A and B contain the same n variables any factor in matrix B that is identical to one of the factors in matrix A should show the same pattern of marker variable loadings as its counterpart in matrix A. Several easy methods can be used to assess the agreement or similarity between factors f_{iA} and f_{jB} in terms of such marker patterns.

To arrive at a simple marker count, each column of matrix A is compared with every column of matrix B. For a particular comparison between two factors f_{iA} and f_{jB} a count is made of the markers of factor f_{iA} loading also factor f_{jB} outside the ±.10 hyperplane. To detect possible reflections of a factor it is convenient to break this total count down into two numbers: the number of out-of-hyperplane loadings agreeing in sign and the number disagreeing in sign. In using these counts for factor identification, as a matter of fact, the total number of markers for each particular factor f_{iA} always has to be taken into account (e.g., expressing the marker counts in percentages of the latter makes them comparable between different rows of matrix C).

Table 3.4 shows an example of a marker count matrix C, the analysis being carried out for a three column matrix A and a four column matrix B. The total number of markers for each of the factors f_{iA} is shown to the right of the corresponding row of the matrix C.

		B				
		1	2	3	4	Total number of markers
	1	1.1	2.1	0.2	0.6	6
A	2	1.0	0.1	0.3	2.1	3
	3	3.0	1.1	0.1	0.0	3

TABLE 3.4

[1] In the case of non-orthogonal factors again the historical problem will arise as to which one of the possible factor matrices is the proper one to use for such factor matching. This controversial issue cannot be dealt with here, and a recent account of this problem has been given elsewhere by Cattell (39). For various reasons (see section 8 of this chapter) usually the reference vector structure matrix will provide the best basis for factor matching.

The first number in each cell is the sign-agreement count, the second number is the sign-disagreement count. Without expressing these counts as percentages it becomes obvious that factor f_{iA} is identical to factor f_{4B}, factor f_{2a} is identical to factor f_{3B}, and factor f_{3A} is identical to factor f_{1B}. Furthermore, we learn from Table 3.4 that factors f_{4B} and f_{3B} are factors f_{1A} and f_{2A}, respectively, in reversed direction.

Compared with actual empirical findings, however, the values in the matrix C shown in Table 3.4 are somewhat idealized. Due to sampling errors, differences between the two samples of subjects, and due to differences in test reliability between the two samples, in empirical marker count matrices for factor identification the highest marker count in a row of matrix C may be considerably lower than the total number of markers for that particular factor--even with factors matching between both studies. Therefore, a statistical test of significance becomes necessary to assess the probability of obtaining certain marker count values by pure chance for otherwise unrelated factors. The salient variable similarity index which will be discussed below provides such a test of significance.

The non-parametric approach to factor identification by means of the marker count is sometimes supplemented by computing within each pair of factors f_{iA} - f_{jB} the average absolute difference in size of loadings for the variables that mark factor f_{iA}. The smaller the average, the better the match between the two factors. At present for this method no statistical test of significance against chance matches has been developed.

(2) Salient Variable Similarity Index

Similar to the marker count, also the salient variable similarity index, developed by Cattell and Baggaley (42), can be regarded as a non-parametric solution of the factor identification problem. In comparing any two factors f_{iA} and f_{jB} the subset of the g variables with highest absolute loadings on factor f_{iA} and the g variables with highest absolute loadings on factor f_{jB} are determined. In the ideal case of complete matching both sets of g variables (marker or salient variables) would be identical; with empirical data, however, the number of variables that show up among the g variables loading highest on factor f_{iA} as well as among the g variables loading highest on factor f_{jB} will be less than g. It can be shown that P_x, the chance probability for obtaining x common variables in both sets of g variables equals to

$$P_x = \frac{\binom{g}{x} \sum_{y=o}^{y=g-x} \left[\binom{n-g}{g-x-y} 2^{g-x-y} \binom{g-x}{y} \right]}{2^g \binom{n}{g}} \qquad (1)$$

where y is a summation index. If c is the number of salients common to both factors the salient variable similarity index s_c gives the probability of obtaining by chance c or more common variables among the g salients selected for each factor; this index s_c is equal to

$$Sc = 1 - \sum_{x = o}^{x = c - 1} Px \tag{2}$$

Thus the salient variable similarity index is a one-sided test of significance and formula (2) above is written for the case where c is less than half of g, which is most likely with empirical data. If c is more than half of g, formula (2) has to be changed into

$$Sc = \sum_{x - c}^{x = g} Px \tag{3}$$

If the salient variable similarity index is used for factor identification between two multi-factor studies A and B, g, the number of salients selected for each factor, is better kept constant for all factors under comparison.

In contrast to the simple marker count method of factor identification, matrix C is a symmetric matrix when the salient variable similarity index is used. If s_c is equal to or below the desired level of significance the match between the two factors is significant at that level. Theoretical consideration as well as practical experience show that the salient variable similarity index is a rather severe statistical test for factor matching.

(3) Correlating Columns of Factor Matrices

In this approach to factor matching typically no distinction is made between marker and non-marker variables for a particular factor. The reduced factor matrices A and B as described in Table 2 are used as the basis for factor matching. In the ideal case of complete factor matching the two column vectors f_{iA} and f_{jB} will be identical; the various coefficients to be described constitute different attempts at assessing such correspondence between any two factors f_{iA} and f_{jB}. The methods differ with regard to the scale properties attributed to the loading coefficients in the factor matrices and with regard to the rationale of the coefficient employed.

In some studies the variables have been ranked separately for each factor according to their loading on it; the degree of correspondence between any two factors has been then expressed by using a rank order correlation coefficient, either Spearman's coefficient rho or Kendall's coefficient tau. The usual test of significance for rank order correlation coefficients is then applied using n, the number of variables common to both matrices A and B, as sample size in this test.

In other studies the coefficients in the factor matrices have been treated as making up an interval scale. The degree of correspondence between any two column vectors of the matrices A and B thus has been expressed in the Pearson product moment correlation between these two columns of loading coefficients. Again a test of significance has been used for this coefficient of factor matching, applying the usual test for product moment correlation coefficients and using n as sample size.

Both approaches have several weaknesses. Since in both the rank order and the product moment correlation coefficient an arbitrary origin of scale is employed, differences in mean loading between the two factor columns under comparison are not taken into account. Because of this very reason loading coefficients near zero might be given a much higher weight than loading coefficients in the neighborhood of .40 or .50, for instance, if the mean loading for a particular factor column happens to be near .40. These considerations merely point out that the loading coefficients in the factor matrices have to be treated as a ratio scale, with the origin being at zero, if some correlational measure is to be applied for the purpose of factor identification.

A coefficient that is widely in use has been suggested by Burt (14), Wrigley and Neuhaus (171), and by Tucker (163); known as the coefficient of congruence, this index avoids the main weakness that is apparent in the rank order and straight forward product moment correlation coefficient. It is the product moment correlation between any two factor columns of matrices A and B, however the computation of the mean loading per column is suppressed by using a zero loading as mean value. Thus, this coefficient is identical to the inner product of the two factor columns under consideration, if they are treated as vectors. Since the inner product of two vectors is equal to the cosine of the angle that separates them in space this coefficient seems at first to provide all the information required for factor matching.

In considering this method it has, however, to be kept in mind, that the spatial interpretation of this adjusted product moment correlation coefficient is only illustrative, but does not give the true spatial relationships between the two sets of factors $f_{.A}$ and $f_{.B}$ one would obtain from projecting both into the same space. This can easily be understood from considering, e.g., that premultiplying a centroid matrix by its transpose does not give a diagonal or even identity matrix, despite the fact that the centroid factors are known to be uncorrelated. So far only Kaiser's new coefficient for factor matching (117) and its generalized formulation by Tucker (164) do provide the true spatial interrelationships between the two sets of factors when projecting them both into the same space. These methods are discussed below.

Elsewhere Cattell (24) has pointed out another criterion for factor identification which also treats the entries of the factor matrices A and B as values with ratio scale properties--the origin of the scale being at zero loading. This is the criterion of proportional profiles according to which a complete match exists between the two factors f_{iA} and f_{jB} if the elements of the first are equal to the elements of the second factor times a constant coefficient of proportionality. In that case matrix A can be expressed as the product of matrix B and a diagonal matrix that contains these coefficients of proportionality. Despite several advantages, however, this criterion has only seldom been used for the purpose of factor identification--in suggesting this criterion, Cattell himself aimed in the main at an analytical solution of rotating two centroid matrices A_o and B_o simultaneously towards two rotated positions A and B that would fulfill the proportionality criterion. So far a solution exists only for the case of orthogonal factors.

(4) Methods That Use Profile Statistics

The column of a factor matrix might also be understood as a profile of loading coefficients over the n variables. The problem of factor identification can then be re-formulated as follows: given a set A of r profiles and a set B of s profiles, which profile out of the latter set shows highest correspondence with or similarity to each of the profiles in set A?

Most of the available statistical indices for comparing profiles have been summarized already by Cronbach and Gleser (77) so that they need not be reported here again. Most of the weaknesses to be encountered with such indices are known. Many of the available statistics for the comparison of profiles are not statistically independent of the number of variables used in the particular profile as well as the metric of the profile values. Different profile comparison measures also give different weights to the three aspects observable in profiles-shape, level, and scatter.

An index that takes these three components equally into account and the range of which extends between +1 and -1 has been suggested elsewhere by Cattell (20, 29, 111) as the pattern similarity coefficient r_p. If n denotes the number of variables and k symbolizes the median chi-square value for a sample of size n, r_p is given by the expression

$$r_p = \frac{2k - \Sigma d^2}{2k + \Sigma d^2} \tag{4}$$

where the sum of d^2 means the squared difference between corresponding elements in the two profiles under comparison, summed over all variables.

Profile comparison indices have only occasionally been used for factor identification. They are generally easy to compute, but for the purpose of factor matching they have to be regarded as more or less approximative procedures the rationale of which is not related to the mathematical properties of the factor matrices A and B under comparison.

6. METHODS OF COMPARING FACTOR ANALYTIC RESOLUTIONS IN SPATIAL REPRESENTATION

It is obvious that a very effective method is possible -- combining both factor-variable comparison and inter-factor angle comparison -- by bringing two studies into a common space. In one sense or another these methods depend upon bringing the test vectors in the two researches into maximum congruence from a common origin, so that the closeness in space can be determined for any two factors f_{iA} and f_{jB}.

Four proposals exist for discussion:

(1) Ahmavaara's transformation analysis,

(2) the Cattell-Hurley Procrustes rotation,

(3) Kaiser's method of relating factors.

(4) Tucker's generalization of Kaiser's method (for matching factors between two or more researches).

In 1939, Mosier in an article entitled "Determining a Simple Structure When Loadings for Certain Tests are Known" (133) developed the mathematical essential for transforming a factor matrix into a new factor position which will be a least-squares fit to another factor matrix containing the same variables. Mosier did not suggest using this procedure for factor identification, his aim was rather to find a method that will help in simple structure rotation whenever the "true" structure of at least part of the variables is known beforehand. The first two methods listed above (Ahmavaara's transformation analysis, the Cattell-Hurley Procrustes rotation) both employ Mosier's mathematical solution, each for a different aim of transformation, and both methods have been developed independently from Mosier's original solution for this general class of rotational problems.

(1) Ahmavaara's Transformation Analysis

Several years ago the Finnish physicist and psychologist Y. Ahmavaara (1) suggested a method of factor matching which he called transformation analysis. He demonstrated this method in a study surveying the factor analytic results in the ability field (2) and in a factor analytic study of questionnaire responses in which personality differences between non-alcoholics and alcoholics were investigated (3). The rationale underlying Ahmavaara's transformation analysis can be briefly described as follows:

Given two factor matrices A and B of the type shown in Table 2, in the transformation analysis one tries to rotate one set of rotated factors (for instance the set of factors $f_{.A}$) into a position as close as possible to the position given by the other set of factors $f_{.B}$. After this rotation has been accomplished an index is used, theoretically distributed -- like a coefficient of correlation -- between +1 and -1, to express for any possible pair of factors f_{iA} and f_{jB} the closeness of their position in the common space. The factor matching matrix C contains these indices as elements.

Ahmavaara defines this matrix C as the transformation matrix λ, then normalized by rows, that will rotate a rotated factor matrix A as close as possible towards the position given by the rotated factor matrix B. Thus this matrix λ is defined by the equation

$$A \, . \, \lambda = B$$

and, with A being non-square, the solution for λ becomes

$$\lambda = (A'A)^{-1}A'B$$

The rows of λ represent the factors $f_{.A}$, the columns represent the factors $f_{.B}$. Ahmavaara then normalizes λ by rows, and it is this matrix which he uses as the matching matrix ("comparison matrix") in the transformation analysis. As can be easily shown, before normalization λ will yield a least-squares fit between both sets of factors, in the sense that the sum of squares of the elements of the matrix $(A \, . \, \lambda - B)$ becomes a minimum.[1]

Ahmavaara suggested this method of relating factors between different studies for both orthogonal and oblique factor matrices. The properties Ahmavaara ascribes to the elements of his factor matching matrix, i.e., the above matrix λ standardized by rows, have been questioned in recent discussions by Bargmann (7) and Kaiser (117). Whereas, for example, Ahmavaara claims transivity of the transformation analytic results, in the sense that rotating A towards B will give factor matching coefficients identical to those yielded from rotating B towards A, the algebra of the transformation analysis does not follow this proposition:

From "rotating A toward B" we obtain

$$\lambda_1 = (A'A)^{-1}A'B$$

and after normalization by rows

$$C_1 = D_2^{-1/2}(A'A)^{-1}A'B$$

[1] Mosier (133) has presented the proof that λ, computed from the above formula, in most cases will only approximate the exact least-squares solution for λ.
The latter solves simultaneously for a transformation matrix λ that fulfills both conditions of
1) a least-squares fit between the matrices $(A \, . \, \lambda)$ and B, and
2) the transformed factors having unit length.
The calculational labor involved in solving for λ, however, is considerably reduced if restriction 2) is first dropped (which yields a solution for λ as given above) and fulfilled afterwards by re-normalizing the obtained λ. The error introduced by using this simplified solution for λ approaches zero when the matrices $(A \, . \, \lambda)$ and B become identical.

where C_1 stands for the final comparison matrix and D_1 is a diagonal matrix, the elements of which are the diagonals of $\lambda_1 \lambda_1'$.
From "rotating B towards A", however, we obtain

$$\lambda_2 = (B'B)^{-1} B'A$$

which becomes after normalization of λ_2

$$C_2 = D_2^{-1/2} (B'B)^{-1} B'A$$

with C_2 being the final comparison resulting from this alternative transformation and D_2 being a diagonal matrix the elements of which are the diagonals of $\lambda_2 \lambda_2'$. It thus becomes evident that, without special assumptions about the matrices A and B, C_2 and C_1 will be different.

As Kaiser (117) has pointed out, normalizing λ by rows will not achieve the desired aim (i.e., to bring the factors back to unit length) if either or both sets of factors $f_{.A}$ and $f_{.B}$ are oblique; in that case pre- and post-multiplying λ by the respective matrices of within study factor intercorrelations would be necessary to normalize the factors again.

From the above discussion it becomes evident that the transformation analysis, in its original formulation (1), should be used only:
1) if both sets of factors $f_{.A}$ and $f_{.B}$ are uncorrelated within each study, and
2) if on a-priori grounds one of the two matrices A and B is to be considered as some kind of a "criterion", so that only one of the two alternative transformations is meaningful and thus the discrepancy between C_1 and C_2 becomes irrelevant.

(2) The Cattell - Hurley Procrustes Transformation

Independently from Ahmavaara, in our laboratory Cattell and Hurley (113) developed a rotational procedure called "Procrustes rotation" which is similar to the transformation analysis in the type of algebraic solution intended. The principle of the Procrustes rotation can be applied to a variety of factor analytic problems; when used for the purpose of matching factors across studies it has some advantages over the transformation analysis.

Whereas in the transformation analysis the rotated factor matrix of one study is rotated as close as possible towards a position of the factors defined as in the rotated factor matrix of the other study, in Procrustes rotation the unrotated (orthogonal) centroid matrix of one study is rotated towards the position of factors given by the rotated factor matrix of the second study. With this rotation accomplished, the best possible representation of the factors of the latter study in the space of the former is obtained; from this a factor matching matrix C can be derived.

To describe the mathematical procedure used in the Procrustes Transformation for factor identification we have to define several new symbols. With two studies under comparison, A_o and B_o shall denote the two (orthogonal) centroid matrices, A and B the two (orthogonal or oblique) factor matrices rotated to simple structure; λ_A and λ_B stand for the transformation matrices used in the two studies, so that the familiar equations

$$A_o \cdot \lambda_A = A \qquad \text{(for study "A")}$$

$$B_o \cdot \lambda_B = B \qquad \text{(for study "B")}$$

are fulfilled.

For the moment we shall assume that matrix A describes a well-established factor structure and therefore the factors $f_{.A}$ may serve as a criterion against which we like to match the factors $f_{.B}$ of matrix B. The first step in Procrustes rotation is to project the "criterion" factors $f_{.A}$ into the space of the factors $f_{.B}$. In other words, we wish to transform the original orthogonal factors of study b (the columns of B_o) in such a way that they match the rotated factors $f_{.A}$ (i.e., the columns of A) as closely as possible. This amounts to finding the transformation λ_P which, when normalized by columns[1] and premultiplied by B_o, will yield the matrix A*

$$B_o \cdot \lambda_P = A^*$$

where A* is the best possible fit to A, in the sense that the sum of the squared elements of matrix (A*-A) is a minimum[2]. The solution for the unnormalized $\lambda_{\dot{P}}$ is

$$\lambda_{\dot{P}} = (B_o' B_o)^{-1} B_o' A$$

which after normalization by columns becomes

$$\lambda_P = \lambda_{\dot{P}} D^{-1/2} = (B_o' B_o)^{-1} B_o' A D^{-1/2}$$

where D is a diagonal matrix, the elements of which are the diagonals of the product matrix $\lambda_{\dot{P}}' \lambda_{\dot{P}}$

---

[1] The normalization by columns is necessary in order to preserve rotated reference vectors of unit length.

[2] See footnote 1) on page 39.

For sake of clarity we shall refer to the unrotated centroid factors in matrix B_o as $f_{.oB}$, to the columns of matrix A* as factors $f_{.A*}$. The latter are not identical with the factors $f_{.A}$, in the same way as A* is different from A; they rather represent the closest possible approximation to the "true" factors $f_{.A}$ when the latter become projected into the factor space of study B and expressed as linear functions of the factors $f_{.Bo}$. Then the elements of matrix λ_P give the cosine of the angle (or the equivalence of the empirically unobservable correlation) between any factor $f_{.Bo}$ and any factor $f_{.A*}$.

To the extent that the factors $f_{.A*}$ approximate the factors $f_{.A}$, the correlation between any two factors f_{iA*} and f_{jB} can be understood as an approximation towards the relationship between the "true" factor f_{iA} and the factor f_{jB}. This substitution of f_{iA} by f_{iA*} in matching the two sets of factors $f_{.A}$ and $f_{.B}$ is an essential part of the Procrustes transformation. As can be seen already, the interpretability of the final matching matrix C depends on how closely the factors $f_{.A*}$ approximate the factors $f_{.A}$. The degree of approximation (or the goodness of fit between $f_{.A*}$ and $f_{.A}$) can be assessed from considering the difference matrix (A*-A). If the factors $f_{.Bo}$, as defined by the n variables common to both study "A" and "B", do not "naturally" lend themselves towards a position given by matrix A, A* will fit A badly. In order to evaluate this fit between A* and A, a procedure would be necessary whereby the elements of (A*-A) can be tested for their statistical significance against a sheer chance departure between A* and A. As yet no final decision has been made among several alternative methods. A simple test of significance, for example, can be carried out as follows:

A bivariate plot is made for the elements of matrix A*, plotting their value in matrix A* along the abscissa, their value in matrix A along the ordinate.[1] A traditional test of significance for the residual variance of the n . r points from the line of regression can then be performed.

The second step in the Procrustes transformation is to obtain the cosine of the angle (or again the empirically unobservable correlation) between any two factors f_{iA*} and f_{jB}. These constitute the final results of this factor identification technique and -- within the limits discussed in the preceeding paragraphs-- they will be an approximation towards the cosine of the angle separating the two factors f_{iA} and f_{jB} in the common space of both studies. This final matrix is obtained from

$$C = \lambda'_B \lambda_P$$

where λ_B is defined as above. The rows of C represent the factors $f_{.B}$, the columns of C represent the factors $f_{.A*}$. Matrix C can also be rewritten as

[1] A similar plot was suggested by Ahmavaara for an analogous problem arising in the transformation analysis.

$$C = \lambda_B{}'(B_o'B_o)^{-1}B_o'AD^{-1/2}$$

and since

$$\lambda_B = (B_o'B_o)^{-1}B_o'B$$

the right hand side can be further expanded to

$$C = B'B_o(B_o'B_o)^{-1}(B_o'B_o)^{-1}B_o'AD^{-1/2}$$

The Procrustes transformation is applicable to both orthogonal and oblique factors. The results as expressed in the final matrix C, however, are not independent of the direction of transformation. Suppose we wish to rotate alternatively the factors $f_{.B}$ into the space defined by the factors $f_{.Ao}$; our new matching matrix $\bar{C}$ with rows representing the factors $f_{.B*}$ and columns representing the factors $f_{.A}$, then becomes

$$\bar{C} = \bar{D}^{-1/2}B'A_o(A_o'A_o)^{-1}(A_o'A_o)^{-1}A_o'A$$

where $\bar{D}$ again denotes a diagonal matrix with elements equal to the diagonal elements in the product matrix obtained after premultiplying the new matrix λ_P by its transpose. From the expanded equations for C and $\bar{C}$ a comparison can be easily made between the alternative factor comparison matrices. We shall use (ℓ_A) and (ℓ_B) for the matrices of latent roots associated with the factors $f_{.A}$ and $f_{.B}$, and L_A and L_B for the matrices of latent vectors associated with the factors $f_{.A}$ and $f_{.B}$. If the factors $f_{.Ao}$ and $f_{.Bo}$ in each case represent principal axis factors, the two matrices C can be rewritten as follows:

$$C = \left[B'L_B(l_B)^{-1}L_B'A\right] D^{-1/2}$$

and

$$\bar{C} = \bar{D}^{-1/2}\left[B'L_A(l_A)^{-1}L_A'A\right]$$

Even if we make the assumption

$$D = \bar{D} = I^{1)}$$

---

[1] This is only fulfilled if $\lambda_{\dot{P}} = \lambda_P$; this condition will be met, if, and only if, B is a true rotational position from A_o and A a true rotational position from B_o, respectively.

C and $\bar{C}$ will only be identical if $L_A = L_B$ and $(l_A) = (l_B)$ which is hardly ever fulfilled with empirical data.

We have discussed the Procrustes transformation at some greater length since it was used considerably in our laboratory over the past years. The problem of non-identity of C and $\bar{C}$ actually never become a true problem in our own studies where there was always only one direction of transformation meaningful, since one of the two factor matrices was typically a "criterion matrix" (obtained from pooling the results of previous researches) and the second matrix constituted the results of a new research in the series.

(3) Kaiser's Method for Relating Factors.

In a recent publication Kaiser(117) discussed several of the available methods for identifying factors across studies and also described a new method for relating factors between studies that are based on different individuals. Given two sets of factors $f_{.A}$ and $f_{.B}$ Kaiser suggests a rigid transformation of both factor matrices that achieves an overall least squares fit between the two sets of factors in terms of the test vectors defining them. Geometrically this results in finding that simultaneous transformation of both sets $f_{.A}$ and $f_{.B}$ that will make the two corresponding sets of test vectors maximally congruent in the space of the study with higher number of dimensions. Having achieved this rotational aim, with the angular separation of corresponding test vectors in study A and study B being a minimum over all common test vectors, for any two factors f_{iA} and f_{jB} the cosine of the angle (which is again equivalent to their empirically unobservable correlation) between them in the larger of the two factor spaces can be determined. These cosine-values represent the final result of this factor identification technique, Kaiser's method for relating factors uses a rigid transformation of both matrices A and B, i.e., the factor-intercorrelations within each of the two studies are left untouched. The quality of over-all fit achieved by this rotation can finally be expressed in a simple index varying between 0 and 1.

The essentials of the mathematics involved in this method can be described briefly, for a more detailed account, however, the reader will have to consult Kaiser's original paper. To explain how a maximum spatial congruence of corresponding test vectors from both studies is sought, consider the case where research study B contains no more factors than study A (i.e., $s \leq r$), so that the s factors $f_{1B}, \ldots, f_{sB}$ will be projected into the r-dimensional space spanned by the factors $f_{1A}, \ldots, f_{rA}$. The desired criterion function for the rotation than becomes

$$\gamma = \sum_{i, j} f'_{iA} f_{jB}$$

(i.e., the sum of the inner products of the factor vectors), and the aim is to find that particular rigid transformation K of both A and B under which γ becomes a maximum. Kaiser's solution for K is

$$K = [(A'B)'(A'B)]^{-1}(A'B)' L (l) L'$$

where (l) and (L) denote the latent roots and vectors, respectively of the product matrix $[(A'B)(A'B)']$. The final factor identification matrix C (with rows representing the factors $f_{.A}$ and columns representing the factors $f_{.B}$) is obtained from

$$C = \lambda'_A K' \lambda_B$$

where λ_A and λ_B are the transformation matrices used in study A and B for obtaining A and B from the two centroid matrices A_o and B_o according to

$$A_o \cdot \lambda_A = A$$

$$B_o \cdot \lambda_B = B.$$

The elements of C are the cosines of the angle separating any two factors f_{iA} and f_{jB} in the common space spanned by the factors $f_{.A}$. By necessity[1] the matrix C, when computed according to the above formula, will always be normalized by rows. Thus, no inference about the absolute goodness of fit between $f_{.A}$ and $f_{.B}$ achieved after rotation K is possible from matrix C. Kaiser showed that the over-all goodness of fit can be expressed in the simple coefficient s, distributed theoretically between 0 and 1, which is given by the formula

$$s = \frac{1}{n} \text{trace} \left[H_A^{-1} A K' B' H_B^{-1} \right]$$

where H_A and H_B are diagonal matrices with elements equal to the square roots of the communalities of the n common tests used in studies A and B, respectively.

Kaiser's method can be used with orthogonal or oblique factors; in the latter case, however, either the orthogonal centroid matrices or the transformation matrices have to be known in order to carry out the above computations. If one of the two factor matrices is a "criterion matrix" of the kind that its elements are loadings averaged over a series of studies, Kaiser's method of relating factors cannot be readily used since no composite centroid or λ is feasible. If the factors in this criterion matrix, however, are known to be only slightly intercorrelated (near orthogonal) Kaiser's technique might still be used, treating the criterion matrix as orthogonal; this will result in an approximation to the true factor interrelationships that will still be helpful for identifying factors across the two matrices. At present no test of significance is available to test for the significance of factor matchings obtained from this method.

---

[1] Consider, for example, the case of $r = s = 2$.

(4) Tucker's Generalization of Kaiser's Method of Relating Factors.

Very recently L. Tucker (164) suggested what appears the most generalized procedure for identifying factors across studies. His approach is not limited to only two factor matrices A and B, but extends the problem of factor matching to N factor matrices (N independent researches) reduced to the n variables, common to all of them. The essential characteristics of Tucker's procedure can be most easily described for the case where only one factor from each of the N factor matrices is considered so that a matrix is obtained as outlined in table 3.5.

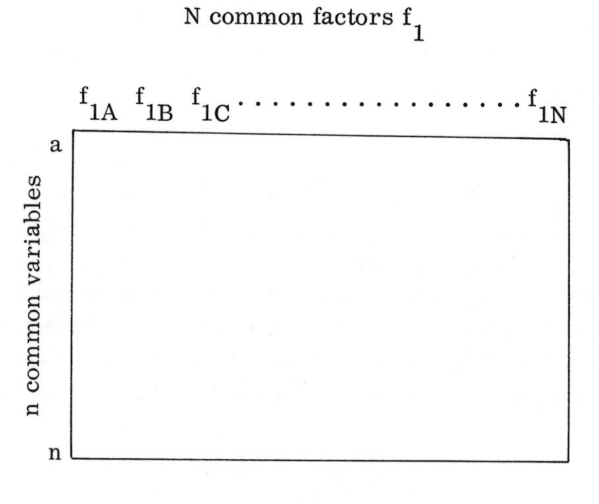

TABLE 3.5

A factor $f_{1.}$ has been selected from each of the N studies. The loadings of each factor on the same n variables are known. Thus the matrix contains N columns (N studies, each represented by one factor) and n rows (variables). We may regard this matrix for the moment as an ordinary analysis-of-variance table with N columns and n rows and a sample size of one per cell. It is easily understood that the higher the match between the N factors under consideration the smaller the mean square within rows will be relative to the mean square between rows. A transformation of the N factors that maximizes the over-all match will have to maximize at the same time a ratio G that can be defined as the ratio of the mean square within rows to the mean square between rows. On this basis a generalized procedure can be worked out for a simultaneous rotation of all N studies towards a maximum over-all match of factors between these studies.

Tucker also shows that for N = 2 studies his procedure will give results identical to Kaiser's solution for relating factors across studies, so that the former actually is a generalization of the latter for the case of more than two studies under comparison.

7. THE USE OF CRITERIA 3, 4, AND 6.

In the foregoing two sections various direct mathematical or statistical methods of factor matching have been reviewed. These methods seek an identification of factors between different studies either by directly comparing the loading pattern between any two factors f_{iA} and f_{jB} (techniques solely based upon the dimension-variable profile - section 5) or from projecting both sets of factors into the same space and assessing their closeness in space after rotation for maximum spatial congruence of corresponding test vectors of both studies (section 6).

The indirect methods of factor matching to be described in this section make use of criteria 3, 4, and 6 mentioned at the beginning of this chapter; thus they rely upon circumstantial or concomitant results of the factor analyses that might also guide towards a factor identification.

(1) Circumstantial Validity.

The term "circumstantial validity" was already introduced earlier in this chapter. Cattell originally (39) suggested the term circumstantial validity for describing a kind of validation procedure that does not attempt to relate one variable with a criterion variable, but in which two variables a and b, for instance, are compared with regard to their correlations with a set of other variables k to n. In so far the concept of circumstantial validity comes close to Brengelmann's (11) concept of internal validity. Applied to the problem of factor matching circumstantial validity means:

If in the set $f_{.A}$ only factor f_{1A} correlates highly positive with factor f_{2A}, which has already been shown to match with factor f_{4B}, another factor f_{3B} that correlates highly positive only with f_{4B} is more likely to match f_{1A} than any other factor f_{jB} that does not correlate with f_{4B}. The implicit assumption underlying the use of the circumstantial validity criterion for factor matching is that there are no serious systematic differences between the groups of subjects A and B so that in both studies the same factors would show the same pattern of factor inter-correlations.

(2) The Variance of a Factor.

Knowing that a particular factor will be present in both studies under comparison and that it will also show the same variance in both groups (as in the case where it is known that the subjects have not been differently selected for this factor in the two groups) the latent root associated with this factor should be equal in both studies within random sampling differences. If it is known, for instance, for study A that the "strongest" factor obtained from factoring the variables a to n is a factor of general intelligence, one will try the hypothesis that the "strongest" factor in the factor analysis B of the same variables a to n is also a factor of general intelligence. Ordering the factors found in both studies according to the latent roots associated with them will provide such a first guide towards factor identification between the two studies.

(3) Factor Identification on the Basis of the Occurrence of Expected Group Differences.

The more research becomes available in a particular variable domain the more knowledge also accumulates on systematic differences between different populations of subjects, in terms of either factor structure or statistical characteristics of factor score distribution. Thus it may be known that a particular factor f_1 shows higher variance in psychotics than nonpsychotic subjects, or a factor f_2 may typically show a certain change in its loading pattern on a standard set of marker variables when changing from non-psychotic to psychotic subjects. In comparing two such groups it is therefore possible to hypothesize certain factor identifications between the two groups from the occurrence of these expected differences between factors present in both studies. The increasing amount of information that is made available by the intensive factor analytic research in several variable domains will make this criterion more helpful and important for future factor identification.

At present these indirect statistical methods for factor matching will often be able to serve only an auxiliary function in factor matching, such as a further substantiation of a match already indicated on direct analytical grounds, etc. Matchings, on the other hand, that first emerged from the use of these indirect methods will still have to be submitted to one of the direct statistical matching procedures. However, with our knowledge becoming more and more comprehensive in the field of human behavior dimensions the usefulness of these indirect methods will continuously increase. Since the more sensitive direct statistical matching methods are generally cumbersome computationwise, it is often desirable to reduce the number of factors that have to be submitted to such a procedure right from the beginning, once some factors could already be identified on other grounds. It is not unlikely that the indirect matching methods will become more and more useful in serving this very purpose of establishing factor matches on the described grounds of circumstantial evidence before the remaining, so far unidentified, factors are submitted to an analytical matching procedure.

8. SUMMARY AND DISCUSSION.

Among the various methods we discussed in this chapter of relating factors found in two different studies on the basis of the same test variables but with different samples of subjects, the direct statistical-mathematical--or, in short, analytical -- techniques discussed in sections 5 and 6 are presumably regarded as the more prominent ones. In section 7 we mentioned briefly some indirect -- and often mainly auxiliary -- statistical methods of factor identification which are based upon the criteria 3, 4, and 6 listed previously (p. 27). The experimental techniques of factor matching, discussed at the beginning of this chapter (p. 27), have as yet been used only very rarely, and apart from their importance in certain special cases of factor identification (such as in the case where the two studies A and B did not only employ different subjects but also have no tests in common) these methods are mathematically less precise than the analytical techniques and typically better suited to the task of exploring the psychological nature of a factor rather than to the aim of factor identification.

Before closing this chapter on factor matching procedures we would like, however, to point out several pitfalls the multivariate experimenter might run into when applying these techniques without watching out rather carefully. In the main there are three such pitfalls: mistaking systematic differences in subject population between the compared studies for indications of a poor factor match, the question of the over-all factor match between two researches, and the problem of how to deal properly with oblique factors.

(1) The Impact of Systematic Population Differences on Factor Matching Results.

Essentially, all analytical methods for matching factors between two researches A and B make the important implicit assumption that the subjects used in the two studies can be regarded as two random samples from the same population. Therefore, factors that match completely between both studies should also show loading patterns that differ only within the range of sampling errors -- assuming that the same criterion for rotation has been used in both studies. Very seldom, however, this ideal case will be fulfilled or even approximated in actual cross-studies factor matching. To the contrary, often the experimenter will choose subjects deliberately from two different populations for the two studies (such as neurotics and normals, children and adults, etc.) with the aim of investigating the stability of a given factor structure over such changes in subject population. On the other hand, if the two samples of subjects A and B are not random samples from the same population, when comparing factors between both studies we would not only expect differences in the loading patterns due to random sampling effects but also systematic differences due to the true psychological differences between both samples of subjects. Systematic differences of that kind are likely to effect one or all of the following parameters:

a) reliability and communality of the variables,
b) latent roots associated with the factors (the relative "strength" of the various factors), and
c) intercorrelations of the factors within each study.

These possibilities will be briefly discussed in the following paragraphs.

(1) If the same variable a has a reliability of +.91 in study A and of +.58 in study B the communality h^2 of this variable is most likely to differ between A and B proportionally. Furthermore, this variable may contribute the highest loading on factor f_{iA} and only a medium loading on factor f_{jB}. Consequently the Burt-Tucker-Wrigley coefficient (see p. 36), for instance, when computed for f_{iA} and f_{jB}, would unduly underestimate the true relationship between these two factors. Before applying this and other analytic matching techniques one therefore should check on each variable for possible differences in reliability or communality between both studies, and apply an appropriate correction of the factor loadings whenever such differences become apparent.

(2) Even if in both groups the same factors are operant, the latent root associated with a particular factor might be different in the two factor analytic solutions. A variable x having its highest loading on factor f_{iA} is less likely to have its highest loading also on factor f_{jB}, if f_{iA} and f_{jB} are a true match, but the latent root of f_{jB} is considerably lower than the latent root of f_{iA}.

(3) Using oblique rotational procedures the two factor solutions under comparison might especially differ in terms of the within-study factor inter-correlation matrices. Two factors might be cooperative factors (29) in one study but not cooperative in the other, or in one research the best simple structure may be a generally more oblique position than in the other research.

At present these possibilities are not generally taken into account when factor matching between different studies is attempted. Elsewhere Cattell (39) has shown in a practical example how important it is to consider such group differences before interpreting the results of any of the above described direct statistical methods for factor identification.

Both Thomson (158) and Thurstone (162) have given classical accounts of the effects of (partial or complete) univariate and multivariate selection of subjects on the final factor analytic results--effects of which the aforementioned ones are only typical and important examples. We cannot regard the factor identification problem as solved until more powerful analytical matching procedures are developed that can take such selection effects into account.

(2) The Over-All Factor Match Between Two Researches.

Given two factor analytic solutions for the same variables, but obtained with different subjects, usually we are not only interested in the best possible pairwise match of factors $f_{.A}$ and $f_{.B}$ but also want to know to what extent the two solutions match in general. Neither of the techniques described in sections 5 and 7 can give a clear answer to this question, only methods that take the spatial representation of the two solutions into account (i.e., the methods discussed in section 6) provide an answer. In the transformation analysis this answer is obtained from the difference matrix $(A \cdot \lambda - B)$, in the Procrustes transformation from the difference matrix $(A^* - B)$, in Kaiser's and Tucker's method the coefficient s expresses the degree of this over-all match between the set $f_{.A}$ and set $f_{.B}$.

In view of the various problems associated with the question of factor identification it is desirable to know the degree of general match of both sets of factors for each comparison of two studies. This would argue that each time at least one of the methods described in section 6 of this chapter should be used.

(3) Special Problems Encountered with Oblique Factors.

Many of the factor identification methods are applicable to both orthogonal and oblique factors. But even if a certain method can be used with oblique factors, special problems are met in interpreting the final matching matrix C. To illustrate these problems let us consider the small example presented in table 3.6.

	f_{1A}	f_{2A}	f_{3A}
f_{1A}	+1.0	+.1	+.4
f_{2A}	+.1	+1.0	-.4
f_{3A}	+.4	-.4	+1.0

Table 6A

	f_{1B}	f_{2B}	f_{3B}
f_{1B}	+1.0	+.2	+.5
f_{2B}	+.2	+1.00	-.3
f_{3B}	+.5	-.3	+1.0

Table 6B

	f_{1B}	f_{2B}	f_{3B}
f_{1A}	+.8		
f_{2A}			+.7
f_{3A}		+.8	

Table 6C

TABLE 3.6

The two small tables 6 A and 6 B show the intercorrelations between three primary factors, table 6 A for the three primaries found in study A, table 6 B for the three primaries found in study B. We shall assume that the true match between the two sets of factors is as described in table 6 C; only the cosines of the angle separating matching factors have been recorded.

Given the information of tables 6 A through 6 C, elementary statistics as well as geometry teach us that for each blank cell in table 6 C we can work out a range within which this particular cosine value (or correlation) will have to lie. The reader familiar with these methods will immediately realize that this is only possible because both sets of primary factors are oblique, i.e., correlated within the studies. And this is the point where the matching problem with oblique factors arises: Even if f_{1A} matches only f_{1B} and is 'in nature' uncorrelated with both f_{2B} and f_{3B}, matrix C will show correlations between f_{1A} and both f_{2B} and f_{3B} if $f_{.A}$ and $f_{.B}$ are oblique, and the size of these "conditional" correlations will depend on the degree of obliquity present in the two studies. Thus, in the example presented in tables 3.6, f_{3A} is likely to correlate positively with f_{1A}, etc.

The solution of this problem has an important bearing on the second question usually arising with matching oblique factors between different studies: Which one of the four matrices available after rotation for oblique simple structure (reference vector structure V_{rs}, reference vector pattern V_{rp}, primary factor structure V_{fs}, primary factor pattern V_{fp})[1] should be used for factor identification? Or in other words: When we previously discussed the "factor matrices" A and B which one of these four "factor matrices" is meant by A and B in the previous formulae if the factors are oblique? The answer to this question is contingent upon a solution for the above stated problem in interpreting the matching matrix C.

In order to draw correct inferences from the factor matching matrix C we seek that transformation of the oblique factors which will partial out from each factor f_{iA} all variance it shares with the remaining factors $f_{.A}$ and from each factor f_{jB} all variance it shares with the remaining factors $f_{.B}$. In other words, we want to express the subject's scores on factor f_{iA} as part scores, with all other factors $f_{.A}$ partialled out (and similarly for factor f_{jB}), so that the correlation between f_{iA} and f_{jB} in the new matching matrix C will be their "true" or "net" correlation, no longer influenced by the within-study factor intercorrelations. Using such part scores for the factors $f_{.A}$ and $f_{.B}$ in the above example (where a given factor f_{iA} correlates with one and only one factor f_{jB}), the matching matrix C would actually contain zeroes for the cells left blank. With empirical data there still will be only a few zeroes in matrix C; these correlations, however, are then no longer due to the obliquity of the factors but represent "true" relationships between a certain factor f_{iA} and several factors $f_{.B}$.[2]

As can be readily shown, and was pointed out recently by White (169) the desired transformation of the primary factors is directly available, the trans-

---

[1] For a discussion of the properties of these matrices see (23, 39, 104)

[2] Practical experience has shown, that finding the appropriate matches between $f_{.A}$ and $f_{.B}$ will then no longer be difficult - granted that there is in principle a one-to-one relationship between factors $f_{.A}$ and $f_{.B}$; a match between any two factors f_{iA} and f_{jB} should only be accepted, if f_{jB} is the best match for f_{iA} and simultaneously f_{iA} is the best match for f_{jB} - or in other words, if reading matrix C by rows and by columns independently results in the same factor identifications.

formed coordinates being the reference vectors: A reference vector v_{iA} represents that portion of the variance of factor f_{iA} which is uncorrelated with the remaining factors $f_{.A}$ and thus represents the desired part-scores on f_{iA}. Using, therefore, reference vector matrices instead of primary factor matrices for A and B will yield a matching matrix C which gives the cross-studies correlations between the two sets of primary factors with the remaining primary factors partialled out within each study.

It is this property of the reference vectors which strongly suggests not employing the factor pattern or factor structure matrices for relating factors between studies. From the two available reference vector matrices, the reference vector pattern and the reference vector structure, the latter should be chosen; it contains for each variable the cosine of the angle separating it from (or its correlation with) each of the reference vectors, which is the information needed for determining the spatial closeness of both sets of reference vectors $v_{.A}$ and $v_{.B}$.

In our own applications of factor identification procedures we consequently have always used reference vector structure matrices for A and B in the above formulae. We regard this as essential when dealing with oblique factors in order to allow for correct inferences from the matching matrix C.

CHAPTER 4

DESCRIPTION OF PREVIOUS STUDIES

CRITERIA OF SELECTION OF STUDIES

Any attempt to synthesize and summarize factor analytic research in regard to personality dimensions is a formidable task. Nevertheless it is the view expressed in this monograph that the time has now come when the initial blind exploratory phase in such research should begin to give way to more sensitive and specific approaches to established dimensions of personality. Research along these lines must, for optimal scientific advancement, be cognizant of relevant details from previous studies. It is our purpose to bring together this information in a manner both detailed enough to serve as a reference source for future research and as a comprehensive summary for the general reader. However it is beyond the scope of this monograph to attempt to synthesize all of the results from previous factor-analytic studies of personality. The specific aim, therefore, has been to present in some detail results from studies satisfying the following criteria.

a. The research must be concerned principally, if not entirely, with objective tests. By an objective test we mean a measure that is both objectively scored and is minimally 'fakable'. Thus in terms of lack of fakability a test should either elicit from the subject a response over which he has little or no voluntary control (e.g., the psychogalvanic skin response) or be a test in which the manifest content is of little relevance to the actual measure of interest to the psychologist (e.g., speed of response in an opinionnaire concerning social issues). Adhering rigidly to this criterion we have excluded all studies involving questionnaire or self-rating devices, in which the main concern is response to content, except where such devices are shown to be relevant to the interpretation of personality dimensions derived from objective tests. A fuller discussion of objective tests may be found elsewhere (32) (151).

b. The research must include a high proportion of variables in common with other factor analytic studies of personality. A constant problem to be faced in any survey of factor analytic research is that of factor identification across a series of studies. The methods and techniques of factor identification now available have been discussed in the previous chapter, and it was pointed out that where different subjects are used from study to study, no quantitative method of identification can be applied without the inclusion of common variables. This criterion stresses the need for the establishment of personality structure through repeatedly confirmed and replicated dimensions, and relationships between such dimensions.

c. The research should contain a wide sampling from the domain of personality measurement. Our concern is with basic personality dimensions that will account for the covariation of personality measures in general, and such dimensions have best opportunity to emerge in unequivocal form when a wide sampling of variables is taken. Limiting the variables to, say, perceptual measures, physiological measures, or purely paper and pencil measures, makes for difficulties in interpreting the relation of any resulting factors to the broader source traits of personality.

d. The studies should involve comparable experimental designs and statistical treatment. The general factor-analytic procedure that has been adopted is as follows: (a) subjects have been tested on a wide range of measures; (b) product moment correlations have been computed, and the resulting correlation matrix factored using the multiple-group, centroid, or principal axes method; (c) the resulting factors have been rotated obliquely to simple structure without regard, or intent to obtain, some predetermined solution. Thus studies involving orthogonal factors, e.g., Guilford (100), or such methods as criterion-analysis, e.g., Eysenck (85), have been excluded from detailed examination. Discussion of the relative merits and demerits of different rotational procedures is available (18) (104) and is not of immediate concern for this chapter. Nevertheless we may emphasize our own position by affirming the belief that only through 'blind' oblique rotation to simple structure, out of the techniques presently available, can the most parsimonious and theoretically acceptable personality dimensions be determined.

The final number of studies selected with regard to the above criteria is quite small, relative to the field as a whole. Thus much good research has received little coverage and the reader must turn elsewhere for such information (91) (100). However, this loss is compensated for by the added clarity and lack of ambiguity that has resulted from such selection.

DISCUSSION OF STUDY DESCRIPTIONS

Chapters 6, 7, and 8 give results from studies selected according to the above criteria. The present chapter, and that following, are devoted to a summary description of these studies. Each study is described under the following headings: (a) subjects, (b) variables, (c) design and method of analysis, (d) identification of factors. In all cases, reference has been made to published material, except in certain cases where the exigencies of space-allotment in professional journals has required us to go farther back to the original data (where this is still available). In order to facilitate the reader's journey through these two chapters, the headings and general content of the study descriptions need some discussion.

A. SUBJECTS: Here are outlined full available details of the sample composition. This involves the number of subjects, sex, age, occupation, educational level, and the like. There is a certain variability in the fullness of this information but in all cases there should be sufficient for most purposes of later researchers.

B. VARIABLES: At this point a basic distinction must be made between a test and a variable. A test refers to the specific vehicle of measurement, e.g., T9 PERSONAL OPINION INVENTORY (a 100 item opinionnaire with Likert-type response alternatives), T 13 KNOWLEDGE OF PERSONAL CHARACTERISTICS (a general fluency test with 32 sections). A variable, on the other hand is the particular method of scoring the test adopted in order to best measure the concept in which the psychologist is interested. For example variable MI. 152 "tendency to agree" is the sum of the agree or strongly agree responses made to T9; variable MI. 193a is a measure of the shift of opinion from one time of responding to the T9 items to another time of responding to the same items (the second time having printed suggestions as to 'desirable' responses). The general fluency test T13 may be scored for such variables as MI. 53 "ratio of self-criticism to self-approval" and MI. 763, which is over-all fluency on all topics. Thus there will tend to be far more variables than tests, as the test name is simply that for the total test stimulus situation confronting the subject, while the variables are the several ways of scoring his responses.

All tests are given T (Test) numbers, while all variables are given MI. (Master Index) numbers, according to a system developed by Cattell (29). A full account of objective tests and their attendant variables is given in a compendium of objective test measurement by Cattell and Warburton (71).

In all descriptions of studies occurring in this and the following chapter reference is made to objective test variables solely in terms of MI. numbers. It should be clear to the reader that the test itself is not of prime concern, but the test numbers can be obtained from Chapters 11 and 12, and Appendices B, C, and D, with the book by Cattell and Warburton (71) giving further details. Whenever variables which do not have MI. numbers have been used in a study, their verbal title is given in full. The verbal titles for all MI. numbers referred to in this monograph also appear in Appendices A and B.

Slight discrepancies between the MI. numbers as listed here and those appearing in the original publications are due to a recent revision of the MI. system (71). However in all cases inspection of the verbal titles will show the variables to be the same. In all cases the more recent MI. system as presented here, and by Cattell and Warburton (71), should be used in any future research.

C. DESIGN AND METHOD OF ANALYSIS: The studies fall into two natural groups, (a) those that employ factor analytic techniques directly to a set of variables, and (b) those that use estimated factor scores or extension analyses (83) (132) in order to examine the association between personality factors and some other set of variables, or to test hypotheses concerning the factors and certain criterion groups. Another way of expressing this is to say that the first group allows for emergence of factors not determined prior to the study, while in the second group the factors are determined and it is their relationship to other variables that is of interest.

The first group requires little comment, except to say that communality estimates are used and the number of factors to be extracted is decided by one or more of several tests for completeness of extraction.[1] In each case the factorization is followed by oblique rotation to simple structure. In more recent studies Bargmann's (6) test for simple structure has been used. Each study description in which factor analysis is involved includes the percentage of variables within the ±.10 hyperplane.

Included in the second group are extension analyses and correlational or experimental studies utilizing factor score estimates in which factor analysis, as such, is not directly employed. By an extension analysis is meant that by using the same sample of subjects correlations may be obtained between factors from an original factor analysis and variables not included in the original factorization[2] (132). This occurs when the experimenter has the results of a factor analysis upon his subjects and is further interested in the relationship of the factors to some specific variable domain. The remainder of the non-factor analytic studies employ factor estimates based upon weighted composites of the salient variables identifying a factor. In many studies these composites are derived from the 1955 Objective-Analytic Battery (27).

Thus a quite common design is to obtain estimated factor scores for each subject and then to correlate these estimated factor scores with criteria of success in different occupational or educational fields, or with classification into clinical categories. Such correlations may be, and often are, expressed in terms of Students 't' ratio.

D. IDENTIFICATION OF FACTORS: The personality dimensions regarded as confirmed over a series of studies have been given U.I. (Universal Index) numbers (30). U.I. 1 is general intelligence, U.I. 2 through U.I. 15 are ability factors, while U.I. 16 through U.I. 36 are more strictly personality or temperamental factors. It is with these last twenty-one factors that we shall be principally concerned. In the factor analysis studies, which appear in the next part of this chapter, each U.I. factor identified in any given study is presented with its column number in the final rotated reference vector structure matrix. In each case the U.I. factors are those identified by the authors of the study from the data then available, and these include even factors regarded as only tentative matches with U.I. factors.

---

[1] Considerably more tests for completeness of factor extraction are now available (153) than at the time when many of these studies were carried out.

[2] In some cases extension analyses have been included with the description of a particular factor analysis. This has occurred when both are included in the same journal article and when the extension variables are not clearly demarked from the factor-analysis variables in terms of content.

DESCRIPTION OF STUDIES: I FACTOR ANALYTIC STUDIES

Th Thornton, G. R. "A Factor Analysis of Tests Designed to Measure Persistence" (1939) (159)

The purpose of this research was to obtain the factor-analytic structure of different measures of persistence.

SUBJECTS: One hundred and eighty-nine undergraduates served as subjects, 135 being male and 54 being female. All but 40 subjects fell within the age range of 18 to 22 years.

VARIABLES: Twenty-two variables were used in all, each of which appeared to exhibit aspects of persistence, and appear in Table 4.1.

Table 4.1: Variables Used in Study Th

MI 45a	MI. 64	MI. 506	MI. 773

Longer total time in breath-holding
More time spent in practicing in aiming test
Shorter distance traced in motor inhibition test
Longer time spent on perceptual ability test
More material read in perceptual ability test
Longer time spent on word building test
Larger number of familiar words written in word building test
Longer total time on pressure test
Longer total time of maintained hand grip
Higher score on Wang Questionnaire on persistence
Higher self-rating on persistence
Higher verbal score on Revised Army Alpha Test
Higher total score for hand grip
Longer time spent on verbal recognition test
Longer reading time in perceptual ability test
Longer time in word construction
Higher self-rating on self-confidence
Higher ascendance score in Allport A-S Reaction Study

DESIGN AND METHOD OF ANALYSIS: R-technique factor analysis was followed, using the centroid method. Six factors were extracted, at which point the residuals were judged as negligible. Eighteen rotations to simple structure were made, approximately 54% of the variables were within the ±.10 hyperplane.

IDENTIFICATION OF FACTORS: Thornton's factors were identified tentatively as F1 (+): withstanding discomfort to achieve a goal (WD), F2 (+): keeping on at a task (PL), F3 (+): sex-strength, F4 (+): feeling of adequacy, F5 (+): mental fluency. The sixth factor was not interpreted. F3 (-) has been interpreted in the Universal Index series as U.I. 22.

Re Rethlingshafer, D. "Relationship of Tests of Persistence to Other Measures of Continuance of Activities" (1942) (143)

SUBJECTS: Thirty-eight undergraduates from the University of North Carolina. The range of intelligence quotients on the Otis Group test was from 99 to 133.

VARIABLES: Twenty-nine variables were used in this study, and appear in Table 4.2.

Table 4.2: Variables Used in Study Re

MI 773 MI 8 MI 506 MI 70

Higher score on anagrams test
Longer time taken on first 10 words of anagram test
Longer time taken on anagrams test
Higher correct score in story reading
Longer time taken to complete first three paragraphs of story-reading
Longer time taken before "giving up" on story-reading
More motor inhibition (Downey Group Will-Temperament Test, adapted)
Longer time of breath holding
Greater strength of grip
Persistence of maintained grip (I)
Persistence of maintained grip (II)
Higher rating on scale of persistence
Faster tempo of tapping
Greater effect of slower intervening rate on tapping tempo I
Greater effect of slower intervening rate on tapping tempo II
Greater ability to shift set
Higher score on Maller and Elkin Attention Test
Larger number of "no" answers from Maller and Elkin Attention Test
Longer time for thermal equilibrium (right and left hands)
Much effect of interruption upon activity
Greater Zeigarnik effect
Higher score, Otis Self-Administering Test, Form A
Higher score, Thurstone's scale on attitude toward constitution
Higher score, Thurstone's scale on attitude toward Communism

DESIGN AND METHOD OF ANALYSIS: The general procedure was R-technique. Seven factors were extracted and rotated. Thirty-three percent of the variables lie between the ±.10 hyperplane bounds.

IDENTIFICATION OF FACTORS: The following interpretations were given for the factors: F1: habit of keeping on at a task once started, F2: physiological inertia, F3: endurance, F4: sex-strength, F5: intelligence, F6: radical-conservatism (?), F7: natural tempo. Similarities between the results of Rethlingshafer's and Thornton's studies have been discussed (18), and Rethlingshafer's F4(-) has been regarded as a precursor of U.I. 22 (+).

T Thurstone, L. L. "A Factorial Study of Perception" (1944) (161)

SUBJECTS: The total number of subjects was 194, most being undergraduate volunteers from the University of Chicago.

VARIABLES: Sixty scores were obtained from each subject, 43 of which were used in a factor analysis. The remaining 17 variables showed relatively low correlations with measures from other tests. All variables appear in Table 4.3.

Table 4.3: Variables Used in Study T

A. Variables Used in the Factor Analysis

MI 7	MI 206	MI 197	MI 64	MI 10
MI 71[1]	MI 94	MI 41	MI 8	

Faster speed of closure (multilated words)
Faster speed of letter comparison
Faster speed of social judgment
Faster speed of gestalt closure (dotted outlines)
Faster speed of closure (hidden digits)
Greater brightness constancy
Wider peripheral visual span
Greater dominance of form over color (Schmidt Ratio)
Larger number of alternatives (Schmidt)
Less brightness contrast
Larger number of different movements perceived in Windmill Illusion
Larger number of alternatives in Windmill Illusion
More illusory perception (Sanders)
More illusory perception (Titchener circle)
More illusory perception (Poggendorff)

[1] Reaction time to light and sound appear as separate variables in Thurstone's tables, but for present purposes they are joined together.

Table 4.3: Variables Used in Study T (Cont)

More illusory perception (Muller Lyer)
More illusory perception (Ehrenstein Square)
More illusory perception (size-weight)
Longer time of decision (size-weight illusion)
Longer time of decision (color-form sorting)
Higher number correct (difficult Gottschaldt figures)
Greater amount of retinal rivalry
Greater shape constancy
Slower speed on mirror tracking
Lower score (Koh's Block Designs)
Higher score, P.M.A. (space Factor S)
Higher score, P.M.A. (Verbal Comprehension Factor V)
Higher score, P.M.A. (Number Factor N)
Higher score, P.M.A. (Word Fluency Factor W)
Higher score, P.M.A. (Reasoning Factor R)
Better memory for both color and form combined
Larger total number of Rorschach responses
Greater tendency to perceive Rorschach stimuli as united wholes

B. Variables Not used in Factor Analysis

MI 39 MI 268

Higher ratio of decision time or easy versus difficult circle size comparisons
Greater preference for favorable than unfavorable social traits
More apparent movement (autokinetic effect)
Higher ratio of form to color recall
Higher Flicker-Fusion frequency (Blue Yellow)
Longer time of spiral after movement
Greater size constancy
Less color-word interference (Stroop ratio)
Higher proportion of social to physical word associations
More weight suggestibility
Rorschach C/D responses
More movement responses (Rorschach)
Rorschach Weight-color
Longer Rorschach C/D time
Longer Rorschach Total time
Longer time of spiral after movement

DESIGN AND METHOD OF ANALYSIS. This study utilizes R-technique, and the factor analysis was made by the multiple-group method. Eleven factors were extracted, and the root mean square of the residual correlations indicated that several residual factors were to be expected. The factors were rotated to simple structure using extended vectors. The final rotated factor matrix showed 66% of the variables to be within the ±.10 hyperplane.

IDENTIFICATION OF FACTORS: Thurstone's perceptual factors were identified as follows:

Factor A: facility in perceptual closure
Factor B: tendency to perceive geometrical designs illusions
Factor C: reaction time
Factor D: oscillation of perception of ambiguous stimuli
Factor E: ability to manipulate two or more configurations simultaneously
Factor F: speed of perception
Factor G: general intelligence
Factor H: (not interpreted with confidence)
Factor J: speed of judgment
Factor K: Rorschach doublet
Factor L: (Residual Factor)

Later work in the temperamental sphere has suggested that factors C, E, and F(-) may be U.I. 22, U.I. 19, and U.I. 17, respectively, as the latter appear in analyses of perception variables.

C_1 Cattell, R. B. "Primary Personality Factors in the Realm of Objective Tests" (1948) (19)

The purpose was to map the dimensional structure of personality in terms of objective tests, bearing in mind for choice of variables (i) personality factors from other measurement media, and (ii) factors emerging previously from analysis of objective tests.

SUBJECTS: Three hundred and seventy college students were tested in this study; one hundred and thirty being male and two hundred and forty being female. All subjects were "slightly selected for psychological interest, indigence, dependability, and leisure, scattered over many academic fields."

VARIABLES: In all one hundred tests were administered to these subjects. A factor analysis of fifty of these measures (including two random variables) is described in the present study. A factor analysis of the remaining variables is reported in C_2. The forty-eight objective test variables used in C_1 appear in table 4.5

Table 4.5: Variables Used in C_1

	MI		
11a	16	27	43
2a, d, g	35	42	22b
1	45a	32	24h
4	28	46b	26
3	21	29	44
6a	9	30	36
7	8	18	40
10	41	33	23a
13a, b, c	14	17	48
31	5	16d	37
12	39	47	19
20a	25	38a	34

DESIGN AND METHOD OF ANALYSIS. The general method was R-technique analysis. The correlation matrix was factored by Thurstone's grouping method (162), the communalities being estimated by Medland's (162) method. Twelve factors were extracted of which only eleven were used for rotation. Tucker's criterion (160) indicated ten factors, and the eleventh factor reduced to a residual during rotation. Eighty-four percent of the variables were obtained between the ±.10 bounds of the hyperplane.

IDENTIFICATION OF FACTORS: The following personality factors were identified: U.I. 16 (1-), U.I. 17 (2+), U.I. 18 (5-), U.I. 19 (7-), U.I. 20 (3+), U.I. 21 (8+), U.I. 22 (4-), U.I. 23 (10+), U.I. 29 (9+). The sixth factor was identified as general intelligence and the eleventh as a residual without significant loadings.

C_2 Cattell, R. B. "A Factorization of Tests of Personality Source Traits" (1951) (22)

This study was a continuation of the research program initiated in C_1.

SUBJECTS: Four hundred and ten college students served as subjects, one hundred and thirty being male and two hundred and eight being female. The average age was 20 years. With the exception of an extra forty male students, the subjects were the same as those studied in C_1.

VARIABLES: Scores on sixty-four tests were available for these students, twenty-two (two per factor) being marker variables carried over from C_1 study. These sixty-four variables appear in table 4.6.

Table 4.6: Variables Used in C_2

MI			
1	37	58	73
2a, d, g	38a	59	74
3	39	60	75
4	41	61	76
5	42	62	77
8	43	63	78
11a	49b	64	79
9	50	65	80
13a, b, c	51	66	86
14	52	67a	81
21	53	68	46a, b
22b	54	88	82
27	55	69	83
34	56	70	84a
35	57	71	90
36	87	72	85

DESIGN AND METHOD OF ANALYSIS: The general method was R-technique analysis. The matrix of correlations was factored by the multiple group centroid method (162). A test of residuals indicated eleven factors, and such was the number extracted. The factors were rotated for simple structure, the eventual rotated reference vector structure matrix showing 57% of the variables to be within the ±.10 hyperplane.

IDENTIFICATION OF FACTORS: The following personality factors were identified, U.I. 16 (3-), U.I. 17 (4+), U.I. 18 (10-), U.I. 19 (5+), U.I. 20 (1+), U.I. 21 (7+), U.I. 22 (6+), U.I. 23 (8+), U.I. 29 (9+).

Factor 2 was identified as general intelligence, factor 10 as being associated with rigidity and low energy, and factor 11 was not identified.

E_2 Eysenck, H. J. "Schizothymia - Cyclothymia as a Dimension of Personality" (1952) (86)

Study E_2 concerns the testing of hypotheses concerning (1) a psychotic-normal continuum, and (2) a schizothyme-cyclothyme continuum.

SUBJECTS: The subjects were 100 normals (soldiers), 50 schizophrenics and 50 manic depressive hospital patients. The average age for the normals was 21 years, for the schizophrenes 28 years, and for the manic-depressives 46 years. All of the normals, 48% of the schizophrenes, and 50% of the manic-depressives, were male.

VARIABLES: Ninety scores were obtained from the subjects, but only 20 measures (see Table 4.7) were reserved for the final analysis. Selection of the 20 tests was made on the basis of size of intercorrelations and experimental independence.

Table 4.7: Variables Used in Study E_2

MI 268	MI 320	MI 8	MI 42

*MI 271 Higher fluency (names of animals)
*MI 67 More neutral responses on questionnaire
*MI 6 Faster speed of reading aloud
*MI 167 Better memory for letters
*MI 1247 Larger size of myokinesis (length of diagonal of squares)
*MI 199 Lower score on work curve (poorest row of addition)
*MI 33 Greater length of writing figures
More over-estimation of distance judgments
Longer time in drawing circles
Better memory for numbers
More alternations in reversible perspective under "don't reverse" instructions
Longer time judged for Track Tracer Test
Larger diameter of coin size estimation
Longer average wave-length of waves
Higher average amplitude of waves
Faster writing speed under "slow" instructions

*Variables marked with an asterisk come from tests that show certain differences in either content or scoring from the M.I. list in Appendices 3 and 4, and therefore both M.I. number and verbal description are given.

DESIGN AND METHOD OF ANALYSIS: The general method used in E_2 is R-technique but modified to accommodate 'criterion analysis.' Two centroid factors were extracted and rotated to maximum correlation with the two criteria. Although not relevant to the purpose of criterion analysis, (there being no concern for simple structure) the percentage of variables within the $\pm.10$ bounds of the hyperplane (normal group only) is 22%.

IDENTIFICATION OF FACTORS: Eysenck's first factor (F1): Psychoticism appears to have a match with U.I. 25: Tense Inflexidia, while F2 has been matched with U.I. 21: Exuberance.

E_3 Eysenck, H. J. "The Scientific Study of Personality" Ch. IV (1952) (87)

Study E_3 forms part of Eysenck's general approach to personality measurement (87), and only a "bare-bones" summary, as required for our present purposes in this chapter, will be presented.

SUBJECTS: The subjects were 96 normal male soldiers[1] with good disciplinary records, and with I.Q.s (estimated from scores on the matrices test of intelligence) of 90 or above.

VARIABLES: Twenty-eight measures obtained on each subject were used in a factor analysis. These variables are listed in Table 4.8.

Table 4.8: Variables Used in Study E_3

MI 277	MI 41	MI 28	MI 167	MI 211a	MI 194
MI 10	MI 42	MI 122			

Higher score on Matrices
Better concentration (numbers)
Better concentration (letters)
Better dexterity (M)
Better dexterity (N)
Better dexterity (O)
More scatter in tapping
Higher score on Mill Hill Vocabulary Test
Higher score on Crown Word Connectrai List
Higher score on Maudsley Medical Questionnaire
Higher score on MMPI Hysteria Scale (MMQ)
Higher O score on MMPI
Higher score on test of worries
Larger number of things disliked
Larger number of things liked
Faster speed of writing symbols
Greater influence of suggestion admitted
Larger number of verbal failures in Association Test
More right hand motor disturbances

[1] A somewhat larger group was actually tested, but the correlation matrix, in general, is based upon an N of 96.

DESIGN AND METHOD OF ANALYSIS: The general procedure herein used was R-technique, but leading to criterion analysis (85). Five centroid factors were extracted and rotated to the neurotic-normal criterion. Although simple structure is not the criterion of rotation an average of 27% of the variables lie within the ±.10 hyperplane.

IDENTIFICATION OF FACTORS: F1 was identified (by definition) as 'neuroticism.' Other factor interpretations were tentative: F2 as a verbal-nonverbal test dichotomy, and F3 as an unidentified intellectual factor. Factors 4 and 5 were not interpreted. U.I. 23 is matched with F1, neuroticism, for reasons outlined in Chapter 7.

Me Meeland, T. "An Investigation of Hypotheses for Distinguishing Personality Factors A, F and H." (1952) (130)

The aim was to clarify and extend knowledge of the concept of extraversion as associated with scales A, F and H of the 16 P.F.

SUBJECTS: The subjects were 102 male undergraduates of the University of Illinois. All were volunteers and members of fraternities.

VARIABLES: Fifty-one variables were used in this study (including a random variable). It should be noted that measures were taken from rather more widely dispersed domains than is usual in factor analysis. The full list of variables is presented below in Table 4.9.

Table 4.9: Variables Used in Me

MI 21(i)	MI 21 (ii)[1]	MI 34	MI 336	MI 26
MI 25a	MI 301	MI 302	MI 303	MI 171
MI 8	MI 110	MI 38	MI 304	MI 487
MI 486	MI 485	MI 122	MI 443	MI 84b
MI 77	MI 43	MI 5	MI 4	MI 74
MI 626	MI 444	MI 506	MI 773	MI 568
Good physical adjustment				
Behavior Rating: A				
Behavior Rating: F				
Behavior Rating: H				
Behavior Rating: L				
16 P.F. Scale: A				
16 P.F. Scale: F				
16 P.F. Scale: H				
16 P.F. Scale: L				

[1] Two similar forms of this test were used.

Table 4.9: Variables Used in Me (Cont)

Greater positive change in pulse rate
Body temperature
PGR latency
Pulse rate
PGR adaptation
Subject number
Time of day
Room temperature
Percent humidity
Barometric pressure
Center of gravity of body

DESIGN AND METHOD OF ANALYSIS: This study used R-technique, and the correlation matrix was factored using the multiple-group method. Eleven factors were extracted. Seventeen rotations to simple structure were carried out, resulting in 61 per cent of the variables being within the ±.10 hyperplane.

IDENTIFICATION OF FACTORS: Only two of the U.I. personality dimensions were identified, namely U.I. 16 (8-) and U.I. 17 (7-).

C_3 Cattell, R. B., Dubin, S.S., Saunders, D.R. "Verification of Hypothesized Factors in One Hundred and Fifteen Objective Personality Test Designs." (1954) (52)

This is a continuation of the C_1 and C_2 research program.

SUBJECTS: One hundred male undergraduate students were used as subjects.

VARIABLES: One hundred and fifteen measures (of which 39 had been markers in either C_1 or C_2) were obtained from the subjects and appear in Table 4.10.[1]

Table 4.10: Variables Used in C_3

MI.			
170	33	101a	145
171	34	102	146b
198	35	291	147
2a	36	192	148
3	38a	104	149
127	38b	105	67b

Table 4.10: Variables Used in C_3 (Cont)

MI.			
175	39	106	150
176	41	144	151
5	42	107	152
177a, b	43	108	153
7	305	109	16a
8	46a	110	155
9	62	111	156
11b	65	112	157
13a, b, c	67a	113	158
15	67b	114	159a
16a	83	193a	159b
21	91	194	161a
22b	92	116a	162b
24b	93	117	163
24c	186	118	164
25a	94	119	165
25b	95	120a, c, e	166
26	96a	121	167a
28	96b	122	169
133	97	123	Random Variable 1
30	98	124	Random Variable 2
31	98b	125a	126
99	100	146b	

[1]The reader will note that the number of variables in Table 4.10 falls short of 115. This is due to the inclusion as separate variables the sub-scores now making up M.I.2a and M.I. 31, and two similar methods of obtaining M.I. 112. The table includes only the composite M.I.s.

DESIGN AND METHOD OF ANALYSIS: The general method was R-technique, using multiple group centroid factor analysis on eighteen clusters selected from the correlation matrix. The factorization was repeated three times in order to obtain communality estimates. One factor was eliminated during rotation due to linear dependence on the others. The final rotated position showed 61 per cent of the variables to be in the ±.10 hyperplane.

IDENTIFICATION OF FACTORS: The following personality dimensions were identified: U.I. 16 (8+), U.I. 17 (11+), U.I. 18 (10+), U.I. 19 (5+), U.I. 20 (2+), U.I. 21 (4+), U.I. 22 (15+), U.I. 23 (7+), U.I. 25 (16-), U.I. 26 (14-), U.I. 27 (17+), U.I. 28 (12-), U.I. 29 (6+), U.I. 31 (1-), U.I. 33(9+). Factor 1 was interpreted as general ability, while Factor 13 was unidentified.

C_4 Cattell, R.B., Dubin, S.S., Saunders, D.R. "Personality Structure in Psychotics by Factorization of Objective Clinical Tests" (1954) (53)

The purpose of this study was to extend the information on the personality structure of normals (gained from C1, C2, and C3) to that of a psychotic population, and to use the results in building up a battery of objective tests.

SUBJECTS: Tests were administered to 100 male psychotics, of whom 5 had only elementary school education, 80 had high school education, and 15 had attended a university. The mean age was 26.9 years with a standard deviation of 4.6 years. The subjects were all patients at a mental hospital, 76 being schizophrenics, 4 severe psycho-neurotics, 1 manic, 7 psychopaths, and 12 unclassified.

VARIABLES: The 104 variables analyzed in this study appear in Table 4.11.[1]

Table 4.11: Variables Used in C4

MI					
157	31	151	116a	21	165
171	96a	24c	117	36	166
158	96b	125b	104	93	150
153	155	152	118	42	67b
16d	5	97	107	94	2a
16a	175	65	104	8	177a, b
305	176	191	198	22c	120a, c, e, g
145a	30	13a	99	46a	167
100	156	119	11b	98a	67a
25a	28	108	101a	92	111
193a	148	114	124	43	126
31	147b	105	122	113	62
194	26	112	98b	83	25b
34	106	109	95	161a	3, 127
35	7	110	91	162b	163
146b	39	133	38b	41	164

DESIGN AND METHOD OF ANALYSIS: The general procedure was R-technique factor analysis. The correlation matrix was factored using the multigroup method, and 18 factors were extracted and rotated for simple structure. 58 per cent of the variables are within the ±.10 hyperplane.

[1] The reader will note that less than 104 variables appear in Table 4.11. This is due to the inclusion within the factor analysis the sub-parts (but not the composite) of M.I. 31 and M.I. 2a. Only the composites are given in this table.

IDENTIFICATION OF FACTORS: The following fifteen personality dimensions were identified: U.I. 16 (16-), U.I. 17 (8+), U.I. 18 (2+), U.I. 19 (12-), U.I. 20 (5-), U.I. 21 (15+), U.I. 22 (17+), U.I. 23 (7+), U.I. 26 (4+), U.I. 27 (18+), U.I. 28 (11-), U.I. 29 (10+), U.I. 30 (14+), U.I. 31 (6+), U.I. 33 (3+). Of the remaining three factors, Factor 1 was identified as general intelligence, and Factors 9 and 13 were unidentified.

Ros Rosenthal, I. "A Factor Analysis of Anxiety Variables." (1955) (146)

The purpose of this study was to make a factor analytic examination of variables associated with anxiety (U.I. 24).

SUBJECTS: The subjects were seventy male college students, of whom ten were graduate students in measurement and prediction of physical fitness, fifteen were sophomores in physical education, and forty-five were freshmen showing lack of proficiency in certain physical activities and upon criteria of physical fitness.

VARIABLES: A total of fifty-four variables were obtained from these subjects (see Table 4.12), including the Taylor M.A.S., and Factors C, F, M, O and Q_4 on the 16 P.F. The remaining forty-eight variables were all objective tests, not all of which have been assigned MI. numbers.

Table 4.12: Variables Used in Ros

MI					
152	219	116	211	7	146b
171	143	2a	153	15	16a
273	5	176	10	177	455b
105	282	260	216	84a	466
444	151	297	41	120a	

Large drop PGR during movie
Large rise in PGR resistance after movie
Large drop PGR while "shock suggestibility test" is being administered
Large drop in resistance during shock trials of conditioning
Large rise in resistance during extinction
Large upward drift PGR when relaxed
Large per cent deflection PGR during startle (represents large drop)
High recovery quotient PGR after startle
High finger temperature
Large amount of conditioning
High extinction after conditioning

Table 4.12: Variables Used in Ros (Cont)

Large mean per cent deflection PGR to shock and startle
Misbelief (quantitative Information)- High Fear
High score on riddles
Justifications-High Fear
High anxiety on Taylor M.A.S.
Factor C on 16 P.F.
Factor F on 16 P.F.
Factor M on 16 P.F.
Factor O on 16 P.F.
Factor Q4 on 16 P.F.
Heart Rate
Word association - High fear
Decrease heart rate after startle
High pulse pressure

DESIGN AND METHOD OF ANALYSIS: The correlation matrix was factored using the centroid method (R-technique). Communality estimates were a modified form (suggested by Burt) of the highest correlation per column method of estimation (23). Using Tucker's criterion for the number of factors, eleven factors were extracted. The Quartimax method of analytical rotation (172) was followed by several graphical rotations. The final simple structure rotated position showed 51 per cent of the variables to be within the ±.10 hyperplane.

FACTOR IDENTIFICATION: The following personality dimensions were identified: U.I. 17 (3+), U.I. 18 (9+), U.I. 19 (8+), U.I. 20 (2+), U.I. 22 (4+), U.I. 24 (1+), U.I. 25 (10+). Factors 6, 7, 11, and 5 could not be adequately identified.

C_5 Cattell, R. B. "Psychiatric Screening of Flying Personnel: Personality Structure in Objective Tests--a study of 1,000 Air Force students in Basic Pilot Training" (1955) (26)

The aim was to accomplish the final stage in the construction of an objective test factor battery by examining the structure of tests previous employed (C1, C2, C3, C4), plus some additional variables, upon a large normal population.

SUBJECTS: The subjects were 500 Air Force basic pilot training students entering training at Greenville Air Force Base, Missouri (1951-2).

VARIABLES: One hundred and twenty six measures were taken from each subject, 103 appearing in the factor analysis (plus a random variable) while 23 were relegated to an extension analysis.

Table 4.13: Variables Used in C_5

FACTOR ANALYSIS VARIABLES

MI					
2a	98b	144	209	249	315
7	105	146b	211a	268	763
8	106	152	212	269	16P.F. A
15	108	167a	213	270	16P.F. C
16a	111	176	215	271	16P.F. E
21	112	193a	216	272	16P.F. F
34	116c	194	219	273	16P.F. G
35	117	171	225	279	16P.F. H
36	118	198	227	280	16P.F. I
40	119	199	229	282	16P.F. L
41	122	200	230	283	16P.F. M
51	133	201	232a	286	16P.F. N
55	30	202	234	288	16P.F. O
67a	38a	203	240	307a	16P.F. Q1
71	39	205	243	308	16P.F. Q2
82	62	206	244	311	16P.F. Q3
83	143	207	246	312	16P.F. Q4

EXTENSION VARIABLES

MI				
31	210	245	113	325
53	237	24d	309	327a
153	82	278	310	328
192	242	284	313	
208	264	292	314	

DESIGN AND METHOD OF ANALYSIS: Using R-technique factor analysis, sixteen factors were extracted by the centroid method. Tucker's criterion (160) indicated that extraction was complete at this point. The highest correlation per column of the correlation matrix was used as a communality estimate, and the procedure was repeated for each extraction. After rotation to simple structure, 67 per cent of the variables were within the ±.10 hyperplane. Extension results are reported as correlations between the rotated factors and the extension variables.

IDENTIFICATION OF FACTORS: The following personality dimensions were identified: U.I. 16 (4+), U.I. 17 (10+), U.I. 18 (16+), U.I. 19 (14+), U.I. 20 (6-), U.I. 21 (3+), U.I. 22 (12+), U.I. 24 (1+), U.I. 25 (11+), U.I. 26 (8+), U.I. 28 (5+), U.I. 29 (13+), U.I. 30 (9+), U.I. 31 (15+), U.I. 32 (7+). Factor 2 was identified as general ability.

C_6 Cattell, R. B. "Psychiatric Screening of Flying Personnel: Personality Structure in Objective Tests -- A Study of 1,000 Air Force students in Basic Pilot Training" (1955) (26)

This study was carried out at the same time, and with the same purpose, as study C5.

SUBJECTS: The subjects were 250 Air Force basic pilot training students entering training at Greenville Air Force Base, Missouri (1951-2).

VARIABLES: Sixty-three objective test measures, plus a random variable were obtained for each subject. These appear in Table 4.14.

Table 4.14: Variables Used in C6

16a	39	35	307a	205	216
15	199	289	288	30	5
249	201	238	24c	763	67a
51	206	213	271	2a	152
225	263	270	273	96a	38a
106	40	269	211a	82	72
112	94	123	283	162b	71
240	7	244	282	232a	192
146b	219	111	105	167a	203
108	246	117	308	176	279
			193a	243	280

DESIGN AND METHOD OF ANALYSIS: An R-technique factor analysis was carried out, using the multiple group method. Communality estimates showed good convergence during four iterations of the multiple group method, and fifteen factors were extracted. After rotation to simple structure 64% of the variables were within the ±.10 hyperplane.

IDENTIFICATION OF FACTORS: The following personality dimensions were identified: U.I. 16 (4+), U.I. 17 (12+), U.I. 18 (13+), U.I. 19 (6+), U.I. 20

(3+), U.I. 21 (1+), U.I. 22 (10-), U.I. 24 (9-), U.I. 26 (14+), U.I. 28 (11+), U.I. 29 (5+), U.I. 30 (7+), U.I. 31 (2-), U.I. 32 (15-). Factor 8 was identified as general ability.

R_1 Scheier, I. H., and Cattell, R. B. "Confirmation of Objective Test Factors and Assessment of their behavior to Questionnaire Factors: A factor analysis of 113 Ratings, Questionnaire and Objective Test Measurements of Personality."(1958) (148)

The purpose of this study was (1) to replicate personality dimensions as they appeared in earlier studies (2) to investigate the relationship between objective test factors and questionnaire factors, and (3) to test hypotheses concerning U.I. 24 (Anxiety).

SUBJECTS: The subjects were 86 University of Illinois male undergraduates, of whom 18 were pre-selected as having high anxiety (defined by the IPAT Anxiety Questionnaire) and 7 were selected for corresponding low anxiety. Also as part of the low-anxiety subgroup were nine university athletes.

VARIABLES: One hundred and thirteen measurements were made on each subject, comprising eighty-one objective tests of personality, two separate parts of each of eight of the 16 P.F. questionnaire factors, two measures on each of five ergic factors, and six ratings of anxiety made by psychiatrists. Details of these variables appear in Table 4.15.

Table 4.15: Variables Used in R_1

MI					
43	116, 229	455	459	211a	470
336	273	456	84a	193a	484
15	108	458	269	276	325
30	443	460	77	450	473
71	42	461	471	451	474
51	23	462	472	452	520
152	199	463	475	453	511
80	33	464	476	478	513
176	5	465	21	234	510
6a	16a	83	39	10	509
2	444	78	146a	479	515
120	445	466	38a	480	457
219	454	467	282	481	459
929a	929b	927a	151	482	468
927b	933a	933b	1716a	1716b	928a
928b					

Table 4.15: Variables Used in R_1 (Cont)

First and second half of 16 P.F. factor A
First and second half of 16 P.F. factor C
First and second half of 16 P.F. factor F
First and second half of 16 P.F. factor H
First and second half of 16 P.F. factor I
First and second half of 16 P.F. factor M
First and second half of 16 P.F. factor O
First and second half of 16 P.F. factor Q4
Psychiatrist I's evaluation of over-all anxiety level
Psychiatrist II's evaluation of over-all anxiety level
Evaluation of "free" anxiety by Psychiatrist II
Evaluation of "bound" anxiety by Psychiatrist II
Evaluation of "situational" anxiety by Psychiatrist II
Evaluation of "characterological" anxiety by Psychiatrist II

DESIGN AND METHOD OF ANALYSIS: R-technique factor analysis was carried out using the centroid method. Tucker's test of the completeness of factor extraction indicated fifteen factors, and such was the number then rotated to simple structure. The final rotated reference vector structure matrix showed 67 per cent of the variables to be within the ±.10 hyperplane.

IDENTIFICATION OF FACTORS: The following personality dimensions were identified: U.I. 16 (12+), U.I. 17 (11+), U.I. 18 (10+), U.I. 19 (14+), U.I. 20 (13+), U.I. 21 (4+), U.I. 22 (6+), U.I. 23 (2+), U.I. 24 (1+), U.I. 25 (7+), U.I. 26 (3+), U.I. 32 (5+), U.I. 34 (8+), U.I. 35 (9+), and U.I. 36 (15-).

R_2 Cattell, R. B. and Scheier, I. H. "Extension of Meaning of Objective Test Personality Factors: especially into anxiety neuroticism, questionnaire and physical factors." (1959) (66)

The purposes of this study were similar to those outlined for R_1.

SUBJECTS: The subjects were 86 University of Illinois undergraduates, and were identical to those used in R_1 above.

VARIABLES: Each subject was measured on 103 variables, 65 of which came from objective tests of personality, 32 were questionnaires (2 parts of each of the 16 P.F. factors) and 6 were measures of ergic factors. Sixty-nine of these variables were common to R_1. The full list of variables appears in Table 4.16.

Table 4.16: Variables Used in R_2

MI					
43	219	444	83	446	490
336	116	445	78	447	73
15	229	454	466	448	491
30	273	455b	467	449	492
71	108	456	469	509	929a
51	443	458	84a	510	929b
152	42	460	269	485	927a
80	23	461	77	486	927b
176	199	462	471	487	933a
6a	33	463	472	74	933b
2	5	464	475	488	
120	16a	465	476	489	

First and second half of the 16 P.F. factor A
First and second half of the 16 P.F. factor B
First and second half of the 16 P.F. factor C
First and second half of the 16 P.F. factor E
First and second half of the 16 P.F. factor F
First and second half of the 16 P.F. factor G
First and second half of the 16 P.F. factor H
First and second half of the 16 P.F. factor I
First and second half of the 16 P.F. factor L
First and second half of the 16 P.F. factor M
First and second half of the 16 P.F. factor N
First and second half of the 16 P.F. factor O
First and second half of the 16 P.F. factor Q1
First and second half of the 16 P.F. factor Q2
First and second half of the 16 P.F. factor Q3
First and second half of the 16 P.F. factor Q4

DESIGN AND METHOD OF ANALYSIS: Following R-technique, centroid factors were extracted from the correlation matrix. Rotation to simple structure was carried out with seventeen factors, this being the number suggested by tests for the completeness of factorization. After rotation 60 per cent of the variables were found to be within the ±.10 hyperplane.

FACTOR IDENTIFICATION: The following personality dimensions were identified: U.I. 16 (5+), U.I. 17 (9+), U.I. 18 (8+), U.I. 19 (11+), U.I. 21 (15+), U.I. 22 (6+), U.I. 23 (17+), U.I. 24 (1+), U.I. 25 (3+), U.I. 26 (14+), U.I. 27 (7+), U.I. 28 (4+), U.I. 29 (16+), U.I. 30 (10+), U.I. 32 (2-). The remaining two factors appear to be concerned with dominance-submission (12+) and physical fitness (13+).

R_3 Cattell, R. B. and Scheier, I. H. "Factors in Personality Change: A discussion of the Condition-Response Incremental Design and Application to 69 Personality Response Measures and Three Stimulus Conditions." (1958) (64) (67)

This study concerns the application of Incremental Condition-Response factor analytic design (Incremental R-technique) to changes in personality 'state' dimensions as these relate to manipulated experimental conditions.

SUBJECTS: The subjects in this study were 86 undergraduates, and identical to those used in both R_1 and R_2 above.

VARIABLES: It will be recalled that 69 of the variables used in R_1 were also in R_2. The difference scores on each variable between the two occasions of testing were used in the present study. The variables giving the 69 difference scores, plus three stimulus condition variables, are listed in Table 4.17.

Table 4.17: Variables (Difference Scores) Used in R_3

MI					
43	336	15	30	71	51
152	80	176	6a	2	120
219	116	229	273	108	443
42	23	199	33	5	16a
444	445	454	455	456	458
460	461	462	463	464	465
83	78	466	467	469	84a
269	77	471	472	475	476
929a	929b	927a	927b	933a	933b

First and second half of 16 P.F. factor A
First and second half of 16 P.F. factor C
First and second half of 16 P.F. factor F
First and second half of 16 P.F. factor H
First and second half of 16 P.F. factor I
First and second half of 16 P.F. factor M
First and second half of 16 P.F. factor O
First and second half of 16 P.F. factor Q4
Imminence of Treadmill Run as an environmental condition varied
Imminence of academic examinations as an environmental condition varied
Questionnaire probe of worrisome matters as an environmental condition varied

DESIGN AND METHOD OF ANALYSIS: Incremental R-technique involves the factor analysis of a matrix containing the intercorrelations of difference scores (as opposed to the raw score intercorrelations used in R-technique). The three stimulus condition variables (treadmill run, examination, and questionnaire probe) are an added refinement allowing the experimenter to relate changes in environmental conditions to personality state factors.

Centroid factor extraction from the 72 x 72 correlation matrix was terminated at 14 factors, using Tucker's criterion. Fifty-nine per cent of the variables were found within the ±.10 hyperplane after rotation to simple structure. This is significant at the .05 level by Bargmann's test of simple structure (6).

IDENTIFICATION OF FACTORS: The following personality dimensions were identified as having a state component: U.I. 17 (6-), U.I. 19 (8-), U.I. 22 (2-), U.I. 23 (3+), U.I. 24 (12+), U.I. 26 (11+), U.I. 27 (7-), U.I. 28 (1-), U.I. 34 (4+), U.I. 35 (10+), U.I. 36 (9-). Of the remaining three factors, one was predominantly associated with physiological variables, one with "self-investment and lack of adaptability to environment", and the last was unidentified (though it was noted to be slightly 'cooperative' with factor 7 (U.I. 27).

H Horn, J. "Structure in Measures of Self-Sentiment, Ego, and Super-Ego Concepts." (1961) (110)

The purpose was to examine the hypothetical integrative concepts of self-sentiment, ego, and superego as measured by objective tests, questionnaire, motivational, and attitudinal variables.

SUBJECTS: There were 137 subjects, composed of 33 male undergraduates, 53 U.S. Air Force enlisted men, and 51 convicts at the Joliet-Stateville Penitentiary. Age ranges were as follows: undergraduates, 18 to 33 years; airmen, 18 years to 24 years; convicts, 19 years to 36 years.

VARIABLES. One hundred and ten variables were used in all, 55 of which appeared in a factor analysis while the remaining 55 were relegated to an extension analysis.

Table 4.18: Variables Used in H

FACTOR ANALYSIS VARIABLES					
MI.					
152	38	246	219	21	35
193a	194	273	191	458	560
167a	192	927	929	933	934

Table 4.18: Variables Used in H (Cont)

Maintain my health attitude: Autism Device
Machiavelli attitude: Autism Device
Parental Sentiment: Information Autism Device
Youthfulness Attitude: Utilities Device
Competitiveness Attitude: Utilities Device
Creativeness Attitude: Utilities Device
Machiavelli Attitude: Utilities Device
Respect Attitude: Preferences Device
Control Attitude: Preferences Device
No Sin Attitude: Preferences Device
Maintain Duty Attitude: Preferences Device
Fluency on Dreams vs. that on others
Acquaintances vs. Friends (Female)
Fluency writing
Willingness to list names of friends and acquaintances
Verbal ability (vocabulary)
Reasoning (letter Series)
Verbal Reasoning (Analogies, 16 P.F.: B)
Number Friends Checked
Number Church Attendances per year
16 P.F. Q2: Self Sufficiency
16 P.F. Q1: Experimenting
16 P.F. L: Suspecting
16 P.F. Q4: Tense
16 P.F. O: Insecure, lack confidence
16 P.F. C: Ego Strength
16 P.F. Q3: Self Sentiment Control
16 P.F. G: Superego Form A
16 P.F. G: Superego Form B
Stability family-physical Environment
Educational-Occupational Status of Parents
Self Educational-Aspirations Level

EXTENSION VARIABLES

MI 35 193a
934 (Information Device)
928 (Information Device)
928 (Autism Device)
Competitiveness Attitude: Autism Device
General Autism
Career Sentiments: Information + Autism Device

Table 4.18: Variables Used in H (Cont)

Sweetheart Sentiment: Information Device
Narcism Erg: Information + Autism Device
Sadism Erg: Information + Autism Device
Maintain my physical health Attitude: Utilities Device
Fluency Writing About Decisions Involving Reference to Self
Fluency Writing about Friends
Number Tried But Missed, P.M.A. (Verbal and Reasoning)
Number People Admired
Number Social Classes Perceived
"Sociability" Rating for Self Relative to Admired Co-worker
"Estimable" Rating for Self Relative to Admired Co-worker
"Dominant-surgency" Rating for Self Relative to Ideal Self
"Wordly Toughness" Rating for Self Relative to Ideal Self
Evaluation Rating for Self Relative to "other"
Potency Rating for Self Relative to "other"
Activity Rating for Self relative to "other"
Stability Rating for Self Relative to "other"
Evaluation Rating for Ideal Self Relative to Beatnik
Potency Rating for Ideal Self Relative to Beatnik
Activity Rating for Ideal Self Relative to Beatnik
Stability Rating for Ideal Self Relative to Beatnik
16 P.F. A: Cyclothymia vs. Schizothymia
16 P.F. E: Dominance vs. Submissiveness
16 P.F. F: Surgency vs. Desurgency (Form A)
16 P.F. H: Parmia vs. Threctia (Form A)
16 P.F. N: Shrewdness vs. Naivete (Form A)
16 P.F. I: Premsia vs. Harria (Form A)
16 P.F. M: Alaxia vs. Praxermia (Form A)
16 P.F. C: Ego Strength (Form B)
16 P.F. Q3: Self Sentiment Control (Form B)
Self Confidence Questionnaire
Independence Questionnaire
Harmoniousness of Relationship with Parents
Usefulness and liking for School
Wealth During Childhood
Stability of Family and Physical Environment during Childhood
Urban Environment During Childhood
Educational Level

"Composed" rating for Self Relative to Admired Co-worker

DESIGN AND METHOD OF ANALYSIS: Following general R-technique, centroid factors were extracted from the correlation matrix. Using Tucker's test for completeness of factor extraction, eighteen factors were extracted and rotated to simple structure. On the final rotation 71 per cent of the variables were within the ±.10 hyperplane.

FACTOR IDENTIFICATION: The following objective-test personality dimensions were identified: U.I. 20 (5+), U.I. 24 (9+), U.I. 28 (3+), and U.I. 36 (1+).

E-D Cattell, R. B., Bjerstedt, A., and Tsujioka, B. "R and Incremental R Study of Elation - Depression" (1962) (44)

This study is part of a larger project on the personality structures involved in elation-depression.

SUBJECTS: There were 139 subjects in all, 78 falling in a clinical group, and 61 in a normal group. All of the clinical patients were in mental hospitals, and were subdivided as follows: DEPRESSIVE GROUP: involutional psychotic reaction with depression (N = 15, 6 males and 9 females), other psychotic depressives (N = 12, 6 males and 6 females), psychoneurosis, depressive reaction (N = 13, 5 males and 8 females); COMPARISON CLINICAL GROUP: schizophrenics, chronic, undifferentiated (N = 15, 8 males and 7 females), manic-depressives (manic type) (N = 13, 6 males and 7 females), psychoneurosis, anxiety reaction (N = 10, 3 males and 7 females). Thus there were 34 males and 44 females in the clinical group.

The normal group was composed of 28 males and 33 females, recruited through an employment bureau and newspaper advertisements.

VARIABLES: Fifty variables were used in the factor analysis, and these appear in Table 4.19.

Table 4.19: Variables Used in E-D

MI	277	763	206	1729
	64	100	271	1730
	2	192	273	1731
	146a	191	307	1732
	146b	159c	236	1733
	8[1]	282	120b	1734
	288	105	227a	1735
	133	109	542	1736
	53	110	269	1737

[1] Two versions of this variable were administered.

Table 4.19: Variables Used in E-D (Cont)

30	112	1725	1738
764	321, 21	1726	1739
316	116b	1727	1740
	152	1728	in-out of hospital

DESIGN AND METHOD OF ANALYSIS: Following R-technique, thirteen centroid factors were extracted from the correlation matrix. The number of factors was obtained by taking the number of eigen-values over +1.00 from the correlation matrix. Following rotation to simple structure, 68 per cent of the variables were within the ±.10 hyperplane.

IDENTIFICATION OF FACTORS: The following personality dimensions were identified: U.I. 17 (4+), U.I. 19 (3+), U.I. 21 (6-), U.I. 25 (14+), U.I. 34 (8+).

R_{10} Cattell, R. B., Damarin, F., Warburton, F. (1962)
"Personality Theory from Multivariate
Experiment" (51)

The aim of this study was to replicate the results from previous studies and in addition to employ a large number of extension variables in order to throw maximum light upon the U.I. factors.

SUBJECTS: A total of 168 subjects were used in R10. Twenty-six were criminals actually in prison at time of testing, and whose crimes tended to be severe. Thirty were classified as institutionalized neurotics, who were being treated for drug addiction and alcoholism. The remaining 112 were University of Illinois undergraduates (normals).

VARIABLES: A total of 265 measures were obtained from these subjects. All measures came from objective tests except for fifteen scales of the 16 P.F. and an Extraversion-Introversion attitude scale. One hundred and eleven variables were used in a factor analysis, while the remaining 154 were analyzed in an extension.[1]

---

[1] A further analysis of the RID data is at present, nearing completion, but, unfortunately, is not available at time of writing. It is not anticipated that there will be any major change in factor loadings.

Table 4.20: Variables Used in R10[1]

FACTOR ANALYSIS VARIABLES

MI

466	965	1471	839	1179	103	219
2a	531	68	1478	1482	191	269
6	535	1064	82	1483	159	270
7	1467	1107	1479	865	105	271
13	1469	1472	703	1165	282	273
15	1351	71	1154	866	108	152
154	493	1473	97	868	112	167
24	1038	1475	123	1160	117	31
42	1041	1128	280	867	120	67
95	1050	1476	1480	1484	134	316
39	1470	1130	852	83	137	143
51	808	1477	1156	1485	146	153
997	1468	72	1481	886	147	194
199	327	460	609	1486	1148	458
1487	796	847	840	1488	853	1489
					1490	1491

Scale of Exviant Attitudes

EXTENSION VARIABLES

MI

1492	682	1521	850
1032	147a	1522	858
1035	147b	939	1167
810	34	938	1183
1493	35	928	902
22c	193a	933	904
1010	1500	1523	203
1011a	1501	1524	120
1012a	1502	863	20
1494	168b	843	266b
1495	807	844	266a

[1] The total count of the variables in Table 4.20 shows this to be less than 265. The difference is made up of variables in which slight modifications in scoring were tried. Such double-entries only appear once in the table.

Table 4.20: Variables Used in R10 (Cont)

MI			
1040	809	845	1530
1496	1503	838	1531
1497	1504	473	283
1146	1505	472	131
1147	1506	723	5
33	1507	1041	33
116	1508	53	42
125a	1509	1525	178
16 P.F.-C	473	1029	113
16 P.F.-L	1510	1030	327a
16 P.F.-O	1511	1033	1532
16 P.F.-Q3	1512	990	1132
16 P.F.-Q4	1043	808	1533
16 P.F.-A	1513	1526	98
16 P.F.-E	1514	1071	273
16 P.F.-F	1515	1527	1115
16 P.F.-H	1516	1528	1125
16 P.F.-Q1	1155	1129	1534
16 P.F. Q2	849	828	1535
16 P.F. M	819	829	1536
16 P.F. G	1101	1133	1142
16 P.F. I	1517	1149	1537
16 P.F. N	1518	1150	1144
530	1177	847	1172
1498	1176	1529	1174
684	1519	853	1538
1499	1520	1157	1113
		1158	1539

DESIGN AND METHOD OF ANALYSIS: R_{10} employed R-technique factor analysis and centroid factors were extracted from the correlation matrix. Twenty-two factors were selected for rotation following Tucker's test for completeness of factor extraction. Forty-nine rotations were made before a satisfactory simple structure was reached. On the final rotation 72 per cent of the variables were within the ±.10 hyperplane. The extension analysis followed the method outlined by Dwyer (83) and Mosier (132).

FACTOR IDENTIFICATION: The following personality dimensions were identified: U.I. 16 (8-), U.I. 17 (19+), U.I. 18 (16-), U.I. 19 (12-), U.I. 23 (13+), U.I. 24 (9+), U.I. 25 (4-), U.I. 26 (22+), U.I. 27 (5-), U.I. 28 (14-), U.I. 30

(20+), U.I. 32 (15-), U.I. 33 (10-), U.I. 34 (3-), U.I. 35 (21-), leaving seven factors as yet unidentified.

DESCRIPTION OF STUDIES II: NON-FACTOR-ANALYTIC STUDIES

R_4 Cattell, R. B., and Scheier, I. H. "Discovery and Development of Measurement Scale for Dimensions of Anxiety" (1951) (63)

The purpose was to examine a set of variables in order to select and develop a more complete battery of tests for the measurement of U.I. 24 (Anxiety).

SUBJECTS: The sample was composed of 187 male undergraduates.

VARIABLES: Twenty-three variables were used, including a U.I. 24 estimated factor score. This factor score was obtained (a) by adding the standard scores on MI. 116 (229), 219, 108, 211, 195, 205, and 454 and (b) adding this composite to the IPAT Anxiety Questionnaire (containing all 5 questionnaire factor markers), giving equal weight to the composite and to the questionnaire.

Table 4.21: Variables Used in R4

MI

116, 229	219	108	211	152	205	454
493	481	506	507			

Confidence in Untried Dangerous and non-Dangerous Performance
Second-Order Motivation Measurement Test
Confidence in Untried dangerous performance
Willingness to risk a decision, "You decide"
Part I of the IPAT Anxiety Questionnaire (MI 454)
Part II of the IPAT Anxiety Questionnaire (MI 454)
4 composites made up of the above tests
U.I. 24 Factor Score

DESIGN AND METHOD OF ANALYSIS: Product moment correlations were computed between the U.I. 24 factor estimate and the 22 other variables. It should be noted that these correlations will be inflated to the extent that the same variable appears in the factor estimate.

AF Cattell, R. B. and Schiff, D. "Psychiatric Screening of Flying Personnel: Prediction of Training Criteria by Objective Personality Factors and Development of the Seven Factor Personality Test." (1953) (69)

The purpose was to examine the relationship between criteria of pilot training success and factor scores derived from objective tests. The study is linked with the C5 and C6 studies.

SUBJECTS: The sample consisted of 1000 U.S. Air Force Officers and basic pilot training students.

VARIABLES: The variables consisted of estimated factor scores for U.I. 16, U.I. 17, U.I. 18, U.I. 19, U.I. 20, U.I. 21, U.I. 22, U.I. 24, U.I. 25, U.I. 26, U.I. 28, U.I. 29, U.I. 30, U.I. 31, U.I. 32 and four criteria of course success. Factor scores were derived from the sum of rescaled raw scores (unit weights) on up to six marker variables. Details on the factor estimates and criteria appear in Table 4.22.

Table 4.22: Variables Used in AF

Predictors:	(i) U.I. 16	MI. 82, 270, 282, 307a, 15,117
	(ii) U.I. 17	MI. 288, 216, 40, 176
	(iii) U.I. 18	MI. 16a, 30, 249, 266
	(iv) U.I. 19	MI. 146b, 16a, 39, 7, 71
	(v) U.I. 20	MI. 152, 38a, 246, 219
	(vi) U.I. 21	MI. 288, 308, 271, 244, 199,152
	(vii) U.I. 22	MI. 176, 5, 282, 280, 263
	(viii) U.I. 24	MI. 211, 152, 219, 205, 55
	(ix) U.I. 25	MI. 7, 199, 279
	(x) U.I. 26	MI. 273, 167a, 283, 105
	(xi) U.I. 28	MI. 67a, 38a, 763, 246
	(xii) U.I. 29	MI. 111, 307a, 308, 112, 72, 71
	(xiii) U.I. 30	MI. 270, 16a, 269, 35
	(xiv) U.I. 31	MI. 176, 280, 243, 203
	(xv) U.I. 32	MI. 108, 16a, 270, 269, 35

Criteria:

(i) The Adjustment Group (AG) Criterion. This was a composite composed of the following:

(a) Objective Items: scores on air crew classification battery, final course outcome, school grades, military conduct grade, flying grade, number of hours of pre-solo dual instruction, number of demerits received for violation of cadet regulations.

(b) Ratings: Military aptitude ratings from classmates, upper classmen, and department instructors.

(c) Clinical evaluation: Rating forms on each subject under headings of ability motivation and personality dimensions by two clinical psychologists. Two psychologists then ranked the candidates in terms of over-all adjustment, and this became the AG criterion.

(ii) The Actuarial Adjustment Rating (AAR). This was (i)(C) Clinical evaluation, above.

(iii) Pass-Fail in Flying School. Of the total 1,000 subjects, 304 failed to complete the course, and the pass-fail dichotomy is used as the third criterion.

(iv) The Oriented Criterion. This is a combination, with equal weights, of the Adjustment Group criterion and the Pass-Fail criterion.

DESIGN AND METHOD OF ANALYSIS: Product moment correlations are presented between the fifteen personality factor estimates and the four criteria of course success for the 1,000 subjects. In addition the same relationships are examined with specific sub-groups within the total sample.

WE Wells, H.P. "Relationships Between Physical Fitness and Psychological Variables" (1958) (166)

The purpose was to examine the relationship between physical fitness measures and personality dimensions from both objective test and questionnaire realms.

SUBJECTS: The subjects were 80 University of Illinois undergraduates, 64 being enrolled in a physical education class, 9 being varsity athletes, and the remaining 7 belonged to no specific sub-group. Seventeen of the 64 P.E. students were classified as 'high anxiety' and seven as 'low anxiety' in terms of their 16 P.F. scores. All of these students also participated in the R_1 and R_2 and R_3 studies.

VARIABLES: The variables fall into the following distinct categories: 38 physical fitness measures, the 16 scales of the 16 P.F., 15 factor score estimates of objective-test dimensions (obtained from the R_1 factorization), 2 ratings of over-all anxiety, and two tests concerning the number of friends of each examinee.

Table 4.23: Variables Used in WE

MI						
492	569	557	506	508	73	491
490	74	558	559	560	561	562
488	563	564	565	566	567	568

Table 4.23: Variables Used in WE (Cont)

1743	570	571	653	654	655	572
573	574	575	576	487	486	485
656	657	658				
The 16 P.F. factor A			U.I. 16		U.I. 24	
The 16 P.F. factor B			U.I. 17		U.I. 25	
The 16 P.F. factor C			U.I. 18		U.I. 26	
The 16 P.F. factor E			U.I. 19		U.I. 32	
The 16 P.F. factor F			U.I. 20		U.I. 34	
The 16 P.F. factor G			U.I. 21		U.I. 35	
The 16 P.F. factor H			U.I. 22		U.I. 36	
The 16 P.F. factor I			U.I. 23			
The 16 P.F. factor L						
The 16 P.F. factor M			Rating of over-all anxiety by Psychiatrist I			
The 16 P.F. factor N						
The 16 P.F. factor O			Rating of over-all anxiety by Psychiatrist II			
The 16 P.F. factor Q1			Number of Friends I			
The 16 P.F. factor Q2			Number of Friends II			
The 16 P.F. factor Q3						
The 16 P.F. factor Q4						

DESIGN AND METHOD OF ANALYSIS: Product moment correlations were computed between (a) the 38 physical fitness variables and (b) the 16 P.F., objective test factors, psychiatrist's ratings, and Friends Tests. The results should be viewed as an extension analysis of the R_1 factorization.

R_6 Scheier, I. H., Cattell, R. B., Horn, J. L. "Objective Test Factor U.I. 23: Its measurement and its relation to clinically - judged neuroticism" (1960) (149)

The general aim of this study was to improve measurement of U.I. 23: High mobilization vs. regression and at the same time clarify interpretation by testing differing subgroups.

SUBJECTS: In this study there were 98 paid subjects, 49 being diagnosed clinically as psychoneurotic (15 Anxiety Reactions, 7 Obsessive-Compulsives, 4 Depressives, 14 in the Psychoneurotic-other category, 2 each of Dissociative Reaction, Conversion Reaction, and Phobic Reaction, and three patients regarded as "mainly psychoneurotic") and 49 normals. The 49 normal and neurotics were matched as follows: 13 male and 36 female in each group; mean age for normals was 32.5 years, for neurotics 32.6 years; age range for both groups

18 to 65 years; mean educational level was 11.4 grades (years) completed for normals, 11.2 for neurotics, both ranging from 8th grade to college graduate level. Standard deviations (as well as means) on the matching variables were almost exactly the same for the two R_6 groups.

VARIABLES: Each subject's score on U.I. 23 was estimated by a weighted combination of his normalized scores on 9 marker tests. These marker tests were: MI. 2a (3), MI. 120 (3), MI. 151 (2), MI. 148 (2), MI. 167a (1), MI. 504b (1), MI. 538 (1), MI. 542 (1), MI. 638 (1). The numbers in parentheses denote the weights. There were 25 variables apart from the marker tests, and these appear in Table 4.24.

Table 4.24: Variables Used in R_6

MI					
608	605a	605b	659	277	967
1416	542	610	638	120	604
504b	596	609	606	2	516
167	613	227	101a	538	151
615					

Few years completed in school
Few write-in answers "What Answer Would You make?"
More "Neurotic" points "Attitudes and Interests" questionnaire
More "Neurotic" points "MacMillan Inventory"
Low proportion disagree "General Decisions: Particulars"
Less compact writing "Writing an Essay"
Few words written "Writing an Essay"
High proportion in-between responses "MacMillan Inventory"
Known marital discord
U.I. 23 Estimated Factor score

DESIGN AND METHOD OF ANALYSIS: This study involved correlating a series of measures hypothetically relevant to U.I. 23 with:

(1) the factor scores as estimated from nine marker tests (see above).
(2) the neurotic-normal dichotomy.

R_8 Scheier, I. H., Cattell, R. B., Horn, J. L. "Objective Test Factor U.I. 23: Its measurement and its relation to clinically-judged neuroticism" (1960)(149)

The purpose was to improve measurement of U.I. 23.

SUBJECTS: The sample consisted of 97 subjects, including 77 Air Force males and 20 undergraduate volunteers from the University of Illinois, 14 of the latter being male and 6 female.

VARIABLES: Each subject's score on U.I. 23 was estimated by a weighted composite of his normalized scores on 9 marker tests. The marker tests were: MI. 542 (2), MI. 504b (2), MI. 516 (1), MI. 120 (3), MI. 2 (3), MI 604 (2), MI. 610 (2), and MI. 609 (2), the numbers in parentheses denoted the respective weights. An additional 44 measures were also obtained on the subjects, and appear in Table 4.25.

Table 4.25: Variables Used in R_8

MI					
542	610	638	120	604	504b
596	609	2a	516	167	613
227a	101a	538	151	605a	1416

High proportion in-between responses "16 P.F." Questionnaire
High proportion in-between responses on Composite Questionnaire
More "neurotic points" "Composite Questionnaire"
Score on 16 P.F. factor A
Score on 16 P.F. factor B
Score on 16 P.F. factor C
Score on 16 P.F. factor E
Score on 16 P.F. factor F
Score on 16 P.F. factor G
Score on 16 P.F. factor H
Score on 16 P.F. factor I
Score on 16 P.F. factor L
Score on 16 P.F. factor M
Score on 16 P.F. factor N
Score on 16 P.F. factor O
Score on 16 P.F. factor Q1
Score on 16 P.F. factor Q2
Score on 16 P.F. factor Q3
Score on 16 P.F. factor Q4

DESIGN AND METHOD OF ANALYSIS: This study involved correlating estimated factor scores (see method above) with a series of variables potentially relevant to strengthening the over-all measurement of U.I. 23.

R9 - Ta[1] (68)

The purpose was to compare scores on objective tests of personality with classification of neurosis.

SUBJECTS: The sample consisted of 54 subjects, including 24 adults diagnosed as neurotic, and 30 normals. All of the subjects, except for 5 normals, were Canadians. Details of matching information is as follows (neurotics vs. normals): age 30.5 years vs. 27.1 years; educational level, 10.4 years vs. 12.6 years; sex, 15 females and 9 males vs. 13 females and 17 males. The neurotic subgroup included "three anxiety states, three hysterical-personality types, two depressive reactions, and one each with trends to obsessive-compulsive, inadequate personality, alcohol addiction, and psychopathic personality" (68).

VARIABLES: Eighteen factor scores were computed for each subject from marker variables, using the method prescribed in the Objective-Analytic Battery Manual (27). The factors estimated were U.I. 16, U.I. 17, U.I. 18, U.I. 19, U.I. 20, U.I. 21, U.I. 22, U.I. 23, U.I. 24, U.I. 25, U.I. 26, U.I. 27, U.I. 28, U.I. 29, U.I. 30, U.I. 31, U.I. 32, U.I. 33, and U.I. 1 (General Intelligence).

DESIGN AND METHOD OF ANALYSIS: The mean factor scores on each of the 18 factors were compared across the neurotic normal groups, using the t-ratio.

R9 - Tb[1] (68)

The aim was to obtain supportive evidence for previous results on comparisons of normals and neurotics in terms of their personality factor scores.

SUBJECTS: The sample consisted of 24 subjects, 5 being neurotic, and 19 normals. Matching details (neurotics vs. normals) are as follows: sex, 3 males and two females, vs. 10 males and 9 females; age, 31.2 years vs. 25.7 years; educational level, 14.4 years of school vs. 10.8 years of school.

VARIABLES: Estimated factor scores on each subject were obtained from standard scores on marker variables for U.I. 16, U.I. 17, U.I. 18, U.I. 19, U.I. 20, U.I. 21, U.I. 22, U.I. 23, U.I. 24, U.I. 25, U.I. 26, U.I. 27, U.I. 28, and U.I. 29. Due to time limitations not all of the marker tests suggested in the Objective Analytic Battery (1955) Manual could be used.

DESIGN AND METHOD OF ANALYSIS:

The neurotic and normal groups were compared, using the t-ratio, on each of the above 14 factors.

---

[1]This research has not yet been fully reported, but a summary of results is available (68). p. 481, 482.

R_7 Scheier, I. H., Cattell, R. B., Mayeske, G.W. "The Objective-Test Factors of Imaginative Tension (U.I. 25) Introversion (U.I. 32), Anxiety (U.I. 24) and Autistic Non-Conformity (U.I. 34): (1) Data on New Factor-measuring tests, and (2) relation of factors to clinically-judged psychosis" (1960) (150)

This study was designed (a) to investigate and confirm new tests for measuring the personality factor-dimensions of Imaginative Tension (U.I. 35), Introversion (U.I. 32), Anxiety (U.I. 24), and Autistic Non-Conformity (U.I. 34), and (b) to determine the relation of score on these factors to clinically judged psychoticism vs. normalcy.

SUBJECTS: One hundred and five adults served as subjects in this study, of which 48 were judged as psychotic on clinical grounds. Characteristics of the sample appear in the following table:

Table 4.26: Characteristics of the R_7 Sample

	MEAN AGE	MEAN EDUC. LEVEL	N
Males, normal	40.7	11.6	31
Males, psychotic	42.8	10.4	28
Females, normal	33.4	12.4	26
Females, psychotic	38.0	12.0	20
Total normal	37.1	12.0	57
Total psychotic	40.4	11.2	48
Total	38.7	11.6	105

N = 105: m = 59: f = 46.

All of the psychotics were in remission but still under treatment, and most were of the affective disorder type.

VARIABLES: Each subject was measured on 113 variables, including four factor estimates (see Table 4.27). The factor scores on U.I. 24 were obtained by summing the stanines on the following subtests (given equal weight); MI. 108, MI. 211, 16 P. F. factor Q4, 16 P.F. factor Q3 (-), and "tendency to agree" derived from a wide variety of items. The following subtests (equal weight) were used as a factor estimate for U.I. 25: MI. 7, MI. 146, MI. 199 ,

MI. 171, MI. 8, and MI. 275. The following subtests (equal weight) were used as a factor estimate for U.I. 32: 16 P.F. factor A(-), 16 P.F. factor F (-), 16 P.F. factor H (-), MI. 316, MI. 282, and MI. 108. Factor scores for U.I. 34 were obtained from the following subtests (numbers in parentheses indicate the weights): 16 P.F. factor M (1), MI. 33 (2), MI. 282 (1).

Table 4.27: Variables Used in R_7

751	685	703	589	752	728
758	686	704	595	753	729
275	687	705	712	754	730
756	685	706	713	939	731
757	689	707	714	938	732
674	690	708	715	928	733
675	691	709	711	933	734
676	692	710	2a	716	735
677	693	743	765	717	736
678	694	744	766	718	737
679	695	745	767	719	738
680	696	746	764	720	739
682	697	747	763	721	740
530	698	748	282	722	741
681	699	327	760	723	742
683	700	583	761	724	Factor Estimate U.I. 25
684	701	587	762	725	Factor Estimate U.I. 32
531	702	588	108	726	Factor Estimate U.I. 24
				727	Factor Estimate U.I. 34

DESIGN AND METHOD OF ANALYSIS: Estimated factor scores (see above) were obtained for the subjects on U.I. 25, U.I. 32, U.I. 24, and U.I. 34. The normal and psychotic groups were compared in terms of their respective factor scores. Correlations were also reported between a series of variables of potential relevance to these factors and the four sets of factor estimates.

N_1 Knapp, R. R. and Most, J. A. "Personality Correlates of Marine Corps Helicopter Pilot Performance." (1960) (121) (124) (123)

This was an examination of relationship between certain personality measures and criteria of helicopter pilot success.

SUBJECTS: Eighty-one qualified Marine Corps officer helicopter pilots acted as subjects, and were selected for testing on the basis of availability during the testing period. The age range was from 21 to 38 years, with a mean age of 25 years. The mean number of years of school completed was approximately 15 years. Seventeen per cent had only high school education while 55 per cent had completed 4 years of college. Approximately 77 per cent were 1st or 2nd lieutenants.

VARIABLES

Predictors: (i) The Minnesota Multiphasic Personality Inventory (MMPI), scales Hs, D, Hy, Pd, Mc, Pa, Pt, Sc, Ma, Si, L, F, K, Ego Strength, Dominance, Responsibility, Manifest Anxiety, and MMPI factors A, R, C and P.

(ii) The Guilford Zimmerman Temperament Survey (GZTS), scales G, R, A, S, E, O, F, T, P, M, ?.

(iii) The Objective-Analytic Personality Test Battery (1955), factors, U.I. 16, U.I. 17, U.I. 18, U.I. 19, U.I. 20, U.I. 21, U.I. 22, U.I. 23, U.I. 24, U.I. 25, U.I. 26, and U.I. 27. Factor scores on the O-A Battery were obtained by summing the standard scores for marker variables for each factor. These marker variables appear in Table 4.28.

Table 4.28: Variables used in the Estimation of U.I. Factor Scores (N1)

MI						
278	282	193	105	134	53	206
125	309	21	67	153	15	146b
307	237	7	29	25	314	51
117	98a	150	266	147	39	159
116	152	308	6	31	275	273
219	113	34	120	330	105	191
246	288	108	151	153	36	125
35	170	9	101	199	29	145
38	271	8	211	7	283	194

Criteria: (i) Peer Ratings (nominations for top or bottom 25% of group) of pilot proficiency (PP).

(ii) Peer Ratings of officer-like qualities (OLQ)

(iii) Peer Ratings of social acceptability (SA)

(iv) Index of Frequency of sick calls (SC)

(v) Aviation Qualification Test (AQT) scores taken prior to air training. This is a measure of general intelligence.

(vi) Flight Aptitude Rate (FAR) scores taken prior to air training. This is a composite of the Mechanical Comprehension Test, the Spatial Apperception Test, and Biographical Inventory.

(vii) Final Flight Grade (FFG) as assigned upon completion of training. This is a composite based upon instructor's ratings.

DESIGN AND METHOD OF ANALYSIS: Product moment correlations were computed between the three personality batteries (MMPI, GZTS, and O-A) and the seven criteria. Three multiple regression analyses were carried out: (a) to predict criterion (i) from U.I. 16, U.I. 17, U.I. 21 and the K scale of the MMPI, (b) to predict criterion (vii) from U.I. 20, U.I. 23, U.I. 25, Pa, Ma, F, and T, and (c) to predict the MMPI factor scale A from A (GZTS), E, P and U.I. 20.

Of particular relevance to this monograph are the correlations between the O-A battery and the criteria (121) (124) and the correlations between the O-A battery and the Guilford-Zimmerman and MMPI scales (123). Also of interest are the correlations between individual O-A variables and both criteria and factor scores (121).

N_2 Knapp, R. R. Criterion Predictions in the Navy from the Objective Analytic Personality Test Battery (1961) (122) (122a)

The purpose is to examine the relationship between personality measures and criteria of military success.

SUBJECTS: The sample consisted of 315 Navy enlisted Submarine School candidates. The age range was from 17 to 35 years with a mean age of approximately 21 years. The range of educational level was from 8 to 16 years with a mean of approximately 11 years.

VARIABLES

Predictors: (i) The Guilford-Martin inventories STDCR, O, Ag. Co, GAMIN, the Guilford-Zimmerman Temperament Survey and the General Classification Test (GCT).

(ii) The Objective-Analytic (O-A) Personality Test Battery (1955), on the complete series of factors, i.e., U.I. 16, U.I. 17, U.I. 18, U.I. 19, U.I. 20, U.I. 21, U.I. 22, U.I. 23, U.I. 24, U.I. 25, U.I. 26, U.I. 27, U.I. 28, U.I.29, U.I. 30, U.I. 31, U.I. 32, U.I. 33. Factor scores were obtained by summing the unweighted stanines on the marker variables for each factor. The marker tests for each factor are described in the test Manual (27), and those for the first 12 factors are listed in Table 4.28.

Criteria:

(1) PASS-DROP: whether the candidate completed the course or was dropped.

(2) CLASS-STANDING: final standing in the class of these successfully completing the course.

(3) CLASS-STANDING WITH INTELLIGENCE PARTIALED OUT. This is the same as criterion (2) except that intelligence as measured by the GCT was partialed out.

DESIGN AND METHOD OF ANALYSIS: Product moment correlations were computed between the Guilford-Martin and O-A battery and the O-A battery and the criteria.

P_1 Pawlik, K. "Educational Prediction from Objective Personality Test Dimensions" (1961) (138)

This research was a further analysis of the R10 data, and explored the relationship between personality factors and college achievement.

SUBJECTS: the subjects were 84 Liberal Arts and Sciences undergraduates at the University of Illinois, and formed a subgroup of the total R10 sample.

VARIABLES: The prediction variables were factor scores (based upon the multiple regression of the 111 variables in R10 upon the sixteen R10 factors which were identified as established personality dimensions), the School and College Aptitude Test (SCAT), and high school percentile rank. The criteria were university grade-point averages.

Table 4.29: Variables Used in P1

PREDICTORS I	Factor Scores on U.I. 16
	Factor Scores on U.I. 17
	Factor Scores on U.I. 18
	Factor Scores on U.I. 19
	Factor Scores on U.I. 23
	Factor Scores on U.I. 24
	Factor Scores on U.I. 25
	Factor Scores on U.I. 26
	Factor Scores on U.I. 27
	Factor Scores on U.I. 28
	Factor Scores on U.I. 30
	Factor Scores on U.I. 32
	Factor Scores on U.I. 33
	Factor Scores on U.I. 34
	Factor Scores on U.I. 35

Table 4.29: Variables Used in P1 (Cont)

PREDICTORS II	SCAT (Verbal Sections) SCAT (Quantitative Sections) SCAT (Total Verbal plus Quantitative Sections)
PREDICTOR III	High School Percentile Rank

Criteria:
FIRST SEMESTER FRESHMAN GRADE POINT AVERAGE
SECOND SEMESTER FRESHMAN GRADE POINT AVERAGE

DESIGN AND METHOD OF ANALYSIS: (1) Product moment correlations were computed between predictors and criteria, (2) Multiple correlations were computed (a) between the predictor sets I, II, and III, and the criteria, (b) between set I (personality factors) and the criteria with the influence of set II (SCAT) partialed out. (3) Two subgroups of the 15 most extreme over- and under-achievers were compared in terms of their fifteen personality factor scores.

R_{10} (1) Cattell, R. B. "Clinical Diagnosis and Prognosis by Objective Personality Factors" (1961) (38)

The purpose of R10 (1) was to compare groups of neurotics, normals, and criminals in terms of their scores on objective test factors.

SUBJECTS: The subjects used in R10 (1) were the same as in R10; namely, 26 criminals, 30 neurotics, and 112 normals (University of Illinois undergraduates).

VARIABLES: Fifteen estimated factor scores (namely for U.I. 16, U.I. 17, U.I. 18, U.I. 19, U.I. 23, U.I. 24, U.I. 25, U.I. 26, U.I. 27, U.I. 28, U.I. 30, U.I. 32, U.I. 33, U.I. 34, and U.I. 35) were used as predictors. The criteria were the three dichotomies normal-criminal, normal-neurotic, and neurotic-criminal.

The estimated factor scores were obtained by the traditional multiple regression procedure, in which a best least squares fit of a linear combination of the tests is used to predict the factor. The variables used to predict the factors were the 111 used in the R10 factor analysis.

DESIGN AND METHOD OF ANALYSIS: Following the computation of factor scores, Students' 't' ratios were computed for the three comparisons normal-criminal, normal-neurotic, and neurotic-criminal on each of the fifteen factors. This study is a further analysis of R10, employing the same variables and subjects.

CHAPTER 5

EXPERIMENTAL FINDINGS ON CHILDREN: LIST OF AVAILABLE RESEARCHES

With the principal researches on adults reviewed in the preceeding chapter, a similar report will be given in this chapter on studies in which objective personality test factors have been investigated in children. In selecting these researches the same restriction applies as has been pointed out in the previous chapter. Since this monograph is limited to factors that have already been replicated over several independent studies, so that there can be no doubt about their "significance", it simultaneously becomes restricted to factor analytic researches which have enough "common ground" in terms of common variables so that factors can be objectively matched between studies.

This restriction limits the number of available researches to seven independent objective personality test factorizations in children, five of which have been carried out in the authors' laboratory. Of the remaining two studies, Brogden's analysis (12) is of particular interest as it represents one of the first attempts towards isolating objective test personality dimensions in children; four of Brogden's factors have been found to match factors now listed in the Universal Index series of personality source traits. In the other research, an analysis by Connor (72), only one of the obtained factors matched with a factor in the U.I. series.

All seven studies to be reported in this chapter are direct factor analyses, extension analyses on specific factors are planned but not completed. With respect to the age range covered, these researches can be divided into three groups: (1) upper grade-school and junior high-school level, late childhood (age range 9-13 years): the studies Bro (12), C 7 (55), and C n (72); (2) lower grade-school level, middle childhood (age range 6-8 years): the studies R 13 (49) and R 15 (56); (3) pre-school level, early childhood (age range 4-6 years): the studies R 12 (60) and R 14 (50). No analysis is as yet available at the high school level (age range 14-18 years). Of the studies in group 1) only C 7 contained all principal salients for factors found in adults; at the present time this study therefore also serves the role of "bridging the gap" between the adult age range and the age period of early and middle childhood.

In reporting these researches the same mode of presentation will be kept as in chapter IV; the studies will be listed in chronological order.

1) Study Bro: Hubert E. Brogden: A Factor Analysis of Forty Character Tests (12)

Historically, Brogden's research is one of the first factorizations of objective personality tests in children. It was designed as a factor analysis of objective test and questionnaire measures of honesty; the selection of variables was largely influenced by the research of Hartshorne and May (105, 106). Sampling of tests from a more general domain of personality traits has not been attempted.

SUBJECTS: 100 sixth grade children, all boys.

VARIABLES: All subjects have been tested on 40 variables, 10 questionnaire and 30 objective test measures; of the latter 11 were intelligence scores from the Otis Intelligence Test. The variables are listed in table 5.1; M.I. (Master Index) numbers are given for those variables that are common to both Brogden's study and the series of analyses from the authors' laboratory.

Table 5.1: Variables Investigated in Study Bro

Var. No. 1	M.I. --	Many problems answered correctly on achievement tests for grades higher than sixth grade
Var. No. 2	M.I. 20a	Much dishonesty (high total score) on motor coordination task with eyes closed
Var. No. 3	M.I. 12	Many fictitious book titles claimed to have read
Var. No. 4	M.I. --	High difference between claimed level of knowledge and actual knowledge
Var. No. 5	M.I. 34	Low suggestibility (derived from four tests, two of which were the two forms of the Otis Suggestibility Test)
Var. No. 6	M.I. --	High persistence in adding
Var. No. 7	M.I. --	High persistence in story completion
Var. No. 8	M.I. --	Less distraction from main task (adding) by interspersed puzzles, jokes, and stories
Var. No. 9	M.I. --	High persistence on picture inhibition test
Var. No. 10	M.I. --	Good knowledge of slang words
Var. No. 11	M.I. --	Many slang expressions selected
Var. No. 12	M.I. 13	Much oscillation of performance
Var. No. 13	M.I. 21	Many questionable reading preferences
Var. No. 14	M.I. --	Many questionable character preferences
Var. No. 15	M.I. 35	Opinion Ballot II (after Hartshorne and May (105,106)); attitude towards authority
Var. No. 16	M.I. --	Opinion Ballots N and VI (after Hartshorne and May): opinion about causes of social success and social failure, and willingness to help others

Table 5.1: Variables Investigated in Study Bro (Cont)

Var. No. 17	M.I. --	Opinion Ballot VIII (after Hartshorne and May): high honesty
Var. No. 18	M.I. --	Opinion Ballot IX (after Hartshorne and May): high sense of duty
Var. No. 19	M.I. 330	Many ethical choices in story identification
Var. No. 20	M.I. --	Evaluation of social and educational institutions (controlled association technique)
Var. No. 21	M.I. 2	Low motor rigidity in SZ Test
Var. No. 22	M.I. 2	Low motor rigidity on V Test
Var. No. 23	M.I. --	Low ideational rigidity on alternative adding and subtracting
Var. No. 24	M.I. 50	High carefulness in obeying directions
Var. No. 25	M.I. --	High deportment grade
Var. No. 26	M.I. 276	High average grade in school subjects
Var. No. 27	M.I. --	Woodworth Personality Inventory: good social adjustment[1]
Var. No. 28	M.I. --	Woodworth Personality Inventory: High self-sufficiency[1]
Var. No. 29	M.I. --	High variability of attainment on the 10 subtests of the Otis Intelligence Test
Var. No. 30-39	M.I. --	Scores from the 10 subtests of the Otis Intelligence Test
Var. No. 40	M.I. --	Total score on the Otis Intelligence Tests

DESIGN AND METHOD OF ANALYSIS: The design was a straight R-technique. The 40 x 40 intercorrelation matrix (Pearson product moment r's) has been factored by Thurstone's centroid analysis. Eight factors have been extracted: from the frequency distribution of the residual correlations the extraction has then been considered complete. The eight centroid factors have been rotated orthogonally for simple structure; only factor 4 has been rotated slightly oblique with regard to factor 5. The total hyperplane count achieved (hyperplane width ±.10) was 43%.

IDENTIFICATION OF FACTORS: Brogden gave the following factor interpretations:

factor 1: high will; a factor similar to Webb's factor w;
factor 2: high honesty;
factor 3: high persistence;

[1]These two scales emerged from an unpublished factor analysis by Brogden of the Woodworth Personality Inventory.

factor 4: Spearman's factor g (154) or Thurstone's factor V (160);
factor 5: high tendency to achieve;
factor 6: high self-control, inhibition, or possibly dutifulness;
factor 7: high willingness to accept, and believe in, moral codes;
factor 8: <uninterpreted>.

On the basis of common marker variables four of Brogden's factors can be identified as the following U.I. factors: factor 1+ as U.I. 16+, factor 2+ as U.I. 20+, factor 3+ as U.I. 26+, and factor 5+ as U.I. 24+.

2) Study C_n: Dave V. Connor: The Effect of Temperamental Traits Upon the Group Intelligence Performance of Children (72).

The objective of this study was to investigate the relationships between various temperament tests and intra-individual variability in intelligence test performance.

SUBJECTS: 229 boys and girls, 11-13 years of age; 53 subjects came from special schools and child guidance clinics and were regarded as maladjusted, the remaining 176 normal children were obtained from primary and secondary schools.

VARIABLES: Four parallel forms have been developed for each of five intelligence tests: abstracting, arithmetic, spatial, general reasoning, and vocabulary; subjects were tested on four occasions (with two weeks interval between any two occasions), each time on a different set of parallel forms of the four tests. From these, four measures of intra-individual performance variability have been derived (variables numbers 15-18 in table 5.2). In addition, 24 personality variables were investigated; only those 16 of the 24 variables which yielded significant differences between normal and maladjusted children were retained for further analysis.

The variables are listed in table 5.2. Equivalent M.I. numbers are given for those variables which correspond to measures used in the authors' laboratory.

Table 5.2: Variables Investigated in Study C_n

Var. No. 1	M.I. 277	
Var. No. 2	M.I. 42	
Var. No. 3	M.I. 122	
Var. No. 4	M.I. --	Magic square
Var. No. 5	M.I. --	Maintained hold (persistence)
Var. No. 6	M.I. 41	
Var. No. 7	M.I. --	Motor perseveration (V test)
Var. No. 8	M.I. --	Worries-and-anxiety questionnaire
Var. No. 9	M.I. --	"Ways to be Different"

Table 5.2: Variables Investigated in Study C_n (Cont)

Var. No. 10	M.I. --	Medical questionnaire
Var. No. 11	M.I. --	Annoyances questionnaire
Var. No. 12	M.I. --	Sentence completion
Var. No. 13	M.I. --	Peer sociometric rating
Var. No. 14	M.I. --	Teachers' rating
Var. No. 15	M.I. --	Day-to-day variability
Var. No. 16	M.I. 13	Within-day variability
Var. No. 17	M.I. --	Inter-test scatter
Var. No. 18	M.I. --	Practice effect
Var. No. 19	M.I. --	Abstraction
Var. No. 20	M.I. --	Arithmetic
Var. No. 21	M.I. --	General reasoning
Var. No. 22	M.I. --	Spatial
Var. No. 23	M.I. --	Vocabulary

DESIGN AND METHOD OF ANALYSIS: The design of this research is an R-technique of factorization (with the exception of the variability measures no. 15-18 which constitute data of the incremental R-technique type). The 23 variables have been completely intercorrelated (Pearson product moment correlation coefficients) and the intercorrelation matrix factor analyzed by Thurstone's centroid method. Six factors have been extracted and rotated orthogonally for both simple structure and optimum correlation with the normal-maladjusted criterion (following Eysenck's (85) procedure of "criterion analysis"). The total hyperplane count finally achieved is 28% (±.10 hyperplane width).

IDENTIFICATION OF FACTORS: Connor interpreted the factors as follows:
factor 1: general intelligence;
factor 2: general stability;
factor 3: self-revealed stability;
factor 4: reputation for stability;
factor 5: persistence;
factor 6: suggestibility.

Factor 4 is now identifiable as source trait U.I. 27.

3) Study C 7: R. B. Cattell and W. Gruen: The Primary Personality Factors in Eleven Year Old Children by Objective Tests (55).

In this study a first attempt was made to investigate at the child level factors found, up to that time, only with adults. Marker variables were included for all U.I. factors then well-replicated in adults.

SUBJECTS: 184 children (87 boys, 97 girls) between 9 and 12 years of age (mean age: 11.2 years), from the Mooseheart Child Community, Illinois.

VARIABLES: A total of 122 objective test variables have been investigated, the M.I. numbers of which are given in table 5.3. In addition, two random variables have been entered into the analysis.

Table 5.3: Variables Investigated in Study C 7
(listed by M.I. numbers)

21	123	8	224	244	112
171	255	143	228	261	2a[1]
4	65	211	120b	80	2d[1]
39	144	35	101a	212	24c
274	245	24d	7	199	13b[2]
64	218	247a	28	299	34
44	41	227a	210	290	250
260	153	96a	296	268	96a
202	219	287	108	43	253
198	256	16a	336	161	257
5	235	231	242	249	82
216	133	193	88	116a	233
2d	106	207	146b	31	24f
276	205	295	278	13b	269
254	122	225	236	99	270
46a	67a	71	2a	271	273
55	246	209	147b	252	275
320	62	15	83	162b	277
262	72	120c	243	263	150
40	111	194	192	191	291
223a	152	214a	264	167a	299

DESIGN AND METHOD OF ANALYSIS: The design was that of a straight R-technique. One hundred and four, out of the total one hundred and twenty-eight variables, have been intercorrelated (product moment correlations) and factored by Thurstone's multi-group method (162). Sixteen factors have been extracted, and the factor extraction has been iterated four times to stabilize the communalities. After thirty oblique visual rotations a total hyperplane count of 67% (hyperplane width: ±.10) has been reached. The loadings of the remaining 24 variables on the rotated factors have been computed by the Dwyer method of extension analysis (83).

[1] Equivalent to M.I. 2a and 2d above, but both scored as a ratio instead of a difference.

[2] Same as M.I. 13b above, but derived from more difficult task.

IDENTIFICATION OF FACTORS: The following personality factors have been identified[1]: U.I. 16(6+), U.I. 17 (14+), U.I. 18 (13+), U.I. 19 (7+), U.I. 20 (4-), U.I. 21 (10-), U.I. 22 (9-), U.I. 23 (5-), U.I. 24 (12+), U. I. 25 (12+), U.I. 26 (11+), U.I. 28 (8+), U.I. 29 (3-), and U.I. 30 (15-). In addition, a general ability factor (U.I. 1 (2+)) has been found. One factor (1) turned out to be an instrument factor, only loaded by PGR measures.

4) Study R 12: R. B. Cattell and D. R. Peterson: Personality Structure in Four and Five Year Olds in Terms of Objective Tests (60).

In study R 12 the research on objective test factors was for the first time extended to the pre-school age level. Many of the marker variables for factors which had been found in adults and were successfully replicated in C 7 had to be especially adapted to meet the specific requirements set by this age group (e.g., only individual tests, only few paper-and-pencil tests, no reading or writing involved, etc.).

SUBJECTS: 80 children (36 boys, 44 girls), average age of 4.7 years. All children attended the University of Chicago Nursery School.

VARIABLES: A total of 81 variables has been investigated, all derived from individual tests. These variables are listed in table 5.4 by their M.I. numbers.

Table 5.4 Variables Investigated in Study R 12
(listed by M.I. numbers)

175	168a	327b	144	205	263
176	218	219	333	123	350
40	21	38b	211a	212	351
5	166	332	330	268	353
263	98a	150	247a	31	352a
335	143	34	342	344	354
71	30	271	340	300a	355
72	29	6c	199	346	945c
307	146b	2b	273	347	356b
270	7	339	161b	348	356a
282	51	227a	343a	24d	2b
336	206	120c	343c	101b	357
105	338	334	341	349	359
				1741	358

[1] The numbers in brackets indicate the number of the rotated factor with which each U.I. factor has been identified.

DESIGN AND METHOD OF ANALYSIS: Study R 12 followed the R-technique design. All 81 variables have been intercorrelated (product moment correlations), and the intercorrelation matrix has been factored by Thurstone's centroid method. Twenty factors have been extracted. The centroid matrix was first submitted to the analytical oblique rotation routine Oblimax (141); the Oblimax solution was then further rotated over 13 visual oblique rotations, after which a total hyperplane count of 68% (hyperplane width: ±.10) had been achieved.

IDENTIFICATION OF FACTORS: The following personality factors have been identified: U.I. 16 (7+), U.I. 17 (12+), U.I. 18 (20+), U.I. 19 (11+), U.I. 20 (14+), U.I. 21 (15+), U.I. 22 (3+), U.I. 23 (6+), U.I. 24 (5+), U.I. 25 (4+), U.I. 26 (19+), U.I. 28 (18+), U.I. 29 (2+), U.I. 30 (8+), U.I. 32 (16+), U.I. 34 (9+), U.I. 35 (17+), in addition a factor of general intelligence U.I. 1 (1+) has been found. Factor 10 has been interpreted as a new factor of Critical Restraint, one factor (13+) has been regarded as an instrument factor (mirror-drawing doublet).

5) Study R 13: R. B. Cattell and R. W. Coan: Objective Test Assessment of the Primary Personality Dimensions in Middle Childhood (49).

This research was designed to represent the hitherto missing link between the studies C 7 (late childhood) and R 12 (early childhood).

SUBJECTS: 164 children (equal numbers from both sexes), ranging in age from 6 years and 3 months to 8 years and 11 months (average age: 7.4 years). The subjects were first and second graders in public schools in East Central Illinois.

VARIABLES: 155 objective personality test variables have been investigated in this study. In the selection of variables special care has been taken to include markers for factors previously found at the adult and child level. The variables are listed by their M.I. numbers in table 5.5.

Table 5.5: Variables Investigated in Study R 13
(listed by M.I. numbers)

360	31	389	286	431	397
113	120d	9	340	435	398
246	375	391	339	152	399
219	309	392	357	436	402
100	377	393	419	437	403
112	378	400	420a	439	109
321	203	401	421	65	408
21	379	404	422	362	410

Table 5.5: Variables Investigated in Study R 13 (Cont)
(listed by M.I. numbers)

108	380	405	101c	365	411
116	206	406	145c	366	28
29	379	271	423	367	45
192	234	273	424	369	415
211a	101b	316	282	373	5
211b	145b	30	105	38b	165
67a	381	407	425	34	416
361	382	409	6b	193	417a
363	143	270	2e	13c	418
364	24d	269	2h	312	170
368	133	412	8	376	432
39	383	413	171	237	433
227a	384	414	7	51	434
370	385	176	146b	307b	438
371	247a	40	426	6a	440
372	386	71	427	390	64
374	387	72	428b	394	277
167a	388	263	429	395	1742
			430	396	441
					442

DESIGN AND METHOD OF ANALYSIS: The first 111 variables have been intercorrelated (product moment correlation), and the resulting matrix of intercorrelations has been analyzed by Thurstone's centroid method. Various criteria for completeness of factor extraction agreed on fifteen "significant" factors. These fifteen factors have been rotated by the analytical oblique rotation procedure Oblimax (141) the results of which have then been rotated visually for oblique simple structure. An additional hyperplane came up in the course of these rotations, so that a sixteenth factor was then added on. In the final rotated reference vector structure matrix, according to Bargmann's test (6), fifteen factors were significant at the 0.001 level, one at the 0.01 level. The total hyperplane count reached was 65% (hyperplane width: ±.10).

The factor loadings of the remaining 49 variables have been estimated from an extension analysis. Estimated factor scores have been computed for all subjects on all sixteen factors (from a complete multiple regression analysis, with the 111 variables being the "predictors", the 16 factors being the "criteria"), and the 49 variables correlated with these estimated factor scores.

IDENTIFICATION OF FACTORS: The following personality dimensions have been identified: U.I. 16 (1+), U.I. 17 (2-), U.I. 18 (12+), U.I. 19 (10-), U.I. 20 (14+), U.I. 21 (3+), U.I. 22 (5+), U.I. 23 (16-), U.I. 24 (6+), U.I.

25 (13-), U.I. 26 (4-), U.I. 28 (9+), U.I. 31 (11+), U.I. 32 (8-), and U.I. 33 (7+). In addition, a factor of general intelligence (U.I. 1 (15+)) has been found.

Recently Pawlik completed a second-order factor analysis from these primary factors.

6) Study R 15: R. B. Cattell and E. Howarth: Verification of Objective Personality Factors in Middle Childhood (56).

This research was designed as a replication of study R 13, with the additional aim of exploring new objective tests which were developed with special reference to the factors previously found in children.

SUBJECTS: 197 grade school children (98 boys, 99 girls), all from public schools in East Central Illinois. Average age: 8.8 years.

VARIABLES: A total of 109 objective test variables have been investigated; in addition, two random variables have been added into the analysis. The variables are listed in table 5.6 by their corresponding M.I. numbers.

Table 5.6: Variables Investigated in Study R 15
(listed by M.I. numbers)

206	120c	1419	7	122	1368
168a	101b	30[2]	146a	42	1427
133	203	385	1355	300b	1428
39	199	24d	339	270	1250
1412	273	143	357	1245	1429
1413	1414	98	176	1421	1430
429	1415	15	175	1352	1433
364	327b	348	40	1422	1372
211a	67a	282	263	1423	1344
359	101b[1]	105	71	1328	1373
212	145b	2a	72	1424	1390
219	1416	280	335	1425	1434
218	193	356b	1363	1364	1435
21	247a	6b	421	1389	1436
309	30	2f	422	1370	1391
382	1417	426	1353	1365	1392
379	1418	428a	1420	1366	609
234	51	430	1354	1426	1437
					1438

[1] Equivalent to M.I. 101b listed before, but obtained from lengthened version of same.

[2] Equivalent to M.I. 30 above, but derived from different test.

DESIGN AND METHOD OF ANALYSIS: The design of this study is a straight R-technique.

All 111 variables have been intercorrelated (product moment correlations) and the resulting matrix of intercorrelations has been factored by Thurstone's centroid method. Twenty-two factors have been extracted; after an initial analytical oblique rotation (Oblimax) twenty-seven visual oblique rotations have been performed. The final rotated position showed good simple structure with a total hyperplane count of 69% (hyperplane width: ±.10).

FACTOR IDENTIFICATION: The following personality factors have been identified: U.I. 16 (1+), U.I. 18 (3+), U.I. 19 (10+), U.I. 21 (6+), U.I. 22 (5+), U.I. 23 (8+), U.I. 24 (9+), U.I. 25 (21+), U.I. 26 (18-), U. I. 28 (13+), U.I. 30 (12-), U.I. 31 (12-) and U.I. 32 (17+). Factors U.I. 17 and 27 could not be identified although markers for these factors have been included; for factors U.I. 29, U.I. 33 and U.I. 36 no markers have been entered into the analysis.

7) Study R 14: R. B. Cattell, F. L. Damarin and J. D. Hundleby: Further Investigation of Objective Personality Test Factors in Early Childhood (50).

This most recent research from the authors' laboratory on objective personality test factors in children was designed to check on the replicability of the results obtained previously with pre-school children (study R 12); in addition, many newly developed tests have been included in the analysis.

SUBJECTS: 129 children (67 boys, 62 girls), varying in age between 3 years and 9 months and 6 years and 10 months (average age: 5.3 years). A relatively heterogeneous sample has been attempted; subjects were children of Air Force enlisted men (from Chanute Air Force Base, Illinois), children (of relatively poor home background) attending a summer camp in northern Illinois, and children from various nursery schools in Champaign, Illinois, and vicinity. Not only a large variability in age, but also in intelligence, social status and home background has thus been achieved.

VARIABLES: 87 variables have been analyzed in this study. The variables are listed by their M.I. numbers in table 5.7.

Table 5.7: Variables Investigated in Study R 14
(listed by M.I. numbers)

175	123	1449	976	422	6c
40	31	1450	1462	430	203
263	227	1410	1463	428	199
270	219	1451	977	42	1456

Table 5.7: Variables Investigated in Study R 14 (Cont)
(listed by M.I. numbers)

282	38c	1452	981	33	835
336	1440	1453	982	1719	152
168a	1443	1411a	983	1720	1465
143	1444	1411b	984	1721	1466
30	1445	1411c	527	1722	1457
146b	1446	1411d	832	1723	1458
327b	1447	950	1464	1724	1459
120c	755	1455	609	1725	1460
359	83	1339	108	1726	1461
273	1448	995	295	277	152[1]
			192	64	211a

DESIGN AND METHOD OF ANALYSIS: The design was a straight R-technique. The first 74 variables have been intercorrelated (product moment correlations) and factor analyzed by Thurstone's centroid method. Twenty-two factors have been extracted and rotated for oblique simple structure. As in the previous researches, the centroid factors have first been rotated analytically by Oblimax; this analytical rotation was followed by 21 visual rotations. The hyperplane count finally reached was 75% (hyperplane width: ±.10).

The loadings of the remaining 15 variables on the rotated factors have been computed by Dwyer's extension analysis (83).

FACTOR IDENTIFICATION: The following factors have been identified: U.I. 19 (16-), U.I. 20 (8+), U.I. 22 (20-), U.I. 24 (7+), U.I. 29 (21+), and U.I. 34 (13+). Factor 12+ was interpreted as a general intelligence factor. Five factors were test-specific or instrument factors, 7 factors were left unidentified.

[1] Equivalent to M.I. 152 above, but scored as a ratio.

[2] The presence of instrument factors in this analysis prompted a re-analysis, and this is at present being carried out. Results so far indicate that any decisions about the personality dimensions are unlikely to be much changed by this further work.

CHAPTER 6

THE MATCHING OF SOURCE TRAITS U.I. 16 to U.I. 36 ACROSS DIFFERENT STUDIES

Each of the twenty-one personality factors indexed as U.I. 16 through U.I. 36, with which this monograph is dealing, has been found in several independent factor analyses. Having described the experimental researches themselves on which these factors rest, we have nevertheless still to examine the evidence for the goodness of matching from research to research. For it is widely agreed that in view of the immense labor in rotating to perfection in simple structure there is always some uncertainty about the description of a factor in a single experiment, and that factor analysis more than most methods must rest the stability of its concepts finally on the ability to demonstrate recurrence of patterns. In short it is essential to investigate the "goodness of replication" for each personality factor before any discussion of the psychological nature of these dimensions. In the present chapter the degree of such matching across researches will be discussed for each factor.[1]

I. THE SOURCES OF EVIDENCE ON CROSS-STUDIES MATCHING OF FACTORS.

The development of techniques for accurate and objective evaluation of the constancy of a factor across the different studies in which it has been found indeed constitutes the indispensable backbone of multivariate experimentation if our search for general dimensions of behavior is not to end in an unintegrated multiplicity of isolated individual research findings. The principal methods of factor matching have already been described in Chapter III. Of these, the salient variable similarity index, the Procrustes transformation, the Burt-Tucker-Wrigley coefficient of congruence, and--most recently--Kaiser's method of relating factors have proved highly valuable in checking on the proper factor identification. In most studies, except the very early ones, at least one, but often several, of these methods have been used to identify the obtained factors against the "model" factor pattern derived from previous studies.

Our present task must be clearly distinguished on the one hand from that of forcing two studies to maximum agreement, as in Tucker's method, and, on the other, to investigate the matching of factors found in a new study, with factors defined in some ideal "criterion matrix" of factor loadings, e.g., as stated by a hypothesis or obtained by averaging across several previous analyses. The

[1]U.I. 36 itself is excluded from discussion in this chapter. See page 322.

former does not test, as here, positions found by some independent procedure in each result to be compared, and the latter assumes some one pattern is the criterion. At this point we rather wish to assess the degree of over-all across-studies consistency of each identified factor. In other words, for each factor we are asking the question: How similar or consistent is the loading pattern of this factor if compared across all the researches in which it has been uniquely rotated and independently identified? In this monograph four different methodological approaches are used, as described below.

(1) Assessing the Factor Match Between Pairs of Studies.

With the exception of Tucker's solution (163), all methods of factor matching reviewed in Chapter III are of the two-studies type, i.e., no more than two sets of loading patterns can be compared at a time. Thus, if a factor has been found in N researches, 1/2N(N - 1) individual factor matching coefficients (salient variable similarity indices, etc.) have to be worked out. The over-all degree of across-studies consistency can then be evaluated from this matrix of study-by-study matching coefficients. Due to the considerable labor involved in thus computing every possible pair we have examined the verdict of this method only in terms of random samples of the possible matching, comparing both asserted matches and asserted non-matches.

(2) Assessing the Factor Match Between Each Study and the Pooled Loading Pattern (Specific Study Excluded).

A factor column of loadings which have been averaged across all N researches in which a factor has been identified will constitute an unbiased estimate of the "true" loading pattern of this factor, as long as the factor identification is correct in each of the N studies. Instead of working through all possible 1/2N (N - 1) comparisons between two studies, as described above, the loading pattern in each study could be compared directly with this pooled factor column. In order to avoid biased comparisons the loading pattern in a given study should be compared with the pooled factor column obtained from averaging loadings only across the remaining N - 1 studies. Such a comparison can then be carried out by any one of the methods described in section 5 of Chapter III. This method has not only the advantage of saving in computing time (only N instead of 1/2N (N-1) comparisons are necessary). In comparing the loading pattern for factor X between studies A and B, the agreement of either with the true pattern will be underestimated, for both studies will (at least within sampling errors) depart from the true loading pattern of X. On the other hand, comparing the loading pattern for factor X between an individual study and the pooled loading pattern will give a more accurate estimate of the replicability of factor X because the pooled loading pattern is a better criterion than the loading pattern of factor X in any single research. Due to changing pooled factor columns for each comparison, only factors which have appeared in relatively few studies were selected to be examined in this way.

(3) Assessing the Correspondence Between Two Pooled Loading Patterns Drawn from a Series of Factor Identifications.

A loading pattern or column of factor loadings found in any one study may be regarded as an estimate of the pattern from a complete population. If such loadings are averaged across a series of studies, then this estimate should be improved. If two such pooled estimates derived from approximately equivalent groups of subjects are then compared, the ensuing indices or coefficients indicate the general degree of agreement or homogeneity that exists in the successive identifications of a factor over a series of researches. This method is somewhat similar to the second method, but differs in that it presents only one summary coefficient.

Coefficients from this method were obtained in the following manner. The list of researches in which a given factor had been identified was inspected, and two population-balanced sets of researches were drawn up. By "balanced", we mean containing approximately similar sub-samples of subjects. Obviously, it would not be fair to compare patterns obtained from different populations, e.g., children and adults, psychotics and normals, for systematic differences should then exist. The composition of these two groups is thus somewhat analogous to the selection of equivalent sub-tests of items on some rational, systematic bases in computing the split-half reliability of a test. On no occasion during the selection of the two sets of researches was any consideration made of the size or scope of actual loadings. Following this, variables were chosen that had appeared in at least four of the researches. Average correlations were then computed for each variable within each set of researches. Finally, the coefficient of congruence was computed for these two sets of averaged correlations.

(4) Assessing the Factor Match Simultaneously Across all N Studies.

Formally, we are dealing with a situation of factor matching as outlined in table 5 of Chapter III; a factor X has been found in N studies and we wish to evaluate the degree of consistency or similarity exhibited in the N loading patterns. One way of assessing this over-all degree of factor matching is directly suggested from Tucker's (164) method of relating factors: The Table of n rows (common variables) and N columns (the different replicative studies) is treated as any analysis of variance table, with n groups (blocks or samples) each of sample size N (or less, if a particular variable is not common to all N studies). In the case of ideal cross-studies consistency all values in a row will be identical, all variation in the table being between-rows variation. In the case of a "zero" match, if N is a large number, the means of the n rows will be identical (and approaching zero average loadings) and all variability in the table is within-rows variation. If we regard this case as a null hypothesis against which we wish to test our actual table of factor loadings, we can directly apply the one-way analysis of variance model to obtain an over-all significance test against zero or chance factor matching. The ratio, $\frac{\text{between-variables mean square,}}{\text{within-variables mean square}}$ can be regarded as an F-ratio as in usual one-way analysis of variance. If F is significant, the within-rows variance is small relative to the between-rows variance and the loading pattern is more consistent across the N studies than expected with pure chance matches; if F is insignificant, the obtained degree of across-studies consistency in loading patterns is not significantly different from chance matches between the N studies.

II. METHODOLOGICAL CONSIDERATIONS IN THE MATCHING OF OBJECTIVE TEST FACTORS.

Before considering the matching of individual U.I. personality factors across different studies, it is necessary to outline certain methodological problems that have direct bearing upon the results obtained. These problems would appear to have particular relevance for factor matching procedures in which the factor is regarded as a trait capable of appearing, though in modified form, in diverse groups of subjects. Certain other problems emerge due to the historical development of research in this field.

(1) The Use of Different Populations.

The measures discussed in this monograph have been administered to widely different groups of subjects, ranging from five-year-old children to adult psychotics. The extent to which such heterogeneity will affect the loading pattern for a variable is in most cases unknown. At least a fair degree of stability must be present, of course, if any objective form of matching is to be obtained between the results from different samples. However, it would be psychologically naive to expect as good a match between factors found in groups of undergraduates and very young children as with different groups of undergraduates. Assuming that sufficient evidence is present, then a systematic linking of studies would promise grounds for judging a factor as present across, say, all age groups, though evidence based solely on the most extreme groups might be quite weak. At present, there is simply not enough accumulated evidence to indicate rigorous bounds for what is meant by sufficient evidence, and decisions of this nature--at least for the next few years--must rest to a regrettable extent upon the wisdom and experience of individual researchers.

(2) The Use of Different Tests at Different Age Levels.

Somewhat similar to (1) above is the problem of evaluating tests which have different content (due to age differences) but appear to measure similar psychological functions. As an example, we may take perceptual-motor rigidity. This has been measured in adults by using the comparison of normal forward writing with a variety of "unnatural" writing forms (e.g., writing backwards, doubling letters, etc.). This test is adequate down to the age of about 8 to 9 years. For children up to this age level a test has been used involving color recognition and reverse color recognition (e.g., saying "blue" when a green stimulus is presented). Although there is sufficient evidence to regard these two tests as measuring the same function, it is not to be expected that they will have identical loading patterns. For quantitative purposes, such variables have been regarded as identical, and this tends to impose an upper bound that is lower than the theoretical upper limit upon matching indices.

In practice, the decremental effect of such true differences between variables that are being for statistical purposes regarded as the same is probably not great. In the first case, they are relatively few in number, and in the second, they have only been regarded as the same if both loading pattern and manifest function have much in common.

(3) Historical Development of Marker Variables.

As an empirical construct in science, any given personality factor is far from static. As hypotheses concerning the factor are tested, and new tests are constructed as improved measures of the factor, so there is a gradual historical development of measures loading the factor. Thus a factor may receive considerable research (e.g., see U.I. 23 and U.I. 24 in Chapter 7), leading to a series of constantly improving tests. Excellent though this undoubtedly is from a broad scientific viewpoint, the unfortunate effect upon matching is often that these newer and better loaded tests are under-represented, due to the relatively few times that each has been used. Thus several of our methods involve the adoption of a lower bound of, say, its use in three or four studies, before a variable is included in the matching analysis. The net result of this is to underemphasize considerably certain recent improved marker tests, and thus to reduce the status of such factors.

(4) The Assumption That Hyperplane Variables May Reflect a True Loading of Zero.

A problem of relevance to use of the coefficient of congruence and the analysis of variance method concerns the extent to which a researcher is willing to assume that variables of low loading are really hyperplane loadings of zero "blurred" by measurement error or imperfect rotation. As most of the researches reviewed in this monograph involve rotation to simple structure--i.e., few high-loading variables and many zero-loading variables--this can be of considerable importance. If we make the assumption that such loadings do reflect random fluctuation around zero, then the effect will be to reduce both the coefficient of congruity and the F ratio. The greater the proportion of variables lying in the hyperplane (i.e., with a true zero loading) the less will be the contribution to any statistic of the high-loading variables. Even though it may be an exaggeration to regard all variables with loadings between +.1 and -.1 as having a population loading of zero, it is undoubtedly true for at least some of such variables, and this may be enough in certain cases to have considerable effect.

(5) Evidence on Matching From Sources Ulterior to the Factor Pattern on Objective Tests.

The decision that factor A in one study is the same personality dimension as factor A' in another study rests on similar arguments to those employed in assessing the construct validity of a test (77a). Evidence from a variety of sources and situations has to be martialled and examined. Evidence on criterion associations (e.g., relationship to clinical diagnosis or academic success), correlations with questionnaire or rating methods of assessment, loadings on second order factors, similar genetic determination or family and environmental correlates, are all legitimate pieces of evidence. In the quantitative matching of objective test factors, however, we have limited consideration solely to objective tests, leaving the reader to incorporate the additional evidence when it is presented in detail in Chapters 7 and 8. Though this has the merit of parsimony and clarity, it does lead to a consistent underevaluation of the extent of match and homogeneity with any given factor.

III. RESULTS ON THE MATCHING OF INDIVIDUAL FACTORS, ARRANGED BY UNIVERSAL INDEX NUMBERS.

In this section the matching of each factor will be examined separately and an illustration of cross-matching of factors between studies C_5 and C_6 will be presented. This will be followed by a brief summary and discussion of results. The method of evaluating by the s or salient variable similarity index is separately described later on page 127, but its conclusions have been focussed in the present accounts.

(1) U.I. 16: Unbound Assertive Ego.

U.I. 16 was the first of the objective test factors to be identified in more than one study. Both the analysis of variance and coefficient of congruence give satisfactory values. As an illustration of the level of values that may be obtained by using the coefficient of congruence, three individual comparisons are also included in Table 6.1.

Table 6.1: Matching Evidence on U.I. 16

A. Results of Analysis of Variance: Over-All Match Across Studies

Source	S.S.	df	M.S.	F	P
Between Variables	3.5226	96	0.0367	1.75	
Within Variables	10.4869	501	0.0209		$<.01$
Total	14.0095	597			

B. Results of Pooled r_c

Researches Group A	Researches Group B	Number of Variables	r_c
C_2 C_4 C_5	C_1 C_3 C_6	68	+.706
R_1 C_7	R_2 R_{10} BRO		

C. Results of Individual r_c Comparisons

Researches	Number of Variables	r_c
C_4 versus C_5	31	+.525
C_1 versus C_2	22	+.771
R_{13} versus R_{15}	37	+.308

(2) U.I. 17: Timid Inhibitedness.

The matching evidence for this factor is rather disappointing, as the analysis of variance results are not significant. The value of +.479 for the pooled coefficient of congruence indicates that at least for this one type of index, the factor can be matched across studies. In part at least, the problem of matching this factor is the dearth of high loading variables that have been used in many studies.

Table 6.2: Matching Evidence on U.I. 17

A. Results of Analysis of Variance: Over-All Match Across Studies

Source	S.S.	df	M.S.	F	P
Between Variables	2.0389	90	0.0226	1.037	$>.05$
Within Variables	9.8960	453	0.0218		
Total	11.9349	543			

Table 6.2: Matching Evidence on U.I. 17 (Cont)

B. Results of Pooled r_c:

Researches Group A	Group B	Number of Variables	r_c
C_1 C_6 Ros R_2	C_2 C_5 R_1 R_{13}	37	+.470
C_7 Th C_3	Me C_4 R_{12}		

(3) U.I. 18: Hypomanic Smartness.

U.I. 18 is significant with regard to the analysis of variance results, but the value of the coefficient of congruence is lower than was to be expected.

Table 6.3: Matching Evidence on U.I. 18

A. Results of Analysis of Variance: Over-All Match Across Studies

Source	S.S.	df	M.S.	F	P
Between Variables	1.8444	27	0.0683	1.967	$<.01$
Within Variables	5.7988	167	0.0347		
Total	7.6432	194			

B. Results of Pooled r_c:

Researches Group A	Group B	Number of Variables	r_c
C_1 C_4 C_5	C_2 C_3 C_6 R_2	91	+.342
R_1 R_{13} C_7	R_{10} R_{15} R_{12}		

(4) U.I. 19: Promethean Will.

In spite of its relationships to various criteria, both clinical and educational, this factor did not yield a significant F ratio. The value of +.451 for the pooled coefficient of congruence suggests that there is sufficient consistency, coupled with evidence from other sources discussed on page 164, to retain this factor in the Universal Index series until more conclusive information is available.

Table 6.4: Matching Evidence on U.I. 19

A. Results of Analysis of Variance: Over-All Match Across Studies

Source	S.S.	df	M.S.	F	P
Between Variables	3.0460	104	0.0293	1.273	$>.05$
Within Variables	14.1531	615	0.0230		
Total	17.1991	719			

B. Results of Pooled r_c:

Researches			
Group A	Group B	Number of Variables	r_c
C_1 C_5 Ros R_2	C_2 C_6 R_1 C_3	57	+.451
R_{10} R_{13} C_7	R_{15} R_{12} C_4		

(5) U.I. 20: Comentive Superego.

Both analyses of variance and the pooled coefficient of congruence agree in the matching of this factor. As with most factors, the match appears to be better with adults than with children.

Table 6.5: Matching Evidence on U.I. 20

A. Results of Analysis of Variance: Over-All Match Across Studies

Source	S.S.	df	M.S.	F	P
Between Variables	2.4392	31	0.0787	1.77	$<.05$
Within Variables	6.7544	152	0.0444		
Total	9.1936	183			

B. Results of pooled r_c:

Researches			
Group A	Group B	Number of Variables	r_c
C_1 C_3 C_6	C_2 C_4 C_5	60	+.599
Ros H_1	R_1 C_7		

(6) U.I. 21: Exuberance

U.I. 21 appears to be fairly consistent over its identification in different researches in terms of both analysis of variance and pooled coefficient of congruence results. It is unfortunate that principal markers have not been included in all studies; otherwise the quantitative evidence would probably be much stronger.

Table 6.6: Matching Evidence on U.I. 21

A. Results of Analysis of Variance: Over-All Match Across Studies

Source	S.S.	df	M.S.	F	P
Between Variables	2.9731	48	0.0619	1.92	$<.01$
Within Variables	9.0853	282	0.0322		
Total	12.0584	330			

B. Results of Pooled r_c:

Researches			
Group A	Group B	Number of Variables	r_c
C_1 C_4 C_5	C_2 C_3 C_6	51	+.472

(7) U.I.22: Cortertia

This factor gives an F value that is significant at a level beyond that to be expected from the relatively modest pooled coefficient of congruence. Such a discrepancy is not too surprising considering the general differences between the two methods.

Table 6.7: Matching Evidence on U.I. 22

A. Results of Analysis of Variance: Over-All Match Across Studies

Source	S.S.	df	M.S.	F	P
Between Variables	3.6063	33	0.1093	2.88	$<.01$
Within Variables	7.6834	203	0.0378		
Total	11.2897	236			

Table 6.7: Matching Evidence On U.I. 22 (Cont)

B. Results of Pooled r_c:

Researches			
Group A	Group B	Number of Variables	r_c
C_1 C_3 C_6	C_2 C_4 C_5	73	+.311
R_2 C_7 R_{15}	Ros R_{12} R_{13}		

(8) U.I. 23: High Mobilization

The matching for this factor has undoubtedly suffered from the exclusion of variables used less than four times from both the analysis of variance and pooled coefficient of congruence methods. Considerable research has been carried out on this factor, and has led to the development of new and potentially good markers for the factor (e.g., as in studies R6 and R8), but these have not yet received widespread enough usage to be included in the matching analysis. The results for both analyses of variance and congruence coefficient should therefore be regarded as strictly lower bounds with every expectation that further research will considerably strengthen these indices.

Table 6.8: Matching Evidence on U.I. 23

A. Results of Analysis of Variance: Over-All Match Across Studies

Source	S.S.	df	M.S.	F	P
Between Variables	1.7841	26	0.0686	2.00	$<.01$
Within Variables	5.0620	148	0.0342		
Total	6.8461	174			

B. Results of Pooled r_c:

Researches			
Group A	Group B	Number of Variables	r_c
C_2 C_3 R_1	C_1 C_4 R_2	54	+.351
R_{10} R_{12} R_{13}	C_7 R_{15}		

(9) U.I. 24: Unbound Anxiety.

U.I. 24 is probably the best matched factor in the Universal Index series according to present evidence. Not only are the analyses of variance and coefficient of congruence results clearly good, but these must be regarded as underestimates as the questionnaire factor (Q data) loadings on U.I. 24 are amongst the highest and most consistent, and these have been eliminated from both analyses.

Table 6.9: Matching Evidence on U.I. 24

A. Results of Analysis of Variance: Over-All Match Across Studies

Source	S.S.	df	M.S.	F	P
Between Variables	3.0584	28	0.1092	3.99	$<.01$
Within Variables	4.7321	173	0.0273		
Total	7.7905	201			

B. Results of Pooled r_c:

Researches			
Group A	Group B	Number of Variables	r_c
C_6 R_{10} R_1	C_5 Ros R_2	48	+.739
C_7 R_{15}	H_1 R_{12} R_{13}		

(10) U.I. 25: Less Imaginative Task-Oriented Realism.

The matching of this factor gave fairly good results for both analysis of variance and pooled congruence coefficient. The match with very young children is rather weak and this tends to affect the over-all results.

Table 6.10: Matching Evidence on U.I. 25

A. Results of Analysis of Variance: Over-All Match Across Studies

Source	S.S.	df	M.S.	F	P
Between Variables	1.2858	27	0.0476	1.55	$<.05$
Within Variables	4.7720	156	0.0305		
Total	6.0579	183			

Table 6:10 Matching Evidence on U.I. 25 (Cont)

B. Results of Pooled r_c:

Researches			
Group A	Group B	Number of Variables	r_c
C_3 Ros R_1 C_7	C_5 R_{10} R_2 R_{13}	45	+.499

(11) U.I. 26: Narcistic Self.

The results for U.I. 26 are definitely disappointing. Analysis of variance results are not significant, though a value of +.483 is reached using the pooled coefficient of congruence. To a large extent these findings are due to the inclusion of only tentative matches at the child level, and the lack of really stable and sizable markers. It may be that this factor, with its interpretation of ego involvement, shows considerable change in loading pattern over different age levels and different samples. Additional support of U.I. 26 as a unitary dimension comes from a variety of criterion correlations.

Table 6.11: Matching Evidence on U.I. 26

A. Results of Analysis of Variance: Over-All Match Across Studies

Source	S.S.	df	M.S.	F	P
Between Variables	2.0578	86	0.0239	1.14	>.05
Within Variables	9.1544	438	0.0209		
Total	11.3122	524			

B. Results of Pooled r_c:

Researches			
Group A	Group B	Number of Variables	r_c
C_5 R_1 Bro	C_6 R_2 C_7	45	+.483
R_{13} C_3 C_4	R_{15} R_{10} R_{12}		

From U.I. 27 onwards, there is insufficient data available for computation of the F ratio. An exception to this is U.I. 28. The reader should be warned, in addition, that for these later factors the congruence coefficient is often based upon small numbers of studies and a corresponding small number of variables.

(12) U.I. 27: Discouraged Skeptical Apathy.

U.I. 27 suffers particularly from not only being identified in relatively few studies, but in having few variables common to many of these studies. Only nine variables were used in the computation of the congruence coefficient.

Table 6.12: Matching Evidence on U.I. 27

Results of Pooled r_c:

Researches			
Group A	Group B	Number of Variables	r_c
$C_4\ R_2$	$C_3\ R_{10}$	9	+.504

(13) U.I. 28: Dependent, Negativistic Asthenia

Analysis of variance results for this factor are quite encouraging, but the pooled congruence coefficient is lower than expected.

Table 6.13: Matching Evidence on U.I. 28

A. Results of Analysis of Variance: Over-All Match Across Studies

Source	S.S.	df	M.S.	F	P
Between Variables	1.5576	23	0.0677	2.43	$<.01$
Within Variables	3.5017	126	0.0277		
Total	7.5613	149			

B. Results of Pooled r_c:

Researches			
Group A	Group B	Number of Variables	r_c
$C_4\ C_5$	$C_3\ C_6$	62	+.370
$H_1\ C_7$	$R_2\ R_{13}$		

(14) U.I. 29: Whole-Hearted Responsiveness.

This factor indicates rather weak matching, due to the lack of a set of high-loading variables characterizing the pattern.

Table 6.14: Matching Evidence on U.I. 29

Results of Pooled r_c:

Researches			
Group A	Group B	Number of Variables	r_c
C_1 C_4	C_2 C_3	61	+.325
C_5 R_2	C_6 C_7		

(15) U.I. 30: Somindence.

A reasonably high pooled coefficient of congruence has been found for this factor, and this is based upon all studies in which it has been identified.

Table 6.15: Matching Evidence on U.I. 30

Results of Pooled r_c:

Researches			
Group A	Group B	Number of Variables	r_c
C_5 R_2 C_7 R_{15}	C_6 R_{10} C_4 R_{12}	24	+.605

(16) U.I. 31: Wary Controlled Steadiness.

The value of the congruence coefficient is rather low for U.I. 31, but is based upon only four studies.

Table 6.16: Matching Evidence on U.I. 31

Results of Pooled r_c:

Researches			
Group A	Group B	Number of Variables	r_c
C_3 C_6	C_4 C_5	26	+.335

(17) U.I. 32: Exvia.

No evidence is presented on the match for this factor in terms of objective tests. In the questionnaire realm, this factor has a clear and sustained pattern, but in terms of objective tests, the loadings have tended to be highly erratic. At present, there appears to be dearth of good markers that have been used in sufficient studies to have influence on matching results. Considerable research is going ahead on this factor, and it appears wise at this stage to wait for new evidence before giving any definite verdict.

(18) U.I.33: Reactive Dismay.

Factor U.I. 33, though having only four independent identifications, has shown such consistency of pattern that method 2 (page 112) was used. This involves the comparison of the factor in any given study with the pooled loadings on the other three factors. Variables had to be present in the given study and in at least two of the studies entering the composite. The s index and coefficient of congruence was used in each case, thus giving eight comparisons. Such comparisons are not, of course, independent, but they serve to illustrate the general procedure, to describe the matching achieved in these studies, and to compare the two indices. Results are presented in Table 6.17. Figures in parentheses following the research identifications in the first two columns indicate the factor number and sign reported by the authors of each research. The number of salient variables (g) used only for the s index, is kept at approximately one-fifth of the number of common variables (n).

The pooled coefficient of congruence, as computed for other factors, is also presented in Table 6.17.

Table 6.17: Matching Evidence on U.I. 33

A. Results of Salient Variable Similarity Indices and r_c Comparisons for U.I. 33

'Test' Factor and Research	Criterion Factor Composite and Researches	Number of Common Variables(n)	Number of Salient Variables(s)	s Probability	r_c
C3 (9+)	C4(3+)R10(10-)R13(7+)	37	7	$<.0008$	+0.425
C4 (3+)	C3(9+)R10(10-)R13(7+)	38	8	$<.003$	+0.409
R10(10-)	C3(9+)C4(3+)R13(7+)	30	6	$<.00004$	+0.331
R13(7+)	C3(9+)C4(3+)R10(10-)	20	4	$<.002$	+0.508

Table 6.17: Matching Evidence on U.I. 33 (Cont)

B. Results of Pooled r_c:

Researches			
Group A	Group B	Number of Variables	r_c
C_3 R_{10}	C_4 R_{13}	15	+.491

(19) U.I. 34: Inconautia and U.I. 35: Stolparsomnia.

These factors are presented together as both have to rely on only two studies for matching evidence and the number of common variables involved is very small. Although both factors give satisfactory pooled coefficients of congruence, the results should not be regarded as more than suggestive.

Table 6.18: Matching Evidence on U.I. 34

Results of r_c:

Researches	Number of Variables	r_c
Ros R_1	6	+.719

Table 6.19: Matching Evidence on U.I. 35

Results of r_c:

Researches	Number of Variables	r_c
R_1 R_{10}	16	+.585

IV. EXAMPLE OF THE USE OF THE INDEX OF SALIENT VARIABLE SIMILARITY (s) IN COMPARING THE FACTORS OBTAINED IN ONE STUDY WITH THE FACTORS OBTAINED IN ANOTHER.

The use of the Index of Salient Variable Similarity (s) in the matching of factors was described in Chapter 3, and some of the practical difficulties were discussed in the first part of the present chapter. The method compares the loadings on a factor in one study with the loadings on a factor in some second study, utilizing a non-parametric test of significance.

The present illustration, reported in study C5 (26), compares 15 factors from C5 with 15 factors from C6, one pair at a time. Table 6.20 contains the results of this comparison, the factors being given in the Universal Index sequence. The probability value is that associated with the given match or better.

Table 6.20: Salient Variable Similarity Indices for Studies C5 and C6

U.I. Factor	C5 Factor Number	C6 Factor Number	S Probability
U.I. 1	2	8	$<.006$
U.I. 16	4	4	$<.006$
U.I. 17	10	12	$<.57$
U.I. 18	16	13	$<.03$
U.I. 19	14	6	$<.003$
U.I. 20	6	3	$<.006$
U.I. 21	3	1	$<.003$
U.I. 22	12	-10	$<.006$
U.I. 24	1	-9	$<.03$
U.I. 26	8	14	$<.003$
U.I. 28	5	11	$<.03$
U.I. 29	13	5	$<.18$
U.I. 30	9	7	$<.18$
U.I. 31	15	-2	$<.18$
U.I. 32	7	15	$<.18$

It is clear that these findings are very good, all but five matches being significant at the $p < .05$ level, and many being significant at $p < .01$ and beyond. There is a slight tendency, as one would expect, for those factors early in the U.I. series to reach higher significance than those late in the series, though an exception to this is U.I. 17. The reader should not suppose, however, that these results are typical for personality factors in general, for it is rare for two studies to contain as many common variables as in this comparison (26). Due to the similarity of the subject groups, occasions and conditions of testing in these two studies, such excellent results would be expected. From Chapter IV the reader will be aware that the research covered in this monograph involves subjects from as widely disparate groups as pre-school children and adult psychotics, and thus less reliance in such cases should be placed upon any index, due to lack of common variables.

V. SUMMARY AND DISCUSSION.

Results so far obtained on the quantitative matching of objective test factors indicate that U.I. 16, 18, 20, 21, 22, 23, 24, 25, and 28 show a pattern which holds up across age ranges and sub-samples within an age range. U.I. 17, 19,

26 and 32 appear to be less stable, and their retention is based upon other evidence as well as objective test measures. The remaining factors, U.I. 27, 29, 30, 31, 33, 34, and 35 have not had sufficient replication for any really complete series of matching techniques to be attempted. Nevertheless these later factors, on present evidence, show every sign of holding up well.

So far as we know this is the first time that conclusions about factor matching in the personality field have been subjected to more than one objective method to evaluate significance. Indeed in the extensive conclusions about personality structure in Eysenck's Structure of Personality as in most other publications in this decade, matching has been concluded from visual inspection. While we feel that more sophisticated methods must be continually developed, in the ways we have indicated in this chapter, we believe that, having regard to (1) the changing samples of variables and persons, (2) the fact that significant congruence correlations will exist (as in cooperative factors) even between two distinct factors, and (3) the fact that the methods outlined in Chapter 3 would have involved prohibitive computing labor for a desk calculator and in most cases relevant programs for a digital computer are not available for some complex methods we would like to use, the above is the best compromise at this present time.

Finally, in regard to central research aims, strategy at this time suggests that the important issue is to marshal sufficient evidence on each U.I. factor to justify its description as a unitary personality dimension, and its continued pursuit in further research. It is of considerably less present importance to assess the accuracy of a particular factor identification originally made in a study some ten or fifteen years ago. A proportion of these earlier studies necessarily suffer from crudities present in earlier stages of factor analytic history. We are orienting clear hypotheses which can now quickly be further checked, with greater nicety in a programmed digital computer age. (In some cases we are even impeded by not all of the necessary information being available from journal articles or original sources.)

In the future we may assume that matching problems will fall into two categories. The first is the matching of factors between a given study and some composite matrix or set of matrices deriving from previous research. The second is the matching of factors between two studies only, presumably in many cases to satisfy certain specific research needs. In both situations it is probably advisable to use more than one method. With the computing facilities soon to be, or presently, available in most research centres, there would appear to be little excuse for the identification of factors in future studies without adequate quantitative support. This counsel is of particular relevance at this time when multivariate analyses of data are increased in both size and frequency of occurrence.

CHAPTER 7

PSYCHOLOGICAL MEANING OF STABLE SOURCE TRAITS
U.I. 16 - U.I. 25

This chapter, and the following, present the accumulated evidence, as of time of writing, on the twenty-one objective test factors. Due to the large amount of material on each factor, the factors have been arbitrarily divided between two chapters-- Chapter 7 containing U.I. 16 - 25 and Chapter 8 containing U.I. 26-36. The division is also an approximate indicator of importance (or at least replicability) for the Universal Index numbers were assigned in serial order as the factors reached status of confirmation.

The factors are dealt with separately in these two chapters, but in each case the evidence is marshalled under specific headings, e.g., questionnaire correlates, criterion relationships, and so forth. In order to make the following pages more readily comprehensible a brief account is now given of the different sections for each factor.

I. PREVALENCE.

This section gives a concise introduction to the factor, indicating the extent to which it has been identified across different age groups and an approximate indication of the surety of matching.

II. QUESTIONNAIRE CORRELATES.

This section contains all evidence on correlations between the factor (or factor estimate) and self-report (Q) measures. The bulk of this information concerns the 16 Personality Factor Questionnaire (16-P.F.), but also includes the Guilford-Zimmerman and Guilford-Martin scales, and a variety of other measures. An argument could be made that factored verbal report measures are objective tests and essentially different from ad hoc self-rating scales. However for the purpose of these chapters we shall include all such measures within the same section. A table of correlations between the U.I. factor and the 16-P.F. factors follows Section VIII in each case.

III. STATE FACTOR MATCHES.

Studies of function fluctuation have shown the presence of several confirmed state factors (35). In some cases these can be directly linked with a personality source trait, and thus throw considerable light upon their operation. Summaries of research on state factors are available (68).

IV. LOADINGS ON SECOND-ORDER OBJECTIVE TEST FACTORS.

Essential to any discussion of the psychological meaning of oblique primary factors is information from higher order factor analyses. Such information is presented in this section for each factor, and a summary appears in Chapter 9.

V. CRITERION CORRELATIONS.

A growing number of research studies have used objective-test factors as predictors in a variety of applied situations. Results are given in this section for such diverse fields as prediction of military success, prediction of academic achievement, and clinical classifications.

VI. NATURE-NURTURE AND AGE-TREND RESULTS.

In this section information is presented (where available) on the relative contribution of heredity and environment to factor scores. Age trends from 9 years to 15 years are available on certain factors, and also appear in this section.

VII. DESCRIPTIVE INTERPRETATION.

One of the principal sources for obtaining the psychological interpretation of a factor is from the matrix of factor loadings. This section is a survey of those variables principally involved in a factor. For the sake of clarity variables have been clustered together in terms of what they appear to have in common from a subjective, surface standpoint. Whenever a variable is referred to in the text it is given its appropriate Master Index (M.I.) number, and the verbal title is adjusted to be in line with the obtained correlation with the factor. An account of the Master Index system is given in Chapter 4, while details of each test from which salient M.I.'s are obtained may be found in Appendix II. No theory is presented in this section, for the intention is to give a verbal account of the types of variables that are associated with the factor. The reader will probably find it advantageous to refer to the table of reference vector correlations (following Part VIII for each factor) as he reads Part VII.

VIII. EXPLANATORY THEORY: HISTORY AND FINAL HYPOTHESES.

This section gives a brief account of historical associations of the factor with psychological theory, and then gives some presently-held theoretical viewpoints on the psychological nature of the factor. Care must be taken to distinguish between Parts VII and VIII. The former gives a verbal description of the factor in terms of salient variables, while the latter involves theory and hypotheses concerning the factor.

In Parts I through VI above considerable care has been taken to present not only positive evidence but also evidence in which no significant relationship has been found. Negative evidence is as important as positive evidence in helping to define a trait, and this maxim has been adhered to. In addition, where no data are available, as for example in nature-nurture ratios on some factors, then this is brought to the readers' attention.

Following Part VIII two tables are presented embodying correlations between (1) 16-P.F. questionnaire factors, and (2) objective tests, with the U.I. factor. The correlations reported are actually between the variable and the U.I. reference vectors.[1]

In such tables of Q and O-T correlations the following design is used:

(1) Each column represents a separate research study. In the box at the top of each column are given, in descending order:

(a) Study identification. This is as used in Chapters 4 and 5 (e.g., C3, R13, H1).

(b) The number of subjects.

(c) Age of subjects (if children).

(d) The Factor Number, with either positive or negative direction, as reported in the study in question.

Within each column are the correlations between the objective test variable (or Q factor) and the U.I. factor (actually reference vector). In each case the positive and negative poles of the factor are as in its title, and the variable is scored as in Appendix III. The test from which the variable is obtained is described in Appendix II. Correlations in parentheses indicate a reversal in sign from that expected.

(2) The adjective preceding the verbal title for each salient Q factor or M.I. variable is that associated with a high positive score on the factor--if the sign of the correlation coefficient is regarded as confirmed. If the correlation is not regarded as confirmed then the adjective associated with a high score on the variable is put in parentheses.

(3) Full data is given on each U.I. factor and each 16-P.F. questionnaire factor. As no selection is used, the 16-P.F. factors are listed in their alphabetical order.

---

[1] Reference vector correlations are proportional to factor loadings. As most readers will be more familiar with tables of correlations than of factor-loadings, this method of presentation has been chosen.

(4) Due to the very large number of objective-test variables that have been involved in the studies reported in this and the following chapter, selection of variables for presentation was inevitable. Accordingly we used the following criteria of choice of variables for the tables in Chapters 7 and 8, and Appendices I, III and IV. First, if a variable gave a correlation with the reference vector greater than ±0.30 on any one occasion, then it was included. Second, if on more than one occasion correlations greater than ±0.15 were reported, then the variable was also included.

The method of selection inevitably led to the inclusion of variables which by no stretch of imagination could be regarded as salient or marking a factor. For example a variable would be included that showed two correlations with a factor of +0.15 and six correlations of zero magnitude. To remove much of this potential confusion each table is split in two; the top half including variables regarded as showing some sort of relationship to the factor, while in the second half are variables regarded as having no relationship to the factor except by chance, or in which the sign direction cannot at present be determined. Variables in the first half of each table are listed in approximate order of saliency, and sign reversals as with the 16 P.F. scales are indicated by parentheses.

For the reader interested in comparing the correlations of a variable with <u>different</u> U.I. factors, then a full table is presented in Appendix I.

U.I. 16 UNBOUND, ASSERTIVE EGO VS. BOUND DISCIPLINED EGO

1. Prevalence

Factor U.I. 16, the first in this series, was independently identified in ten factor analytic researches at the adult age level and in four studies at the child level. Additional evidence is available from Wells' extension analysis on adult subjects and from Brogden's research on children, one of his factors matching U.I. 16 closely.

U.I. 16 ranks among the best confirmed personality factors found in objective tests. In most studies U.I. 16 has a large factor variance (or large associated latent root) and usually its place is among the first three or four factors in an analysis.

2. Questionnaire Correlates

Evidence on questionnaire factor correlates of U.I. 16 is available from five studies (see table 7.1). U.I. 16 correlates consistently with factor I- (Harria: tough, realistic) and, less marked, with factor N+ (Shrewdness: sophisticated, polished). This suggests an interpretation of U.I. 16 in terms of these characteristics: realistic, self-assertive, fact-oriented, tough-minded rather than tender-minded, self-determined, and more sophisticated (or "high-brow") in tastes and values.

The correlations, reported by Knapp in the two recent studies N1 (123) and N2 (123) on the relationship between first-order objective test factors and various questionnaire and inventory scales, are in agreement with this interpretation. Of the Guilford-Martin scales, T (Thinking Introversion; r = +.16) G (General Activity; r = +.26), and A (Ascendance; r = +.18) correlated significantly with U.I. 16. Of the Guilford-Zimmerman scales, G (General Activity; +.22), A (Ascendance; r = +.32), and S (Sociability) had significant correlations with this factor. Of the MMPI scales, Mf (Femininity of Interests; r = +.32), Sc (Schizophrenia; r = +.22), and L (Lie Scale; r = -.23) correlated significantly, the latter one indicating that U.I. 16 correlates negatively with the tendency to select the socially desirable item responses; the scale Do (Dominance), derived from the MMPI item pool by Gough, McClosky, and Meehl (98), correlated +.30 with U.I. 16.

Of the Kuder interest scales only Literary Interests correlated significantly with U.I. 16 (r = +.24) (138). Psychiatric anxiety ratings, available in study R 1, did not load on the factor.

3. State Factor Matches

None of the twelve state factors (P.U.I. 1 through P.U.I. 12), so far identified in the objective personality test realm, resembles the psychometric pattern of U.I. 16 closely enough to justify a match, nor was U.I. 16 found in the incremental R-technique study R 3. Thus, on the basis of presently available empirical evidence, U.I. 16 has to be understood as a more or less pure trait factor, with hardly any temperamental state variance involved.

4. Loadings on Second-Order Objective Test Factors

Factor U.I. 16 loads only one second-order objective test factor of which it is the best marker (average loading of +.35); this factor F (T) II (Expansive Ego vs. History of Difficulties in Problem Solving) has been interpreted as a second-order trait of ego-expansiveness.

5. Criterion Correlations

a) Clinical Criteria

In both studies R9-Ta (68, p. 481f) and R10 (I) (38) neurotics scored significantly lower than normals on U.I. 16. Besides U.I. 25, U.I. 16 is also the only other factor that differs significantly between neurotics and criminals (38), criminals scoring significantly higher than neurotics.

No results are as yet available on the correlation of U.I. 16 with the normal-psychotic dichotomy since this factor was not measured in R 7.

b) School and Academic Achievement

No significant relationship has been found in study P 1 (138) between U.I. 16 and college achievement, high-achievers, however, scored higher on U.I. 16 than low-achievers.

c) Military Criteria

In study AF (69) on the prediction of pilot training criteria, U.I. 16 correlated significantly (+.16) with the "actuarial adjustment rating"[1]. In Knapp's study N1 (121) the factor correlated +.37 with the total score on the AQT (Aviation Qualification Test), but negatively (-.39) with peer ratings of pilot proficiency; Knapp also found a positive correlation of +.52 with sick call frequency.

[1] Two clinical psychologists rated each airman for his adjustment to pilot training on a 24-item rating scheme

In N2 (122), the second one of Knapp's two criterion studies, factor U.I. 16 correlated significantly with both the Pass-Fail criterion (r = +.23) and the Class Standing criterion (r = +.22) in naval submarine training.

These results indicate a general competence, efficiency, and determinedness as characteristic of the positive factor pole, showing in better personal adjustment to, and qualification for, pilot and submarine training. There is, however, no evidence that the U.I. 16 person would also show a better actual on-the-job performance in military settings; the correlations between U.I. 16 and objective flight performance measures are insignificant in both studies AF and N1. The significant negative correlation with peer ratings of pilot proficiency probably indicates low over-all sociometric status of the U.I. 16 person rather than actually poor performance as a pilot. This interpretation seems most likely in the light of the assertiveness, dominance, and determinedness associated with U.I. 16.

6. Nature-Nurture and Age Trend Results

Among the ten personality factors U.I. 16, 17, 19, 20, 21, 22, 23, 26, 28, and 29 for which nature-nurture results are available, U.I. 16 is the factor most strongly determined by environmental influences (70). Since these nature-nurture data were obtained with children of an average age of 12 years this very marked environmental determination of U.I. 16 must therefore date from the early and middle childhood period, in which case the psychological influences originating in the home environment (parents, sibs) and in social inter-actions with same-age playmates will probably account for the main part of the nurture variance in this factor.

With hardly any hereditary source of variance in U.I. 16, the assumption of an early environmental determination is further strengthened from the fact that, of all ten factors listed above, U.I. 16 shows least, if any, change over the age range from 9 to 15 years (29, p. 616f.).

7. Descriptive Interpretation.

At least four main attributes of U.I. 16 emerge from a closer consideration of the objective test variables loading this factor (see table 7.2):

1. Fast speed and tempo

In the psychometric pattern of U.I. 16 we find a total of 21 variables which all indicate fast tempo (i.e., fast "natural" rate of performance) and fast speed (i.e., fast top rate of performance). These encompass a wide range, from tempo of physical movements (M.I. 270: fast arm-shoulder tempo; M.I. 269: fast leg-circling tempo), through psychomotor and "ideomotor" speed and tempo (M.I. 268: fast tapping tempo; M.I. 264: fast tapping speed; M.I. 272: fast speed of dotting; M.I. 9: fast ideomotor tempo in writing, drawing, etc.;

M.I. 6: fast ideomotor speed; M.I. 335: fast reaction time under complex instructions), speed on simple motor tasks (M.I. 82: fast speed on finger maze; M.I. 379: fast pencil maze performance; M.I. 340: fast speed of repetitive form board performance; M.I. 278 and M.I. 511: fast tempo of reading), to perceptual speed (M.I. 307: fast speed of letter comparison; M.I. 308: fast speed of number comparison; M.I. 309: fast speed of line judgment; M.I.7: fast speed of perceptual Gestalt completion) and speed of judgment and decision (M.I. 244: fast speed of judgment - "hard-headed realism" test; M.I. 378: fast speed and high accuracy in quantity judgments; M.I. 382: fast speed of evaluative judgment; M.I. 153: fast speed of decision - CMS).

Since the fast speed and tempo extends over this broad range of widely different performances (from simple physical movements M.I. 269, 270 to judgments on complex social issues M.I. 244) any interpretation in terms of sheer "fast over-all speed" on the part of the extreme U.I. 16 individual seems rather doubtful. The above mentioned variables cut across several well-known speed factors (144) which are practically uncorrelated; therefore "fast speed" should be regarded as a "symptom" of the U.I. 16 person -- for which a proper casual explanation will have to be sought -- rather than as a primary characteristic in itself.

2. High self-assertiveness

Common experience shows high self-assertion to be associated, amongst others, with fast speed of decisions, high endurance, less fluctuation of performance quality over time, and less readiness to change one's opinion when presented with the opinion of an "authority". Fast speed of judgment on complex social issues (M.I. 244) and fast speed of decision (M.I. 153) have already been mentioned as marking U.I. 16. In addition, this factor correlates positively with several other variables which strengthen an interpretation of U.I. 16 in terms of high self-assertiveness: a person scoring high on U.I. 16 shows high endurance on tiring tasks (M.I. 346), less oscillation of performance (M.I. 13), less attitude shift toward the attitude endorsed by authorities (M.I. 35); he is positive and optimistic about his future (M.I. 112: more favorable than unfavorable self-reference in events; M.I. 212: many distant goals considered attainable), and does not change his opinion readily when presented with additional arguments (M.I. 34: less "immaturity of opinion"). "Harric assertiveness" probably also accounts for this person's higher level of aspiration (M.I. 101a and M.I. 101b), his carefulness in following instructions (M.I. 50 and M.I. 51) and in obeying rules (M.I. 98a), as well as his tendency to orient his tastes and cultural preferences after those endorsed by the upper social classes. Thus U.I. 16 is correlated with more "high-brow" tastes (M.I. 117), more rejection of questionable books and stories (M.I. 21), and more sense of poetic aptness (M.I. 118) -- loadings, which all tie in well with the questionnaire evidence on higher shrewdness (N+) at the U.I. 16+ pole.

3. Less impairment of performance by frustration

There are four variables (M.I. 96a, 165, 465, 61) in the pattern of U.I. 16 which consistently indicate less impairment of performance under frustration, disapproval, or distraction conditions. The extreme U.I. 16 person is less sensitive to such unfavorable conditions -- distraction, criticism, and emotional resentments are less likely to result in a decrease of speed or accuracy of performance. Subjects scoring at the extreme positive pole of this factor do not "give in" easily, are more endurant, and try hard to give a "good performance". In fact, it may be this very characteristic of the assertive individual which explains also the slightly better scholastic achievement of the U.I. 16 student to which we referred above (section 5).

4. "Strong" physique

The assertive psychological properties in U.I. 16 are to some extent "replicated" in the U.I. 16 individual's physique. Already years back, when correlations between body build and factor U.I. 16 were still lacking, we expected a positive relationship between this factor and measures of physical size ("assertive" bodily characteristics). More recent studies have now verified this hypothesis. At its positive pole U.I. 16 is characterized by a generally "big" body, longer and thicker bones (M.I. 487) and muscles (M.I. 486) and a larger amount of fatty tissue (M.I. 485). In addition, our results indicate a higher excitational level at the U.I. 16+ pole (M.I. 444: higher systolic blood pressure; M.I. 78: higher involuntary muscle tension in right arm), a kind of enduring physical tenseness.

The negative correlation between U.I. 16 and the endurance time on an exhausting treadmill run (M.I. 492) could be due to a tendency to avoid bodily harm, possibly arising from an over concern about one's health. Such an interpretation would also agree with Knapp's finding of a positive correlation between this factor and sick call frequency in a sample of naval helicopter trainees (study N 1). Both results, however, may also simply point out poorer physical health at the positive pole of U.I. 16. In Knapp's study direct measures or ratings of physical health were not available; in view of the higher physical strength correlated with U.I. 16, the former interpretation is more consistent with the general pattern of this factor.

8. Explanatory Theory: History and Final Hypotheses

A personality trait of assertiveness, defined in terms of objective tests, was new at the time it was first found in study C1. Several of its attributes, however, have been fully recognized since the early beginnings of research on individual differences. Our "descriptive interpretations" has probably reminded the reader of W. James' classical hypotheses about a tough- vs. tender-mindedness trait, and the concept of self-assertion (and ego-restriction, at the U.I. 16- pole) has received much attention in psychoanalytic theory and subsequent clinical psychology. More recently, in their research on "need for achievement", McClelland, Atkinson, and others (129, 4) investigated personality characteristics which, at least in part, resemble closely some of the attributes of the U.I. 16+ assertiveness.

Any final hypothesis about factor U.I. 16 will have to take into account, besides the sole psychometric loading pattern, the very strong environmental determination of this factor. The -- obviously constitutional -- "assertive" physical characteristics in U.I. 16+ can therefore only be ascribed a "facilitating" role in the development of this pattern. On our present evidence, the formation of this pattern must take place in early and middle childhood. During later childhood and puberty U.I. 16 hardly shows any change in the sense of age development, and neither of the six available analyses on trait fluctuations over time in adults revealed a state factor that could be matched with U.I. 16. If one furthermore considers the large latent root typically associated with U.I. 16, all evidence points into the direction of U.I. 16 being a potent, high stable personality factor of early environmental determination.

At the sheer descriptive level, the main psychological attributes of U.I. 16 are high assertiveness, high decisiveness, fast speed of performance, high resistance to frustration and distraction, and upper social class tastes and values. At the explanatory level, our hypothesis about factor U.I. 16 can be most briefly expressed by the term "unbound vs. bound ego". At its positive pole, this factor carries the main characteristics of unrestricted assertiveness -- of a person trusting in himself, who is quick in his decisions, highly self-determined and not easily frustrated. These attributes represent main ego-functions, whose pervasive potency or expansiveness (vs. restriction, at the U.I. 16- pole) is the content of U.I. 16 as a personality dimension. Our hypothesis further assumes, that this factor should be correlated positively with the degree of liberal permissiveness and agreement experienced as child from parents and sibs, and correlated negatively with the amount of frustration met in early childhood.

This interpretation is strengthened from the results on second-order objective test factors. U.I. 16 loads only factor F (T) II which is a second-order trait of ego-expansiveness, further characterized by high intelligence (U.I. 1), high will-power (U.I. 19), high "neural reserves" (U.I. 23), high self-sentiment (U.I. 36) and high thoroughness (U.I. 18-).

Table 7.1
U.I. 16: Assertive Ego vs. Disciplined Ego

Q-Factor	Factor Title	Factor Identification (Research, Sample Size, Age of Subjects, Factor Number in Study)				
		Me 102 Adult (8-)	C5 500 Adult (4+)	R1 86 Adult (12+)	R2 86 Adult (5+)	R10 168 Adult (8-)
A	(higher) Cyclothymia	-09	+05	-17	-03	-01
B	(higher) Intelligence				+15	
C	(higher) Ego Strength		-01	+04	-12	00
E	(higher) Dominance		+10		-01	+06
F	(higher) Surgency	+20	-02	-02	-04	+11
G	(higher) Super Ego Strength		+06		+13	00
H	(higher) Parmia	+07	-02	-16	00	+09
*I	higher Harria (tough, realistic)		-35	-23	-05	(+08)
L	(higher) Protension	+09	+01		+06	+10
M	(higher) Alaxia		+04	-06	+12	+14
*N	higher Shrewdness (sophisticated, polished)		+23		+03	+14
O	(higher) Timidity		+05	+10	+04	+07
Q1	(higher) Radicalism		+02		-09	+09
Q2	(higher) Self-Sufficiency		+03		-02	+17
Q3	(higher) Self Sentiment Control		-04		00	-01
Q4	(higher) Ergic Tension		+04	00	+01	+07

U. I. 16: ASSERTIVE EGO VS. DISCIPLINED EGO (page 1)

Master Index Number	Variable Title	Factor Identification (Research, Sample Size, Age of Subjects, Factor Number in Study)															
		C1	C2	Me	C3	C4	C5	C6	R1	R2	R10	We	BRO	C7	R12	R13	R15
		370	410	102	100	100	500	250	86	86	168	80	100	184	80	164	197
		Adult	Adult	Adult	Adult	Adult	Adult	Adult	Adult	Adult	Adult	Adult	11-12	9-12	4-5	6-9	7-10
		(1-)	(3-)	(8-)	(8+)	(16-)	(4+)	(4+)	(12+)	(5+)	(8-)	--	(1+)	(6+)	(7+)	(1+)	(1+)
21	few questionable reading preferences	+26	+58	+49	+31	+22	+18		+15				+31	+14	(-04)	+03	(-07)
35	less suggestibility to authority	-16	-49		-26	-04	-08	(+07)			-11		-53	(+09)			
15	more use of circles -- CMS				+04		+28	+38	+22	+36	+11			+08			+01
143	higher total score -- CMS						+40				+44			(-08)	+00	+33	+12
34	less immaturity of opinion	-12	-22	(+07)	-06	-14	-11				-02		-53	-10	-14		
270	faster arm-shoulder tempo						+38	+39			+00		+43	+43	+02	+22	+03
269	faster leg-circling tempo						+28	+37	+03	+03	+01			+10		+06	
2a-f	less motor rigidity	-06	-00		-01	(+10)	-21	-13	(+01)	-14	-15		-40	(+06)	(+05)	-07	-18
82	greater distance covered (faster speed) on finger maze		+00				+52	+24			(-03)			+03			
117	many responses indicative of "highbrow" taste				+26	+48	+47	+12			+17						
9	faster ideomotor tempo	+52	+55		+31											+35	
6	faster ideomotor speed	+22							+11	(-01)	+19				+00	+24	(-07)
98a	larger proportion correct decisions -- CMS				+53	+05					+25				+05		(-03)
278,511	faster tempo of reading	+53					+64		+34					+10			
120a-g	lower ratio of accuracy to speed				-05	-20			-09	(+19)	-00			-05	(+01)	(+05)	-79
13a,b,c	less oscillation of performance	-26	-35		-09	-02					(+27)			-14			
282	many objects perceived in unstructured drawings						+35	+34	+15		+26				(-05)	+08	+07
307	faster speed of letter comparison						+17	+56						+15	(-05)		
96a	less impairment of reading speed by frustrated preference				+51	+05		+20						+02			
206	greater perceptual accuracy on Gottschaldt figures						+12	+17							+20	+35	(-02)
51	more carefulness in following detailed instructions (higher index of carefulness)		(-10)				+00	+22	+26	(-14)	+22				(-03)	+37	+28
116a,b	less critical severity in judgments on social issues				-27	-10	-16		(+03)	(+05)	+00			-13			
268	faster tapping tempo						+38							+77	+22		
234	more inaccuracy on pencil mazes						+30									+37	+68
171	less ideational rigidity (more hidden objects correctly seen)			+21			+30							+01			
118	more sense of poetic aptness				+38	+21	+29										
84a	greater increase in heart rate after startle		+54	+53					(-10)	(-07)							
316	higher fluency on own than other people's personal characteristics								+39	+05	+12					+12	
487	greater length and girth of bones			+36						+60		+05					
486	greater length and girth of muscles			(-09)						+55		+07					
485	larger amount of fatty tissue			(-13)						+45		+10					
98b	higher absolute number of correct decisions -- CMS				+40	+03	+13										
24d	higher ratio of final (fast) to initial (slow) CMS total score						+37							+03	(-03)	+09	+14
41	fewer correct movements in two-hand co-ordination	+00	-03		(+08)	-14	-20							-22			

U. I. 16: ASSERTIVE EGO VS. DISCIPLINED EGO (page 2)

Master Index Number	Variable Title	RESEARCH															
		C1	C2	Me	C3	C4	C5	C6	R1	R2	R10	We	BRO	C7	R12	R13	R15
65	less logical consistency of attitudes		+10		-04	-19								-16			
271	higher total verbal fluency on topics						+16	+01			+61			(-10)	+05	+14	
7	faster speed of perceptual Gestalt completion	+03			(-03)	(-08)	+22	+04			+33			(-05)	(-14)	(-01)	+01
106	more unreflective acceptance of unqualified statements				(-03)	+09	(-02)	+15						+36			
112	higher ratio of favorable to unfavorable self-reference in events				+06	(-06)	+09	+37			+05			(-06)		(-02)	
309	faster speed of line length judgment						+63									+68	(-02)
153	faster speed of decision -- CMS				(-06)	+05					+44						
99	higher ratio of verbal to numerical ability				+38	+35								(-08)			
125a, b	higher ratio of personal to institutional values				+60	(-11)					+14						
273	lower relative fluency on self						-06	-05			-55			(+01)	(+01)	-01	(+01)
55	lower fluency of association on emotional relative to non-emotional stimulus words		-32				(+07)							-25			
247a	greater expansiveness of copied design													+36		+29	(-03)
199	better computational skills						(-01)	+16	+09	+34	+10			(-29)	(-08)		(-07)
283	higher proportion of fluency on dreams						+11	+29			(-20)						
144	more acceptance of aphorisms						(-06)							+04	+48		
379	faster speed and higher accuracy of pencil maze performance															+71	+52
308	faster speed of perceptual judgment (number comparison)						+16	+52									
244	faster speed of judgment ("hard-headed realism" test)						+26							+17			
150	less agreement with obvious remarks				-33	-07											
509	good articulatory efficiency (normal reading)								-03	-35							
492	shorter endurance time on treadmill run									-38		-07					
212	higher number of distant goals considered attainable													+09	+51		
933b	lower self-sentiment erg (less desire to avoid damage to sense of self-respect)								-35	-09							
165	less impairment of classification performance by disapproval				(+08)	-41											
465	less decrement in coding performance with anxiety sound distraction								(+11)	-30							
78	involuntary muscle tension in right arm		(-07)						(-03)	+31							
219	fewer frailties admitted						(+07)	+00	-26	-03	(+02)			-19	(+04)	-05	-09
444	higher systolic blood pressure			(-14)					+39	+20							
14	fewer jokes considered funny	-35	-04														
50	higher alertness in following directions		+10										+40				
340	faster speed of repetitive form board performance														(+03)	-40	
382	faster speed of evaluative judgment															+46	(-01)
264	faster speed of tapping													+35			
272	faster speed of dotting						+29										
335	faster reaction time under complex instructions														-31		
375	greater accuracy in circle cancellation															+45	

U. I. 16: ASSERTIVE EGO VS. DISCIPLINED EGO (page 3)

Master Index Number	Variable Title	RESEARCH															
		C1	C2	Me	C3	C4	C5	C6	R1	R2	R10	We	BRO	C7	R12	R13	R15
378	faster speed and higher accuracy in quantity judgments															+44	
79	shorter duration of eidetic images		-55														
61	less impairment of word judgment performance by frustration		-39														
237	more slowing of speed on pencil mazes with increasing difficulty						+46										
346	higher will-endurance (less decrease in leg persistence over time)														+35		
101a, b	higher level of aspiration in coding														+46		
716	higher total number of words remembered (on test of simultaneous word learning and word associating)										+36						
1146	faster speed of checking things disliked										+35						
839	slower speed of checking things liked than things disliked										-39						
63	more femininity of interests (Terman-Miles Test)		-31														
5	higher ratio of regularly to irregularly warned reaction time	+16	+11	+13	(-10)	(-05)		(-10)	+15	+01	+03			(-28)	+02		
30	higher ratio of self-criticism to criticism of others	(-14)			+11	+23	+03	+03	+33	+02					(-21)	+07	+11
38b	higher ratio of consonant to dissonant recall (uncorrected for tendency to agree)			+40	(-02)	+24									+08		
263	(smaller) variability of simple reaction times							+02						+02	-15	-30	+14
461	(more) tendency to overestimate length of fear periods								+45	-26							
71	(greater) number of errors of reaction under complex instructions		-34				+03	+09	+20	-02	-07			+24	-02	-07	+08
42	(more) body sway suggestibility	+06	+10		+22	+13			-29	-05	-04						+08
8	(higher) frequency of alternating perspective	+07	+30	+01	+00	-05	+04							+06		-02	
39	(higher) ratio of color to form in sorting	+13	+20		+01	+16	+10	+12	-02		-17			-09		-18	+10
62	(faster) reading speed for emotional vs. non-emotional material		-29		+16	+03	+07							-03			
167a, b	(better) immediate memory				-10		+20	+08			+17			-19		-13	
176	(slower) irregularly warned reaction time				+21	+22	-01	+01	+07	-32					-24	-28	+03
198	(more) hidden words found				-14	-15	+21							+11			
227a	(more) color choices in pictures relative to form choices						-15							+17	-07	-04	

U.I. 17: TIMID INHIBITEDNESS VS. LACK OF INHIBITION

1. Prevalence

At the adult level this factor has been identified in thirteen factor analytic studies, at the child level in three studies. In addition, extension results on U.I. 17 are available from Wells' study. Since this factor is a very well established pattern and could be identified in all but three of the independent factor analyses which are covered in this monograph, it is ranked second in our series. U.I. 17 was also found in the incremental R-technique study R 3.

2. Questionnaire Correlates

Evidence on the loading of questionnaire factors, measured in the 16 P.F. Test, is available from five R-technique studies (TM, C 5, R 1, R 2, and Ros) and from the incremental R-technique research R 3 (see table 7.3). Across these six studies U.I. 17 does not yield any consistent correlations with questionnaire factors. There is an indication of a slight positive correlation with B (higher General Intelligence), but factor B has been measured in only one study. Therefore, with the present empirical evidence, U.I. 17 has its place among the few objective test factors which are practically uncorrelated with primary questionnaire factors of the 16 P.F. Test.

In Knapp's researches N 1 and N 2 (123) U.I. 17 correlated significantly with the five Guilford-Martin questionnaire factors D (Depression; r = +.11), C (Cycloid Disposition; r = +.11), Ag- (lack of Agreeableness; r = -.14), Co- (lack of Cooperativeness; r = -.19), and N- (lack of Calmness; r = -.16), and with the two Guilford-Zimmermann scales T- (lack of Thoughtfulness; r = .32) and P- (lack of Personal Relations; r = -.26). Of the MMPI scales, U.I. 17 correlated significantly with Sc (Schizophrenia; r = +.24) and Ma (Hypomania; r = +.21); the scale Re (Responsibility), which has been derived by Gough, McClosky, and Meehl (98) from the items used in the MMPI, correlated -.27 i.e., in the direction of "lack of Responsibility" with U.I. 17.

No significant correlations have been found between U.I. 17 and the Kuder interest scales (138). Psychiatric anxiety ratings (study R 1) loaded on U.I. 17 as follows: Both psychiatrists' ratings on over-all anxiety loaded "unsignificantly"; of the specific anxiety ratings given by psychiatrist I, two yielded out-of-hyperplane loadings: the rating on free anxiety loaded -.24, the rating on bound anxiety +.15.

3. State Factor Matches

There is no match for U.I. 17 among the eleven state factors found in straight P-technique analyses. However, a factor matching U.I. 17 very closely was identified in the incremental R-technique study R 3; it was interpreted as "cautious mood" and was given the joint label U.I. 17 - P.U.I. 12[1]. Thus there is no definitive answer on whether or not -- or to which extent -- U.I. 17 contains state variance as well as trait variance. Presumably U.I. 17 is mainly a trait factor with only little state fluctuation (or state fluctuation in only certain types of subjects); this would explain its emergence in study R 3 and its absence in all five P-technique analyses.

4. Loadings on Second-Order Objective Test Factors

U.I. 17 is the top marker (average loading: +.36) of the second-order factor F (T) V which was interpreted as "History of Inhibiting, Restraining Environment"; factor F (T) V further loads the primaries U.I. 23+ (High Mobilization) and U.I. 31+ (Wary, Controlled Steadiness). Neither of the remaining six second-order factors loads on U.I. 17.

5. Criterion Correlations

a) Clinical Criteria

No significant differences have been found on this factor between normals and neurotics in R 9-Ta (68). In R 7 (comparison between normals and psychotics) U.I. 17 has not been measured, in R 10 the factor has not been identified.

b) School and Academic Achievement

M.I. 276 (scholastic achievement) does not load U.I. 17. In P 1 factor U.I. 17 has not been measured.

---

[1]It is this factor from R3 that has been entered in table 8.3.

c) Military Criteria

In study AF by Cattell and Schiff (69) U.I. 17 correlated significantly (-.12) with the Pass-Fail criterion of pilot training success, in Knapp's research N 1 -.26 with peer ratings of pilot proficiency. No significant criterion correlations have been found for U.I. 17 in N 2 (naval submarine training).

6. Nature-Nurture and Age Trend Results

The nature-nurture findings on U.I. 17 are practically identical to those obtained for factor U.I. 19. Both are factors with a slightly stronger environmental than hereditary determination; and in both factors the preponderance of environmental over constitutional variance is more pronounced in the "between-families" than the "within-families" variance (70).

Over the age range 9 to 15 years U.I. 17 shows a marked rise in mean score to the extent of about one raw score standard deviation (29).

7. Descriptive Interpretation

The loading pattern of factor U.I. 17 is given in table 7.4. There are three main attributes, which we consider important for understanding of this factor and which are themselves closely interrelated: timidity, cautiousness, and inhibitedness.

1. Timidity

U.I. 17 loads positively on a series of variables which measure various aspects of fearfulness or timidity. Of these the most prominent timidity-"indicator" is variable M.I. 43, high magnitude of mean PGR deflection to threat, which is a direct measure of the amplitude of a subject's autonomic reactions to stimuli provoking primary fear. Fearfulness or timidity is furthermore expressed in the loadings of the following variables: M.I. 336 (high absolute number of threatening objects perceived in unstructured drawings), M.I. 105 (high percentage of threatening objects perceived in unstructured drawings), M.I. 1734 (high proportion of sad, fearful ideas given), M.I. 374 (little preference for disturbing sounds), M.I. 44 (more preference for safe rather than dangerous situations), M.I. 427 (more attention paid to non-aggressive rather than aggressive pictures), M. I. 428 (more attention paid to non-disturbing rather than disturbing pictures), M.I. 429 (more preference for non-aggressive rather than aggressive pictures), and M.I. 430 (more preference for non-disturbing rather than disturbing pictures).

2. Cautiousness

Clinical experience usually shows high timidity to be associated with high cautiousness -- and in fact, the loading pattern of U.I. 17 contains, several variables which are illustrative of a somewhat hesitating and cautious behavior, a tendency to "play safe", to avoid risks. Thus a person high on U.I. 17 works slow on a test of perceptual Gestalt completion (M.I. 7), if warning signals are given at regular rather than irregular intervals it does not speed up his reaction times (M.I. 5), more complex instructions increase his reaction time (M.I. 72), he is slow in identifying objects under dark adaptation conditions (M.I. 10), is rather slow in his judgments (M.I. 3, M.I. 303, M.I. 304), and shows slow alternating perspective (M.I. 8). This higher cautiousness[1] expresses itself also at the broader level of behavior within given social contexts: The extreme U.I. 17+ individual gives fewer questionable preferences when choosing between book titles (M.I. 21), is more restrained in his reading preferences (M.I. 321), shows rather highbrow taste (M.I. 117), good knowledge of social etiquette (M.I. 107), is willing to accept remarks and propositions presented to him (M.I. 150), and avoids extreme responses (M.I. 67b).

3. Inhibitedness

Both timidity and cautiousness are frequently observed to result in an increased tendency towards inhibiting overt behavior. This need not necessarily imply a generally restrained behavior; but upon meeting a potentially or actually threatening situation the timid individual will typically react with a withdrawal-response rather than an approach-reaction. We use the more common term "inhibitedness" although "inhibitability" -- i.e.: ability or tendency to react by inhibiting overt behavior -- would be a more correct term.

Higher inhibitedness (or: "inhibitability"), as an attribute of U.I. 17+, is inferred from such variables as M.I. 46a (much reduction of maze activity by shock), M.I. 96 (much reduction of reading speed by frustration), M.I. 475 (little action impetus), and M.I. 40 (few false reactions to irrelevant stimuli in reaction time test). What these four variables have in common is a readiness to "withhold" overt behavior. By means of a slight exaggeration we might even speak of a tendency to "respond by not reacting". It is this very personality characteristic which we tried to express in the term "inhibitability". The reader will notice that this inhibition only acts upon frequency and amplitude (or over-all amount) of reactions (M.I. 46a, 96) and does not affect relative accuracy and quality of performance (M.I. 93, 166) -- an important distinction when it comes to separate the inhibitability from sheer "low frustration tolerance", the latter typically affecting both speed and relative accuracy of

[1] There is strong evidence against interpreting these loadings as indicating sheer slowness of performance itself, rather than slowness due to cautiousness: the main markers for alertness and speed of performance (which mainly load on U.I. 22), such as simple reaction time, speed on various routine performances (cancellation, classification, etc.), and others, do not correlate with factor U.I. 17.

performance (e.g., see U.I. 16-). The poorer articulation in reading and speaking (M.I. 509a, 509b), loading positively on U.I. 17+, can be well understood as a further "symptom" of this inhibitedness -- from the common observation that inhibited persons often show various articulatory speech difficulties.

The general description of U.I. 17+ as timid, cautious inhibitedness is further specified and amplified by several loadings which have not been discussed as yet. For example, the extreme U.I. 17+ individual is rather optimistic (M.I. 108) and unsuspicious (M.I. 91), and is self-confident as far as his knowledge and his skills are concerned (M.I. 325). These loadings indicate the absence of any paranoic, pessimistic or inferiority complex attributes in U.I. 17+ -- attributes which one otherwise might be inclined to ascribe to a personality trait of inhibition. The loadings of the variables M.I. 126 (More female than male person choices) and M.I. 63 (more feminine than masculine on the Terman-Miles Interest Test) seem to line up well with the inhibitedness hypothesis.

8. Explanatory Theory: History and Final Hypotheses

The two main descriptive attributes of U.I. 17+, timidity and inhibitedness, have both been given much attention in various fields of psychological research and theory. In a recent review Cattell and Pawlik (139) discussed three different modes or conceptual contexts in which "inhibitedness" is currently used; a brief summary of these will be given here:

a) "Inhibition" as a descriptive concept in clinical diagnosis: A person is described as more inhibited if his behavior lacks free expression, his (especially social) reactivity is reduced, and his emotionality is restrained. Diagnostically, the term "inhibition" is quite often used somewhat loosely. A premetric assessment of individual differences in inhibitedness is obtained either from behavior observations and interviews or from projective techniques (experience-type in the Rorschach test, etc.).

b) "Inhibition" as an explanatory concept in learning and personality theory: Inhibiting neuro-psychological processes, as opposed to excitatory processes, have been hypothesized already in early theories of verbal learning (134, 135); they gained broader significance for theories of behavior in the work of Pavlov (137), Hull (112), and other learning theorists, as well as in neurophysiological research proper (97, see also 108). Recently, in an attempt towards a unifying theory bridging the gap between the thinking in traditional learning and personality theory, Eysenck (88, 89) suggested a re-interpretation of the classical extroversion-introversion dimension in terms of a proponderance of either inhibitory or excitatory processes. All these approaches have in common that "inhibition" has the status of an "intervening variable", hypothesized to account for certain experimental findings; typically the question whether or not "inhibition" can be regarded as a unitary concept was less important and only seldom investigated.

c) "Inhibition" as unitary personality trait: Due to the properties of factor analytic methodology, our concept of "inhibition" (or "inhibitedness") as a personality source trait, as demonstrated in factor U.I. 17, is distinct from the previous ones in several respects. We think of "inhibition" in terms of a unitary dimension underlying individual differences in overt behavior, measurable from objective tests, with "inhibition" being the hypothetical construct accounting for the particular variable pattern by which the factor is defined.

From the descriptive interpretation we gave of the inhibitedness factor U.I. 17 in the previous section, the reader may wonder if the positive pole of this factor should not better be interpreted in terms of general anxiety or the introvert pole of the familiar extroversion-introversion dimension.

Actually, in one of the researches (C 3) which preceded study C 5, in which the independent anxiety factor U.I. 24+ was found for the first time, U.I. 17+ was tentatively interpreted as anxiety. Now, ten years later, several reasons have become apparent which definitely exclude such an interpretation of U.I. 17.

First of all, there cannot be any doubt that it is factor U.I. 24+ which represents the personality trait of general "unbound" anxiety. Beyond the evidence available from the loading pattern of objective tests, this interpretation of U.I. 24 is fully substantiated from clinical validation data (correlation with psychiatric rating of anxiety[1] in study R 1) and from its questionnaire correlates. The well-replicated second-order questionnaire anxiety factor in the 16 P.F. Test (characterized by the primaries C-, H-, L+, M+, O+, Q3-, Q4+) (28, 29, 34, 120) correlates only with factor U.I. 24. Similarly the Taylor MAS and an anxiety self-checklist load highly on U.I. 24 and give zero-loadings on U.I. 17 (see discussion of U.I. 24, p. 219 ff). Secondly, factor U.I. 17 not only lacks these questionnaire and rating loadings in its loading pattern also the main objective test markers of free anxiety are missing -- such as high over-all annoyability, high emotional tension, social seclusiveness, and others. As was mentioned earlier, there is also no significant difference between normals and neurotics in the mean score on U.I. 17 -- as there should be if U.I. 17 were general trait anxiety, since all clinical experience points in the direction of neurotics being more anxious than normals. That factor U.I. 17 is quite distinct from the anxiety factor U.I. 24 is furthermore indicated by the fact that these two first-order OT factors do not load the same second-order OT factor. Thus all available evidence describes U.I. 17+ as a personality dimension distinctly different from a factor of free anxiety.

---

[1] In R1 the ratings of free anxiety by psychiatrist II actually correlated negatively (-.24) with U.I. 17+, indicating less free anxiety in U.I. 17+.

There still remains the possibility, however, of mistaking this factor for introversion. As will be shown in the next chapter, factor U.I. 32, Exvia vs. Invia, is the closest representation of the familiar extroversion-introversion dimension so far found in the objective personality test realm. Factor U.I. 32 also correlates highly with the second-order questionnaire factor of extroversion in the 16 P.F. Test (characterized by the primaries A+, E+, F+, H+, Q2+) (28, 29, 34, 120). At present there is no evidence that this U.I. 32- introversion trait may be associated with timidity or inhibitedness -- nor does the psychometric pattern of U.I. 17 contain any of the typical objective-test introversion markers (such as low ideational fluency, low social interests, low suggestibility, etc.). Furthermore, U.I. 17 does not load on any of the questionnaire first-order factors that constitute the second-order questionnaire extraversion factor, and U.I. 32 and U.I. 17 load on different second-order OT factors. These results clearly indicate that U.I. 17+ (inhibitedness) and U.I. 32- (introversion) do in fact represent two different personality dimensions, the factors certainly not being "cooperative" (29).

The results of this comparison between U.I. 17 and both U.I. 24 and U.I. 32 require an explanation of factor U.I. 17 which restores it as a personality dimension quite apart from anxiety and introversion. Our present hypothesis of this factor can be briefly summarized as follows.

U.I. 17+ is a personality dimension characterized, at its positive pole, by a strong tendency to cautiously inhibit overt behavior in potentially threatening or simply difficult situations. This readiness to react by "not responding" is a mainly learned personality characteristic, i.e., to a large extent determined by a particular environment which constantly reinforces, or asks for, personal restraint. The signs of fearfulness or timidity which we observed in table 8.3 indicate that the increased inhibitability at the U.I. 17+ pole either serves as a mechanism of adjustment to higher timidity "per se" or tends to leave feelings of fear unreduced (if not increased) as the individual refrains from overt reaction.

The described dynamics of U.I. 17+ explain the preponderance of environmental forces over hereditary forces in the determination of the factor. Rules and standards prevalent in our culture apparently ask, to a certain extent, for an ability to inhibit outward-directed action, which is also shown in the fact that the mean score on U.I. 17 rises considerably over the age range from 9 to 15 years -- a period during which the individual more and more internalizes cultural standards and gets confronted with increasing environmental demands.

As yet no research has been done on the relationships between objective test factors and variables describing a person's early home environment. We expect that U.I. 17+ would be associated with a more restraining home environment which exercises stronger demands upon the child and discourages him frequently. Since such an atmosphere is more typical of middle class families, a curvilinear correlation is predicted between U. I. 17 and social status of parents, yielding higher mean factor scores in children from middle class families than in children from upper and lower class homes.

Table 7.3

U.I. 17: Timid Inhibitedness vs. Lack of Inhibition

Q-Factor	Factor Title	Factor Identification (Research, Sample Size, Age of Subjects, Factor Number in Study)					
		Me 102 Adult (7-)	C5 500 Adult (10+)	Ros 70 Adult (3+)	R1 86 Adult (11+)	R2 86 Adult (9+)	R3 86 Adult (6-)
A	(higher) Cyclothymia	+08	+14		-02	+01	+09
*B	higher Intelligence					+24	
C	(higher) Ego Strength		+08	-08	+02	-06	+18
E	(higher) Dominance		-04			00	
F	(higher) Surgency	+07	00	+03	-07	+04	-13
G	(higher) Super Ego Strength		+15			-04	
H	(higher) Parmia	+09	+03		-01	-15	+22
I	(higher) Premsia		-02		+18	-11	+08
L	(higher) Protension	+05	-07			-04	
M	(higher) Alaxia		+01	+27	-01	-06	-19
N	(higher) Shrewdness		+12			-06	
O	(higher) Timidity		-02	-03	00	-03	+06
Q1	(higher) Radicalism		+09			-02	
Q2	(higher) Self-Sufficiency		-03			-12	
Q3	(higher) Self Sentiment Control		-03			+05	
Q4	(higher) Ergic Tension		-05	+21	+03	+04	-02

U. I. 17: TIMID INHIBITEDNESS VS. LACK OF INHIBITION (page 1)

Master Index Number	Variable Title	Factor Identification (Research, Sample Size, Age of Subjects, Factor Number in Study)																
		Th2	C1	C2	Me	C3	C4	C5	C6	Ros	R1	R2	R3	E-D1	We	C7	R12	R13
		290	370	410	102	100	100	500	250	70	86	86	86	139	80	184	80	164
		Adult	Adult	Adult	Adult	Adult	Adult	Adult	Adult	Adult	Adult	Adult	Adult	Adult	Adult	9-12	4-5	6-9
		(F-)	(2+)	(4+)	(7-)	(11+)	(8+)	(10+)	(12+)	(3+)	(11+)	(9+)	(6-)	(4+)	--	(14+)	(12+)	(2-)
21	fewer questionable reading preferences		+47	+65	+26	+23	(-10)	+21			+18					+13	+35	+62
7	slower speed of closure in Gestalt completion	-53	-15			-20	-19	(+07)	(+05)	-07						(+07)	-29	-00
43	higher mean percentage PGR deflection due to threatening stimuli		+32	+34	+29	+15	+15				+09	+11	+09			+10		
5	higher ratio of regularly warned to irregularly warned reaction time		+07	+46	+15	+18	+10		+08	+21	+12	+05	+24			(-01)	+11	
282	higher total number of objects perceived in unstructured drawings							+00	+19	+11	+36			+04			+40	+01
105	greater proportion of threatening objects seen in unstructured drawings					+44	+40	(-01)	+20	+31				+15			+02	+07
336	larger absolute number of threatening objects seen in unstructured drawings				+11						+54	+11	+28			+21	+38	
112	more adverse than favorable self-reference in events					+06	+34	+17	+16					+02		+11		+19
72	more slowing of reaction time under complex instructions (higher ratio of complex to simple reaction time)			+44					+08							+13	+02	+11
133	more criticalness of evaluation					+22	+01	+10						+27		+09		+02
8	lower frequency of fluctuation in alternating perspective		(+04)	-27	-23	-20	-04	-06						-13		(+09)		-09
77	higher salivary ph (more alkalinity of saliva)			+06	+16					+32	+26	+04	+12					
78	higher involuntary muscle tension			+33							+10	(-02)	+11					
74	higher basal metabolic rate			+38	+05							+00			+01			
40	fewer false reactions in reaction time experiments		-03					-32	-09							(+08)	(+03)	-02
3, 127	slower speed of judgment	-39	-02	(+01)		-13	-06									(+09)		
46a	much impairment of maze performance (reduction of distance covered) by shock punishment		(-01)			+42	+18									+31		
117	more responses indicative of "highbrow" taste					+33	(-11)	+15	+28									
176	slower irregularly warned reaction time					(-05)	(-04)	+29	+06	+32							(-17)	+03
51	higher index of carefulness			+54				(-12)	(-03)		+09	(-05)	(-03)				+11	
10	slower time of dark adaptation	+61	+11							+27								
150	more acceptance of obvious remarks					+54	+07									+10		
464	greater average handwriting pressure										+06	+34	+04					
108	more confident assumption of skill in untried performance					+03	-12	-05	+08		+30	+08	-02			+13		-26
25a	better recall of emotional relative to non-emotional words		+06		+48	+00												
216	less (slower) shock suggestibility							+31	+57							(-03)		
288	faster speed of judgment in evaluating others' performance							+40	+15					(-06)				
41	few correct movements in two-hand co-ordination		(+02)	-08		-11	(+12)	-11		-22						-22		
62	faster reading speed for emotional vs. non-emotional material			+15		(-05)	+28	+01								+01		
106	more unreflective acceptance of unqualified statements					(-07)	+25	+02	+22							+17		
455a, b	greater volume of saliva secreted									+21	+01	+01	+18					

U. I. 17: TIMID INHIBITEDNESS VS. LACK OF INHIBITION (page 2)

Master Index Number	Variable Title	RESEARCH																
		Th2	C1	C2	Me	C3	C4	C5	C6	Ros	R1	R2	R3	E-D1	We	C7	R12	R13
82	faster speed of maze performance (greater distance covered)			(-05)				+21								+43		
485	smaller amount of fatty tissue				(+04)							-40			-18			
486	smaller length and girth of muscles				-03							-48			(+10)			
487	smaller length and girth of bones				(+13)							-30			-02			
467	more distraction from aesthetic material in numerical and verbal tasks										+33	(-04)	+01					
321	more restrained reading preferences													+21				+54
166	less impairment of classification performance by shock					-24	-23											
107	more knowledge of etiquette					+27	+24											
509	higher articulatory efficiency (normal reading)										-29	-33						
126	lower ratio of male to female person choices					-06	-30											
475	less action impetus											-36	-23					
218	more willingness to play practical jokes and tease															+50	+34	
93	less reduction of perceptual accuracy under movement restraint					(-06)	+48											
91	less autistic suspicion					(+01)	-53											
490	smaller T-wave amplitude (ECG)											-51			(+10)			
124	less tendency to agree with optimistic statements (corrected for general optimism-pessimism)						-39					(+02)						
67b	less extremity of viewpoint on aphorisms					-34	(+07)											
429	more preference for non-aggressive rather than aggressive pictures																	-72
430	more preference for non-disturbing rather than disturbing pictures																	-65
303	slower speed of decision on "whole" judgments				-63													
29	less mischievousness of humor																	-51
374	less preference for disturbing sounds																	-53
400	more preference for safe rather than dangerous situations																	-52
427	more attention to non-aggressive rather than aggressive pictures																	-50
304	slower speed of decision on "detail" judgments				-56													
159c	greater inaccuracy of other-referent and self-referent time estimates													+49				
63	more femininity of interests (Terman-Miles Test)			-46														
428b	more attention to non-disturbing rather than disturbing pictures																	-40
96a	more impairment of reading speed by frustrated preference								-31									
159a	less inaccuracy of other-referent time estimates					-33												
353	less variability of arm-circling tempo																-32	
352a	greater variability in number of objects seen in different unstructured drawings																+31	

U. I. 17: TIMID INHIBITEDNESS VS. LACK OF INHIBITION (page 3)

Master Index Number	Variable Title	RESEARCH																
		Th2	C1	C2	Me	C3	C4	C5	C6	Ros	R1	R2	R3	E-D1	We	C7	R12	R13
211a	less susceptibility to annoyance							-19	-08	(+15)	-25					-03	(+05)	-03
269	slower leg-circling tempo							-17	(+13)		-02	(+04)	-21			-08		(+02)
515	less increase in sound pressure of voice from normal to delayed feedback reading										-30							
1716b	lower appeal erg (less desire to heed parents' advice)										-33							
1734	higher proportion of sad, fearful ideas given													+30				
2a-g	(more) motor rigidity		-09	+02		-05	+02	+08	-05	-42	+01	-16	+06	+05		+01	-03	-13
84a	(greater) increase in heart rate after startle			+07	-03					+29	-24	-02	+25					
120a-c	(higher) ratio of accuracy to speed					-08	+50				-25	+05	-15	-06		-07	+05	+11
118	(more) sense of poetic aptness					+30	-17											
83	(higher) fidgetometer frequency			+09		+39	-12	-14			+01	-02	-31			+09		
456	(more) slowing of reaction time when electric shock is applied										+03	+25	-36					
460	(greater) preference for familiar relative to strange in written material										-33	+21	+12					
23a	(better) immediate memory for words		+11								-11	+33	-47					
110	(higher) anteversion/retroversion ratio				+26	+02	-16							-16				
30	(more) criticism of self relative to criticism of others		+00			+11	-13	+03	-26		-05	-08	-23	+28			+09	-08
16a	(more) slanting lines crossed in CMS		+03			+09		-27	+05	+12	-06	+07	+18			-06		
35	(more) suggestibility to authority		+06	+09		+01		-08	+11							-33		
39	(higher) ratio of color to form in sorting		-08	-19		+07	+21	-01	-06		-02					+19		-11
122	(greater) static ataxia				+17	-03	+07	+13								-18		
193a	(more) shifting of attitudes towards those of successful people					-09		+02	+30		-28					+15		-05
198	(more) hidden words found					-22	+30	+07	+09							-05		
219	(more) common frailties admitted							+03	+22	-08	+17	+14	-07			-03	-08	-15
263	(greater) variability in simple reaction times								+16							+05	-30	+03

U.I. 18: HYPOMANIC SMARTNESS VS. SLOW THOROUGHNESS

1. Prevalence

This factor has been identified in nine factor analyses with adults and four with children. In addition an extension analysis on adults by Wells (166) examined the relationship between this factor and certain physical fitness, body-build, and physiological measures. The match across studies for both adults and children is good, but continues to rest on rather fewer tests (such as the Cursive Miniature Situation Test) than is usually found in the Universal Index.

2. Questionnaire Correlates

Earlier discussion of the relationship between objective test and 16 P.F. questionnaire factors suggested that an identity might be established between U.I. 18 and N(+): SHREWDNESS (Sophisticated, Polished), evidence coming from both Q (questionnaire) and L (rating) data. Further likely-looking 16 P.F. factors were L(+): PROTENSION (Suspecting, jealous) and H(+): PARMIA (Adventurous, "thick-skinned"). More recent evidence from R1, R2, and R10 has tended to throw doubts upon the importance of both N and H, though confirming the direction of correlation, and L now appears unlikely as a correlate.

Apart from N and H, 16 P.F. factors which show some potential for future research on U.I. 18 are F(+): SURGENCY (Enthusiastic, talkative), Q1(+): RADICALISM (Experimenting, critical), and M(+): ALAXIA (Bohemian, unconcerned). In general, however, it can be said that at the present time due to low correlations and sign-reversals no 16 P.F. factor can be designated as a consistent marker for U.I. 18.

In his study of objective-test factors and questionnaire measures, Knapp (123) found no significant correlation between U.I. 18 and the Guilford STDCR and Guilford-Martin O, Ag, Co, and GAMIN scales with a sample of 315 Navy enlisted men. On 81 officer helicopter pilots, using the Guilford-Zimmerman (GRASEOFTPM?) and M.M.P.I. scales plus E_S (Ego Strength), Do (Dominance), and Re (Responsibility), the correlations were again non-significant. These measures include the MMPI Hypomania scale which one would have anticipated as correlating positively with this factor. The only measures approaching significance were M (Masculinity) and Pd (Psychopathic Deviate).

No significant correlations have been found between U.I. 18 and the Taylor MAS scale (146) (123) or the IPAT Anxiety Scale. Correlations with the Kuder Preference Record are also non-significant (138).

In general it seems that little or no association has been found between U.I. 18 and questionnaire or self-report measures of personality and interests, though there has been ample opportunity for such cross-media correspondence to appear. Clearly at the present time we must look elsewhere for information of aid in the interpretation of U.I. 18.

3. State Factor Matches

No state factor has been identified as corresponding to U.I. 18.

4. Loadings on Second-Order Objective Test Factors

U.I. 18 appears in three second-order objective test factors, F(T)II(-): History of Difficulty in Problem Solving vs. Expansive Ego, F(T)IV(+): High Educated Self-Consciousness vs. Low Educated Self-Consciousness, and F(T)VII(+): High Tension to Achieve, Controlled Drive Tension Level vs. Low Tension to Achieve (57). These results suggest ego-weakness and desire for social success and approval (the latter possibly being a compensatory device for the former) as being important for our understanding of U.I. 18.

5. Criterion Correlations

a) Clinical Criteria

Three studies, R9-Ta, R9-Tb, and R10 have compared groups of normals and neurotics in terms of factor scores on U.I. 18. In no case was a significant difference obtained, and the differences are not consistent in sign. In spite of this evident freedom from any direct relationship to neurosis, psychiatrists' ratings of anxiety correlate negatively with this factor -- this being markedly so for ratings of over-all anxiety, and less so for 'bound', 'situational', and 'characterological' anxiety. That not too much weight be placed upon the psychiatrists' judgments alone, it may be necessary to remind the reader that an essentially zero relationship has been found with self-report measures of anxiety (see section 2).

b) School and Academic Achievement

Evidence on school and college achievement comes from C7, R1 and P 1, and in each case no association with this factor was demonstrated. Pawlik's results indicated that U.I. 18+ may be accompanied by over-achievement (138).

(c) Military Criteria

U.I. 18 appears to have some association with military training success. In the C 5 study of Air Force pilot trainees, positive correlations were found with all four criteria, though significance was only reached with the oriented criterion (a composite assessment including course results, and a variety of ratings and adjustment measures). Knapp's (122) study of Navy enlisted men also indicated a significant positive correlation with class standing in Submarine School. However with helicopter pilots Knapp found a non-significant correlation with Final Flying Grade and low non-significant negative correlations with peer ratings of pilot proficiency, officer-like qualities, and social acceptability. In general it seems that U.I. 18 may be a predictor of training success in terms of relatively objective achievement measures, but that this potential is less likely to be reflected in rating assessments by supervisors or peers.

6. Nature-Nurture and Age Trend Results

At present no evidence is available on the relative contribution of heredity or environment to this factor, and no research has been carried out on age trends of factor scores.

7. Descriptive Interpretation

The variables loading U.I. 18 may be grouped together under four headings: Speed on perceptual motor tasks, Superficiality, Insecurity, and Desire for social success. In addition there is a complex relationship between the factor and certain acquiescence and recall measures.

Speed on Perceptual-Motor Tasks. Associated with U.I. 18 is fast performance on many perceptual-motor tasks. Higher total score in CMS (MI. 143), more decisions made (MI. 153) and circles used (MI. 15) in CMS, faster simple reaction time (MI. 4), more accuracy in rapid shape comparison (MI. 385), greater speed on finger maze (MI. 82), all have positive loadings on this factor. However, absent are significant loadings on many variables such as speed of gestalt completion, and tasks more cognitive in nature. This suggests that the speed aspect of U.I. 18 may be strictly limited to certain tasks in which little loss in total score is incurred by erroneous actions--as in maze performance or simple reaction time.

Superficiality. A tendency for rushing through a test, and making what might be called 'superficial' judgments would inevitably lead to certain error scores. These do occur in more slanting lines crossed in CMS (MI. 16a) and in lower proportion correct in gestalt completion (MI. 146b). A possible interpretation suggests that this mode of response in the test situation seems to appear only when the subject may regard the 'pay-off' for a rapid but not error-free performance as being greater than that for a meticulous but slower performance. Presumably the 'pay-off' for a rapid but erroneous response in complex reaction time is not regarded in this light. The higher ratio of color to form in sorting

(MI. 39) suggests that there may be a more basic general tendency to react in terms of 'obvious' cues or initial impressions. This also would appear in more unreflective acceptance of unqualified statements (MI. 106). If this view is correct then one may also anticipate a sensitive 'feed-back' mechanism that slows down U.I. 18 performance after a certain level has been reached where no gain is to accrue, and loss will appear, through extra speed. This would account for the absence of loadings on error measures where the task is more difficult or more highly structured.

Insecurity. What appears to be a sense of personal insecurity also appears in U.I. 18, with higher ratio of self-criticism to criticism of others (MI. 30), lower proportion of fluency on self-relative to total verbal fluency (MI. 273), less aspiration for improvement in coding (MI. 148), more self-reference seen in events (MI. 111), higher ratio of self-criticism to self-approval (MI. 53), and more excess of unpleasant to pleasant comment on self (MI. 1418).

Social Success. Susceptibility to social success has been suggested (29) as one aspect of U.I. 18(+). On present evidence this appears principally in the shifting of attitudes towards those of successful people (MI. 193a), and in the general shift measure of ego weakness (MI. 115). That the loading on MI. 193a is rather specific to this form of suggestion is indicated by the absence of any substantial shift of attitude away from neurotics (MI. 194) or towards those of authority figures (MI. 35).

Somewhat conflicting loadings appear on the 'acquiescence' variables-- less tendency to agree with optimistic statements (MI. 124), more unreflective acceptance of unqualified statements (MI. 106), and essentially zero loadings on the general tendency to agree (MI. 152). This is not too surprising from the present argument, as one might expect a greater endorsement of 'agree' responses from a superficial approach to the items, but also the occasional operation of a more discriminating secondary approach acting as a counterbalance. As supportive evidence for this it is interesting at this point to note that, relative to other individuals, a person with high endowment of U.I. 18 is likely to recall statements previously disagreed with rather than those agreed with (MI. 38a).

Also loading U.I. 18 are much oscillation of performance (MI. 13a) and high fidgetomotor frequency (MI. 83), and both add to the picture of restlessness.

The only physical fitness variable appearing consistently with U.I. 18 is high score on the Schneider Index (MI. 73).

8. Explanatory Theory: History and Final Hypotheses

There is no direct counterpart to U.I. 18 in general psychological theory, and the factor does not appear to have been reported elsewhere in the literature. This may well be due to the peculiar pattern of speed and errors on relatively simple tasks, flavored by some sense of insecurity and possibly need for social success. Variables measuring these aspects are unlikely to appear together in many analyses, and this reduces the probability of the emergence of identification of U.I. 18.

At this point it is necessary to raise an issue which is of paramount importance to any discussion of this factor. This issue concerns the view, recognized for some time (Cattell, 1957), that U.I. 18 may not be a personality source trait but an 'instrument factor' of the Cursive Miniature Situation Test.

Our knowledge of instrument factors, response sets, test-form factors, and the like has increased considerably over recent years (75) (165) (15) (114) (37). In brief, when more than one measure (even though these be algebraically independent) is obtained from the same test or situation, or the same general test format is used, or style of response is required, then a source of variation may emerge which is due to the exigencies of the particular test situation but which may, mistakenly on occasion, be regarded as a more fundamental personality attribute of greater generality. That such sources of variation may be essential parts of some broader unit is clear enough, and there are many examples of their use in this way (e.g., the "tendency to agree" (M. I. 152) measure in U.I. 20 and U.I. 24). Clearly the point is not that such factors should be automatically removed or avoided, but that they should be known and their implications acted upon in a broader context.

Inspection of Table 7.6 shows that most of the consistent and high loadings on U.I. 18 come from five measures taken from the Cursive Miniature Situation Test, namely: faster speed of decision, CMS (MI. 153), greater use of circles, CMS (MI. 15), higher total score, CMS (MI. 143), more slanting lines crossed, CMS (MI. 16a), and lower ratio of initial to final performance, CMS (MI. 24d). This in itself is sufficient for examining the possibility that U.I. 18 may be a CMS instrument factor. The lack of any appreciable correlation with non-objective test measures (see section 2) and among criterion comparisons--with the possible exception of military success--would also be expected more from an instrument factor than from a source trait. However, strong arguments exist for retention of U.I. 18 as a source trait. First, from Table 7.6 it is clear that though CMS variables tend to dominate the scene, other variables quite disparate in nature from the CMS also have consistent loadings on this factor. Second, the five CMS variables themselves are not conceptually consistent as an instrument factor. Thus we find high total score, CMS (MI. 143) and many slanting lines crossed, CMS (MI. 16a) in which the latter, a penalized response, will tend if anything to diminish total score. Further, the lower ratio of initial to final performance, CMS (MI. 24d), indicates higher score on the second half of the test than on the first, while a high total score would be anticipated from someone who does equally well on both parts. Thirdly, U.I. 18 has been identified with a fairly consistent pattern of non-CMS variables when only two, one, or as in C2, no CMS variables were present in the analysis. Fourthly, certain CMS variables, such as more cheating on instructions CMS (MI. 20), higher proportion of correct decisions CMS (MI. 98), and aspiration level CMS (MI. 17), are absent from Table 7.6 or show low inconsistent loadings. Bearing these arguments in mind, the present decision is to retain U.I. 18 as a personality source trait, though noting its undue dependence upon one test.[1]

The salient variables of U.I. 18 present a pattern of rapid performance on perceptual motor tasks accompanied by a certain proneness for error, personal insecurity, ego weakness, and restlessness. It was suggested in Section 7 that the U.I. 18(+) person tends to respond to the obvious in the test situation, gaining high scores when cursory inspections and rapid 'snap' decisions have to be made. However this need not be characteristic of all U.I. 18(+) behavior, for when problems become more difficult (more cognitive?), structured, or the penalty for error more apparent, it seems likely that a more controlled manner of responding may emerge.

This response to the obvious without waiting for full assimilation of all information - a form of superficiality - is regarded as central to the interpretation of this factor. That this runs deeper than simply a mode of response is implied by loadings on many of the self-depreciatory and ego-weakness variables among the objective tests and the presence of U.I. 18 in second-order factors of ego-weakness, self-awareness and need for social approval and achievement. (The presence of need for achievement is supported by Pawlik's findings on over-achievement). It is our present hypothesis that U.I. 18(+) involves a basic ego-weakness that is compensated for by the slick, perhaps over-expressive behavior outlined above. In addition this ego weakness does not enter the individual's awareness of himself except for the self-depreciation found among the objective tests and possibly a felt need for social success. Apart from the need for achievement it seems unlikely that ego-weakness will find its way directly into self-report measures. This may well be a case in which the individual's perception of himself (as revealed by questionnaires, etc.) when taken on face value and in isolation from other evidence, gives a somewhat distorted picture. It is particularly unfortunate that age trends are not available for this factor as we would certainly expect a monotonic increase during childhood and early adolescence.

Anxiety - if present at all in this factor - appears from psychiatrists' ratings to belong with U.I. 18 (-). This is not unreasonable for with U.I. 18 (-) there is a slow adjustment and a plodding lack of spontaneity which probably accounts for the ratings of high-over-all anxiety.

Description of U.I. 18 (+) test behavior shows certain characteristics that could be regarded as hypomanic, and this accounts for the title of Hypomanic Smartness. So far there is no data to support a direct tie-up with hypomania, but this will not be discarded as a possible future hypothesis.

This factor, though one of the earliest in the Universal Index series, is also one upon which relatively little information of a positive nature has been established. We must therefore await further evidence before placing too much reliance on theoretical interpretations.

---

[1] At the moment of writing, data is under analysis including all markers for U.I. 18 and a large number of new measures constructed from hypotheses concerning the theoretical implications of U.I. 18. In this way it is hoped that much of the dependence of U.I. 18 upon the CMS test will be reduced.

Table 7.5

U.I. 18: Hypomanic Smartness vs. Slow Thoroughness

Q-Factor	Factor Title	Factor Identification (Research, Sample Size, Age of Subjects, Factor Number in Study)			
		C5 500 Adult (16+)	R1 86 Adult (10-)	R2 86 Adult (8+)	R10 168 Adult (16-)
A	(higher) Cyclothymia	+01	+02	+08	+02
B	(higher) Intelligence			+03	
C	(higher) Ego Strength	+19	+05	-07	-05
E	(higher) Dominance	-11		+09	+04
*F	higher Surgency (enthusiastic, talkative)	(-04)	+23	+05	(-04)
G	(higher) Super Ego Strength	-07		-28	+02
*H	higher Parmia (adventurous, "thick-skinned")	(-01)	+35	(-05)	(-02)
*I	(higher) Premsia	+02	+27	-02	-09
L	(higher) Protension	-09		-03	+13
*M	higher Alaxia (bohemian, unconcerned)	(-07)	(-08)	+23	+09
N	(higher) Shrewdness	-04		+19	00
O	(higher) Timidity	-10	+10	-17	+03
*Q1	higher Radicalism (experimenting, critical)	00		+40	+09
Q2	(higher) Self-Sufficiency	-09		-09	00
Q3	(higher) Self Sentiment Control	00		-02	+07
Q4	(higher) Ergic Tension	-13	-04	-04	00

U. I. 18: HYPOMANIC SMARTNESS VS. SLOW THOROUGHNESS (page 1)

Master Index Number	Variable Title	Factor Identification (Research, Sample Size, Age of Subjects, Factor Number in Study)													
		C1	C2	C3	C4	C5	C6	R1	R2	R10	We	C7	R12	R13	R15
		370	410	100	100	500	250	86	86	168	80	184	80	164	197
		Adult	Adult	Adult	Adult	Adult	Adult	Adult	Adult	Adult	Adult	9-12	4-5	6-9	7-10
		(5-)	(10-)	(10+)	(2+)	(16+)	(13+)	(10-)	(8+)	(16-)	--	(13+)	(20+)	(12+)	(3+)
153	faster speed of decision -- CMS			+69	+41	+25				+29		+10			
15	greater use of circles -- CMS			+07		+31	+23	+32	+10	+42		+52			
16a	more slanting lines crossed -- CMS	+09		+49	+01	+27	+41	+09	+19	+26		+49			
143	higher total score -- CMS			+44		+18				+00		+61	+14	+19	+23
24d	higher ratio of final (fast) to initial (slow) total score -- CMS					+45						+40	+40	+05	(-08)
83	higher fidgetometer frequency		+42	+01	(-03)	+02		+21	+22	+04		+04			
193a	more shifting of attitudes towards those of successful people			+08	+15	+15	+38			(-10)		+04		+10	+04
38a	lower ratio of consonant to dissonant recall (corrected for tendency to agree)	-41	-60	-09		-03	-10	-20							
39	higher ratio of color to form in sorting	+32	+32	+41	+30	+03	(-06)	+08		(-04)		+00		+06	+07
30	more criticism of self relative to criticism of others	(-02)		+15	(-04)	+21	+47	(-08)	(-35)				(-08)	+52	+15
269	faster leg-circling tempo					(-04)	(-01)	+15	+33	+06		+16		+02	
25a	less recall of emotional relative to non-emotional words	-21	-03	-33	-20										
13a	more oscillation of performance	+03	+03	+31	+23					+02		(-07)			
106	more unreflective acceptance of unqualified statements			+10	+17	+22	(-09)					+07			
5	higher ratio of regularly warned to irregularly warned reaction time	-04	-09	(+08)	-09		(+01)	-32	-18	-03		-07	-16		
146b	lower proportion correct in perceptual closure			-03	-27	(+12)	-04			-33		-02	-01	-13	
98b	higher absolute number of correct decisions -- CMS			+44	+19	(-06)									
16d	more excess use of circles -- CMS	+11			+77										
96a	less impairment of reading speed by frustrated preference			(-01)	+24							+24			
8	faster rate of alternating perspective	+00	+07	+04	+17	+04						+19		+10	
273	lower proportion of fluency on self relative to total verbal fluency					-15	(+04)	(+07)	-40	(+01)		-16	-23	(+27)	-24
82	greater distance covered on finger maze		+58			(-08)	+05			(-05)		+20			
73	higher score on Schneider index		+45						+02		+14				
385	more accuracy in rapid shape comparison													+43	+44
263	less variability in simple reaction times						-30					-11	-01	(+06)	-09
96b	less effect of frustrated preference on computational speed			+23	+32										
77	higher salivary ph (more alkilinity)		+09					+03	+38						
111	more self-reference seen in events			(-06)	+40	+04	+05					+02			
53	higher ratio of self-criticism to self-approval		+04			+59				(-09)					
124	less tendency to agree with optimistic statements			-15	-40				(+02)						
265	more decrement in coding performance with anxiety sound distraction							+23	+20						
148	less aspiration for improvement in coding			-18	-17										
4	faster average reaction time	(+02)	-41												
229	less severe standards					-09		+17	-29			-07			

U. I. 18: HYPOMANIC SMARTNESS VS. SLOW THOROUGHNESS (page 2)

Master Index Number	Variable Title	RESEARCH													
		C1	C2	C3	C4	C5	C6	R1	R2	R10	We	C7	R12	R13	R15
1716a	higher appeal erg (more desire to serve God)							+50							
1418	more excess of unpleasant to pleasant comment on self														-47
115	little independence through ego strength (much shift)									-42					
1487	less cautious (relative to others) attitudes to automobile driving after seeing horrifying pictures									-39					
428b	less attention to disturbing relative to non-disturbing pictures													-34	
274	lower verbal ability											-33			
56	more increase in emotional associations after fear story		+32												
66	fewer correct picture titles chosen		-32												
515	more increase in sound pressure from normal to delayed feedback reading							+32							
1128	smaller proportion of words used to describe people in horrifying than pleasant									+32					
65	less logical consistency of attitudes		-30												
609	good spatial integration														+30
219	(more) willingness to admit common frailties					-06	-21	-05	+08	+04		-05	-10	+07	+31
152	(more) tendency to agree			+00	-33	+07	-01	-08	+02	+07		-01		+09	
108	(more) assumption of skill in untried performance			+00	+45	-11	-05	-08	-01	-02		+13		-19	
43	(higher) magnitude of mean PGR deflection to threatening stimuli	-01	-33	+03	-08			-04	+03			+10			
116a	(higher) critical severity			-16	+33	+03		+17	-29	-10		-01		-02	
309	(faster) speed of line length judgment													+22	-48
202	(more) willingness to take a chance in answering questions					+15						-19			
94	(higher) mean frequency of flicker fusion				-31		+18								
227a	(more) color choices relative to form choices in picture preference											-03	+05	-35	
17	(higher) aspiration level -- CMS	+03								-34					
105	(higher) proportion of threatening objects seen in unstructured drawings			-03	-03	+05	+13			-33			+01	+04	+07
51	(more) carefulness in following instructions (index of carefulness)		-06			+01	+05	-14	+30	+05			-05		+11
927a	(higher) sex erg (more desire to satisfy sexual needs)							(-02)	+33						
247b	(more) expansiveness of copied design											+13	+34	-17	-03
3	(faster) speed of judgment	-02	-19	+09	+32										
7	(faster) speed of Gestalt closure	+14		-09	+17	+02	+22			-34		-08	+03	+03	-04
21	(fewer) questionable reading preferences	+10	+03	+01	-08	+03		-16				+08	+16	-06	-05
33	(larger) size of myokinetic movement	-10		+23				+15	-23	+03					
42	(more) body sway suggestibility	-03	-23	+26	-19			+10	-04	-04					+00
113	(more) acceptance of reality principle			-10	-03	+18				-17				+03	
147b	(greater) breadth of experience and accomplishment			-40	+18					+06		+12			
270	(faster) arm-circling tempo					-17	-07			-03		+26	-05	+16	+03

U.I. 19: PROMETHEAN WILL VS. SUBDUEDNESS

1. Prevalence

Factor U.I. 19 has been identified in thirteen factor analyses with adults, and five with children. In addition there are results from an extension analysis by Wells (166) on adults. The main loadings on Thurstones' E Factor, "suppressive manipulation of configurations" are also included in Table 7.8, though the variable domain in this case is limited to measures of perception.

2. Questionnaire Correlates

Cross media comparisons between U.I. 19 and the 16 P.F. are available from C5, R1, R2, R3, Ros and R10. The present position, considering all previous studies, is that H(+): PARMIA, Adventurous, Thick-Skinned, is the best correlate, followed with less conviction by M(+): ALAXIA, Bohemina, Unconcerned, A(-): SCHIZOTHYMIA, Aloof, Cold, and possibly N(+): SHREWDNESS, Sophisticated, Polished.

Knapp's (123) comparison of the Guilford-Martin scales and U.I. 19(+) on Navy Submarine School candidates showed only one significant correlation, that with C(-): Lack of Cycloid Disposition (r = -.12). Significant correlations with the Guilford-Zimmerman scales and MMPI, on officer pilots, were with G(+): General Activity (r = +.26), T(+): Thoughtfulness (r = +.30), and L(-): Low score on Lie Scale (r = -.23).

U.I. 19(+) has been correlated with questionnaire and self-report measures of anxiety in five studies (R1, R2, R3, Ros and N1). Four of the correlations are positive, but only in R3 (using incremental R technique) is the value significant.

The only significant correlation between U.I. 19+ and Kuder Preference Record indicates a negative association (r = -.23) with computational interests (138). In general a pattern emerges of a free-thinking, active, rather unstable individual with a certain imperviousness and coldness towards the perceptions and behavior of others. These questionnaire findings are consonant with those from objective tests, and add particular confirmation in a more social context to the criticalness and aloofness that appears to characterize this factor.

3. State Factor Matches

U.I. 19+ has been matched, though the match is only tentative at the moment, with P.U.I. 11(-): Promethean Will (Egoistic, Critical Mood) vs. Subduedness (Resigned, Cowed Mood). P.U.I. 11(-) has appeared in one P-technique study and one incremental R-technique (R 3). Among high loading variables are: slower ideomotor speed, good memory, higher critical severity, less fluency in self-criticism, more alkalinity of saliva, more increase of heart rate after startle, and higher pulse-pressure (170) (68).

4. Loadings on Second-Order Objective Test Factors

In second-order objective test factorizations, U.I. 18(+) appears with F(T)I-: Absence of Cultural Introjection vs. Tied Socialization or Superego, F(T)II+: Expansive Ego vs. History of Difficulty in Problem Solving, F(T)III+: Temperamental Ardor vs. Temperamental Apathy, and with reduced loadings on F(T)VII: High Tension to Achieve Controlled Drive Tension Level vs. Low Tension to Achieve (57).

5. Criterion Correlates

a) Clinical Criteria

In the R9-Ta comparison of normals and neurotics, normals were found to have a significantly higher score on U.I. 19+. However in R9-Ta and R10 (I) the differences were non-significant. Psychiatrists' ratings of Over-all Anxiety and Situational Anxiety (148) correlate negatively with U.I. 19+.

b) School and Academic Achievement

Three results of comparisons of U.I. 19 and scholastic achievement have been reported (R 1, C 7, and P 1). In both C 7 and Pawlik's analysis, U.I. 19+ was significantly positively related to grade-point average. The R 1 data is in conflict, however, for a -0.30 correlation was reported. These results are puzzling and further research is needed. Considering all evidence we may regard U.I. 19 as being probably positively related to achievement -- though awaiting further confirmation.

c) Military Criteria

Evidence on the relationship between U.I. 19 and military success comes from C5 and Knapp's studies (N1, N2) of helicopter pilots and submarine school candidates. In general correlations with criteria in these studies are essentially zero, the only exception being with the submarine school candidates which indicated a positive relationship with pass-drop (r = +.15) and class standing (r = +.27) criteria. With the helicopter pilots a significant correlation was observed with AQT, an intelligence test used as a predictor of course success.

6. Nature-Nurture and Age Trend Results

Nature-nurture information indicates that U.I. 19 is about evenly determined by both heredity and environment, and there is the further suggestion by Cattell, Stice, and Kristy (70) that environmental influences may be greater on those below average on the factor. Factor scores show a steady rise from the age of nine to eleven years of age when a general flattening out occurs.

7. Descriptive Interpretation

In spite of its identification in many studies, the variables that have loaded U.I. 19 -- apart from the principal markers -- show no great tendency to group together in relation to known and clearly defined psychological or psychometric concepts. Nevertheless certain aspects of U.I. 19 test performance are fairly clear, but these still leave a rather large residue of somewhat isolated variables that emphasize the need for further research.

Accurate, competent performance. The first grouping is very broad, including a large number of competency measures, usually of a perceptual or perceptual-motor kind, showing exactness, control, and low error scores. Among the accurate competent performances are found: higher proportion correct in perceptual closure (MI. 146b), large number correct in perceptual closure (MI. 146a), higher accuracy in perceptual closure on Gottschaldt figures (MI. 206), lower rigidity (MI. 2), higher score on Index of Carefulness (MI. 51) and many correct movements in two-hand coordination (MI. 41). Avoidance of errors appears in less proneness to false reactions in reaction time (MI. 40), fewer erroneous reactions when maintaining complex mental sets (MI. 71), fewer slanting lines crossed, CMS (MI. 16a), and less use of circles, CMS (MI. 15). There is no evidence to support the view that over-scrupulousness in avoiding errors leads to low scores. Indeed in spite of very few errors in complex reaction time, the actual time itself is fast (MI. 176). It seems that the high U. I. 19 person keeps up a high rate of performance commensurate with few errors.

Ability to Concentrate. An interesting and probably significant aspect of U.I. 19(+) performance is the ability to concentrate on problems with either little support from the environment or with actual distraction. Examples of such behavior are found in less distraction by aesthetic material in verbal and numerical tasks (MI. 467), less distractability in picture inspection task (MI. 426), more ability to do numerical problems in one's head (MI. 476), and more efficient speed articulation under delayed reading conditions (MI. 510). It is noteworthy that U.I. 19 is associated with a high score on the ability to do mathematical problems in one's head (or with distraction) without there being any real evidence for high mathematical or computational skill as such. Presumably the solution of problems in one's head without the support of pencil and paper implies high competence in avoiding mind-wandering and distractions from the environment. Less impairment of classification performance by shock (MI. 166) suggests that good performance is retained under more severe stress, but confirmation is lacking from all other measures involving shock, stress and punishment.

A certain criticalness of others while maintaining a rather more complacent view of oneself also appears in this factor. There is relatively little criticism of self compared to criticism of others (MI. 30), more pleasant than unpleasant self comment (MI. 141), lower ratio of self-criticism to self approval (MI. 53), and less willingness to admit common frailties (MI. 219). That this may be related to a more general criticalness of non-self things and events may be inferred from the critical hostility of judgment in MI. 116a, b, but this needs further confirmation. It is scarcely surprising to find a higher ratio of number of acquaintances to number of friends (MI. 472) as high endowment of U.I. 19 may imply the setting of rather exact and vigorous standards as to who could be called a friend!

Logical Flexibility. A somewhat surprising characteristic of U.I. 19 is what might be called mental flexibility, appearing in greater number of riddles solved (MI. 26), more immaturity of opinion (MI. 34), and higher percentage of choice of unusual names (MI. 865), as well as the good perceptual closure and lack of rigidity mentioned above. Particularly relevant may be the absence of all shift measures (i.e., shift to successfuls (MI. 193a), shift from neurotics (MI. 194), and shift to authority (MI. 35) and the presence of much logical consistency of attitudes (MI. 65), little fluctuation of attitudes in MI. 31. This implies that though flexible in avoiding response or mental set perseveration in free response tasks, or when good logical arguments suggest a change of opinion, the U.I. 19(+) person takes little heed of prestige or social suggestion.

Conservative Estimates of Own Performance. A tendency to give conservative estimations of present and future personal performance also appears in this factor, though it may be a product of the general control and exactness mentioned above. Here are found less considered possible in given time for self (MI. 192), less excess of aspiration over performance in coding and mazes (MI. 101a, b), and lower ratio of estimated to actual time for ergograph work (MI. 1518). The rather low loadings on these variables suggest that the U.I. 19(+) person probably is an accurate rather than a pessimistic estimater.

Motivation measures present a pattern which combines high sex erg (Want to Satisfy Sexual needs) (MI. 927a), Low Fear Erg (Does not want protection against atomic terror) (MI. 929b), and Low Self-Sentiment Erg (Does not want good control over mental processes) (MI. 933a).

Finally there are some loadings on physiological and body-build measures which, though not at present giving a concise and readily interpretable facet of U.I. 19, are of considerable interest for the future. These measures include less rapid PGR upward drift (MI. 80), greater amount of GSR conditioning (MI. 469), lower absolute level of GSR (MI. 443), higher salivary pH (MI. 77), greater total physical strength (MI. 557).

8. Explanatory Theory: History and Final Hypotheses

From Table 7.8 it can be seen that U.I. 19 is a well established personality factor. However it does not appear to have emerged as such prior to 1948 in the C1 study (19). Indications are that it probably appeared in splintered form in several of the early studies of perception and temperament employing a rather narrow sampling of variables. Conceptual agreement between certain aspects of this factor and Thurstone's 'E' (161), plus the sharing of certain common markers, justifies the inclusion of the latter in Table 7:8.

The evidence so far accumulated on U.I. 19 may be summarized as follows:

(1) Objective tests indicate that the U.I. 19(+) person is characterized by (a) exactness, control, low error scores, and general good performance in a variety of tasks, but principally in the area of perception, (b) ability to concentrate on 'problems in one's head' and to remain relatively unaffected by distraction, (c) self-complacency, relatively critical of others, yet not over-confident, (d) a degree of flexibility in changing responses, or adapting to, problems involving competence, but unaffected by any form of prestige suggestion.

(2) Questionnaire correlates of U.I. 19(+) suggest a person who is active and free-thinking, yet perhaps rather cold and distant in his relationship with other people.

(3) In general criterion results indicate a rather loose relationship to achievement in the military and educational spheres. U.I. 19(-) is related to neurosis, but not markedly so, and is regarded as a neurotic contributory factor. Questionnaire measures of anxiety show no definite relationship to this factor.

(4) P.U.I. 11(-) is probably the state factor attached to U.I. 19. Second-order objective test analyses confirm the general character of independence, control, and egoism.

(5) Heredity and environment appear to play about equal parts in the determination of U.I. 19.

At present the evidence on U.I. 19 continues to make interpretation beyond the descriptive level a difficult procedure. Nevertheless certain inferences may be drawn as to the interaction of the U.I. 19 (+) person and his social environment. The critical, free-thinking, and perfectionistic aspects of U.I. 19 (+) coupled with high ability could produce the rather uncompromising, highly efficient leader, whose lack of immediate warmth and individual sympathy for other people is balanced by considerable drive and determination. Such a pattern fits several of the 19th century reformers (perhaps Florence Nightingale and Lord Shaftesbury) and many religious, and military figures. Impatience with compromise, and the ability to concentrate on one major problem to the exclusion of all others, would lead to success in one field but also the preclusion of success in high executive positions involving a wide variety of issues and the inevitability of compromise decisions. Thus where the issue is one of social ethics the response of the U.I. 19 (+) person would be toward society in general, and not toward specific individual members. Coupled with relatively low general intelligence one would expect a plodding exactness leading to competence in some routine occupation and a general lack of involvement in social affairs.

The determination, independence, and 'thick-skinnedness' of U.I. 19 (+) is absent, of course, in U.I. 19 (-). This probably accounts, at least in part, for the association between U.I. 19 (-) and neurosis, for here there is no ready-made channel of activity to sublimate conflicting drives and general inadequacy. U.I. 19 (-) has been called Resignation - Subduedness and this appears to fit very well the rather colorless negative pole of the factor.

As a pattern of behavior U.I. 19 appears to be consistent and relatively unambiguous from the objective test evidence. However, once we progress beyond the descriptive level and attempt to integrate U.I. 19 within general theory, in terms of the development of the factor and its relation to other factors, the task becomes more complex. There appear to be no immediately available concepts from psycho-analysis, learning theory, or general personality theory that coincide with this factor. Such absence of correspondence is not in any way disturbing, and is, in any case, to be expected from use of factor analysis in the context of present personality theory. Certain theoretical issues may be discussed, however, and a tentative hypothesis suggested as to the nature of U.I. 19.

There are aspects of U.I. 19, such as control and perfectionism, that appear close to the psycho-analytic concept of the Superego, but two points militate against this interpretation. The first is lack of supportive evidence from the questionnaire realm. The second is the substantial hereditary determination and the definite implication that U.I. 19 is relatively 'free' of the environment, which would not be expected from traditional views on the Superego.

The determination, exactness, and independence of U.I. 19 also suggest a relationship to development of the self-sentiment. Certainly this is no self-sentiment factor as such, for there are substantial negative loadings on the Self-Sentiment Erg. Nevertheless it may be that U.I. 19 is dependent upon a defective self-sentiment growth that leads to both lack of self-awareness and lack of awareness of self in relation to others. Concomitantly, of course, this would also involve lack of sympathy and sensitiveness towards others. This leads to our final, albeit tentative, hypothesis. This is that hereditary endowment accounts for the determination, control and generally efficient performance of U.I. 19 (+), particularly in the perceptual realm; while lack of affection in the early years leads to defective self-sentiment development. Age trend results suggest that by the middle school years the pattern of U.I. 19 has been established and remains constant, and this fits in very well with this general hypothesis. The unconscious egoism that appears in the U.I. 19 (+) person will lead him to be often at variance with his environment, but the absence of need for affection or support (or severe repression of such a need) enables him to continue his course without the anxiety (and possibly later conformity) that would otherwise result.

Table 7.7
U.I. 19: Promethean Will vs. Subduedness

Q-Factor	Factor Title	Factor Identification (Research, Sample Size, Age of Subjects, Factor Number in Study)					
		C5 500 Adult (14+)	Ros 70 Adult (8+)	R1 86 Adult (14-)	R2 86 Adult (11+)	R3 86 Adult (8-)	R10 168 Adult (12-)
*A	higher Schizothymia (aloof, cold)	-11		-05	-06	(+02)	-05
B	(higher) Intelligence				-09		
C	(higher) Ego Strength	+04	-28	-04	-16	00	+16
E	(higher) Dominance	+09			-04		+05
F	(higher) Surgency	+13	-06	+23	00	-06	+03
G	(higher) Super Ego Strength	-07			-11		00
*H	higher Parmia (adventurous, ("thick-skinned")	+11		+23	(-13)	+02	+23
*I	higher Premsia (sensitive effeminate)	+33		(-02)	(-05)	(-04)	+14
L	(higher) Protension	-08			-01		-05
*M	higher Alaxia (bohemian, unconcerned)	+10	+13	+06	+08	00	+09
*N	higher Snrewdness (sophisticated, polished)	+25			+05		(-04)
O	(higher) Timidity	-06	-03	+08	00	00	-20
Q1	(higher) Radicalism	+08			+04		+13
Q2	(higher) Self-Sufficiency	-06			-01		-16
Q3	(higher) Self Sentiment Control	-07			+11		+26
Q4	(higher) Ergic Tension	-01	-05	+01	+13	+08	-12

U. I. 19: PROMETHEAN WILL VS. SUBDUEDNESS (page 1)

Master Index Number	Variable Title	Factor Identification (Research, Sample Size, Age of Subjects, Factor Number in Study)																		
		T2	C1	C2	C3	C4	C5	C6	Ros	R1	R2	R3	R10	E-D1	We	C7	R12	R13	R15	R14
		190	370	410	100	100	500	250	70	86	86	86	168	139	80	184	80	164	197	129
		Adult	Adult	Adult	Adult	Adult	Adult	Adult	Adult	Adult	Adult	Adult	Adult	Adult	Adult	9-12	4-5	6-9	7-10	3-7
		E	(7-)	(5+)	(5+)	(12-)	(14+)	(6+)	(8+)	(14-)	(11+)	(8-)	(12-)	(3+)	--	(7+)	(11+)	(10-)	(10+)	(16-)
146b	higher proportion correct in perceptual closure				+55	+21	+33	+48					+01	+51		+12	+38	+13		+32
206	higher accuracy in perceptual closure on Gottschaldt figures	+37					+25	+33		+29				+14			+09	+34	+29	
51	higher score: index of carefulness			(-03)			+37	+32		+04	+22	+01	+13				+35		(-12)	
8	faster rate of alternating perspective	+06	(-05)	+32	+26	+21	+15							+30		+20		+08		
30	less criticism of self relative to criticism of others		(+01)		-38	-18	(+11)	-05		-30	+00	-30	-33	-01			-11	-08	-11	-39
146a	larger number correct in perceptual closure								+35	+29				+59				+13	+53	
71	fewer erroneous reactions under complex instructions			-58			-13	-17		-18	-31	-02	-06			(+14)	-40	-04	(+08)	
2a,b,e	lower motor (and motor-perceptual) rigidity		(+01)	(+04)	+00	-18	-20	-32	(+21)	-04	+00	-06	-22	-04		-22	-16	-56	-18	
116a,b	higher severity of judgment				+57	+13	+03		(-14)	+23	(-13)	+30	+17	+03		+10		+14		
7	faster speed of perceptual closure	+06	(-06)		+08	+25	+24	+46	+00				(-01)			(-02)	+00	+14	+63	
16a	fewer slanting lines crossed -- CMS		-11		(+07)	-04	-23	-34	-28	-03	-17	-21	(+01)			(+06)				
41	more correct movements in two-hand co-ordination	+59	+34	+01	+40	+10	+04		+14							(-01)				
39	higher ratio of color to form in sorting		+07	+33	+11	(-16)	+31	+12		+02			(-06)			+36		(-14)	(-11)	
176	faster irregularly warned reaction time				-26	-52			-14	-32	(+07)	(+02)					(+05)	(+11)	-10	
21	more questionable reading preferences		+06	+22	(-22)	+02	+14			+01				+18		+12	+05	(-04)	+20	
80	less rapid PGR upward drift			-42						-10	-24	(+17)				-13				
219	less willingness to admit common frailties						-08	(+05)	-28	-01	-10	-05	-17			-23	-07	-05	-08	-09
15	less use of circles -- CMS		-28		-04	(+09)	-09	-21	-32	-16	(+01)	(+01)	-04			-08	+00		(+01)	
34	more immaturity of opinion		+01	+38	(-25)	+18	+15						+04			+04	(-03)			
466	lower frequency of hand tremor								-21	-06	-49	(+06)	-21							
40	less proneness to false reactions in reaction time		-10				-05	-04					(+14)			(+22)	-36	-27	-04	-13
282	greater number of objects seen in unstructured drawings						+00	+07	+17				(-03)	+27			+12	+04	+08	+16
469	greater amount of GSR conditioning									+13	+32	+31								
65	more logical consistency of attitudes			+21	+32	+23										+03				
99	higher ratio of verbal to numerical ability				(-01)	+28										+33				
476	more ability to do numerical problems in one's head									-06	-36	-23								
467	less distraction by aesthetic material in verbal and numerical tasks									-01	-28	-31								
9	faster ideomotor tempo		+00	+37	(-16)													+24		
198	more hidden words found				+19	+49	+06									+00				
170	more hidden pictures seen correctly	+47							+22											
117	more highbrow tastes				(-04)	+17	(-02)	+19					+08							

U. I. 19: PROMETHEAN WILL VS. SUBDUEDNESS (page 2)

Master Index Number	Variable Title	RESEARCH																		
		T2	C1	C2	C3	C4	C5	C6	Ros	R1	R2	R3	R10	E-D1	We	C7	R12	R13	R15	R14
22a-c	higher ratio of chance to purposeful observation and memory		+35	+18	+07	+04							(-06)							
927a	higher sex erg (desire to satisfy sexual needs)									+51	+18	(-07)								
288	slower speed of judgment						-04	-08						-35						
64	male sex	+36		+22										+04		+37		(-24)		(-05)
111	less self-reference seen in events				-30	-02	-04	(+10)								-22				
53	lower ratio of self-criticism to self-approval			-30			(+10)						-32	+00						
472	higher ratio of acquaintances to friends									+00	+49	+09	(-02)							
454	more anxiety-tension symptoms checked									+01	+09	+34								
38a	lower ratio of consonant to dissonant recall (corrected)		(+01)	-01	-25		+00	(+10)		-01							-23			
933a	lower self-sentiment erg (good control over mental processes)									-36	(+04)	-07	-10							
84b	more increase of pulse-rate in stress			+02					+08	(-05)	+05	+41								
929b	lower fear erg (desire for protection against atomic terror)									(+04)	-20	-24								
263	less variability in simple reaction time							-16								-31	-10	(+13)	+00	-20
201	higher ability on number series						+07	+32												
107	more knowledge of social etiquette				+03	+57														
26	greater number of riddles solved				+01	+50														
77	higher salivary ph			+18					(-20)	(-07)	+02	+40								
443	lower absolute level of GSR									-06	-30	-02								
92	less readiness to imitate animal sounds				+42	+07														
166	less impairment of classification performance by shock				-15	-25														
461	higher ratio of frightening to non-frightening estimates of passages in film strips									(-01)	+42	+14								
155	smaller range of flicker fusion				-09	-32														
101a,b	less excess of aspiration over performance (coding, mazes)				-20	-18	(+07)									(+05)		-14	(+04)	
277	higher age													(-09)		+34				+07
426	less distractibility in picture inspection task																	-40	-02	
156	less lag of flicker fusion decision				-06	-30														
171	more hidden objects seen in pictures				(-26)		+03		+22							+07		+18		
192	less considered possible in given time for self				-07	-57	-14	(+05)								-02		(+09)		(+02)
920	lower average amplitude of hand tremor									-06	-49	(+06)								
37	higher ability to suggest classifications		+03	+33																

U. I. 19: PROMETHEAN WILL VS. SUBDUEDNESS (page 3)

Master Index Number	Variable Title	RESEARCH																		
		T2	C1	C2	C3	C4	C5	C6	Ros	R1	R2	R3	R10	E-D1	We	C7	R12	R13	R15	R14
1518	lower ratio of estimated to actual time for ergograph work				(+02)	-40							-01			(+07)	-02			
509	more efficient speech articulation (normal reading)									(-04)	+37									
78	more involuntary muscle tension			(-16)						+30	+05	+14								
428b	less attention to disturbing vs. non-disturbing pictures																	-42	(+06)	(+02)
5	higher ratio of regularly to irregularly warned reaction time		+00	+04	+23	+08		+05	+17	(-03)	(-02)	+04	+01			(-04)	+06			
112	more favorable relative to unfavorable self-reference				+02	+18	(-02)	+15					(-03)	+03		+07		+01		
143	higher total score -- CMS						(-06)		(-03)				+04			+18	(-09)	+18	+11	+17
67a,b	less extremity of viewpoint			-01	-20	(+02)	(+01)	(+01)					-01			-07		-35	-05	
120a-g	lower ratio of accuracy to speed in mazes				-03	-14			+00	-05	(+09)	-24	(+01)			-22	-02	(+01)	-07	(+01)
31	less fluctuation of attitudes		(+04)		(+05)	-36	-12						+00				(+02)			-03
1410	less tolerance for interruptions of story																			+52
159a,c	more variability in other-referent time estimates				+45															
79	shorter duration of eidetic images			-44																
865	higher percentage of choice of unusual names												+39							
1041	fewer persons arousing hostility												-36							
61	higher influence of frustration on judgments			+36																
510	more efficient speech articulation (delayed feedback)										+36									
231	longer distance travelled on mazes															+35				
557	greater total physical strength (back, leg, hand)														+35					
1351	lower percentage of morally unacceptable solutions declined												-34							
50	higher alertness in following instructions			+32																
1029	fewer admissions of trouble and conflict												-32							
1440	more lability in perceptual preferences																			+32
1414	higher speed on letter cancellation																		+30	
1418	more pleasant vs. unpleasant self comment																		+30	
493	less readiness to commit oneself to a course of action												-30							
1339	greater pleasantness of home atmosphere																			+30
133	(more) criticalness of judgments				+12	-07	-10									-27	-02	+32	-13	
211a	(more) susceptibility to annoyance						+11	+00	-05	-03						-43	-18	-13	+00	-02
35	(more) suggestibility to authority		+02	-05	+07	-32	+11	+07		+09			+02			-14				
175	(slower) regularly warned reaction time		+10	+17	+31	-49					+07	+02	-06			-34	+07		+02	+06
147b	(greater) estimated breadth of experience and accomplishment				-14	+22							-01			+17				
36	(higher) ability to state logical assumptions		-14	-12	-16	+27	+00													

U. I. 19: PROMETHEAN WILL VS. SUBDUEDNESS (page 4)

Master Index Number	Variable Title	RESEARCH																		
		T2	C1	C2	C3	C4	C5	C6	Ros	R1	R2	R3	R10	E-D1	We	C7	R12	R13	R15	R14
73	(higher) Schneider index			+16							-22				-15					
105	(higher) proportion of threatening objects seen in unstructured drawings				+37	+14	+10	+08	-06				-08	+14		+05	-44	-11	+17	
463	(greater) acceleration to a competitive situation									+42	-09	-21								
465	(more) decrement in coding due to anxiety sound distraction									+26	-08	-53								
82	(greater) distance covered on finger maze			-11			+13	-15					-02			+41				
6a,b,c	(faster) ideomotor and motor speed		+01						+31	+11	+03	-47	+12			-01	-07	-33	-01	
276	(higher) academic achievement									-30						+30				
203	(more) confidence in numerical ability						-03	+10					+02				+19		-15	+18
42	(more) body sway suggestibility		+08	+07	+14	-27				+10	+02	-02	-13						+18	+03
108	(more) confident assumption of skill in untried performance				-22	+02	-02	+17		+02	+21	-06	+01			-01		+02		+13
150	(more) acceptance of obvious aphorisms				-13	+11										-14	+41			
152	(more) tendency to agree				+20	+04	+02	+04	-11	+05	-05	-19	-07	+01		+08		+03		-06
193a	(more) shifting of attitudes towards those of successful people				-32		+17	+02		+09			+04			-03				

U.I. 20: COMENTIVE SUPEREGO (DEVELOPMENT) VS. ABCULTION

1. Prevalence

U.I. 20 has been identified as such in nine factor analyses with adults and in five with children. Similarity between this factor and one found earlier by Brogden and others accounts for the BR column of average loadings in Table 7.10. An extension analysis by Wells (166) examined correlations of a U.I. 20 factor estimate with physical fitness variables. The matching of factors across studies is excellent and appears to continue through all age levels.

2. Questionnaire Correlates

U.I. 20 was identified in three studies (C 5, R 1, and Ros) also containing the 16 P.F. scales, but no established questionnaire correlates of this factor emerged. Possible further correlates appear to be A (-): Schizothymia (aloof, cold) and O (+): Timidity (insecure, anxious), but both of these questionnaire factors show too low an association to exert much influence on discussion of U.I. 20 at present.

Knapp (123) found low but significant positive correlations between U.I. 20 (+) and R (+): Rhathymia (r = +.11) and M (+): Masculinity (r = +.11), of the Guilford-Martin scales with 315 Naval enlisted men. With 81 officer helicopter pilots the significant correlations were with E (-): Emotional Instability (r = -.27), O (-): Lack of Objectivity (r = -.25), of the Guilford-Zimmerman scales, Pd (+): Psychopathic Deviate (r = +.23), Ma (+): Hypomania (r = +.23), L (-): Low Score on Lie Scale (r = -.36), and K (-): Little Test Defensiveness (r = -.31), of the MMPI.

Correlations with measures of anxiety show a consistent positive relationship with U.I. 20 (+). Thus in Ros and Knapp (123) correlations of +0.20 and +0.25 were found with the Taylor MAS, and +0.35 with the IPAT Anxiety Scale (R 1). However it is important to note that with the exception of O (+), no association emerges with those first-order 16 P.F. factors entering into the second-order 16 P.F. factor of Anxiety. The absence of these 16 P.F. associations is one of the main known differences between this factor and U.I. 24: Anxiety.

An important point has to be borne in mind, however, before placing too much reliance on the bulk of the self-report evidence on U.I. 20 which comes from Knapp's two studies. This is that the factor was measured in these two groups by unweighted sums of stanines for the U.I. 20 tests contained in the 1955 Objective-Analytic Personality Battery (27). Now U.I. 20 and U.I. 24 are 'co-operative' factors, and the very close similarity between the U.I. 20 and U.I. 24 results as reported by Knapp suggests that the U.I. 20 factor scores may have been impure and contaminated by U.I. 24. This being the case, Knapp's results for this factor should be regarded with caution pending later confirmation.

In general it appears that U.I. 20 is lacking in any firm relation with questionnaire measures, and that what tenuous links there are do not present a very cohesive pattern. An exception to this is the low but consistent association with self-report measures of anxiety and the essentially zero association with the 16 P.F. second-order factor of anxiety.

3. State Factor Matches

No state form of U.I. 20 has as yet been discovered.

4. Loadings on Second-Order Objective Test Factors

U.I. 20+ appears in two second-order objective test factors, F (T) I (+): Tied Socialization or Superego vs. Absence of Cultural Introjection, and F (T) III (+): Temperamental Ardor vs. Temperamental Apathy, with somewhat higher loadings on the former.

F(T)I is the largest of the second-order objective test factors, and it is hypothesized that it "represents the extent to which the individual has accepted the culture patterns and standards of the group" (57). Neurotics are significantly higher than normals on this factor (57). The place of U.I. 20 (+) within F(T) III is conceptually not too clear, except that it endorses the generally genetic determination of this second-order factor. Hospitalized neurotics have significantly higher F (T) III scores than do normals.

One important finding is that U.I. 20 and U.I. 24 do not appear together in any second-order objective test factor. U.I. 28: Dependent Negativistic Asthenia, which may have some theoretical tie with U.I. 20, also appears in F(T)I.

5. Criterion Correlations

a) Clinical Criteria

Comparisons between normal and neurotic groups suggest that neurotics may score slightly higher than normals on U.I. 20+, (R9-Ta, R10 (I), R9-TB), but in no case has a significant difference been found.

Ratings by psychiatrists give negative correlations between U.I. 20 (+) and Overall Anxiety, Free Anxiety, Bound Anxiety, Situational Anxiety, and Characterological Anxiety (148).

b) School and Academic Achievement

With regard to academic achievement there appears to be no relationship to grade point average (BR, C 7, R 1).

c) Military Criteria

U.I. 20(+) has shown a consistent positive relationship to criteria of military success, but the actual size of the correlations has usually been small and of borderline significance. In AF a significant correlation was found with the Oriented Criterion (a composite of final pass-fail and course adjustment and achievement measures) among pilot trainees, and Knapp (121) (122) found a significant correlation with both Final Flying Grade for helicopter pilots and class standing of enlisted Submarine School Candidates. This last correlation however dropped below the level of significance when intelligence was partialed out.

6. Nature-Nurture and Age-Trend Results

Hereditary variance is found to be four times greater than environmental variance for U.I. 20. This predominance of heredity is found both between and within families (70). Age trend results show a steady rise from 9 years of age to 15 years (29).

7. Descriptive Interpretation

Acquiescence

A central aspect of this factor is the tendency to respond with agreement to questionnaire statements of a wide variety of content. This appears in more tendency to agree (MI. 152), more tendency to agree with optimistic statements (MI. 124), more unreflective acceptance of unqualified statements (MI. 106), and more agreement with platitudinous thinking (MI. 144). There are no acquiescence variables used in these studies which have failed to load U.I. 20. Present also is greater recall of statements agreed with than statements disagreed with (MI. 38a, b, c).

Conformity

As to whether such variables as "willingness to admit common frailties" (MI. 219) "absence of questionable reading preferences" (MI. 21), and more authority submission (MI. 246) relate to basic honesty or uprightness, rather than the desire to please or conform at least in the test situation (even if this means admitting guilt!) remains to be seen. All three variables are good markers for U.I. 20 but the second (absence of questionable reading preferences) is poor for children, probably due to measurement difficulties at the low age ranges. Willingness to admit common frailties (MI. 219) may well be related to the low lie score, L (-), of the MMPI (see Section 2).

Suggestibility

A definite influence upon response of suggestion from a wide variety of sources is found in U.I. 20 (+). Among the more personal and direct influences are more agreement with both authority and sample (MI. 69), and more body sway suggestibility (MI. 42). Rapid appearance of a negative after-image (MI. 70) may also fall here as a rapid response may be regarded as the desired response, though no such suggestion is made directly. Less personal influences are found in more suggestibility to authority (MI. 35). However it is important to note that apart from MI. 35 there is no evidence that shift measures (a shift of opinion from one time of testing to another in line with suggestion of a preferred response), such as shift in attitudes to those of successful people (MI. 193a), immaturity of opinion (MI. 35), and shift in attitudes away from those endorsed by neurotics (MI. 194), are at all involved in this factor.

Sensitivity to Punishment

It appears that verbal punishment rather than praise affects the performance of an individual with a high factor score on U.I. 20 (+). This shows in lower ratios of performance on both tests of classification and perceptual closure under approval to disapproval conditions (MI. 165, and MI. 163), but somewhat inconsistent findings appear for the ratio of cancellation performance under approval to disapproval (MI. 161). The presence of lower ratio of performance on both classification and perceptual closure under normal to shock conditions (MI. 164, and MI. 166) implies that the shock may be regarded as punishment for poor performance. Nevertheless the reader should be warned that such ratio measures as these may also be interpreted as little impairment due to shock (perhaps as an ability to withstand or ignore such treatment) rather than as a response aimed at improving performance to an un-punished level, and further evidence is needed on this point. Support for the view that U.I. 20 (+) involves a general sensitivity to punishment is found in much awareness of error (MI. 169) and much PGR upward drift after shock (MI. 80).

Low Reactivity

Physiological and physical measures give a picture of slow reactivity to stimulation and a low level of 'alertness' of the central nervous system. Present are slower regularly and irregularly warned reaction times (MI. 175, and MI. 176), less increase in metabolic rate with stimulation (MI. 75), fewer PGR deflections during nonsense reading (MI. 291), lower basal metabolic rate (MI. 74), less involuntary muscle tension (MI. 78), and more static ataxia (MI. 122).

Hostility

Finally, there is evidence, though this is not completely clear, for a certain degree of hostility in judgment, shown in higher over-all annoyability (MI. 211) and critical severity (MI. 116). However it should be noted that these loadings are relatively low in value, compared with those for U.I. 24, a factor 'cooperative' with U.I. 20.

8. Explanatory Theory: History and Final Hypotheses

Early studies by Brogden (12), Rethlingshafer (143), and others, suggested the presence of an 'honesty' factor involving willing acceptance of social and ethical norms of behavior. The apparent truthfulness and conforming aspects of U.I. 20, plus the sharing of a few important marker variables, led to a tentative identification with this factor. However, as the pattern of relevant variables for U.I. 20 was more clearly defined, it became clear that altruism or honesty as such is simply one of several interpretations of this factor, and probably not the most likely.

The high factor loadings of 'tendency to agree' or acquiescence variables suggests a fairly close, but probably complex, relationship between U.I. 20 and the response set of acquiescence (74) (76) (73) (131). It is our view that this response facet distributes its variance over three personality traits, U.I. 20, U.I. 24, and U.I. 28, and that this emerges from factor analyses based on a sampling of variables from a wide domain of objective personality measures and using rotation for simple structure.

Inspection of the evidence on U.I. 20 that has so far accumulated suggests that this is a very complex pattern, and difficult to place under any one unitary concept at present in psychological literature. Individual aspects of this factor fit psychological theory quite well, but when joined together they present a definite challenge to future research. At least three paradoxes are involved in U.I. 20.

The first paradox is that in spite of sharing many of the principal marker variables of U.I. 24: (anxiety), and showing positive correlations with self-report measures of anxiety, U.I. 20 is not Anxiety - at least in the clinical sense, or as measured by U.I. 24. It is clear that U.I. 20 is co-operative with U.I. 24, but both factors have been found together in sufficient studies for them to be regarded as separate personality dimensions and both do not appear in the same second-order factors. The correlation with self-report measures of anxiety is countered by lack of correlation with the 16 P.F. second order Anxiety factor, negative correlations with psychiatrists' ratings of anxiety, and the only slight and non-significant relation to neurosis.

The second paradox is that in spite of the strong suggestion from objective tests of high acculturation, acquiescence, and conformity, there is a complete absence of any supportive questionnaire evidence. Correlations would be expected with G (+): Super Ego Strength, Q 1 (-): Conservatism, and Q 2 (-): Group Dependence in the 16 P.F., Ag (+): Agreeableness, Co (+): Co-operativeness, S (+): Sociability, and F (+): Friendliness, of the Guilford-Martin and Guilford-Zimmermann scales, and Pd (-): Low score on Psychopathic Deviate scale, L (-): Low Score on Lie Scale, and K (-): Little test defensiveness, of the MMPI. Apart from the last two, L (-) and K (-), and the anticipated results from anxiety measures, no such cross-media correspondence appears - indeed a correlation appears with Pd (+)! Admittedly the cooperativeness of U.I. 20 and U.I. 24 tends to bias scores from factor estimates, but the questionnaire results still remain puzzling.

The third paradox of U.I. 20 is that though the objective test evidence points towards considerable sensitivity to the environment (acquiescence, conformity, etc.) the nature-nurture data clearly indicates that the factor is predominantly hereditarily determined.

HYPOTHESIS I: U.I. 20 as honesty or altruism

This early notion of U.I. 20 has been essentially discarded as the salient variables for this factor clearly indicate it to be more complex than simple altruism, and to be closer to social acceptance and compliance. That honesty may be a by-product or effect of this complex pattern appears, in certain circumstances, to be likely, but the causal network between the two is far from being fully understood. Unfortunately due to measurement difficulties there is little direct evidence on the association of measures of honesty and U.I. 20, apart from Brogden's early work with children.

HYPOTHESIS II: U.I. 20 as Bound Anxiety

"One can define an anxiety which is 'bound' in the sense of being a reaction occurring only in a specific situation or involving only a specific response as in some phobic or obsessional - compulsive behavior" (68, page 16). Bound anxiety is not to be regarded as being confined to pathological behavior. Inspection of many of the high markers for U.I. 20 suggests a type of conforming behavior that could be regarded as a form of defense against anxiety and thus possibly as bound anxiety. The strong hereditary determination of U.I. 20 implies that the factor would, in this case, have to be regarded as a 'constitutional tendency to bind'. Against this interpretation of U.I. 20 is the rating of bound anxiety by psychiatrists, which correlates with U.I. 20 (-), the non-conforming pole of this factor.

HYPOTHESIS III: U.I. 20 as desire to please one's fellows

Almost all of the principal marker tests for U.I. 20 could be interpreted as involving a general desire to please and cooperate with others, - at least in the test situation. Acquiescence, willingness to admit common frailties, susceptibility to direct personal suggestion as opposed to the more indirect suggestion of the 'shift' measures, and much influence of verbal punishment, all point in this direction. To take this hypothesis further would be to imply gregariousness and sociability, but here the lack of questionnaire correlates becomes even more troublesome.

HYPOTHESIS IV: U.I. 20 as resulting from deep unconscious anxiety

Here it is suggested that U.I. 20, as a pattern of behavior, emerges as a defense against anxiety and is so successful that the usual behavioral symptoms of anxiety do not appear. In other words certain modes of response - acquiescence, conformity, sociable willingness, and so forth, - have been integrated into the individual's behavioral interaction with his environment so as to avoid situations leading to conscious recurrence of anxiety. The implication is of a constitutional capacity to adopt the norms of one's reference group and to be somewhat acquiescent and compliant in all situations. This view would account for the lack of anxiety responses on the 16 P.F., and to some extent the negative correlations with anxiety ratings. Further, one would expect that if the tight defenses were not sufficient in the face of severe stress then a neurotic breakdown might well occur, and this is supported by the slight association of U.I. 20 (+) with neurosis.

In terms of development it would be anticipated that the mechanism of U.I. 20 (+) would grow out of initial anxiety and appear as a desire to please (as in Hypothesis III) and a steady adoption of the norms and standards of the peer-group and family. As U.I. 20 (+) increases, one would expect U.I. 24 (+) to decrease. Here we have the emergence of standards and conscience as a direct product of interaction with the social environment and group attachment. Support for this interpretation appears in the presence of U.I. 20 (+) in the second-order factor of Tied Socialization or Superego. Thus, depending upon the social group, U.I. 20 (+) might be found in groups of criminals and among the most law-abiding citizens, the suggestion being that forms of behavior will be adopted that avoid conflict with one's fellows or inner structure of beliefs, the latter in turn being derived from the individual's inter-personal history.

SUMMARY

Due to the subtle nature of this factor the level of explanation is necessarily more suggestive than conclusive. Four hypotheses have been discussed, and preference is shown to the final one, Hypothesis IV.

Table 7.9
U.I. 20: Comentive Superego (Development) vs. Abcultion

Q-Factor	Factor Title	Factor Identification (Research, Sample Size, Age of Subjects, Factor Number in Study)			
		C5 500 Adult (6-)	Ros 70 Adult (2+)	R1 86 Adult (13+)	HI 137 Adult (5+)
*A	higher Schizothymia (aloof, cold)	-18		-11	
B	(higher) Intelligence				
C	(higher) Ego Strength	00	+14	-04	00
E	(higher) Dominance	+01			
F	(higher) Surgency	+03	+02	-01	
G	(higher) Super Ego Strength	-03			+18
H	(higher) Parmia	00		-04	
I	(higher) Premsia	+04		-02	
L	(higher) Protension	-03			+13
M	(higher) Alaxia	-03	+15	+02	
N	(higher) Shrewdness	-10			
*O	higher Timidity (insecure, anxious)	(-04)	+26	+02	+03
Q1	(higher) Radicalism	-12			-04
Q2	(higher) Self-Sufficiency	+03			00
Q3	(higher) Self Sentiment Control	+04			+07
Q4	(higher) Ergic Tension	-05	00	00	+05

U. I. 20: COMENTIVE SUPEREGO (DEVELOPMENT) VS. ABCULTION (page 1)

Master Index Number	Variable Title	Factor Identification (Research, Sample Size, Age of Subjects, Factor Number in Study)														
		C1 370 Adult (3+)	C2 410 Adult (1+)	C3 100 Adult (2+)	C4 100 Adult (5-)	C5 500 Adult (6-)	C6 250 Adult (3+)	Ros 70 Adult (2+)	R1 86 Adult (13+)	HI 137 Adult (5+)	We 80 Adult --	BRO 100 11-12 (2+)	C7 184 9-12 (4-)	R12 80 4-5 (14+)	R13 164 6-9 (14+)	R14 129 3-7 (8+)
152	more tendency to agree			+10	+39	+62	+74	+33	+20	+66			+67		+17	+02
38a,c	higher ratio of consonant to dissonant recall (corrected for general tendency to agree)	+13	+64	+23		+53	+71		+45						+07	+40
219	more willingness to admit common frailties					+27	+36	+39	+08	(-09)			+47	+34	+03	+47
211a	higher over-all annoyability					+04	+10	+20	+24				+21	+13	+09	+28
21	more absence of questionable preferences in reading	+25	+57	+12	+11	+15			+09	+10		+34	+15	+00	+00	
35	more suggestibility to authority	+35	+04	+29	+22	+44	+36			+15		+01	(-16)			
246	more authority submission					-18	-48			-01			-49		-07	
106	more unreflective acceptance of unqualified statements			+14	+61	+02	+07						+11			
42	more body sway suggestibility	+10	+09	+33	+29				+14							+29
38b	higher ratio of consonant to dissonant recall (not corrected for general tendency to agree)			+17	+39					+49				(-03)		
36	less ability to state logical assumptions	-44	-51	-03	-22	-03										
116a	higher severity of judgment			(-06)	+11	(-06)		+48	+11				+56		+21	
327a	less logical consistency of attitude					+39								+31		+00
34	less immaturity of opinion	-09	-04	(+12)	-21	-35						-12	-18	-17	(+08)	
113	less acceptance of reality principle control			-33	(+02)	-49									(+10)	
175	slower regularly warned reaction time			+34	+28									+05		(-05)
165	lower ratio of performance (classification) under approval to disapproval			-56	-31											
33	larger size of myokinetic movement	(-03)		+07					+31							+27
163	lower ratio of performance (perceptual closure) under approval to disapproval			-50	-07											
167a	better immediate memory	+00		+11		(-07)	+06		+40	+20			(-16)		+06	
74	lower basal metabolic rate		-45					-09			-05					
164	lower ratio of performance (perceptual closure) under normal to shock conditions			-26	-21											
78	less involuntary muscle tension		+23						+35							
122	more static ataxia			+28	+27	(-08)							+12			
291	fewer PGR deflections during nonsense reading												-21	-22		
46a,b	lower ratio of performance (mazes) under normal relative to shock conditions	-03	(+16)	-61	(+18)								-02			
55	lower ratio of emotional to unemotional association		-47			-02										
166	lower ratio of performance (classification) under normal to shock conditions			-30	-02											
144	more agreement with platitudinous thinking (aphorisms)			(-05)		+11							+37	(-04)		
110	more future relative to past associations			+34	+07											
205	more emotionality of comment					(-01)	+17						+20	+00		
101a,b	less excess of aspiration over performance in coding, mazes			+41	+00										+07	

U. I. 20: COMENTIVE SUPEREGO (DEVELOPMENT) VS. ABCULTION (page 2)

Master Index Number	Variable Title	RESEARCH														
		C1	C2	C3	C4	C5	C6	Ros	R1	HI	We	BRO	C7	R12	R13	R14
14	more jokes considered funny	+00	+30													
124	more tendency to agree (optimistic statements)			(-17)	+68											
80	more PGR upward drift after shock		(-05)						+52							
176	slower irregularly warned reaction time			+47	+27	(-04)	(-05)	+10	(-01)					+01	(-02)	
348	more critical rejection vs. uncritical acceptance of generalizations													+63		
20a	more dishonesty (cheating)											-59				
75	less increase in metabolic rate with stimulation		-51													
1463	more imaginative falsification in memory for pictorial details															+49
70	more rapid appearance of negative after-image		-43													
79	longer duration of eidetic images		+41													
422	greater height of single tower constructed															+39
470	slower rate of PGR conditioning								-35							
59	less effect of tempting distraction upon recall		-35													
76	higher pitch of voice		+33													
69	more tendency to agree with authority and sample		+31													
393	greater preference for crayoning original (S's own) than provided drawings														+31	
976	fewer perceptions of self as different from others															-36
169	more awareness of error			+26												
13a-c	(more) oscillation of performance	+03	+02	-30	-01								+01			
161a	(higher) ratio of cancellation performance under approval relative to disapproval			-28	-20								+15	+46		
193a	(more) shifting of attitude towards those of successful people			-09	-09	-38	+25		-01	-01			-09		-01	
5	(higher) ratio of regularly warned to irregularly warned reaction time	+31	+02	-21	-12		-01	+24	+08				+20	+05		
67a,b	(more) extremity of viewpoint		+01	-04	+03	-05	+01						+38	-22	+18	
198	(more) hidden words found in anagrams			-43	-01	+10							+00			
120a-c	(higher) ratio of accuracy to speed			-56	+06			-13	+01				+03	+09	+05	+05
64	(male) sex		-51										+13			+32
270	(faster) tempo of arm-shoulder motion					-05	-03						+28	-19	-07	+31
282	(more) objects seen in unstructured drawings					+06	-11	-03	-31					+21	+13	+00
286	(higher) ratio of reaction time to auditory relative to visual stimuli					-06									+35	
65	(more) logical consistency of attitudes		-03	+00	+33								-64			
7	(faster) speed of Gestalt closure	-18		+13	-01	+07	-09	+15					+18	-01	+03	
146b	(lower) percentage correct in Gestalt closure			+02	-28	+08	-17						+02	+11	-04	-29
8	(higher) frequency of alternating perspective	+00	+08	-08	-16	+05							-02		+28	
15	(more) use of circles -- CMS			-22		+00	-03	+10	+16				-10			
41	(more) correct movements in two-hand co-ordination	+15	+16	-01	+06	-02							-07			
117	(more) highbrow tastes			+04	-30	+11	-15									

U.I. 21: EXUBERANCE VS. SUPPRESSIBILITY

1. Prevalence

U.I. 21 has been identified in ten factor analyses with adults and four factor analyses with children. In addition column TXXVII in Table 7.12 contains the mean loadings of a factor known as "fluency of association", among other titles, in a series of earlier factor analyses discussed by Cattell (18). Also included is an extension analysis by Wells (166) examining physiological and physical fitness correlates of this factor. The match across studies for adults is good, but that with children (excepting study C_7) is not so clear.

2. Questionnaire Correlates

Correlations between the 16 P.F. and U.I. 21(+) were obtained in studies C5, R1, and R2. These confirm earlier findings (Cattell, 1957) that F (+): SURGENCY (Enthusiastic, Talkative) is positively, though not highly, related to this factor. Other 16 P.F. factors which show some potential as correlates are: M(+): ALAXIA (Bohemian, Unconcerned), O(-): CONFIDENCE (Confident, Unshakable) and Q4(+): HIGH ERGIC TENSION (Tense, Excitable), but the loadings are too low for high confidence at the present time.

Knapp's (123) study of 315 Naval Submarine School candidates presents significant positive correlations of U.I. 21(+) with G(+): General Activity (r = +.22), Ag(-): Low score on Agreeableness (r = -.12), and A(+): Ascendance (r = +.11) of the Guilford-Martin scales. Significant positive correlations on a sample of officer helicopter pilots were found with G(+): General Activity (r = +.32), A(+): Ascendance (r = +.30), and S(+): Sociability (r = +.38) of the Guilford-Zimmermann, and L(-): Low score on Lie Scale (r = -.24) and Do(+): Dominance (r = +.23), of the MMPI.

No significant relationship has been observed between U.I. 21(+) and questionnaire and self-report measures of anxiety (R1, R2, and N1).

Evidence from different questionnaires is in agreement in characterizing a high U.I. 21 (+) individual as enthusiastic, energetic, dominant, and excitable. There is no direct questionnaire evidence for any relationship with anxiety or deep emotional instability.

3. State Factor Matches

No factor from analyses of psychological states by P-technique or incremental R-technique has been found.

4. Loadings on Second-Order Objective Test Factors

U.I. 21 appears in only one second-order factor, F(T)III(+): Temperamental Ardor vs. Temperamental Apathy, in which it has the highest average loading(57). This second-order factor is rather difficult to interpret, but it contains first-order factors with relatively high hereditary determination and has a central character of "willful exuberance and ardor of temper" which fits well with U.I. 21(+).

5. Criterion Correlations

a) Clinical Criteria

Comparisons of groups of normals and neurotics shows U.I. 21(+) to be of some potential value in the prediction of neurosis. In study R9-Ta, using estimated factor scores based on previously established marker variables, a significant ($P < .01$) negative correlation was found with clinical diagnosis of neurosis. A reversed, but non-significant result was found in R9-Tb.

Low non-significant negative correlations were found in study R1 between U.I. 21(+) and psychiatrists' ratings of over-all anxiety and bound anxiety.

b) School and Academic Achievement

The relationship between U.I. 21(+) and academic and school achievement was assessed in studies R1 and C7 (Undergraduates and 11-year old children) and low negative correlations were found.

c) Military Criteria

The potential of U.I. 21 as a predictor of military success has been reported in three studies, C5, N1 and N2. With all four criteria of pilot training and a future prognosis used in C5 this factor shows consistent positive but non-significant correlations. In N1 a non-significant correlation was found by Knapp (121) with Final Flying Grade for helicopter pilots, but a significant negative correlation appeared with peer ratings of pilot proficiency. A significant positive correlation was found with AQT, a measure of general ability. A significant positive correlation (+.27) was reported in N2 by Knapp (122) of U.I. 21(+) with class-standing among Naval Submarine School candidates. A marked similarity may be observed between military criteria results for U.I. 21(+) and

U.I. 18 (+): HYPOMANIC SMARTNESS, the only discrepancy being the positive correlation of +0.25 of number of sick-calls (helicopter pilots), with U.I. 21(+), while the correlation of this variable with U.I. 18(+) is zero.

6. Nature-Nurture and Age-Trend Results

U.I. 21 is predominantly an inherited source trait (70). However, both heredity and environment appear to have equal weight within families suggesting that families with generally high endowment of U.I. 21(+) tend to develop an environment more favorable to further development of the trait. A parallel has been drawn between the development of U.I. 21(+) and that of general intelligence (29).

U.I. 21(+) declines steadily with age (29), and apart from the slight decline of U.I. 28, is the only U.I. factor to show this characteristic.

7. Descriptive Interpretation

Recent work on U.I. 21(+) has filled out and integrated the earlier observed general picture of high energy and mental power appearing as a form of energetic zest and exuberance for most activities. There is definite evidence that performance and opinion are not influenced by social suggestion--which may well be a lack in perception of such influences rather than the taking of an independent stand. High speed of judgment, with verbal and ideational fluency, appear to be fairly central. A generally low estimate of one's own capabilities, backed up by a tendency to make errors, may be contrasted with a performance that, though erratic, tends to be at a fairly good level. Consideration of physiological variables indicates that there is much reaction to stimulation or threat as well as a generally high level of activity. Finally there is the suggestion of rather small body build.

Imperviousness to Social Suggestion.

The relative imperviousness of U.I. 21(+) to social suggestion (at least in paper-and-pencil tests) is exemplified by little change of opinion or attitude in the various 'shift' measures--less suggestibility to authority (MI. 35), less shifting of attitudes away from those of neurotics (MI. 194), and less shift of attitude toward successful people (MI. 193a). The loading on "less immaturity of opinion" (MI. 34) in which the subject sticks to his opinion in spite of mature, far-seeing arguments that may suggest an alternative answer, fits into this same general category. Fewer overt facial reactions to jokes (MI. 157) may also, in rather different context, be an expression of the same tendency.

Speed of Social Judgment.

In something of the same vein as imperviousness to social suggestion is high speed of judgment on social situations or tasks and performances involving other people. Thus U.I. 21 is associated with the making of more rapid decisions on tests of hard-headed realism (MI. 244), social judgment (MI. 168a), criminal punishment (MI. 289), and evaluation of the performances of others (MI. 288). It would appear reasonable to associate high endowment with a lack of concern for, and involvement with, social pressures and problems. It is surprising at first that several of the 'tendency to agree' or acquiescence variables--more tendency to agree (MI. 152), more unreflective acceptance of unqualified statements (MI. 106), more tendency to agree with platitudes (MI. 144)--appear consistently, though with relatively low factor loadings, with U.I. 21. However it is not unreasonable to suppose that the high speed of judgment on attitude and opinion items may in itself predispose toward agreement responses (or, to be more precise, away from disagreement responses).

Speed of Perceptual Judgment.

That speed of judgment on questionnaire statements might be a facet of a more general speed of decision is suggested by faster speed of perceptual judgment in comparing numbers (MI. 308), faster speed of line judgment (regardless of accuracy) (MI. 309), and faster speed of letter comparison (MI. 307). However, it should be noted that such decisions are relatively simple and specific to the perceptual realm. Until more evidence is available on more complex judgmental situations, it seems wise to keep these two speed of judgment characteristics as separate aspects of U.I. 21.

Verbal Fluency.

An important characteristic of U.I. 21(+) is higher verbal fluency on varied topics (MI. 271). There is a strong suggestion that this involves not just speed of expression, which is certainly involved in this factor, but also ideational fluency. Contributory evidence in terms of perceptual and ideational richness comes from a variety of measures, including more hidden objects correctly seen in pictures (MI. 170), greater number of objects seen in unstructured pictures (MI. 282), and more perceptions of aggressive implements (MI. 425). However the little accuracy in perceptual closure (MI. 146b) and less ability to suggest classifications (MI. 37) point in the other direction, and certain variables which would be expected to confirm the ideational aspect of such fluency are absent from Table 7.12.

Fast Tempo.

Considering the speed element which appears in the preceding three paragraphs, it is not surprising to find that this is probably more than reaction to the challenge of a test situation. Faster tempo of tapping (MI. 268) and faster reading tempo (MI. 278) indicate a habitually fast mode of reaction for the U.I. 21(+) person.

Errors in Perceptual Tasks.

That U.I. 21(+) at times involves speed at the price of accuracy is indicated by many errors in shape comparisons (MI. 350) and little accuracy in perceptual closure (MI. 146b). On the other hand with reaction time there are fewer errors under complex instructions (MI. 71), and there is an absence of any significant loadings on such error variables as the number of slanting lines crossed: C.M.S. (MI. 16a).

Low Self-Estimation.

A fairly large group of variables associated with U.I. 21(+) involve a generally low estimate of one's own capabilities. Not only is a low estimate given of prowess in past activities, but this is carried forward into the future. Thus we find less self-confidence regarding untried performance (MI. 108), lower level of estimate of experience and accomplishment (MI. 147b), less excess aspiration over performance (MI. 101a, b), more long-term life goals (MI. 458), less considered possible for self (MI. 192), and lower estimation of personal prowess (MI. 104). Support for this appears in quite young children, with less belief in attainability of goals (MI. 212).

General Competence.

It should be noted that this personal under-rating of U.I. 21(+) does not appear to be justified on the grounds of competence in perceptual motor or cognitive tasks, at leas in the test situation. Perceptual-motor and fluency performances have already been discussed, but other competences include better immediate memory (MI. 167a), better memory for names (MI. 249), higher numerical ability (MI. 199), higher ability to do problems in one's head (MI. 476), higher total number correct in letter exercises (MI. 1735), and less initial difficulty in re-adaptation (MI. 1736).

Sensitivity to Threat and Emotional Stimulation.

In general, shock and stress lead to a marked decrement of performance on a variety of simple tasks. This group of variables contains more decrease in myokinesis under threat (MI. 95), more effect of restraint upon performance (MI. 93), more slowing of reaction time due to shock (MI. 456), and more impairment of performance by fright (MI. 46a, b). There is no clear evidence on the relative effects of praise and punishment. An accompanying physiological reaction to that of overt behavior in the stress situation is suggested by more increase of pulse-rate under stress (MI. 84b) and more metabolic rate change with stimulation (MI. 75). Somewhat surprising is the loading for less pupil dilation with stress (MI. 445). Additional confirmation to the implication that U.I. 21(+) is associated with a sensitivity to threat and emotional stimulation comes from more attention to disturbing vs. non-disturbing pictures (MI. 428b), better recall of emotionally interesting relative to dry material (MI. 87), better recall of frightening than non-frightening film-strip material (MI. 459), and higher absolute number of aggressive implements perceived (MI. 425). A low and somewhat inconsistent loading appears for the proportion of threatening objects seen in drawings (MI. 105).

Physiological Activity.

In general physiological measures present a pattern of high activity. Among such variables are higher magnitude of mean PGR deflection to threatening stimuli (MI. 43), higher basal metabolic rate (MI. 74), and higher systolic blood pressure (MI. 444). Also involved in U.I. 21(+) are less involuntary muscle tension (MI. 76), less PGR conditioning (MI. 469), more static ataxia (MI. 122) and smaller area under pulse wave EKG (MI. 491). Possibly also related to these measures, and indicating a somewhat erratic level of performance, is more oscillation (variability) in performance (MI. 13).

Slight Body Build.

Body-build measures, mainly from Wells' extension analysis but also partly from the R2 factor analysis, indicate that the U.I. 21(+) individual tends to be lower on mesomorphy MI. 486), and to have lower physical weight (MI. 506), smaller shoulder width (MI. 576) and lower score on a muscular index.

8. Theoretical Interpretation: History and Final Hypotheses.

Early research, mainly concerned with limited domains of temperament, intelligence, or perception, indicated a group of factors described as 'fluency'. In particular, and relevant for U.I. 21, is a sub-group of these factors involving fluency of associations (under restrictions) (18). Salient variables for these factors were Finishing Drawings, Free Associations, Word-Building speed, and Tempo of Tapping among temperament analyses (159) (103) (115) and Words per Minute and Finding Rhymes for Words in the abilities field (160). These factors, such as Carroll's "A" and Thurstone's "W" appear to be close enough to specific aspects of U.I. 21 to be brought together and regarded as evidence of U.I. 21 as it appears from the sampling of a limited domain of variables. Also of relevance is a factor found by Eysenck (86) which appears to contain several of the U.I. 21 markers.

Recent research has retained the general speed and fluency characteristics from the earlier studies, but added imperviousness to social suggestion, higher speed of judgments on social issues, higher speed of perceptual judgment, faster tempo, proneness to errors, lower self-confidence, general efficiency and good memory, performance much affected by shock and stress, high physiological activity and smaller body build. The present breadth of U.I. 21 makes it difficult to do more than just mention its rather fragmentary historical antecedents.

Before presenting hypotheses attempting to account for the mechanism of U.I. 21 it would appear appropriate to summarize briefly the main points and cross-implications of the previous sections.

1. There is agreement of both questionnaire and objective test evidence on the energetic, active, excitable aspects of U.I. 21 (+), as well as on the independence and 'sticking to one's opinion'.

2. Not directly in the objective test loadings, but contained in the questionnaire and criteria data (peer ratings) is the implication that in spite of his energy and capabilities the U.I. 21(+) person is unlikely to be popular.

3. Found only in the objective test evidence is speed of judgment, fluency, a rather low estimation of personal capabilities, and sensitivity to physical threat. The small body build, though of considerable interest, requires further confirmation.

4. U.I. 21(+) is related negatively to neurosis, but little if at all to anxiety.

5. U.I. 21(+) plays a major role in the second-order objective test factor of Temperamental Ardor.

6. U.I. 21 is mainly hereditarily determined and declines with age.

7. The correlation of U.I. 21(+) with achievement in both the military and educational spheres (particularly the latter) is less than one would expect from general accomplishment in objective tests.

Two theoretical interpretations of U.I. 21 have been considered (68). The first is that the negative pole represents a form of inhibition, perhaps bound anxiety; while the positive pole represents lack of inhibition (uninhibitedness?). The second is that U.I. 21(+) is a form of nervous energy, while U.I. 21(-) is absence of such energy through constitutional rather than environmental sources.

The first hypothesis is rather unsatisfactory for though it accounts for much of the data presented above, such as the relationship to neurosis, it is in open conflict with certain established facts. Most immediately apparent is the assumption of considerable environmental influence which is not borne out by genetic research. The age trend data does not appear to support the notion of U.I. 21 as any form of anxiety (or freedom therefrom) or inhibition, for why should it decline so sharply with age? Further, it should be noted that the sole direct evidence for a linkage with anxiety comes from the very modest loadings of psychiatrist's ratings of anxiety on U.I. 21(-). A last point, but one worth considering, is that U.I. 17 appears to account for the form of inhibition under discussion.

The second and preferred hypothesis fits the available evidence quite closely. However the concept of a constitutional nervous energy requires further amplification and here we suggest that this nervous energy is tied closely to high general activity of the central nervous system, sensitivity of the sympathetic nervous system, and in particular to metabolic rate. A further implication is that the boisterous impetuousness of U.I. 21 (+) declines with age partly due to the slowing down of body mechanisms in general, but also due to a lack of support from a necessarily stimulating yet permissive environment.

The interaction of environment with U.I. 21 may be viewed in the following way. Given a child highly endowed with U.I. 21(+) certain overt behaviors will emerge which appear as youthful zest, enthusiasm and apparent independence. In certain families these behaviors will be strictly controlled or even punished, leading to a diminution of U.I. 21 factor scores. In other families in which there is a constant undercurrent of excitement, sense of adventurousness, or the non-family environment is particularly stimulating, these behaviors are more likely to be retained, though modified in shape by the passage through adolescence to adulthood. There is definite agreement here from genetic studies (70). As modern society is not always too tolerant of the over-enthusiastic or over-active, this may lead to unpopularity and the lack of confidence in personal capabilities described in the previous section. That this treatment from society does not lead to maladjustment may be accounted for by the general activity which drives the individual onwards (similar to the resilence to punishment and pain observable in certain children) switching from one task to the next, and also probably by a lack of social sensitivity (as evidenced by both questionnaire and objective test variables). This lack of sensitivity may itself, of course, be a defense against criticism, but it seems more appropriate to regard it as part of the general boisterousness.

As earlier suggested (29), U.I. 21 (+) should be related to success in a life of action, and given the necessary environment could lead to a Churchill or a John Paul Jones - and regarding children perhaps we could add Huckleberry Finn to the list!

U.I. 21(-) and its relation to neurosis poses a particular problem as it may be regarded (29) as either a cause of neurosis through poor adaptability and learning, or as a consequence of neurosis through some form of neural exhaustion. There is insufficient evidence to lay any great emphasis upon either view, but the former seems to be the natural counter-part to our preferred interpretation of U.I. 21(+). In other words due to his slowness, inhibitedness, and lack of self determination, a U.I. 21(-) person is open to considerable conflicts, and lacks the mercurial quality of U.I. 21 (+) as an aid in their solution.

Further evidence is urgently needed upon the genesis and early history of U.I. 21. In particular we need further confirmation of its hereditary determination and the forms of child-rearing most advantageous to its full development. Significant findings should also emerge from occupational choice and occupational success.

Table 7.11
U.I. 21: Exuberance vs. Suppressibility

Q-Factor	Factor Title	Factor Identification (Research, Sample Size, Age of Subjects, Factor Number in Study)		
		C5 500 Adult (3+)	R1 86 Adult (4+)	R2 86 Adult (15+)
*A	higher Cyclothymia	+14	+14	(-13)
B	(higher) Intelligence			-01
C	(higher) Ego Strength	-02	+07	+02
E	(higher) Dominance	-08		+04
*F	higher Surgency (enthusiastic, talkative)	+05	+26	(-12)
G	(higher) Super Ego Strength	+09		-08
H	(higher) Parmia	-02	+08	+08
I	(higher) Premsia	+10	-03	-04
L	(higher) Protension	+05		-01
M	(higher) Alaxia	-08	+17	+05
N	(higher) Shrewdness	+06		-01
*O	higher Confidence (confident, unshakable)	(+02)	-24	(00)
Q1	(higher) Radicalism	-08		+02
Q2	(higher) Self-Sufficiency	-07		+04
Q3	(higher) Self Sentiment Control	+01		+06
Q4	(higher) Ergic Tension	-03	+06	+15

U. I. 21: EXUBERANCE VS. SUPPRESSIBILITY (page 1)

Master Index Number	Variable Title	Factor Identification (Research, Sample Size, Age of Subjects, Factor Number in Study)															
		E2	Txxvii	C1	C2	C3	C4	C5	C6	R1	R2	E-D1	We	C7	R12	R13	R15
		200	100	370	410	100	100	500	250	86	86	139	80	184	80	164	197
		Adult	Adult	Adult	Adult	Adult	Adult	Adult	Adult	Adult	Adult	Adult	Adult	9-12	4-5	6-9	7-10
		(2+)	--	(8+)	(7+)	(4+)	(15+)	(3+)	(1+)	(4+)	(15+)	(6-)	--	(10-)	(15+)	(3+)	(6+)
271	higher total verbal fluency on topics	+54	+55					+32	+35			+39		+13	+27	+32	
34	less immaturity of opinion			-25	-42	-56	-66	-08						-43	-02		
167a	better immediate memory	+41				+03	+47	+13	+44					+06		+20	
35	less suggestibility to authority			-23	-46	-07	-28	-08	-13					-26			
244	faster speed of judgment in test of hard-headed realism		+50					+48	+70					+41			
108	less self-confidence regarding untried performance					-34	(+01)	-15	-16	-59	-30			-06		(+04)	
146b	lower proportion correct in perceptual closure					-03	-09	-24	-13			-08		-49	-01	(+14)	
199	higher numerical ability	+35						+33	+35	+10	+12			+09	(-03)		+00
282	greater number of objects seen in unstructured drawings							+04	(-04)	(-06)		+27			+09	+73	+24
152	more tendency to agree					+15	+06	+37	+24	+05	+27	+02		+07		(-09)	
288	faster speed of evaluating others' performance							+51	+70			+44					
307	faster speed of letter comparison							+46	+36			+44			+28		
308	faster speed of perceptual judgment in comparing numbers		+59					+48	+44								
13a	more oscillation			+02	+30	+21	+41							+12			
71	fewer erroneous reactions under complex instructions				-30			(+08)	-08	-10	(+09)			-02	-02	-03	-24
33	larger size of myokinetic movement	+45		(-01)		+10				+21	+19						
22a-c	higher ratio of chance to purposeful observation and memory			+04	+13	+15	+24										
193a	less shifting of attitudes towards those of successful people					(+07)	(+14)	-06	-09	-05				-54			-08
268	faster tempo of tapping		+54					+14						(-15)	+34		
106	more unreflective acceptance of unqualified statements					+10	+04	+26	+08					+12			
168a	faster speed of social judgment														+48		+15
147b	lower level of estimate of experience and accomplishment					-05	-26							-18			
95	more decrease in myokinesis under threat					+57	+20										
144	more tendency to agree with platitudes (aphorisms)					+15		+10						(-08)	+19		
24c	lower ratio of final to initial performance, backward reading			-03		-17	-17							(+14)			
38a	higher ratio of consonant to dissonant recall (corrected)			(-05)	(-06)	+48		+30	+13	(-02)							
177a,b	faster motor speed			+07		(-10)	+23				+01					+33	(-06)
84b	more increase of pulse-rate in stress				+53					(-06)	+11						
64	female sex				-09							(+22)		-18			
62	faster reading speed for emotional relative to non-emotional material				+19	+20	+02	(-13)						+09			
38b	lower ratio of consonant to dissonant recall (uncorrected)					-12	(+13)								-47		
74	higher basal metabolic rate				+43						+25		(-18)				
486	less mesomorph										-14		-36				
309	faster speed of line judgment (regardless of accuracy)							+54								+11	
428b	more attention to disturbing relative to non-disturbing pictures															+08	+39

U. I. 21: EXUBERANCE VS. SUPPRESSIBILITY (page 2)

Master Index Number	Variable Title	RESEARCH															
		E2	Txxvii	C1	C2	C3	C4	C5	C6	R1	R2	E-D1	We	C7	R12	R13	R15
466	higher magnitude of hand tremor									+35	+28						
249	better memory for names							+09	+38								
101a,b	less excess aspiration over performance					-46	-15	-11							-10		(+10)
444	higher systolic blood pressure									+09	+32						
122	more static ataxia					+21	(-09)	+06						+19			-02
157	fewer overt facial reactions to jokes					-38	-08										
445	less pupil dilation at stress									-34	-08						
491	smaller area under curve of pulse wave (EKG)										-04		-31				
476	higher ability to do problems in one's head									-37	-04						
458	more long term life goals									+01	+36						
93	more effect of restraint on performance					-01	-34										
456	more slowing of reaction time due to shock									+05	+30						
212	less belief in attainability of goals							(+05)						-08	-30		-09
43	higher magnitude of mean PGR deflection to threatening stimuli		+30	+05	(-05)	+25	+12			+00	+10			(-02)			
78	less involuntary muscle tension				+10					(-06)	+42						
194	less shifting of attitudes away from those of neurotics					-06		-05						-22			
104	lower estimation of personal prowess					-26	-08										
46a,b	more impairment of performance by fright			+05	+30	+04	+04							(-04)			
175	slower regularly warned reaction time					(-13)	+06								+05		+36
192	less considered possible for self in given time					-34	(+04)	-02	-02					-02		(+08)	
469	less PGR conditioning									(+07)	-44						
37	less ability to suggest classification			(+05)	-30												
459	better memory for fearful rather than neutral material									+35	(-09)						
1735	higher total number correct in letter exercises											+69					
289	faster speed of judgment on criminal punishment								+63								
278	faster reading tempo							+59									
75	more increase of metabolic rate with stimulation				+56												
425	higher absolute number of aggressive implements perceived															+52	
1736	less initial difficulty in re-adaptation											+50					
170	more hidden objects correctly seen in pictures					-47											
513	louder speaking voice (high sound pressure)									+41							
63	more masculine than feminine interests				+40												
87	better recall of emotionally interesting relative to dry material				+34												
350	more errors in shape comparisons														+32		
506	lower physical weight												-31				
242	higher ratio of social relative to non-social annoyances													-31			
76	higher pitch of voice				+30												
347	higher readiness to imitate animal sounds														+30		

U. I. 21: EXUBERANCE VS. SUPPRESSIBILITY (page 3)

Master Index Number	Variable Title	RESEARCH															
		E2	Txxvii	C1	C2	C3	C4	C5	C6	R1	R2	E-D1	We	C7	R12	R13	R15
576	smaller shoulder width												-30				
28	(higher) dynamic momentum	+16	+38	-04		-08	-15							+16			
7	(faster) perceptual speed of closure			+03		-03	-21	-18	-07					-34	+45	+55	-24
143	(higher) total score -- CMS							+34						-03	-14	+07	-02
15	(more) use of circles -- CMS					-04		+28	+07	+08	+03			-08			-23
243	(higher) ratio of purposeful to non-purposeful annoyances							-18	+03					+29			
105	(higher) proportion of threatening objects seen in drawings					+02	+07	-13	+26			+01			-06	+48	+23
83	(higher) fidgetometer frequency				+03	+27	+20	-11		-23	-31			-03			
82	(greater) distance covered in mazes				-39			+15	+14					+06			
161a	(higher) ratio of performance under approval relative to disapproval					-01	+20							-21	+41		
2a-h	(more) motor rigidity			-12	-05	+00	-06	+07	+14	+03	-15	+07		-11	-01	+24	-04
171	(more) hidden objects perceived					-40	-04	-01						-05		+58	
67a	(more) extremity of viewpoint				-06	-20	-09	-13	+00					+09	-09	-05	+18
39	(higher) ratio of color to form in sorting			-01	+10	+11	+17	+03	-09	-43				-21		-20	+10
16a	(more) slanting lines crossed -- CMS			+08		+03		+25	+05	-17	-05			-03			
263	(more) variability in simple reaction time								-21					+10	-06	-02	+27
219	(more) honesty in admitting common frailties							-08	-04	+16	-05			+10	+07	+03	+26
5	(higher) ratio of regularly to irregularly warned reaction time			-07	+00	-05	+00		-16	-23	-22			+01	-05		
211a	(more) susceptibility to annoyance							-10	+06	+32				+06	-04	-03	-09
206	(greater) accuracy on Gottschaldt figures							+05	-02		+06	+38			-03	+13	-18
120	(higher) ratio of accuracy to speed					-06	+01			+19	+06	+43			+08	+03	-09
8	(faster) alternating perspective			-06	+06	+17	-08	-10				+45		-07		+12	
113	(more) acceptance of reality principle					-31	+06	-04								+05	

U.I. 22: CORTERTIA VS. PATHEMIA

1. Prevalence

A very stable and well replicated pattern, this factor has been identified in ten factor analytic researches at the adult age level (including the incremental R-technique study R3) and in five researches at the child level. In addition to one extension analysis (Wells), further evidence on U.I. 22 is available from studies by Thornton and Ryan (143, 159; Combined as T-R) and by Thurstone (161; study T2). It is the "persistence" factor of Thornton and Ryan and Thurstone's factor C that match factor U.I. 22 closely and have therefore been included in table 7.14.

2. Questionnaire Correlates

Evidence on the 16 P.F. Test questionnaire factor loadings of U.I. 22 is available from five studies (C5, R1, R2, R3, and Ros; see table 7.13. Six questionnaire factors correlate consistently with U.I. 22+: C+ (high Ego Strenth: mature, calm), I- (high Harria: tough, realistic), M- (high Praxernia: conventional, practical), N+ (high Shrewdness: sophisticated, polished), O- (high Confidence: confident, unshakable), and Q4- (low Ergic Tension: phlegmatic, composed).

If this pattern is reflected in signs -- i.e., changed into the structure C-, I+, M+, N-, O+, and Q4+ -- it resembles closely the third second-order questionnaire factor F (Q) III which is called "Pathemia" (28, 29) and which has been known for sometime to relate negatively with the objective test factor U.I. 22+. These characteristics of low Ego Strength (emotionally unstable), Premsia (sensitive, effeminate), Alaxia (unconcerned), Naivete (less sophisticated), Timidity (insecure, anxious) and high Ergic Tension (tense, excitable) have led to interpreting Pathemia as a personality dimension involving high affectivity of imagination and overt response. Theoretically, Pathemia has been explained as a preponderance of subcortial (mainly hypothalamic) over cortical control.

The negative correlation between this second-order questionnaire dimension F(Q)III+ and the objective test first-order factor U.I. 22+ (Cortertia) is well substantiated from the correlations set out in table 8.14. As to the psychological interpretation, a description of U.I. 22- in terms of Pathemia is in excellent agreement with the objective test loadings of this factor.

In the studies N1(123) and N2(123) Knapp found significant correlations between U.I. 22 and two of the Guilford-Martin factors: S+ (Social Introversion; r = +.13) and M+ (Masculinity; r = +.12). No significant correlations have been obtained by Knapp between U.I. 22 and the Guilford-Zimmerman scales; of the MMPI scales only Mf (Femininity of Interests) correlated significantly with U.I. 22 (+.26). The latter result is in agreement with the negative loading of M.I. 64 (male sex) on this factor (see table 8.13), i.e., with the finding that a high score on U.I. 22+ is more frequent in female than male subjects; it disagrees, however, with the above reported positive correlation between U.I. 22 and the Guilford-Martin scale M and with the positive loading of M.I. 63 (more masculine than feminine interests on the Terman-Miles Interest Test) (see table 8.13) on this factor. Whereas the correlation between U.I. 22 and female physical sex is well substantiated, obviously no conclusions can be drawn at present as to the correlation between this factor and measures of male vs. female interests.

No results are available on the correlation between U.I. 22 and the Kuder interest scales (138) because the factor has not been found in R10. In R1 the psychiatric anxiety ratings did not load on this factor.

3. State Factor Matches

The state factor P.U.I. 2+ matches the R-technique factor U.I. 22- very closely; this state factor has been found in four P-technique analyses (47, 58, 107, 170) and in the incremental R-technique study R3 (where it was jointly identified as P.U.I. 2+ and U.I. 22-). Factor P.U.I. 2+ is a state pattern of Desurgency or Pathemia and its current interpretation has much common ground with the familiar mood dimension of depression (P.U.I. 2+ pole) vs. elation (P.U.I. 2- pole).

The patterns of both the state factor P.U.I. 2- and the trait factor U.I. 22+ resemble each other so closely that we have to regard U.I. 22 as a personality dimension with a large proportion of state variance.

4. Loadings on Second-Order Objective Test Factors

Factor U.I. 22 loads only one second-order objective test factor: F (T) IV: high Educated Self-Consciousness vs. Low Self-Consciousness. This second-order factor has its highest and most consistent loading on U.I. 22+ (average correlation: +.31); other first-order OT factors contributing to F (T) IV are, in descending order of loadings: U.I. 18+, U.I. 25+, U.I. 36+, U.I. 30-, U.I. 29-, and U.I. 33+. Besides high Cortertia, factor F(T) IV is thus characterized by higher "Hypomanic Smartness", more composed realism, and higher self-sentiment.

5. Criterion Correlations

a) Clinical Criteria

In study R9-Ta (68) a significant difference was found between normals and neurotics on this factor, neurotics scoring significantly lower over U.I. 22+ than normals. In the research R10, U.I. 22 was not identified; therefore, no cross-check on this finding is available as yet. In R7 (difference between normals and psychotics) U.I. 22 was not measured.

b) School and Academic Achievement

The variable M.I. 276 (scholastic achievement) does not load on U.I. 22 (see table 7.14). In P1 (138) the factor has not been measured.

c) Military Criteria

In the Cattell and Schiff study AF (69) on the prediction of pilot proficiency, of all factors (including U.I. 1, general intelligence) U.I. 22 yielded the highest correlations with both the primary-training-success criterion[1] (+.31) and the adjustment-group-rating criterion[2] (+.26). The high "cortical alertness" of U.I. 22+ apparently represents an essential personality characteristic of success in pilot training.

In Knapp's research N1 (121) U.I. 22 did not correlate significantly with the final flight grade and even negatively (-.29) with a flight-aptitude rating. Since these correlations, however, were based on a considerably smaller sample (N = 48) than study AF (N = 1,000) they are less reliable. The only other significant criterion correlation of U.I. 22 in Knapp's analysis was with sick-call frequency (+.41); as in the case of U.I. 16, it is difficult to ascertain whether this positive correlation expresses actually poorer physical health of U.I. 22+ persons or simply more concern with one's health.

In study N2 (success in submarine training course) (122) no significant criterion correlations were found with U.I. 22.

6. Nature-Nurture and Age Trend Results

Factor U.I. 22 shows stronger environmental than hereditary determination (70). The preponderance of environment-due over heredity-due variance is more pronounced in within-family than between-families variability in U.I. 22.

[1] This is the final pass-fail criterion, obtained at the end of the flight training course.

[2] The adjustment-group-rating criterion grades each pilot trainee on a 6-point scale; it was introduced as a measure of a trainee's over-all adjustment to flight training. The score on this criterion was derived from the trainee's scores on Air Force aptitude and achievement tests, ratings (by instructors and peers), and a clinical evaluation (obtained from two clinical psychologists who rated each trainee on the basis of clinical test results and an interview).

The inference from this result is that environmental influences will determine this factor to a larger extent among siblings than among unrelated (and thus genotypically more different) children.

Of all ten personality factors, measured in the one available study on the age development of personality dimensions (29), U.I. 22 shows by far the biggest change in mean score over the age span from 9 to 15 years: Mean scores on this factor increase over this period by 3 1/2 standard deviation units. From the extent of this change with age one can assume that the increase in Cortertia presumably accounts for a major part of the change in personality over this period.

7. Descriptive Interpretation

Our present interpretation of U.I. 22 does in no major aspect depart from the hypotheses raised for this factor in previous publications (29, 68). Even with the many more researches available now than there have been for previous summaries (29), the original interpretation of U.I. 22+ as a personality pattern characterized by high speed of basic neural processes or an increased "cortical alertness" (which led to the term "Cortertia") seems still the most appropriate one.

There are at least seven variables in the psychometric pattern of U.I. 22 which indicate fast speed of performance: three reaction time variables (M.I. 175, 176, 335), fast ideomotor speed and tempo (M.I. 6a, b, c, M.I. 9), fast speed of maze performance (M.I. 231), and fast speed of formboard performance (M.I. 340). The manifestation of this "energetic alertness" attribute of U.I. 22+ extends, however, by far beyond the behavioral aspect of sheer fast speed of performance; therefore, any interpretation which regards U.I. 22+ as mainly a "speed factor" would be much too specific and would not account for the remaining loadings which do not involve tempo or speed.

Thus, besides fast speed of performance, the high cortical alertness in U.I. 22+ results in, what we might call, a "tense reaction-impetus" or over-readiness to respond. What is meant by this interpretation will become apparent from considering the following test loadings: At its positive pole this factor is characterized by high restlessness (M.I. 83: high fidgetometer frequency) and increased involuntary muscular tension (M.I. 78: higher involuntary muscle tension in right arm), by higher action impetus (M.I. 475), larger average amplitude of conditioned galvanic skin reactions (M.I. 469), and more oscillation of performance over time (M.I. 13). This "over-readiness to respond" is not always a "good" attribute: the positive loading of variable M.I. 40 shows that in a reaction time test a subject scoring high on U.I. 22+ more frequently reacts to occasionally interspersed false stimuli, instead of waiting for the actual stimulus as he has been instructed to do. The hypothesized high alertness in U.I. 22+ manifests itself, in addition to the performance modalities already discussed, also in tests of perception (M.I. 94: high critical flicker fusion frequency; M.I. 79: much eidetic imagery; M.I. 8: fast alternations on a test of reversible perspective), imagination (M.I. 282: many objects perceived in unstructured drawings), word fluency (M.I. 1: high fluency of associations), and plasticity of thinking (M.I. 37: many classifications found in object sorting test).

Whereas the test performance at the U.I. 22+ pole is relatively unaffected by physical discomfort (M.I. 93, 166), it decreases very much after disapproval (M.I. 343a) and threat (M.I. 95). When presented with highly fatiguing (M.I. 45) or increasingly more difficult tasks (M.I. 28) the highly corticalert person is also less endurant, and under complex instructions his number of incorrect reactions increases more (M.I. 71). Our interpretation of these findings is in terms of an inability of the U.I. 22+ individual to maintain his high degree of alertness over a longer period of time (cf. also M.I. 13), especially with increasing difficulty of the task or when his performance meets criticism.

U.I. 22 is one of the few sex-correlated factors in this series of personality source traits, a high U.I. 22+ score being more frequently encountered with female than male subjects (M.I. 64).[1] On measures of motivation U. I. 22 yielded two consistent loadings: U.I. 22+ is associated with lower fear erg (M.I. 929b) and higher sex erg (M.I. 927a).

8. Explanatory Theory: History and Final Hypotheses

As was mentioned in the beginning of this discussion, factors resembling U.I. 22 very closely have been found previously by Thurstone (161) and Thornton and Ryan (143, 159). It was not before sampling test variables from a less restricted area of behavior, however, that the general pattern of this trait became fully apparent. Thus it is quite conceivable that aspects or "facets" of U.I. 22 were also obtained in some of the researches which found a general speed factor or a specific factor of performance speed within a restricted variable domain. The decision as to whether or not such a speed factor may be partial representation of Cortertia would only become possible, however, if these researches had included at least some of the other salients of U.I. 22.

The theory of U.I. 22 as a personality source trait of high cortical alertness (Cortertia) vs. more subcortical, hypothalamic integration of behavior (Pathemia), which was extracted from the evidence on objective test loadings, is well substantiated from the correlations of this factor with questionnaire primaries and second-order objective test factors, which have been reviewed above. The Cortertia-Pathemia interpretation provides also our explanation for the very marked increase in mean score in U.I. 22 during the age span 9 to

---

[1]The single positive loading of M.I. 63 (more masculine than feminine interests) is less convincing than M.I. 64 which has four "significant" loadings. At present we have no evidence of how to account for the loading of M.I. 63.

15 years. During later childhood and puberty the individual's behavior gets more "corticated" and brain stem processes typically lose influence upon the control of overt responses; ergic tension from unreduced drives decreases since the individual learns more and more to integrate his needs and desires. Also the finding that neurotics score significantly lower than normals on U.I. 22 is understandable from this interpretation -- in the sense that the neurotics behavior is more emotional-effective than rational-effective.

The notion of Cortical Alertness vs. Pathemia led us to consider U.I. 22 as a possible personality trait of generally higher vs. generally lower cortical arousal level. The recent theories on cortical arousal level and its implication on behavior (9, 82, 128) have typically been applied to intra-individual response variability only. Assuming that different individuals will differ in terms of their habitual cortical arousal level makes these theories, however, readily applicable to inter-individual response variability. And in fact, very recently R. Berry (10) has shown that the hypothesis, for example, of an inverted U-relationship between arousal level and performance also holds with inter-inter-individual differences in both variables. Of the variables used in the reported factor analyses, fidgetometer frequency (M.I. 83) and involuntary muscle tension (M.I. 78) can be regarded as measures of inter-individual differences in arousal level, and their positive loading on U.I. 22 supports the hypothesis that this factor is a personality trait of high (vs. low) habitual cortical arousal level. This interpretation would also explain the low endurance found in persons scoring high on this factor.

If this last hypothesis is correct, from the work of Lindsley and others a non-linear correlation would have to be expected between measures of performance level and scores on U.I. 22. The linearity of these correlations has not been tested in the reported factor analyses. In a recent research by Pawlik and Cattell (140), for the first time, the correlation between characteristics of the alpha-rhythm in the individual EEG and factor U.I. 22 has been investigated, in order to allow for a more "direct" test of this hypothesis. The findings of this study gave strong support to the suggested interpretation of U.I. 22.

Among all the evidence on factor U.I. 22 there is only one result which does not readily fit this interpretation -- namely, the larger environmental than hereditary variance in U.I. 22. Alpha frequency in the resting EEG was found by Pawlik and Cattell (140) to load positively on U.I. 22+ -- but twin studies (126, 142) showed that alpha frequency is to a large extent determined by heredity. A possible resolution of this discrepancy may lie in the methodology of the determination of the nature-nurture ratios themselves. The nature-nurture results on the objective test factors have been obtained from a special statistical analysis described elsewhere by Cattell (36), which avoids some of the shortcomings of the classical twin method which has been used in the genetic investigation of EEG characteristics.

Table 7.13
U.I. 22: Cortertia vs. Pathemia

Q-Factor	Factor Title	Factor Identification (Research, Sample Size, Age of Subjects, Factor Number in Study)				
		C5 500 Adult (12+)	Ros 70 Adult (4+)	R1 86 Adult (6+)	R2 86 Adult (6+)	R3 86 Adult (2-)
A	(higher) Cyclothymia	-01		+14	-21	+10
B	(higher) Intelligence				+04	
*C	higher Ego Strength (mature, calm)	+15	+15	+08	+12	+03
E	(higher) Dominance	-13			-01	
F	(higher) Surgency	-09	+06	+08	-08	+01
G	(higher) Super Ego Strength	+08			-11	
H	(higher) Parmia	-02		+20	-24	-01
*I	higher Harria (tough, realistic)	(+04)		-15	-36	-04
L	(higher) Protension	-19			-08	
*M	higher Praxernia (conventional, practical)	(+05)	(+09)	-04	-25	-07
*N	higher Shrewdness (sophisticated, polished)	+03			+23	
*O	higher Confidence (confident, unshakable)	-01	-05	-04	-32	(+06)
Q1	(higher) Radicalism	+08			00	
Q2	(higher) Self Sufficiency	-03			-01	
Q3	(higher) Self Sentiment Control	+07			+17	
*Q4	lower Ergic Tension (phlegmatic, composed)	-04	-27	(+03)	-15	-10

U. I. 22: CORTERTIA VS. PATHEMIA (page 1)

Master Index Number	Variable Title	Factor Identification (Research, Sample Size, Age of Subjects, Factor Number in Study)																	
		T2	T-R	C1	C2	C3	C4	C5	C6	Ros	R1	R2	R3	We	C7	R12	R13	R15	R14
		190	189	370	410	100	100	500	250	70	86	86	86	80	184	80	164	197	129
		Adult	Adult	Adult	Adult	Adult	Adult	Adult	Adult	Adult	Adult	Adult	Adult	Adult	9-12	4-5	6-9	7-10	3-7
		(3-)	(4-)	(4-)	(6+)	(15+)	(17+)	(12+)	(10-)	(4+)	(6+)	(6+)	(2-)	--	(9-)	(3+)	(5+)	(7+)	(20-)
176	faster irregularly warned reaction time	-71				-48	-19	-25	-56	-34	-31	-35	-34			-44	-68	-64	
5	higher ratio of regularly to irregularly warned reaction time			+07	+17	(-10)	+38		+64	+54	+04	+38	+15		+31	+01			
6a,b,c	faster ideomotor speed		+30	+26		+20	+15			+26	+68	+13	+00		+19	+28	+00	(-04)	
40	more false responses to irrelevant signals in reaction time experiment			+16				+22	+02						+38	+23	+57	(-10)	+00
282	greater number of objects perceived in unstructured drawings							+24	+27	+28	+43					+00	+12	(-07)	+34
8	higher frequency of fluctuation in alternating perspective test		+31	+33	+31	+20	(-06)	+07							+17		+14		
83	higher fidgetometer frequency				+43	+08	+41	+14			+09	(-13)	+16		+08				+02
64	female sex	-22	-50		-25										(+07)				-01
13a-c	more oscillation of performance			+43	+03	+18	+10								+07				
72	more slowing of reaction time under complex instructions (higher ratio of simple to complex reaction time)				+29				+08						(-32)	(-04)	+38	+49	
71	greater number of errors of reaction under complex instructions				(-02)			+04	(-12)		+00	+05	+34		+20	+33	+53	+06	
43	smaller mean percentage PGR deflection to threatening stimuli			(+06)	-23	-36	-05				(+12)	-13	(+01)		-06				
219	fewer common frailties admitted							(+05)	(+05)	-12	-24	-21	-46		-09	-30	-12	-13	(+09)
80	less recovery (upward drift) of GSR when relaxed from shock				(+07)						(+08)	-44	-30		-11				
175	faster regularly warned reaction time					-61	(+01)									-40		-73	-47
28	less endurance of difficulty (lower "dynamic momentum")		-46	-02		-05	-24								-28				
263	less variability in simple reaction times								-39						-63	-52	-31	-38	-49
116	less critical severity of judgment					(+02)	(+11)			-27	-33	-02	-03		-06		-08		
94	higher mean critical flicker fusion frequency	+11				+52	+50		+11										
212	higher number of distant goals considered attainable							+09							+01	+16		+31	
9	faster ideomotor tempo			+08	+34	+19											(-07)		
78	higher involuntary muscle tension in right arm				+17						(-10)	+12	+33						
469	higher amplitude of conditioned GSR									+00	(-09)	+16	+43						
39	lower ratio of color to form in sorting			-02	-07	-00	-00	-38	(+14)		-01				(+06)		(+05)	(+15)	-17
55	lower fluency of association to emotional relative to non-emotional stimulus words				-38			-09							-04				
234	more carelessness in pencil maze performance										+30						+30	+00	
929b	lower fear erg (less desire for protection against atomic terror)										-08	-10	-43						
927a	higher sex erg (more desire to satisfy sexual needs)										+30	+05	+26						

U. I. 22: CORTERTIA VS. PATHEMIA (page 2)

Master Index Number	Variable Title	RESEARCH																	
		T2	T-R	C1	C2	C3	C4	C5	C6	Ros	R1	R2	R3	We	C7	R12	R13	R15	R14
26	less capable to deal with surprises (smaller number of riddles solved)			(+02)		-38	-02												
3	speed of judgment			+03	+27	+20	(-04)												
36	higher logical ability			+13	+21	+18	(-09)	(-07)											
4	faster average reaction time			-08	-16										-72				
33	smaller size of myokinetic movement			(+08)		-20					-22	(+03)	-01						
162b	more impairment in correct cancelling by distraction					+26	+15		(-03)						+02				
273	higher proportion of fluency on self							+06	(-01)	+07					+01	+35	(-07)	(-01)	+41
475	more action impetus										(-01)	+36	+31						
340	faster speed of repetitive form board performance															+58	+20		
93	less reduction of perceptual accuracy under movement restraint					-25	-39												
335	faster reaction time under complex instructions															-45		-19	
95	more decrease in size of myokinetic movements under threat					+03	+38												
151	slower speed of decision on principals than on particulars					-12	-30												
155	larger range in successive critical flicker fusion frequency measurements					+00	+39												
92	less readiness to imitate animal sounds (longer time taken to begin imitation)					+35	+15												
166	less impairment of classification performance by shock					(+04)	-35												
45	less endurance of shock and fatigue		-61	(+07)															
1	higher fluency of association			(-04)	+36														
37	more classifications suggested in object sorting test			(-02)	+34														
325	higher total level of self-estimated experience in a range of skills							+44											
1434	smaller number of aggressive picture interpretations																	-40	
343a	higher ratio of speed under approval relative to disapproval (form board performance)															+39			
474	higher total number of acquaintances recalled on fluency test										+39								
63	more masculine than feminine interests				+38														
1439	higher absolute verbal frequency on self																		+41
231	faster speed of maze performance (longer distance travelled)														+37				
79	more eidetic imagery (longer duration of images)				+37														
1719	higher general intelligence (scale I, subscale 1 of Cattell Culture Fair Intelligence Test)																		+32
609	greater accuracy (on "Where Do the Lines Cross?" test)																		+30

U. I. 22: CORTERTIA VS. PATHEMIA (page 3)

Master Index Number	Variable Title	RESEARCH																	
		T2	T-R	C1	C2	C3	C4	C5	C6	Ros	R1	R2	R3	We	C7	R12	R13	R15	R14
53	lower ratio of self-criticism to self-appreciation				-34														
70	longer average time interval between disappearance of positive and appearance of negative after image				+30														
336	(higher) absolute number of threatening objects perceived in unstructured drawings										+35	-14	-27		-10	-04			+24
30	(more) criticism of self relative to criticism of others			+04		-08						-41				+02	+10	+01	
199	(higher) computational skills							-09	-07		+42	-06	+07		+00	+06		+09	-01
120a-c, g	(higher) ratio of accuracy to speed					+07	-04			-04	-05	+21	-04		-20	+49	+03	-08	-13
77	(higher) salivary ph				+19					-35	+20	+02	-09						
67a, b	(more) extremity of viewpoint				-16	-01	+01	-04	-06						+07		+30		
316	(higher) relative fluency on own vs. other people's personal characteristics										+07	-40	+37				+07		
933b	(higher) self-sentiment erg (desire to avoid damage to sense of self-respect)										-30	+12	+04						
920	(higher) average amplitude of hand tremor										-13	-13	+34						
143	(higher) total score -- CMS							-06		-02					+02	+19	+12	-03	+21
108	(more) confident assumption of skill in untried performance					+02	-19	-12	+19		-02	+00	-14		-10		-02		+22
203	(more) confidence in one's numerical ability							-24	+02								+10	+07	+25
51	(higher) index of carefulness				-15			+12	+15		+10	+04	-10			-02		+00	
15	(more) use of circles -- CMS					+26		-22	-11	-15	-05	-02	+26		+06			+00	
62	(faster) speed of reading emotional relative to non-emotional material				-07	+01	-15	+11							-18				
152	(more) tendency to agree					+07	-03	-14	+19	+15	-10	+00	+05		-04		-04		+01
270	(faster) tempo of arm-circling							-10	+06						+21	-25	+05	+10	+01
271	(higher) total verbal fluency							-10	-17						+09	+18	+08		
466	(higher) frequency of hand tremor									-06	-13	-13	+34						

U.I. 23: HIGH MOBILIZATION VS. NEUROTIC REGRESSIVE DEBILITY (OR REGRESSION)

1. Prevalence

U.I. 23 has been identified in ten factor analyses with adults and four factor analyses with children. In addition there is evidence from Wells' (166) study of physical fitness and body-build characteristics concerning the relationship between such variables and U.I. 23. A further two analyses reported as R6 and R8 in Table 7.16, using a composite of U.I. 23 marker variables as a criterion, report a series of correlations with tests specifically designed to measure this factor. In general the match of factors across all studies is very good, and in particular this is true for adults (upon whom more intensive research has been concentrated).

2. Questionnaire Correlates

U.I. 23 has been compared with scores from the 16 P.F. in five studies (R1, R2, R3, R8, R10). Results indicate that at the present time no questionnaire factor is consistently and highly related to U.I. 23. Factor H(-): Threctia, Timid, Shy shows a moderate association, but the sign of correlation is not completely consistent. Factor B(+) (Intelligence) correlated +0.54 with the U.I. 23 factor estimate composite in R8, but the size of such a correlation is probably due to the factorially impure nature of the composite (i.e., it may well have included intelligence as well as U.I. 23). Factor C(+): High Ego Strength, Mature, Calm has also shown some promise as a correlate.

Knapp's studies of Submarine School candidates and officer helicopter pilots (123) show no significant correlations between U.I. 23 and any of the Guilford-Martin, Guilford-Zimmerman, and MMPI scales. Moderately low negative correlations are reported with an anxiety-tension check list (MI. 454) in R1 and R3, but this was not confirmed in R2 or by Knapp (using the Taylor MAS). In R6 and R8 negative correlations are found with a neurotic symptom check list (MI. 605a) and the Macmillan Inventory.

Significant correlations were found in R10 between this factor and more Computational Interests ($r = +.22$), more Artistic Interests ($r = +.24$), fewer Scientific Interests ($r = -.25$), and fewer Literary Interests ($r = -.22$) as measured by the Kuder Preference Record (138).

3. State Factor Matches

Of relevance to U.I. 23 as a source trait is the finding of P.U.I. 8 (Good Mobilization vs. Overwroughtness and Regressiveness of Interests), a state dimension regarded as the state counterpart of U.I. 23. The factor has been located in two P-technique and one incremental R-technique factor analyses (58, 107, 64). It is regarded as "an inner security, coherence, and capacity to mobilize as opposed to over-wrought, distracted, inaccurate reactions to many outside stimuli, along with indications of ergic regressions from adaptive interests." (68, p. 166). Principal loading variables are long hours of sleep the previous night, quick reaction, high endurance, high fluency, low rigidity, high ratio of accuracy to accomplishment.

4. Loadings on Second-Order Objective Test Factors

U.I. 23 appears in two second-order objective test factors, negatively with F(T)II Expansive Ego vs. History of Difficulty in Problem Solving, and positively with F(T)V: History of Inhibiting, Restraining Environment vs. Laxness (57).

5. Criterion Correlations

a) Clinical Criteria

In four studies, R9-Ta, R9-Tb, R10 (I), and R6, reported by Cattell and Scheier (68) and Cattell (38), comparison was made between U.I. 23 factor scores for normals and neurotics. With the exception of one study only, R9-Tb, results showed neurotics to be significantly lower than normals on the factor. However, the R9-Tb comparison is the least satisfactory being based on only 24 cases (19 normals and 5 neurotics). Further subdivision of R10 (I) data showed normals to be higher than criminals on U.I. 23, and both higher than neurotics. No significant correlations have been reported between U.I. 23 and psychiatrists' ratings of anxiety (R1).

b) School and Academic Achievement

No substantial correlations were reported between this factor and school or college achievement. However, in R1, C7, and P1 there are indications, as one would expect, that high achievement is more likely to accompany U.I. 23(+).

c) Military Criteria

U.I. 23(+) was found by Knapp (121) to play a part in the prediction of training success for helicopter pilots. His results show positive (but not significant) correlations between U.I. 23 and ratings of Pilot Proficiency, Officer-Like Qualities, and Social Acceptability. With Final Flying Grade the correlation was +0.353 ($p < .01$). However correlations with course success in Submarine School (122) were non-significant.

In general it seems that U.I. 23 is highly involved in the development of neurosis, but its association with other life criteria of military and educational success is by no means as clear.

6. Nature-Nurture Ratio

In 1951 Eysenck and Prell reported a predominance of heredity over environment in the determination of Eysenck's 'neuroticism' factor (regarded as similar to U.I. 23) (85a). Conflicting results to this were obtained by Cattell, Stice and Kristy (70) who found environment to be the principal contributor to U.I. 23. In discussion of this difference, Cattell, Stice and Kristy point out the weaknesses of the twin method as used by Eysenck and Prell, and the relatively small size of their sample. For these reasons preference is given to the later result, but clearly further research is needed on this problem of prime importance to the clinician.

Age trend results with children indicate a fairly rapid early rise gradually slowing down until by the age of 14-15 years a plateau is reached (29).

7. Descriptive Interpretation

Lower Rigidity

A predominant characteristic of U.I. 23(+) is flexibility and the facility to switch or reverse responses with minimal decrement to performance. Most noticeable here are consistently lower rigidity (MI. 2a, e, f and MI. 2h) and better two hand co-ordination (MI. 41) scores of U.I. 23(+). At present lower rigidity is one of the two best markers for this factor.

General Competence

It is clear even from only a superficial glance at Table 7.16 that U.I. 23(+) is highly related to competence in a variety of problem and test situations, many of them of a very general kind. Such variables include: Higher ratio of accuracy to speed (MI. 120), higher numerical ability (MI. 199), faster speed of coding (MI. 6a) more items checked correctly in proofreading figures (MI. 606). This is not the whole picture however, for as was observed in the previous section, little relationship has been found between U.I. 23(+) and scholastic achievement or verbal ability. Further there are certain variables noticeably missing--arithmetic reasoning, CMS Total Score and reaction time, among others. Also contrary to expectation are less ability to suggest classifications (MI. 37) and lower logical consistency of attitudes (MI. 65).

Less Dependence on Environment

Further insight into the specialized functioning of U.I. 23 appears in high loadings of variables that involve manipulation and retention of symbols without direct support from the environment--in a phrase, "doing problems in one's head." Higher scores on WHERE DO THE LINES CROSS? (MI. 609), UPSIDE-DOWN DRAWINGS (MI. 610), WHERE DO YOU LAND? (MI. 605), FINDING THE LONGEST LINE (MI. 615), multiplying in one's head (MI. 542), doing arithmetical and logical problems in one's head (MI. 476), and alphabet skipping (MI. 504b), all fall within this category. Whether these tests are important because U.I. 23(-) is associated with (i) a need for environmental support (given in the test situation by pencil and paper) as such, or (ii) a general susceptibility to distraction leading to difficulties in concentrating upon any task, remains unclear. That mathematical reasoning and certain speed components of these tests are not involved is implied by the mainly zero relationship of these components to U.I. 23.

Body-Sway Suggestibility

One of the oldest markers for U.I. 23, lower body-sway suggestibility (MI. 42), and lower shock suggestibility (MI. 216), support the view of a general suggestibility characteristic to U.I. 23. However this is negated by positive loadings on measures of the effect of verbal suggestion upon questionnaire response as in much shift to successfuls (MI. 193a) and much shift from neurotics (MI. 194). At present there seems no alternative to concurrence with Cattell and Scheier (64a) in their view that something rather specific to the body-sway measure itself appears to be involved.

Less Extremity of Viewpoint

Within the realm of questionnaire responses it appears that choice of the 'middle of the road' and avoidance of extreme categories is related to U.I. 23. Evidence here is for less extremity of viewpoint (MI. 67a), fewer deviant questionnaire responses (MI. 439), and many "in between" responses on a neurotic checklist (MI. 605a). Apart from the less excess of aspiration over performance in coding (MI. 101), there is no real evidence for a more general cautiousness of approach.

Reading Speed

Linguistic competence appears to be associated with this factor, and can be observed in faster speed of reading (MI. 516 and MI. 511) and higher total fluency on completing words (MI. 597). The absence of many traditional fluency measures implies that this facility with words is probably not higher verbal fluency as it is usually regarded, but is characterized by a set of highly controlled verbal skills.

Endurance of Stress

Certain variables concerning endurance of, or resistance to, difficulty load U.I. 23. Among them are higher dynamic momentum (MI. 28), lower ratio of cancellation performance under normal to shock conditions (MI. 162b), and faster correct word rate for reading under delayed feedback conditions (MI. 510). However there are many similar variables that show no such relationship to U.I. 23. It may be that in relatively few of the tests so far used has the difficulty reached such a level as to enable the fatigue effect, long believed to be concerned in U.I. 23(-) to appear. Also present is little physiological reactivity following stimulation, to be seen in little increase in pulse and heart rate due to stress (MI. 84), and less pupil dilation at stress (MI. 445). However again certain absences from the list of variables in Table 7.16 and the high positive correlation with metabolic rate change with stimulation (MI. 75) make interpretation difficult.

Certain Variables Not Falling in the Above Categories

More preference for color over form in picture preference (MI. 227a, b) has appeared consistently with this factor, and particularly in studies with children. Ratio of color to form in sorting (MI. 39), however, has no interpretable sign relationship. Measures of motivation, used in R1, R2, and R3, indicate that U.I. 23(+) is associated with lower sex erg (less desire to satisfy sexual needs) (MI. 927a), higher sex erg (greater desire for romantic love) (MI. 927b), and lower appeal erg (less desire to heed parents advice) (MI. 1716b). The relationship between ergic components and U.I. 23 is not yet clear enough to warrant further discussion.

No body-build or physical fitness correlates of U.I. 23 have been found. Physiological measures in general show rather low loadings, but of interest are lower absolute level of GSR resistance (MI. 443), less involuntary muscle tension (MI. 78), and lower ratio of PGR responses to mental vs. physical stimuli (MI. 305).

8. Explanatory Theory: History and Final Hypotheses

Historically, research on U.I. 23 has been closely tied to the development of metric approaches to neurosis. Early intuitive work in this area had led to the broad classification (with sub-classifications) of a large number of behavioral disorders as neurosis. Classification was based upon subjective rating, and this in turn being due to the clinician's background, training, personal predilections, and so forth. With the emergence of a quantitative approach in psychology, and in particular the use of factor analysis as a research tool, the door was opened to the scientific study of neurosis. There have been two general approaches to this area, that of Cattell, and that by Eysenck. Both have much in common, but also certain critical differences emerge that are of profound theoretical importance.

Eysenck's findings on his dimension of 'neuroticism' are based upon the thinking underlying what has been called 'criterion analysis' (85). Groups of 'normals' and groups rated by clinicians as neurotic are tested on various objective measures. Using those measures that significantly differentiate the groups, a factor analysis is carried out. Rotation of factors is aimed at producing a factor which is maximally discriminating between neurotics and normals. In brief, the procedure starts with a neurotic-normal classification based upon ratings, and ends with a set of loadings on a factor of neuroticism.

The approach by Cattell and his co-workers is quite different, and is in many ways the reverse of that by Eysenck. Starting with successive sets of objective measures, theoretically relevant to the broad domain of personality, Cattell extracts a larger number of factors and rotates these to simple structure. The relationship to clinically rated neurosis is then assessed by means of analysis of variance or discriminant function techniques. Thus the ratings are used as a final criterion (one among many) and not, as in Eysenck's work, the initial jumping-off ground. Many of the variables found by Eysenck in his neuroticism factor also appear in U.I. 23, but many other variables fall in other U.I. factors. This accounts for the classification by Cattell and Scheier (68) of U.I. 16(-), 22(-), 23(-), 24(+) and 29(-) as neurotic process factors (i.e., intimately concerned in classification of neurosis) and U.I. 1(-): Low Intelligence, 19(-), 21(-), 25(-), 32(+), and 34 (+) as neurotic-contributory factors (i.e., less intimately concerned). Thus opposed to the unitary dimension of neuroticism proposed by Eysenck, Cattell has several factors predictive of neurosis. Though similar in terms of many variables, neuroticism and U.I. 23 are certainly not the same. The theoretical discussion that follows will deal solely with U.I. 23, and Eysenck's findings will be mentioned only when they are strictly relevant.

There is little doubt as to the overt characteristics of U.I. 23 as it is presently measured, and these have been outlined in the previous section. Consideration of these characteristics, with questionnaire and criterion evidence and the presence of the state factor P.U.I. 8, leads to a number of hypotheses concerning the nature of U.I. 23 in a more profound theoretical sense.

The first hypothesis, attractive in its simplicity and directness, is that U.I. 23 is a hereditarily determined debility or susceptibility to neurosis. That not all individuals with very low scores on the factor are classifiable as neurotic would be accounted for by differential environmental stresses. Against this view is the evidence for a fair proportion at least of the variance in U.I. 23 being due to environmental determination, and the indication that more factors than U.I. 23 are needed to account for classification as neurotic.

A second hypothesis, somewhat similar to the first, is that U.I. 23 is the general neurotic disintegration itself. Against this is the need for more than U.I. 23 to account for classification as neurotic, and the presence of a state counterpart to the trait factor. In addition such a view is tautologous unless some consistent pattern of relationship between U.I. 23 and the stresses of an environment is explicitly proposed.

The third, and preferred, hypothesis is that U.I. 23- represents the result of prolonged conflict, perhaps accompanying neurotic disintegration, and appearing in a form of ergic regression similar to neurasthenia. Neurasthenic symptoms - inability to concentrate, poor memory, lack of continued effort in a prolonged task, relatively low competence in many performances, - all describe U.I. 23(-) performance, and it seems desirable at present to avoid in any way regarding U.I. 23 as <u>the</u> neurosis factor. This interpretation also fits in more satisfactorily with the state factor evidence.

If U.I. 23(-) signifies a history of unresolved and prolonged conflict, leading to ergic regression and incapacity to mobilize mental (and probably physical) resources, then the age trend curve for this factor (somewhat similar to that for intelligence) suggests a maturational trend of importance to developmental psychology. In addition data presented by Cattell and Scheier (67) shows that U.I. 23+ increases during stress (or immediate anticipation of such stress), and gives certain implications for research upon therapy.

Table 7.15
U.I. 23: High Mobilization vs. Neurotic Regressive Debility (or Regression)

Q-Factor	Factor Title	Factor Identification (Research, Sample Size, Age of Subjects, Factor Number in Study)				
		R1 86 Adult (2+)	R2 86 Adult (17+)	R3 86 Adult (3+)	R10 168 Adult (13+)	R8 97 Adult --
A	(higher) Cyclothymia	+05	00	00	-08	+04
*B	higher Intelligence (bright)		(-01)			+54
*C	higher Ego Strength (mature, calm)	+07	+02	+21	+03	+04
E	(higher) Dominance		-03		-17	+29
F	(higher) Surgency	-02	-07	+05	+09	-04
G	(higher) Super Ego Strength		00		+04	+05
*H	higher Threctia (timid, shy)	(+12)	-19	-12	-24	(+07)
I	(higher) Premsia	-01	+01	+15	+06	-07
L	(higher) Protension		+06		00	+10
M	(higher) Alaxia	-08	+01	00	+04	-10
N	(higher) Shrewdness		-01		-04	+12
O	(higher) Timidity	-18	-05	+03	+11	-05
Q1	(higher) Radicalism		00		+08	+16
Q2	(higher) Self-Sufficiency		-06		+02	+18
Q3	(higher) Self Sentiment Control		+15		+09	-32
Q4	(higher) Ergic Tension	+02	+05	-14	+09	00

U. I. 23: HIGH MOBILIZATION VS. NEUROTIC REGRESSIVE DEBILITY (OR REGRESSION) (page 1)

Master Index Number	Variable Title	Factor Identification (Research, Sample Size, Age of Subjects, Factor Number in Study)																
		E1	E3	C1	C2	C3	C4	R1	R2	R3	R10	We	R6	R8	C7	R12	R13	R15
		105	100	370	410	100	100	86	86	86	168	80	98	97	184	80	164	197
		Adult	Adult	Adult	Adult	Adult	Adult	Adult	Adult	Adult	Adult	Adult	Adult	Adult	9-12	4-5	6-9	7-10
		--	--	(10+)	(8+)	(7+)	(7+)	(2+)	(17+)	(3+)	(13+)	--	--	--	(5-)	(6+)	(16-)	(8+)
2a,e,f	lower rigidity (perceptual motor)	-42		-15	-16	-58	-19	-39	-18	-30	-28		-51*	-23*	-41	-25	-02	-15
42	less body-sway suggestibility	-64	-12	-20	-05	-26	-12	-15	-32	-10	-01							-08
120	higher ratio of accuracy to speed	+40				+20	+29	+38	+36	+40	+36		+36*	+57*	+36	+30	+19	+05
199	higher score on numerical ability							+39	+27	+07	+15				+25	+08		+20
6a	higher speed of coding							+19	+18	(-01)	+35		+43	+61				
609	greater accuracy in spatial judgment										+41		+57	+38*				
41	better two-hand co-ordination		+42	+02	+06	(-15)	+37								+36			
516,511	higher speed of reading to one's self							+44					+26	+44*				
28	higher dynamic momentum	+50	+16	(-01)		+12	+36								+00			
84	less increase in pulse and heart rate due to startle				-15			-01	-57	-10								
101a,b	less excess of aspiration over achievement in coding	-17		-03		-29	-01						(+16)*		-56	-37	(+10)	-05
162b	higher ratio of cancellation performance under normal to shock conditions					+26	+46								+26			
476	less mind wandering vs. ability to do problems in one's head							-41	-28	-06								
8	higher speed of alternating perspective			(-01)	+31	(-21)	+13								+20		+15	
443	lower absolute level of GSR resistance							-31	-11	-18								
610	higher number of correct answers in reversed drawings												+56	+60*				
445	less pupil dilation at stress							-05	-34	-07								
604	more correct answers "where do you land?"												+55	+56*				
542	higher correct score, multiplying in one's head												+47*	+61*				
596	faster speed on word completion												+39	+52				
504b	higher correct score: "alphabet skipping"												+30*	+53*				
606	more items checked correctly in proofreading figures												+46	+32*				
67a,b	less extremity of viewpoint				-22	(+04)	-31				-28				(+09)		-07	(+03)
218	much willingness to play practical jokes and tease															+27		+26
151	higher ratio of decision time on principles vs. particulars					+31	+27						(-06)*					
605a	lower score on neurotic symptom checklist												-27	-20				
356b	more errors in color naming															+50	+10	+02
65	lower logical consistency of attitudes				-30	-18									+00			
110	less future relative to past associations					-20	-16											
21	fewer questionable reading preferences			+01	(-02)	+01	(-05)	+10							+18	(-02)	+29	+12
167a,b	better immediate memory	+00	+33			+14	(-01)				+00		+34*		+01		+16	
927b	higher sex erg (greater desire for romantic love)							(-04)	+23	+46								
927a	lower sex erg (less desire to satisfy sexual needs)							(+08)	-10	-39								
216	less shock suggestibility		-15												-17			

U. I. 23: HIGH MOBILIZATION VS. NEUROTIC REGRESSIVE DEBILITY (OR REGRESSION) (page 2)

Master Index Number	Variable Title	RESEARCH																
		E1	E3	C1	C2	C3	C4	R1	R2	R3	R10	We	R6	R8	C7	R12	R13	R15
638	higher absolute level of aspiration in coding												+47*	+59		(-37)		
454	lower score on anxiety-tension checklist							-15	(+01)	-20								
78	less involuntary muscle tension				-27			-15	-06	(+05)								
194	more shifting of attitudes away from those of neurotics					+03	+32				+01							
37	less ability to suggest classifications			-05	-34													
193a	more shifting of attitudes towards those of successful people						+34								+04			
7	faster speed of Gestalt closure			(-03)		+19	+38				+08				(-07)	(-02)	(-02)	(-02)
112	higher ratio of favorable to unfavorable self-reference					(-05)	+35				+01				+19		+01	
305	lower ratio of PGR responses to mental rather than physical stimuli					-31	-09											
36	more ability to state assumptions			+08	+00	+33	(-01)											
75	more increase in metabolic rate with stimulation				+65													
2h	low rigidity: proportion incorrect in reversed color naming															-63		
510	more articulatory efficiency under delayed feedback conditions								+57									
1366	less doing of unpleasant activities																	-52
965	much consistency in serial ratings of ideal self										-45							
605b	more "in between" responses on neurotic symptom checklist												+44					
1490	much accuracy in novel sound identification										+45							
615	higher proportion correct "finding the longest line"												+43					
352a	greater variability in number of objects seen in unstructured drawings															+42		
58	greater myokinesis drift				+41													
388	greater expansiveness in drawing others relative to drawing self			-05	-34													
407	slower speed of decision in paired associations																+38	
1489	more accuracy in recalling horrifying rather than pleasant details										+38							
439	fewer deviant questionnaire responses																+35	
1716b	lower appeal erg (less desire to heed parents' advice)							-36										
171	large number of years completed in school												+36					
202	less willing to take a chance														-34			
1530	higher accuracy in pitch discrimination										+31							
597	more letters repeated "completing words"												+31					
409	faster decision speed with many rather than few alternatives																+30	
602	faster speed of inventing answer responses												+30					
613	faster speed in design copying												+30					
51	(higher) index of carefulness				-63			+03	+36	+05	+16					+05		+05
3,127	(faster) speed of judgment			+06	-18	+30	+10											
34	(more) immaturity of opinion			+03	+05	-16	+08				+16				-15	+07		
219	(more) willingness to admit common frailties							-02	+21	+00	+09				+03	-03	-41	+15
77	(higher) salivary ph				-19			+20	-28	+00								

U. I. 23: HIGH MOBILIZATION VS. NEUROTIC REGRESSIVE DEBILITY (OR REGRESSION) (page 3)

Master Index Number	Variable Title	RESEARCH																
		E1	E3	C1	C2	C3	C4	R1	R2	R3	R10	We	R6	R8	C7	R12	R13	R15
471	(more) reluctance to enter fear situation							-11	-15	+21								
71	(more) errors of response in reaction time under complex instructions				+13			+05	+00	-21	-27				-03	-03	+01	-02
146b	(higher) proportion correct in Gestalt closure					+13	+14				+12				-32	-01	+05	
39	(higher) ratio of color to form in sorting			-03	+01	-11	-17	+04			+22				-02		-47	+08
6b	(faster) ideomotor speed (color naming)							+19	+18	-01						-05	-07	-05
143	(higher) total score -- CMS										+31				+04	+05	-02	-08
114	(greater) underestimation of time estimates for performance					+11	-42											
464	(greater) handwriting pressure							+01	-37	+06								
5	(higher) ratio of regularly to irregularly warned reaction time			+00	-07	-08	-08	-01	-02	+26	+07				+08	-16		
13a-c	(more) oscillation of performance			-02	+00	-03	-07				-07				+30			
30	(more) criticism of self relative to others			-03		-15	-18	+12	-04	-03						+03	-08	+09
33	(larger) size of myokinetic movement			-03		-03		+02	+05	+26	-18							
227a,b	(more) preference for color over form in picture preference												-20		+36	-40	-04	
133	(more) criticalness of evaluation					-02	-16								+08		+01	-16
282	(greater) number of objects seen in unstructured drawings							+17			+06					+02	+01	-17

* A composite of these variables was used to determine the estimated U. I. 23 factor scores in R6 and R8.

U.I. 24: HIGH UNBOUND ANXIETY VS. GOOD ADJUSTMENT

1. Prevalence

Factor U.I. 24 was identified in eight factor analytic researches (including the incremental R-technique study R3) using adult subjects, and five studies at the child level. For the adult age range extension results are contributed by three studies (R4, R7, Wells), two of which (R4, R7) have been especially designed as extension analyses on this factor. In addition, some results on U.I. 24 are available from a study by Brogden (12), one of his factors matching U.I. 24.

2. Questionnaire Correlates

In several researches on the second-order factor structure of the primary questionnaire factors measured in the 16 P.F. Test, a very clear second-order factor F(Q)II of general anxiety has been found (28, 29, 34, 120), in both adult subjects and children. This factor F(Q)II typically loads on C-, H+, O+, Q3-, and Q4+, and its loading structure is very consistent when compared across all available questionnaire second-order analyses.

The factor U.I. 24+ is the only first-order objective test factor that correlates highly positively with F(Q) II: Anxiety. In table 7.15 the loadings of the sixteen primary questionnaire factors on U.I. 24+ are summarized; the evidence comes from seven factor analytic studies (including the incremental R-technique study R3) in which the 16 P.F. Test (or parts of it) and objective tests have been included in the same factor analysis. All above mentioned principal salients of F(Q)II load U.I. 24+ in the expected direction; in addition, also L+ and M+ yield consistent loadings.

Thus, the complete primary questionnaire factor pattern of U.I. 24+ comprises low Ego Strength (emotional, unstable; C-), high Threctia (timid, shy; H+), high Protension (suspicious, jealous; L+), high Autia (bohemian, unconcerned; M+), high Timidity (insecure, anxious; O+), low Integration (lax, unsure; Q3-), and high Ergic Tension (tense, excitable; Q4+). These questionnaire factors describe well-known aspects of free anxiety: the high timidity and anxiousness, the high ergic tension (presumably due to unreduced drives and needs), the low self-integration and ego strength, with a general tendency towards aggressive projection (L+). Only the loading of M+ (high Autia) is at first unexpected since highly anxious persons typically present themselves as rather acquiescent and show a strong "tendency to please." There seem to be two alternative explanations for the M+ component in the questionnaire pattern of

U.I. 24: The high Autia may indicate either simple withdrawal from social interaction or actual negativistic disregard of societal standards; both would result in a high score on questionnaire factor M+, and both could be conceived of as an adjustment mechanism that will reduce fear arising from social contacts (such as fear of not fulfilling given social norms, fear of failing in social competition, etc.).

In study N2 (123) Knapp found significant correlations between U.I. 24+ and the following factor scales from the Guilford-Martin Personality Inventory: T+ (high Thinking Introversion: +.19), D+ (high Depression: +.13), C+ (high Cycloid Disposition: +.18), O- (low Objectivity: -.13), Ag- (low Agreeableness: -.15), G+ (high General Activity: +.17), and N- (low Calmness: -.13). Some of these correlations are in good agreement with the correlations between U.I. 24 and scales from the 16 P.F. Test-despite the apparent differences between both questionnaires in terms of construction and of properties of scales. Thus the correlations with T+, Ag-, G+, and N- in the Guilford-Martin Personality Inventory, for example, compare well with the loadings found for the factors A-, M+, and Q4+, respectively, in the 16 P.F. Test.

In the smaller sample available for analysis N 1 (123) Knapp obtained significant correlations of U.I. 24+ with the scales E- (low Emotional Stability: -.24) and O- (Low Objectivity: -.24) of the Guilford-Zimmerman Temperament Survey and scales L- (low Lie Scale: -.48) and K- (low Test Defensiveness: -.44) of the MMPI. The latter two correlations indicate that the highly anxious person is less eager to choose the sociably more desirable item responses and is very critical of himself. These findings are in excellent agreement with similar results obtained with objective tests.[1]

Knapp also reported a positive correlation of +.25 between U.I. 24+ and the Taylor Manifest Anxiety Scale; Rosenthal (study Ros), who used the Taylor MAS as a variable in her factor analysis, similarly found a high positive loading (+.85) of this questionnaire scale on U.I. 24+. A self-checklist on anxiety-tension symptoms showed consistent positive loadings on U.I. 24+ in four factor analyses (R1, R2, R3, R4). Thus, U.I. 24+ does not only correlate with questionnaire traits traditionally regarded as attributes underlying manifest anxiety, but also with direct self-ratings on free anxiety.

If our interpretation of U.I. 24 as a personality dimension of free anxiety (vs. good adjustment) is correct, this factor should also correlate with clinically judged level of anxiety. Some results of research R1 are pertinent to this question: The subjects of this study have been interviewed independently by two psychiatrists who rated all subjects on level of "global anxiety". In addition, one of the two psychiatrists rated the subjects also specifically on "free anxiety", "situational anxiety", "bound anxiety", and "characterological anxiety". The six ratings, thus available for each subject, were entered into the factor analysis as separate variables. The ratings by the two psychiatrists on "global

[1] They also demonstrate the methodological need to investigate such artificially isolated concepts as "social desirability" or "acquiescence" within a broader variable domain - in order that cross-relationships with other traits not be lost!

anxiety" loaded +.30 and +.36, respectively, on factor U.I. 24+. Of the specific ratings on free, situational, bound, and characterological anxiety only the first two loaded on U.I. 24 (+.42 and +.26); the rating on bound anxiety loaded mainly on factors U.I. 18- and U.I. 20-, the rating on characterological anxiety mainly on U.I. 20-.

In summarizing all available evidence on questionnaire correlates of U.I. 24 we conclude: The objective test factor U.I. 24 correlates positively with self-evaluated and clinically judged level of free anxiety. It is closely related to the second-order anxiety factor in the 16 P.F. Test and correlates also with several scales in Guilford's series of personality inventories. The main questionnaire attributes of U.I. 24 are: high timidity and insecurity (16 P.F.T.: H+, O+), low ego strength and integration (16 P.F.T.: C-, Q3-; GZTS: E-), high suspiciousness and autism (16 P.F.T.: L+, M+; Guilford-Martin: Ag-, and possibly T-), and high level of unreduced drive level (16 P.F. Test: Q4-; Guilford-Martin: G+, N-).

Regarding interest correlates of U.I. 24, Pawlik (138) found significant correlations between this factor and two of the Kuder interest scales: Persuasive Interests correlated +.22 with U.I. 24, Musical Interests -.24.

3. State Factor Matches

Factor U.I. 24 is one of the seven (or possibly eight) first-order objective test factors with known match among state factors. There is a good positive match between U.I. 24+ and P.U.I. 9+ which has been interpreted as a state dimension of high anxiety and high general autonomic activity. Factor P.U.I. 9 was identified in two P-technique analyses (one of which was a "stimulus controlled" P-technique experiment (99, 170)) and in the incremental R-technique research R3 in which it was jointly identified with U.I. 24+. The fact that the objective test pattern of U.I. 24 also emerges as a state factor indicates a double nature of this factor as both a trait and a state dimension.

4. Loadings on Second-Order Test Factors

U.I. 24 is top salient of the second-order OT factor F(T) VII which was interpreted as "high Tension to Achieve". Other first-order OT factors with consistent loadings on F(T)VII are U.I. 18+ (high Hypomanic Smartness), U. I. 30- (less Aloof Independence), U.I. 25- (less Accurate Realism), and U.I. 19+ (high Promethian Will).

5. Criterion Correlations

a) Clinical Criteria

In both studies R9-Ta (68) and R10(I) (38) a positive significant difference was found on U.I. 24 between neurotics and normals. This result is in good agreement with clinical research findings of an increased anxiety level in neurotics. In R10(I) Cattell also found a significant difference between normals and criminals on this factor, the criminals scoring on the average higher on the anxiety factor than the normals; this finding, which stands in sharp contrast to the every-day life notion of the "bold and daring" delinquent, supports modern clinical views on delinquency according to which the delinquent is indeed highly "anxious" -- not in the sense of high "fearfulness", but on the basis of high and unreduced drive strength (high ergic tension), low ego integration, and low sociability.

The difference between normals and psychotics in R7 was not significant, but was in the expected direction, i.e., the psychotic subjects scored on the average higher on U.I. 24+ than the normal subjects.

b) School and Academic Achievement

The results on the relationship between U.I. 24 and school achievement are conflicting (cf. M.I. 276, Table 8.16). Brogden found a high positive correlation of +.40 between U.I. 24+ and elementary school achievement; in study C7 this correlation dropped to +.18. In college students (R1) M.I. 276 loaded only +.12 on U.I. 24, and in a recent analysis on the relationship between objective test first-order factors and college-achievement Pawlik (study P1) found a negative relationship, both low-achievers and under-achievers scoring higher on U.I. 24+ than high-achievers and over-achievers, respectively.

c) Military Criteria

In neither of the two studies AF (69) and N1 (121) did U.I. 24 yield any significant correlations with pilot success; the only significant correlation Knapp (121) reports is with peer ratings of social acceptability as a pilot (-.26) -- presumably an indication of a slight negative correlation between U.I. 24 anxiety and sociometric status. In study N2 (122), however, Knapp found a significant positive correlation of U.I. 24 with both the Pass-Fail (+.26) and the Class Standing criterion (+.12) in naval submarine training. This result would be in support of the recently proposed hypothesis that anxiety, increased general drive strength, has a facilitating effect upon learning processes. As will be discussed in the theoretical section on this factor, this interpretation of anxiety is, however, not in full agreement with the empirical evidence on the correlation between U.I. 24 and scholastic achievement in general.

6. Nature-Nurture and Age Trend Results

In neither of the two studies on nature-nurture ratios (70) and age trends (29), respectively, U.I. 24 was measured.

7. Descriptive Interpretation

During the past three years in the work of this laboratory extensive research has been directed towards the intensification of measurement and further clarification of interpretation of this factor. It is notably the work of Cattell and Scheier (in the researches R1 through R7) in which a large-scale exploration of all recognized manifestations of anxiety was undertaken and which furnished the main interpretative evidence on factor U.I. 24 (68, 65). In terms of objective test loadings of this factor, as they are set out in Table 7.16, there seem to be four aspects or implications of general anxiety around which the various test variables with 'significant' loadings cluster.

1. Anxiety, manifested in increased annoyance and embarrassment

From the above reported correlations between U.I. 24+ and self-evaluated as well as clinically judged anxiety the high positive loadings of the various measures of susceptibility to annoyance (M.I. 211a, 211b, 359, 243, 767) and embarrassment (M.I. 481) become very well understandable. Common clinical experience already describes the highly anxious person as easily embarrassed, as reacting readily with anticipatory fear to stimulus situations which may possibly involve danger or threat. The variables M.I. 243, 767, and 211b further specify this overall susceptibility to embarrassment and annoyance: such anticipatory fear reactions (manifesting themselves as annoyance or embarrassment) will occur more readily in purposefully rather than non-purposefully annoying instances (M. I. 243), easier with social than non-social annoyances (M.I. 767), and will in particular develop in situations which the subject will interpret as ego-threatening (M.I. 211b). Presumably these loadings do not only indicate that the extremely anxious person is more annoyed and embarrassed than persons scoring low on this factor, but that the highly anxious individual also perceives more situations as potentially threatening or planned to be harmful and thus annoying.

2. Insecurity, guilt, and self-depreciation

Clinical observation traditionally views manifest anxiety as closely linked with feelings of insecurity and guilt and with ideas of self-depreciation. Of the variables loading U.I. 24 several confirm this important aspect of anxiety. The anxious person admits more common frailties (M.I. 219) -- or "sins", as we might as well say -- than the average subject; appearing in the context of several other variables indicating feelings of self-depreciation and insecurity this loading of M.I. 219 can be best understood as expressing increased guilt proneness. This interpretation is substantiated through the loadings of the variables M.I. 246 (much authority submission), M.I. 108 (less self-confident regarding untried performance), and M.I. 147a (less self-confident relative to opportunity) which clearly illustrate the anxious person's ideas of self-depreciation, his tendency to undervalue his own capabilities, his feelings of insecurity and thence his pronounced submissiveness to authority.

Insecurity also may serve as a common denominator in the loadings of M.I. 152 (high tendency to agree), M.I. 144 (much acceptance of aphorisms), and M.I. 294 (little contact with reality). If these loadings are actually due to increased insecurity -- or doubts about one's being right or wrong -- one would predict subjects scoring high on U.I. 24+ to develop a strong (however superficial !) tendency to conform with social standards. This tendency is in fact expressed in the pattern of U.I. 24: The anxious person admits fewer questionable reading preferences (M.I. 21) and shows good ethical choices in a story test (M.I. 330). There are two loadings which suggest that this insecurity is not restricted to self-perception but does extend into the broader field of social contacts. The anxious individual lists fewer friends (M.I. 473) and shows low fluency on personal characteristics (M.I. 763). Since U.I. 24+ correlates positively with M.I. 271 (total verbal fluency) these loadings cannot be due to a generally low ability to express oneself verbally; they rather indicate little interest in, and active withdrawal from, social contacts which in itself is well understandable viewed against a background of high insecurity feelings.

3. High ergic tension

Increased ergic tension, which we mentioned already when reviewing the evidence on questionnaire correlates of U.I. 24, is also clearly expressed in the objective test pattern of this factor. The anxious individual is more emotional in his comments (M.I. 205), is more fluent in his associations to emotional than to non-emotional stimuli (M.I. 55), and is less long-circuited (M.I. 458), i.e., life goals are perceived as less distant in time (which suggests a striving for more immediate gratification). This increased emotionality, as a direct resultant of high ergic tension, is also known by the clinician as a typical symptom of unbound anxiety. The loadings of M.I. 327a, c (many logical inconsistencies in attitudes) and M.I. 67a (much extremity of viewpoint) can be understood from this high ergic tension -- in the sense that the anxious person will react more emotionally to opinionnaire type items.

An interpretative problem, not fully solved as yet, arises only with regard to the loadings of M.I. 116a, b (high critical severity), M.I. 133 (more critical in evaluating performance of others), and M.I. 595 (high percentage of jokes considered funny on Humor Factors #6, 7, and 8). First of all, it might puzzle the reader to think of the U.I. 24+ person as being very humorous (M.I. 595). This apparent inconsistency can be easily resolved; The Humor Test factors 6, 7, and 8 all cluster around a kind of hostile, aggressive, and cynical humor (Factor 6+: hostile derogation; Factor 7+: cold cynicism; Factor 8+: ponderous humor). Thus the loading of M.I. 595 simply describes the anxious person as more cynical, hostile, and critical. This puts M.I. 595, together with M.I. 116 and 133, into one cluster of variables. And in this context the above mentioned interpretational problem becomes evident: Are we to infer that the anxious individual is more aggressive or do these variables suggest a projection mechanism, such that the anxious individual projects his insecurity and self-depreciation into his evaluation of other people?

Cattell and Scheier, in a previous publication (65), have favored the projection-interpretation. Even with the higher number of researches available now, on U.I. 24, it is still difficult to decide between the two alternative hypotheses. Both would fit the anxiety concept equally well. The questionnaire loadings discussed above (L+ in the 16 P.F. Test) and the test results reviewed in the preceding section are somewhat in favor of the projection-hypothesis; in favor of the aggression-hypothesis is the evidence on high ergic tension in U.I. 24+.

The kind of cynicism or critical severity encountered here should not be mistaken, however, for extremistic tough-mindedness. As shown in the loading of M.I. 383, the person scoring high on U.I. 24+ will reduce his criticism readily, when anticipating the possibility he might have to defend his critical remarks against the ones he criticized -- a behavior not expected in the case of the typically rather out-spoken, tough-minded personality.

4. Asthenic physique

A fourth aspect of U.I. 24+ anxiety concerns physical characteristics. In very general terms these can be subsumed under the notion of "asthenic physique". The factor correlates negatively with the Larson C-VJ-D Index (i.e., a person scoring high on U.I. 24+ can only perform few "chins", few vertical jumps, and few "dips") (M.I. 560, 657) which indicates both low physical strength and endurance; also the loading of handwriting pressure is negative (M.I. 464).

These somewhat asthenic characteristics are blended with bodily characteristics of increased tension level. The anxious individual has a high systolic blood pressure (M.I. 444) and is more suggestible in his involuntary movements (high body sway suggestibility, M.I. 42). Unexplained, however, is the discrepancy between the results for variables M.I. 269 (slow leg-circling tempo) and M.I. 270 (fast arm-circling tempo).

8. Explanatory Theory: History and Final Hypotheses

Anxiety, both as a descriptive and explanatory clinical concept, has a long history that partly reflects the historical development of clinical psychology itself, of which it has been a core concept for a long time. In the field of experimental psychology, especially in studies on animal learning, anxiety has been assigned the role of an intervening variable, and has been conceptualized as a secondary or learned drive (conditioned fear). Evidence on anxiety as a unitary personality trait, on the other hand, is comparatively rare; due to their more restricted variable sampling, factor analytic studies done outside the authors' laboratory typically did not identify an anxiety factor.

In a recent monograph, Cattell and Scheier (65) summarized the empirical evidence on factor U.I. 24 in a set of ten hypotheses. As the researches that have been completed since then do not ask for any major changes in Cattell and Scheier's original interpretation of this factor, we need not discuss it here at greater length and a brief summary of the two theoretically most important aspects will suffice.

1. U.I. 24+: a unitary personality trait of conscious, free, anxiety

This interpretation is fully supported by the positive loadings of self-rated and psychiatrically judged free anxiety on U.I. 24+ as well as by the evidence on the various questionnaire correlates of the factor; it also explains many of the objective test loadings[1] and the obtained differences between criterion groups.

Our hypothesis is that high unbound anxiety, as defined in U.I. 24+, originates in a state of continuously unreduced emotional tensions and unsatisfied drives and needs -- particularly, if environmental pressure and/or already internalized cultural standards request an overt suppression of important ergs. The amount of parental demands and restrictions to which an individual becomes exposed during early and middle childhood is very likely to constitute a major part of this environmental determination of free anxiety. From a developmental point of view, unreduced (and possibly repressed) emotions and unsatisfied ergs will not only result in increased ergic tension, but this frustration, if persistent over a long enough period of time, will also reduce ego-strength, self-confidence, and self-sentiment control. It will make a person more irritable and restless and lower his general frustration tolerance -- all of these being well-known "symptoms" of manifest anxiety.

Such an "environmentalistic" hypothesis about the development of U.I. 24+ anxiety assumes, as a matter of fact, a larger environmental than hereditary determination of this factor. As yet no direct results are available for U.I. 24 on nature-nurture ratios. From a genetic analysis of several primary questionnaire factors (45), however, some indirect evidence can be obtained. Of the questionnaire correlates of U.I. 24, C, Q3, and Q4 are in fact more environmentally determined; only H is mainly due to heredity (L, M, and O were not included in the genetic analysis).

2. U.I. 24 and the concept of generalized drive level

In motivation research, following the conceptual frame-work of classical learning theory, anxiety (as secondary fear drive) is typically conceived of as general drive level (92, 93, 155). As Cattell and Scheier pointed out elsewhere (65, 68) it is theoretically odd to identify all drive with anxiety ! Moreover, our present results show that the U.I. 24+ anxiety trait does not have the relations one would expect for total ergic drive. There is, however, some indirect evidence (29) that one of the five identified second-order ergic factors, a factor called Ergic Expression (Ergic Release) vs. Ergic Suppression (Ergic Control),

---

[1] The only objective test loading which does not seem to fit this interpretation is the negative loading of a measure of fear erg on U.I. 24+ (see Table 8.16). Cattell and Scheier (65) discussed four possible explanations for this isolated finding. Presumably the most satisfactory explanation is one that recognizes that only a small percentage of the variance of fear erg is dependent upon U.I. 24, and that this fraction of the fear erg "is the effect of fear in its instrumentality of producing inhibition and the psychological development of sentiments" (65, p. 371).

might correlate slightly with U.I. 24+ since two (sex erg, fear erg) out of the total five markers of the ergic repression factor load slightly (+.18, -.09) and in expected direction on U.I. 24. Certainly no definitive answer can be given, however, in view of the small size of these correlations.

Closely related to the notion of anxiety as general drive state is the hypothesized relationship between intra- as well as inter-individual differences in anxiety and rate of learning (e.g. 93). Starting from Hull's classical formulation of the excitatory potential E_r of a response r being a multiplicative function of both the general drive level D of the individual and his habit strength H_r with regard to this response r, a very large number of researches investigated the rate at which a person will learn a response as a function of his general anxiety level, the latter typically being measured by Taylor's MAS (157). No review or theoretical exploitation of these studies shall be attempted here; however, we wish to discuss briefly to what extent our results can contribute to this theoretically interesting problem.

In the research R1 a typical GSR conditioning experiment was also administered; only rate of conditioning loaded factor U.I. 24, the correlation being +.25,[1] whereas both amplitude of conditioned GSR and rate of extinction had insignificant loadings. This indicates that more anxious subjects learn faster in simple conditioning experiments. As was already mentioned above, there is, however, no general relationship between U.I. 24 and such a broad and complex measure of learning ability as school achievement. The obtained correlations vary considerably, in particular with the type of school: at the elementary school level U.I. 24 tends to correlate positively with school achievement, but in college undergraduates this relationship is reversed. Of the three studies on the prediction of military training criteria only one yielded a significant and positive correlation between U.I. 24 and training success. No significant correlations have been found between this factor and general intelligence, specific verbal ability (M.I. 274), however, loads positively on U.I. 24 and Knapp's study (N2) found a significant and positive correlation between U.I. 24 and the Navy General Classification Test.

The conclusion from these findings is that manifest anxiety, as defined in factor U.I. 24+, does in fact relate positively to rate of simple learning and to success in certain training programs, however no general relationship can be inferred between this factor and various scholastic achievement criteria or rate of learning in general.

---

[1] This loading was not included in Table 8.17 since it did not fulfill our initial requirement (either one loading of .30 or above, or two loadings of .15 or above).

Table 7.17
U.I. 24: Unbound Anxiety vs. Good Adjustment

Q-Factor	Factor Title	Factor Identification (Research, Sample Size, Age of Subjects, Factor Number in Study)						
		C5 500 Adult (1+)	Ros 70 Adult (1+)	R1 86 Adult (2+)	R2 86 Adult (1+)	R3 86 Adult (12+)	R10 168 Adult (9+)	HI 137 Adult (9+)
A	(higher) Cyclothymia	+01		-19	00	+06	-03	
B	(higher) Intelligence				+12			
**C	lower Ego Strength (emotional, unstable)	-56	-46	-48	-23	-29	-15	-57
E	(higher) Dominance	+21			-12		-16	
F	(higher) Surgency	+17	+11	+01	+04	+01	-05	
G	(higher) Super Ego Strength	+10			-30		+09	-08
**H	higher Threctia (timid, shy)	-33		-36	-23	(+04)	-09	
I	(higher) Premsia	-16		+03	+03	-07	-14	
**L	higher Protension (suspecting, jealous)	+54			+15		+17	+52
*M	higher Autia (bohemian, unconcerned)	+46	+24	+14	+11	+04	(-18)	
N	(higher) Shrewdness	-01			+04		-14	
**O	higher Timidity (insecure, anxious)	+66	+84	+32	+30	+02	+12	+58
Q1	(higher) Radicalism	+03			-05		-13	-09
Q2	(higher) Self-Sufficiency	+06			+14		-09	+01
**Q3	lower Integration (lax, unsure)	-60			-53		-08	-56
**Q4	higher Ergic Tension (tense, excitable)	+74	+70	+61	+50	+40	+13	+65

U. I. 24: UNBOUND ANXIETY VS. GOOD ADJUSTMENT (page 1)

Master Index Number	Variable Title	Factor Identification (Research, Sample Size, Age of Subjects, Factor Number in Study)																	
		C5	C6	Ros	R1	R2	R3	R10	HI	We	R4	R7-Ps	R7-No	BRO	C7	R12	R13	R15	R14
		500	250	70	86	86	86	168	137	80	187	48	57	100	184	80	164	197	129
		Adult	Adult	Adult	Adult	Adult	Adult	Adult	Adult	Adult	Adult	Adult	Adult	11-12	9-12	4-5	6-9	7-10	3-7
		(1+)	(9-)	(1+)	(1+)	(1+)	(12+)	(9+)	(9+)	--	--	--	--	(5+)	(12+)	(5+)	(6+)	(9+)	(7+)
219	more common frailties admitted	+42	+19	+38	+37	+33	+11	+09	+43		+59				+34	+21	+03	(-01)	+19
152	more tendency to agree	+24	+63	+26	+17	+07	+11	+66	+13		+29	*	*		+39		+01		+24
211a	more over-all susceptibility to annoyance	+52	+39	+49	+15						+48	*	*		+08	+81	+52	+82	+20
108	less confident assumption of skill in untried performance	-11	-03		-27	-21	-35	-52			-19	*	*		-23		-09		-04
116a,b	higher critical severity (hard-headed cynicism)	+28		+33	+11	+18	+04	+15			+15				+37		+12		
21	fewer questionable reading preferences	+33			(-02)				(-13)					+36	+06	+36	+14	(-02)	
205	more emotionality of comment	+35	+13								+27				+05	+11			
454	more anxiety-tension symptoms checked on self-checklist				+56	+53	+41				+57								
176	slower irregularly warned reaction time	+06	+11	+06	+22	+06	+07	+17								(-05)	(-05)	+07	
270	faster arm-circling tempo	+05	(-08)					(-09)							(-08)	+10	+35	(-02)	+26
2a-f	lower motor rigidity	-03	-04	-11	-05	-03	-01	-17				(+13)	-17	-02	(+08)	-02	-06	(+04)	
120a,b	higher ratio of accuracy to speed			+11	+13	+04	(-04)	+00							+36	+08	+04	+04	+01
67a	more extremity of viewpoint	+08	+06					(-05)							+24		+18	+10	
269	slower leg-circling tempo	-04	-03		-29	-20	-03	-02							(+02)		(+18)		
199	lower numerical ability	-11	-20		-00	(+04)	-07	(+02)	(+03)							-10			
133	more criticalness of evaluation	+11													(-10)	+00	+46	+12	
271	higher total verbal fluency on topics	+02	+08					+00							+26	+20	(-01)		
458	less long-circuited: life goals less distant in time				(+16)	-03	-32	-15	(+06)										
359	more extreme annoyance responses															+78		+78	+04
327a,c	more logical inconsistencies in attitudes (on double presentation of same items, once inverted)	+51										(-07)	(-09)						+30
243	higher ratio of purposeful to non-purposeful annoyance	+26	+62												+17				
276	higher grade point average				+12									+40	+18				
464	lower average handwriting pressure				-05	-26	-30												
763	lower total fluency on own and other people's personal characteristics								-24			-25	-15						
473	lower total number of friends recalled on fluency test				-27			-15					-30						
246	more authority submission	(+05)	(+06)												-39		-36		
444	higher systolic blood pressure			(-07)	+10	(-07)	+30												
5	higher ratio of regularly to irregularly warned reaction time		+12	+26	(-01)	+09	(-15)	+08							+05	+01			
42	more body sway suggestibility				+40	(-02)	+02	(-10)										(-05)	+06
929b	lower fear erg (less desire for protection against atomic terror)				-29	-16	-09												
927a	higher sex erg (more desire to satisfy sexual needs)				+24	+07	+20												
927b	higher sex erg (more desire for romantic love)				+41	+09	+05												

U. I. 24: UNBOUND ANXIETY VS. GOOD ADJUSTMENT (page 2)

Master Index Number	Variable Title	RESEARCH																	
		C5	C6	Ros	R1	R2	R3	R10	HI	We	R4	R7-Ps	R7-No	BRO	C7	R12	R13	R15	R14
144	more acceptance of aphorisms	+10													+47	(-01)			
712	higher percentage of rhyme associations given											+45	+36						
481	higher susceptibility to embarrassment				+24						+38								
595	higher percentage of jokes considered funny											+54	+12						
274	higher verbal ability													+55	+13				
674	lower accuracy in checking numbers											-17	-34						
699	fewer attempts to identify real and nonsense stimuli											-31	-22						
767	greater number of social relative to non-social annoyances											-14	-33						
330	better ethical choices in story completion													+44		(-02)			
719	smaller number of association words intruded in recall of original words											-21	-25						
740	more slowing down of speed in word matching when simple copying is not allowed											+18	+16						
55	greater fluency of association to emotional relative to non-emotional stimulus words	+37														(-08)			
96a	more impairment of reading speed by frustrated preference		-30												(+01)				
764	lower ratio of criticism to approval of self and others											(+01)	-30						
64	female sex														(+03)				-36
718	higher ratio of number of words remembered correctly to total remembered (combined word recall-word association test)											+33	(-04)						
761	smaller proportion of animate objects seen in unstructured drawings											(+13)	-30						
--	higher anxiety: Taylor Manifest Anxiety Scale			+85															
211b	higher susceptibility to annoyance involving ego threats																+50		
113	less acceptance of reality principle	-43																	
1447	less capacity to mobilize response																		-45
147a	less self-confidence relative to opportunity							-39											
657	smaller number of dips subject can do									-36									
383	more reduction of criticism when anticipating public discussion of one's critical remarks																+33		
245	less exactness of time estimates														-32				
982	longer time required to form objects with putty																		+36
560	smaller total number of chins, vertical jumps, and dips subject can do (Larson's C-VJ-D index)									-31									
1366	less tendency to do unpleasant activities																	-31	
1450	more work done during uninterrupted than interrupted periods																		+31

U. I. 24: UNBOUND ANXIETY VS. GOOD ADJUSTMENT (page 3)

Master Index Number	Variable Title	RESEARCH																	
		C5	C6	Ros	R1	R2	R3	R10	HI	We	R4	R7-Ps	R7-No	BRO	C7	R12	R13	R15	R14
282	(greater) number of objects perceived in unstructured drawings	+03	+24	-27	-05		-07				+10	-11				+23	+06	-18	+01
71	(greater) number of erroneous reactions under complex instructions	+13	+07		-07	-16	+07	+21							-06	-01	+13	-01	
336	(larger) absolute number of threatening objects seen in unstructured drawings				+01	-20	+04								+22	+22			+00
455a	(greater) volume of saliva secreted in 30 seconds			-05	+10	-39	+27												
31	(more) fluctuation of attitudes	-06						+04							-36	-05	+04		+10
465	(more) decrement in coding performance with anxiety sound distraction				+18	+02	-26												
472	(higher) ratio of acquaintances to friends				+30	+08	-21												
475	(higher) action impetus					+35	-31												
682	(higher) total synesthesia											+16	-33						
684	(faster) aesthetic decision time											+22	-45						
736	(higher) proportion of items answered on test "Which Is Larger?"											+16	-22						
741	(more) obtrusion by immediately adjoining letters											+16	-38						
742	(greater) distance of obtrusion (i.e., from which an adjoining stimulus word is copied as response)											-21	-34						
67b	(greater) extremity of response on aphorisms														+24	-28			
35	(more) suggestibility to authority	-06	-15					-14	-03					+34	+00				
80	(more) PGR upward drift when relaxed than under shock				+16	-19	+05								-02				

* Study R7: In addition to the scores Q_3- and Q_4+ from the 16 P. F. Test the three variables marked by an asterisk have been used for estimating factor scores on U.I. 24.

U.I. 25: LESS IMAGINATIVE, TASK-ORIENTED REALISM VS. TENSE INFLEXIDIA

1. Prevalence

Factor U.I. 25 was identified in seven factor analytic researches at the adult level, and in four studies so far available at the child level. Two studies (R7, Wells) contribute extension results for the adult age range. Also included in Table 7.20 are the results that Eysenck (86) obtained for his "Psychoticism" factor which matches U.I. 25- (columns E2 in Table 7.20).

2. Questionnaire Correlates

From the presently available evidence (see Table 7.19) factor U.I. 25 appears to be rather specific to objective test performance. Of the primary questionnaire factors of the 16 P.F. Test, only O+ (high Timidity: insecure, anxious) and Q4+ (high Ergic Tension: tense, excitable) load on U.I. 25. According to Knapp's results (N1, N2) U.I. 25 does not correlate significantly with any of the Guilford-Martin and the MMPI scales; of the scales in the Guilford-Zimmerman Temperament Survey only T+ (Thoughtfulness) correlates significantly (+.25) with this factor.

Of the psychiatric anxiety ratings analyzed in study R1 only one yielded a "significant" loading on U.I. 25: the rating on "characterological anxiety" loaded +.17. Significant correlations have been obtained between this factor and four of the Kuder interest scores (138): low Scientific Interests ($r = -.21$), low Persuasive Interests ($r = -.29$), low Artistic Interests ($r = -.25$), and higher Musical Interests ($r = +.21$).

3. State Factor Matches

No match can be obtained for U.I. 25 among the state factors known at present. Factor U.I. 25 also could not be identified in the incremental R-technique study R3. From these negative findings we can conclude that U.I. 25 is largely, if not exclusively, a trait factor with little or no state variance.

4. Loadings on Second-Order Objective Test Factors

U.I. 25 loads on three second-order OT factors, F(T)I, F(T)IV, and F(T)VII. Its main loading is on factor F(T)I (Tied Socialization or Superego vs. Absence of Cultural Introjection), which is further characterized by U.I. 20+ (Comentive Superego), U.I. 28+ (Asthenia), U.I. 1- (low General Intelligence), U.I. 35+ (Stolparsomnia), and U.I. 32+ (Extraversion). On both F(T)V (Educated Self-Consciousness) and F(T)VII (Tension to Achieve, Controlled Drive Tension Level) U.I. 25 loads negatively (average loadings of -.17 and -.18, respectively).

5. Criterion Correlations

a) Clinical Criteria

In study R9-Ta (68) no significant difference has been found on this factor between normals and neurotics. In the analysis R10(I) (38) delinquents scored significantly lower on U.I. 25 than sociopathic neurotics, and both groups significantly lower than non-delinquent normals. U.I. 25 is the only other factor besides U.I. 16 which thus differentiates significantly between delinquents and neurotics.

The difference between psychotics and normals was insignificant in R7, however in the expected direction (psychotics scoring lower on U.I. 25 than normals).

b) School and Academic Achievement

Scholastic achievement (variable M.I. 276) does not load on U.I. 25. Also in study P1 (138) no relationship has been found between this factor and college achievement.

c) Military Criteria

In the research AF (69) on the prediction of pilot proficiency U.I. 25+ correlated significantly with good adjustment to flight training (Adjustment Group Rating; r = +.09) and with higher over-all training success (Pass-Fail criterion; r = +.12). However, in study N1 which is based on a relatively small sample of 48 Naval helicopter pilot trainees, Knapp (121) found a negative correlation of -.32 between U.I. 25+ and final flight grade. In N2 (122) this factor was uncorrelated with the Pass-Fail criterion in a naval submarine training course, but correlated significantly with the Class Standing criterion (+.14).

Disregarding the results of N_1, which are less reliable due to the small sample size, a positive relationship can be concluded between this factor and success in military pilot and submarine training.

6. Nature-Nurture and Age Trend Results

Factor U.I. 25 has not been measured in the genetic study (70) and the research on age development (29).

7. Descriptive Interpretation

The objective test loadings of U.I. 25, in the main, "cluster" around the following four distinct psychological attributes:

1. Less imaginative cognition

Several loadings indicate slow speed and low productivity in perceptual tasks which either involve an imaginative re-interpretation of ambiguous stimulus patterns or ask for sensory after-effects after a direct stimulation has already ceased. The extreme U.I. 25+ individual attempts only few items on a gestalt completion test (M.I. 7), and his responses are largely inaccurate (M.I. 146b and M.I. 146a); in unstructured drawings he perceives only few objects (M.I. 282), he reports fewer alternations (per unit time) on a test of reversible perspective (M.I. 8), and gives only few correct identifications after distorted acoustic presentations of real and nonsense words (M.I. 696, 698).

This cognitive-perceptual "syndrome" becomes more characteristic if one considers that U.I. 25+ otherwise loads positively on various speed and tempo variables and several accuracy measures, which will be discussed below. Apparently we are dealing in U.I. 25+ with a relative unimaginitiveness and a lack of phantasy which will only become apparent in comparatively unstructured tasks in which either the stimulus pattern itself is rather unorganized or the subject cannot base his responses on direct stimulation. This lack of phantasy (in the broader meaning of the word) or playful imagination seemed to us an important characteristic of a reality oriented personality -- a line of interpreting U.I. 25+ which is going to be further substantiated by the remaining variables loading this factor.

2. High accuracy and speed in well-structured tasks

In contrast to perceptual-cognitive tasks that ask for imagination or phantasy, U.I. 25+ correlates positively with good (i.e., fast and accurate) performance on well-structured physical or psychological tasks. This is evidenced by a series of loadings: The extreme U.I. 25+ individual obeys more strictly the rules on the CMS test (i.e., he crosses fewer slanting lines; M.I. 16a), is highly skilled on computational tasks (M.I. 199), is fast and accurate on various speeded tasks (speeded color naming: M.I. 356a; checking numbers: M.I. 674, 120b, c; rapid calculations: M.I. 240; letter cancellation: M.I. 1414; letter exercises: M.I. 1735; memory for figures: M.I. 689), shows fast ideomotor tempo (M.I. 6a, b, c) as well as fast physical tempo (M.I. 269, 270), and has a short reaction time in tests of simple reaction (M.I. 176).

U.I. 25 is certainly not associated with a general lack of accuracy in perceptual tasks (as one might otherwise infer from M.I. 7 and 146), since accuracy on tests of well-structured or "explicit" observation (M.I. 356a; 120b, c; 674; 1414) loads positively. Apparently the U.I. 25+ person is highly efficient in tasks which can be solved by using rules and knowledge learned previously (cf. M.I. 199: high computational skill; M.I. 275: high arithmetic reasoning ability) but is somewhat "helpless" whenever such acquired knowledge does not apply (see also M.I. 1736). This interpretation is well in line with the positive loadings of two measures of ideational rigidity on U.I. 25+ (M.I. 170, 198).[1] As indicated by the variables M.I. 715, 271, and 680 the efficiency of the U.I. 25+ person also covers the verbal domain, in the sense that he is highly fluent.

An additional insight into this personality dimension arises from the loading of M.I. 476: The person scoring high on U.I. 25+ is less internally distracted (shows less "mind-wandering") and thus performs well when he has to solve numerical problems without the use of paper and pencil.

3. Reality-directed attitudes (or "realism")

Attributes, such as less imagination, higher efficiency on structured rather than on unstructured tasks, and others, that have been pointed out above, suggest a generally more realistic personality pattern. And there are, in fact, several loadings that would explicitly suggest such an interpretation of U.I. 25+.

The extreme U.I. 25+ individual has good memory for proper names (M.I. 249), copies stimulus figures (M.I. 247a, b) and draws figures (M.I. 386) more appropriately (see also M.I. 389: gives more whole-person than part-of-person drawings); he can think of a whole variety of solutions when presented with novel situations (M.I. 808), tends to identify a previously learned stimulus figure (e.g., a rough drawing of a man) by the most realistic drawing out of a series of drawings (M.I. 691), and prefers the more familiar over the more strange (and unusual) in stories (M.I. 460). The realism interpretation also would account for this person's readiness to cheat (!) in reporting his success in a game where there is ample possibility of cheating (M.I. 1179), his unwillingness to answer prying questions (M.I. 1351), as well as his less eccentric ideal values (M.I. 1513).

4. Reduced emotional tensions

In our present understanding of U.I. 25 we are inclined to "explain" the U.I. 25+ person's "healthy realism" on the basis of a tendency towards more immediate discharge of emotions which will eventually result in a more successful emotional integration -- this at the cost of imaginative, creative productivity. We infer this type of adjustment from U.I. 25+ loading on such vari-

[1]Note that classical motor rigidity (M.I. 2), however, does not yield a consistent loading on U.I. 25.

ables as "few admissions of personal troubles and conflicts" (M.I. 1029) and "few extreme mood states reported" (M.I. 1421). The U.I. 25+ person apparently acts out his emotional tensions immediately (M.I. 43), does not repress his emotions -- and maybe achieves thus a better ergic integration. At least we do not find any signs of anxiety or aggression in the pattern of U.I. 25-, signs otherwise indicative of repressed (or at least unreduced and unintegrated) ergic tension. On the contrary, the U.I. 25+ individual is less impaired in his performance by shock (M.I. 162b), unusual and stressing situations (M.I. 510) nor by increasing difficulty of the task (M.I. 24d).

Of the Humor Factors, Factor 2 (M.I. 583) loads positively on U.I. 25, in the sense that a person scoring high on U.I. 25+ prefers good-natured playful humor over dry wit and critical humor; this result confirms the above mentioned ergic-integration hypothesis. In this context the positive loading of Q4 on U.I. 25 presumably indicates a higher general drive (or motivation) level, rather than unreduced or even repressed ergic tension.

8. Explanatory Theory: History and Final Hypotheses

The identification of this factor in our series of factor analytic studies is of considerable interest in the light of Eysenck's results on a general "psychoticism" factor (86), which matches factor U.I. 25 closely in reversed direction (i.e., U.I. 25-). It is true that the obverse match between Eysenck's psychoticism factor and this factor U.I. 25 cannot be fully assessed since there are only a few variables common to Eysenck's studies and the researches carried out in our own laboratory (see table 7.20) -- but at least 4 out of the 5 common variables are main markers of both Eysenck's psychoticism factor and of U.I. 25-. The criterion data so far available on U.I. 25, according to which normals and psychotics differ only insignificantly, would not necessarily imply this interpretation of U.I. 25 -- the fact, however, that Eysenck obtained his psychoticism factor from a criterion-rotation approach (which made his factor maximally correlated with the normal-psychotic criterion) strongly suggests, that this personality dimension might be one of the (presumably several!) personality source traits which lie at the heart of the normal-psychotic distinction. More research certainly is needed to decide this question. The non-significant difference between normals and psychotics in Scheier's study R7 may in part be due to his using only a small number of variables for estimating factor scores on U.I. 25 (since no factor analysis proper was carried out in R7); further-more it is quite possible, that this factor may "distinguish certain kinds of psychotics from normals, a discrimination which is blurred in...the mixed-type sample of psychotics" (150, p. 8) used in the R7 study.

The principal attributes of U.I. 25+, as inferred from the objective test loadings, are less imaginative cognition, high accuracy and speed in well-structured tasks, reality-directed attitudes, and reduced inner tension. According to our theory it is the latter two attributes which provide the key to an understanding of this factor. Our hypothesis is that a person with a high score on U.I. 25+ has acquired his "realism" from well-adjusted emotional development. He was ready to integrate his emotions and desires within the framework of norms and standards prescribed by society and thus is more relaxed. He did not accumulate this inner tension which typically lies at the very heart of (quite often productive) imagination. This person's view of life is a rather unphilosophical one, he is practical and shows a good sense of what he is expected to do.

This interpretation explains the difference in level of performance between less structured and well-structured tasks which we described above as a genuine characteristic of the U.I. 25+ personality. Little can be said about the specific dynamic mechanisms which produce this personality pattern. From Eysenck's findings on the "psychoticism" factor (86) a larger hereditary than environmental determination of U.I. 25 is very likely -- unfortunately, however, no direct nature-nurture results are available yet. We typically regarded this factor as less liable to environmental influences, as a trait relatively stable over time,[1] which could well be primarily hereditary in nature.

If the suggested explanatory hypothesis is reversed, so that it will fit the U.I. 25- pole, it resembles indeed several features well-known in the development of psychoses. The U.I. 25- person is more imaginative, performs well on unstructured tasks, poorly on structured tasks, is unrealistic and day-dreaming, easily distracted in his work by his own ideas, and more tense. These characteristics provide, at least in part, also an explanation for the low average score of delinquents on this factor. From the second-order factor loadings of U.I. 25 we saw that the degree to which an individual internalizes cultural standards is positively related with this factor. At its negative pole, U.I. 25 therefore implies less readiness to integrate personal motives into prescribed norms; if we add on the increased inner tension and the more unrealistic directions of attitudes observed in U.I. 25-, we obtain a personality pattern from which extra-social and even anti-social behavior is to be expected.

---

[1] U.I. 25 has no match among the state factors.

Table 7.19

U.I. 25: Less Imaginative, Task-Oriented Realism vs. Tense Inflexidia

Q-Factor	Factor Title	Factor Identification (Research, Sample Size, Age of Subjects, Factor Number in Study)				
		C5 500 Adult (11+)	Ros 70 Adult (10+)	R1 86 Adult (7+)	R2 86 Adult (3+)	R10 168 Adult (4-)
A	(higher) Cyclothymia	+15		-01	-01	+15
B	(higher) Intelligence				-08	
C	(higher) Ego Strength	+02	+07	-03	+05	+21
E	(higher) Dominance	-01			+25	-15
F	(higher) Surgency	+01	-10	+06	+19	-06
G	(higher) Super Ego Strength	-05			+06	+05
H	(higher) Parmia	-06		-02	+19	-09
I	(higher) Premsia	-02		-04	-19	+04
L	(higher) Protension	+08			+22	-17
M	(higher) Alaxia	-04	-06	+01	-14	-19
N	(higher) Shrewdness	+09			+05	-04
*O	higher Timidity (insecure, anxious)	(-01)	+06	+47	(-03)	(-08)
Q1	(higher) Radicalism	+08			+08	+01
Q2	(higher) Self-Sufficiency	+04			+17	+08
Q3	(higher) Self Sentiment Control	+09			-07	+14
*Q4	higher Ergic Tension (tense, excitable)	(-04)	+20	+26	+10	(-05)

U. I. 25: LESS IMAGINATIVE, TASK-ORIENTED REALISM VS. TENSE INFLEXIDIA (page 1)

Master Index Number	Variable Title	Factor Identification (Research, Sample Size, Age of Subjects, Factor Number in Study)														
		E2	C3	C5	Ros	R1	R2	R10	E-D1	We	R7-Ps	R7-No	C7	R12	R13	R15
		105	100	500	70	86	86	168	139	80	48	57	184	80	164	197
		Adult	Adult	Adult	Adult	Adult	Adult	Adult	Adult	Adult	Adult	Adult	9-12	4-5	6-9	7-10
		(1+)	(16-)	(11+)	(10+)	(7+)	(3+)	(4-)	(14-)	--	--	--	(12+)	(4+)	(13-)	(21+)
199	higher computational skill	+41		+35		+19	+58	+26			**	**	+29	+02		+16
7	slower speed of perceptual Gestalt completion		-58	-32	-44			-13			**	**	-36	(+03)	-02	-02
6a,b,c	faster ideomotor speed	+41	+14*	+03*	+27*	(-02)	+61	+26						+84	+16	(-02)
146b	lower percentage correct on perceptual Gestalt completion		-34	-21				-21	-34				-15	-00	+01	
270	faster tempo of arm-shoulder motion			+16				+27					+31	+03	+02	(-12)
247a,b	less expansiveness of copied design	-61											-15	-02	-32	-04
8	lower frequency of fluctuation in alternating perspective	-29	-16	-18					(+09)		**	**	-04		-18	
72	more slowing of reaction time under complex instructions							+10					+05	-02	+34	+15
273	lower proportion fluency on self			-00	-17			-05	-01				-01	-27	-18	-13
176	faster irregularly warned reaction time		-17	(+07)	-01	-09	-04	-04						(+10)	-33	-04
282	fewer objects perceived in unstructured drawings			-01	-22	-53		(+10)	(+01)					-10	-02	-09
269	faster leg-circling tempo			+21		(-07)	+01	+25	(-04)				+19		+07	
263	less variability of simple reaction times												-12	(+01)	-38	-13
271	higher total verbal fluency on topics			+06				+19	+25				+19	+32	(-03)	
336	larger absolute number of threatening objects seen in unstructured drawings					(-31)	+27						+12	+03		
24d	lower ratio of initial (slow) to final (fast) performance -- CMS			-06				-05					-03	-13	-31	(+10)
206	greater accuracy on Gottschaldt figures			(-12)					+16					+21	(-08)	+17
146a	lower absolute accuracy on perceptual Gestalt completion				-69	-49			-39		**	**			(+01)	(+09)
43	higher mean percentage PGR deflection to threatening stimuli		+20			+06	+36						(-10)			
715	greater frequency of associations							+42			+06	+33				
120b,c	higher ratio of accuracy to speed in checking numbers								+31		+16	+36				
194	more shifting of attitudes away from those of neurotics			+01				+22						+17		
198	fewer hidden words found in anagrams (higher ideational rigidity)			-02	-30								-03			
16a	fewer slanting lines crossed -- CMS		(+06)		(+04)	-42	(+05)	-15					-05			
691	much regression (towards the "real", intended object) in figure recognition										+35	+39				
356a	more correct responses on speeded color naming test													+81		+02
476	better ability to do numerical problems in one's head (less mind-wandering)					-09	-46									
162b	less impairment of cancellation performance by noise distraction		-34										-23			
674	higher accuracy in checking numbers										+31	+23				
696	fewer real word stimuli identified correctly										-36	-17				
288	faster speed of evaluative judgment			+02					+50							
758	larger absolute vertical deviation ("drift") in myokinesis test										+32	+20				
65	more logical consistency of attitudes		+28								+08	-08	+18			
171	fewer hidden pictures seen		-35	-23	-30								-02		-04	
316	higher ratio of fluency on own to other people's personal characteristics					+18	+32		+00							

U. I. 25: LESS IMAGINATIVE, TASK-ORIENTED REALISM VS. TENSE INFLEXIDIA (page 2)

Master Index Number	Variable Title	RESEARCH														
		E2	C3	C5	Ros	R1	R2	R10	E-D1	We	R7-Ps	R7-No	C7	R12	R13	R15
692	more distortion in figure recognition										+33	+16				
583	more preference for good-natured, playful humor than dry wit (higher humor factor 2)										+29	+18				
321	fewer restrained reading preferences								-38						-08	
689	more figures recognized correctly										+29	+15				
698	lower total number of word stimuli (real and nonsense) identified correctly										-25	-20				
486	smaller length and girth of muscles						-28			-14						
487	smaller length and girth of bones						-30			-12						
320	shorter estimate of time taken working on mirror drawing	-33											-13			
680	larger number of newly devised words used										+08	+30				
510	higher articulatory efficiency (speaking and reading) under delayed feedback conditions					+06	+30									
249	better memory for proper names			+18									+22			
690	more simplification in figure recognition										+35	+02				
1735	higher total correct in letter exercises								+48							
1029	fewer admissions of trouble and conflict							-41								
1414	higher accuracy on letter cancellation															+41
389	greater tendency to draw whole rather than part of human figures														+40	
1107	less hesitance (faster speed) on shuffle-board							+40								
460	greater preference for familiar than strange in written material						(-03)	+38								
386	less expansiveness in human figure drawings														-35	
240	faster speed on rapid calculations			+35												
4	faster average reaction time												-35			
1179	more cheating in reporting success of risks taken							+35								
110	lower anteversion/retroversion ratio		-33						-03							
1736	more initial difficulty in re-adaptation in letter exercises								+32							
1351	less readiness to answer prying questions							-32								
808	more solutions presented in novel situations							+31								
275	higher arithmetic reasoning ability										**	**	+30			
170	fewer hidden objects seen correctly (higher ideational rigidity)				-30						**	**				
125a	lower ratio of personal to institutional values							-30								
1513	less cultural eccentricity of ideal values							-30								
1421	fewer extreme mood states (highly elated or depressed) reported															-30
51	(higher) index of carefulness in observation			-03		+28	-13	+11						+24		-30
2a-f	(higher) motor rigidity		+03	-08	-01	-01	+02	+08	+13		+07	-10	+06	+11	+06	+09
143	(higher) total score -- CMS			-01	-01			-08					-02	-15	+19	+29
211a	(more) susceptibility to annoyance			+08	+15	-07							-01	+06	-20	-01
466	(greater) average amplitude of hand tremor				+27	-11	+24	-02								

U. I. 25: LESS IMAGINATIVE, TASK-ORIENTED REALISM VS. TENSE INFLEXIDIA (page 3)

Master Index Number	Variable Title	RESEARCH														
		E2	C3	C5	Ros	R1	R2	R10	E-D1	We	R7-Ps	R7-No	C7	R12	R13	R15
927b	(higher) sex erg (desire for romantic love)					-33	+34									
42	(higher) body sway suggestibility		-13			+01	-08	+24								-22
30	(more) criticism of self relative to criticism of others		-21	+08			+02		+48					+06	-07	-03
34	(more) immaturity of opinion		-16	+00									+29	-09		
116a,b	(higher) severity of judgment		-03	-08	+15	+10	-11	+12					-01			
152	(more) tendency to agree		-17	+06	+28	+00	+00	-03	+46				-15		+02	

* Actually M.I. 177a,b: faster motor speed.

** These six variables have been used in study R7 for computing estimated factor scores on U.I. 25.

CHAPTER 8

PSYCHOLOGICAL MEANING OF STABLE SOURCE TRAITS U.I. 26 - U.I. 36

In this chapter the psychometric description and psychological interpretation of the personality source traits in objective tests is continued. Several of the eleven factors discussed in the present chapter are either presented here for the first time or have already been reported in earlier publications (29, 68), but their psychological nature has been less clear previous to the more recent researches. The same mode of presentation is kept in this chapter as in the preceding one.

U.I. 26: NARCISTIC SELF vs. LOW SELF COMMAND

1. Prevalence

The factor U.I. 26 has been identified in eight factor analytic studies with adults after 1954, and four factor analytic studies with children. In addition results from an earlier series of studies: Brogden (12), Crutcher (78), Rethlingshafer (143), Ryans (147), and Thornton (159) employing a more limited domain of variables, appear as mean values in column (BRO) of Table 8.2. An extension analysis by Wells (166) examined correlations between a large number of physical fitness variables and U.I. 26.

2. Questionnaire Correlates

Correlations between U.I. 26 and the 16 P.F. are found in five studies (C5, R1, R2, R3, and R10). Apart from M(-): PRAXERNIA, (conventional, practical), and O(-): CONFIDENCE, (confident, unshakable) there are no consistent correlates. This is surprising due to our expectancy that U.I. 26(+) would correlate highly with C(+): HIGH EGO STRENGTH, G(+): HIGH SUPER EGO STRENGTH, and Q3: SELF-SENTIMENT CONTROL, but there is no supportive evidence for this as yet.

Correlations between U.I. 26 and the Guilford-Martin scales are reported by Knapp (123) using Naval Submarine School candidates as subjects. Only one significant correlation was found--that with Ag(+): Agreeableness ($r = +.14$). Correlations between U.I. 26 and the Guilford-Zimmerman and MMPI scales have also been reported (123) using helicopter pilots as subjects, and in no case was a significant correlation found.

No relationship has been found between self-report measures of anxiety and U.I. 26 (R1, R2, R3, N1). However it should be noted that M(+) and O (-) of the 16 P.F. fall into the second-order 16 P.F. factor of Anxiety, and that in later research some slight association between U.I. 26(+) and lack of anxiety may emerge.

Correlations with the Kuder Preference Record (138) show U.I. 26 to be significantly correlated with Computational Interests ($r = +.21$) and Lack of Persuasive Interests ($r = -.22$).

In general it seems that only confidence and conventionality, out of the overt signs of controlled self-sentiment development, have appeared in the cross-media comparisons examined up to the present time. Information from other sources, coupled with inspection of the salient loading variables and their theoretical implications suggest that questionnaire and self-report correlations of this factor should soon emerge in a more comprehensive fashion--but probably evincing a quite complex relationship.

3. State Factor Matches

P.U.I. 4: Effort Stress vs. Repose has been regarded as the state equivalent of U.I. 26. Evidence here is from a series of five P-technique and one (R-3) incremental R-technique study (47, 58, 107, 170, 64, 99). P.U.I. 4 is regarded as a physiological stress reaction separable from that of anxiety. It involves "high physiological stress with high emotional control and conscientious, high-striving performance, rather than with high emotionality and impulsiveness" (68, p. 165).

The response is regarded as being increased by extra stress due to the need for higher control. Included among the important marking variables are high concentration in memorizing, lower rigidity, fewer circles in CMS, and increase in 17-OH corticosteroids in urine.

4. Loadings on Second-Order Objective Test Factors

U.I. 26 appears in only one second-order objective test factor, F(T)VI(+): Narcistic Development vs. Environmental Contact and Investment, which it dominates (57).

5. Criterion Correlations

a) Clinical Criteria

Prediction of clinical criteria has in general shown U.I. 26 to differentiate between normals and neurotics. Specifically, in the R9-Ta and R10 (I) studies, U.I. 26(+) was significantly higher in normals than neurotics, but in R9-Ta (a relatively small group) the difference is in the other direction, but not significantly so. Also in R10 (I), criminals were found to be significantly lower on U.I. 26(+) than normals, and about the same as neurotics. With regard to psychiatric evaluations of anxiety (R1) no relationship has been found with this factor.

b) School and Academic Achievement

Results from the BRO composite of studies, R1, and C7 all show a definite positive relationship between achievement (as measured by grade point average) and U.I. 26(+). A more recent comparison of factor scores and college achievement (P1) not only confirms this but also indicates that U.I. 26(+) may be associated in particular with over-achievement.

c) Military Criteria

Evidence on the relationship between U.I. 26 and military success is to be found in three studies (AF) (N1) (N2) and no significant correlations have been reported with course success. However Knapp (124) reports a significant positive correlation between U.I. 26 and social acceptibility (r = +.218) (derived from peer ratings) and a negative correlation between U.I. 26 and number of sick calls (r = -.273), the subjects in both instances being helicopter pilots. A further significant positive correlation was with FAR.

6. Nature-Nurture and Age-Trend Results

Present evidence (70) suggests that environment is between two and four times as important as heredity in the determination of U.I. 26. Age trend results (29) indicate a steady rise through childhood to the age of 11 years and then an accelerated rise to the age of 15 years.

7. Descriptive Interpretation

Sophisticated Competence

A pervasive efficiency and sophistication of response appears throughout the test performance of a person highly endowed with U.I. 26(+). Examples are better immediate memory power for words (MI. 167b), better immediate memory for attitudes checked (MI. 167a), higher ability to state logical assumptions (MI. 36), higher proportion correct in gestalt closure (MI. 146b), better articulatory efficiency (MI. 509), faster ideomotor speed with adult subjects (MI. 6a), higher dynamic momentum (MI. 28), and more good taste in color blending (MI. 119). Such measures suggest a relationship with general ability and more particularly with verbal ability (MI. 274), and there is some evidence in support of the latter. The inconsistent loadings on computational skill (MI. 199), the higher sense of poetical appropriateness (MI. 118), and the suggestion of a higher ratio of verbal to numerical ability (MI. 99) add confirmation to the view that linguistic skills and accomplishments are deeply involved with the outward expression of U.I. 26(+).

Persistence in the Face of Difficulty

A second persistent and distinct characteristic of this factor is the capacity to mobilize reserves when faced with an increasingly difficult problem. This appears to amount to a 'shifting of gears' in performance to that required for competent completion of a task. Direct confirmatory evidence comes from higher ratio of final to initial performance on a variety of tasks (MI. 24a, c, d), and fewer errors in reaction time under complex instructions (MI. 71); while at the child level there is less decrease in persistence over time (MI. 346). High competence in articulation under impeded (delayed feed back) conditions (MI. 510) also fits this interpretation, as does the evidence for little effect of frustration and threat upon a wide variety of performances--less effect of frustrated preference on computing speed (MI. 96b), and higher ratio of performance under discomfort to normal conditions (MI. 162b). More persistence of an old response in an unrewarding situation (MI. 475) further emphasizes the determined nature of U.I. 26(+) behavior. To what extent the loadings on lower perceptual-motor rigidity (MI. 2a, e, f) particularly with children, belong to this group of measures rather than to the general competency and flexibility of U.I. 26(+) is not clear.

Higher Fluency on Self Relative to Other Topics

U.I. 26(+) is associated with a particular pattern among the various fluency measures, namely higher proportion of fluency on self (MI. 273), lower total fluency on non-self topics (MI. 271), and lower proportion of fluency on dreams (MI. 283). That this is a highly controlled and non-complacent self-concern is implied by the higher ratio of impersonal to personal annoyances (MI. 242), lack of any clear association with the amount of self-reference seen in events (MI. 111) and a rather low estimate of personal capabilities.

Lower Self-Evaluation

The characteristic of lower self-evaluation appears in lower estimation of personal prowess (MI. 104), lower amount considered possible in a given time for self (MI. 192), lower estimated breadth of skill and accomplishment (MI. 147b) and higher ratio of self-criticism to criticism of others (MI. 30). Such loadings may well indicate an avoidance of over-estimation rather than under-estimation, and this interpretation would be more in line with the present argument. Certainly there is no suggestion of pessimism as such being associated with U.I. 26.

Sensitivity to Indirect Threat

That U.I. 26(+) is related to a sensitivity to threatening or emotional stimuli of an indirect nature rather than to immediate physical threat is suggested by the higher proportion of threatening objects seen in unstructured drawings (MI. 105), higher ratio of frightening to non-frightening material time estimates (MI. 461), higher ratio of emotional to non-emotional recall (MI. 25a), and perhaps higher emotionality of comment (MI. 205). Missing completely is evidence of any undue reaction to direct threat or pain and there is some evidence to the contrary in less reluctance to enter fear situation (MI. 471) and less increase in tempo under threat (MI. 158).

Relaxed Control

Several measures indicate that the overt behavior of U.I. 26(+) is in general calm, relaxed and well under control. Such measures are lower fidgetometer frequency (MI. 83), lower oscillation (MI. 13a), and lower ideomotor tempo (MI. 9). A connection here with physiological correlates is suggested for there is lower systolic blood pressure (MI. 444) and less upward drift of GSR when relaxed after shock (MI. 80).

Certain Variables Not Falling in the Above Categories

Finally certain measures need to be mentioned which, though showing relevance to U.I. 26, do not fit completely into the present argument. First there is a consistent preference for form over color in sorting (MI. 39). Admittedly this is consonant with the general control and somewhat inhibited aspects of U.I. 26(+), but preference for form over color in picture preference (MI. 227a, b) is absent, and further the sensitivity to emotional stimuli discussed above might suggest preference for color--color being regarded by some writers as more 'emotional'. Second, there is higher performance under approval relative to disapproval (MI. 161a, b) which, with higher ratio of performance under disapproval to control conditions in cancellation (MI. 260), implies that the U.I. 26(+) person may be affected by both praise and punishment, and mainly by the former. The evidence needs further confirmation, but it does imply that the standards of performance which appeared to be self-imposed may be determined to no little extent by immediate external pressures.

8. Explanatory Theory: History and Final Hypotheses

A considerable number of early studies, reviewed by Cattell in 1955 (25) contain many of the characteristics and variables that presently make up U.I. 26. These studies (12, 78, 143, 147, 159) usually contained variables from a rather limited domain and extracted factors variously named Persistence, Self-Control, Willingness to Withstand Discomfort, Dynamic Momentum, Cosation, and Endurance. The similarity between average loadings on these factors and U.I. 26 is quite marked, as can be observed in column BR of Table 8.2.

Apart from confirmation of the general self-control and endurance of difficulty, more recent research has added certain new characteristics, described in the previous section, of linguistic skill, general efficiency, higher fluency on self, conservative estimates of own competence, sensitivity to associative emotional stimuli, and smoothness of performance. Armed also with information on cross-media comparisons, criteria correlations, and higher-order and state factor relationships, we are now in a position to make definite statements concerning U.I. 26, even at the cost of repetition.

(a) The characteristics of the objective tests loading U.I. 26 present a varied but highly consistent pattern which is meaningful on the descriptive level at even a superficial inspection, and which integrates well with early research.

(b) This factor has few correlates among questionnaire measures (apart from modest associations with confidence, conventionality, and agreeableness) which is in itself a surprising finding.

(c) U.I. 26(-) appears to accompany neurosis and criminality.

(d) U.I. 26(+) has little relationship to success in military training schools, but is a substantial predictor of school and college achievement.

(e) U.I. 26 is predominantly environmentally determined and increases up to the age of 15 years.

(f) It has a state factor and appears importantly in one second-order objective test factor.

Certain hypotheses may now be entertained as to the nature and development of U.I. 26.

HYPOTHESIS 1. U.I. 26 (+) as Persistence or Determination

This is the old concept of U.I. 26 and seizes upon one of its central characteristics as a form of explanation. Undoubtedly the U.I. 26(+) person is persistent, and such behavior could be due to early up-bringing. Criterion data fits well, except for the lack of correlation with military success. However, to uphold this hypothesis also involves discarding or ignoring many other characteristics--such as conservative self-estimation--outlined above. Unless further research casts doubt upon the relevance of these other characteristics it would appear wise to discard this hypothesis.

HYPOTHESIS 2. U.I. 26(+) as the Result of a Family Environment with High Educational and Socio-Economic Level.

The environmental determination of U.I. 26 predisposes towards a social learning explanation, and Hypothesis 2 suggests that a favored environment automatically leads toward behavior indicative of this factor. The general sophistication, competence, high academic achievement, and perhaps ability to withstand difficulty (at least in the test situation) are in agreement, but the presence of a state factor and the pronounced relationship to neurosis would be unexpected and, as in Hypothesis 1, many other characteristics indicated by salient marker variables have to be ignored. If one amends the family or general past environment in order to include specific forms of child development and upbringing then the implications become much wider than a demographic hypothesis, and lead directly to Hypothesis 3.

HYPOTHESIS 3. U.I. 26(+) as Narcistic Self-Sentiment Development

Hypothesis 3 combines parts of the previous two hypotheses and binds them together in terms of development of the self-sentiment. In brief we suggest that certain environmental conditions combine together to shape development of the self-sentiment in a manner leading to the behavioral characteristics, such as persistence and competence, discussed above. Central to this development is a gradual setting up of self-standards--ways of behaving relative to the 'ideal' self (29). It is proposed that this process springs directly from certain environmental conditions which lead to, or encourage, the setting up of a rigorous set of standards in terms of personal efficiency, and a rather conservative and self-contained approach to the more complex areas of emotional adjustment and social interaction. The behavior of U.I. 26(+) is aimed at being as close as possible to that of the ideal self, and when discrepancies occur then either the actual behavior is modified (e.g., intensified in the realm of problem-solving), or the ideal self is modified, or the individual departs from the potentially conflicting situation. The elaborate structure of U.I. 26(+) is seen as being built up by such mechanisms as sublimation, regression, and possibly repression. The whole development appears to continue at an unconscious level until adulthood, when one would anticipate a reserve of behaviors that, for the individual, are optimally appropriate for most situations.

These standards clearly involve efficient and sustained performance in any situation even loosely containing competence. In opinions and attitudes there may be both an unwillingness to go 'out on a limb' and an unwillingness to appear as having no opinions. The extremity of viewpoint measures show neither positive nor negative relationships to this factor, and there is a tendency to agree with platitudinous statements. The lower estimate of personal capabilities is particularly interesting as it suggests that past experience has given reward to absence of over-confidence--in the present view this would constitute little discrepancy between ideal-self behavior and actual behavior. It seems likely that an over-estimate would be much more disturbing than a corresponding degree of under-estimation. The sensitivity to emotional associative stimuli, and not to direct shock or threat, indirectly reinforces the view that where disturbance appears in U.I. 26(+) it is likely to be a reaction to threat to the ideal self (i.e., danger of a discrepancy between ideal self and actual behavior), and not to any direct physical stimuli.

Granting that such self-investment rules of behavior can be set up, two rather crucial problems still remain: (1) What determines whether standards are set up at all? (2) Why do the standards discussed above appear in this particular form? Clearly the answers to both problems are highly inter-related, and will be found mainly in the individual's past history and development. Unfortunately there is as yet no early history data which could be used to show linkage with U.I. 26. Findings from developmental psychology (tentative though these may be) would perhaps suggest a delicate balance of non-permissiveness and parental affection, in addition to a home atmosphere emphasizing a striving for high educational and occupation accomplishments.

The absence of expected questionnaire correlates is still puzzling, though it may be that the facade presented by U.I. 26(+) acts as a shield against self-report measures. Certainly confidence (in the sense of being unshakable) and conventionality appear as reasonable correlates, and the indications of some degree of social success from the Guilford-Martin scale and peer-ratings (123) (124) would be expected. In general criterion correlations support this hypothesis, again with the possible exception of military course success. The presence of U.I. 26(+) in the second-order objective test factor of Narcistic Development, in the company of U.I. 27 and U.I. 34 is at first surprising for here there is the suggestion of a "false ego development, a moving out of contact with reality" (57). However the rigid structure of behavior and value systems associated with U.I. 26 has, in order to maintain maximal internal consistency, to deviate from the environment in certain respects. Thus U.I. 26 through either modifying the concept of the ideal self, or removal from a potentially threatening situation, is decreasing environmental contact and investment. Even in terms of changing levels of response, behavior such as over-persistence (as in MI. 475) has about it an unhealthy air of too much self-absorption. Life is not as smooth and orderly as would be required for U.I. 26(+) to keep in close contact with reality. The trio of U.I. 26(+), U.I. 27(+), and U.I. 34(+) suggests that we may have here a partial answer to the second problem above, in that these factors may be different modes of expression of the developing self-sentiment, each with its own specific developmental history.

Table 8.1
U.I. 26: Narcistic Self-Sentiment (Development) vs. Low Self Command

Q-Factor	Factor Title	Factor Identification (Research, Sample Size, Age of Subjects, Factor Number in Study)				
		C5 500 Adult (8+)	R1 86 Adult (3+)	R2 86 Adult (14+)	R3 86 Adult (11+)	R10 168 Adult (22+)
A	(higher) Cyclothymia	-04	+19	-15	+05	+06
B	(higher) Intelligence			+07		
C	(higher) Ego Strength	+13	-03	+06	-07	-12
E	(higher) Dominance	-12		-08		+02
F	(higher) Surgency	00	-06	-04	+06	-07
G	(higher) Super Ego Strength	+07		-02		+10
H	(higher) Parmia	+01	+05	-02	-16	00
I	(higher) Premsia	-01	+01	+01	+03	+12
L	(higher) Protension	-13		-18		+10
*M	higher Praxernia (conventional, practical)	-16	(+02)	-02	-17	-14
N	(higher) Shrewdness	-09		00		+06
*O	higher Confidence (confident, unshakable)	-15	(+11)	-03	-35	(+09)
Q1	(higher) Radicalism	-03		+04		-07
Q2	(higher) Self-Sufficiency	-04		-04		-08
Q3	(higher) Self Sentiment Control	+14		-09		-05
Q4	(higher) Ergic Tension	-15	+04	+07	-02	+15

U. I. 26: NARCISTIC SELF VS. LOW SELF COMMAND (page 1)

Master Index Number	Variable Title	Factor Identification (Research, Sample Size, Age of Subjects, Factor Number in Study)													
		C3	C4	C5	C6	R1	R2	R3	R10	We	BRO	C7	R12	R13	R15
		100	100	500	250	86	86	86	168	77	100	184	80	164	197
		Adult	Adult	Adult	Adult	Adult	Adult	Adult	Adult	Adult	11-12	9-12	4-5	6-9	7-10
		(14-)	(4+)	(8+)	(14+)	(3+)	(14+)	(11+)	(22+)	--	(3+)	(11+)	(19+)	(4-)	(18-)
273	higher proportion of fluency on self			+51	+62				+22			+03	+03	+28	+20
2a	lower motor rigidity	+00	-04	(+09)	-14	-00	-18	-21	(+05)		-33	-25	-34		+00
39	more preference for form over color in sorting	-03	-23	-01	-21	-11			-29			-01		-08	(+16)
167a	better immediate memory for attitudes checked	(-04)	(-22)	+30	+13				+30			+32		+17	
167b	better immediate memory power for words					+56	+17	+15							
71	fewer errors in reaction time under complex instructions			(+03)	-12	-31	-26	-05	-19			-21	(+03)	-35	-04
24d	higher ratio of final to initial performance -- CMS			(-02)							+53	+09	+50	+19	+20
83	lower fidgetometer frequency	-13	-36	-03		-50	(+05)	+01	-08			-07			
105	higher proportion of threatening objects perceived in unstructured drawings	+22	(-14)	+19	+20				(-03)				+28	+05	+08
24a,c	higher ratio of final to initial performance: backward writing and reading	+35	+24		+24				+21			+04			
205	more emotionality of comment			+21	+03							+32	(-01)		
36	higher ability to state logical assumptions	+32	+17	+10					+11						
162b	higher ratio of cancellation performance under discomfort relative to normal conditions	+16	+12		+07							+31			
13a	lower oscillation	-25	-27						(+12)		-52	-05			
276	higher achievement (grade point average)					+34					+37	+17			
146b	higher proportion correct in perceptual closure	(-05)	+15	+17	+04				(-02)			+08	+41		
283	lower proportion of fluency on dreams			-47	-56				(+03)						
271	lower total fluency on topics			-24	-06				-02			+00	-05	-20	
2e,f	lower rigidity (reverse color naming)												-55	-12	-29
192	lower amount considered possible in given time for self	+21	+27						+07						
6b,c	slower ideomotor speed (color naming)												-31	-11	-18
461	higher ratio of frightening to non-frightening material time estimates					+10	+08	+30							
161a,b	higher performance under approval relative to disapproval	(-08)	+34									+43	+07		
119	more good taste in color blending	+11	+17	+16											
153	higher total number of decisions made -- CMS	(-03)	+13	(-02)					+27			+32			
118	higher sense of poetical appropriateness	+00	+19	+22											
444	lower systolic blood pressure					-01	-14	-26							
21	fewer questionable reading preferences	-19	-01	(+01)		-14						+00	-05	-16	(+06)
6a	faster ideomotor speed					+29	+05	+01	+15						
77	higher salivary ph (more alkalinity)					+24	+12	+01							
34	more immaturity of opinion	+16		+10					+11		+15	+07	(-01)		
80	less PGR upward drift when relaxed after shock					-15	-05	(+11)				-24			
120a-g	higher ratio of accuracy to speed	+00	+05			+36	+14	+13	+03			+09	(-04)	+00	+02

U. I. 26: NARCISTIC SELF VS. LOW SELF COMMAND (page 2)

Master Index Number	Variable Title	RESEARCH													
		C3	C4	C5	C6	R1	R2	R3	R10	We	BRO	C7	R12	R13	R15
113	more break down of reality principle	-26	-23	-17					(+11)					-03	
25a	higher ratio of emotional to non-emotional recall	+28	+40												
242	higher ratio of impersonal to personal annoyances			+14								+52			
147b	lower estimated breadth of skill and accomplishment	-26	(+02)						-27			(+01)			
475	more persistence of old response in unrewarding situation						+16	+23							
65	lower logical consistency of attitudes	-28							-29						
509	better articulatory efficiency, normal reading					+27	+42								
80	less upward drift of GSR when relaxed after shock					-15	-06	(+11)				-24			
286	higher ratio of reaction time to auditory relative to visual stimuli			+17										+18	
219	more willingness to admit common frailties			+16	+20	+05	(-02)	(-01)	+13			+14	+02	+02	(-11)
104	lower estimation of personal prowess	-22	-16												
152	more tendency to agree	+21	+24	(-06)	+00	+00	(-12)	(-03)	(-07)			+05		+26	
110	more future relative to past associations	+16	+18												
158	less increase of tempo under threat (myokinesis)	-33	-08												
46a	more impairment of pencil maze performance by distraction		+34						+06						
111	more self-reference seen in events	+07	+23	(-18)	+03							+29			
472	higher ratio of acquaintances to friends					+44	+15	(-06)	+06						
510	better articulatory efficiency, delayed feedback					(-01)	+58								
30	higher ratio of self-criticism to criticism of others	+06	+02	+03	+08	(-08)	+15	(-14)					+00	+30	+05
471	less reluctance to enter fear situation					-37	-04	(+02)							
9	slower ideomotor tempo												-31	-04	
476	less mind-wandering vs. ability to do numerical problems in one's head					-31	-03	(+02)							
28	higher dynamic momentum	(-07)	(-04)								+69	+11			
96b	less effect of frustrated preference on computing speed	+06	+71												
144	more agreement with platitudinous thinking (aphorisms)	(-03)		+15								(-10)	+18		
2h	lower rigidity (reverse color naming, proportion incorrect)												-43		
1421	higher elation-depression: extremes														+46
1245	higher elation-depression: mood swings														+44
355	higher caution in Gestalt completion												+42		
474	larger number of acquaintances recalled					+41									
274	higher verbal ability											+37			
260	higher ratio of cancellation performance under disapproval relative to control											+33			
102	lower tolerance for obvious remarks	-33													
346	less decrease in persistence over time												+30		
212	(greater) belief in attainability of goals			+16								-24	-07		+11
108	(more) self-confidence regarding untried performance	+01	-18	-16	+05	+04	+05	-19	-19			+05		+01	
67a,b	(more) extremity of viewpoint	-05	-12	+16	+01				-00			+07		-18	+11
72	(more) slowing of reaction time by complex instructions				+16	-30			-05			-04	+15	-25	+30

U. I. 26: NARCISTIC SELF VS. LOW SELF COMMAND (page 3)

Master Index Number	Variable Title	RESEARCH													
		C3	C4	C5	C6	R1	R2	R3	R10	We	BRO	C7	R12	R13	R15
43	(higher) magnitude of mean PGR deflection to threatening stimuli	-05	+03			-19	+23	-13				+00			
193a	(more) shifting of attitudes towards those of successful people	+07	-39						+27						
35	(more) suggestibility to authority	-04	-26	+10	+01				+24			+14			
42	(more) body sway suggestibility	+02	+24			-15	-08	-12	-10						-26
25b	(better) recall of words from emotionally interesting than emotionally dull stories	+33	-19												
51	(higher) index of carefulness			+06	+07	-02	+15	-20	+07				+05		-10
443	(greater) absolute level of GSR					+13	-21	-16							
33	(larger) size of myokinetic movements	+08				+14	+40	-21	-06						
456	(greater) slowing of reaction time due to shock					-22	+39	-02							
15	(more) use of circles -- CMS	-07		-09	-02	+07	+00	-36	-11			-06	+03		-03
211a	(more) susceptibility to annoyances			+14	-10	+06						+36	-11	-01	-07
99	(higher) ratio of verbal to numerical ability	-12	+09									+32			
40	(more) false reactions in reaction time			+01	+04							-11	+03	-42	+04
171	(more) hidden objects seen in pictures								-22					+15	
168a	(faster) speed of social judgment												-30		+02
199	(higher) numerical ability			-10	-01	+20	-00	+05	+33			+27	-28		-26
16a	(more) slanting lines crossed in CMS	-03	+13	-05	+08	-41	+10	+03				+03			
458	(more) long term life goals					+33	-06	-02	+02						
445	(larger) pupil diameter at stress					+31	-07	-06							
269	(faster) leg-circling tempo			-08	-05	-31	-06	-01	+03			+11		+07	
133	(higher) criticalness of evaluation	-57	+04	-03								+13		+10	-05
38b	(higher) ratio of consonant to dissonant recall (not corrected for tendency to agree)	-20	+16										-13		
62	(faster) reading speed for emotional relative to non-emotional material	+22	-20	-01								-11			
116a	(higher) severity of judgment	-24	-10			-03	+06	+10	+24			+17			
176	(slower) irregularly warned reaction time	+20	-07		+00	+06	-26	-04					-20	+17	+09

U.I. 27: DISCOURAGED, SKEPTICAL APATHY VS. UNGRUDGING INVOLVEMENT

1. Prevalence

Factor U.I. 27 has been found in five independent factor analyses, four of which used adult subjects and one children (study Cn). Despite the fact that the main markers of U.I. 27 have been included in all researches from study C3 onwards, this factor could only be identified in so few a number of studies, and in none of the other five researches on the personality structure in children, that have been carried out in this laboratory. This indicates that U.I. 27 apparently is a less easily identifiable, more subtle personality pattern.

2. Questionnaire Correlates

Evidence on the relationship between U.I. 27 and primary questionnaire factors, as measured in the 16 P.F. Test, comes from two studies: R2 and R10 (see Table 8.3). On these results U.I. 27 correlates with none of the 16 questionnaire factors to any considerable degree; there is an indication of slightly higher A+ (Cyclothymia: warm, sociable) and O- (Confidence: confident, unshakable) in U.I. 27+, but even these correlations are low.

In study N2 (N = 315 Navy Submarine School candidates) Knapp (123) found significant correlations between two of the Guilford-Martin scales and this factor; C (Cycloid Disposition)[1] correlated -.13 with U.I. 27, Ag (Agreeableness) +.11. In the smaller sample available in N1 (N = 81 naval helicopter pilot trainees) Knapp (123) obtained a significant correlation of +.21 between the MMPI scale Sc (Schizophrenia) and U.I. 27; the correlations with the scales of the Guilford-Zimmerman Temperament Survey were all insignificant.

Using data of the R10 study, Pawlik (138) found a significant correlation of +.24 between U.I. 27 and the Kuder scale Computational Interest.

Summarizing the available questionnaire results on this factor, we conclude that U.I. 27 is mainly an objective test personality dimension, with very little questionnaire-related variance.

---

[1] Guilford-Martin's factor C is more a measure of emotional stability than cycloid disposition per se. Therefore the positive loading of the 16 P.F. Test factor A and the negative correlation with the Guilford-Martin scale C are not necessarily contradictory.

Since U.I. 27 was not identified in R1 no results are available on the loading of psychiatric anxiety ratings on this factor.

3. State Factor Matches

U.I. 27 has not been identified in the incremental R-technique study R3, nor is there a clear match between this factor and any of the state factors obtained from direct P-technique analyses. The factors P.U.I. 3 (General Diurnal Fatigue States) and P.U.I. 5- (low Adrenergic or Sympathetic Autonomic Response), which do not match any other trait factor, are in content rather similar to U.I. 27 -- in terms of analytical factor matching criteria, however, neither of the two can be identified as a state correlate of U.I. 27. Our conclusion is that if U.I. 27 does include state variance, its corresponding state factor has not been found as yet.

4. Loadings on Second-Order Objective Test Factors

Factor U.I. 27 contributes to two second-order OT factors. It loads positively (average loading: +.30) on factor F(T) VI (Narcistic Development vs. Environmental Contact and Investment), together with U.I. 26+ (Narcistic Self-Will) and U.I. 34+ (Inconautia). In addition, U.I. 27 loads negatively (average loading: -.19) on F(T)III (Temperamental Ardor vs. Temperamental Apathy) the main salients of which are U.I. 21+ (Exuberance), U.I. 20+ (Comentive Superego), U.I. 1- (low General Intelligence), U.I. 19+ (Promethean Will), and U.I. 32+ (Extraversion).

5. Criterion Correlations

a) Clinical Criteria

In neither of the two studies R9-Ta (68) and R10(I) (38) significant criterion relationships have been found.

b) School and Academic Achievement

The only positive finding comes from Pawlik's study P1 on personality correlates of college achievement (138); collegiate high-achievers scored lower on U.I. 27+ than collegiate low-achievers. Variable M.I. 276 (scholastic achievement) has not been included in any of the studies in which U.I. 27 emerged.

c) Military Criteria

According to the results of N1 (121) U.I. 27 is not related to success in pilot training. However, the factor has not been measured in study AF (69) so that no cross-validation of this negative finding is available. In N2 (122) U.I. 27 correlated significantly (+.12) with the Class Standing criterion of success in naval submarine training.

6. Nature-Nurture and Age Trend Results

No results are available as yet since U.I. 27 has not been measured in the genetic (70) and age trend study (29).

7. Descriptive Interpretation

The objective test pattern of factor U.I. 27 (see Table 8.4) contains as a principal characteristic of this factor, several signs of low-self-sentiment. A person scoring high on U.I. 27+ is less confident in his skills on untried performances (M.I. 108), is more critical about himself than about other people (M.I. 30), and believes various future events will effect him unfavorably rather than favorably (M.I. 112). This low self-sentiment occurs, however, in a setting of increased self-concern -- this person endorses more personal than institutional values (M.I. 125a). What here appears to be a discrepancy could, on the other hand, well be the result of the long-term dynamic process. Being overly concerned about himself, this individual responded to the various restrictions, forced upon him by his social environment, by a gradual disregard of social demands and -- in the process of dealing with the resulting frustrations -- increasingly lower self-esteem might have developed.

In the testing situation, the U.I. 27+ person appears as little achievement motivated, or at least little ego-involved. He shows much oscillation of performance quality over time (M.I. 13a), his aspirations exceed his actual performance only by a small amount (M.I. 101a), and in a novel task he learns slowly (M.I. 24c); paying special attention to a given task does not improve his observation and memory over the score obtained from incidental observation and memory (M.I. 22c), and he is less ambitious to invent many solutions for various novel situations (M.I. 808).

It is at first difficult to separate this syndrome from sheer low capability; the fact, however, that this person is otherwise careful (M.I. 51) and makes only fewer erroneous reactions when working under complex instruction (M.I. 71) seems to point out that we are obviously not dealing with incapability _per se_, but rather with low motivation.

This pattern of a general "apathy" explains also the U.I. 27+ person's dryness with regard to jokes (M.I. 157) as well as his high body sway suggestibility (M.I. 42), which presumably is mainly another sign of indifference towards the testing situation as a whole and of less readiness to accept external control.

In study R2 also three of the known motivation factors (29) loaded on U.I. 27; according to these results this factor is characterized by low fear erg (M.I. 929a), high sex erg (M.I. 927a), and low self-sentiment (M.I. 933a) at its positive pole. Considering also the 16 P.F. Test correlates of U.I. 27+ (A+, O-), Cattell and Scheier (68) inferred from these loadings that U.I. 27+ implies a higher disregard of various social demands (lower fear erg, higher sex erg, more cyclothyme and emotionally unstable); this interpretation would agree with the described objective test pattern of apathy and low self-sentiment in U.I. 27+.

Important for a theoretical explanation of this factor is also the positive correlation between U.I. 27+ and two variables indicating scepticism (M.I. 867, 178). Despite the lack of any paranoic tendencies (M.I. 91); the U.I. 27+ person is sceptical as to the factors determining success in higher occupational groups (M.I. 867), and agrees less with the majority opinion (M.I. 178). The implication of these results will be discussed in the following paragraph.

8. Explanatory Theory: History and Final Hypotheses

Elsewhere (29) Cattell has briefly mentioned three hypotheses in connection with this factor: U.I. 27+ may express a state dimension of either increased fatigue or increased depression, or a trait factor of apathy and discouragement. It is for two reasons that we prefer the last over the former two hypotheses. First of all, as discussed above under 3), our present results do not indicate a one-to-one match between U.I. 27 and any of the known P-technique factors, nor was this factor identified in the incremental R-technique study R3. Secondly, Connor (72) found in his study a correlation of -.39 between this factor and the average sociometric rating the subject is given by his peers -- a result which certainly does not fit any interpretation of U.I. 27 in terms of a state factor. Thus, by excluding the fatigue and depression hypotheses we shall consider more closely Cattell's third hypothesis: U.I. 27+ being a trait factor of apathy or discouragement.

A personality dimension, resembling factor U.I. 27 in psychological content, has not been found in factor analytic researches outside the authors' laboratory. The fact that up to the present this factor has been identified in no more than five analyses points out the subtlety of this source trait -- which cannot be expected to emerge from analyses more restricted in terms of both the number of factors extracted and the breadth of variable population sampled.

The objective test evidence on U.I. 27 can be summarized in the following attributes (phrased for the U.I. 27+ pole): less regard of social demands, low self-sentiment despite much self-concern, little ego-involvement and low motivation in the testing situation, and more scepticism; high emotional instability is added to these characteristics from the questionnaire correlations of U.I. 27.

Our theory on factor U.I. 27 rests to a considerable degree on its loadings on the two second-order OT factors F(T)VI, Narcistic Development, and F(T)III, Temperamental Apathy. Notably from the fact that U.I. 27 has not been identified in any of the studies on the personality structure in children carried out in the authors' laboratory, we concluded that this factor, as defined in adults, may represent a kind of end stage of an adjustive development -- a stage, which typically is not reached to its full extent before early adulthood. If our principal hypothesis about factor interpretation in general is correct, namely, that at each hierarchical level a factor represents a cause common to the variates (of the next lower stage) which load this factor, then U.I. 27 can be understood as a personality pattern growing from double causation: low Temperamental Ardor (F(T)III-) or high emotional apathy, and high Narcism (F(T)VI+). The above mentioned adjustive development, of which U.I. 27+ is the result, can then be briefly described in the following hypothesis about the factor.

U.I. 27 is primarily characterized by a narcistic direction of emotions and needs. Indications of this, such as putting personal values before institutional values, are still recognizable even in the adult loading pattern. By its very nature, primary narcism is a premature need state and undergoes a further development during later childhood. In the first-order OT personality dimensions U.I. 26, U.I. 27, and U.I. 34 we apparently have met three distinct adjustment "formulae" to primary narcism. The adjustment mechanism shown in factor U.I. 27 is based on a prevailing temperamental apathy,[1] and it is the latter which obviously determined the direction of adjustment: neglect of external controls and standards.

Thus U.I. 27 does not represent sheer "apathy" in the usual sense, but an interesting "blend" of apathy with frustrated (or discouraged) narcism. The latter is clearly demonstrated by the several signs of low self-sentiment in Table 8.4, the low ego-involvement, and the little regard for social demands. It is the latter characteristic which U.I. 27 apparently shares with U.I. 34.

---

[1]Note that this second-order factor F(T)III is primarily constitutional, i.e., determined by heredity (57).

Table 8.3

U.I. 27: Discouraged, Sceptical Apathy vs. Ungrudging Involvement

Q-Factor	Factor Title	Factor Identification (Research, Sample Size, Age of Subjects, Factor Number in Study)	
		R2 86 Adult (7+)	R10 168 Adult (5-)
*A	higher Cyclothymia (warm, sociable)	+25	+07
B	(higher) Intelligence	-14	
C	(higher) Ego Strength	-02	-01
E	(higher) Dominance	-02	+05
F	(higher) Surgency	+11	+09
G	(higher) Super Ego Strength	-12	+04
H	(higher) Parmia	+07	-09
I	(higher) Premsia	+16	-11
L	(higher) Protension	+05	+04
M	(higher) Alaxia	-03	+05
N	(higher) Shrewdness	00	-08
*O	higher Confidence (confident, unshakable)	-21	(+04)
Q1	(higher) Radicalism	-09	+04
Q2	(higher) Self-Sufficiency	-04	+14
Q3	(higher) Self Sentiment Control	-12	-03
Q4	(higher) Ergic Tension	-07	+10

U. I. 27: DISCOURAGED, SCEPTICAL APATHY VS. UNGRUDGING INVOLVEMENT (page 1)

Master Index Number	Variable Title	Factor Identification (Research, Sample Size, Age of Subjects, Factor Number in Study)				
		C3 100 Adult (17+)	C4 100 Adult (18+)	R2 86 Adult (7+)	R10 168 Adult (5-)	Cn 229 11-13 (4+)
42	more body sway suggestibility	+51	+66	+45	+20	+16
13a	more oscillation of performance	+27	+01		+22	+22
122	greater static ataxia	+55	+35			+25
194	more shifting of attitudes away from those of neurotics	+28	+12		+24	
125a	higher ratio of personal to institutional values	+10	+25		+16	
116	less severity of judgment	-05	-22	-14	(+07)	
108	less confident assumption of skill in untried performances	(+06)	-15	-16	-10	
112	more unfavorable than favorable self-reference in events	(+02)	-00		-49	
145	higher responsiveness of aspiration level to actual performance (coding)	+51	+14			
101a	less excess of aspiration level over performance level (coding)	-22	-29			
305	higher PGR deflection to mental than physical stimuli	-03	-39			
24c	larger ratio of final to initial novel performance (backward reading) (less gain from practice)	-21	-14			
157	less overt laughter at jokes	-07	-29			
118	more sense of poetic appropriateness	+14	+18			
91	less autistic suspicion	-21	-12			
71	fewer erroneous reactions under complex mental sets			-25	-09	
26	greater number of riddles solved	+15	+12			
30	higher ratio of self-criticism to criticism of others	+17	+12			
51	higher index of carefulness in observation			+25	+02	
8	higher frequency of fluctuation on alternating perspective	+31	(-07)			
929a	lower fear erg (less fear of accidents and diseases)			-49		
927a	higher sex erg (more desire to satisfy sexual needs)			+47		
927b	higher sex erg (more desire for romantic love)			+35		
933a	lower self-sentiment erg (less desire for good control over mental processes)			-34		
865	greater preference for unusual names				+32	
867	more suspicion towards higher occupational groups				+30	
22c	higher ratio of incidental to purposeful observation and memory				+26	
808	fewer solutions presented in novel situations				-25	
178	less agreement with majority				-24	
153	(faster) speed of decision -- CMS	+16	+15		-18	
193a	(more) shifting of attitudes towards those of successful people	+47	-20		-10	

U.I. 28: DEPENDENT, NEGATIVISTIC ASTHENIA VS. UNDISCIPLINED SELFASSUREDNESS

1. Prevalence

Factor U.I. 28 has been identified in eight factor analytic studies at the adult age level (including the incremental R-technique study R3) and in four studies carried out at the child level. Our present results, however, indicate that this personality trait is more strongly represented among adults than children; whereas in study C7 (the subjects being children between 9 and 11 years) the loading pattern still matches closely the one found for adults, the identification of factor U.I. 28 in the remaining three child studies is less consolidated. As for the researches R12 and R15, the match should be considered as tentative only.

2. Questionnaire Correlates

In five of the eight studies in which factor U.I. 28 was identified, the 16 P.F. Test (or parts of it) has been included in the analysis (see Table 8.5). The following primary questionnaire factors loaded on U.I. 28: H+ (high Parmia: adventurous, "thick-skinned"), L+ (high Protension: suspecting, jealous), M+ (high Autia: bohemian, unconcerned), Q1- (high Conservativism: conservative, accepting), and Q4+ (high Ergic Tension: tense, excitable).[1]

In N2 (123) Knapp reported significant correlations between U.I. 28+ and the Guilford-Martin scales C+ (higher Cycloid Disposition; r = +.12), O- lack of Objectivity; r = -.12), Ag- (lack of Agreeableness; r = -.11), Co- (lack of Cooperativeness; r = -.12), and A- (lack of Ascendance; r = -.11). No results are available on the correlations of U.I. 28 with the Guilford-Zimmerman and the MMPI scales because the factor has not been measured in research N1 (123). Of the Kuder scales the score Musical Interests correlates significantly (-.28) with this factor (138).

The loadings of psychiatric anxiety ratings on U.I. 28 are not known as this factor was not found in R1.

---

[1] Both Q1 and Q4,, however, each contain one out-of-hyperplane loading with reversed sign.

3. State Factor Matches

The state factor P.U.I. 10 (Less Rigid Superego vs. Increased Superego Demands) matches U.I. 28-. P.U.I. 10 was found in one P-technique analysis (170) and in the incremental R-technique study R3 in which it was identified jointly with U.I. 28-. This result indicates that U.I. 28 shows significant function fluctuation over time, and that its variance is partly state variance.

4. Loadings on Second-Order Objective Test Factors

Factor U.I. 28 loads on only one second-order OT factor: F(T)I, Tied Socialization or Superego vs. Absence of Cultural Introjection (average loading: +.26). The principal primary factor salients of F(T)I, besides U.I. 28, are U.I. 20+ (Comentive Superego), U.I. 1- (low General Intelligence), U.I. 19- (Subduedness), U.I. 25+ (Realism), and U.I. 32+ (Extraversion).

5. Criterion Correlates

a) Clinical Criteria

In study R9-Ta (68) neurotics scored significantly higher on U.I. 28 than normals, and in R10(I) (38) both delinquents and sociopathic neurotics (drug addicts, alcoholics) scored significantly lower on U.I. 28 than non-delinquent normals. In R7 (comparison between normals and psychotics) the factor was not investigated.

b) School and Academic Achievement

Pawlik (138) found no difference between collegiate high- and low-achievers on U.I. 28, under-achievers, however, scored significantly higher on U.I. 28 than over-achievers. Variable M.I. 276 (scholastic achievement) did not load the factor in C7.

c) Military Criteria

According to the Cattell and Schiff study AF (69) U.I. 28 is not related to pilot proficiency; no cross-check on this negative finding is available from Knapp's research N1 (121) since the factor has not been measured in that study. In study N2 (122) Knapp found a low but significant correlation ($r = +.12$) between U.I. 28 and the Class-Standing criterion of success in naval submarine training.

6. Nature-Nurture and Age Trend Results

U.I. 28 is more environmentally determined than constitutional (70), and the preponderance of environmental over constitutional variance is larger between families than within families. This result indicates that differences in extra-familial environment, given a certain home background, are less crucial in the determination of this factor than differences between different home atmospheres and families.

Over the age range from 9 to 15 years the mean score on U.I. 28 decreases by about 3/8 of the within-year standard deviation (29). This result is of special interest, since U.I. 28 is the only other factor besides U.I. 21 that decreases over this age period.

7. Descriptive Interpretation

From the loading pattern of U.I. 28+, as set out in Table 8.6, two main attributes of this factor can be inferred: low psycho-physical momentum, and insecurity and lack of self-confidence. Both of these attributes express, to a varying degree, personality characteristics which generally are interpreted as signs of asthenia.

1. Lower Psycho-Physical Momentum

In the perception of the extreme U.I. 28+ person time elapses quicker (M.I. 97), especially when working (M.I. 123); consequently he expects of himself (M.I. 192) as well as of others (M.I. 295) to get less done in a given time. This person is only quick on perceptual tasks which rely more upon imagination (M.I. 7, 8) but even then he is rather rigid (M.I. 170, 171); otherwise his speed of performance is slow (M.I. 335, 339, 379), and he makes more errors of response when working under complex instructions (M.I. 71).

Probably due to the slow speed, however, this person is still relatively more accurate than quick (M.I. 120a, b, c); in view of the total pattern of the factor this result seems to suggest personal insecurity and cautiousness rather than a determined striving for accuracy.

Despite a strong physique (M.I. 486: higher length and girth of bones) and a higher physical strength (M.I. 489), the extreme U.I. 28+ individual actually shows a low autonomic activation level (M.I. 443: lower absolute PGR resistance level; M.I. 83: lower fidgetometer frequency). However, his performance is little impaired by shock (M.I. 164) or disapproval (M.I. 343) which may indicate a higher stress and frustration tolerance.

2. Insecurity and Lack of Self-Confidence

There are several test variables in the loading pattern of factor U.I. 28 which indicate insecurity and reduced self-confidence at the positive pole of this factor. A person scoring high on this factor is highly submissive towards authority (M.I. 246), is less self-confident of his skills in untried performances (M.I. 108), socially less secure (M.I. 107: less knowledge of social etiquette), and is easily influenced in his attitudes when presented with statements of how other groups of people responded to the same opinionnaire items (M.I. 35: much shift of attitude toward the attitude endorsed by successful people; M.I. 194: much shift of attitude away from the attitude endorsed by neurotics).

Although the U.I. 28+ person, on the one hand, develops an acquiescent tendency to agree with statements presented to him (M.I. 152), he is on the other hand, more critical in his judgments on social topics (M.I. 116a, b) and often more extreme in his viewpoints (M.I. 67a). We shall consider this puzzling "conflict" later in the theoretical discussion of this factor; for the purpose of a descriptive interpretation, the latter two loadings might be understood as a symptom of negativism, possibly developed as a form of reaction formation in response to the self-experienced insecurity or its causes.

Our reasons in choosing the term "asthenia" as the principal descriptive label for this factor will be obvious to the reader from the above reported results. In summarizing our descriptive interpretation of U.I. 28 we conclude: At its positive pole this factor is characterized by a low "psycho-physical momentum", self-experienced insecurity, lack of self-confidence, and negativism; this characterization is further augmented by such attributes as good resistance to stress and frustration, instability of views and opinions, and low autonomic activation level.

8. Explanatory Theory: History and Final Hypotheses

There can be no doubt that the psychological characteristics of U.I. 28 are internally conflicting. In the objective test medium we found the puzzling discrepancy that U.I. 28+ implies both asthenic qualities and negativism, the latter expressed in a tendency towards extreme responses and higher criticalness. The same type of "conflict" becomes also evident from the questionnaire correlates of U.I. 28. In the 16 P.F. Test the discrepancy is between Q1- (Conservativism) on the one hand, and H+ (Parmia) and M+ (Autia) on the other hand; in the correlations with the Guilford-Martin scales this discrepancy lies between A- (lack of Ascendence) as contrasted with Ag- (lack of Agreeableness), O- (higher Subjectivity), and Co- (lack of Cooperativeness).

If we want to put this conflict or internal discrepancy by way of a simple "formula" we might say: U.I. 28+ is characterized by attributes of both dependent asthenia and negativistic subjectivity. Knowing that this factor is largely environmentally determined, especially by differences between different home atmospheres, we hypothesized that this psychological discrepancy in U.I. 28+ could well be a result of a true conflict in the individual's development. From the content of the factor such a conflict is most likely to have occurred in the socialization process. The close relation of U.I. 28 to aspects of the socialization process is further indicated from its positive loading on F(T)I, a second-order OT factor of internalized cultural standards (vs. absence of cultural introjection). These considerations result in the following theory on factor U.I. 28.

The psychological characteristics of U.I. 28+ originated in a conflict between severe, strict parental socialization practices and the growing individual's own need for self-realization. The extreme U.I. 28+ person has originally fully accepted the demands put on him, the criticisms and requests which he met in a more "authoritarian" environment. We regard the asthenic attributes, which after all account for the major part of the objective test loadings, as a developmental result of the former, and consider the negativistic subjectivity in U.I. 28+ as a kind of denial mechanism or reaction formation in response to the self-perceived insecurity. The observed decline of U.I. 28 from 9 to 15 years could be well understood from this hypothesis: as the individual more and more grows out of the parental family, the influence that the latter can exert upon him will also decrease, and the mean score on U.I. 28+ would be expected to decline.

In a recent publication (40), Cattell presented a more complete development of this theory than can be presented here. In future research on this factor special attention should be given to variables describing an individual's early home environment in order to allow for an empirical test of these hypotheses. However tentative this theory may appear at present, it does not only provide an explanation of the objective test and questionnaire loadings of U.I. 28 but also explains the obtained criterion relationships -- the significantly higher mean score of neurotics, the significantly lower mean score of both delinquents and sociopaths, and the negative correlation with collegiate over-achievement. A true ego-superego conflict, originating in severe standards, is frequently observed with neurotics, whereas the absence of cultural introjection (together with "asthenic" personality characteristics and high self-esteem) at the U.I. 28- pole explain the low score of delinquents and sociopaths on this factor. The high score on U.I. 28 found in college under-achievers (as compared with over-achievers) can be understood from the asthenic insecurity and lack of self-confidence (discouragement) in U.I. 28+ which will make a student perform poorer in college than predicted from his actual ability.

Table 8.5
U.I. 28: Dependent, Negativistic Asthenia vs. Undisciplined Selfassuredness

Q-Factor	Factor Title	Factor Identification (Research, Sample Size, Age of Subjects, Factor Number in Study)				
		C5 500 Adult (5+)	R2 86 Adult (4+)	R3 86 Adult (1-)	R10 168 Adult (14-)	HI 137 Adult (3+)
A	(higher) Cyclothymia	-03	+06	-05	+02	
B	(higher) Intelligence		-19			
C	(higher) Ego Strength	+02	-17	-13	+01	-02
E	(higher) Dominance	-01	+03		-03	
F	(higher) Surgency	+17	-02	-19	+06	
G	(higher) Super Ego Strength	-20	+12		-14	00
*H	higher Parmia (adventurous)	+25	+01	+06	+04	
I	(higher) Premsia	+13	-01	+03	+11	
*L	higher Protension (suspecting, jealous)	+15	+11		+03	+21
*M	higher Autia (bohemian, unconcerned)	(-05)	+21	(-04)	+15	
N	(higher Shrewdness	+16	+04		-09	
O	(higher) Timidity	-23	+01	+07	+06	-03
*Q1	higher Conservativism (conservative, accepting)	-15	-21		-01	(+23)
Q2	(higher) Self-Sufficiency	+01	-20		-11	+12
Q3	(higher) Self Sentiment Control	+25	-03		-21	+09
*Q4	higher Ergic Tension (tense excitable)	(-17)	+26	+24	+14	+01

U. I. 28: DEPENDENT, NEGATIVISTIC ASTHENIA VS. UNDISCIPLINED SELFASSUREDNESS (page 1)

Master Index Number	Variable Title	Factor Identification (Research, Sample Size, Age of Subjects, Factor Number in Study)											
		C3 100 Adult (12-)	C4 100 Adult (11-)	C5 500 Adult (5+)	C6 250 Adult (11+)	R2 86 Adult (4+)	R3 86 Adult (1-)	R10 168 Adult (14-)	HI 137 Adult (3+)	C7 184 9-12 (8+)	R12 80 4-5 (18+)	R13 164 6-9 (9+)	R15 197 7-10 (13+)
152	more tendency to agree	+25	+35	+28	+33	+53	+28	(-01)	+13	(-03)		+01	
120a-c	higher ratio of accuracy to speed	+05	+05			+27	+01	(-01)		+17	+20	+39	+09
7	faster speed of perceptual Gestalt completion	(-01)	+19	+27	+20			+08		+09		+04	+02
67a	more extremity of viewpoint	(-01)	(-14)	+30	+33			+16		+04	+17	+13	+13
123	longer time estimated for working relative to idle periods	+05			+52			+61		+64	+08		
192	less considered possible in given time for self	-46	-27					-38	-04	-35		-18	
116a	higher critical severity of judgment	(-08)	+46	+22		+20	+31	(-01)		(-09)		+27	
38a	higher ratio of consonant to dissonant opinion recall	+18	(-02)	+28	+20				+01		+03		
35	more suggestibility to authority	+27	+34	+29	(-09)			(-02)	+57	+20			
108	less confident assumption of skill in untried performance	-31	-09	(+03)	(+15)	-25	-11	(+03)		-08		-08	
71	greater number of errors of response under complex instructions			(-12)	(-01)	+30	+19	(-08)		+24	+04	+12	+00
193a	more shifting of attitudes towards those of successful people	(-04)	+10	+32	(-01)			(-09)	+05	+18			
194	more shifting of attitudes towards those of neurotics	+16	(-04)	+38				(-04)	+23	(-04)			
211a	more susceptible to annoyance			+28	+12					+10		+04	+01
16a	more slanting lines crossed -- CMS	+01	+02	(-06)	(-03)	+33	+29	(-04)		+06			
97	greater length of passing time estimates	+00	+51					+59		+76			
191	less considered possible in given time for others	-16	-17					-15	-19	-41			
280	lower accuracy of time interval estimates			-18	-11			-52					-10
246	more authority submission			-27	-26					-00		-04	
212	fewer distant goals considered attainable			+06						+35	+06		+11
15	more circles used -- CMS	+11		(-09)	+08	+06	+02	+13		+01	+30*		+02
21	fewer questionable reading preferences	+02	+20	+01					(-30)	(-14)	+01	+10	+07
171	more total number of hidden objects seen (lower ideational rigidity)	+57	+07	+17									
763	more fluency on people's personal characteristics			+33	+23				+20				
111	less self-reference in events	(+04)	-37	-02	(+10)					-09			
357	higher total distance covered (more venturesomeness) in mirror drawing performance										(-26)	+45	+67
339	slower speed of mirror drawing performance										(-16)	+46	+68
316	higher fluency on own than other people's personal characteristics					(-06)	+30					+32	
170	more hidden objects correctly seen (lower ideational rigidity)	+36	(-08)							+16			
125a	lower ratio of personal to institutional values	-33	(+18)					-05					
443	lower absolute level of skin resistance (PGR)					-15	-57						
107	less knowledge of social etiquette	-22	-27										
101a,b	more excess aspiration over performance (coding and mazes)	-13	-25							-07	-04	-15	+00
113	more acceptance of reality principle	+24	(-15)	+59				+10				(-10)	

U. I. 28: DEPENDENT, NEGATIVISTIC ASTHENIA VS. UNDISCIPLINED SELFASSUREDNESS (page 2)

Master Index Number	Variable Title	RESEARCH											
		C3	C4	C5	C6	R2	R3	R10	HI	C7	R12	R13	R15
176	faster irregularly warned reaction time	(+13)	+00		-02	+00	-04				-03	-16	-28
219	less willingness to admit common frailties			-08	-26	-07	-20	(+01)	-05	-16	(+04)	(+02)	(+01)
945c	better consonant recall										+43		+13
155	larger range of successful flicker fusion frequency measures	(-02)	+38										
379	slower speed (and less accuracy) of pencil maze performance											(+08)	-35
462	greater preference for stronger than weaker smells					(+03)	-33						
929b	lower fear erg (less desire for protection against atomic horror)					-32	(+03)						
164	less impairment of word completion performance by shock	-31	(+08)										
1160	less suspicion towards occupations							-39					
886	smaller size of drawings of trees and people							-38					
489	greater total physical strength					+38							
491	larger area under curve of pulse wave (ECG)					+38							
275	lower total correct on arithmetic reasoning										-34		
335	slower reaction time under complex instructions												+34
486	higher length and girth of muscles					+34							
375	greater accuracy in circle cancellation											+33	
343a	less reduction of speed of form board performance by disapproval										-32		
8	(higher) frequency of fluctuation on alternating perspective	-32	-03	+11						+03		+04	
83	(higher) fidgetometer frequency					+10	-36						
136	(higher) color/form ratio in sorting	-00		-30	+14								
36	(higher) ability to state logical assumptions	+23	-21	-11									
927a	(higher) sex erg (desire to satisfy sexual needs)					+22	-26						
96a	(less) impairment of reading speed by frustrated preference	+40			-13					-14			
30	(more) criticism of self relative to others	-20	+22	+01	-03	+11	-22				-21	+25	+00
39	(higher) ratio of color to form in sorting	+07	+12	-30	+14			+04		+06		-09	-04
51	(higher) index of carefulness			+06	-17	+11	-20	-01			+05		+17
72	(higher) ratio of complex to simple reaction time				+17			-11		+05	-13	+10	-19
271	(higher) total verbal fluency on topics			+15	+21			-01		+08	-05	-04	

* In Study R12 this variable was scored as 'more circles <u>and</u> more slanting lines'.

U.I. 29: WHOLE-HEARTED RESPONSIVENESS VS. DEFENSIVE COMPLACENCY

1. Prevalence

U.I. 29 has been found in seven factor analyses with adults and in three with children. The matching of factors across studies is fairly good, but does not have the clarity to be seen in most of the earlier factors in the U.I. series.

2. Questionnaire Correlates

16 P.F. Questionnaire correlates of U.I. 29 are available from studies C5 and R2. For no questionnaire factor is the evidence strong enough for confidence in suggesting a relationship. However the best correlates so far are G(+): High Superego Strength (conscientious, persistent) and I(-): Harria (tough, realistic), but their implications for U.I. 29 are not clear.

Knapp's study of the Guilford-Martin questionnaire factors (123) on Navy enlisted men presents significant correlations between U.I. 29(+) and G(+): Agreeableness (r = +.18), A(+): Ascendance (r = +.15), C(-): Lack of Cycloid Disposition (r = -.12), D(-): Lack of Depression (r = -.11), T(+): Thinking Introversion (r = +.11), and S(-): Lack of Social Introversion (r = -.11).

There appears at present to be little common ground between the 16 P.F. and Guilford-Martin correlates of U.I. 29, and neither battery gives much information of aid in discussing this factor. However it must be borne in mind that there is evidence from only three sources at the present moment and that further replication will probably clarify the position.

There is little information on the association between U.I. 29 and questionnaire measures of anxiety. Relevant data is only available from R2, using an anxiety-tension checklist (MI. 454), and the correlation was zero.

3. State Factor Matches

No state factor match has been established for U.I. 29, though a similarity has been noticed (68) to P.U.I. 10: Guilt or Superego Activity. This state factor however, has been matched with U.I. 28. A further possible state factor match with U.I. 29 is P.U.I. 3: Diurnal Fatigue.

4. Loadings on Second-Order Objective Test Factors

U.I. 29 appears in only one second-order objective test factor, F(T)IV(-): Low Educated Self-Consciousness vs. High Educated Self-Consciousness (57).

5. Criterion Correlations

a) Clinical Criteria

Clinical evidence shows U.I. 29 to be an important discriminator between neurotic and non-neurotic groups. In both R9-Ta, and R10(I) normals were significantly ($p < .001$) higher than neurotics on U.I. 29(+). The small R9-Tb group comparison, however, showed a non-significant difference in the other direction. No significant correlations have been reported between U.I. 29 and psychiatrists' ratings of anxiety (R1).

b) School and Academic Achievement

There are indications of a negative correlation between scholastic achievement and U.I.29(+) but the evidence so far is based upon 11 year old children only (C7), and is therefore not conclusive.

c) Military Criteria

In AF low (non-significant) negative correlations were obtained between this factor and criteria of pilot training success. Knapp (122) reports positive correlations between U.I. 29 and (a) Pass-Drop criteria and (b) Class-Standing Criteria for enlisted Submarine School Candidates. Both correlations were significant, but the second ceased to be significant when intelligence as measured by the GCT was partialed out. No further evidence for military success associations is presently available.

6. Nature-Nurture and Age Trend Results

Of all the U.I. factors on which nature-nurture ratios have been computed, U.I. 29 shows the highest environmental determination, thus making it extremely difficult to uphold any constitutional theory as to the development of this factor (70). Factor scores on U.I. 29 show a slow rise from the age of 9 years to that of 13 years. From 13 years to 15 years the scores remain level (29).

7. Descriptive Interpretation

The speed and co-operativeness of responses of U.I. 29 is well illustrated by high scores on CMS variables such as total score (MI. 143), and larger percentage of correct decisions (MI. 98a). With rigidity measures there is again an apparent rising to the occasion, and a correspondingly lower score on rigidity (MI. 2a). Faster ideomotor tempo (MI. 9) and tempo of tapping (MI. 268) are present, as is faster speed on such measures as letter-comparison (MI. 307). Important too are better immediate memory scores (MI. 167a) and lower oscillation (MI. 13), suggesting a steady concentration. Missing however, are many measures of speed and accuracy on such perceptual tasks as gestalt completion and the whole realm of fluency measures. It may be that certain tasks are more interesting and challenging to a person high on U.I. 29, and it is upon these that he expends most effort. There are indeed indications of a responsiveness to the exotic and away from the mundane and colorless in such variables as better recall of words from emotionally interesting than in emotionally dry stories (MI. 25b), higher sense of poetical appropriateness (MI. 118), less preference for familiar relative to strange in written material (MI. 460), and more tendency to consider remarks 'obvious' (MI. 102).

In general, frustration, threat, and pain do not affect performance for we find higher ratio of shock to normal cancellation performance (MI. 261), and less impairment of performance by discomfort and threat (MI. 46a, b). Here it might be suggested that such stimuli may act as a spur to even better performance if the task is made more challenging. However just increasing the difficulty of a test does not always appear to have this effect, as is shown by lower ratio of regular to irregular reaction time (MI. 5).

The tendency to over-respond, or respond too quickly, observed in earlier studies does not appear at present to play such an important part in discussion of this factor. Nevertheless the larger PGR upward drift when relaxed (MI. 80), many reactions to false signals in reaction time (MI. 40), less slowing of reaction time by complex instructions (MI. 72), and more increase in basal metabolic rate after stimulation (MI. 75), suggest that this interpretation should be borne in mind.

8. Explanatory Theory: History and Final Hypotheses

There is no account of any factor similar to U.I. 29 being described in the literature prior to the C1 study. However it is probably involved in Eysenck's 'neuroticism' factor, though U.I. 23 has always been regarded as more central to the 'neuroticism' factor.

In discussion of U.I. 29 it is important to bear four things in mind. Firstly, it is primarily an environmentally determined dimension. Secondly, it is cooperative (in the sense of sharing somewhat similar marker variables) with U.I. 23. Thirdly, U.I. 29(-) is related to neurosis, and is regarded as a neurotic process factor. Finally, U.I. 29(+) does not appear to be positively correlated with success in the military and educational fields, and may even be negatively correlated.

U.I. 29, in spite of its clinical importance, is in need of much further research. In particular it needs high-loading marker variables, based on hypotheses concerning its psychological implications, which will successfully split it away conceptually from certain other factors, notably U.I. 23.

There are two principal hypotheses concerning this trait. The first is that it is 'some form of high neuroendocrinal energy reserves' (68) leading to rapid and effective interaction with the environment. This is rather close to a comparative freedom from fatigue, leading to responsive, determined grappling with problems at the positive pole, and weary, apathetic, withdrawn behavior at the negative pole. Under such an hypothesis one would expect all-round competence on criteria such as success in military training courses or school achievement to appear with U.I. 29(+), but as was observed above, this is not the case. Indeed the pattern of marker variables (and absences from the list), plus the criteria data, argue for a lack of both concentrated efforts in certain response channels, and 'staying power' over a longer period of time. The presence of positive correlations with Thurstone's PMA points up the fact that the individual highly endowed in U.I. 29(+) does not appear to be deficient in the requisite abilities.

The second, and slightly preferred, hypothesis considers U.I. 29(+) as being strength of will or ego strength, enabling the individual to mobilize his responses rapidly and effectively in dealing with his environment. At this point there is little difference between this and the previous hypothesis. However, considering arguments against the first hypothesis leads us to suggest that this is not ego-strength as the term is normally used in clinical and psycho-analytic literature, but that it is a short-term strength of will enabling the individual to function well in specific situations but devoid of the long-term strength needed for success in a job or course of instruction. Essentially this appears to be a strength of will without long-term purpose and concentrating on certain tasks in an almost capricious manner. Nevertheless the general responsiveness of U.I. 29(+) to the environment would enable a co-ordinated and usually competent set of performances in the test situation to emerge. Indeed providing that there is not too much responsibility involving strategic planning, and a not too constant environment is provided, then U.I. 29 might well be related to success in a variety of social areas. In college one would anticipate study to be confined to the night before examinations, and success in chemistry, medicine or engineering would appear unlikely!

The largely environmental determination of this factor suggests that U.I. 29(+) may be associated with a history of a permissive environment with the individual constantly cushioned against adversity. U.I. 29(-) on the other hand would emerge from a history of conflict and traumatic experience as a general exhaustion leading in the extreme to neurasthenic symptoms and absence of even momentary interest and enthusiasm. This development may well involve heightened inhibition of the central nervous system and generally lowered reactivity. It is in this way that U.I. 29(-) is regarded as an effect rather than a cause of the development of neurosis. As such it should be modifiable by a change to a more rewarding environment as in therapy, changing one's job, educational success and encouragement, and so on.

It is in the notion of the willed response that the main difference lies between this factor and U.I. 23. U.I. 23(-) involves a general incapacity to mobilize reserves in order to carry out all manner of mental and physical tasks. U.I. 29(-) on the other hand shows a lack of conscious willed direction in dealing with immediate environmental pressures. It seems likely that U.I. 29(-) would respond more rapidly to therapy than U.I. 23(-).

Table 8.7
U.I. 29: Whole-Hearted Responsiveness vs. Defensive Complacency

Q-Factor	Factor Title	Factor Identification (Research, Sample Size, Age of Subjects, Factor Number in Study)	
		C5 500 Adult (13+)	R2 86 Adult (16+)
A	(higher) Cyclothymia	-13	-01
B	(higher) Intelligence		+07
C	(higher) Ego Strength	-11	-08
E	(higher) Dominance	+12	+07
F	(higher) Surgency	-01	-02
*G	higher Super Ego Strength (conscientious, persistent)	+05	+26
H	(higher) Parmia	-03	+03
*I	higher Harria (tough, realistic)	-23	-02
L	(higher) Premsia	+09	-05
M	(higher) Alaxia	+01	-06
N	(higher) Shrewdness	-19	+02
O	(higher) Timidity	+05	+13
Q1	(higher) Radicalism	+10	-04
Q2	(higher) Self-Sufficiency	+23	+00
Q3	(higher) Self Sentiment Control	-02	+01
Q4	(higher) Ergic Tension	+03	+02

U. I. 29: WHOLE-HEARTED RESPONSIVENESS VS. DEFENSIVE COMPLACENCY (page 1)

Master Index Number	Variable Title	Factor Identification (Research, Sample Size, Age of Subjects, Factor Number in Study)									
		C1	C2	C3	C4	C5	C6	R2	C7	R12	R14
		370	410	100	100	500	250	86	184	80	129
		Adult	Adult	Adult	Adult	Adult	Adult	Adult	9-12	4-5	3-7
		(9+)	(9+)	(6+)	(10+)	(13+)	(5+)	(16+)	(3-)	(2+)	(21+)
5	lower ratio of regular to irregular reaction time	-18	-03	-01	(+09)		-30	-18	-46	(+08)	
2a-h	lower motor rigidity	(+09)	-03	-15	-14	-16	-20	-54	-36	-04	
143	higher total score -- CMS					+27			+31	+44	+35
268	faster tempo of tapping			+47	+20	+05	+12		+36		
108	more assumption of skill in untried performance			+07	+25	+17	+19	+49	(-15)		+20
25b	better recall of words from emotionally interesting than emotionally dry stories	+03	+34	+30	+53						
13a,b	less oscillation	-15	-05	-17	-22				-15		
176	slower irregularly warned reaction time			+19	+00	+13	(-09)	+13		-60	
80	larger PGR upward drift when relaxed		+77					+31	+25		
167a	better immediate memory			+47	+20				+10		
46a,b	less impairment of performance by discomfort and threat	-01	-13	-46	-40				(+07)		
83	lower fidgetometer frequency		-08	-14	-20	-18		(+26)	-08		-10
98a	larger percentage of correct decisions -- CMS			+30	+07	(-01)				+54	
72	less slowing of reaction time by complex instructions		-06				-56		(+12)	-56	
9	faster ideomotor tempo	+06	+35	+43							
118	higher sense of poetical appropriateness			+03	+27	+19					
111	larger amount of self-reference seen in events			+08	(-09)	+22	+30		(-13)		
40	more reactions to false signals in reaction time	+07				+08	+61		(-08)		(-09)
67a,b	less extremity of viewpoint		-24	-17	-17	(+17)	(+08)		-08		
43	higher mean PGR deflection to threat	-02	-06	(+17)	-07			-33	-09		
102	greater tendency to consider remarks 'obvious'			+44					+23		
51	higher index of carefulness		+16			+03	+06	+23		(-29)	
133	less criticalness of judgment					-14			-57		
3	higher speed of judgment	(-08)	+33	+32	+10						
307	faster speed of letter comparison					+32	+13				
11b	higher intelligence (PMA Verbal and Numerical)			+31	+10						
37	greater ability to suggest classifications	+02	+33								
147b	greater estimated breadth of experience and accomplishments			-32	(+04)				-03		
192	less considered possible in given time for self			(+14)	-45						-04
74	higher basal metabolic rate		+69					(-29)			
165	higher ratio of classification performance under approval relative to disapproval			(-09)	+53						
21	more questionable reading preferences	-01	-05	-25	(+05)	-20			-05	-03	
71	greater number of reaction time errors under complex instructions		+00			+08	+58	+07	+05	(-09)	
270	faster tempo of arm-circling					+19	+12		(-01)	+15	(-04)

U. I. 29: WHOLE-HEARTED RESPONSIVENESS VS. DEFENSIVE COMPLACENCY (page 2)

Master Index Number	Variable Title	RESEARCH									
		C1	C2	C3	C4	C5	C6	R2	C7	R12	R14
4	slower average reaction time	+24	+15						+11		
119	better taste in color blendings			+23	(-14)	+16					
148	higher aspiration for improvement in coding			-02	+34						
16b	less excess use of circles and slanting lines -- CMS									-52	
341	less relative accuracy under approval relative to disapproval									-43	
75	more increase in basal metabolic rate after stimulation		+39								
460	less preference for familiar relative to strange in written material								-38		
1455	greater preference for tidiness in drawings										+40
261	higher ratio of cancellation performance under shock relative to normal conditions								+36		
359	more extremity of viewpoint in test of annoyances										+30
112	(more) favorable relative to unfavorable self-reference			-01	-28	+22	+24		-12		
82	(greater) distance covered in finger maze					-19	+09		-16		
28	(faster) dynamic momentum	-06		-07	+39						
126	(higher) ratio of male to female person choices			+18	-33						
24c	(higher) ratio of initial to later performance, reading backward and color naming			-15	+21						-16
7	(faster) speed of perceptual Gestalt completion	-02		+04	+01	+00	+04		-57		
120a-g	(higher) ratio of accuracy to speed			+06	-06			+17	+10	+05	-25
211a	(lower) susceptibility to annoyance					+13	+08		-19	+03	-34
39	(higher) ratio of color to form in sorting	+06	-06	-19	+09	+19	+07		+01		
62	(faster) reading speed for emotional relative to non-emotional material		-31	+14	+22	+10					
175	(slower) regularly warned reaction time			-09	+05					-58	+05
193a	(more) shifting of attitudes towards those of successful people			+30		-07	-15		+04		

U.I. 30: SOMINDENCE VS. DISSOFRUSTANCE

1. Prevalence

Factor U.I. 30 was found in five independent factor analytic researches with adult subjects, and in three studies at the child level. In general, this factor is less well established with children than adults, two of the three child researches (R12, R15) yielded only a tentative match.

2. Questionnaire Correlates

Evidence on the loadings of primary questionnaire personality factors, as measured in the 16 P.F. Test, comes from the three studies C5, R2, and R10 (see Table 8.9). Factor U.I. 30 loads F- (high Desurgency: glum, silent), G- (low Superego Strength: casual, undependable), N- (low Shrewdness: simple, naive), Q1- (high Conservativism: conservative, accepting), and to a lesser degree L- (low Protension: trustful, adaptable).

In N2 (123) Knapp obtained significant correlations between U.I. 30 and several scales of the Guilford-Martin personality inventories; U.I. 30 correlated with S- (less Social Introversion; r = -.21), D- (less Depression; r = -.18), C- (lower Cycloid Disposition; r = -.17), O+ (higher Objectivity; r = +.18), Co+ (higher Cooperativeness; r = +.19), G+ (higher General Activity; r = +.13), A+ (higher Ascendance; r = +.22), I+ (higher Confidence; r = +.19), and N+ (higher Calmness; r = +.18). In addition, U.I. 30 is the only other factor besides U.I. 33, that correlated significantly with the number of "don't know" and "neither-nor" responses, summed over-all items in the Guilford-Martin scales (r = -.18). According to the results of a recent study by Becker (8) these correlations would indicate a positive correlation between U.I. 30+ and a second-order extraversion factor in the Guilford-Martin scales, as well as a negative correlation with a second-order anxiety factor in these scales.

Since in Becker's analysis, however, rotations have stopped at the position arrived at by the analytical rotation procedure Oblimax (141), without further rotations for maximum simple structure, this interpretation in terms of second-order factors of the Guilford-Martin scales can only be regarded as tentative. Furthermore, as will be noted from comparing Table 8.9 with Table 7.15 and 8.13 respectively, the salients of the well-replicated 16 P.F. Test second-order factors F (Q) II: Anxiety and F (Q) I: Extroversion do not appear among the 16 P.F. Test factors loading U.I. 30 (except F and N, which are, however, reversed in sign).

U.I. 30 has not been included in Knapp's analysis N1 (123); the correlations of this factor with the Guilford-Zimmerman Temperament Survey and the MMPI scales are therefore not known. Using data of the R10 study Pawlik (138) obtained significant correlations between U.I. 30 and three of the Kuder interest scales: U.I. 30 correlated positively (r = +.25) with Persuasive Interests, and negatively with both Computational Interests (r = -.26) and Clerical Interests (r = -.43).

The correlations between this factor and psychiatric ratings of anxiety are not known because U.I. 30 has not been identified in study R1.

3. State Factor Matches

U.I. 30 was not identified in the incremental R-technique study R3 and does not match any of the known P-technique factors. The conclusion is that U.I. 30 is primarily a trait dimension, with little, if any, state variance.

4. Loadings on Second-Order Objective Test Factors

Typically, factor U.I. 30 yields relatively low correlations with other primary OT factors, and thus contributes only little to second-order OT factors. U.I. 30 loads on the average r = -.16 on F(T)IV (high Educated Self-Consciousness), which is mainly loaded by U.I. 22+ (Cortertia), U.I. 18+ (Hypomanic Smartness), U.I. 25- (Imaginative Tension), and U.I. 36+ (high Self-Sentiment); in addition, U.I. 30 also loads negatively (average loading: -.19) on F(T)VII (High Tension to Achieve, Controlled Drive Tension Level) whose principal primary factor salients are U.I. 24+ (Free Anxiety), U.I. 18+ (Hypomanic Smartness), and U.I. 25- (Imaginative Tension).

5. Criterion Correlations

a) Clinical Criteria

In both studies R9-Ta (68) and R10(I) (38) U.I. 30 did not differ significantly between normals and neurotics. A significant difference, however, was obtained in R10(I) between delinquents and non-delinquents, with the criminals scoring lower on U.I. 30 than the non-delinquent control subjects.

In R7 (comparison between psychotics and normals) the factor has not been measured.

b) School and Academic Achievement

Variable M.I. 276 (scholastic achievement) which was included in study C7 does not load on U.I. 30. In study P1 (138) the factor was not related to collegiate high-achievement and over-achievement.

c) Military Criteria

No significant correlations have been found in study AF (69) between this factor and criteria of success in pilot training, and Knapp's results in research N2 (122) indicate that U.I. 30 is also unrelated with success in naval submarine training. In N1 (121) U.I. 30 has not been measured.

6. Nature-Nurture and Age Trend Results

Factor U.I. 30 has not been measured in the genetic study (70) and the age trend research (29).

7. Descriptive Interpretation

When this factor was found for the first time it was descriptively interpreted as "Independent Super-Ego Stolidity" (53). In a later publication (29), with more empirical evidence available, Cattell described this factor as a personality pattern mainly characterized by a tendency towards attitudinal and emotional independence and by slow speed (stolidity). This interpretation became fully verified in the more recent studies, which then added the additional attributes of aloofness and desurgency. Desurgency and a tendency towards personal independence appear now as the main concepts underlying the psychometric pattern of U.I. 30+.

1. Stolid independence

The stolid independence of U.I. 30+ becomes evident in three "manifestations": as slow tempo and speed, less carefulness, and as attitudinal independence. The extreme U.I. 30+ person shows slow psychomotor speed and tempo throughout a wide variety of tasks (M.I. 268, 269, 270, 1414, 1416), he is less careful in his decisions (M.I. 98b) and in his performance (MI. 16a) on the CMS test, and his work lacks neatness (M.I. 1426). This is of special interest, if we further consider that this person's aspiration level is high relative to his performance (M.I. 101a, b), that his "dynamic momentum" (more endurance of difficulty) (M.I. 28), and that his physical speed is very low despite a healthy and thus less easily fatigued physique (M.I. 73). The central explanation of this pattern seems to lie in a low will endurance (M.I. 300a) of the U.I. 30+ individual -- a characteristic which might be the key concept for understanding this stolidity.

The independence in U.I. 30+ is not only manifested in less care for proper execution of assigned tasks, but extends also into the broader area of attitudes. Subjects scoring high on this factor are more stable in their attitudes, i.e., less easily influenced by statements about how other people reacted to the same opinionnaire items (M.I. 31), and they are less suggestible to authority (M.I. 35).

2. Aloof desurgency

This second main attribute of factor U.I. 30+ had not become fully evident before the more recent research results on this dimension. These results describe the extreme U.I. 30+ subject as personally "dry" rather than emotional (M.I. 55: greater fluency of association to non-emotional than emotional stimuli; M.I. 109: more unpleasant than pleasant associations given; M.I. 205: less emotionality of comment), as more retrovert in his thinking (M.I. 110), and more critical (M.I. 133). This person likes few people (M.I. 1429) and is less willing to go along in a game situation (M.I. 347). Also the lower imaginative ability (M.I. 282) fits well into this pattern.

A description in terms of "aloof desurgency" is further substantiated from the negative loading of questionnaire factor F (Surgency vs. Desurgency) on U.I. 30. This finding describes the extreme U.I. 30+ individual as more glum and silent and less enthusiastic -- temperamental characteristics which confirm the picture of U.I. 30+ as described above on the basis of objective test loadings.

8. Explanatory Theory: History and Final Hypotheses

As a personality source trait, U.I. 30 is more prominent in adults than children, and as yet this factor has not been reported by other investigators working in the field of objective test factorizations. Little can be said at present in terms of a theoretical explanation of this source trait, going beyond the above descriptive interpretation.

From the fact that U.I. 30 is also less easily identifiable in younger children than in adults, a dynamic explanation of this factor becomes very likely -- in the sense that the pattern of U.I. 30 is the product of a psychological development which is not completed before later childhood or the first post-puberty years. Our hypothesis is that factor U.I. 30+ represents a personality dimension of mature independence -- which is also expressed in the title "Somindence" (sober mature independence) vs. "Dissofrustance" (dissociative rejection of frustrating ideas). This interpretation is in accordance with the loadings of U.I. 30 on second-order OT factors; it assumes that this independence is an adjustment mechanism which partly reduces anxiety and "anxiousness" (negative loading of U.I. 30 on F(T)VII) by "going at one's own pace" and rejecting external interference. By contrast, the personality pattern found at the U.I. 30- pole is characterized by higher willingness to live up to requirements, more carefulness, increased dependence on external control, and more emotionally toned social behavior.

Table 8.9
U.I. 30: Somindence vs. Dissofrustance

Q-Factor	Factor Title	Factor Identification (Research, Sample Size, Age of Subjects, Factor Number in Study)		
		C5 500 Adult (9+)	R2 86 Adult (10+)	R10 168 Adult (20+)
A	(higher) Cyclothymia	-03	+04	-10
B	(higher) Intelligence		+18	
C	(higher) Ego Strength	-01	-04	+03
E	(higher) Dominance	-04	-06	+16
*F	higher Desurgency (glum, silent)	-08	-44	-09
*G	lower Super Ego Strength (casual, undependable)	-32	-08	(+06)
H	(higher) Parmia	-01	-13	+15
I	(higher) Premsia	+05	+13	+13
L	(higher) Protension	-13	-16	-10
M	(higher) Alaxia	-07	+01	+10
*N	lower Shrewdness (simple, awkward)	-28	-17	(+03)
O	(higher) Timidity	+07	-01	-01
*Q1	higher Conservativism (conservative, accepting)	-27	-02	(+07)
Q2	(higher) Self-Sufficiency	-09	+06	+01
Q3	(higher) Self Sentiment Control	+04	00	-06
Q4	(higher) Ergic Tension	+07	-06	+01

U. I. 30: SOMINDENCE VS. DISSOFRUSTANCE (page 1)

Master Index Number	Variable Title	Factor Identification (Research, Sample Size, Age of Subjects, Factor Number in Study)							
		C4 100 Adult (14+)	C5 500 Adult (9+)	C6 250 Adult (7+)	R2 86 Adult (10+)	R10 168 Adult (20+)	C7 184 9-12 (15-)	R12 80 4-5 (8+)	R15 197 7-10 (12+)
269	slower leg-circling tempo		-36	-73	-42	-27	-04		
270	slower arm-shoulder tempo		-39	-79		-21	-01	-15	(+03)
42	higher body sway suggestibility	(-11)			+32	+27			+26
282	smaller number of objects seen in unstructured drawings		-13	-03				-37	-35
31	less fluctuation of attitudes	-16	-04				-55	-04	
101a,b	more excess of aspiration over performance	-22	-10				-02		-18
35	less suggestibility to authority	-04	-05	-31		-00	(+07)		
268	slower tapping tempo		-32				(+09)	-25	
98b	smaller absolute number of correct decisions -- CMS	-38	(+09)						-49
205	less emotionality of comment		(+06)	-00			-33	-01	
133	more critical of evaluation	(-13)	+00				+13		+30
55	greater fluency of association to non-emotional relative to emotional stimulus words		-01				-44		
1428	lower fluency concerning successful tasks								-63
94	higher critical flicker fusion frequency	+30		+12					
117	more highbrow tastes	+20	(-02)	+03		+22			
1250	less successful (mean self-rating) on liked tasks								-61
1429	fewer people listed as liked								-51
155	larger range of successive critical flicker fusion measures	+48							
300a	less prolonged will-endurance (lower leg persistence)							-46	
109	lower ratio of pleasant to unpleasant associations	-45							
287	more awareness of error on two-hand co-ordination test (higher proportion of errors corrected)						+44		
22a	lower ratio of incidental to purposeful observation and memory					-42			
1416	slower speed on coding								-42
1414	slower speed on letter cancellation								-40
1426	smaller total number of items completed (less personal care and neatness)								-38
347	less readiness to imitate animal sounds							-36	
462	greater preference for stronger than weaker smells				-36				
73	higher Schneider index				+36				
28	higher dynamic momentum (more endurance of difficulty)	+36							
448	greater versatility of interest				+34				
110	lower anteversion/retroversion ratio	-33							
945c	poorer consonant recall								-31
16a	more slanting lines crossed -- CMS		(-02)	+31			(-06)		
15	(more) circles used -- CMS		+12	+12	+18	-02	-05		-05

U. I 30: SOMINDENCE VS. DISSOFRUSTANCE (page 2)

Master Index Number	Variable Title	RESEARCH							
		C4	C5	C6	R2	R10	C7	R12	R15
143	(higher) total score -- CMS		-04			-04	-10	+48	
112	(higher) ratio of adverse to favorable self-reference in events	-38	-09	+04		+01	+25		
246	(less) authority submission		-30				+11		
6	(faster) ideomotor speed				+27			-03	-19
16b	(more) excess use of circles and slanting lines -- CMS							-43	
39	(higher) ratio of color to form in sorting	-19	+04	+03		-02	-20		+10
67a,b	(greater) extremity of viewpoint	+05	+26	-01		+10	-22		
116a,b	(higher) severity of judgment	+13			-23	+11	+15		

U.I. 31: WARY, CONTROLLED STEADINESS VS. IMPULSIVE VARIABILITY

1. Prevalence

Factor U.I. 31 was found in six independent factor analyses (four studies at the adult age level, and two studies at the child level). No specific extension analyses have as yet been carried out on this factor.

2. Questionnaire Correlates

Evidence on questionnaire correlates of U.I.31 with the 16 P.F. Test is available from only one study (C5; see Table 8.11); only two loadings are outside the ±.10 hyperplane (A+, Q2-) and even these are too low to claim "significance". In Knapp's study N2 (123) the correlations between U.I. 31 and the Guilford-Martin questionnaire factors were all insignificant; in the research N1 (123) (relationship with the Guilford-Zimmerman and MMPI scales) U.I. 31 has not been measured. The correlations of U.I. 31 with the Kuder interest scales and psychiatric anxiety ratings are not known, since the factor has not been identified in R10 and R1, respectively.

Thus, at present no questionnaire correlates of U.I. 31 have been found.

3. State Factor Matches

Neither of the known state factors can be considered as a match of U.I. 31; nor was the factor found in the incremental R-technique research R3. We have to conclude that this factor presumably contains little, if any, state variance, i.e., is mainly a trait factor.

4. Loadings on Second-Order Objective Test Factors

Factor U.I. 31 loads on only one second-order OT factor: F(T)V, History of Inhibiting, Restraining Environment vs. Laxness (average loading: +.16). Factor F(T)V loads only two other first-order objective test factors, namely U.I. 17+ (Inhibitedness) and U.I. 23+ (high Neural Reserves).

5. Criterion Correlations

a) Clinical Criteria

No significant differences have been found on this factor in R9-Ta (68) between normals and neurotics. In R7 and R10(I) the factor has not been measured.

b) School and Academic Achievement

Variable M.I. 276 (scholastic achievement) was included in R13 but did not load on U.I. 31. In P1 (138) the factor has not been measured.

c) Military Criteria

In N1 (121) U.I. 31 has not been measured; in N2 (122) the correlations between the factor and criteria of success in naval submarine training were insignificant. In the Cattell and Schiff study AF (69) U.I. 31 correlated significantly (r = +.11) with the "Oriented Criterion" of pilot training success, which was a combination of the "Adjustment Group Rating" and the actual flight-training Pass-Fail criterion.

6. Nature-Nurture and Age Trend Results

The factor has not been measured in the genetics study (70) and the research on age development (29).

7. Descriptive Interpretation

The objective test evidence on U.I. 31 (see Table 8.12) allows for three, mutually interrelated, descriptive hypotheses about this factor.

1. Caution or wariness

There are several indications of increased cautiousness (or wariness) in the psychometric structure of this personality factor. A person scoring at the extreme positive pole of U.I. 31 is less extreme in his views and opinions (M.I. 67b, 150), less decided on a range of opinions (M.I. 121), is cautious in not accepting too readily various unqualified statements (M.I. 106) or platitudes (M.I. 144), and avoids choosing questionable reading material (M.I. 21). What appears in variable M.I. 113 as less reality-oriented (or more autistic) attitude can probably also be understood on this basis rather than as an actual escape from reality, for which there would be no further confirmation from the remaining variables.

2. Controlled self-determinedness

This second attribute of U.I. 31 is a very interesting characteristic -- more so in view of the high cautiousness in U.I. 31+. We infer it from the U.I. 31+ person's accurate (and thus more "realistic") time estimations (M.I. 192), his stable attitudes (M.I. 31), and a group of three variables (M.I. 363, 364, 371) which all indicate a more self-determined and self-controlled temperament. Such emotional stability, which is already suggested from the loading of M.I. 31, is further expressed in M.I. 211a, a lower susceptibility to annoyance on the part of the U.I. 31+ individual. Together with the high cautiousness this self-determinedness opens up several hypotheses about this personality trait. It may be that the wariness of U.I. 31+ is only a kind of safe-guarding mechanism which gradually allows for a better integration of this self-determined realism; or the latter may be best understood as a reaction formation in response to the former. Our present results do not provide sufficient evidence to decide between these two hypotheses.

3. Slow and less accurate performance

Several variables in Table 8.12 indicate low accuracy (M.I. 356b, 71, 385) and slow speed of performance (M.I. 177a, b; 41, 269). Whereas the slow speed of movement and psychological performance could well be explained from the cautiousness of the U.I. 31+ person, no immediate explanation is available for the low accuracy. All three accuracy measures are obtained from highly speeded tests, i.e., from tests in which the subject is asked to perform at top speed -- a condition which may be more of a hindrance to the extreme U.I. 31+ subjects so that his accuracy decreases particularly on such tasks (in the same way as the U.I. 31+ person has low shock tolerance (M.I. 166)).

The available objective test evidence on U.I. 31+ can thus be summarized in the following attributes: high cautiousness or wariness, much self-determinedness and self-control, more stable attitudes, and slow performance.

8. Explanatory Theory: History and Final Hypotheses

A personality dimension similar to U.I. 31 has not been identified as yet by other researchers in the field, which may be partly due to the fact that this factor shares hardly any variance with known questionnaire dimensions but is practically restricted to objective behavior measures. Since the loading pattern of U.I. 31 differs little with the age of the subjects and can be traced back to middle childhood (7-8 years), any theory on its development has either to assume a mainly constitutional source of this source trait or a very early environmental determination. As yet we do not know the nature-nurture ratios for this factor. However the only loading of U.I. 31 at the second-order OT factor level is on F(T)V, the remaining two first-order salients of which are both largely environmentally determined. Thus, we shall consider only the second alternative for the present, namely that U.I. 31 is mainly due to early environmental influences.

Our hypothesis is that factor U.I. 31 represents a personality source trait of high vs. low ego-control; from the content of F(T)V we assume that high ego-control (U.I. 31+) originates in a moderately restraining, effective rather than affective environment whereas low ego-control (U.I. 31-) appears to result from a more relaxed, less restraining, more affective environment. This hypothesis could explain the controlled, wary steadiness at the U.I. 31+ pole, and the impulsive unsteadiness or variability in U.I. 31-. Self-determinedness and self-control, which load positively on this factor, thus appear as the principal attributes of U.I. 31+. The wariness or cautiousness in U.I. 31+ may be viewed as a safeguarding mechanism resulting from more intensive and more foresighted self-control--a personality mechanism, which by its very nature in turn will tend to indirectly reinforce emotional and motivational steadiness and stability.

Table 8.11
U.I. 31: Wary, Controlled Steadiness vs. Impulsive Variability

Q-Factor	Factor Title	Factor Identification (Research, Sample Size, Age of Subjects, Factor Number in Study)
		C5 500 Adult (15+)
A	(higher) Cyclothymia	+12
B	(higher) Intelligence	
C	(higher) Ego Strength	-02
E	(higher) Dominance	-07
F	(higher) Surgency	-01
G	(higher) Super Ego Strength	-05
H	(higher) Parmia	-05
I	(higher) Premsia	-06
L	(higher) Protension	+06
M	(higher) Alaxia	+07
N	(higher) Shrewdness	-02
O	(higher) Timidity	-10
Q1	(higher) Radicalism	-08
Q2	(higher) Self-Sufficiency	-11
Q3	(higher) Self Sentiment Control	-07
Q4	(higher) Ergic Tension	-06

U. I. 31: WARY, CONTROLLED STEADINESS VS. IMPULSIVE VARIABILITY (page 1)

Master Index Number	Variable Title	Factor Identification (Research, Sample Size, Age of Subjects, Factor Number in Study)					
		C3 100 Adult (1+)	C4 100 Adult (6+)	C5 500 Adult (15+)	C6 250 Adult (2-)	R13 164 6-9 (11+)	R15 197 7-10 (18+)
192	more considered possible in given time for self	+06	+40	+20	+81	+10	
203	less confidence in one's own correctness in computations			-40	-80	-12	-20
67b	less extremity of viewpoint on aphorisms	-64	-40	-05	-06	-11	
280	higher accuracy of time interval estimates			-35	-70		-21
21	fewer questionable reading preferences	+01	+21	+08		+24	+10
211a	less susceptibility to annoyance			-04	-16	-15	-02
31	less fluctuation of attitudes	-57	-48	-02		(+20)	
106	less unreflective acceptance of unqualified statements	-25	-10	(+14)	-17		
113	less acceptance of reality principle (more autistic)	-30	-25			(+09)	
41	fewer correct movements on two-hand co-ordination	-26	-24	(+08)			
71	greater number of errors of reaction under complex instructions			+29	(-03)	+23	+04
364	more "internal-control" than "external-control" choices in story completion					+61	+12
150	less acceptance of "obvious" remarks	-31	-10				
166	more impairment of classification performance by shock	+01	+39				
144	less agreement with aphorisms	-27			-17		
430	greater preference for non-disturbing than disturbing pictures					-38	-03
385	less accuracy in rapid shape comparison					-16	-24
356b	higher total number of errors on speeded color naming						+63
121	greater indecisiveness of opinion	+62					
363	more "ego-control" than "malevolent-intervention" choices in story completion					+60	
361	less confident assumption of knowledge					-36	
371	more "ego-control" than "benevolent-intervention" choices in picture interpretation					+32	
177a,b	(faster) motor speed	+06	+18			+07	-65
269	(slower) leg-circling tempo			+19	-05	-21	
146a	(greater) absolute accuracy on perceptual Gestalt completion	+07	-19	+19	+00	+04	
35	(more) suggestibility to authority	-22	+17	+10	+08		
108	(more) confident assumption of skill in untried performance	+02	+15	-03	+13	-22	
39	(higher) ratio of color to form in sorting	+03	+22	+15	-08	-05	-17

U.I. 32: EXVIA VS. INVIA

1. Prevalence

Factor U.I. 32, ranking rather late in our series, has independently emerged in five factorizations at the adult level and in three factor analytic researches at the child level. For the adult age range, extension results are available from two studies (R7, Wells).

2. Questionnaire Correlates

In several studies (28, 29, 34, 120) on the second-order structure of the primary questionnaire factors, measured in the 16 P.F. Test, consistently a very clear second-order questionnaire factor of extraversion-introversion has been found, in both children and adults, and typically with a large factor variance. The principal first-order salients of this Factor F(Q)I are A+, E+, F+, H+, M-, and Q2-. Evidence on the loadings of primary questionnaire factors on U.I. 32 is available from four factor analyses (see Table 8.13). In these all markers of the second-order questionnaire extraversion factor but M load consistently, and in expected direction, on U.I. 32; in addition, also N+ (high Shrewdness: sophisticated) loads slightly positive. From these results a high positive correlation can be inferred between the objective test first-order factor U.I. 32 and the second-order questionnaire factor F(Q)I, Extraversion vs. Introversion.

On the basis of these 16 P.F. Test loadings U.I. 32+ can be described as more cyclothyme (warm, sociable; A+), more dominant (dominant, aggressive; E+), more surgent (enthusiastic, talkative; F+), more adventurous and bold (high Parmia; H+), more shrewd (sophisticated, polished; N+), and more group dependent (dependent, imitative; Q2-). This personality pattern represents the principal characteristics of extraversion (vs. introversion), such as more outward-going, more social and group dependent, more emotional, and more daring. In fact, the interpretation of factor U.I. 32+ as Exvia (or extraversion) relies to a considerable extent on these questionnaire loadings.

There is only little evidence on questionnaire correlates of U.I. 32 with other than the 16 P.F. Test factors. In Knapp's study N2 (123) U.I. 32 correlated insignificantly with all of the Guilford-Martin scales,[1] only the correlation with R (Rhathymia) is near significant and in expected direction (+.10). No results are as yet available on the correlation between U.I. 32 and the Guilford-Zimmerman and MMPI scales because this factor has not been measured in Knapp's study N1 (123). Significant correlations exist between U.I. 32 and two of the Kuder interest scales (138): the factor correlates positively with Artistic Interests (r = .21) and negatively with Clerical Interests (r = -.33).

In study R1 two anxiety ratings by psychiatrist I loaded on U.I. 32: the rating on free anxiety loaded negatively (-.28), the rating on situational anxiety positively (+.15).

3. State Factor Matches

No state factor resembling U.I. 32 is known as yet. Since U.I. 32 has not been found in the incremental R-technique research R3 either, we shall conclude that this factor is mainly, if not exclusively, a trait dimension.

4. Loadings on Second-Order Objective Test Factors

In the five available analyses on second-order objective test factors the communality of U.I. 32 with the remaining primary OT factors was on the average relatively low. There is certainly no second-order factor of extraversion in the medium of objective tests. U.I. 32 rather appears in the loading pattern of two, practically independent, second-order OT factors: F(T)I: Tied Socialization or Superego vs. Absence of Cultural Introjection (average loading: +.19), and F(T)III: Temperamental Ardor vs. Temperamental Apathy (average loading: +.16).

5. Criterion Correlations

a) Clinical Criteria

In both studies R9-Ta (68) and R10(I) (38) factor U.I. 32 differentiated significantly between normals and neurotics, the latter being more introverted (U.I. 32-). In addition, in R10(I) also a significant difference between delinquents and non-delinquents was found in this factor: non-delinquents were more extravert (U.I. 32+) than criminals.

Psychotics and normals did not differ significantly in this factor in study R7.

---

[1]This negative finding is puzzling because several of the scales in the Guilford-Martin Inventories usually contribute a strong second-order extraversion factor.

b) School and Academic Achievement

No relationship was found between U.I. 32 and school or college achievement in R1, R13, and P1 (138).

c) Military Criteria

According to study AF (69) this factor is not related to success in pilot training. No cross-validation of this negative finding is available as yet because U.I. 32 has not been measured in N1 (121).

In N2 (122) Knapp found a significant negative correlation (r = -.12) between extraversion (U.I. 32+) and the Class Standing criteria of success in naval submarine training.

6. Nature-Nurture and Age Trend Results

Factor U.I. 32 has not been included in the genetics research (70) and the study on age development (29).

7. Descriptive Interpretation

Besides the evidence on questionnaire correlates, the descriptive interpretation of U.I. 32 as extraversion-introversion is based, in the main, on the following three objective test characteristics of this factor.

1. Optimistic, self-confident socio-orientedness

The individual scoring high on U.I. 32+ is fluent on (own and other people's) personal characteristics (M.I. 763), and more so on his own than on other people's characteristics (M.I. 316); this fluency on self is also high relative to his general verbal fluency (M.I. 273, 283). Since the principal marker for general verbal fluency (M.I. 271) does not load on U.I. 32, it cannot simply be general verbal fluency which accounts for these salients of extraversion; the U.I. 32+ person is only fluent on topics of specific social or personal relevance -- a kind of attitude and interest we intended above in the term "socio-orientedness". The lack of any general verbal fluency distinguishes this factor also very clearly from other primarily fluency loaded factors, such as U.I. 21 (Exuberance).

According to our results the extreme extravert is also more optimistic (M.I. 112 when presented with various events that might occur to him, he believes they will affect him favorably rather than unfavorably; M.I. 449: less self-sacrifice believed necessary to achieve life goals), satisfied with and confident in his capacities (M.I. 108: more self-confident regarding success chances on various untried performances) and rather self-willed (M.I. 246: little authority submission; M.I. 35: little authority suggestibility, M.I. 152: less tendency to agree).

In his actual performances this individual is less cautious than others (M.I. 421, 423), and in his self-evaluation not too critical (M.I. 219: few common frailties admitted).

On the basis of this evidence the extravert individual cannot necessarily be regarded the "well-adjusted" personality 'per se'. An extended interpretation of extraversion as "sociable willingness" is certainly not corroborated from our results, and can only arise from an undue extension of the specific extraversion pattern towards the pattern of factors U.I. 20 and/or U.I. 24-, which have already been discussed above and which are not significantly correlated with U.I. 32.

Carrigan, in her recent review of the extraversion concept (16), arrived at the same conclusion and pointed out that extraversion and general social adjustment must be regarded as different personality dimensions; whenever an extraversion factor is found in an analysis typically also a separate (adjustment" factor (anxiety, "neuroticism", etc.) is identified from the same analysis.

From what our results indicate in this connection, it is not a general "social well-adjustment" but a "being oriented towards topics of social impact" that characterizes U.I. 32; in addition, the extravert is optimistic, less cautious, less critical regarding himself and somewhat self-willed. It is the latter aspects of extraversion which have occasionally been referred to as "rhathymia" (101). These "happy-go-lucky" attributes of the extravert might in part also explain the unselfishness (M.I. 332) which loads positively on U.I. 32+ at the child level ("live and let live"!).

2. Less accurate, more fluent perception and thinking

As to his cognitive characteristics, the extravert person is less accurate (M.I. 146a) but highly fluent in his perceptions (M.I. 282) (both of which together might indicate a slight confabulatory tendency). As has been known for a long time for mania, the pathologically extreme case of extraversion, also the "normal" extravert gives more superficial (namely: alliterative and rhyme) associations in word association tests (M.I. 714). In his thinking the extravert is realistic (M.I. 696) and efficient (M.I. 275). If there is possibility for interference between "the old" and "the new", older habits interfere strongly with new ones (M.I. 695). If misspelled words have to be learned, e.g., "pensil", the correct spelling intrudes frequently when the subject has to reproduce the misspelled words in the recall section of the test.

These results are well in line with the general notion of the extravert mode of perception and thinking. On the one hand they suggest a cognitive plasticity, in the sense that the extravert reacts abundantly to stimuli. On the other hand they describe an efficient and realistic mind which perseveres easily with what has been learned previously.

3. Pyknic (endomorph) physique

From the work of Kretschmer (125), Sheldon (152) and others a positive correlation would be expected between pyknic (endomorph) physique and extraversion. In Table 8.14 we indeed find a positive correlation with an endormorphy index (M.I. 485). The higher systolic blood pressure (M.I. 444) of the extravert and his lower hand writing pressure (M.I. 464) are well in line with this physique correlation.

In addition to these three main characteristics of U.I. 32+ Extraversion, our results indicate various specific attributes. Whereas, for instance, factor U.I. 32 is not correlated with any general speed measures, the extravert seems to be specifically fast on tiresome performances (M.I. 420a, 738, 684) -- maybe, in order to 'get done' with them. This interpretation seems likely on the basis of several results which indicate a low endurance; the extravert gives up early on a tiring physical task (treadmill run, M.I. 492) or constructive task (tower construction, M.I. 422) and does not spurt up (M.I. 24d). A reduced tendency to achieve might well be associated with, or even be the cause of, this low endurance.

8. Explanatory Theory: History and Final Hypotheses

Factorization of personality inventories typically yields clear evidence of an extraversion-introversion factor in the questionnaire realm (e.g. 5, 127, 136). In the modality of objective behavior tests only studies from Eysenck's laboratory (e.g., 87, 109) and the researches carried out in the authors' laboratory (see Table 8.14) have identified such a personality dimension. This apparent difficulty of isolating a source trait in objective tests which apparently has very big variance in questionnaire data is indeed very puzzling. Only studies in which the behavioral measures were sampled from a wide domain succeed at all in identifying an objective test extraversion factor, but even there the OT extraversion factor has typically a small factor variance (in the sense of a small associated latent root) and a relatively wide hyperplane. This difference between the questionnaire and the objective test medium with regard to the identifiability of an extraversion-introversion factor is furthermore brought out in the fact that at the primary questionnaire factor level several extraversion-contributing factors can be isolated which yield a large second-order questionnaire extraversion factor, whereas in objective tests only a small-variance first-order extraversion factor exists and no second-order OT extraversion factor can be found (27).

The most likely explanation of this result can be expressed in two hypotheses.

Hypothesis I:

Questionnaire and objective test factors of same numerical order actually belong to different hierarchical levels, the Q first-order factors paralleling the variable level in OT data, the Q second-order factor paralleling OT first-order factors, etc. The reason for this hierarchical difference between Q and OT factors lies in the higher specificity of questionnaire items as compared with objective test items.

This hypothesis is confirmed for four of the OT primaries: U.I. 19, U.I. 22, U.I. 24, and U.I. 32 (see the discussion of these factors), which in fact exhaust all well-replicated second-order Q factors.

No results are as yet available on third-order Q factors; from the above hypothesis these are expected to match some of the second-order OT factors.[1] As can be seen already now, OT data apparently sample a much wider domain of personality-due behavior variance; this is also illustrated in the larger number of first-order factors found in objective tests than in questionnaires. From this hypothesis the segment of the personality sphere (17) accessible to Q measures would be considerably restricted in comparison to the more exhaustive OT measures. Extraversion, Anxiety, Pathemia and Promethean Will would be the principal personality source traits covered in Q data, and therefore an extraversion factor is more readily identifiable in Q measures than OT measures.

Hypothesis II:

In questionnaire data some segments of the total personality sphere are more adequately represented than in objective test data -- in particular, social behavior is poorly sampled in objective tests. Since extraversion-introversion is largely loaded by measures of either direct or symbolic social behavior, our present repertoire of objective tests is less likely to yield a strong extraversion-introversion factor.

A proper explanation of the problem of why extraversion is less strongly represented in objective test data than in questionnaire data can be gained from considering both hypotheses together. Questionnaire instruments, by their very nature, give only a partial representation of the total personality sphere, and the segment they cover contains amongst others the source trait of extraversion; in Q data, therefore, extraversion accounts for a higher percentage of the total variance sampled than in OT data. Our hypothesis is that the factorial representation of extraversion in objective tests can be strengthened by a more intensive coverage of social behavior in the OT medium. Research studies are presently under way to investigate this proposition.

As a concept in personality theory, extraversion-introversion has been given very much attention. In fact, this personality trait is among the few traits that had already been recognized in a pre-metric (and even pre-scientific) psychology and are still kept today. Originally this trait was typically conceived

---

[1] For a fuller discussion of this hierarchical-structure hypothesis regarding Q and OT data the reader is referred to chapter 10.

of as a type continuum rather than a trait continuum; already in the ancient "personology" of Hippocrates it can be detected as one of the classificatory principles underlying the molar type scheme, and as Rohracher (145) has pointed out several years ago, most of the modern typologies still imply the notion of an extraversion-introversion continuum. C.G. Jung (116) contributed not only the now familiar verbal term for this trait but also developed an extensive theoretical framework within which extraversion-introversion became a theoretically well-defined concept. Other researchers, like Kretschmer (125) and Sheldon (152), introduced new verbal labels for what partly is the same underlying trait and at the same time investigated the relationship between this personality dimension and body build.

It was subsequent to Jung's classical theoretical formulations that the concept of extraversion-introversion was more and more extended and "stretched", both by psychologists and laymen. Soon it had "grown" unduly into a most general (and consequently less meaningful) personality trait into which social adjustment, anxiety, disposition towards neurosis, and others have been subsumed. If extraversion-introversion is to be restored as a useful concept in personality theory it has to be re-distillated as a functionally unitary personality source trait, disclad of the superposed characteristics which do not stand empirical verification. We regard the two related factors F(Q)I and U.I. 32 as a close enough representation of Jung's original notion of extraversion-introversion to justify our factor interpretation but called the factor Exvia vs. Invia to avoid confusion with the now less clear term Extraversion vs. Introversion.

Manifold research efforts have been devoted to investigating behavioral attributes associated with, and criterion performances predictable from, this trait, but less attention has been given to the theoretical exploitation of the source characteristics, the basic "behavioral formula", underlying this personality dimension. Jung suggested an explanation in terms of libido direction: the libido being consciously outward directed in extraversion, consciously inward directed in introversion. Our theory of the source trait Exvia vs. Invia is based in the main upon three sources of evidence: the objective test loading pattern of U.I. 32, the salients of F(Q)I Extraversion-Introversion, and the loadings of U.I. 32 on F(T)I and F(T)III.

From the projections of U.I. 32 on the second-order OT factors F(T)I and F(T)III a "two-factor" theory of Exvia can be formulated. Exvia originates in ready introjection of social values (F(T)I) and higher temperamental ardor (more intensive emotions which are readily overtly expressed (F(T)III). Invia, on the other hand, is caused by little readiness to internalize cultural standards and higher temperamental apathy (emotions are less intensive and frequent and are very seldom overtly expressed). Factor U.I. 32 thus represents a source trait which is a joint effect of two causes, introjection of social values and temperamental ardor. In combining both, Exvia can be understood as <u>externally controlled extrojection</u> (or tendency to react "outwardly"), Invia as <u>internally controlled introjection</u> (or tendency to react "inwardly").

This last formulation presents our present theory on factor U.I. 32. At the positive, exvious pole of this factor, for example, the higher interest in people, the higher sociability, surgency, group dependence, and abundancy of response appear as manifestation of higher external (and less internal) control,[1] while the higher adventurousness and dominance, the lower attitude conformity, accuracy and endurance appear as manifestations of the stronger extrojective tendency.

---

[1]See also M.I. 364 in table 8.14 which illustrates this notion of Exvia directly.

Table 8.13
U.I. 32: Exvia vs. Invia

Q-Factor	Factor Title	Factor Identification (Research, Sample Size, Age of Subjects, Factor Number in Study)			
		C5 500 Adult (7+)	R1 86 Adult (5+)	R2 86 Adult (2-)	R10 168 Adult (15-)
**A	higher Cyclothymia (warm, sociable)	+39	+53	+50	+07
B	(higher) Intelligence			-06	
C	(higher) Ego Strength	+06	-11	+07	+04
**E	higher Dominance (dominant, aggressive)	+46		+16	+11
**F	higher Surgency (enthusiastic, talkative)	+46	+11	+10	+12
G	(higher) Super Ego Strength	-05		+12	-07
**H	higher Parmia (adventurous)	+43	+16	+39	+09
I	(higher) Premsia	+01	+04	+05	+17
L	(higher) Protension	+12		-25	+03
M	(higher) Alaxia	+10	+01	-22	+12
*N	higher Shrewdness (sophisticated, polished)	+16		+21	(-05)
O	(higher) Timidity	-18	+05	+14	+03
Q1	(higher) Radicalism	+01		-07	+04
**Q2	higher Group Dependence (dependent, imitative)	-25		-41	-06
Q3	(higher) Self Sentiment Control	-07		+03	-08
Q4	(higher) Ergic Tension	-01	+09	-14	+04

U. I. 32: EXVIA VS. INVIA (page 1)

Master Index Number	Variable Title	Factor Identification (Research, Sample Size, Age of Subjects, Factor Number in Study)										
		C5	C6	R1	R2	R10	We	R7-Ps	R7-No	R12	R13	R15
		500	250	86	86	168	80	48	57	80	164	197
		Adult	Adult	Adult	Adult	Adult	Adult	Adult	Adult	4-5	6-9	7-10
		(7-)	(15-)	(5-)	(2+)	(15-)	--	--	--	(16+)	(8-)	(17+)
282	greater number of objects perceived in unstructured drawings	+09	+49	+04		+34		*	*	+02	+12	(-01)
316	higher fluency on own relative to other people's personal characteristics			+26	+13	+50		*	*		+13	
763	higher total fluency on own and other people's personal characteristics	+16	+45					+25	+26			
24d	lower ratio of final (speeded) to initial (slow) total score -- CMS					-08				-01	-24	-42
5	higher ratio of regularly to irregularly warned reaction time		+05	+42	(-01)	(-04)				+25		
108	more confident assumption of skill in untried performance	+10	+30	+10	+14	(-01)		*	*		+10	
146a	lower absolute accuracy in perceptual Gestalt completion		-32			-20				(+04)	-04	-05
152	less tendency to agree	(+09)	-19	(+06)	-31	-05					(+05)	
273	higher proportion of fluency on self	+00	(-08)			+30				+20	+06	+00
219	fewer common frailties admitted	-03	(+09)	(+05)	-01	-07				-01	-34	-04
38b	lower ratio of consonant to dissonant recall (corrected for tendency to agree)	-03	-35			-04						
422	lower height of single tower constructed (in small children)										-52	-51
460	greater preference for strange rather than familiar in written material			+24	+15	+21						
283	higher proportion of fluency on dreams	+13	+21			+28						
112	higher ratio of favorable to unfavorable self-reference in events	(-04)	+19			+00					+20	
246	less authority submission	+05	+22								+20	
684	faster aesthetic reaction time							+19	+26			
263	smaller variability in simple reaction times		-02							-32	(+10)	-13
16a	fewer slanting lines crossed -- CMS	-10	-31	(+29)	-05	(+08)						
35	less suggestibility to authority	-25	(+06)			-04						
421	less cautious anticipation in tower construction										-21	-57
464	lower handwriting pressure			-31	(+10)							
695	larger proportion of correct letters inserted							+34	+17			
707	fewer items completed on word classification							-17	-32			
364	less internal relative to external control in story completion										-23	-23
444	higher systolic blood pressure			+25	+19							
706	more words grouped together on word classification (higher average inclusiveness)							+09	+34			
714	higher proportion of alliterative and rhyming associations given							+20	+25			
927b	higher sex erg (more desire for romantic love)			+08	+34							
696	higher number of real word stimuli identified correctly							+12	+28			
485	greater length and girth of muscles				+24		+18					
492	shorter endurance time on treadmill run				-24		-16					
713	lower proportion of alliterative associations given							-05	-32			
737	more figures scanned on figure comparison test							+32	+09			

U. I. 32: EXVIA VS. INVIA (page 2)

Master Index Number	Variable Title	RESEARCH										
		C5	C6	R1	R2	R10	We	R7-Ps	R7-No	R12	R13	R15
738	more figures checked on figure comparison test							+27	+11			
767	greater number of non-social relative to social annoyances							+30	+06			
733	lower proportion of items attempted (on absurdly difficult questions)							-01	-30			
275	higher total correct in test on arithmetic reasoning and logic							(-12)	+46			
686	higher ratio of aesthetic to synaesthetic reasoning speed					(-03)		+31	(-02)			
717	higher number of words recalled correctly on combined word recall-word association test							(-03)	+32			
423	less planfulness in bridge construction										-46	
420a	faster speed in single tower construction										-42	
332	much willingness to forego prize for those in need (more altruism)									+36		
1489	less accuracy in recalling details from horrifying than pleasant pictures					+36						
853	more concreteness in aesthetic completion					+33						
886	larger size of drawings of trees and people					+33						
867	more suspicion towards higher occupational groups					+32						
449	lower amount of self-sacrifice believed necessary to achieve life goals				-33							
167a, b	(better) immediate memory	+02	+12	-21	+18	+17					-08	
84a	(greater) increase of heart rate after startle			+24	-16							
472	(higher) ratio of number of acquaintances to number of friends recalled			-22	+16	+08						
510	(more) articulatory efficiency under delayed feedback			-36	+16							
120a-c	(higher) ratio of accuracy to speed			-22	+03	+02		+38	-12	+06	+13	-07
30	(higher) ratio of self criticism to criticism of others	-14	+13	+44	-02	+50				+09	-11	-27
199	(higher) numerical ability	+00	-07	+06	-05	-11				+34		+02
105	(greater) proportion of threatening objects seen in unstructured drawings	-03	-09			+32				-02	-06	+06
193a	(more) shifting of attitudes toward those of successful people	-20	-03	-30		+25					+05	
40	(more) reactions to irrelevant signals in reaction time	+01	-01							-16	+08	+15
51	(higher) index of carefulness	+01	+02	-06	+15	+05				+01		+18

* Study R7: In addition to the scores A+, F+, and H+ from the 16 P. F. Test the three variables marked by an asterisk have been used for estimating factor scores on U.I. 32.

U.I. 33: REACTIVE DISMAY VS. SANGUINENNESS

1. Prevalence

U.I. 33 has been identified in four studies, three being with adults and one with eleven year old children. Despite the small number of replications it retains a distinctive cohesive quality that is psychologically of considerable interest. The matching of factors across studies is very good.

2. Questionnaire Correlates

Correlations are available between U.I. 33 and all factors (except B) of the 16 P.F. from Study R10. Results show U.I. 33(+) to be positively correlated with Q3 (-): Lax, Unsure, (Low Integration), Q2(-): Dependent, Imitative, and E(-): Submissive, Mild.

The thirteen factors of the Guilford (1940) Inventory of Factors STDCR, the Guilford-Martin (1943) Inventory of Factors GAMIN, and the Guilford-Martin (1943) Personnel Inventory were correlated with U.I. 33(+) by Knapp (N2) using a sample of 315 Navy enlisted men. Significant negative correlations were found with Co (Co-operativeness) (r = -.31), A (Ascendence) (r = -.26), I (Confidence) (r = -.26), O (Objectivity), N (Calmness), G (General Activity), Ag (Agreeableness), R (Rhathymia) (r = -.11), and T (Thinking Introversion) (r = -.11). Significant positive correlations were found with S (Social Introversion) (r = +.22), D (Depression) (r = +.22), ? (Question marks) (r = +.22), and C (Cycloid Disposition) (r = +.18).

The 16 P.F. and Guilford-Martin results agree that U.I. 33(+) involves lack of confidence, dependence, and submissiveness. Of interest, however, is the additional information from the Guilford-Martin scales on unco-operativeness, disagreeableness, depression, and social introversion. Clearly the results make psychological sense and, as will be seen later, fit very appropriately the interpretation based on objective tests alone.

Knapp's results are particularly encouraging for of the eighteen objective test factors studied, U.I. 33 had by far the largest number of significant correlations with questionnaire traits. The prognosis is therefore very good that after a few more replications a solid link will be established between this factor and factors from the questionnaire realm.

Recent data on the Kuder Preference Record and objective test factors gives a negative correlation between U.I. 33(+) and persuasive interests (r = -.25) and a positive correlation with clerical interests (r = +.24) (138).

3. State Factor Matches

At present there is no state factor match for U.I. 33.

4. Loadings on Second-Order Objective Test Factors

Second order data on U.I. 33 is available from the N1 study only, and the factor had a low positive loading on F(T)IV: High Educated Self-Consciousness vs. Low Educated Self-Consciousness. (57).

5. Criterion Correlations

a) Clinical Criteria

Comparatively little is known of relationships between U.I. 33 and clinical criteria. Evidence from R9-Ta and R10(I) suggests that normals may be higher than neurotics on U.I. 33(+) though neither difference reaches statistical significance. Normals, however, were found to have significantly higher factor scores than criminals in R10 (I).

b) School and Academic Achievement

Data upon academic achievement (P1) showed no significant difference between high and low achievers in terms of this factor.

c) Military Criteria

The only information on military achievement is Knapp's study of Naval Submarine School candidates (N1), and here non-significant correlations were found between U.I. 33(+) and criteria of Pass-Fail and Class Standing.

6. Nature-Nurture and Age-Trend Results

No nature-nurture or age-trend results are presently available for U.I. 33.

7. Descriptive Interpretation

Pessimism

A pervasive pessimism, not only concerning oneself, but of events in general, is symptomatic of a high factor score on U.I. 33(+). This pessimism extends to less confident assumption of skill in untried performance (MI. 108), higher ratio of adverse to favorable self-reference seen in events (MI. 112), more pessimism over doing good (MI. 100), less considered possible in a given time for self (MI. 192) and less belief in early maturity (MI. 1478). Of interest to the clinician is the choice in a problem situation, by young children, of pictures suggesting that the central figure becomes the victim of a malevolent external agent rather than obtaining mastry through his own efforts (MI. 372). This picture of a depressed lack of confidence contains also the suggestion of a limited hostility as shown by higher over-all annoyability (MI. 211a).

Timidity

U.I. 33(+) is also associated with a conservative and fearful approach to the environment. Especially prevalent is fear or withdrawal from the new or strange, with less preference for dangerous vs. safe situations (MI. 400), strange rather than familiar pictures (MI. 384), competitive vs. non-competitive situations (MI. 401). Interestingly enough there is no evidence for a decline in performance due to the application of shock, punishment, or frustration; which suggests that it may be the fear of a stimulus, rather than the stimulus itself, that is important. There is contributory evidence for this view in less impairment of maze performance by shock (MI. 46a, b), and less impairment of classification by shock (MI. 166). The conservative, 'middle of the road,' somewhat inhibited, aspect of U.I. 33(+) appears in adults with consistently low scores on extremity of viewpoint measures (MI. 67a) and in children with less irrelevant marking of test papers (MI. 437), less untidiness of coloring (MI. 391), and lower absolute number of correct decisions made in C.M.S. test (MI. 98b). Additional confirmation of conservatism and low extremity of viewpoint comes from the positive correlation with question-mark responses (?) on the Guilford-Martin (see section 2).

Cognitive Ability

It appears that U.I. 33(+) may be related to comparatively high scores on cognitive tasks for there is higher verbal and numerical ability on P.M.A. (MI. 11b), more logical consistency in reasoning about emotional topics (MI. 327d), rather than on perceptual or perceptual-motor activities. However, a consistent relationship with low motor rigidity (MI. 2a) is also found.

Perseverence

The association of U.I. 33(+) with a low ratio of initial to final performance on reading backward (MI. 24c), and C.M.S. (MI. 24d), lower motor rigidity (MI. 2a), and less impairment of maze (MI. 46a, b) or classification (MI. 166) performance by shock, suggests competence in dealing with tasks demanding concentrated and sustained effort--in other words determination and staying power.

8. Explanatory Theory: History and Final Hypotheses

U.I. 33 is a comparative late-comer in the Universal Index series, but in spite of few replications its loading pattern, from a psychological point of view, is quite distinct. To our knowledge this pattern has not been found elsewhere among objective tests. A certain similarity appears between part of the U.I. 33 pattern (that involving pessimism and depression) and the depression factor in questionnaire responses found by Guilford (99a), and others.

Perhaps the most important information to appear since previous writing on this factor (29) is the very clear indication of linkage with self-report measures. As outlined in Section 2, U.I. 33(+) correlates with lack of confidence, dependence, and submissiveness (16 P.F. and Guilford-Martin) and lack of objectivity and calmness, low general activity, care-wornness, social introversion and depression (Guilford-Martin). These findings fit almost exactly the objective test data on pessimism, and to a large extent the conservatism and fearfulness discussed in section 7 above. Even the higher annoyability (MI. 211), implying hostility, is supported by correlations with C_o(-) Lack of Cooperativeness and Ag(-): Disagreeableness, and the lower extremity of viewpoint (MI. 67a) with Question Marks (?) on the Guilford-Martin.

Objective-test information not immediately mirrored in questionnaire responses is particularly illuminating. First there is the suggestion that the fearfulness is a form of anxiety relating to future, impending troubles and not a reaction to the onslaught of pain or frustration. The evidence is quite clear here, for in spite of correlations with expressed preference for safe, known situations, there is apparent resistance to pain or shock itself--or at least no diminution of performance occurs under these circumstances. This aspect of U.I. 33(+) may, of course, be reflected in the negative correlation with Rhathymia (Freedom from Care). Unfortunately there is no direct information with regard to established anxiety scales, though from the correlations with Q3(-), Q2(-) and E(-) of the 16 P.F. a correlation would be expected with the 16 P.F. second order factor of Anxiety. As U.I. 33 was not identified in R1, R2, or R3 there is no evidence on any relationship to fear ergs or drives, but such would also be anticipated.

Emerging from objective test analyses but showing no questionnaire counterpart are variables categorized as indicating "staying power or determination." Expected questionnaire correlates would be Q2(+): Self-Sentiment Control, G(+): Super Ego Strength, and any factors involving persistence, but this is not supported by the data. A likely explanation is that the all-embracing pessimism extends so far into the verbal self-report realm that it gives no opportunity for the more sterling qualities of U.I. 33(+) to appear. Thus though a person high on U.I. 33(+) may work steadily and competently through a test even under pain or distraction, he probably views himself as failing miserably!

Several hypotheses suggest themselves as accounting for the clearly defined behavior of U.I. 33. However two broad regions of emphasis appear, one suggesting a relationship with clinical depression, and the other to a history of early frustration and disappointment. Undoubtedly environmental effects play some part in shaping U.I. 33 whatever hypothesis is finally adopted.

HYPOTHESIS I: U.I. 33(+) as the depressive pole of a manic-depressive continuum.

Many of the symptoms of clinical depression appear in U.I. 33, mainly concerned with pessimism and withdrawal. On the other hand several of the pathological symptoms of depression do not appear in U.I. 33(+), namely slower motor speed, slower speed of talking and writing, and general apathy and exhaustion. A counter argument here is that with the possible exception of C4, no advanced pathological cases appear in the four studies identifying U.I. 33, and that the behavior retardation associated with depression and the illogicality and egocentricity of mania may not appear at the extreme ends of the dimension as so far explored. As the bulk of the subjects were "normal" then the marker variables would only be indices for the normal range, and severe disturbance beyond this point might well change the saliency of certain variables. It is particularly unfortunate that a nature-nurture ratio has not, as yet, been established for this factor, for Fuller and Thompson's (96) synthesis of findings in psychological genetics suggest a high hereditary determination of clinical depression.

HYPOTHESIS II: U.I. 33(+) as a learned reaction to a history of unsuccessful striving for self and social recognition.

The view here is that U.I. 33(+) is a closely integrated set of habits learned during a long series of disappointments and frustrations. Such disappointments concern not only social behavior with other people but also perception of self and the development of self-sentiment. Tinged with some aggression, as would be expected, these habits include overt anticipation that the worst is likely to happen and that nothing can be done by any personal intervention to avoid the onslaught of environmental pressures. Along with this, to be consistent with Table 8.16 there has to be a dour determination (presumably completely at a non-conscious level) to at least keep going on any task at hand. The determination to retain a satisfactory level of performance does not imply, of course, any interest or inspiration that may lead to a higher level of performance. This probably accounts for the near zero association of achievement with U.I. 33(+), for in spite of good scores on ability measures this plodding, inhibited form of behavior could scarcely lead to a high gradepoint average.

An interesting and important finding from R10(I) is the higher scores by normals than criminals on U.I. 33(+). This may be due to the freedom from early frustration and punishment at the negative pole of this factor leading to a euphoric absence of fears about the future. Coupled with a socially undesirable environment this could lead to major criminal actions--and indeed this was the case with the R10(I) sample. Crime, if existent at all with U.I. 33(+), would probably be confined to petty spite, as the fear of punishment would be great and the subjective probability of being convicted near to a certainty. This association of U.I. 33(-) with criminality also fits the first hypothesis as the manic pole would be characterized by aggression, emotionality, and lack of control.

No preference is shown at the present time for either of the hypotheses outlined above, and both must await further experimental evidence. The most crucial information lacking at present is that on nature-nurture determination, for the first hypothesis is largely genetic and the second environmental. Also desirable for both hypotheses would be some body-build and physiological correlates, for Kallman's (118) (119) research suggests an association of the manic-depressive condition with mesomorphy-endomorphy, and certain bodily characteristics may be more conducive to insult and criticism than others.

Table 8.15
U.I. 33: Reactive Dismay vs. Sanguineness

Q-Factor	Factor Title	Factor Identification (Research, Sample Size, Age of Subjects, Factor Numbers in Study) R10 168 Adult (10-)
A	(higher) Cyclothymia	00
B	(higher) Intelligence	
C	(higher) Ego Strength	-12
*E	higher Submissiveness (more submissive, mild)	-18
F	(higher) Surgency	-09
G	(higher) Super Ego Strength	00
H	(higher) Parmia	-06
I	(higher) Premsia	-10
L	(higher) Protension	-01
M	(higher) Alaxia	+02
N	(higher) Shrewdness	-04
O	(higher) Timidity	+03
Q1	(higher) Radicalism	-13
*Q2	higher Group Dependence (dependent, imitative)	-18
*Q3	lower Integration (lax, unsure)	-19
Q4	(higher) Ergic Tension	+05

U. I. 33: REACTIVE DISMAY VS. SANGUINENESS (page 1)

Master Index Number	Variable Title	Factor Identification (Research, Sample Size, Age of Subjects, Factor Number in Study)			
		C3 100 Adult (9+)	C4 100 Adult (3+)	R10 168 Adult (10−)	R13 164 6-9 (7+)
112	lower ratio of favorable to adverse self-reference	-52	-38	-01	-34
108	less confident assumption of skill in untried performance	-18	-01	-23	-42
24c,d	higher ratio of final to initial performance (reading and writing backward, CMS)	-18	-27	-39	-07
100	more pessimism over doing good	+51	+25		+07
67a	lower extremity of viewpoint	-11	-36	-12	
192	less considered possible in given time for self	+00	-44	-49	-41
46a,b	less impairment of maze performance by shock punishment	-32	-29	-03	
2a	lower motor rigidity (writing backwards)	-05	-55	-14	
166	less impairment of classification performance by shock	-15	-31		
67b	lower extremity of viewpoint	-11	-36		
11b	higher verbal and numerical ability (PMA)	+36	+02		
305	lower ratio of PGR deflection to mental than physical threatening stimuli	(+01)	-31		
159c	less inaccuracy of time estimated for self and others			-42	
437	less irrelevant marking of test papers				-38
391	less untidiness of coloring				-38
211a	more susceptibility to annoyances				+34
1478	less belief in early maturity			-33	
327d	more logical consistency in reasoning about emotional topics			+33	
401	less preference for competitive vs. non-competitive situations				-32
384	less preference for strange rather than familiar pictures				-31
372	less ego control relative to malevolent external intervention				-30
98b	lower absolute number of correct decisions -- CMS				-30
400	less preference for dangerous vs. safe situations				-29
99	(higher) ratio of verbal to numerical ability	-13	+31		
113	(more) acceptance of reality principle	+02	-11	-01	+33

U.I. 34: INCONAUTIA VS. PRACTICALNESS

1. Prevalence

Factor U.I. 34 was identified in four factor analytic researches at the adult age level, and further investigated in two extension analyses (R7, Wells). As yet this factor has been found only twice in children (studies R12 and R14), and even these matches are somewhat doubtful since some of the major markers of U.I. 34 were not included in these studies.[1] It is for this reason that our discussion will in the main be restricted to results found with adult subjects.

2. Questionnaire Correlates

A main support towards an interpretation of factor U.I. 34 has become available from its consistent loading on questionnaire factor M+(bohemian, unconcerned Alaxia or Autia; R1: +.40, R3: +.38, Ros: +.45; see Table 8.17). Most of the characteristics of factor M, such as the bohemian unconcernedness, the non-conformity, the more unconventional attitudes, and the less rational and more autistic thinking, can be well re-identified in the objective test pattern of U.I. 34 (see Table 8.18). To a lesser degree U.I. 34 also is loaded by the 16 P.F. Test factors A+ (high Schizothymia: aloof, cold) and C+ (higher Ego Strength: mature, calm). In Knapp's researches N1 (123) and N2 (123) on the questionnaire correlates of objective test factors U.I. 34 has not been measured; its correlations with the Guilford-Martin, the Guilford-Zimmerman, and the MMPI scales are therefore not known.

In data from the R10 study, significant correlations were obtained between this factor and two of the Kuder interest scales: U.I. 34 correlated +.30 with Persuasive Interests and +.28 with Artistic Interests.

In the research R1 the anxiety ratings by psychiatrist I loaded "insignificantly" on this factor, the rating on over-all anxiety by psychiatrist II, loaded +.37 on U.I. 34.

3. State Factor Matches

Factor U.I. 34 does not match any of the known state factors and was not identified in the incremental R-technique study R3. This indicates that the factor is largely a trait dimension.

---

[1] Also the identification of U.I. 34 in study Ros is not fully substantiated on the basis of objective test loadings alone; since the 16 P.F. Test, however, has also been used in this research, factor U.I. 34 could be unmistakably identified from its high loading on questionnaire factor M+. (See section on questionnaire correlates.)

4. Loadings on Second-Order Objective Test Factors

U.I. 34 loads on only one second-order OT factor: F(T)VI, Narcistic Development vs. Environmental Contact and Investment (loading of +.51 in R1, not available in remaining four second-order analyses). Factor F(T)VI is in addition loaded by U.I. 26+ (Narcistic Self-Will) and U.I. 27+ (Discouraged, Sceptical Apathy).

5. Criterion Correlations

a) Clinical Criteria

In R10(I) (38) no significant criterion correlations have been found for U.I. 34. Normals and psychotics do not differ significantly in this factor (R7). In study R9-Ta (68) U.I. 34 has not been measured.

b) School and Academic Achievement

U.I. 34 correlates negatively with college achievement. This result has been obtained in two studies: In R1 variable M.I. 276 (scholastic achievement) loaded negatively on this factor; in P1 (138) again a negative correlation was found between U.I. 34 and college achievement -- in the sense of both high-achievement and over-achievement.

c) Military Criteria

Factor U.I. 34 has not been measured in any of the three studies AF(69), N1(121), and N2(122).

6. Nature-Nurture and Age Trend Results

Factor U.I. 34 has not been included in the genetics research (70) and the study on age development (29).

7. Descriptive Interpretation

What appears to be a central attribute of U.I. 34+, in summarizing the objective test evidence on this factor (Table 8.18), might be called "tendency towards more emotional, less rational reasoning". Several variables (M.I. 681, 685, 687) indicate that persons scoring high on U.I. 34+ are quicker and more correct in emotional, synaesthetic, and aesthetic judgments than in logical judgments; in completing stories they are less concerned about logical sequence (M.I. 711). Consistent with these characteristics is the high imaginative fluency in U.I. 34+ (M.I. 282) and, on the other hand, the low carefulness (M.I. 51) and high inaccuracy of performance relative to speed (M.I. 120a, b, c).

The second interesting feature of U.I. 34+ is an increased interest in the unusual, extreme or exaggerated. The U.I. 34+ person prefers stronger rather than weaker smells (M.I. 462), shows more interest in stories about strange and unusual happenings than familiar and more common topics (M.I. 460), and selects more questionable books and stories (M.I. 21).

The less accurate performance and lower carefulness in U.I. 34+ may, at least in part, also indicate a certain indifference. Such a descriptive interpretation would be confirmed by two loadings (M.I. 731, 732) which both show that the U.I. 34+ person may be less concerned about possible consequences of his actions and thus is more ready to commit himself to a particular course of action. Also the more frequent choice of questionable reading material (M.I. 21), already mentioned above, could be partly explained from this interpretation -- in the sense that persons scoring high on U.I. 34+ are more indifferent with regard to existing "good taste" and to what is generally considered appropriate or inappropriate. Less concern about tact and other people's feelings would be indicated further by the negative loading of Humor Factor 5 (M.I. 587) on this factor: persons scoring at the positive pole of this factor consider hostile, derogative jokes as funnier than urbane, pleasant or placid jokes. At the child level this loading is paralleled by more mischievous humor (M.I. 29) in U.I. 34+.

As far as autonomic responses are concerned, U.I. 34+ correlates positively with four measures indicating a higher vegetative arousal level: basal metabolic rate (M.I. 74), volume of secreted saliva (M.I. 455a), extent of gross behavior during forced quiet period (M.I. 1448), and mean PGR deflection to threat and startle (M.I. 43). This increased level of autonomic activity suggests that U.I. 34 might correlate positively with fear and anxiety. Besides the loading of M.I. 43 itself, there are three other loadings which do in fact strengthen this hypothesis: the rating on over-all anxiety by psychiatrist II (R1, see above -- section 2) and a measure of bound fearfulness (M.I. 336: more threatening objects seen in unstructured drawings) both loaded positively on U.I. 34+, and in a reaction time test the U.I. 34+ person slows down more in his reaction time after shock (M.I. 456).

In children U.I. 34+ is loaded positively by verbal fluency (M.I. 271). This does not load the factor in adults, however.

From the above discussion the following main descriptive characteristics of U.I. 34+ can be summarized: more emotional than logical-rational reasoning; interest in, and preference for, the unusual and extreme; indifference regarding external standard; social aggressiveness; higher vegetative arousal level and anxiety.

8. Explanantory Theory: History and Final Hypotheses

A personality dimension similar to U.I. 34 in content and meaning has not been found by other researchers in the area of objective personality test factorization, despite the fact that this personality trait has been recognized for a long time by both professional psychologists and laymen -- namely as a personality dimension of bohemian ("arty") vs. socially adjusted behavior. The following explanatory theory of this factor is based, besides the objective test loading structure, largely on the questionnaire correlates and on the loading on second-order objective test factors.

Our hypothesis is that factor U.I. 34 represents a personality source trait of indifference and unconcernedness, further characterized by more emotional and idiosyncratic reasoning and higher (bound?) anxiety; at its negative pole, U.I. 34 manifests itself in higher group dependence, more logical and strict thinking and reduced anxiety. Especially the low readiness in U.I. 34+ persons to accept external control over their behavior and the described features of unconcerned independence led to the descriptive terms chosen for this factor: Inconautia (i.e., "incontinent", or less controlled and organized, autia) vs. (disciplined) Practicalness. This interpretation also accounts for the positive questionnaire loadings M+ and A+ as well as the finding that U.I. 34 is negatively related to academic achievement, even after intelligence is partialled out of the latter.

From the positive loading of this factor on a second-order OT factor of narcistic development (F(T)VI) we formed the theory that U.I. 34 reflects one of several adjustive directions originating in primary narcism.[1] In fact, we think that U.I. 34, as compared with U.I. 26 and U.I. 27, results from a personality development in the course of which primary narcistic motives have been less reduced and thus led the individual into voluntarily preserved isolation from general norms and demands -- an adjustment process which satisfies the narcistic motivation and keeps it persistent at the same time. The higher anxiety in U.I. 34+ may be a by-product of this withdrawal from external control, but it is equally possible that in fact the latter is adopted because of the former.

---

[1]See also the theoretical discussions on factors U.I. 26 and U.I. 27.

Table 8.17
U.I. 34: Inconautia vs. Practicalness

Q-Factor	Factor Title	Factor Identification (Research, Sample Size, Age of Subjects, Factor Number in Study)		
		R1 86 Adult (4+)	R3 86 Adult (4+)	ROS 70 Adult (6+)
*A	higher Schizothymia (aloof, cold)	-13	-22	
B	(higher) Intelligence			
*C	higher Ego Strength (mature, calm)	(-02)	+01	+21
E	(higher) Dominance			
F	(higher) Surgency	+01	+10	+10
G	(higher) Super Ego Strength			
H	(higher) Parmia	-07	+03	
I	(higher) Premsia	+18	+02	
L	(higher) Protension			
**M	higher Autia (bohemian, unconcerned)	+40	+20	+45
N	(higher) Shrewdness			
O	(higher) Timidity	+05	+08	-05
Q1	(higher) Radicalism			
Q2	(higher) Self Sufficiency			
Q3	(higher) Self Sentiment Control			
Q4	(higher) Ergic Tension	+10	+17	+04

U. I. 34: INCONAUTIA VS. PRACTICALNESS (page 1)

Master Index Number	Variable Title	Factor Identification (Research, Sample Size, Age of Subjects, Factor Number in Study)								
		Ros 70 Adult (6+)	R1 86 Adult (8+)	R3 86 Adult (4+)	E-D1 139 Adult (8+)	We 80 Adult --	R7-Ps 48 Adult --	R7-No 57 Adult --	R12 80 4-5 (9+)	R14 129 3-7 (13+)
120a-c	lower ratio of accuracy to speed	-18	-20	-40	-36				-01	-43
282	greater number of objects perceived in unstructured drawings	+24	+23		+28		*	*	+31	+06
336	larger absolute number of threatening objects seen in unstructured drawings		+15	(-01)					+35	+08
83	lower fidgetometer frequency		-06	-30						-54
33	larger size of myokinetic movement		+04	+39			*	*		+38
455a	higher volume of saliva secreted in 30 seconds	+45	+10	+03						
43	higher mean percentage PGR deflection to threatening stimuli	+09	+04	+30						
227a	lower color/form ratio in picture preferences				-03				-34	-06
763	more fluency concerning people's personal characteristics				+45		(-18)	+06		
116b	less severity of judgment (more indulgent standards)	(+07)	-11		-54					
51	lower index of carefulness in observation		-22	-21					(+02)	
271	higher total verbal fluency on topics				+29				+30	
711	smaller number of logical sequences maintained						-10	-42		
462	greater preference for stronger than weaker smells		-17	-34						
732	more items answered on test of readiness to commit oneself to a course of action						+28	+21		
74	higher basal metabolic rate	+02				+34				
731	higher readiness to commit oneself to a course of action						+29	+12		
456	greater slowing of reaction time when electric shock is applied		+26	+10						
704	more items completed of figure classification test						+05	+29		
586	more hostile derogation than urbane pleasantness (high humor factor 5)						+28	+11		
681	higher ratio of total synaesthesia to total reasoning correct						+35	+02		
718	higher percentage of words recalled correctly on combined word recall-word association test						+20	+15		
685	higher ratio of synaesthetic-aesthetic decision time to total reasoning correct						+32	+01		
687	higher ratio of number aesthetic problems attempted to total reasoning correct						+22	+02		
719	higher number of associated words intruded in recall of original words						+36	(-07)		
460	greater preference for strange rather than familiar in written material		(+10)	-34						
705	higher proportion of items completed (relative to total attempted) on figure classification test						(-02)	+30		
21	more questionable reading preferences		-30						(+03)	
515	less increase in sound pressure from normal to delayed feedback reading		-50							
72	more slowing of reaction time under complex instructions								-49	
641	faster speed of shape comparison								+49	
335	faster complex reaction time								-48	
513	higher sound pressure of voice in speaking and reading (normal conditions)		+42							
24d	lower ratio of initial (slow) to final (fast) total score -- CMS								-36	

U. I. 34: INCONAUTIA VS. PRACTICALNESS (page 2)

Master Index Number	Variable Title	RESEARCH								
		Ros	R1	R3	E-D1	We	R7-Ps	R7-No	R12	R14
1452	less awareness of own willingness to perform self-helped tasks									-33
1733	higher total imaginative fluency				+35					
29	much mischievousness of humor								+35	
1448	less gross behavior during forced quiet period									-29
276	lower academic achievement		-31							
1728	greater preference for symmetric rather than non-symmetric designs				+30					
530	(faster) speed of decision on synaesthetic than reasoning problems						+28	-13		
71	(greater) number of erroneous reactions under complex instructions		+16	-17						
692	(more) distortion on figure recognition						+18	-19		
713	(higher) percentage of alliterative associations given						+18	-25		
152	(more) tendency to agree	+14	+09	+01	-30					+03

* The variables marked by an asterisk, together with factor M+ (Autia) of the 16 P. F. Test, have been used in R7 for computing estimated factor scores on U.I. 34.

U.I. 35: STOLPARSOMNIA VS. EXCITATION

1. Prevalence

U.I. 35 has been identified in three factor analyses with adults (including R3, using incremental R-technique) and one factor analysis with children. An extension analysis by Wells (166) examined the relationship between the factor and physical fitness measures. The matching of factors with adults is very good, but that at the child level can only be regarded as tentative.

2. Questionnaire Correlates

Correlations between U.I. 35(+) and the 16 P.F. scales are available from three studies (R1, R3, and R10). In R10 all sixteen scales were used, but in R1 and R3 only A, C, F, H, I, M, O, and Q4 were tested. Only F(+): Surgency (Enthusiastic, Talkative) appears to have moderate and consistent correlations. M(-): Praxernia (Conventional, Practical) and O(-): Confidence (Confident, Unshakable) have low correlations, but are indicated by other evidence as being possible correlates. Questionnaire correlates do not integrate clearly with objective test findings, and further research is needed on this relationship. A significant negative correlation was found in R10 between Literary Interests, as measured by the Kuder Preference Record, and U.I. 35(+) ($r = -.21$).

3. State Factor Matches

The state factor P.U.I. 1 Unreactiveness (Torpor) vs. Sensitive, Overactive State shows considerable similarity to U.I. 35, and is regarded as its state equivalent (47, 58, 107, 170). High loading variables are: Larger magnitude of percentage GSR deflection, higher ataxic sway suggestibility, tendency to overestimate fear periods, higher level of electrical skin resistance, poorer deliberate immediate memorizing, higher self sentiment. Discussion of this factor by Cattell and Scheier (68) suggests a close relationship to the cholinergic or vagatonic factor discovered in analyses of physiological measures.

4. Loadings on Second-Order Objective Test Factors

U.I. 35 appears in only one second-order objective test factor: F(T)I: Tied Socialization or Superego vs. Absence of Cultural Introjection. The loading is positive (57).

5. Criterion Correlations

a) Clinical Criteria

In a comparison of normals, neurotics, and criminals (R10(I)), criminals were found to have significantly higher factor scores than normals on U.I. 35 (+). Neurotics had scores slightly lower than criminals, but were not significantly different from either of the other two groups. Positive correlations were found in R1 between this factor and psychiatrist's ratings of situational, free, and over-all anxiety.

b) School and Academic Achievement

U.I. 35 (+) has been found to have a marked relationship to both under-achievement and low achievement among university undergraduates (P1).

c) Military Criteria

No evidence is available on the relationship between U.I. 35 and military criteria.

6. Nature-Nurture and Age Trend Results

No information is available at present on either nature-nurture ratios or age-trend results for this factor.

7. Descriptive Interpretation

Lower Competence

There is no evidence that U.I. 35(+) is related to 'good' performance on any of the variables used in the four factor analyses. Further, definitely poor performance appears in lower numerical ability (MI. 199), poorer immediate memory for words (MI. 167, MI. 23a), smaller breadth of classification (MI. 703), higher degree of poor planning in drawing layout (MI. 847) and more errors of omission in C.M.S. (Child Form) (MI. 354). Certain motor and perceptual tasks, gestalt completion, rigidity, and several measures involving speed, and indeed some fluency and linguistic tests, though present in the studies do not appear to have any relationship to the factor.

Torpid Reaction

A second characteristic of U.I. 35(+) is generally sluggish, torpid behavior, lacking incisiveness. This appears in slower irregularly warned reaction time (MI. 176), slower tempo of leg-circling (MI. 269), and lower average writing pressure (MI. 464). In overt behavior it seems that an individual with a high score on this factor would be slow off the mark and make rather pondorous movements without too much fine control, as is found in larger size of myokinetic movement (MI. 33). Many gross movements would be anticipated when carrying out activities at high speeds, but unfortunately no tests of this have as yet been used.

Personal Disillusionment

A degree of personal disillusionment appears in the negative loading for the average time anticipated to elapse before attaining one's life goals (MI. 458). This is not pessimism as such for, apart from less confidence of skill in untried performance (MI. 108), other variables concerned with pessimism do not appear. The reaction appears rather to be a stolid yet realistic appraisal and acceptance of the individual's own capabilities. Indirect support for this comes in higher consistency of aspiration level (MI. 349), less fluctuation of attitudes (MI. 31), and less increase in the ratio of accuracy to speed in moving from an easy to a more difficult task (MI. 334). Such variables show a definite consistency of behavior from one moment to the next, and in the case of aspiration level show no evidence that this is low relative to performance.

Parasympathetic Dominance

Certain physiological measures are related to U.I. 35: Higher magnitude of mean PGR deflection to threat (MI. 43), higher absolute level of GSR (MI. 443), lower systolic blood pressure (MI. 444), and more involuntary muscle tension (MI. 78). These variables, though having modest loadings, contribute to the general interpretation of this factor and are of considerable relevance to the accompanying state factor P.U.I. 1.

Variables Not Included in the Above Categories

A miscellany of variables complete the pattern of U.I. 35(+), including higher ratio of acquaintances to friends (MI. 472)--probably due to regarding few people as friends, and higher ratio of time estimates for frightening vs.

non-frightening passages in film strips (MI. 461). An expressed preference for strange over familiar in written material (MI. 460) appears to be a consistent marker, but its psychological implications for this factor remain obscure.

Various motivation measures appear as correlates of U.I. 35(+), namely lower appeal erg (less desire to be in touch with God) (MI. 1716a), lower appeal erg (less desire to heed parent's advice) (MI. 1716b), and higher sex erg (more desire to satisfy sexual needs) (MI. 927a). The lower appeal scores suggest a degree of independence and self-reliance, while the higher sex erg fits in well with the general parasympathetic character of this factor.

In summary we find in U.I. 35(+) a pattern of sluggish stolidity in behavior, that lacks in inspiration but includes perhaps a not unrealistic self-appraisal. This is accompanied by a set of physiological correlates that suggest parasympathetic dominance. The total picture at its extreme seems not unlike the Fat Boy of the "Pickwick Papers," but unfortunately the requisite supporting evidence from Wells' study on body build is not in agreement!

8. Explanatory Theory: History and Final Hypothesis

U.I. 35 comes late in the U.I. series, and provides relatively little in the way of criterion relationships. However its interest comes from a possible relationship to factors emerging from analyses of physiological variables--though such analyses have been few, in spite of their promise for psychological theory.

Confirmation exists for a dimension directly involving the action of the autonomic nervous system from research by Darrow and Heath (81), Darling (80), Freeman and Katzoff (94), and Wenger (167), among others. The suggestion by Wenger was of a general balance in the population between the parasympathetic (or cholinergic) and sympathetic (or andronergic) systems. Any individual was likely to be in a state of imbalance--i.e., either of parasympathetic dominance or sympathetic dominance. There appears to be little further evidence concerning this dimension, though Eysenck (90) has discussed the possibility that such imbalance may be related to his factors of neuroticism and extraversion.

The relevance of a parasympathetic factor to interpretation of U.I. 35 rests upon the similarity between loadings of physiological measures on the two factors. This resemblance is particularly clear for the state factor P.U.I. 1., but also appears less clearly for the source trait U.I. 35. The view expressed here is that U.I. 35 may well be the parasympathetic factor from physiological studies as it emerges from analyses of tests from a broader domain. Any one-to-one match is not possible as in no case were the non-physiological measures ever the same. However, from general interpretation of the non-physiological correlations, the likelihood of such a match is strengthened. Further research is needed on this issue, in particular using factor analyses including a wider range of physiological variables than has been used so far with U.I.

35, and sufficient non-physiological marker variables from the objective test and questionnaire realms.

Unfortunately nature-nurture ratios and age trend results are not available for this factor. However if the present view is correct then U.I. 35 should be predominantly hereditarily determined. One would also expect consistent correlations with anxiety, and thus that U.I. 35 could be considered as a neurotic contributory factor, but not a neurotic process factor.

An alternative view of U.I. 35 is that it principally involves 'long-circuiting,' defined as "the renunciation of immediate satisfaction in the interests of attaining relatively remote goals" (68). The present view does not conflict with this but regards the 'long-circuiting' as being only one by-product of the trait.

U.I. 36: FORE-SIGHTED SELF-SENTIMENT VS. LOW FORE-SIGHTED SELF-SENTIMENT

A factor which appeared in studies R1, R3, and H1 was interpreted as being central to the concept of the self-sentiment, and was matched across the three studies on the basis of inspection. Since (a) both R1 and R3 involve the same subjects, (b) R3 is not properly a trait study as incremental-R technique factor analysis is used, and (c) both R1 and H1 have but few variables in common, this factor is not regarded as confirmed in the same quantitative sense that this term may be applied to other factors. On the basis of present evidence quantitative forms of matching are not feasible and thus no report on this factor is given in Chapter 6. However the potential theoretical importance of such a dimension, coupled with preliminary results of research at present being carried out, argue for its inclusion in this survey. In order to stress that this factor is at the moment lacking any form of quantitative assessment, we have abjured our usual method of presentation in favor of a simple short summary.

Little evidence is available on questionnaire correlates of U.I. 36, and so far no substantial relationships with questionnaire dimensions have emerged. No information is available on criterion relationships, nature-nurture ration, or on age-trends in factor scores. A state factor was identified in R3 as U.I. 36, and was named P.U.I. 6 Assured Self-Regard. U.I. 36 appears with positive sign in two second-order objective test factors: F(T)II Expansive Ego, and F(T)IV High Educated Self-Consciousness.

The core of this factor, in terms of marker measures, is the self sentiment as it is assessed in the dynamic or motivation mode of measurement. This is reflected in a +.24 average loading on M.I. 933a (greater desire to have good control over one's own mental processes) and a +.38 loading on M.I. 933b (greater reluctance to damage one's sense of self-respect). Details of the loading pattern of U.I. 36 upon other variables may be obtained from Appendices 1, 2, and 3.

Table 8.19
U.I. 35: Stolparsomnia vs. Excitation

Q-Factor	Factor Title	Factor Identification (Research, Sample Size, Age of Subjects, Factor Number in Study)		
		R1 86 Adult (9+)	R3 86 Adult (10+)	R10 168 Adult (21-)
A	(higher) Cyclothymia	+04	+02	-05
B	(higher) Intelligence			
C	(higher) Ego Strength	+07	-02	-04
E	(higher) Dominance			+12
*F	higher Surgency (more enthusiastic, talkative)	+12	+23	+17
G	(higher) Super Ego Strength			00
H	(higher) Parmia	-07	-03	+04
I	(higher) Premsia	+08	+07	-01
L	(higher) Protension			+11
*M	higher Praxernia (more conventional, practical)	(00)	-22	-03
N	(higher) Shrewdness			+12
*O	higher Confidence (more confident, unshakable)	-05	-11	-08
Q1	(higher) Radicalism			+02
Q2	(higher) Self-Sufficiency			-04
Q3	(higher) Self Sentiment Control			+05
Q4	(higher) Ergic Tension	-04	+01	-05

U. I. 35: STOLPARSOMNIA VS. EXCITATION (page 1)

Master Index Number	Variable Title	Factor Identification (Research, Sample Size, Age of Subjects, Factor Number in Study)				
		R1 86 Adult (9+)	R3 86 Adult (10+)	R10 168 Adult (21-)	We 80 Adult --	R12 80 4-5 (17+)
458	more long term life goals	+37	+19	+40		
199	lower numerical ability	-25	-28	-18		-32
460	less preference for familiar over strange in written material	-26	-10	-22		
33	larger size of myokinetic movement	+25	+27	+08		
464	lower average writing pressure	-29	-28			
43	higher magnitude of mean PGR deflection to threat	+21	+32			
167	poorer immediate memory for words	-05	-35	-10		
176	slower irregularly warned reaction time	+10	+27	+06		
269	slower tempo of leg-circling		-30	-05		
108	less confident of skill in untried performance	-04	-20	-04		
443	higher absolute level of GSR	+12	+19			
461	higher ratio of time estimates for frightening vs. non-frightening passages	+04	+39			
444	lower systolic blood pressure	-27	-04			
78	more involuntary muscle tension	+08	+21			
927a	higher sex erg (desire to satisfy sexual needs)	+31	+05			
472	higher ratio of acquaintances to friends	+18	+09			
334	less relative accuracy in difficult relative to easy mazes					-43
1716a	lower appeal erg (desire to be in touch with God)	-42				
531	quicker aesthetic-emotional than cognitive-logical decision time			+40		
31	less fluctuation of attitudes					-39
1716b	lower appeal erg (desire to heed parents' advice)	-38				
703	smaller breadth of classification			-37		
354	more errors of omission in CMS (Child Form)					+36
847	higher degree of poor planning in drawing layout			+34		
473	lower total number of friends	-34				
349	higher consistency in aspiration in maze task					+31
866	less preference for negative arguments			-30		
530	slower synaesthetic than cognitive-logical decision time			-30		
327b	more logical inconsistency of response					+30
316	(more) fluency concerning own than other people's personal characteristics	+35		-06		
123	(higher) ratio of working time estimate to relaxing time estimate			+15		-41
211a	(more) susceptibility to annoyance	+41				-14

U. I. 35: STOLPARSOMNIA VS. EXCITATION (page 2)

Master Index Number	Variable Title	RESEARCH				
		R1	R3	R10	We	R12
42	(more) body sway suggestibility	+03	+31	-25		
933b	(higher) self sentiment erg (less desire to damage sense of self respect)	-09	+34			

CHAPTER 9

MULTIVARIATE PERSONALITY RESEARCH IN THE OBJECTIVE TEST REALM: INTEGRATION AND FUTURE RESEARCH

In the preceding Chapters 4 through 8 the reader has been familiarized with the body of results originating from a twenty years' program of research on objective personality test factors. It will be our aim in this chapter to integrate the major findings into a more comprehensive structural view on personality measurement and an attempt towards a multivariate personality theory. In the third section of this chapter a brief survey will be presented of important theoretical problems which have not been tackled in the past and should therefore be given special consideration in future research.

I. PERSONALITY TRAITS: MODALITIES AND DOMAINS OF MEASUREMENT

1. Media, Modes, and Domains of Measurement

Any given response r_{ijk}, of individual i to "stimulus" j on occasion k (18, 29), can be further classified according to the kind of quality of "stimulus" j; the three principal dimensions of this classification will be called medium, mode, and domain of measurement.

Different media of measurement differ with regard to the nature of the stimulus to which the individual is responding. In personality measurement, typically three media are distinguished (18): behavior ratings (BR), self-ratings or questionnaires (Q), and objective tests (OT).

By mode of measurement we refer to a distinction in terms of different stimulus-response relationships.[1] The three principal modes of measurement are ability measures, temperament measures, and dynamic (or motivation) measures. In pure ability measures, the extent of variability between different individuals in terms of their responses is a (curvilinear) function of only the difficulty or complexity of the stimulus. In pure dynamic measures, the extent of this inter-individual response variability is a (curvilinear) function of only the degree of (actual or potential) drive reduction inherent in a given stimulus. By contrast, a variable is a measure of temperament if the extent

[1] For a more detailed discussion the reader is referred to (18).

of inter-individual response variability stays unaffected by both changes in the difficulty (or complexity) and the drive reducing properties of the stimulus. Whereas a given variable can be easily and uniquely classified as to the medium of measurement to which it belongs, typically no unique classification is possible as to the mode of measurement which it expresses. The latter is due to the familiar factorial heterogeneity of most observable variables which renders a classification in terms of mode of measurement into an assessment of the degree to which each mode is represented in a given variable.

Different domains of measurement differ with respect to the behavioral (surface) content of both stimulus and response. Thus, social behavior, perceptual responses, learning ability, etc., would constitute different domains of measurement.

2. The Position of the Known Objective Personality Test Factors with Regard to Other Media of Personality Measurement

If personality factors, found independently in the different media of measurement, do in fact represent general, functionally unitary dimensions underlying overt behavior, a considerable parallelity is to be expected between the three media in terms of the factors obtained in each. This important question had been recognized by Cattell already some ten years ago, and since then special attention has been given to this problem of inter-media matching of factors (43, 61, 62).

In principle, either one of the following two designs of analysis can be used in an inter-media matching study:

(1) For the same group of subjects measurements are obtained on factors identified in different media, and the factor scores are intercorrelated across the media (e.g., the cyclothymia factor in ratings is correlated with the cyclothymia factor in questionnaire responses).

(2) A factor analysis is designed to include marker variables for factors found independently in the different media; a single analysis is then carried out over all two (or three) media.

The BR-Q matching has mainly been investigated by the first design, the Q-OT matching mainly by the second. From these studies the following conclusions can be drawn with respect to the inter-media matching of factors.

(a) BR-factors and Q-factors intercorrelate substantially across media, and for most of the factors a "point-to-point" correspondence is obtained in comparing BR and Q media (29).

(b) Several OT primaries correlate consistently with Q primaries, but -- with the exception of U.I. 34 -- no simple "point-to-point" relationship seems to exist between first-order factors in Q and OT media. In fact, the major Q-OT matches are between second-order Q and first-order OT factors (see discussion of OT primaries U.I. 19, 22, 24, 32); all four well-replicated second-order Q factors are matched by OT primaries. A similar relationship holds between BR-factors and OT-factors.

These results do not leave any doubt about the behavioral generality of factors found in different media. On the other hand, however, a theoretically important limitation of BR and Q data can be inferred: In comparison with objective tests, in behavior ratings and questionnaires a smaller and/or more specific segment of the total behavioral variance is sampled. This explains (1) the appearance of new factors in OT responses which are not present in BR and Q data, and (2) the apparent difference between OT data and Q as well as BR data in terms of the hierarchical order of primary factors (OT primaries are equivalent to Q and BR second-order factors). Not only are BR and Q media more limited as to variable domain sampled, but in BR and Q data the first-order factors are also more specific than in objective tests. The latter can be easily understood from the fact that the first-order factor analysis is based upon individual item intercorrelations in BR and Q, and on test intercorrelations in OT.

3. The Position of Objective Personality Test Factors with Regard to the Three Modes of Personality Measurement

In pre-metric personality theories not infrequently the view is held that the causal entities underlying human behavior are various skills and abilities, temperamental characteristics, and dynamic (or motivational) attributes -- the three sets of entities typically being regarded as mutually interacting, but conceptually distinct (and distinguishable). With regard to factor analytically derived personality source traits, the extent of such "modal" purity of underlying dimensions becomes a direct function of the way in which the researcher samples his variables. If the variables are deliberately sampled from a wide domain of interindividual behavior differences the resulting dimensions are <u>not</u> pure as to the mode of measurement, but typically are loaded by variables from all three modes; and the question as to whether a factor should be interpreted as an ability, temperament, or dynamic source trait becomes a matter of degree. In other words, adequate broad variable sampling results in personality factors that cut across the three modes of personality measurement.

In the discussions of the first-order OT factors in the foregoing two chapters the reader will find several typical examples substantiating this thesis. Factors U.I. 22 and U.I. 16, for instance, contain both ability and temperament qualities, and factor U.I. 24 is loaded by both temperament and dynamic surface traits.

This fact should be kept in mind when comparing, for example, Thurstone's primary mental abilities with the primary OT factors. What appeared in Thurstone's work to be a pure ability factor, due to his restricted variable sampling (only ability-type variables!) may well be a broader personality source trait, when variables are chosen from a wider domain -- i.e., a factor of which the ability component is only one aspect. We actually have two interesting examples of this effect in the U.I. factor series. Both Thurstone's perceptual speed factor and fluency factor are actually much more general personality dimensions. Perceptual speed and verbal fluency convey only part of the nature of U.I. 17 and 21, respectively, when these factors are extracted from a more representative matrix of behavioral variability.

4. The Question of Representative Variable Sampling

Given the fact that the results of any factor analysis will heavily depend upon the principles on which the researcher selected the variables for his analysis, a brief discussion of the procedures of variable sampling which led to the discovery of the present twenty-one OT personality factors seems necessary at this point.

Historically, the principles of variable selection have undergone some changes during the course of the research programs on objective test factors in the authors' laboratory. Looking back, two "stages" can be described.

(1) During the initial phase of research the variable selection was guided by two principles:
   (a) the attempt to represent each surface concept in Cattell's original "personality sphere" (17, 18) by at least one objective test variable, and
   (b) to construct at least one objective test for each of the principal personality factors found up to that time in ratings and questionnaires.

(2) After the major OT factors had been replicated over two or three studies, a second phase began. In each new analysis the principal salients of all hitherto identified OT factors were included, together with new tests which were constructed with the specific aim of:
   (a) testing interpretative hypotheses about the factors already known, and
   (b) exploring tests from variable domains which have not been represented in previous studies (e.g., physiological measures in R1, R2, R3, and Wells; special child tests in R12 and R13, etc.).

The degree to which these efforts towards a widely representative variable sampling have been successful is difficult to evaluate other than by continuously observing actual real-life behavior and checking back whether or not a test of this particular trait has already been tried. Due to its specific purpose, in this monograph little space is devoted to a description of the objective test variables that have been tried (see Appendix A and B). To get a full picture of the population of behavioral variability covered by these variables the reader is referred to Cattell and Warburton's recent Compendium of Objective Personality Tests (71). In all more than a thousand different OT variables have been tried in the various factor analyses; from an intuitive psychological point of view -- since no objective method of assessment is available! -- all surface traits considered important in traditional personality theory and clinical psychology seem to be equally well represented in this variable selection. In the course of future research new tests for additional, more specific, behavioral domains may be added to this sample of variables, and they may also give rise to the discovery of new personality source traits. With the wide variety of test variables already tried the present twenty-one OT factors, however, are most likely to actually represent the major general personality dimensions.

5. The Generality of Objective Personality Test Factors

In factor analysis, the term "generality" is used in two ways:

(1) with regard to the hierarchical level that a factor occupies (general factor, common factors, test-specific factors), and

(2) with respect to the percentage of the subject population in which it can be identified (a factor being the more "general" the larger the percentage of subjects from the total unselected population in which it exists).

In this context we shall be concerned with this latter meaning of "generality" of a factor. Among the many differences in subject populations that may produce "group specific" factors and suppress factors found in other subject groups, presumably the following two dimensions of differential subject selection have been given most frequent consideration:

(1) differences in terms of "normality" of subjects, i.e., ranging from normal adult subjects to neurotics, psychopaths, delinquents, psychotics, and other clinical groups;

(2) differences in terms of age.

With respect to the second of the above two definitions, a factor can be called "general" if it was consistently identified in separate analyses despite gross differences between these analyses in the kind of subjects tested -- in particular, differences along the two continua normality and age. From the present evidence (cf. chapters VI and VII) there can be no doubt that the described OT personality source traits are indeed very "general" in this sense. These factors have been found in adults as well as children, and within adults in such widely different groups as undergraduate students, Air Force Cadets, psychotics, delinquents, and neurotics! Whereas our results do not necessarily exclude the existence of less general personality factors specific to particular subjects groups only, most factors described in the U.I. series apparently represent relatively general dimensions of behavior in that they could be successfully re-identified in different studies despite major changes in subject population.

II. THEORETICAL PSYCHOLOGICAL INTEGRATION OF THE KNOWN 21 OBJECTIVE TEST TRAITS

So far in this chapter we have described the different measurement modalities in personality research and the extent to which confidence may be felt that such measures do in fact representatively sample the totality of behavior in the personality domain. It is now time to turn specifically to the twenty-one dimensions described in Chapters 7 and 8 in order to place these dimensions into an integrated behavioral system.

Space does not permit a full and detailed exposition of the known and hypothetical interrelationships between the dimensions and their development under given genetic and environmental conditions, and more complete accounts may be obtained elsewhere (29) (68). Nevertheless the reader has so far been exposed only to the empirical facts and theoretical implications of the dimensions in isolation, as it were, and without the benefit of suggestions as to how the dimensions develop together in human personality. Accordingly, in the next few pages the overall picture of nature-nurture findings will be discussed, results and implications of higher-order factorizations will be described, and a proposed model of personality development will be outlined.

1. The relative contribution of heredity and environment to the personality structure.

Behavior, in general, has been properly regarded by psychologists as being a product of both genetic and environmental influences. However, apart from lip-service there has been a tendency to concentrate research almost wholly upon environmental determiners. A recent survey (96) shows that in spite of many references, genetic influences upon behavior have been much neglected in psychological research. When one turns, therefore, to <u>factors</u> rather than isolated tests, the number of genetic studies that show relevance becomes very small indeed.

Present evidence (70) regarding the twenty-one objective test dimensions suggests that approximately seventy percent of personality factor variance is environmentally determined, leaving thirty percent for constitutional determination. This figure can only be tentative at the moment as it rests upon one study investigating only eleven dimensions (U.I. 1, U.I. 16, U.I. 17, U.I. 19, U.I. 20, U.I. 21, U.I. 22, U.I. 23, U.I. 26, U.I. 28, and U.I. 29). Comparison of within-family variance to between-family variance indicates that the former is rather more important, and this is of considerable significance in any discussion of the specific environmental contributors to factor variance. Later research will broaden the range of information on the factors, and should show to what extent factors (not variables) <u>should</u> represent pure determination by either nature or nurture.

2. Higher order dimensions of objective tests.

a) Second order dimensions.

In the same way that primary factors are essential in order to clarify and systematize the results from surface trait correlations, second- or higher-order factorizations may be turned to as integrative and to some extent explanatory concepts for lower level findings. Evidence from second-order factor analyses of C5, C6, R1, R2, and N1 has been presented elsewhere (57) and (68), but will be outlined here in order to pull together the scattered results reported in Chapters 7 and 8.

Seven factors have emerged from such analyses, and are as follows:

F(T)I: TIED SOCIALIZATION VS. ABSENCE OF CULTURAL INTROJECTION.

The first-order factors loading F(T)I are, in order of saliency:

U.I. 20 (+): Comentive Superego,
U.I. 28 (+): Dependent, Negativistic Asthenia,
U.I. 1 (-): Lower intelligence,
U.I. 19 (-): Subduedness,
U.I. 25 (+): Task oriented realism,
U.I. 35 (+): Stolparsomnia,
and U.I. 32 (+): Exvia.

This factor is dominated by U.I. 20 and U.I. 28, and appears to express the extent to which the individual has adopted the standards set by his social environment. Leaving aside the lower intelligence, the results express different phases or expressions of acceptance of social norms. Bearing in mind the theoretical discussions of Chapters VII and VIII, U.I. 20 and U.I. 28 both appear distinctly as shaped by the environment. The former shows general acquiescence and desire to do the "right thing" with the latter as an asthenic reaction to over-expressive early discipline. The formlessness of U.I. 19(-) -- in the sense of absence of critical and demanding standards -- would suggest a person who adheres to the most expedient course of action rather than that suggested by inner (and perhaps somewhat idiosyncratic) standards of conduct. The realism of U.I. 25 (+) and the overt behavior of U.I. 32(+) may both be regarded as acceptable and conforming behavior in our society. The presence of U.I. 35(+), a complex and as yet not too well understood dimension, may well be as a denial of erratic, 'excitable' behavior in favor of torpid resignation.

F(T)II: EXPANSIVE EGO VS. HISTORY OF DIFFICULTY IN PROBLEM SOLVING

The first-order factors loading F(T)II are;

U.I. 16 (+): Assertive Ego,
U.I. 19 (+): Promethean Will,

U.I. 36 (+): Foresighted Self-Sentiment,
U.I. 1 (+): Higher Intelligence,
U.I. 23 (-): Regression,
and U.I. 18 (-): Slow Thoroughness

though the last three do not have substantial values. The central core of this factor is of strong ego development, and the assertion and self-determination of U.I. 16 and U.I. 19, in combination with the high intelligence imply a forceful and strong-willed approach to life's problems. The association with U.I. 36 corroborates the strong suggestion of ego-involvement.

The presence of U.I. 23(-) and U.I. 18(-) is not clear at the present time.

F(T)III: TEMPERAMENTAL ARDOR VS. TEMPERAMENTAL APATHY.

This factor has loadings from

U.I. 21 (+): Exuberance,
U.I. 20 (+): Comentive Superego,
U.I. 1 (-): Lower Intelligence,
U.I. 19 (+): Promethean Will,
U.I. 27 (-): Ungrudging Involvement,
and U.I. 32 (+): Exvia

F(T)III is perhaps the most difficult to interpret of the second-order objective test factors. It appears to be unique in possessing factors with high heredity determination (57) and has a general character of enthusiastic expressiveness. The presence of U.I. 20(+) and absence of U.I. 29(+) is rather surprising, and the latter may imply that long-term, resilient, ardor is involved.

F(T)IV: HIGH EDUCATED SELF-CONSCIOUSNESS VS. LOW EDUCATED SELF-CONSCIOUSNESS

Salient primary factors for F(T)IV are

U.I. 22 (+): Cortertia,
U.I. 18 (+): Hypomanic Smartness,
U.I. 25 (-): Tense Inflexidia,
U.I. 36 (+): Foresighted Self-Sentiment,
U.I. 30 (-): Dissofrustance,
U.I. 29 (-): Defensive Complacency,
and U.I. 33 (+): Reactive Dismay

This second-order factor, in contrast to F(T)III, contains primary factors that are primarily environmentally determined.

An alert, shrewd responsiveness appears to typify this factor, and it has been suggested (68) that the pattern may emerge from an exacting and competitive early home atmoshpere.

F(T)V: HISTORY OF INHIBITING, RESTRAINING ENVIRONMENT VS. LAXNESS.

Only three primary factors show any considerable loadings on this factor: U.I. 17(+): Timid Inhibitedness, U.I. 23(+): High Mobilization, and U.I. 31(+): Wary, Controlled Steadiness. The high loadings on U.I. 17, plus the general character of this factor, suggest that F(T)V emerges from a strict, inhibiting environment. The primary factors imply high control and inhibition without any suggestion of any accompanying disintegrative process. Indeed the presence of U.I. 23 and U.I. 31 is perhaps an indication that a cautious passivity rather than timidity is the central feature.

F(T)VI: NARCISTIC DEVELOPMENT VS. ENVIRONMENTAL CONTACT AND INVESTMENT.

This factor is dominated by the primary U.I. 26(+): Narcistic Self-Sentiment, but is also associated with U.I. 27(+): Discouraged Skeptical Apathy, and U.I. 34: Inconautia. It seems clear that we have here a form of self-sentiment development, but with certain rather unhealthy aspects. The striving nature of U.I. 26, apathy of U.I. 34, and possible bohemianism or 'autia' of U.I. 34 suggest that these may be three possible emergents from a history of disturbed ego development, possibly related to sibling competitiveness or high parental expectancies.

F(T)VII: HIGH TENSION TO ACHIEVE VS. LOW TENSION TO ACHIEVE

The salient primary factors involved in F(T)VII are U.I. 24(+): Unbound Anxiety, U.I. 18(+): Hypomanic Smartness, U.I. 30(-): Dissofrustance, U.I. 25(-): Tense Inflexidia, and U.I. 19(+): Promethean Will. U.I. 24 and U.I. 18 tend to dominate this factor and imply a high reactive tension. The loadings on factors other than U.I. 24 certainly show that F(T)VII is more than anxiety as such, and that it may be "total drive tension as it is oriented and controlled toward achievement" (57). However the absence of several primary factors that seem to be more intimately concerned with achievement or adaption (in one's own eyes or the eyes of society) as in U.I. 20 and U.I. 26 make this interpretation tentative at present.

b) Third order dimensions.

At present there is only one study reporting a third order factorization of objective tests (140b). Three principal axis factors were extracted from the 7 x 7 matrix of averaged correlations between 2nd-order factors obtained from R1 (148), R2 (66) and N2 (121) and reported elsewhere (57). The three rotated third order factors are as follows:

F(T)A: IMMATURE SELF-CENTERED TEMPERAMENT VS. MATURE ENVIRONMENT-ORIENTED STOLIDITY

The second-order factors entering the interpretation of F(T)A are:

F(T)III(+): Temperamental ardor
F(T)IV(-): Low self-consciousness
F(T)VI(+): Narcistic development

The clearest features of this factor appear to be a lack of maturity and control coupled with increased self-concern.

F(T)B: RESTRAINED ACCEPTANCE VS. UNRESTRAINED NEGLECT OF EXTERNAL NORMS

This second factor at the third-order-level has salient loadings on:

F(T)I(+): Tied socialization
F(T)IV(-): Low self-consciousness
F(T)V(+): History of inhibiting, restraining environment

Central to this factor is dependence upon the environment and considerable internalization of standards and mores, and not surprisingly, this is associated with lower ego strength and greater caution.

F(T)C: HIGH SELF-ASSERTION VS. LOW SELF ASSERTION

Salient loadings on this factor are:

F(T)II(+): Expansive ego
F(T)V(-): Laxness
F(T)VII(+): Tension to achieve

Dominated by F(T)II(+), this factor implies high self-assertion, with controlled drive and less inhibition.

c) Implications of higher order analyses.

It is perhaps unnecessary to point out that interpretation at any higher level is dependent upon the accuracy of measurement and interpretation at lower levels. Thus considerably more research is needed before an empirical framework of inter and intra factorization levels, and its psychological implications, can be regarded as confirmed. Indeed we may anticipate that eventually fourth order levels of factorization will be needed before a truly comprehensive picture emerges.

It must be noted that in general as we move from test intercorrelations to primary factor intercorrelations, on to second-order, and finally to third order, the correlations tend to diminish in absolute size. This suggests that it is unlikely that it will be either necessary or desirable for much research to go beyond third (or possibly fourth) orders in the future, even though the size of future studies is likely to increase tremendously with computing progress. Due to the relatively low correlations between oblique primary factors,[1] and the representative sampling of the initial variable domain, the U.I. factors can be seen as standing more or less "on their own feet" (i.e., having a large proportion of specific factor variance in higher level analyses). Nevertheless it is of great importance to the scientist in the field of personality to develop techniques for delineating the multiple causal network accounting for individual differences from factor analytic evidence at all levels of factoring.

III. THE DEVELOPMENT OF PERSONALITY

At birth we may assume the presence of certain propensities in terms of personality dimensions. As maturation proceeds a multiple personality appears (i.e. can be measured), deviations on environmentally determined dimensions can be recorded, and modifications take place on dimensions regarded as the product of both heredity and environmental influences. A model is therefore needed to account for the mutual interaction between, and resulting change upon, both the multiple personality and the multiplicity of courses of action, barriers, conflicts, and the like, presented by the environment. That this is a two-way, or 'feed-back' process should be clear enough, for possession of certain factor scores will predispose the individual towards certain situations (and courses of action within such situations), while at the same time success or failure will tend to modify factor scores.

A theoretical formulation of this interactional process has been outlined by Cattell (21a), and Cattell and Scheier (68). In the latter publication an Adjustment Process Analysis (APA) Chart is presented, with specific reference to the development of anxiety and the prediction of neurosis. To deal with this complex analytical procedure at length would be outside the scope of this monograph, and the reader is referred to the two above-mentioned publications.

In brief, the APA Chart assumes a given drive level (or impetus to action) within the individual, and a particular situation in which this drive is operating. Various choice points are indicated, leading to specific courses of action. There is no assumption of any 'conscious' aspects to decision at choice points, as such points merely indicate that a series of behavioral paths, usually, but not always, mutually exclusive, and available to the individual. Each path has an associated coefficient for each personality dimension, denoting the likelihood, given the individual's factor score, that the path will be chosen. For example U.I. 17(+) would not be associated with choice of paths loading to barriers or potential punishment, while the opposite is probably true for U.I. 21(+). Repeated traversement of particular paths will lead to modifications in factor score for those dimensions associated with environmental determination. Thus

[1] It is rare for a correlation between primary factors to exceed ±0.50, and many such correlations are close to orthogonality.

the decline in U.I. 21 during late childhood and adolescence may be due, at least in part, to repeated set-backs and frustrations. The narcistic development of U.I. 26 is likely to follow from systematic elimination of paths leading to potential loss of self-esteem.

Choice points may be related to either 'external' barriers, threats, and immediate gratifications, or to 'internal' conflicts and frustrations. It seems likely that after the first few years of life the choice-points relating to external barriers will have little effect upon personality change, but they may be of extreme importance in early infancy. It is interesting to note that the factors which appear, on theoretical grounds, to be associated with particular paths bear some similarity to the groupings within the second-order factors.

IV. AIMS OF FUTURE RESEARCH

In the present and preceding two chapters the empirical evidence on the major twenty-one source traits in objective personality tests have been presented and theoretically integrated. At this point, therefore, it is desirable to outline in a more systematic fashion the aims and strategies of multivariate research within the framework of these personality dimensions in the years to come. There can be no doubt that the factor analysis of variables specifically chosen to give denser representation of hitherto less explored subdomains of the total personality sphere may eventually lead to the discovery of new personality factors. The writers recognize the importance and necessity of such investigation, but at the present time would give primacy to more intensive research upon the factors so far replicated. It is within this context that the following outline should be understood.

In principle three different aims of future research can be distinguished: (1) the testing of specific hypotheses on individual factors, (2) examining the dynamic and functional relationships of, as well as interrelationships between, personality source traits, and, (3) investigating the relationships between the source traits and various external criteria.

1. The Testing of Specific Hypotheses on Individual Factors.

In the discussion of each source trait in Chapters 7 and 8, Sections 1 through 7 summarized the empirical evidence, and in Section 8 a theoretical integration was attempted and various hypotheses were discussed. These hypotheses generally involve the relationship between a factor and certain sociological, physiological, and psychological variables, its developmental history, and a wide range of specific home background associations.

2. The Examination of the Dynamic and Functional Relationships of, as well as Interrelationships Between, Personality Source Traits.

At the time of writing a special research project is being planned which would provide, in a much more comprehensive way than previously attempted, the following information on each factor:

(a) Nature-nurture evidence,

(b) Cross-cultural comparisons between different national and ethnic groups,

(c) Age trends from childhood to late adulthood.

In addition, specific studies are necessary to examine the 'behavior' of certain factors in specific situations such as psycho-physical stress, frustration, etc. Also of interest in the relationship with such bodily changes as we induced by hormonal processes, drugs, brain damage, etc. In fact the research goals outlined in this section aim at projecting the personality source traits into the broader matrix of variables known to affect intra- and inter-behavior differences.

3. The Investigation of Relationships Between the Source Traits and Various External Criteria.

The applied psychologist might be interested in the predictive power of the source traits with respect to a wider range of achievement, military, clinical, and various occupational criteria than has hitherto been investigated. Of such criterion relationships perhaps the most demanding is that of differentiating between normals and certain specific pathological groups. Whereas initially the primary aim was to distinguish between such broad categories as normals, neurotics and psychotics, further research has to concentrate now upon narrower nosological syndromes, such as the different neuroses and psychoses.

CHAPTER 10

MEASUREMENT OF PERSONALITY TRAITS U.I. 16 - U.I. 36: THE BEST CHOICE OF TESTS

I. Test Selection for the Measurement of Psychological Traits: The Five Principal Settings of Personality Measurement

Several criteria have to be considered in selecting tests for the purpose of measuring the discussed twenty-one personality source traits. These criteria will become more apparent from a brief review of the principal research settings in which test selection procedures may be applied.

In most general terms, five different types of psychological measurement can be distinguished if the distinction is drawn with respect to both the aim of measurement and the source and nature of validity data upon which the measurement is based. Below these five types of measurement will be presented in ascending order of complexity of the measurement principles involved - an order, which at the same time also represents a line of historical development in psychological measurement.

1) Univariate measurement - not pre-validated

In this - most unsophisticated - type of measurement the researcher wishes to measure a certain quality or (surface) trait which in itself is so little explored that its correlations with observable test responses are unknown. Under these circumstances, the test selection will largely depend upon related previous research findings and may often become a matter of "intuition." The validity of the experimenter's choice of tests remains still to be ascertained before psychological conclusions can be drawn from the results obtained with the tests selected.

Whereas this type of univariate measurement is rather typical of the exploratory stage of research in an entirely new field, it should be considered an exception beyond this stage since, at the time of test selection, no objective data are available to evaluate the appropriateness of the tests chosen.

2) Univariate measurement - pre-validated

In this second type of measurement a single test is to be selected for the assessment of a single trait, but correlations between this trait and a series of tests are known. Typically, the test yielding the highest correlation will then be chosen. Instead of the raw test-trait correlations, frequently correlations corrected for unreliability of the test are used as the basis of test selection; having made his choice, the experimenter then also aims at increasing the reliability of the selected test (by increasing its length, from an analysis of internal test consistency, etc.).

Pre-validated univariate test selection has been widely used. Its major drawback lies in the empirical fact that, in general, a single test represents a rather inadequate measurement instrument of those more complex functions of behavior in which psychologists typically are interested. As a result, univariate measurement usually is confined to the assessment of broad surface traits the internal complexity of which is unknown and quite often underestimated.

3) Multivariate measurement of not necessarily functionally unitary traits

In the most general sense, we are applying the term "multivariate" to any measurement approach which employs several tests for the assessment of a particular trait. Within the realm of multivariate measurement the actual assessment operations differ, besides other things, with the nature of the trait which is to be measured, i.e., whether or not the chosen trait is a functionally unitary dimension (such as a factor obtained from a factor analysis). In this paragraph we shall consider the case where the functional unity of the trait has not been proved (and, as a consequence, is very often also not fulfilled). Typical examples of such multivariate measurement are: 1) the measurement of an hypothesized source trait and, 2) the measurement of a complex life criterion. An example of the former might be a test battery constructed for measuring an hypothesized general trait of social adjustment, the latter is illustrated by the many researches on the prediction of external criteria such as pilot proficiency, academic achievement, accident proneness, etc. from a battery of psychological tests.

Principles of test selection differ between these two cases. The multivariate measurement of complex external criteria usually employs a multiple regression approach. A large series of tests, considered prospective predictors of the criterion chosen, are completely intercorrelated as well as correlated with measures of the criterion; a prediction equation is then derived which maximizes the multiple correlation between criterion estimates, obtained from a weighted composite of all test scores, and actual criterion measures. Analytical methods have been developed (156, 168) allowing for an optimal test selection from the set of tests initially tried, such that the number of test predictors is minimized while the composite predictive accuracy is maintained.

By contrast, the multivariate measurement of hypothesized source traits (i.e. case 1 above) faces several difficulties. No direct test validity figures are available at the time of test selection - due to the very circumstance that the particular source trait has not been demonstrated as a factor common to a set of tests, but has been postulated at the outset and tests for its measurement have been constructed thereafter. In essence, therefore, this type of multivariate measurement is analogous to the not prevalidated univariate measurement described above. Test selection has to be based largely upon "intuition" and upon - often unsystematic - evidence from previous researches. Because of these very difficulties, the desired source trait is sometimes assumed to be highly correlated with certain external criteria; the observable correlations between certain tests and these criteria may then be regarded as approximating the required test-source trait correlations, which cannot be obtained directly since the source trait is not empirically defined.

The multivariate measurement of complex traits for which functional unity has not been proved is certainly justifiable from the framework of the applied psychologist, if such a trait represents an important external criterion and its prediction is the main aim of a research study. Relating external criteria directly to specific tests instead of relating them to broader, functionally unitary behavior dimensions need not result in a loss of statistical predictive power; and as long as the applied psychologist is mainly interested in the latter, he will be satisfied with his measurement model.

By the time, however, when also a theoretical-psychological understanding of a particular criterion behavior is sought, this mode of measurement turns out to be less satisfactory, and what previously might have been rejected as an unnecessary "detour" (namely: predicting criterion behavior not directly from single tests but from integrated dimensions of behavior) will then appear the more fruitful approach. This is due to the fact that, in general, criterion correlations with specific test behavior are theoretically more difficult to deal with, less easily interpretable, than criterion correlations with factor-analytically derived behavior dimensions - since, as a rule, the psychological interpretation of individual test responses is less substantiated and less clear than the interpretation of more general source traits.

As to the multivariate measurement of empirically undefined, i.e. only hypothesized source traits, little theoretical advancement seems to result from such measurement devices. Not only is the degree unknown to which each selected test actually measures this source trait, but later research usually reveals that such test batteries measure not only one, but in fact, several different source traits (or factors) which are contaminated in the suggested total score.

4) Multivariate measurement of a single source trait at a time

By the term "source trait" we are always referring to a trait of known functional unity; without exception "source trait" therefore refers to a factor analytically isolated behavior dimension.

Measuring a single source trait at a time is a relatively infrequent case of multivariate measurement. It arises primarily in those instances where an intercorrelation matrix has rank 1 and the single common factor is to be measured. With the usual broad variable sampling in modern factor analysis this case will hardly ever happen and thus is restricted to special analyses of relatively narrow variable subdomains.

In such cases, the test selection is based upon the factor loadings of the investigated variables which may be treated - for the purpose of this selection - like criterion correlations.

5) Multivariate measurement of several source traits at a time

It is this most complex case of multivariate measurement with which we are concerned when selecting tests for the assessment of the twenty-one personality source traits U.I. 16 - U.I. 36. In contrast to the four types of measurement discussed above, test selection in this case faces the great difficulty of considerable factorial complexity of observable test variables - a difficulty unknown to univariate and simple multivariate measurement, because the functional complexity of variables is not brought to light in these measurement approaches. In addition, the nature of the data on which the choice of variables is to be based does not allow the application of any of the analytic-statistical methods of test selection (Wherry-Doolittle method, etc.). This is due to the following three characteristics of the basic data on variable-factor relationships which are typical of replicated factorizations in general:
1) The replicated test-factor correlations are obtained from different studies which differ as to the test intercorrelations.
2) The inter-study variability in terms of the loadings of a variable j on a factor p is due also to a variability between these studies in the spatial position of factor p.
3) Not all markers of a given factor have been included in all studies in which this factor had emerged.

Under these circumstances, a set of special criteria of test selection had to be worked out which - in the absence of analytical test selection methods - would still provide for valid measurement of each factor by a minimum number of variables, and at the same time avoid undue correlation between different factors due to highly correlated marker variables. As the present chapter is only dealing with the <u>selection</u> of suitable test variables, we need not go into the question of how to compute estimated factor scores from selected marker variables; these statistical problems will be discussed in chapter XI. For the present it will therefore suffice to review briefly the criteria of test selection which have been observed throughout this chapter.

II. The Measurement of the Twenty-One Objective Personality Test Factors: Principles of Test Selection

The major rules adopted for test selection can be summarized under the following five criteria:

1. The Factor Loadings of the Variables

Only variables are to be selected which

a) correlate consistently with the factor in question, and

b) do not load on any other factor.

It is the second of these rules which is sometimes difficult to fulfill since highly reliable variables often are factorially complex. For such variables the following requirements have to be met in order to be included into the battery without creating too much spurious correlation between different factors:

a) The particular variable loads higher on factor A, for which it is to be selected than on any other factor B, ...K.

b) If a variable i has been chosen for the measurement of factor A but also loads on factor B, it is desirable to include into the battery for factor A another j which loads on A in the same direction as variable i but whose loading on factor B is opposite in sign to the loading of variable i (so that variable j will act as a suppressor variable with regard to factor B).

c) If no such variable j exists, no other variable must be chosen for the measurement of factor A which would also load consistently on factor B.

In Appendix I the principal evidence is presented on the variable-factor relationships upon which the test selection was based. The rows of this extensive table represent the test variables; a variable is entered into this table if it occurred in at least one of the 21 individual factor tables (see chapters VII and VIII). The columns represent the personality factors U.I. 16 - U.I. 36. A blank space either indicates that this variable has not been used in any of the researches in which this factor has been identified or that the variable has been measured in one or more researches which yielded this factor, but that its loadings have been too low in order to be included into the individual table for this factor. For all remaining variables two entries are given per column:

1. Average Factor Loading. This is the first entry from the left. The averages are weighted for the number of cases in each research, Fisher's z transformation having been used. For a given factor the average is computed from all reference vector correlations reported for the variable in previous studies. No differentiation is made between children and adults, nor between different adult populations. Any sign reversals of the correlations away from the expected direction are, of course, retained in the average.

It is probably wise at this point to emphasize that the variables having values in the columns of Appendix 1 are by no means all to be considered as marker variables. Our criteria of inclusion were such as to necessarily include certain variables with essentially zero correlations along with the higher correlations of the marker variables.

2. Total Number of Researches. This is the second entry and appears within brackets. Recorded is the total number of studies on which the above average is based. The reader interested in results from different sub-groups or in the total number of subjects reflected in the average correlations should turn to the individual factor tables in Chapters 7 and 8.

Whereas the test selection has to be done separately for the adult and the two childhood age ranges, table I in the appendix summarizes the results across all age levels. Otherwise it contains all information on the variable-factor relationships essential for test selection.

As to a lower limit in absolute size of average factor loadings, required for a variable to be accepted into the battery, no general rules have been set. Most variables selected had average factor correlations of .20 or above, but in the case of factors with small factor variance occasionally also variables had to be included into the battery with an average loading below .20.

2. The intercorrelations of the variables

Complete intercorrelation matrices are not available from each research for all variables that have been selected for the measurement of a particular factor, for certain variables have only been included in the more recent studies. Therefore, as a first approximation, the required variable intercorrelations have been averaged across all available analyses. In order to maximize the power of factor measurement, the selected variables had to be those out of the salients of a factor which showed lowest intercorrelations.

3. Consistency of the battery across age levels

Special care seemed necessary to keep the selected test variables as consistent as possible across the various age levels. No complete consistency of this kind can be achieved, as a matter of fact, but the selection of tests for the adult age range was also contingent upon the best factor salients in children, and vice versa. A high consistency between the factor batteries for the different age levels, both in terms of content and format of tests chosen, seemed essential for future applications of these batteries, e.g., in research on the genetics and age development of personality source traits.

In designing these factor batteries the following three age levels have been considered: adult age range (18 years and onwards), late childhood (9 - 13 years), and middle childhood (7 - 9 years). The factor battery for middle childhood is still of a somewhat tentative nature for some of the factors, until the present choice of tests is confirmed by later studies.

At the present time, no battery will be suggested for the early childhood or pre-school level (4 - 5 years). As yet most of the factors have been identified in only one study at this age level (research R12): in view of the special problems met in this age group this was considered an insufficient basis for proposing a factor battery. Most tests to be administered to these children are different in format from the tests used with adults, in the sense that no reading or writing can be involved and that the test content has to be specifically adapted. Also, as experience showed, tests of equal length are less reliable in young children than in adults. The reader interested in working with children of this age group will find all the empirical evidence, prerequisite to constructing a factor battery, in the factor tables of chapters VII and VIII. The writers will present a final test battery for this age level in the near future, which will be based upon broader evidence than reported in this book.

4. Experimental independence of different factor scales

When dealing with the variable-factor relationship as a criterion of test selection we mentioned certain requirements which have to be met in order to keep direct spurious correlation as low as possible between different factor scales. Now we shall consider briefly experimental dependence as an additional important indirect source of spurious correlation between the scales for two factors A and B.

Let us assume that two variables a and b are obtained from the same test; a may be a speed measure, b an accuracy measure. We shall further assume that variable a loads only on factor A, and variable b only on factor B. If a and b are included into the battery for factors A and B, respectively, the two factor scales may be spuriously correlated due to possible experimental correlation (and correlated error of measurement) between variables a and b.

Since, as a rule, one test yields several variables with different factor composition, different factor scales are likely to share common tests even if there is no overlap between these scales in terms of actual variables. In order to guard against undue spurious correlation of the described nature we placed the following additional restriction upon test selection: The sets of variables chosen for any two factors should have no more than two tests in common.

5. The heterogeneity of a factor scale in test content and format

Quite in contrast to previously held views about internal homogeneity of a psychological scale is this last criterion of test selection. Tests should be chosen for the measurement of a given factor in such a way that the resulting factor scale is internally highly heterogeneous as to both content and format of selected tests. This rule is of particular importance if instrumental (device or method) variance is not to be contaminated with a source trait measure. Let us take a simple example: Among the many variables with consistent loadings on factor U.I. 16 (see table 7.2) a considerable number represent speed measures (sheer physical speed, perceptual speed, speed of decision and judgment). As evidenced from the total structure of this factor, however, fast speed is only one aspect of this personality dimension. If a test constructor were to select his measures of U.I. 16 mainly from these speed variables he is very likely to end up with a specific speed factor rather than this much broader source trait.

No general rules can be given to guard against such a mis-choice of tests -- as the degree of homogeneity of a factor scale in test content and test format can only be subjectively evaluated. The multivariate researcher, however, should keep this potential danger in mind and aim at a rather large variability in format and content among the tests chosen for a particular factor scale.

III. The Measurement of the Twenty-One Objective Test Factors: Best Choice of Tests[1]

In this section three test batteries will be given for each factor, except for those that have not been identified at all three age levels (7 - 9 years, 9 - 13 years, adults); these three batteries will be called 8-year battery, 11-year battery, and adult battery. The scales have been compiled with the aim of fulfilling each of the above requirements and criteria optimally. Each factor scale contains between 5 and 10 variables; for practical purposes of test administration the number of individual tests has always been kept as small as possible.

For each factor a table will be given listing the selected variables
1) by their respective M.I. (Master Index) number,
2) by their verbal title (preceded by the corresponding test title), and
3) by the T number of the test from which the variable is measured.

In addition, a distinction is made in these tables between group administrable (paper and pencil) tests (G) and individual tests (I). The latter usually also require some apparatus. For a short description of the tests the reader is referred to Appendix II. In the column "Total Test Administration Time" the time for administering each test is given in minutes; these times include actual testing time as well as time needed to give the proper test instructions.

For each variable selected the average factor loading on the particular factor will be reported. The right hand columns in each table represent the batteries for the different age levels. An x in these columns indicates that the variables is to be used for measuring the factor at the given age level. Whenever such an entry reads "xm" instead of "x" the particular test is used in a modified version that makes it suitable for this age group (child versions of adult tests or adult versions of child tests).

If a variable is consistent marker at at least one age level but has not been used in studies at the remaining age levels, an asterisk is used instead of an x. This indicates that the variable is <u>expected</u> to load also at this age level, but this hypothesis is still unconfirmed. Such variables are not recommended for use in a measurement battery at this age level but should be considered in factor analytic studies as possible marker variables.

Each factor battery will be given a brief discussion which is preceded by a table listing its general characteristics (number and type of tests selected, total

[1] No test battery is recommended here for U.I. 36. However a battery based upon current research results may be obtained from the author. See page 322.

administration time, and overlap between different age forms in terms of common measures).

Factor U.I. 16: Unbound, Assertive Ego vs. Bound, Disciplined Ego

1. Characteristics of U.I. 16 Battery (table 10.1)

	Adult Form	11-Year Form	8-Year Form
number of variables	10	6	7
number of group tests	8	4	6
number of individual tests	1	2	1
total administration time	42 min.	26 min.	27 min.

Overlap between forms: adult - 11-year: 4 variables
adult - 8-year: 4 variables
11-year - 8-year: 3 variables

2. Discussion

For the two child forms only 6 and 7 variables, respectively, could be selected. In each age form the time of individual testing needed is small compared to the group testing time.

Variable M.I. 50 has been chosen for the 11-year battery although its average factor loading is higher on U.I. 19 than on U.I. 16. Since the loading on U.I. 19, however, is only in adults and the loading on U.I. 16 is in children higher than the former this choice seemed justifiable.

As regards the 8-year battery, a modified child version has to be given of test T 50.

Table 10.1. Test Battery for Factor U.I. 16

Variable	Test	G or I	Variable Title	Test Administration Time	Average Factor Loading	Selected For		
						Adult Battery (18y. --)	11-Year Battery (9-13y.)	8-Year Battery (7-9y.)
M.I. 9	T50	G	Ideomotor Tempo: faster ideomotor tempo	4:00	+.49	x	*	xm
M.I. 270	T138	I	Arm Circling: faster-arm-shoulder tempo	2:00	+.27	x	x	x
M.I. 117	T27	G	Highbrow Tastes: more responses indicative of "highbrow" taste	6:00	+.34	x	*	
M.I. 278 & M.I. 511	T6	G	Reading Tempo and Memory for Interesting Material: faster tempo of reading	5:00	+.57	x	x	*
M.I. 282	T20	G	Unstructured Drawings: greater number of objects perceived in unstructured drawings	5:00	+.25	x		
M.I. 268	T136	I	Tapping: faster tapping tempo	3:00	+.49	x	x	*
M.I. 234	T42	G	Pencil mazes: more inaccuracy on pencil mazes	2:00	+.41	x	*	x

Table 10.1. Test Battery for Factor U.I. 16 (Continued)

Variable	Test	G or I	Variable Title	Test Admin-stration Time	Average Factor Loading	Selected For		
						Adult Battery (18. --)	11-Year Battery (9-13y.)	8-Year Battery (7-9y.)
M.I. 309	T45	G	Line Length Judgment: faster speed of line length judgment	3:00	+.52	x	x	x
M.I. 118	T259	G	Poetic Appropriateness: more sense of poetic appropriateness	6:00	+.29	x		
M.I. 125a	T9*)	G	Opinion Inventory X: higher ratio of personal to institutional values	6:00	+.22	x	*	
M.I. 247a	T117	G	Drawing - Expansiveness of Copying: greater expansiveness of copied design	7:00	+.21		x	x
M.I. 382	T150	G	Design Evaluation Speed: faster speed of evaluative judgment	5:00	+.22			x

*) Only one section of T9 is to be used.

Table 10.1. Test Battery for Factor U.I. 16 (Continued)

Variable	Test	G or I	Variable Title	Test Admin-stration Time	Average Factor Loading	Selected For		
						Adult Battery (18. --)	11-Year Battery (9-13y.)	8-Year Battery (7-9y.)
M.I. 375	T280	G	Cancellation of Circles: greater accuracy in circle cancellation	4:00	+.45			x
M.I. 50	T378	G	Following Directions: higher alertness in following directions	6:00	+.16		x	

Factor U.I. 17: Timid Inhibitedness vs. Lack of Inhibition

1. Characteristics of U.I. 17 Battery (table 10.2)

	Adult Form	11-Year Form	8-Year Form
number of variables	9	6	6
number of group tests[1]	4(5)	3(4)	5(6)
number of individual tests[1]	5(4)	3(2)	1(0)
total administration time	46 min.	39 min.	32 min.

Overlap between forms: adult - 11-year: 6 variables
adult - 8-year: 3 variables
11-year - 8 year: 3 variables

2. Discussion

In general, the batteries for factor U.I. 17 contain a comparatively large number of individual tests which cannot be replaced by other group administrable tests if the factor validity is not to be lowered. However, for at least one of these individual tests (T 122: Reaction Times) a newly developed group form can be substituted for which no apparatus other than a tape recorder is needed. The resulting changes in the number of group and individual tests have been indicated in brackets in the above table.

Of the variables selected for the 11-year form M.I. 336 has not been measured in C7. However, since the highly related score M.I. 105 loaded sizably in this study the selection of this variable for the age group 9-13 years seemed justified. Modified child versions have to be given at this age level of tests T24 and T18.

[1]The numbers in brackets are obtained if a recently developed group form of T122 is to be used.

Table 10.2. Test Battery for Factor U.I. 17

Variable	Test	G or I	Variable Title	Test Administration Time	Average Factor Loading	Selected For		
						Adult Battery (18y. --)	11-year Battery (9-13y.)	8-Year Battery (7-9y.)
M.I. 43	T128	I	Psychogalvanic Reflex: higher mean percentage PGR deflection to threatening stimuli	8:00	+.24	x	x	*
M.I. 336	T20	G	Unstructured Drawings: larger absolute number of threatening objects perceived in unstructured drawings	5:00	+.38	x	x	x
M.I. 112	T24	G	Unusual Events: more adverse than favorable self-reference in events	4:00	+.16	x	xm	xm
M.I. 72	T122*)	I	Reaction Time: more slowing of reaction time under complex instructions	8:00	+.24	x	x	x
M.I. 46a	T129	I	Mazes: more impairment of maze performance by shock punishment	5:00	+.16	x	x	*
M.I. 10	T179	I	Dark Adaptation: slower dark adaptation	4:00	+.35	x	*	

Table 10.2. Test Battery for Factor U.I. 17 (Continued)

Variable	Test	G or I	Variable Title	Test Admini-stration Time	Average Factor Loading	Selected For		
						Adult Battery (18y. --)	11-year Battery (9-13y.)	8-Year Battery (7-9y.)
M.I. 150	T18	G	Aphorisms: more acceptance of obvious remarks	9:00	+.22	x	xm	
M.I. 216	T135	I	Shock Suggestibility: less shock suggestibility	3:00	+.33	x		
M.I. 303	T362	G	Whole-Detail Speed: slower speed of decision on "whole" judgements	5:00	-.63	x		
M.I. 29	T40	G	Criticalness in humor: less mischievousness of humor	4:00	-.51		*	x
M.I. 429	T143	G	Picture Inspection: more preference for non-aggressive than aggressive pictures	6:00	-.72			x
M.I. 374	T295	G	Disturbing Sounds: less preference for disturbing sounds	5:00	-.53	*	*	x

*) Only part of T122 has to be given; thus the administration time can be reduced to 8 minutes (instead of 12 minutes for the whole test T122).

Factor U.I. 18: Hypomanic Smartness vs. Slow Thoroughness

1. Characteristics of U.I. 18 Battery (table 10.3)

	Adult Form	11-Year Form	8-Year Form
number of variables	9	5	5
number of group tests	7	4	4
number of individual tests	1	0	0
total administration time	49 min.	21 min.	36 min.

Overlap between forms:
adult - 11-year: 3 variables
adult - 8-year: 1 variable
11-year - 8 year: 1 variable

2. Discussion

Two variables from T121, the Cursive Miniature Situation, are included in all three forms. These variables involve quite different aspects of performance, and this should reduce to a minimum any specific C.M.S. test variance that may enter into the factor score. T299 may be replaced by a modification of M.I. 96b (T283) Frustration Tolerance: Less Impairment of Computing Speed by Frustrated Preference at the test administrator's discretion.

Table 10.3. Test Battery for Factor U.I. 18

Variable	Test	G or I	Variable Title	Test Admini-stration Time	Average Factor Loading	Selected For		
						Adult Battery (18. --)	11-Year Battery (9-13y.)	8-Year Battery (7-9y.)
M.I. 15	T121	G	C.M.S.: more use of circles	7:00	+.30	x	x	
M.I. 16a	T121	G	C.M.S.: more slanting lines crossed	7:00	+.28	x	x	*
M.I. 39	T113	G	Color-Form Sorting: higher ratio of color to form in sorting	4:00	+.24	x		
M.I.*96a	T299	G	Reading Speed: less impairment by frustrated preference	4:00	+.26	x	x	*
M.I. 83	T99	I	Fidgeting: higher score	3:00	+.21	x		
M.I. 193a	T10	G	Opinion Inventory Y: more shifting of attitudes towards those of successful people	12:00	+.13	x		
M.I. 30	T13	G	Criticalness of Self vs. Others: more criticism of self relative to criticism of others	10:00	+.18	x	*	x

M.I. *96b T283 Frustration Tolerance: less impairment of computing speed by frustrated preference may be used instead of M.I. 96a.

Table 10.3. Test Battery for Factor U.I. 18 (Continued)

Variable	Test	G or I	Variable Title	Test Administration Time	Average Factor Loading	Selected For		
						Adult Battery (18y. --)	11-Year Battery (9-13y.)	8-Year Battery (7-9y.)
M.I. 106	T21	G	Risk Taking in Unqualified Statements: more unreflective acceptance of unqualified statements	4:00	+.21	x		
M.I. 385	T185	G	Shape Comparison: more accuracy	4:00	+.44	*	*	x
M.I. 465	T49	G	Letter Placement: more decrement in coding performance with anxiety sound reaction	5:00	+.22	x	*	
M.I. 82	T129	G	Mazes: greater distance covered	3:00		x		
M.I. 143	T121	G	CMS: higher total score	7:00				x
M.I. 247b	T229	G	Drawings: Greater expansiveness	7:00			x	x

Table 10.3. Test Battery for Factor U.I. 18 (Continued)

Variable	Test	G or I	Variable Title	Test Administration Time	Average Factor Loading	Selected For		
						Adult Battery (18y. --)	11-Year Battery (9-13y.)	8-Year Battery (7-9y.)
M.I. 1418	T368	G	Pleasant vs. Unpleasant Comments on Self and Others: lower ratio of pleasant to unpleasant comments on self	8:00				x

Factor U.I. 19: Promethean Will vs. Subduedness

1. Characteristics of U.I. 19 Battery (table 10.4)

	Adult Form	11-Year Form	8-Year Form
number of variables	10	4	6
number of group tests	8	4	6
number of individual tests	2	0	0
total administration time	58 min.	19 min.	34 min.

Overlap between forms: adult - 11-year: 3 variables
adult - 8-year: 3 variables
11-year - 8 year: 2 variables

2. Discussion

U.I. 19 is one of the most frequently identified factors, yet presents certain difficulties in measurement. The main problem is that apart from such markers as M.I. 146b there is a tendency for the factor to enter many variables whose main loadings are upon other factors. This called for considerable care in the selection of variables at all three age levels.

The reader will observe that M.I. 30 (T13) less criticism of self vs. criticism of others and M.I. 116a (T9) higher severity of judgment have rather lower average loadings than is customary. Their inclusion, rather than that of certain other variables, is due to an attempt to represent the different facets of U.I. 19 in as varied a fashion as possible and not to rely too heavily, for instance, upon tests of perceptual closure.

Unfortunately only M.I. 146a (not M.I. 146b) has been used with 8-year-old children, thus reducing the overlap of variables among the different age levels. However there is considerable evidence to suggest that for this factor these two measures are essentially interchangeable.

Although M.I. 206 (higher accuracy in perceptual closure on Gottschaldt figures) has not been used with 11-year-old children, there is high presumptive evidence from all other age levels that its inclusion in the 11-year form would have been justified. Nevertheless adhering to the policy outlined in the introduction to this chapter we are awaiting empirical confirmation at each age level before suggesting the inclusion of a test.

Table 10.4. Test Battery for Factor U.I. 19

Variable	Test	G or I	Variable Title	Test Administration Time	Average Factor Loading	Selected For		
						Adult Battery (18y.--)	11-Year Battery (9-13y.)	8-Year Battery (7-9y.)
M.I. 146b	T2	G	Gestalt Closure: greater percentage correct	3:00	+.33	x	x	*
M.I. 206	T37	G	Gottschaldt Perceptual Analysis: greater accuracy	5:00	+.26	x	*	x
M.I. 71	T122	I	Reaction Times: fewer errors under complex instructions	12:00	-.19	x		
M.I. 51	T114	G	Observation: more carefulness in following detailed instructions	4:00	+.17	x		
M.I. 8	T3	G	Alternating Perspective: higher frequency of fluctuation	3:00	+.17	x	x	
M.I. 30	T13	G	Criticalness of Self vs. Others: less criticism of self relative to criticism of others	10:00	-.09	x	*	xm
M.I. 116a	T9	G	Opinion Inventory X: higher severity of judgment	6:00	+.13	x	x	xm

Table 10.4. Test Battery for Factor U.I. 19 (Continued)

Variable	Test	G or I	Variable Title	Test Admini-stration Time	Average Factor Loading	Selected For		
						Adult Battery (18y. --)	11-Year Battery (9-13y.)	8-Year Battery (7-9y.)
M.I. 467	T364	G	Distraction by Aesthetic Material: less distraction in numerical and verbal tasks by aesthetic material	8:00	-.21	x	*	*
M.I. 41	T126	I	Two-hand Co-ordination: many correct movements	3:00	+.18	x		
M.I. 2e	T142	G	Color Naming: less rigidity	5:00	-.14		x	x
M.I. 426	T143	G	Picture Inspection: less distractibility	5:00	-.20			x
M.I. 472	T64	G	Friends and Acquaintances: more acquaintances relative to friends recalled	4:00	+.19	x	*	
M.I. 146a	T2	G	Gestalt Closure: greater absolute accuracy	3:00				x

Factor U.I. 20: Comentive Superego (Development) vs. Abcultion

1. Characteristics of U.I. 20 Battery (table 10.5)

	Adult Form	11-Year Form	8-Year Form
number of variables	10	5	
number of group tests	6	3	
number of individual tests	3	1	
total administration time	75 min.	53 min.	

Overlap between forms: adult - 11-year: 3 variables
adult - 8 year: -- variables
11-year - 8-year: -- variables

2. Discussion

Due to the co-operativeness existing between U.I. 20, U.I. 24, and U.I. 28, considerable care has been taken to make the two forms for this factor as factorially pure as possible. This accounts for the absence of such markers as M.I. 219 and M.I. 211a, and the inclusion of M.I. 55 which should act as a suppressor (at least with regard to U.I. 24).

The reader will note that no 8-Year Form is presented for this factor. U.I. 20 has been identified only once at this age level (R13), and the identification (being tentative) needs further replication before a battery can be presented with confidence. For factor analysis purposes table 7.9 gives information as to choice of marker variables with young children.

Table 10.5. Test Battery for Factor U.I. 20

Variable	Test	G or I	Variable Title	Test Administration Time	Average Factor Loading	Selected For		
						Adult Battery (18y. --)	11-Year Battery (9-13y.)	8-Year Battery (7-9y.)
M.I. 152	T9	G	Opinion Inventory X: more tendency to agree	39:00	+.52	x	x	
M.I. 38a	T9	G	Opinion Inventory X: higher ratio of consonant to dissonant recall (corrected for tendency to agree)		+.34	x		
M.I. 35	T10	G	Opinion Inventory Y: more suggestibility to authority	6:00	+.25	x		
M.I. 246	T34	G	Authoritarianism: more submission	4:00	-.26	x	x	
M.I. 36	T11	G	Logical Assumptions: higher logical ability	5:00	-.40	x		
M.I. 165	T139	I	Classification: lower ratio of performance under approval relative to disapproval	4:00	-.45	x	*	

Table 10.5. Test Battery for Factor U.I. 20 (Continued)

Variable	Test	G or I	Variable Title	Test Admini-stration Time	Average Factor Loading	Selected For		
						Adult Battery (18y. --)	11-Year Battery (9-13y.)	8-Year Battery (7-9y.)
M.I. 106	T21	G	Risk Taking in Unqualified Statements: more unreflective acceptance of unqualified statements	5:00	+.11	x	x	
M.I. 116a	T9	G	Opinion Inventory X: higher severity of judgment		+.14		x	
M.I. 70	T130	I	After Images: faster arrival of negative after-image	4:00	-.43	x	*	
M.I. 78	T177	I	Muscle Tension: less involuntary muscle tension	4:00	+.24	x		
M.I. 55	T14	G	Association of Emotional Words: lower fluency of association on emotional relative to non-emotional words	4:00	-.24	x		
M.I. 291	T128	I	PGR: fewer deflections during nonsense readings	5:00	-.21		x	

Factor U.I. 21: Exuberance vs. Suppressibility

1. Characteristics of U.I. 21 Battery (table 10.6)

	Adult Form	11-Year Form	8-Year Form
number of variables	10	6	5
number of group tests	8	6	5
number of individual tests	1	0	0
total administration time	62 min.	47 min.	28 min.

Overlap between forms:
adult - 11-year: 5 variables
adult - 8-year: 2 variables
11-year - 8-year: 1 variable

2. Discussion

The 8-year child form of this battery is somewhat shorter, in terms of tests, than is really desirable, and should be regarded as strictly tentative at the present moment. M.I. 282 and M.I. 425, both from T20 appear better on this factor with children than with adults, and there are also lower loadings from other factors at this age level. Due to the interrelationship between M.I. 282 and M.I. 425 the administrator may decide to omit one of these two measures.

The inclusion of M.I. 193a in the 11-year form is due to an increased loading (-.31) at this level.

The reader should note that either T9 or T118 may be used to obtain the immediate memory score of 167. When more than one factor is being measured there are advantages in favor of T9, but for the single factor U.I. 21 there is considerable saving in time through use of T118.

Table 10.6. Test Battery for Factor U.I. 21

Variable	Test	G or I	Variable Title	Test Administration Time	Average Factor Loading	Selected For		
						Adult Battery (18y. --)	11-Year Battery (9-13y.)	8-Year Battery (7-9y.)
M.I. 271	T43	G	Fluency: higher total fluency on topics	9:00	+.35	x	x	xm
M.I. 34	T10	G	Opinion Inventory Y: less immaturity of opinion	12:00	-.27	x	x	
M.I. 244	T361	G	Hard-Headed Realism Decisions: faster speed of judgment	6:00	+.60	x	x	
M.I. 288	T8	G	Criticalness of Evaluation: faster speed of judgment	4:00	+.56	x		
M.I. 308	T44	G	Number Comparison: faster speed	7:00	+.48	x	*	
M.I. 33	T124	I or G	Myokinesis: larger size of myokinetic movement	5:00	+.16	x	*	*
M.I. 146b	T2	G	Gestalt Closure: lower percentage correct	3:00	-.29	x	x	*
M.I. 282	T20	G	Unstructured Drawings: greater number of objects seen	5:00	+.20			x

Table 10.6. Test Battery for Factor U.I. 21 (Continued)

Variable	Test	G or I	Variable Title	Test Administration Time	Average Factor Loading	Selected For		
						Adult Battery (18y. --)	11-Year Battery (9-13y.)	8-Year Battery (7-9y.)
M.I. 193a	T10	G	Opinion Inventory Y: less shifting of attitudes towards those of successful people	12:00	-.12		x	
M.I. 168a	T360	G	Speed of Social Judgment: faster speed of socio-emotional judgment	4:00	+.28	*	*	x
M.I. 95	T124	I	Myokinesis: more decrease of movements under threat	5:00	+.41	x	*	*
M.I. 147b	T22	G	Skills: greater breadth of experience and accomplishment	5:00	-.17	x	x	*
M.I. 425	T20	G	Unstructured Drawings: higher absolute number of implements perceived	5:00	+.52			x
M.I. 167a M.I. 167b	T9 T118	G	Opinion Inventory X: better immediate memory Memory: higher total score	39:00 10:00	+.25	x		xm

Factor U.I. 22: Cortertia vs. Pathemia

1. Characteristics of U.I. 22 Battery (table 10.7)

	Adult Form	11-Year Form	8-Year Form
number of variables	9	6	6
number of group tests	5	3	3
number of individual tests[1]	2	1	1
total administration time	40 min.	27 min.	25 min.

Overlap between forms:
adult - 11-year: 6 variables
adult - 8-year: 5 variables
11-year - 8-year: 5 variables

2. Discussion

Each of the three batteries for U.I. 22 contain three variables (M.I. 175, M.I. 40, and M.I. 263) which are obtained from the same test (T122: Reaction Times). Special care has been taken to select, out of the several reaction time variables marking this factor, those that are least interrelated both experimentally and statistically. M.I. 175 has been chosen instead of M.I. 176 for its lower loadings on other factors. Although M.I. 175 has not been used in C7, its selection was regarded justifiable.

a) from the otherwise high across-age consistency of this variable (good loadings in Adults, R14, and R15), and
b) because the related variable M.I. 176 loaded sizably in C7.

No special child forms are needed for any of the tests. In adults, the measurement of U.I. 22 can be further strengthened if physical sex (M.I. 64) is used as an additional marker of the factor.

[1] Since 3 variables are obtained from test T122 (Reaction Times) the total number of tests is smaller than the number of variables chosen.

Table 10.7. Test Battery for Factor U.I. 22

Variable	Test	G or I	Variable Title	Test Administration Time	Average Factor Loading	Selected For		
						Adult Battery (18y. --)	11-Year Battery (9-13y.)	8-Year Battery (7-9y.)
M.I. 175	T122	I	Reaction Times: faster regularly warned reaction time	12:00	-.48	x	x	x
M.I. 40	T122	I	Reaction Times: more false reactions to irrelevant signals	12:00	+.20	x	x	x
M.I. 263	T122	I	Reaction Times: less variability in simple reaction times	12:00	-.40	x	x	x
M.I. 6a	T49	G	Ideomotor Speed: faster ideomotor speed	5:00	+.20	x	x	x
M.I. 8	T3	G	Alternating Perspective higher frequency of fluctuation in alternating perspective	3:00	+.21	x	x	x
M.I. 28	T51	G	Endurance of Difficulty: less endurance of difficulty	7:00	-.20	x	x	*
M.I. 94	T134	I	Flicker Fusion: higher mean critical flicker fusion frequency	4:00	+.25	x	*	*

*) Only part of this test has to be given.

Table 10.7. Test Battery for Factor U.I. 22 (Continued)

Variable	Test	G or I	Variable Title	Test Administration Time	Average Factor Loading	Selected For		
						Adult Battery (18y. --)	11-Year Battery (9-13y.)	8-Year Battery (7-9y.)
M.I. 55	T14	G	Association to Emotional Words: lower fluency of associations to emotional relative to non-emotional stimuli	4:00	-.20	x		
M.I. 325	T22	G	Skills: higher total level of self-estimated experience in a range of skill	5:00	+.44	x		
M.I. 1434	T171*)	G	Picture Interpretation and Recall: smaller number of aggresive picture interpretations	5:00	-.60			x

*) Only part of this test has to be given.

Factor U.I. 23: High Mobilization vs. Neurotic Regressive Debility

1. Characteristics of U.I. 23 Battery (table 10.8)

	Adult Form	11-Year Form	8-Year Form
number of variables	9	5	
number of group tests	7	4	
number of individual tests	2	1	
total administration time	46 min.	27 min.	
Overlap between forms:	adult -- 11-year: 5 variables adult - 8-years: -- variables 11-year - 8-year: -- variables		

2. Discussion

Most research on U.I. 23 has been concentrated at the adult level. This has been of considerable benefit to the adult form but has made for difficulties at the young child level where there are few measures apart from M.I. 2f (T288), M.I. 120, and M.I. 8 (T3) that appear strong enough to be put forward in a test battery, and therefore only an adult and 11-year form are presented. For factor analysis purposes the reader is referred to the principal markers given in table 7.16.

Although M.I. 120 can be obtained specifically from T4, research has shown that a more reliable measure is to be obtained from a composite of accuracy to speed ratios derived from a variety of tests such as T4, T1, T120, and T126.

Table 10.8. Test Battery for Factor U.I. 23

Variable	Test	G or I	Variable Title	Test Administration Time	Average Factor Loading	Selected For: Adult Battery (18y. --)	Selected For: 11-Year Battery (9-13y.)	Selected For: 8-Year Battery (7-9y.)
M.I. 2a, f	T1	G	Backward Writing: less motor rigidity	12:00	-.28	x	x	
M.I.42	T127	I	Body Sway Suggestibility: less swaying	3:00	-.16	x		
M.I. 120	T4	G	Cancellation of Letters: greater accuracy relative to speed	4:00	+.31	x	x	
M.I. 609	T112	G	Spatial Judgment: greater accuracy	8:00	+.45	x	*	
M.I. 516	T299	G	Reading Speed: faster rate of reading to oneself	4:00	+.45	x	*	
M.I. 227a	T116	G	Picture Preferences: fewer color choices relative to form choices	4:00	-.25	x	x	
M.I. 162b	T120	G	Cancellation: less impairment in correct performances by noise distraction	5:00	-.32	x	x	

Table 10.8. Test Battery for Factor U.I. 23 (Continued)

Variable	Test	G or I	Variable Title	Test Administration Time	Average Factor Loading	Selected For		
						Adult Battery (18y. --)	11-Year Battery (9-13y.)	8-Year Battery (7-9y.)
M.I. 604	T200	G	Complex Task: higher number of correct responses	4:00	+.55	x	*	
M.I. 41	T126	I	Two-Hand Co-Ordination: more correct movements	2:00	+.13	x	x	

Factor U.I. 24: Unbound Anxiety vs. Good Adjustment

1. Characteristics of U.I. 24 Battery

	Adult Form	11-Year Form	8-Year Form
number of variables	9	6	5
number of group tests	9	6	5
number of individual tests	0	0	0
total administration time	36 min.	31 min.	21 min.

Overlap between forms:
adult - 11-year: 4 variables
adult - 8-year: 2 variables
11-year - 8-year: 1 variable

2. Discussion

Good representation of the central pattern of factor U.I. 24 could be achieved in both the adult and 11-year battery, but less well in the 8-year form. The latter has comparatively little overlap with the other two age forms in terms of common test variables and can at present only be considered a tentative test battery.

Most of the six tests selected for the 11-year and 8-year forms have to be given in modified child versions. Variable M.I. 246 is actually a U.I. 20 marker in adults; it has been included into the U.I. 24 8-year battery because its principal loading at that age level is on U.I. 24 rather than on U.I. 20.

Table 10.9. Test Battery for Factor U.I. 24

Variable	Test	G or I	Variable Title	Test Administration Time	Average Factor Loading	Selected For		
						Adult Battery (18y.--)	11-Year Battery (9-13y.)	8-Year Battery (7-9y.)
M.I. 219	T41	G	Honesty in Admitting Frailties: more common frailties admitted	4:00	+.29	x	xm	
M.I. 211a	T38	G	Annoyances: more over-all susceptibility to annoyance	3:00	+.52	x	*	xm
M.I. 108	T22	G	Skills: less confident assumption of skill in untried performance	5:00	-.18	x	xm	*
M.I. 116a	T9*)	G	Opinion Inventory X: higher critical severity	6:00	+.22	x	xm	xm
M.I. 205	T36	G	Emotionality of Comment: more emotionality of comment	4:00	+.24	x		
M.I. 473	T64	G	Friends and Acquaintances fewer friends recalled	4:00	-.21	x		
M.I. 481	T272	G	Embarrassing Situations: higher susceptibility to embarrassment	3:00	+.34	x		

*) Only one section of test T9 has to be given.

Table 10.9. Test Battery for Factor U.I. 24 (Continued)

Variable	Test	G or I	Variable Title	Test Administration Time	Average Factor Loading	Selected For		
						Adult Battery (18y.--)	11-Year Battery (9-13y.)	8-Year Battery (7-9y.)
M.I. 55	T14	G	Association to Emotional Words: greater fluency of association to emotional relative to non-emotional stimuli	4:00	+.37	x		
M.I. 144	T31	G	Aphorisms: more acceptance of aphorisms	3:00	+.19	x	xm	
M.I. 330	T47	G	Ethical Choices: better ethical choices in story completion	6:00	+.24		x	*
M.I. 245	T19	G	Time Estimates for Everyday Tasks: less exactness of time estimates	7:00	-.32	*	x	*
M.I. 133	T8	G	Criticalness of Evaluation: more criticalness of evaluation	4:00	+.14 **)		*	xm
M.I. 1366	T163	G	Compliance: less tendency to do unpleasant activities	4:00	-.31		*	x

*) Only one section of test T9 has to be given.

**) Average loading for 8-Year level alone: +.26

Table 10:9. Test Battery for Factor U.I. 24 (Continued)

Variable	Test	G or I	Variable Title	Test Administration Time	Average Factor Loading	Selected For		
						Adult Battery (18y.--)	11-Year Battery (9-13y.)	8-Year Battery (7-9y.)
M.I. 246	T34	G	Authoritarianism: more authority submission	4:00	-.09***)			xm

***) Loading for 8-Year level: -.36

Factor U.I. 25: Less Imaginative, Task-Oriented Realism vs. Tense Inflexidia

1. Characteristics of U.I. 25 Battery (table 10.10)

	Adult Form	11-Year Form	8-Year Form
number of variables	7	4	
number of group tests	7	4	
number of individual tests	0	0	
total administration time	39 min.	22 min.	

Overlap between forms:
adult - 11-year: 3 variables.
adult - 8-year: -- variables
11-year - 8-year: -- variables

2. Discussion

Only two age forms could be constructed for this factor. For the 8-year level no sufficient number of pure measures of U.I. 25 is indicated from R13 and R15; therefore this age form has been dropped entirely. Even the 11-year form for U.I. 25 is somewhat tentative insofar as the number of measures suitable for inclusion is short of the desired minimum of five. No special child forms are needed of any test.

Table 10.10. Test Battery for Factor U.I. 25

Variable	Test	G or I	Variable Title	Test Administration Time	Average Factor Loading	Selected For		
						Adult Battery (18y.--)	11-Year Battery (9-13y.)	8-Year Battery (7-9y.)
M.I. 199	T35	G	Numerical Ability: higher computational skill	8:00	+.30	x	x	
M.I. 7	T2	G	Gestalt Closure: slower speed of perceptual Gestalt completion	3:00	-.25	x	x	
M.I. 6a	T49	G	Ideomotor Speed: faster ideomotor speed	5:00	+.19	x	x	
M.I. 715	T224	G	Psychotic Skidding: greater frequency of associations	5:00	+.35	x	*	
M.I. 671	T242	G	Designs -- Simplification: more regression towards the real object in figure recognition	7:00	+.37	x	*	
M.I. 696	T164	G	"Auditory Hallucinations": fewer real word stimuli identified correctly	5:00	-.26	x		

*) Cattell Humor Test Battery

Table 10.10. Test Battery for Factor U.I. 25 (Continued)

Variable	Test	G or I	Variable Title	Test Administration Time	Average Factor Loading	Selected For		
						Adult Battery (18y.--)	11-Year Battery (9-13y.)	8-Year Battery (7-9y.)
M.I. 583	*)	G	Humor Factor 2: more preference for good-natured, playful humor than dry wit	6:00	+.23	x		
M.I. 249	T118	G	Memory for Names and Objects: better memory for proper names	6:00	+.19		x	

*) Cattell Humor Test Battery

Factor U.I. 26: Narcistic Self vs. Low Self-Command

1. Characteristics of U.I. 26 Battery (table 10.11)

	Adult Form	11-Year Form	8-Year Form
number of variables	6	5	5
number of group tests	5	4	4
number of individual tests	1	1	1
total administration time	40 min.	28 min.	41 min.

Overlap between forms: adult - 11-year: 3 variables
adult - 8-year: 3 variables
11-year - 8-year: 2 variables

2. Discussion

The adult form contains two tests for M.I. 167, either of which may be used at the administrator's discretion. T9 is very long, but also includes several other measures that may be important if more than one factor is to be measured. T118 is recommended if the research is based solely upon U.I. 26.

Modified versions of T43, T9, T118, and T121 are used in the child forms.

M.I. 205 (T36) is included in the 11-year form as it has a higher loading on U.I. 26 at this age level than on U.I. 24 (the factor with which it is usually associated in adults).

Table 10.11. Test Battery for Factor U.I. 26

Variable	Test	G or I	Variable Title	Test Administration Time	Average Factor Loading	Selected For		
						Adult Battery (18y.--)	11-Year Battery (9-13y.)	8-Year Battery (7-9y.)
M.I. 273	T43	G	Fluency: higher proportion of fluency on self relative to total verbal fluency	9:00	+.33	x		xm
M.I. 167a	T9	G	Opinion Inventory X: better immediate memory	40:00	+.31	x	xm	xm
M.I. 167b	T118	G	Memory: higher total score	10:00	+.31	x	xm	xm
M.I. 161a,b	T123	I	Cancellation Under Disapproval: higher ratio of performance under approval relative to disapproval	4:00	+.25	x	x	*
M.I. 119	T115	G	Color Blending: higher aesthetic score as evaluated by artists	5:00	+.15	x	*	
M.I. 24a-d	T121	G	C.M.S.: higher ratio of final (fast) to initial (slow) total score	7:00	-.16	x	x	xm

Table 10.12. Test Battery for Factor U.I. 26 (Continued)

Variable	Time	G or I	Variable Title	Test Administration Time	Average Factor Loading	Selected For		
						Adult Battery (18y.--)	11-Year Battery (9-13y.)	8-Year Battery (7-9y.)
M.I. 105	T20	G	Drawing (Unstructured): greater proportion of threatening objects seen	5:00	+.12	x		
M.I. 30	T13	G	Criticalness of Self Versus Others: more criticism of self relative to criticism of others	10:00	+.13		*	x
M.I. 242	T38	G	Annoyability: higher ratio of social relative to non-social annoyance	3:00	+.20		x	
M.I. 2f	T288	I	Color Naming: less rigidity	5:00	-.28		*	x
M.I. 205	T36	G	Emotionality of Comment: more emotionality	4:00	+.19		x	*

Factor U.I. 27: Discouraged, Sceptical Apathy vs. Ungrudging Involvement

1. Characteristics of U.I. 27 Battery (table 10.12)

	Adult Form	11-Year Form	8-Year Form
number of variables	6		
number of group tests	4		
number of individual tests	2		
total administration time	41 min.		

Overlap between forms:
adult - 11-year: -- variables
adult - 8-year: -- variables
11-year - 8-year: -- variables

2. Discussion

Only an adult form is recommended for this factor since U.I. 27 has so far been reliably replicated only in adults. Even this form is a provisional battery only (with the small number of chosen tests) and a research study is presently being carried out containing a comprehensive extension analysis specifically on this factor.

Table 10.12. Test Battery for Factor U.I. 27

Variable	Test	G or I	Variable Title	Test Admini-stration Time	Average Factor Loading	Selected For		
						Adult Battery (18y.--)	11-Year Battery (9-13y.)	8-Year Battery (7-9y.)
M.I.42	T127	I	Body Sway Suggestibility: more body sway suggestibility	5:00	+.35	x		
M.I. 194	T9*) & T10	G	Opinion Inventory X and Y: more shifting of attitudes away from those of neurotics	12:00	+.22	x		
M.I. 145a	T17	G	Aspiration Level: higher responsiveness of aspiration level to actual performance	8:00	+.34	x		
M.I. 305	T128	I	Psychogalvanic Reflex: higher PGR deflection to mental than physical stimuli	8:00	-.22	x		
M.I. 865	T93	G	Name Choosing: greater preference for unusual names	4:00	+.32	x		
M.I. 13e	T4	G	Cancellation of Letters: more oscillation of performance	4:00	+.20	x		

Factor U.I. 28: Dependent, Negativistic Asthenia vs. Undisciplined Selfassuredness

1. Characteristics of U.I. 28 Battery (table 10.13)

	Adult Form	11-Year Form	8-Year Form
number of variables	7	5	
number of group tests	5	4	
number of individual tests	0	0	
total administration time	64 min.	57 min.	

Overlap between forms: adult - 11-year: 4 variables
adult - 8-year: -- variables
11-year - 8-year: -- variables

2. Discussion

Only an adult and an 11-year form are suggested for this factor as the presently available evidence from R13 and R15 is not comprehensive enough for constructing an 8-year form properly overlapping with the other two forms. Special care has been taken in the construction of the two batteries to adequately suppress "latent ties" with factors U.I. 20 and U.I. 28, resulting from the co-operativeness of these factors. The reader might ask if it is justified to include as many as 4 variables (M.I. 67a, 97, 35, 193a in adults) obtained, at least in part, from the same test. Actually, variable M.I. 97 is completely independent of the remaining three measures. M.I. 35 and M.I. 193a are each based upon 20 different items which are grouped together into the same tests for no other than practical reasons. Only variable M.I. 67a involves, besides 60 other items, also the 40 items from which the shift measures M.I. 35 and 193a are scored. However, with the marked difference in scoring procedures, no direct experimental or statistical correlation should result from this.

Of all tests chosen for the 11-year form modified child versions have been developed which should be used instead of the adult versions.

Table 10.13. Test Battery for Factor U.I. 28

Variable	Test	G or I	Variable Title	Test Administration Time	Average Factor Loading	Selected For: Adult Battery (18y.--)	Selected For: 11-Year Battery (9-13y.)	Selected For: 8-Year Battery (7-9y.)
M.I. 67a	T9	G	Opinion Inventory X: more extremity of viewpoint	30:00	+.22	x		
M.I. 97	T9	G	Opinion Inventory X: greater length of passing time estimates	30:00	+.52	x	x	
M.I. 35	T9 & T10 *)	G	Opinion Inventories X & Y: higher suggestibility to authority	11:00	+.24	x	xm	
M.I. 193	T9 & T10 *)	G	Opinion Inventories X & Y: more shifting of attitudes toward those of "succesful" people	11:00	+.17	x	xm	
M.I. 191	T19	G	Time Estimates for everyday Tasks: less considered possible in given time for others	7:00	-.27	x	xm	
M.I. 171	T33	G	Hidden Pictures: larger total number of hidden objects identified	6:00	+.34	x	*	

*) [illegible] of T10 have to be given to obtain M.I. 35 and M.I. 193a. The administration time for these two

Table 10.13. Test Battery for Factor U.I. 28 (Continued)

Variable	Test	G or I	Variable Title	Test Administration Time	Average Factor Loading	Selected For		
						Adult Battery (18y.--)	11-Year Battery (9-13y.)	8-Year Battery (7-9y.)
M.I. 763	T13	G	Criticalness of Self vs. Others: higher fluency on people's personal characteristics	10:00	+.31	x		
M.I. 212	T39	G	Goal Seeking: fewer distant goals considered attainable	3:00	+.13**)		xm	

**) Loading in 11-Year old children alone: +.35

Factor U.I. 29: Whole-Hearted Responsiveness vs. Defensive Complacency

1. Characteristics of U.I. 29 Battery (table 10.14)

	Adult Form	11-Year Form	8-Year Form
number of variables	5	5	
number of group tests	4	4	
number of individual tests	1	1	
total administration time	34 min.	42 min.	

Overlap between forms:
adult - 11-year: 3 variables
adult - 8-year: -- variables
11-year - 8-year: -- variables

2. Discussion

The salient variables appearing in U.I. 29 exhibit a definite tendency to load other factors in addition to U.I. 29 -- in particular U.I. 16 and U.I. 17. This has had effect upon the choice and number of tests, and at present five tests are suggested in both the adult and 11-year forms.

Modifications of tests appropriate for the 11-year age level are found in T8 and T18.

Table 10.14. Test Battery for Factor U.I. 29

Variable	Test	G or I	Variable Title	Test Administration Time	Average Factor Loading	Selected For		
						Adult Battery (18y.--)	11-Year Battery (9-13y.)	8-Year Battery (7-9y.)
M.I. 25b	T6	G	Reading: better recall of emotionally interesting relative to dry material	7:00	+.25	x	*	
M.I. 80	T128	I	P.G.R: more upward drift when relaxed than under shock	10:00	+.62	x	x	
M.I. 111	T24	G	Unusual Event: more self reference	4:00	+.16	x		
M.I. 133	T8	G	Criticalness of Evaluation: less criticalness	4:00	-.27	x	xm	
M.I. 102	T18	G	Aphorisms: more tendency to consider remarks "obvious."	9:00	+.30	x	xm	
M.I. 5	T122	I	Reaction Times: lower ratio of regularly to irregularly warned reaction time	12:00	-.17		x	
M.I. 143	T121	G	Cursive Miniature Situation: higher total score	7:00	+.23		x	

Factor U.I. 30: Somindence vs. Dissofrustance

1. Characteristics of U.I. 30 Battery (table 10.15)

	Adult Form	11-Year Form	8-Year Form
number of variables	7	3	4
number of group tests[1]	5	3	4
number of individual tests	2	1	0
total administration time	38 min.	20 min.	24 min.

Overlap between forms:
adult - 11-year: 1 variable
adult - 8-year: 1 variable
11-year - 8-year: 0 variables

2. Discussion

Although well measurable in adults, this factor is extremely difficult to measure in children on the basis of the existing results. Both the present 11-year and the 8-year form are tentative, the former more so than the latter. Each of the two child batteries also overlaps in only one variable with the adult form. The battery for 11-year old children has only been suggested because all three selected tests load the factor .40 or above. Modified child versions of T9 and T10 should be used in the 11-year form, of T131 in the 8-year form.

The two variables M.I. 109 and M.I. 110, chosen for the adult battery, are scored from the same test (T23) but practically independent. Therefore the inclusion of both seemed justifiable.

[1] The two variables M.I. 109 and M.I. 110 are obtained from the same test; two tests (part of T9 and T10) are to be administered for variable M.I. 31.

Table 10.15. Test Battery for Factor U.I. 30

Variable	Test	G or I	Variable Title	Test Admini-stration Time	Average Factor Loading	Selected For		
						Adult Battery (18y.--)	11-Year Battery (9-13y.)	8-Year Battery (7-9y.)
M.I. 269	T137	I	Leg Circling: slower leg-circling tempo	2:00	-.41	x		*
M.I. 31	T9 & T10 *)	G	less fluctuation of attitudes	12:00	-.16	x	xm	*
M.I. 98b	T131	G	C.M.S.: smaller absolute number of correct decisions	8:00	-.12	x	*	xm
M.I. 155	T134	I	Flicker Fusion: larger range of successive critical flicker fusion frequency measures	4:00	+.48	x	*	*
M.I. 109	T23	G	Associations: lower ratio of pleasant to unpleasant associations	6:00	-.45	x	*	*
M.I. 110	T23	G	Associations: lower anteversion-retroversion ratio	6:00	-.33	x	*	

*) Only one part is used of each test T9 and T10.

Table 10.15. Test Battery for Factor U.I. 30 (Continued)

Variable	Test	G or I	Variable Title	Test Administration Time	Average Factor Loading	Selected For		
						Adult Battery (18y.--)	11-Year Battery (9-13y.)	8-Year Battery (7-9y.)
M.I. 448	T297	G	Information: greater versatility of interest	6:00	+.34	x	*	*
M.I. 287	T126	I	Two-hand Coordination: more awareness of error	3:00	+.44	*	x	
M.I. 55	T14	G	Association to Emotional Words: greater fluency of association to non-emotional than emotional stimuli	5:00	-.13 **)		x	
M.I. 1428	T167	G	Fluency Concerning Successful Tasks: lower fluency concerning successful tasks	4:00	-.63	*	*	x
M.I. 1429	T370	G	Respect for People: fewer people listed as "liked"	4:00	-.51		*	x
M.I. 1416	T17	G	Aspiration Level in Coding: slower speed on coding	8:00	-.42	*	*	x

**) Factor loading for 11-Year level alone: -.44

Factor U.I. 31: Wary, Controlled Steadiness vs. Impulsive Variability

1. Characteristics of U.I. 31 Battery (table 10.16)

	Adult Form	11-Year Form	8-Year Form
number of variables	7		4
number of group tests	5[1]		4
number of individual tests	0		0
total administration time	69 min.		47 min.

Overlap between forms:

adult - 11-year: -- variables
adult - 8-year: 2 variables
11-year - 8-year: -- variables

2. Discussion

No 11-year form can be made available for this factor because U.I. 31 has not been identified in study C7. Although four variables (M.I. 250, 113, 121, and 31) are, at least in part, scored from the same test T9 their joint choice will not introduce "instrument" variance for these variables are scored from different parts of the test.

With only four tests, the 8-year form for U.I. 31 is only a preliminary test battery whose overlap with the adult form is also smaller than desired.

[1] Four variables (M.I. 280, 113, 121, and 31) are obtained from the same test (T9); however, for scoring variable M.I. 31 in addition part of test T10 has to be given.

Table 10.16. Test Battery for Factor U.I. 31

Variable	Test	G or I	Variable Title	Test Admini-stration Time	Average Factor Loading	Selected For		
						Adult Battery (18y.--)	11-Year Battery (9-13y.)	8-Year Battery (7-9y.)
M.I. 192	T19	G	Time Estimates for Everyday Tasks: more considered possible in given time for self	7:00	-.38	x		*
M.I. 703	T35	G	Numerical Ability: less confidence in one's own correctness in computations	8:00	-.45	x		x
M.I. 280	T9	G	Opinion Inventory X: higher accuracy of time interval estimates	30:00	-.42	x		x
M.I. 121	T9	G	Opinion Inventory X: greater indecisiveness of opinion		+.62	x		*
M.I. 113	T9	G	Opinion Inventory X: less acceptance of reality principles		-.11*)	x		
M.I. 31	T9 & T10**)	G	Opinion Inventory X and Y: less fluctuation of attitudes	***) 8:00	****) -.11	x		

*) Average factor loading for adults alone: -.26.
**) Only one part is used of each test T9 and T10.
***) Time is only the required additional time for administering one part of T10.

Table 10.16. Test Battery for Factor U.I. 31 (Continued)

Variable	Test	G or I	Variable Title	Test Administration Time	Average Factor Loading	Selected For		
						Adult Battery (18y.--)	11-Year Battery (9-13y.)	8-Year Battery (7-9y.)
M.I. 150	T18	G	Aphorisms: less acceptance of "obvious" remarks	9:00	-.21	x		
M.I. 364	T149	G	Story Completion: more "internal-control" than "external-control" choices in story completion	5:00	+.37			x
M.I. 361	T151	G	Knowledge: more confident assumption of knowledge	4:00	-.36			x

Factor U.I. 32: Exvia vs. Invia

1. Characteristics of U.I. 32 Battery (table 10.17)

	Adult Form	11-Year Form	8-Year Form
number of variables	7		
number of group tests	6		
number of individual tests	1		
total administration time	41 min.		

Overlap between forms: adult - 11-year: -- variables
adult - 8-year: -- variables
11-year - 8-year: -- variables

2. Discussion

Only an adult form is suggested for factor U.I. 32. The factor has not been identified in C7 (11-year old children), and for the 8-year level not enough strong markers can be obtained if we are not to select experimentally interdependent scores. The reported adult battery comprises all important aspects of extraversion as defined in the loading pattern of U.I. 32.

Table 10.17. Test Battery for Factor U.I. 32

Variable	Test	G or I	Variable Title	Test Admini-stration Time	Average Factor Loading	Selected For		
						Adult Battery (18y.--)	11-Year Battery (9-13y.)	8-Year Battery (7-9y.)
M.I. 316	T13	G	Criticalness of Self vs. Others: higher fluency on own relative to other people's personal characteristics	10:00	+.28	x		
M.I. 444	T304	I	Physiological Measures: higher systolic blood pressure	2:00	+.23	x		
M.I. 460	T111	G	Stories: greater preference for strange than familiar in written material	6:00		x		
M.I. 714	T224	G	Psychotic Skidding: higher proportion of alliterative and rhyming associations given	3:00	+.23	x		
M.I. 1489	T71	G	Horrifying Pictures: less accuracy in recalling details from horrifying than pleasant pictures	10:00	+.36	x		
M.I. 853	T88	G	Aesthetic Judgment: more concreteness in aesthetic completion	6:00	+.33	x		

Table 10.17. Test Battery for Factor U.I. 32 (Continued)

Variable	Test	G or I	Variable Title	Test Administration Time	Average Factor Loading	Selected For		
						Adult Battery (18y.--)	11-Year Battery (9-13y.)	8-Year Battery (7-9y.)
M.I. 449	T181	G	Abnegation: less self-sacrifice believed necessary to achieve life goals	4:00	-.33	x		

Factor U.I. 33: Reactive Dismay vs. Sanguineness

1. Characteristics of U.I. 33 Battery (table 10.18)

	Adult Form	11-Year Form	8-Year Form
number of variables	7		5
number of group tests	5		5
number of individual tests	2		0
total administration time	34 min.		26 min.

Overlap between forms:
adult - 11-year: -- variable
adult - 8-year: 3 variables
11-year - 8-year: -- variables

2. Discussion

Due to the existence of only one research on children (R13) in which this factor has been identified, the 8-year form is regarded as tentative.

Three tests (T24, T22 and T19) have modified versions appropriate for the eight-year-old.

The administrator has a choice of either T194 or T121 in order to obtain M.I. 24. The former is recommended as it takes less time and gives no indication of having a lower correlation than the latter with U.I. 33.

Table 10.18. Test Battery for Factor U.I. 33

Variable	Test	G or I	Variable Title	Test Administration Time	Average Factor Loading	Selected For: Adult Battery (18y.--)	Selected For: 11-Year Battery (9-13y.)	Selected For: 8-Year Battery (7-9y.)
M.I. 112	T24	G	Unusual Events: less favorable relative to unfavorable self reference	4:00	+.28	x		xm
M.I. 108	T22	G	Skills: less confident assumption of skill in untried performance	5:00	-.25	x		xm
M.I. 24^{c}_{d}	T194	G	Reading Backward: higher ratio of final to initial novel performance	4:00	-.24	x		*
			-or-					
	T121	G	C.M.S.: higher ratio of final (fast) to initial (slow) total score	7:00				
M.I. 100	T16	G	Pessimism About Events: more pessimism over doing good	5:00	+.25	x		
M.I. 192	T19	G	Time Estimates for Everyday Tasks: less considered possible for self in given time	7:00	-.45	x		xm

Table 10.18. Test Battery for Factor U.I. 33 (Continued)

Variable	Test	G or I	Variable Title	Test Administration Time	Average Factor Loading	Selected For		
						Adult Battery (18y.--)	11-Year Battery (9-13y.)	8-Year Battery (7-9y.)
M.I. 46a	T129	I	Mazes: less impairment of performance (reduction of distance covered) by shock punishment	5:00	-.18	x		*
M.I. 166	T119	I	Classification: less impairment by shock	4:00	-.23	x		*
M.I. 391	T196	G	Crayoning: less untidiness	5:00	-.38			x
M.I. 401	T197	G	Social Activity Preference: less preference for competitive situations than non-competitive situations	5:00	-.32	*		x

Factor U.I. 34: Inconautia vs. Practicalness

1. Characteristics of U.I. 34 Battery (table 10.19)

	Adult Form	11-Year Form	8-Year Form
number of variables	7		
number of group tests	6		
number of individual tests	1		
total administration time	36 min.		

Overlap between forms:
adult - 11-year: -- variables
adult - 8-year: -- variables
11-year - 8-year: -- variables

2. Discussion

As to the present, factor U.I. 34 has not been identified in 8- and 11-year old children; so only an adult battery can be suggested.

Table 10.19. Test Battery for Factor U.I. 34

Variable	Test	G or I	Variable Title	Test Administration Time	Average Factor Loading	Selected For		
						Adult Battery (18y.--)	11-Year Battery (9-13y.)	8-Year Battery (7-9y.)
M.I.120e	T4	G	Cancellation of Letters: lower ratio of accuracy to speed	4:00	-.31	x		
M.I. 33	T124	G*)	larger size of myokinetic movement	6:00	+.30	x		
M.I. 711	T250	G	Story Completion: smaller number of logical sequences maintained	5:00	-.28	x		
M.I. 462	T240	I	Smell Preferences: greater preference for weaker than stronger smells	4:00	-.25	x		
M.I. 731	T283	G	Difficult Task: higher readiness to commit one-self to a course of action	5:00	+.20	x		
M.I. 681	T55	G	Decisiveness: higher ratio of total synaesthesia to total reasoning correct	7:00	+.18	x		
M.I. 586	**)	G	Humor Factor 5+ more hostile derogation than urbane pleasantness	5:00	+.19	x		

*) The test now exists in a group administrable form.

**) Cattell Humor Test.

Factor U.I. 35: Stolparsomnia vs. Excitation

1. Characteristics of U.I. 35 Battery (table 10.20)

	Adult Form	11-Year Form	8-Year Form
number of variables	7		
number of group tests	5		
number of individual tests	2		
total administration time	45 min.		

Overlap between forms:
adult - 11-year: -- variables
adult - 8-year: -- variables
11-year - 8-year: -- variables

2. Discussion

This factor has not been identified in analyses at either the 11-year or 8-year child level, and therefore only an adult battery is presented.

Table 10.20. Test Battery for Factor U.I. 35

Variable	Test	G or I	Variable Title	Test Administration Time	Average Factor Loading	Selected For		
						Adult Battery (18y.--)	11-Year Battery (9-13y.)	8-Year Battery (7-9y.)
M.I. 458	T110	G	Goal Seeking: more long term life goals	5:00	+.34	x		
M.I. 464	T211	I	Writing Pressure: less hand writing pressure	2:00	-.29	x		
M.I. 43	T128	I	P.G.R: higher mean percentage deflection to threatening stimuli	10:00	+.26	x		
M.I. 461	T363	G	Memory for Film Strip Material: higher ratio of time estimates for frightening vs. non-frightening passages	8:00	+.22	x		
M.I. 531	T55	G	Decisiveness: faster aesthetic-emotional relative to logical decision time	5:00	+.40	x		
M.I. 199	T35	G	Numerical Ability: lower score	8:00	-.25	x		
M.I. 703	T84	G	Classification Breadth: less breadth	7:00	-.37	x		

CHAPTER 11

THE DESIGN OF THE OBJECTIVE-ANALYTIC (O-A) PERSONALITY FACTOR BATTERIES

A great deal of scientific work depends on the exact reproduction of experimental conditions and measurements. The continuation of the present research on personality structure and development hinges on studies to check the factor structure obtained over the various age ranges, to investigate fresh hypotheses about the meaning of factors, and, especially, to investigate the dynamics of personality by developmental studies of particular influences upon the personality factor levels. The spawning of psychological tests in huge numbers on very inadequate research foundations has unfortunately brought the construction of psychological tests into low repute. Yet the publication of psychological tests which are based upon thorough research into personality structure, rather than upon popularity and sales, is an extremely important contribution to science. It is a task which has been quite inadequately supported in certain instances, since research foundations, on the one hand, may consider it as an applied or even commercial scientific undertaking, while the commercial publishers and test specialists are likely to reject such propositions as not having the profit necessary for business maintenance compared to simple tests of a popular nature.

These difficulties have arisen in carrying the basic research on personality structure reported here through to the stage of an immediately applicable test battery. Yet without such batteries being available, progress cannot go forward to the important research objectives described above. (It is out of the question for the slender resources of an individual research professor to face the heavy clerical and printing costs necessary to respond to the letters of other researchers in the field requesting copies of administration and scoring instructions for the tests reported in the scientific literature.) In these circumstances we have received help from two sources, namely, the University of Illinois Press, Urbana, and the Institute for Personality and Ability Testing, Champaign. The former has undertaken the large volume by Cattell and Warburton (71) in which particulars are given of test administration and scoring, together with two or three test item examples sufficient for an investigator to continue test construction, for some four hundred tests which have been referred to in this analysis and various other articles and monographs. The Institute for Personality and Ability Testing, which is not subsidized, has undertaken to make available, at a moderate cost in relation to the specialist labors involved, routinely administrable test batteries, of appropriate length, for the chief personality factors here studied. This construction has lead to batteries at three distinct age levels as follows:

> The O-A Battery #1, measuring 14 factors, for adults, from from seventeen years and upward.
> The O-A Battery #2, measuring 11 factors for ten through twelve years of age.
> The O-A Battery #3, measuring 8 factors for six through nine year old children.

The age divisions among these batteries cannot simply be drawn according to school administrative divisions. They are based on the fact that scientific research shows that essentially the same <u>type</u> of personality test loads much the same factors for children of eleven to seventeen as for adults, so that only modifications of the content of the actual items is really necessary as between the adult and this age range. Nevertheless, since the tests in the adult and child batteries have not been tried out for the adolescent years, it seemed most appropriate to construct batteries for adults of seventeen years and upwards, children between 10 and 12 years, and children between 6 and 9 years. Such batteries would be based upon the results from specific studies at different age levels and would therefore avoid any dangers of fluctuations in test loadings within the 13 to 17 year age span. Admittedly there is considerable ground for expecting that the pattern of loadings during adolescence will be similar to that at earlier and later stages, and an experimenter may wish to bridge the gap by using such tests as are common to the adult and 11 year old batteries. However, the evidence in support of such action would be purely presumptive. The problems of battery construction at the pre-school level were outlined in the previous chapter, and no multi factor battery is here presented for children below the age of six.

In general for the multi factor batteries, as for the unifactor batteries, attempt is made to preserve the same style of tests throughout the different age levels. However, due to fluctuations in the loading pattern for certain variables, and certain natural difficulties in extending tests down to young children, new tests at times enter the picture for the 11-year and 8-year batteries -- particularly the latter. One obvious cause of division is the lack of dependable reading ability below eight years of age. This involves the use of modified forms of almost all verbal tests at this level. In addition, it is necessary to confine tests at the 8-year level to relatively small groups of subjects, and several tests usually thought of as being group administerable must be given on an individual basis.

Battery Number 1, for adults, is completely group administerable. Battery Number 2, for 11-year olds, has a majority of group tests but does contain individual tests. With the relatively few tests per factor at this age level it became imperative for some factors (but not all) to retain individual tests. Battery Number 3, for 8-year olds, has rather more individual tests than at the 11-year level and rather simpler language requirements. Thus, the curve of growth of intelligence and cognitive skills to some extent dictates that the number of years over which a battery can be applied will be short in the earlier ages and of increasing span as the later batteries are reached. The differences in actual form of test at the lower age levels may perhaps in twenty or thirty years time be overcome by the discovery of tests in some way continuous in style with those of a different age which nevertheless load the factors sufficiently. At present, the summed specifics when the sub-tests are added together for a particular battery, will be somewhat different at the different age levels, but this is a trivial matter in comparison with the fact that the shared common factor variance generates measurement of the same personality factor. The above batteries at present have only an A form, though equivalent B forms are in process of construction. Generally there is no problem about using the same form for re-testing individuals, providing a lapse of at least two or three weeks has occurred since the last testing.

It might seem that once the choice of the best loaded test for each factor at each age level from the evidence of accumulated researches has been made, as in Chapter 10 above, the task of constructing a battery would be quite simple. But this is far from true, for the construction of a test battery is almost a work of art, and requires a great number of special skills and statistical and psychological considerations, which need intensive study in themselves. Among the considerations which need to be brought into balance in a complex outcome, if success is to be achieved, are the following:

(1) Are the same variables (i.e., M.I.s) occasionally to contribute to more than one factor score? There exist a number of variables sufficiently loaded on two different factors to perform this function, but the score will add the same specifics and unique error to both of the factors and cause a slight spurious correlation between the battery scores for the two factors. On the other hand, much time may be saved by using certain variables in this way.

(2) A distinct but related problem concerns not the use of the same identical variable in two factors, but the use of the same test, from the performance on which two quite distinct scores (i.e., variables) are derived. In this case, the common elements contributed to the two factors may be quite negligible, and we have not hesitated to use tests in this way to save testing time, though we have only used the very same score, i.e., M.I. number, in different factors on comparatively rare occasions.

(3) When tests load on other factors besides the wanted factor, the ideal test construction will cause suppressor action on the unwanted factors, by having one sub-test loaded positively and the other negatively on the unwanted factor. This has been discussed in precise fashion elsewhere (70a). Where such relationships are known they have been utilized in the batteries.

(4) How many tests are necessary to contribute a sufficiently high validity and reliability to each factor measurement? The answer to this depends entirely upon the user's judgment of how much extra testing time he is prepared to give for the reliability that he requires. Here we have tried to cater for two levels of taste, one of which we perhaps share with about a quarter of the psychological world. In our opinion, important research, or routinely, applied work seriously affecting the career or clinical status of an individual, should not be based on fewer than ten sub-tests per factor. Preferably it should be based on perhaps twenty-sub-tests per factor, because, at the present stage of science, reliabilities and validities around 0.9 cannot be obtained with less. On the other hand, a survey of opinion shows that psychologists in the applied field, particularly, are not prepared to give more time than is required to give about half a dozen tests in the battery for each factor. Our compromise has been to construct the complete factor battery, for eleven and eight factors in 11 year and 8 year old children, respectively, and fourteen factors in adults, on the shorter time for each factor, i.e., six sub-tests per factor, but to make available batteries for single factors which cover ten tests. The single factor batteries were presented in the previous chapter. Thus the researcher can take the single factor batteries, adding one to another and test as many factors as he requires. The battery with six sub-tests per factor is, however, fitted together like a watch, to operate as a whole. It is true that the individual, if he so desires, can take single factors out of this battery, using only six sub-tests, but these six sub-tests are not chosen by us ideally to measure the one factor. They are chosen, as we have indicated by the simile of the watch, to go together, i.e., ideally, with the other tests in a combination which will yield the full number of factor measurements with a minimum total testing time. Due to the arrangement of tests, and the relative difficulty or ease of measuring a factor, the number of variables per factor fluctuates between five and seven.

(5) In this construction of the multi-factor battery, to give the minimum total time in regard to the number of tests, we have utilized the same test and occasionally the same M.I. performance for more than one factor contribution, but have always done so with the restriction that no two factors shall share more than one test score in common. This puts a limit to the amount of interfactor correlation that might arise from common scores through specifics.

(6) The choice of which factors to include in the child and adult batteries has to be made again, on fairly complex considerations. In the first place, the choice has been in terms of the factors most clearly replicated and for which tests of substantial loading have been demonstrated several times. Secondly, however, we have to consider the question of greatest usefulness of the factor in various theoretical and applied fields. For example, the anxiety factor, U.I. 24, the general inhibition factor, U.I. 17, the regression factor, U.I. 23 (Eysenck's "neuroticism"), are obviously essential in relation to the major issues in present psychological research. However, no sharp line can be drawn in such a series and individual researchers may well wish to add markers for

factors not included in the batteries, and these are given in the individual factor tables in Chapters 7 and 8. Considerable caution should be used in the choice of variables for factors not included in the batteries, particularly if unit weight factor scores are contemplated. One other consideration here was that, for developmental research, the factors measured in the child batteries should also be found in the adult battery, and this has resulted in some modifications in the judgments that would have been made from the other two principles.

(7) It would be a mistake to assume that the division between group tests and individual tests is one between pencil and paper tests and apparatus tests, though there is substantial overlap of these qualities for the reason that we have tried to make the administration of the group test as free of apparatus as possible. However, the group administration of tests requires a projector and slides as well as a loud speaker system and a few other minor pieces of apparatus such as a stop watch or metronome. In this connection since we believe that the advantages from the automation of test instruction by a magnetic tape, e.g., in accuracy of timing and tone of voice, far outweigh any shortcomings through the absence of a personal touch, we hope that in time the administration of all these tests, at present set down on paper for the examiner to read out, will be fully automated.

(8) The scoring of the tests is not yet arranged for IBM answer sheets, but individual experimenters can easily develop this. Nor are the scores at the moment transformable to standardized scores, and it may well take some years to produce such standardizations. A more important theoretical, psychometric issue is whether the sub-tests should be added in their raw score form or multiplied by certain weights to bring them more closely to the beta weights derived from the correlations of the sub-tests with the factors. This latter cannot, of course, be properly done until the standardization is carried out, because it depends upon the standard deviation of the raw score of each sub-test. However, there is no doubt that a more accurate result would be obtained from weighting the tests according to the beta weights instead of accepting the accidental weight given to them by the ranges of their raw scores. These beta weights are in the process of being worked out from the preliminary standardization.

Anything satisfying all the above scientific conditions, and trying to meet the differing tastes of various kinds of psychologists, must necessarily be a little complex. The batteries for the single factors are perhaps comparatively straightforward, but the multi-batteries have involved a good deal of thought in terms of the sequences in which the sub-tests shall be arranged, the sequences of instructions, and, especially the instructions to scores in putting together the different test scores, to add up in the correct way.

The average time for the administration of a single factor battery (see Chapter 10) with adults is about 47 minutes. The time for the adult multi-factor battery is 6 hours and 11 minutes. The 11-year and 8-year single factor batteries for children average 33 and 31, respectively, per factor. The 11-year multi-factor battery takes 3 hours and 30 minutes, while the 8-year battery takes 3 hours and 13 minutes. There are, of course, fewer factors in the two child batteries, but the conditions of testing usually demand longer time per test. The multi-factor batteries are best broken down into periods of two or three hours. However, there are certain passages of time between earlier and later tests in the battery which need to be kept within limits, in ways described in the particulars of the battery. One of the limitations of objective personality tests at present is that they cannot be given to individuals who are sub-literate or borderline mental defective, and of course, it may take several years to adapt these tests to really low levels of intellectual capacity.

The test numbers (T), variable numbers (M.I.) and titles in direction of a positive score on the factor (direction of scoring), U.I. factors involved, and the appropriate duration of the tests, are set out in tables 11.1, 11.2, and 11.3 for the different age levels. Table 11.4 contains lists of tests and variables used for the measurement of each factor in turn. However, any more detailed description of the batteries, the apparatus required, etc., is transferred to the Handbook of the Objective-Analytic Personality Factor Batteries, which contain full instructions for research and routine use (40a).

The multi-factor battery for adults (table 11.1) contains measures on all factors except U.I. 27, U.I. 29, U.I. 31, U.I. 33, U.I. 34, U.I. 35, and U.I. 36. Overlap between variables (i.e., the same variables contributing to two separate factor scores) is very slight, and occurs only three times. No specific order of administration is strictly necessary, except that T9 and T10 must be given on separate occasions.

The battery for 11-year old children (table 11.2) contains measures on U.I. 16, U.I. 17, U.I. 18, U.I. 19, U.I. 20, U.I. 21, U.I. 22, U.I. 23, U.I. 24, U.I. 26 and U.I. 28. The overlap of variables is rather more than that with adults, and occurs five times. U.I. 19 is the factor mainly concerned in such overlap, and this may be omitted from the final analysis if the researcher so wishes. It would certainly be of doubtful wisdom to perform a factor analysis that included scores on U.I. 19 derived in this way, due to the spurious correlations that would emerge of U.I. 19 with other factors.

The battery for 8-year old children (table 11.3) contains measures on U.I. 16, U.I. 17, U.I. 18, U.I. 19, U.I. 21, U.I. 22, U.I. 24 and U.I. 26. There are three overlapping variables. The batteries for U.I. 19 and U.I. 21 are not as strong as is desirable, and are best regarded as tentative pending further confirmation.

Table 11.1.
The Multi-Factor Battery for Adults (No. 1): U.I. 16, 17, 18, 19, 20, 21, 22, 23, 24, 25, 26, 28, 30, 32

Test	MI	Title	Time	U.I. Factor Measured By The Variable
T1	2	Backward Writing: less motor rigidity	12:00	23
T2	7	Gestalt Closure: slower speed of perceptual Gestalt completion	3:00	25
	146b	Gestalt Closure: greater percentage correct		19
T3	8	Alternating Perspective: higher frequency of fluctuation in alternating perspective	3:00	22
T4	120	Cancellation of Letters: greater accuracy relative to speed	4:00	23
T6	278	Reading Tempo and Memory for Interesting Material: faster tempo of reading	5:00	16
	25b	Reading: better recall of emotionally interesting relative to dry material		29
T8	288	Criticalness of Evaluation: faster speed of judgment	4:00	21
	133	Criticalness of Evaluation: less criticalness		29
T9	152	Opinion Inventory X: more tendency to agree	39:00	20
	38a	Opinion Inventory X: higher ratio of consonant to dissonant recall (corrected for tendency to agree)		20
	34	Opinion Inventory Y: less immaturity of opinion		21
	116a	Opinion Inventory X: higher critical severity		24
	167a	Opinion Inventory X: better immediate memory		26
	194	Opinion Inventory X and Y: more shifting of attitudes away from those of neurotics		27
	97	Opinion Inventory X: greater length of passing time estimates		28
	31	Less fluctuation of attitudes		30
	67a	Opinion Inventory X: more extremity of viewpoint		28

Table 11.1. (Continued)

Test	MI	Title	Time	U.I. Factor Measured By The Variable
	125a	Opinion Inventory X: higher ratio of personal to institutional values		16
T10	193a	Opinion Inventory Y: more shifting of attitudes towards those of successful people	31:00	18,28
	35	Opinion Inventory Y: more suggestibility to authority		20,28
	34	Opinion Inventory Y: less immaturity of opinion		21
	194	Opinion Inventory X and Y: more shifting of attitudes away from those of neurotics		27
	31	Less fluctuation of attitudes		30
T11	36	Logical Assumptions: higher logical ability	5:00	20
T13	30	Criticalness of Self vs. Others: less criticism of self relative to criticism of others	10:00	19
	316	Criticalness of Self vs. Others: higher fluency on own relative to other people's personal characteristics		32
	763	Criticalness of Self vs. Others: higher fluency on people's personal characteristics		28
T18	150	Aphorisms: more acceptance of obvious remarks	9:00	17
	102	Aphorisms: more tendency to consider remarks "obvious"		29
T19	191	Time Estimates for Everyday Tasks: less considered possible in time for others	7:00	28
T20	282	Unstructured Drawings: greater number of objects perceived in unstructured drawings	5:00	16

Table 11.1. (Continued)

Test	MI	Title	Time	U.I. Factor Measured By The Variable
	336	Unstructured Drawings: larger absolute number of threatening objects perceived in unstructured drawings		17
	105	Drawings (Unstructured): greater proportion of threatening objects seen		26
T21	106	Risk Taking in Unqualified Statements: more unreflective acceptance of unqualified statements	5:00	20
T22	108	Skills: less confidence assumption of skill in untried performance	5:00	24
	147b	Skills: greater breadth of experience and accomplishment		21
	325	Skills: higher total level of self-estimated experience in a range of skill		22
T23	109	Associations: lower ratio of pleasant to unpleasant associations	6:00	30
	110	Associations: lower anteversion-retroversion ratio		30
T24	112	Unusual Events: more adverse than favorable self reference in events	4:00	17
	111	Unusual Event: more self-reference		29
T27	117	Highbrow Tastes: more responses indicative of "highbrow" taste	6:00	16
T33	171	Hidden Pictures: larger total number of hidden objects identified	6:00	28
T34	246	Authoritarianism: more submission	4:00	20
T35	199	Numerical Ability: higher computational skill	8:00	25
T36	205	Emotionality of Comment: more emotionality of comment	4:00	24
T37	206	Gottschaldt Perceptual Analysis: greater accuracy	5:00	19
T38	211a	Annoyances: more overall susceptibility to annoyance	3:00	24
T41	219	Honesty in Admitting Frailties: more common frailties admitted	4:00	24
T42	234	Pencil Mazes: more inaccuracy on pencil mazes	2:00	16
T43	271	Fluency: higher total fluency on topics	9:00	21

Table 11.1. (Continued)

Test	MI	Title	Time	U.I. Factor Measured By The Variable
	273	Fluency: higher proportion of fluency on self relative to total verbal fluency		26
T44	308	Number Comparison: faster speed	7:00	21
T45	309	Line Length Judgment: faster speed of line length judgment	3:00	16
T49	6a	Ideomotor Speed: faster ideomotor speed	5:00	25, 22
	465	Letter Placement: more decrement in coding performance with anxiety sound reaction		18
T50	9	Ideomotor Tempo: faster ideomotor tempo	4:00	16
T51	28	Endurance of Difficulty: less endurance of difficulty	7:00	22
T64	473	Friends and Acquaintances: fewer friends recalled	4:00	24
	472	Friends and Acquaintances: more acquaintances relative to friends recalled		19
T71	1489	Horrifying Pictures: less accuracy in recalling details from horrifying than pleasant pictures	10:00	32
T88	853	Aesthetic Judgment: more concreteness in aesthetic completion	6:00	32
T99	83	Fidgeting: higher score	3:00	18
T111	460	Stories: greater preference for strange than familiar in written material	6:00	32
T112	609	Spatial Judgment: greater accuracy	8:00	23
T113	39	Color-Form Sorting: higher ratio of color to form in sorting	4:00	18
T114	51	Observation: more carefulness in following detailed instructions	4:00	19
T115	119	Color Blending: higher aesthetic score as evaluated by artists	5:00	26
T116	227a, b	Picture Preferences: fewer color choices relative to form choices	4:00	23
T120	162b	Cancellation: less impairment in correct performance by noise distraction	5:00	23
T121	15	C.M.S.: more use of circles	7:00	18

Table 11.1. (Continued)

Test	MI	Title	Time	U.I. Factor Measured By The Variable
	16a	C.M.S.: more slanting lines crossed		18
	24d	C.M.S.: higher ratio of final (fast) to initial (slow) total score		26
T122	72	Reaction Time: more slowing of reaction time under complex instructions	8:00	17
	71	Reaction Times: fewer errors under complex instructions		19
	40	Reaction Times: more false reactions to irrelevant signals		22
	175	Reaction Times: faster regularly warned reaction time		22
	263	Reaction Times: less variability in simple reaction times		22
T124	33	Myokinesis: large size of myokinetic movement	5:00	21
T131	98b	C.M.S.: smaller absolute number of correct decisions	8:00	30
T164	696	"Auditory Hallucinations": fewer real word stimuli identified correctly	5:00	25
T181	449	Abnegation: less self sacrifice believed necessary to achieve life goals	4:00	32
T224	715	Psychotic Skidding: greater frequency of associations	5:00	25
	714	Psychotic Skidding: higher proportion of alliterative and rhyming associations given		32
T242	691	Design-Simplification: more regression towards the real object in figure recognition	7:00	25
T297	448	Information: greater versatility of interests	6:00	30
T299	96a	Reading Speed: less impairment by frustrated preference	4:00	18
	516	Reading Speed: faster rate of reading to oneself		23
T361	244	Hard Headed Realism Decisions: faster speed of judgment	6:00	21

Table 11.1. (Continued)

Test	MI	Title	Time	U.I. Factor Measured By The Variable
T362	303	Whole-Detail Speed: slower speed of decision on "whole" judgments	5:00	17
T364	467	Distraction by Aesthetic Material: less distraction in numerical and verbal tasks by aesthetic material	8:00	19

TOTAL NUMBER OF TESTS: 56

TOTAL TESTING TIME: 6 hours 11 minutes

Table 11.2.
The Multi-Factor Battery for 11-Year Old Children (No. 2): U.I. 16, 17, 18, 19, 20, 21, 22, 23, 24, 26, 28

Test	MI	Title	Group or Individual	Time	As For Adults U.I.
T1	2a	Backward Writing: less motor rigidity	G	12:00	23, 19
T2	146b	Gestalt Closure: greater percentage correct	G	3:00	19
		smaller percentage correct			21
T3	8	Alternating Perspective: higher frequency of fluctuation in alternating perspective	G	3:00	19, 22
T4	120	Cancellation of Letters: greater accuracy relative to speed	G	4:00	23
T6	278	Reading Tempo and Memory for Interesting Material: faster tempo of reading	G	7:00	16
T9	116a	Opinion Inventory X: higher severity of judgment	G	6:00	19, 24
	152	Opinion Inventory X: more tendency to agree			20
	116a	Opinion Inventory X: higher severity of judgment			20
	34	Opinion Inventory Y: less immaturity of opinion			21
	167a	Opinion Inventory X: better immediate memory			26
	35	Opinion Inventories X and Y: higher suggestibility to authority			28
	97	Opinion Inventory X: greater length of passing time estimates			28
T10	34	Opinion Inventory Y: less immaturity of opinion	G	12:00	21
	193a	Opinion Inventory Y: more shifting of attitudes towards those of successful people			21, 28
	35	Opinion Inventories X and Y: higher suggestibility to authority			28
T18	150	Aphorisms: more acceptance of obvious remarks	G	9:00	17
T19	245	Time Estimates for Everyday Tasks: less exactness of time estimates	G	7:00	24
	191	Time Estimates for Everyday Tasks: less considered possible in given time for others			28

Table 11.2. (Continued)

Test	MI	Title	Group or Individual	Time	As For Adults U.I.
T20	336	Unstructured Drawings: larger absolute number of threatening objects perceived in unstructured drawings	G	5:00	17
T21	106	Risk Taking in Unqualified Statements: more unreflective acceptance of unqualified statements	G	4:00	20
T22	147b	Skills: greater breadth of experience and accomplishment	G	5:00	21
	108	Skills: less confident assumption of skill in untried performance			24
T24	112	Unusual Events: more adverse than favorable self-reference in events	G	4:00	17
T31	144	Aphorisms: more acceptance of aphorisms	G	3:00	24
T34	246	Authoritarianism: more submission	G	4:00	20
T36	205	Emotionality of Comment: more emotionality	G	4:00	26
T38	242	Annoyability: higher ratio of social relative to non-social annoyance	G	3:00	26
T39	212	Goal Seeking: fewer distant goals considered attainable	G	3:00	28
T41	219	Honesty in Admitting Frailties: more common frailties admitted	G	4:00	24
T43	271	Fluency: higher total fluency on topics	G	9:00	21
T45	309	Line Length Judgment: faster speed of line length judgment	G	3:00	16
T47	330	Ethical Choices: better ethical choices in story completion	G	6:00	24
T49	6a	Ideomotor Speed: faster ideomotor speed	G	5:00	22
T51	28	Endurance of Difficulty: less endurance of difficulty	G	7:00	22
T116	227a,b	Picture Preferences: fewer color choices relative to form choices	G	4:00	23
T117	247a	Drawing-Expansiveness of Copying: greater expansiveness of copied design	G	7:00	16
T120	162b	Cancellation: less impairment in correct performance by noise distraction	G	5:00	23

Table 11.2. (Continued)

Test	MI	Title	Group Or Individual	Time	As For Adults U.I.
T121	15	C.M.S.: more use of circles	G	7:00	18
	16a	C.M.S.: more slanting lines crossed			18
	24d	C.M.S.: higher ratio of final (fast) to initial (slow) total score			26
T122	72	Reaction Times: more slowing of reaction time under complex instructions	I	8:00	17
	175	Reaction Times: faster regularly warned reaction time			22
	40	Reaction Times: more false reactions to irrelevant signals			22
	263	Reaction Times: less variability in simple reaction times			22
T123	161a, b	Cancellation Under Disapproval: higher ratio of performance under approval relative to disapproval	I	4:00	26
T126	41	Two-Hand-Coordination: more correct movements	I	2:00	23
T128	43	Psychogalvanic Reflex: higher mean percentage PGR deflection to threatening stimuli	I	8:00	17
	291	P.G.R.: fewer deflections during nonsense readings			20
T129	46a	Mazes: more impairment of maze performance by shock punishment	I	5:00	17
	82	Mazes: greater distance covered			18
T136	268	Tapping: faster tapping ratio	I	3:00	16
T138	270	Arm Circling: faster arm-shoulder tempo	I	2:00	16
T229	247b	Drawings: greater expansiveness	G	7:00	18
T299	96a	Reading Speed: less impairment by frustrated preference	G	4:00	18
T361	244	Hard-Headed Realism Decisions: faster speed of judgment	G	6:00	21
T378	50	Following Directions: higher alertness in following directions	G	6:00	16

TOTAL NUMBER OF TESTS: 39

TOTAL TESTING TIME: 3 hours 30 seconds

Table 11.3.
The Multi-Factor Battery for 8-Year Old Children (No. 3): U.I. 16, 17, 18, 19, 21, 22, 24, 26

Test	MI	Title	Group Or Individual	Time	As For Adults U.I.
T2	146a	Gestalt Closure: greater absolute accuracy	G	3:00	19
T3	8	Alternating Perspective: higher frequency of fluctuation in alternating perspective	G	3:00	22
T8	133	Criticalness of Evaluation: more criticalness of evaluation	G	4:00	24
T9	116a	Opinion Inventory X: higher severity of judgment	G	6:00	19, 24
	167a, b	Opinion Inventory X: better immediate memory			21, 26
T13	30	Criticalness of Self vs. Others: more criticism of self relative to criticism of others	G	10:00	18
		less criticism of self relative to criticism of others			19
T20	336	Unstructured Drawings: larger absolute number of threatening objects perceived in unstructured drawings	G	5:00	17
	282	Unstructured Drawings: greater number of objects seen			21
	425	Unstructured Drawings: higher absolute number of implements perceived			21
T24	112	Unusual Events: more adverse than favorable self-reference in events	G	4:00	17
T34	246	Authoritarianism: more authority submission	G	4:00	24
T37	206	Gottschaldt Perceptual Analysis: greater accuracy	G	5:00	19
T38	211a	Annoyances: more over-all susceptibility to annoyance	G	3:00	24
T40	29	Criticalness in Humor: less mischieviousness of humor	G	4:00	17
T42	234	Pencil Mazes: more inaccuracy on pencil mazes	G	2:00	16
T43	271	Fluency: higher total fluency on topics	G	9:00	21

Table 11.3. (Continued)

Test	MI	Title	Group Or Individual	Time	As For Adults U.I.
	273	Fluency: higher proportion of fluency on self relative to total verbal fluency			26
T45	309	Line Length Judgment: faster speed of line length judgment	G	3:00	16
T49	6a	Ideomotor Speed: faster ideomotor speed	G	5:00	22
T50	9	Ideomotor Tempo: faster ideomotor tempo	G	4:00	16
T113	30	Criticalness of Self vs. Others: more criticism of self relative to criticism of others	G	4:00	26
T117	247a	Drawing-Expansiveness of Copying: greater expansiveness of copied design	G	7:00	16
T121	143	C.M.S.: higher total score	G	7:00	18
	24d	C.M.S.: higher ratio of final (fast) to initial (slow) total score			26
T122	72	Reaction Times: more slowing of reaction time under complex instructions	I	8:00	17
	175	Reaction Times: faster regularly warned reaction time			22
	40	Reaction Times: more false reactions to irrelevant signals			22
	263	Reaction Times: less variability in simple reaction times			22
T138	270	Arm Circling: faster arm-shoulder tempo	I	2:00	16
T142	2e	Color Naming: less rigidity	G	5:00	19
T143	429	Picture Inspection: more preference for non-aggressive than aggressive pictures	G	5:00	17
	426	Picture Inspection: less distractibility			19
T150	382	Design Evaluation Speed: faster speed of evaluation judgment	G	5:00	16
T163	1366	Compliance: less tendency to do unpleasant things	G	4:00	24
T171	1434	Picture Interpretation and Recall: smaller number of aggressive picture interpretations	G	5:00	22

Table 11.3. (Continued)

Test	MI	Title	Group Or Individual	Time	As For Adults U.I.
T185	385	Shape Comparison: more accuracy	G	4:00	18
T229	247b	Drawings: greater expansiveness	G	7:00	18
T280	375	Cancellation of Circles: greater accuracy in cicle cancellation	G	4:00	16
T288	2f	Color Naming: less rigidity	I	5:00	26
T295	374	Disturbing Sounds: less preference for disturbing sounds	G	5:00	17
T360	168a	Speed of Social Judgment: faster speed of socio-emotional judgment	G	4:00	21
T368	1418	Pleasant vs. Unpleasant Comments on Self and Others: lower ratio of pleasant to unpleasant	G	8:00	18

TOTAL NUMBER OF TESTS: 33
TOTAL TESTING TIME: 3 hours 13 minutes

Table 11.4.
Tests and Variables Entering into the Measurement of Each Factor at Each Age Level

Battery 1: Adults

U.I. 16		U.I. 17		U.I. 18		U.I. 19		U.I. 20		U.I. 21	
Test	MI	Test	MI	Test	MI	Test	MI	Test	MI	Test	MI
T50	9	T20	336	T121	15	T2	146b	T9	152	T43	271
T27	117	T24	112	T121	16a	T37	206	T9	38a	T10	34
T6	278	T122	72	T113	39	T122	71	T10	35	T361	244
T20	282	T18	150	T299	96a	T114	51	T34	246	T8	288
T42	234	T362	303	T99	83	T13	30	T11	36	T44	308
T45	309			T10	193a					T124	33
T9	125a										

U.I. 22		U.I. 23		U.I. 24		U.I. 25		U.I. 26		U.I. 28		U.I. 30		U.I. 32	
Test	MI	Test	MI	Test	MI	Test	MI	Test	MI	Test	MI	Test	MI	Test	MI
T122	175	T1	2a	T41	219	T35	199	T43	273	T9	67a	T137	269	T13	316
T122	40	T4	120	T38	211a	T2	7	T9	167a	T10	35	T10	31	T224	714
T3	8	T112	609	T22	108	T49	6a	T115	119	T10	193a	T131	98b	T71	1489
T51	28	T299	516	T9	116a	T224	715	T121	24d	T9	97	T23	109	T88	853
T134	94	T116	227a	T36	205	T242	691	T20	105	T19	191	T297	448	T181	449
		T120	162b	T64	473	T164	696			T33	171				

Table 11.4. (Continued)

Battery 2: 11-year Old Children

U.I. 16		U.I. 17		U.I. 18		U.I. 19		U.I. 20		U.I. 21	
Test	MI	Test	MI	Test	MI	Test	MI	Test	MI	Test	MI
T138	270	T128	43	T121	15	T2	146b	T9	152	T43	271
T6	278	T20	336	T121	16a	T3	8	T34	246	T10	34
T136	268	T24	112	T299	96a	T9	116a	T21	106	T361	244
T45	309	T122	72	T129	82	T1	2a	T9	116a	T2	146b
T117	247a	T18	150	T229	247b			T128	291	T10	193a
T378	50	T129	46a							T22	147b

U.I. 22		U.I. 23		U.I. 24		U.I. 26		U.I. 28	
Test	MI	Test	MI	Test	MI	Test	MI	Test	MI
T122	175	T1	2a	T41	219	T9	167a	T10	35
T122	40	T4	120	T22	108	T123	161a	T10	193a
T122	263	T116	227a	T9	116a	T121	24d	T9	97
T3	8	T120	162b	T31	144	T38	242	T19	191
T51	28	T126	41	T47	330	T36	205	T39	212
T49	6a			T19	245				

Table 11.4. (Continued)

Battery 3: 8-Year Old Children

U.I. 16		U.I. 17		U.I. 18		U.I. 19		U.I. 21	
Test	MI	Test	MI	Test	MI	Test	MI	Test	MI
T50	9	T20	336	T13	30	T37	206	T43	271
T138	270	T24	112	T185	385	T13	30	T20	282
T42	234	T122	72	T121	143	T9	116a	T360	168a
T45	309	T40	29	T229	247b	T142	2e	T20	425
T117	247a	T143	429	T368	1418	T143	426	T9	167a
T150	382	T295	374			T2	146a		

U.I. 22		U.I. 24		U.I. 26	
Test	MI	Test	MI	Test	MI
T122	175	T38	211a	T43	273
T122	40	T9	116a	T9	167a
T122	263	T8	133	T121	24d
T3	8	T163	1366	T13	30
T49	6a	T34	246	T288	2f
T171	1434				

CHAPTER 12

SUMMARY

The primary objectives of this monograph are in essence fourfold:

1. to reformulate both the methodology and psychological foundations of multivariate personality researches from a two-decade's experience of research in this field;
2. to give an exhaustive presentation of all accumulated experimental findings on twenty-one best confirmed source traits in objective behavioral tests;
3. to venture, on this basis, interpretative hypotheses for the obtained personality factors and an outline or framework for integrating these into a multivariate theory of personality -- the latter aim being pursued with particular reference to the most recent findings on higher-order personality factors;
4. to select, for three of the four age levels that have been investigated as yet, a battery of tests for measuring all personality factors that have been substantiated for a given age level.

1. METHODOLOGICAL AND PSYCHOLOGICAL FOUNDATIONS OF MULTIVARIATE PERSONALITY RESEARCH

Multiple factor analysis represents the core method, but no ultimate goal in itself, in multivariate psychological research. As a heuristic technique, factor analysis is highly powerful for abstracting from a set of observations those underlying dimensions or source traits which are fewer in number than the observable variables and explain the observed interindividual differences in a set of test variables, both in a mathematical and a causal-theoretical sense. Full theoretical utilization of such source traits, as obtained from replicative factor analytic studies, is contingent, however, upon the experimenter's ingenuity in designing specific multivariate experiments to test his hypotheses about the factors and accumulate additional empirical evidence beyond the sheer loading pattern of a factor. In other words, a well-replicated loading pattern does not constitute the final goal in understanding a psychological factor, but the start-off point for investigating the theoretical properties of such a dimension.

Leaving aside the question which of the proposed mathematical and statistical methods should be used in actually carrying out a factor analysis (see Chapter 1), the general strategy of multivariate personality research can be described as a three-stage procedure:

1) Factor Discovery: Each factor analysis, carried out on reliable data, will yield replicable factors, but the theoretical usefulness of the latter will depend upon the experimenter's plans in choosing his test variables. A broader, more general behavioral relevance of the discovered personality factors can only be expected if the chosen set of variables constitutes a representative sample from the total population or "domain" of variables which are of possible relevance to interindividual personality differences at large. Results of analyses on samples of variables which belong to limited subsets from this total domain are usually difficult to interpret, as to both the hierarchical order of the obtained factors and their theoretical properties (i.e. the extent to which the chosen variables do exhaust the unknown pattern of a factor).
2) Factor Replication and Matching: No generality can be claimed for factors which have not been shown to stand successfully the empirical test of replicability. The adequacy of this request can be easily seen from considering the large number of factors, each found once in a specific analysis, unrelated across studies and often uninterpretable. This second stage of multivariate personality research asks for careful planning of the replicative factor analytic experiments. The principal salient variables for each originally discovered factor have to be carried over into the replicative analysis, and at the same time the experimenter should try to extend his variable sample into hitherto uncovered variable areas in order to increase the behavioral generality of the factors and to be able to test his initial hypotheses regarding the interpretation of the factors. Furthermore, replicative analysis should be carried out with different subject samples than the original analysis (different age and educational level, normals and abnormals, etc.) so that the generality of a factor in terms of the total subject population can be evaluated later. As far as the actual factorization is concerned, special care has to be taken in matching factors between replicative analyses (see Chapter 3).
3) Factor Interpretation: As has been said before, the interpretation of a factor should rest upon not only the replicated loading pattern, but also on additional experimental evidences, extraneous in method of collection to the factor analytic procedure. Such evidence may come from observed correlations between the factor in question and various external life criteria, from genetic analyses of this source trait, its age development, from multivariate experiments in which this factor served as one of the independent variables, etc.

2. EMPIRICAL FINDINGS ON THE TWENTY-ONE BEST CONFIRMED OBJECTIVE PERSONALITY TEST FACTORS

Due to our request for careful replication of a factor before considering it as "discovered", the number of factor analytic studies of objective personality tests becomes reduced to those that have a fair proportion of principal variables in common. This restriction limits the researches to be considered from outside the author's laboratory to some studies by Thurstone and Eysenck and a few isolated analyses. In all, a total of 26 factor analytic researches on objective personality tests is covered in this monograph, 8 of these being carried out with children, the remainder with adults. In addition five extension analyses are available on certain factors in adults, and seven researches on criterion correlations of the factors. Nature-nurture ratios and age development (between 9 and 15 years) are known for eleven of the twenty-one factors, all from one study. The relationship between these factors, all obtained from R-technique experimental designs, and the state factors found in P-technique analyses, can be evaluated from six independent researches. Second-order factorizations of the twenty-one primary factors, yielding seven second-order factors, are available from five analyses; a factorization of these second-order factors, resulting in three third-order factors, has been undertaken in one study in which data have been combined from three independent researches.

Thus the total number of studies reported in this monograph is 50. These researches are described in chapters IV and V, the loading pattern of the twenty-one best confirmed primary personality factors in objective test data are presented in chapters VII and VIII, together with a description for each factor. The matching of these factors across studies is reported in chapter VI.

3. THEORETICAL INTERPRETATION OF THE TWENTY-ONE PERSONALITY SOURCE TRAITS.

Besides the actual loading pattern, as obtained from the replicative researches, the interpretation of a factor has been based on the following additional information whenever available for the factor in question:

1. the correlation with other primary objective personality test factors;
2. the correlation with primary questionnaire personality factors and (unfactored) familiar questionnaire scales;
3. the pattern of a factor in terms of second-order OT personality factors;
4. the relationship between the objective personality test state factors obtained from P-technique factorizations;
5. the correlation with external criteria;
6. the evidence upon nature-nurture variance ratios available from the genetic analysis of a factor;
7. the age development of the factor during pre-puberty and puberty (between 9 and 15 years).

The factors were given, besides a verbal title, a Universal Index (U.I.) number which starts at U.I. 16, thus containing the series of well-replicated source trait factors after the fifteen ability factors distinguished by French (95). The additional evidence available on each factor, together with a theoretical interpretation of each factor, is presented in Chapters 7 and 8. Chapter 9 gives a "synoptic" integration of these first-order personality factors, both from the psychometrist's and the personality theorist's point of view.

The following is a list of the twenty-one primary personality factors in objective behavior tests:

U.I. 16: Unbound, Assertive Ego vs. Bound, Disciplined Ego
U.I. 17: Timid Inhibitedness vs. Lack of Inhibition
U.I. 18: Hypomanic Smartness vs. Slow Thoroughness
U.I. 19: Promethean Will vs. Subduedness
U.I. 20: Comentive Superego vs. Abcultion
U.I. 21: Exuberance vs. Suppressibility
U.I. 22: Cortertia vs. Pathemia
U.I. 23: High Mobilization vs. Neurotic Regressive Debility (or Regression)
U.I. 24: Unbound Anxiety vs. Good Adjustment
U.I. 25: Less Imaginative, Task-Oriented Realism vs. Tense Inflexidia
U.I. 26: Narcistic Self-Sentiment (Development) vs. Low Self Command
U.I. 27: Discouraged, Sceptical Apathy vs. Ungrudging Involvement
U.I. 28: Dependent, Negativistic Asthenia vs. Undisciplined Selfassuredness
U.I. 29: Whole-hearted Responsiveness vs. Defensive Complacency
U.I. 30: Somindence vs. Dissofrustance
U.I. 31: Wary, Controlled Steadiness vs. Impulsive Variability
U.I. 32: Exvia vs. Invia
U.I. 33: Reactive Dismay vs. Sanguineness
U.I. 34: Inconautia vs. Practicalness
U.I. 35: Stolparsomnia vs. Excitation
U.I. 36: Foresighted Self-Sentiment vs. Low Foresighted Self-Sentiment

4. THE SELECTION OF A BATTERY OF OBJECTIVE TESTS FOR THE MEASUREMENT OF THE CONFIRMED PERSONALITY SOURCE TRAITS.

Several of the primary personality factors (e.g. U.I. 16, 20, 32, etc.) refer to personality dimensions which are widely used in personality theory. Although they represent familiar concepts to the theorist, their functional unity as source traits has not been demonstrated previously and, with the necessary factor analytic evidence lacking, the researcher intending to actually experiment with these dimensions (and thus measure them) had no objective empirical data to rely upon in his choice of test variables.

In order to give those who wish to do research on these personality dimensions a suitable measuring instrument and to have an established basis for both relating and integrating future research on personality source traits, it seemed desirable to select for each factor a short battery of tests which in turn can be used also for marking this factor in future factor analytic studies. For each factor a set of tests, mostly group administerable, has been chosen; these factor scales have been designed in three "editions", corresponding to the three different age levels they were aimed at (adults, junior high-school children, and grade-school children). The principles of test selection adhered to in the design of these factor batteries are listed in Chapter 9, the results of the test selection are reported in Chapters 10 and 11.

BIBLIOGRAPHY

1. Ahmavaara, Y. Transformation analysis of factorial data. Helsinki: Ann Ac. Sci. Fenn. B, 88, 1954.

2. Ahmavaara, Y. The unified factor theory of mind. Helsinki: Ann. Ac. Sci. Fenn., 1957, 3, 106.

3. Ahmavaara, Y. and Markkanen, T. The unified factor model: its position in psychometric theory and application to sociological alcohol study. Helsinki: Finnish Foundation for Alcohol Studies, 1958.

4. Atkinson, J. W. Motives in fantasy, action, and society. Princeton: D. Van Nostrand, 1958.

5. Baehr, M. A factorial study of temperament. Chicago: Univer. of Chicago, 1951.

6. Bargmann, R. Signifikanz Untersuchungen der einfachen Struktur in der Faktorenanalyse. Mitt. Bl. Math. Stat., 1955, 1-24.

7. Bargmann, R. Review of Ahmavaara's "on the unified factor theory of mind." Psychometrika, 1960, 25, 105-109.

8. Becker, W.C. A comparison of the factor structure and other properties of the 16 P.F. and the Guilford-Martin personality inventories. Ed. psychol. Measmt., 1961, 21, 393-404.

9. Berlyne, D. E. Conflict, arousal, and curiosity. New York: McGraw-Hill, 1960.

10. Berry, R. N. Skin conductance levels and verbal recall. Paper presented at 1961 M.P.A. Annual Convention in Chicago.

11. Brengelmann, J. C. Spaltungsfaehigkeit als Persoenlichkeits-merkmal. Z. exp. angew. Psychol., 1954, 2, 454-494.

12. Brogden, H. E. A factor analysis of forty character tests. Psychol. Mon., 1940, 234, 35-55.

13. Burt, C. L. The factorial analysis of emotional traits. Char. and Pers., 1939, 7, 238-254, 285-299.

13a. Burt, C. L. The factors of the mind. London: Univer. of London Press, 1940.

14. Burt, C. L. The factorial study of temperamental traits. Brit. J. Psychol., Stat. Sec., 1948, 1, 178-203.

15. Campbell, D. T., and Fiske, D. W. Convergent and discriminant validation by the multitrait-multimethod matrix. Psychol. Bull., 1959, 56, 81-105.

16. Carrigan, P. M. Extraversion-introversion as a dimension of personality: a re-appraisal. Psychol. Bull., 1960, 57, 329-360.

17. Cattell, R. B. The principal trait clusters for describing personality. Psychol. Bull., 1945, 42, 129-161.

18. Cattell, R. B. The description and measurement of personality. Yonkers, New York: World Book Co., 1946.

19. Cattell, R. B. Primary personality factors in the realm of objective tests. J. Pers., 1948, 16, 459-487.

20. Cattell, R. B. r_p and other coefficients of pattern similarity. Psychometrika, 1949, 14, 279-298.

21. Cattell, R. B. A note on factor invariance and the identification of factors. Brit. J. Psychol., Stat. Sec., 1949, 2, 134-139.

21a. Cattell, R. B. Personality: a systematic theoretical and factual study. New York: McGraw-Hill, 1950.

22. Cattell, R. B. A factorization of tests of personality source traits. Brit. J. Psychol., Stat. Sect., 1951, 4, 165-178.

23. Cattell, R. B. Factor analysis. New York: Harpers, 1952.

24. Cattell, R. B. Factor rotation for proportional profiles: analytical solution and example. Brit. J. Psychol., Stat. Sec., 1955, 8, 83-92.

25. Cattell, R. B. The principal replicated factors discovered in objective personality tests. J. abnorm. soc. Psychol., 1955, 50, 291-314.

26. Cattell, R. B. Psychiatric screening of flying personnel: personality structure in objective tests--a study of 1,000 Air Force students in basic pilot training. Report No. 9, Project No. 21-0202-007. Randolph Field, Texas: U.S.A.F. School of Aviation Medicine, 1955.

27. Cattell, R. B., et al. The Objective-Analytic (O-A) Personality Factor Batteries. 1602 Coronado Drive, Champaign, Ill.: Instit. for Pers. Abil. Testing, 1955.

28. Cattell, R. B. Second-order personality factors in the questionnaire realm. J. consult. Psychol., 1956, 20, 411-418.

29. Cattell, R. B. Personality and motivation structure and measurement. New York: World Book Co., 1957.

30. Cattell, R. B. A universal index for psychological factors. Psychologia, 1957, 1, 74-85.

31. Cattell, R. B. A need for alertness to multivariate experimental findings in integrative surveys. Psychol. Bull., 1958, 55, 253-256.

32. Cattell, R. B. What is "Objective" in "objective personality tests"? J. counsul. Psychol., 1958, 5, 285-289.

33. Cattell, R. B. Extracting the correct number of factors in factor analysis. Ed. Psychol. Measmt., 1958, 4, 791-838.

34. Cattell, R. B. Anxiety, extraversion and other second-order personality factors in children. J. Pers., 1959, 27, 464-476.

35. Cattell, R. B. The dimensional (unitary-component) measurement of anxiety, excitement, effort stress, and other mood reaction patterns. In Uhr, L. and Miller, J. G. Drugs and behavior. New York: John Wiley and Sons, 1960, Pp. 437-462.

36. Cattell, R. B. The multiple abstract variance analysis. Equations and solutions for nature-nurture research on continuous variables. Psychol. Rev., 1960, 67, 353-372.

37. Cattell, R. B. Theory of situational, instrument, second-order, and refraction factors in personality structure research. Psychol. Bull., 1961, 58, 160-174.

38. Cattell, R. B. Clinical diagnosis and prognosis by objective personality factors. Paper read at annual meeting of the A.P.A. in New York, September, 1961.

39. Cattell, R. B. The basis of recognition and interpretation of factors. Ed. psychol. Measmt., 1962, 22, 667-697.

40. Cattell, R. B. The parental early repressiveness hypothesis for the "authoritarian" personality factor U.I. 28. J. genet. Psychol., 1964, 106, 333-349.

40a. Cattell, R. B., et al. Handbook for the Objective-Analytic Personality Factor Batteries. 1602 Coronado Drive, Champaign, Ill.: Instit. for Pers. and Abil. Testing (In preparation).

41. Cattell, R. B. Essentials of personality theory. (In preparation).

42. Cattell, R. B. and Baggaley, A. R. The salient variable similarity index for factor matching. Brit. J. Stat. Psychol., 1960, 13, 33-46.

43. Cattell, R. B. and Beloff, H. Le structure factorielle de la personalite des enfants de onze ans a travers trois types d'epreuves. Rev. Psychol. Appl., 1956, 6, 65-89.

44. Cattell, R.B., Bjerstedt, A., and Tsujioka, B. The measurement of Elation-Depression in terms of objective tests. (in preparation)

45. Cattell, R. B., Blewett, D. B. and Beloff, H. The inheritance of personality: a multiple variance analysis determination of approximate nature-nurture ratios for primary personality factors in Q-data. Amer. J. Hum. Genet., 1955, 7, 122-146.

46. Cattell, R. B. and Butcher, J. Prediction of achievement and creativity. Indianapolis, Ind.: Bobbs Merrill, (in press)

47. Cattell, R. B., Cattell, A.K.S. and Rhymer, R. M. P-technique demonstrated in determining psycho-physiological source traits in a normal individual. Psychometrika, 1947, 12, 267-288.

48. Cattell, R. B. and Coan, R. W. Personality dimensions in the questionnaire responses of six and seven-year-olds. Brit. J. Educ. Psychol., 1958, 28, 232-242.

49. Cattell, R. B. and Coan, R. W. Objective-test assessment of the primary personality dimensions in middle childhood. Brit. J. Psychol., 1959, 50, 235-252.

50. Cattell, R. B., Damarin, F. L. and Hundleby, J. D. Further investigation of objective personality test factors in early childhood. (In preparation)

51. Cattell, R. B., Damarin, F., and Warburton, F. W. Personality theory from multivariate experiment. (In preparation)

52. Cattell, R. B., Dubin, S. S. and Saunders, D. R. Verification of hypothesized factors in one hundred objective personality test designs. Psychometrika, 1954, 3, 209-230.

53. Cattell, R. B., Dubin, S. S., and Saunders, D. R. Personality structure in psychotics by factorization of objective clinical tests. J. ment. Sci., 1954, 100, 154-176.

54. Cattell, R. B. and Foster, M. J. The rotoplot program for multiple, single-plane, visually-guided rotation. Behav. Sci., 1963, 8, 156-165.

55. Cattell, R. B. and Gruen, W. The primary personality factors in 11-year-old children by objective tests. J. Pers., 1955, 23, 460-478.

56. Cattell, R. B. and Howarth, E. Verification of objective test personality factor patterns in middle childhood. J. genet. Psychol., 1964, 104, 331-349.

57. Cattell, R. B., Knapp, R. R. and Scheier, I. H. Second-order personality factor structure in the objective test realm. J. consult. Psychol., 1961, 25, 345-352.

58. Cattell, R. B. and Luborsky, L. B. P-technique demonstrated as a new clinical method for determining personality and symptom structure. J. genet. Psychol., 1950, 42, 3-24.

59. Cattell, R. B. and Muerle, J. L. The "Maxplane" program for factor rotation to oblique simple structure. Ed. psychol. Measmt., 1960, 20, 569-590.

59a. Cattell, R. B. and Pawlik, K. The use of algebraically derived variables in factor analyses. (in preparation)

60. Cattell, R. B. and Peterson, D. R. Personality structure in four and five year olds in terms of objective tests. J. clin. Psychol., 1959, 15, 355-369.

61. Cattell, R. B. and Saunders, D. R. Interrelation and matching of personality factors from behavior rating, questionnaire and objective test data. J. soc. Psychol., 1950, 31, 243-260.

62. Cattell, R. B. and Saunders, D. R. Beitraege zur Faktorenanalyse der Personnlichkeit. Z. exp. angew. Psychol., 1955, 2, 325-357.

63. Cattell, R. B. and Scheier, I. H. Discovery and development of measurement scales for the dimensions of anxiety. Report on Department of the Army Contract NO. DA-49-007-MD-620. Dayton, Ohio: (Document Service Center, Knott Bldg.) Armed Services Technical Information Agency, 1957.

64. Cattell, R. B. and Scheier, I. H. Factors in personality change: a discussion of the condition-response incremental design and application to 69 personality response measures and three stimulus conditions. Urbana, Ill.: Lab. of Pers. Assess. and Group Behavior, Advance Publication No. 9, 1958.

64a. Cattell, R. B. and Scheier, I. H. The objective test measurement of neuroticism, U.I. 23(-): a review of eight factor analytic studies. J. Indian Psychol., 1958, 33, 217-236.

65. Cattell, R. B. and Scheier, I. H. The nature of anxiety: a review of thirteen multivariate analyses comprising 814 variables. Psychol. Reports, 1958, 4, 351-388.

66. Cattell, R. B. and Scheier, I. H. Extension of meaning of objective test personality factors: especially into anxiety, neuroticism, questionnaire, and physical factors. J. gen. Psychol., 1959, 61, 287-315.

67. Cattell, R. B. and Scheier, I. H. Stimuli related to stress, neuroticism, excitation and anxiety response patterns: illustrating a new multivariate experimental design. J. abnorm. soc. Psychol., 1960, 60, 195-204.

68. Cattell, R. B. and Scheier, I. H. The meaning and measurement of neuroticism and anxiety. New York: Ronald Press, 1961.

69. Cattell, R. B., Schiff, H., et al. Psychiatric screening of flying personnel: prediction of training criteria by objective personality factors and development of the seven factor personality test. Report No. 10, Contract No. AF 33)038)-19569, Project No. 21-0202-0007, Randolph Field, Texas: USAF School of Aviation Medicine, 1953.

70. Cattell, R. B., Stice, G. F. and Kristy, N. F. A first approximation to nature-nurture ratios for eleven primary personality factors in objective tests. J. abnorm. soc. Psychol., 1957, 54, 143-159.

70a. Cattell, R.B., and Tsujioka, B. The importance of factor-trueness and validity versus homogeneity and orthogonality, in test scales. Educ. psychol. Measmt, 1964, 24, 3-30.

71. Cattell, R. B. and Warburton, F.W. Principles of personality measurement and a compendium of objective tests. Urbana, Ill.: Univer. of Ill. Press, 1963 (In press).

72. Connor, D. V. The effect of temperamental traits upon the group intelligence test performance of children. Doctoral dissertation, University of London Library, 1952.

73. Couch, A. and Keniston, K. Agreeing response set and social desirability. J. abnorm. soc. Psychol., 1961, 62, 175-179.

74. Cronbach, L. J. Studies of acquiescence as a factor in the true-false test. J. educ. Psychol., 1942, 33, 401-415.

75. Cronbach, L. J. Response sets and test validity. Educ. psychol. Measmt., 1946, 6, 475-494.

76. Cronbach, L. J. Further evidence on response sets and test design. Ed. psychol. Measmt., 1950, 10, 3-31.

77. Cronbach, L. J. and Gleser, G. C. Assessing similarity between profiles. Psychol. Bull., 1953, 50, 456-473.

77a. Cronbach, L.J. and Meehl, P.E. Construct validity in psychological tests. Psychol. Bull., 1955, 52, 281-302.

78. Crutcher, R. An experimental study of persistence. J. appl. Psychol., 1934, 18, 409-417.

79. Cureton, T. K. Physical fitness appraisal and guidance. St. Louis: The C.V. Mosby Co., 1947.

80. Darling, R. P. Autonomic action in relation to personality traits of children. J. abnorm. soc. Psychol., 1940, 35, 246-260.

81. Darrow, C. W. and Heath, L. L. Reaction tendencies relating to personality. In K. S. Lashley (Ed.), Studies in the dynamics of behavior. Chicago: Univer. of Chicago Press, 1932.

82. Duffy, E. The psychological significance of the concept of "arousal" or "activation." Psychol. Rev., 1957, 64, 265-275.

83. Dwyer, P. S. The determination of the factor loadings of a given test from the known factor loadings of other tests. Psychometrika, 1937, 2, 173-178.

84. Eysenck, H. J. Dimensions of personality. London: Kegan Paul, 1947.

85. Eysenck, H. J. Criterion analysis--an application of the hypothetico-deductive method to factor analysis. Psychol. Rev., 1950, 57, 38-53.

85a. Eysenck, H. J., and Prell, D. B. The inheritance of neuroticism: an experimental study. J. ment. Sci., 1951, 97, 441-465.

86. Eysenck, H. J. Schizothymia-cyclothymia as a dimension of personality. II. Experimental. J. Pers., 1952, 30, 345-384.

87. Eysenck, H. J. The scientific study of personality. London: Routledge and Kegan Paul, 1952.

88. Eysenck, H. J. Cortical inhibition, figural after-effect, and the theory of personality. J. abnorm. soc. Psychol., 1955, 51, 94-106.

89. Eysenck, H. J. Reminiscence, drive and personality theory. J. abnorm. soc. Psychol., 1956, 53, 328-333.

90. Eysenck, H.J. The structure of human personality. 2nd Edition: London: Methuen and Co., 1960.

91. Eysenck, H. J. Handbook of abnormal psychology. New York: Basic Books, 1961.

92. Farber, I. E. Anxiety as a drive state. In M. R. Jones (Ed.) Current theory and research on motivation, Nebraska Symposium on Motivation. Lincoln, Nebr.: Univer. of Nebraska Press, 1954. Pp. 1-46.

93. Farber, I. E. and Spence, K. W. Complex learning and conditioning as a function of anxiety. J. exp. Psychol., 1953, 45, 120-125.

94. Freeman, G. L. and Katzoff, E. T. Individual differences in physiological reactions to stimulation and their relation to other measures of emotionality. J. exp. Psychol., 1942, 31, 527-537.

95. French, J. W. The description of personality measurements in terms of rotated factors. Princeton: Educational Testing Service Report, 1953.

96. Fuller, J. L. and Thompson, W. R. Behavior genetics. New York: John Wiley and Sons, 1960.

97. Fulton, J. F. Physiology of the nervous system. 3rd Edition. London: Oxford Univer. Press, 1949.

98. Gough, H. G., McClosky, M., and Meehl, P. E. A personality scale for social responsibility. J. abnorm. soc. Psychol., 1952, 47, 73-80.

99. Grinker, R., et al. (unpublished, reported as study MR in (68), p. 475 ff.)

99a. Guilford, J. P. and Zimmerman, W. S. Fourteen dimensions of temperament. Psychol. Monogr., 1956, 70, No. 10 (Whole No. 417).

100. Guilford, J. P. Personality. New York: McGraw Hill, 1959.

101. Guilford, J. P. and Guilford, R. B. Personality factors D, R, T, and A. J. abnorm. soc. Psychol., 1939, 34, 21-26.

102. Guttman, L. Some necessary conditions for common factor analysis. Psychometrika, 1954, 19, 149-161.

103. Hargreaves, H. L. The "Faculty" of imagination. Brit. J. Psychol., Monogr. Suppl., 1927, 3, 10.

104. Harman, H. M. Modern factor analysis. Chicago: Univer. of Chicago Press, 1960.

105. Hartshorne, M., May, M. A. and Maller, J. B. Studies in service and self-control. New York: MacMillan, 1929.

106. Hartshorne, M. and May, M. Studies in deceit. New York: MacMillan, 1930.

107. Haverland, E. M. An experimental analysis by P-technique of some functionally unitary varieties of fatigue. M.A. thesis, Univer. of Illinois Library, 1959.

108. Hebb, D. O. Organization of behavior. A neuropsychological theory. New York: John Wiley and Sons, 1949.

109. Hildebrand, M. P. A factor study of introversion-extraversion. Brit. J. Psychol., 1958, 49, 1-11.

110. Horn, J. Structure in measures of self-sentiment, ego and super-ego concepts. Unpublished Master thesis. Univer. of Illinois, 1961.

111. Horn, J. L. Significance tests for use with r_p and related profile statistics. Ed. psychol. Measmt., 1961, 21, 363-370.

112. Hull, C. L. Principles of behavior. An introduction to behavior theory. New York: Appleton-Century-Crofts, 1943.

113. Hurley, J. R. and Cattell, R. B. The Procrustes program: producing direct rotation to test a hypothesized factor structure. Behav. Sci., 1962, 7, 258-262.

114. Jackson, D. N., and Messick, S. Content and style in personality assesment. Psychol. Bull., 1956, 55, 243-252.

115. Johnson, D. M. and Reynolds, F. A factor analysis of verbal ability. Psychol. Rev., 1941, 4, 183-195.

116. Jung, C. G. Psychologische Typen. Zuerich: Rascher and Cie., 1921.

117. Kaiser, H. F. Relating factors between studies based upon different individuals. Preliminary draft, July 15, 1960.

118. Kallman, F. J. The genetics of psychotic behavior patterns. Proc. Assoc. Res. Nerv. Ment. Dis., 1954, 33, 357-366.

119. Kallman, F. J. Heredity in health and mental disorder. New York: Norton, 1953.

120. Karson, S. and Pool, K. B. Second-order factors in personality measurement. J. consult. Psychol., 1958, 22, 299-303.

121. Knapp, R. R. and Most, J. A. Personality correlates of marine corps helicopter pilot performance. U.S.N. Med. Fld. Res. Lab. Rep., 1960, No. 18 01 09.1.3.

122. Knapp, R. R. Criterion predictions in the navy from the objective analytic personality test battery. Paper read at the annual meeting of the A.P.A., New York, September, 1961.

122a. Knapp, R. R. The validity of the Objective-Analytic Personality Test Battery in Navy settings. Educ. psychol. Measmt. 1962, 22, 379-387.

123. Knapp, R. R. The nature of primary personality dimensions as shown by relations of Cattell's objective personality test factors to questionnaire scales. Mimeographed report, 1960.

124. Knapp, R. R. Objective personality test and sociometric correlates of frequency of sick bay visits. J. appl. Psychol., 1961, 45, 104-110.

125. Kretschmer, E. Koerperbau and Charakter. 21 Edition. Berlin: Springer, 1955.

126. Lermot, W. G., Gibbs, E. L. and Gibbs, F. A. The brain wave pattern, an hereditary trait. J. Hered., 1945, 36, 233-243.

127. Lovell, C. A study of the factor structure of thirteen personality variables. Ed. psychol. Measmt., 1945, 5, 335-350.

128. Malmo, R. B. Activation: a neurophysiological dimension. Psychol. Rev., 1959, 66, 367-386.

129. McClelland, D. C. The achievement motive. New York: Appleton-Century-Crofts, 1953.

130. Meeland, T. An investigation of hypotheses for distinguishing personality factors A, F and H. Unpublished doctoral dissertation, Univer. of Illinois, 1952.

131. Messick, S. and Jackson, D. N. Acquiescence and the factorial interpretation of the M.M.P.I. Psychol. Bull., 1961, 58, 299-304.

132. Mosier, C. I. A note on Dwyer: the determination of the factor loadings of a given test. Psychometrika, 1938, 3, 297-299.

133. Mosier, C. I. Determining a simple structure when loadings for certain tests are known. Psychometrika, 1939, 4, 149-162.

134. Muller, G. E. and Pilzecker, A. Experimentelle Beitraege zur Lehre vom Gedaechtnis. Z. Psychol. Ergbd., 1900, 1, 1-288.

135. Muller, G. E. and Schumann, F. Experimentelle Beitraege zur Untersuchung des Gedaechtnisses. J. Psychol., 1894, 6, 81-190.

136. North, R. D. An analysis of the personality dimensions of introversion-extraversion. J. Pers., 1949, 17, 352-367.

137. Pavlov, I. P. Conditioned reflexes. (Transl. by G. V. Anrep). London: Oxford Univer. Press, 1927.

138. Pawlik, K. Educational Prediction from objective personality test dimensions. Paper read at the annual meeting of the A.P.A., New York: September, 1961.

139. Pawlik, K. Inhibition as a personality source trait. (In preparation)

140. Pawlik, K. and Cattell, R. B. The relationship between certain personality factors and measures of cortical arousal. Neuropsychologia, in press.

140a. Pawlik, K. and Cattell, R. B. Third-order factors in objective personality tests. Brit. J. Psychol., 1964, 55, 1-18.

141. Pinzka, C. and Saunders, D. R. Analytic rotation to simple structure, II: Extension to an oblique solution. Research Bulletin RB-54-31. Princeton, New Jersey: Educational Testing Service, 1954.

142. Raney, E. Brain potentials and lateral dominance in twins. J. exp. Psychol., 1939, 24, 21-39.

143. Rethlingshafer, D. The relation of tests of persistence to other measures of continuance of action. J. abnorm. soc. Psychol., 1942, 37, 71-82.

144. Rimoldi, H. J. A. Personal tempo. J. abn. soc. Psychol., 1951, 46, 283-303.

145. Rohracher, H. Kleine Charakterkunde. 7 Ed. Wien: Urban and Schwarzenberg, 1956.

146. Rosenthal, Irene. A factor analysis of anxiety variables. Unpublished doctoral dissertation, Univer. of Illinois, 1955.

147. Ryans, D. G. An experimental attempt to analyze persistent behavior. J. gen. Psychol., 1938, 19, 333-353.

148. Scheier, I. H. and Cattell, R. B. Conformation of objective test factors and assessment of their relation to questionnaire factors: a factor analysis of 113 rating, questionnaire and objective test measurements of personality. J. ment. Sci., 1958, 104, 608-624.

149. Scheier, I. H., Cattell, R. B. and Horn, J. L. Objective test factor U.I. 23: its measurement and its relation to clinically-judged neuroticism. J. clin. Psychol., 1960, 16, 135-145.

150. Scheier, I. H., Cattell, R. B. and Mayeske, G. W. The objective-test factors of imaginative tension (U.I. 25), introversion (U.I. 32), anxiety (U.I. 24) and autistic non-conformity (U.I. 34): (1) Data on new factor-measuring tests, and (2) relation of factors to clinically-judged psychosis. Urbana, Ill.: Lab. of Pers. Assess. and Group Behavior, Advance Publ. No. 10, 1960.

151. Scheier, I. H. What is an "objective test". Psychol. Rept., 1958, 4, 147-157.

152. Sheldon, W. M. The varieties of temperament. New York: Harper, 1942.

153. Sokal, R. E. A comparison of five tests for completeness of factor extraction. Trans. Kansas. Acad. Sci., 1959, 62, 141-152.

154. Spearman, C. The abilities of man. London: MacMillan and Co., 1932.

155. Spence, K. W. Behavior theory and conditioning. New Haven: Yale Univer. Press, 1956.

156. Stead, W. M. and Shartle, C. L. et al. Occupational Counselling techniques. New York: American Book Co., 1940.

157. Taylor, J. A. A personality scale of manifest anxiety. J. abnorm. soc. Psychol., 1953, 48, 285-290.

158. Thomson, G. M. The factorial analysis of human ability. 5th Ed. New York: Houghton Mifflin Co., 1951.

159. Thornton, G. R. A factor analysis of tests designed to measure persistence. Psychol. Monogr., 1939, 51, 1-42.

160. Thurstone, L. L. Primary mental abilities. Chicago: Univer. of Chicago Press, 1938.

161. Thurstone, L. L. A factorial study of perception. Chicago: Univer. of Chicago Press, 1944.

162. Thurstone, L. L. Multiple factor analysis. Chicago: Univer. of Chicago Press, 1947.

163. Tucker, L. R. A method of synthesis of factor analysis studies. Dept. of the Army, A.G.O. Personnel Res. Sec., Rep. No. 984, 1951.

164. Tucker, L. A new method of relating factors between studies. Personal communication, 1961.

165. Vernon, P. E. Educational testing and test-form factors. Educational Testing Service Bulletin (RB-58-3). Princeton: Educational Testing Service, 1958.

166. Wells, H. P. Relationships between physical fitness and psychological variables. Unpublished doctoral dissertation, Univer. of Illinois, 1958.

167. Wenger, M. A. Studies of autonomic balance in Army Air Force Personnel. Comp. psychol. Monogr., 1948, 101, 1-111.

168. Wherry, R. J. Test selection and suppressor variables. Psychometrika, 1946, 11, 239-247.

169. White, O. Some properties of three factor contribution matrices. Unpublished manuscript, 1961.

170. Williams, H. V. A determination of psychosomatic functional unities in personality by means of P-technique. J. soc. Psychol., 1954, 25-45.

171. Wrigley, C. and Neuhaus, J. O. The matching of two sets of factors. Amer. Psychol., 1955, 10, 418-419.

172. Wrigley, C., Saunders, D. R., and Neuhaus, J. O. Application of the quartimax method of rotation to Thurstone's primary mental abilities study. Psychometrika, 1958, 23, 151-170.

APPENDIX 1

LOADINGS OF SALIENT VARIABLES ON FACTORS U.I. 16 - U.I. 36

Master Index Number	U.I. 16	U.I. 17	U.I. 18	U.I. 19	U.I. 20	U.I. 21	U.I. 22	U.I. 23	U.I. 24	U.I. 25
1						+09(2) +09(2)	+18(2) +36(1)			
2a-h	-11(13) -13(11)	-03(14) -03(14)		-14(16) -21(13)		+04(2)		-28(15) -28(15)	+04(10) +08(8)	+03(12)
3, 127		-09(6) -17(4)						-01(4)		
4			-22(2) -41(1)							
5	+02(11) +11(7)	+18(12) -30(11)	-03(10)		+09(9)	+01(7)	+25(11) +28(9)		-04(8) -12(4)	
6a-c	+14(7) +20(5)			-03(9) -03(9)			+20(12) +25(11)	+52(2) +52(2)		+19(11) +23(9)
7	+08(10) +13(5)	-11(11) -24(8)		+20(10) +27(7)		-04(9)		+04(8) +11(5)		-25(7) -25(7)
8		-09(9) -15(7)		+17(8) +22(7)		+03(7)	+21(8) +22(7)	+14(6) +24(4)		-13(6) -18(5)
9	+49(4) +49(4)			+21(3) +21(3)			+17(4) +21(3)			
10		+35(3) +35(3)		+21(3) +21(3)						
11b										
13a-c, g	-23(5) -23(5)		+07(6) +07(6)		+00(5)	+19(3) +19(3)	+19(5) +19(5)			
14	-20(2) -20(2)				+16(2) +16(2)					
15	+16(11) +20(10)		+30(10) +30(10)	-13(11) -16(8)		+09(10)				
16a			+28(7) +28(7)	-15(11) -20(8)						-10(5) -25(2)
16b										
16d										
17										
20a					-60(1)					
21	+25(12) +30(10)	+39(10) +41(9)		+10(11)	+22(11) +25(10)				+12(8) +34(5)	
22a-c				-25(2) -25(2)		+11(14) +11(4)				
23a		+03(4)								
24a, c, d			+24(6) +24(6)		+02(4)	-09(4) -09(4)				-07(5) -13(4)
24e										
25a		+13(3) +13(3)	-15(4) -15(4)							
25b										
26				+27(2) +27(2)			-07(3) -21(2)			
28							-20(5) -20(5)	+15(5) +31(4)		
29		-51(1) -51(1)								
30	+02(8)	+01(9)		-09(14) -18(12)		+04(9)	-00(5)			
31				-12(3) -45(1)	+23(1) +23(1)				-06(4)	
33					+04(4)	+16(6) +24(5)		-00(7)		
34	-11(11) -18(9)			+13(8) +16(6)	+05(8)	-27(8) -31(7)		-00(7)		
35	-17(10) -21(8)			+01(9)	+25(9) +29(7)	-24(8) -24(8)				
36				-06(5)	-40(4) -40(4)			-00(4)		
37				+19(2) +19(2)		-14(2) -30(1)	+17(2) +34(1)	-21(2) -21(2)		
38a, c			-24(8) -28(6)	-04(5) -07(4)	+34(5) +36(5)	-14(5) -14(4)				
38b	+00(10) +09(6)				+53(6) +53(6)	+26(4) +26(4)				
39			+24(11) +26(9)	+11(11) +18(7)		-03(6)	-09(9) -11(7)	-03(6)		
40		-12(6) -16(4)		-05(9) -10(7)			+20(9) +20(9)			+04(7) +04(7)
41				+18(7) +20(6)				+13(6) +16(5)		
42	+06(7)				+16(6) +16(6)			-16(12) -16(12)	+01(6) +16(3)	+00(6)
43		+24(9) +24(9)	-10(7) -10(7)			+04(8) +05(7)	-11(6) -17(5)			+08(4) +21(3)
45a							-19(2) -61(1)			
46a, b		+16(4) +31(3)			-08(4) -13(3)	+30(1) +30(1)				
47										
50	+16(2) +16(2)			+32(1) +32(1)						
51	+11(7) +14(5)	+13(7) +46(3)	-01(5)	+17(9) +28(7)				-28(5)		-02(5) -02(5)
53			+31(3) +39(2)	-25(3) -25(3)			-34(1)			
55	-14(3) -30(2)				-24(2) -24(2)		-20(3) -20(3)		+32(2) +37(1)	
56			+32(1) +32(1)							
57										
58								+41(1) +41(1)		
59					-25(1) -35(1)					
61	-39(1) -39(1)			+36(1) +36(1)						
63	-31(1) -31(1)	-46(1) -46(1)				+40(1) 40(1)	+38(1) +38(1)			
64				+12(5)	-33(3)	-12(6) -19(3)	-22(6) -26(5)		-15(2) -39(1)	
65			-33(1) -33(1)	+18(3) +18(3)	-15(4)			-21(3) -21(3)		
66			-32(1) -32(1)							
67a, b		-15(2) -34(1)		+11(4)	-11(6)	+03(7) +03(7)	-02(5)	-13(7) -23(4)	+10(8) +11(7)	
69					+31(1) +31(1)					
70					-43(1) -43(1)		+30(1) +30(1)			
71	-02(9)			-19(11) -25(9)		-08(9) -16(7)	+10(10) +18(8)	-02(8)	-06(10)	
72		+24(5) +24(5)					+20(6) +30(4)			+16(5) +14(5)
73			+36(3) +36(3)	+06(3)						
74		+26(5) +26(5)			-35(3) -35(3)	+33(3) +41(2)				
75					-51(1) -51(1)	+56(1) +56(1)				
76					+33(1) +33(1)	+30(1) +30(1)		+65(1) +65(1)		
77		+12(6) +12(6)	+13(3) +13(3)	+15(4) +19(3)			+09(5)	-13(4)		
78	-01(3) +31(1)	+23(4) +26(3)		-02(4)	+24(2) +24(2)	+13(3) +16(2)	+15(4) +19(3)	-19(4) -22(3)		
79	-55(1) -55(1)			-44(1) -44(1)	+41(1) +41(1)		+37(1) +37(1)			
80				-25(5) -31(4)	+06(2) +52(1)		-08(6) -25(4)			

Appendix

Master Index Number	U.I. 26		U.I. 27		U.I. 28		U.I. 29		U.I. 30		U.I. 31		U.I. 32		U.I. 33		U.I. 34		U.I. 35		U.I. 36	
1																						
2a-h	-24(4)	-24(4)					-11(8)	-16(7)							-24(3)	-24(3)						
3, 127																						
4																						
5							+17(9)	+19(7)					+09(5)	+17(3)								
6a-c	-03(3)	-03(3)							-04(3)													
7					+16(7)	-17(6)	-09(5)															
8			+12(2)	+31(1)	+03(5)																	
9	-13(2)						+25(3)	+25(3)														
10																						
11b							+21(2)	+21(2)							+20(2)	+20(2)						
13a-c, g	-15(5)	-24(4)	+20(4)	+20(4)			-21(3)	-21(3)														
14																						
15	-06(11)				+02(10)	+08(8)			-00(7)													
16a	-09(5)	-09(5)			+09(5)	+16(4)			+u6(3)	+32(1)			-02(5)	-18(3)								
16b							-52(1)	-52(1)														
16d																						
17																						
20a																						
21	-03(5)				+00(8)	+05(6)					+11(5)	+11(5)					-15(2)	-30(1)				
22a-c			+26(1)	+26(1)					-42(1)	-42(1)												
23a																			-16(3)	-16(3)		
24a, c, d	+01(7)	+01(7)	-18(2)	-18(2)			-04(3)						-23(4)	-23(4)	-24(4)	-24(4)	-36(1)	-36(1)				
24e																						
25a	+34(2)	+34(2)																				
25b	+09(2)						+25(4)	+25(4)														
26	+33(1)	+33(1)	+14(2)	+14(2)																		
28	+19(4)	+35(2)					+02(3)		+36(1)	+36(1)												
29																						
30	+13(6)	+13(6)	+14(2)	+14(2)									+01(9)									
31									-16(4)	-16(4)	-11(4)	-18(3)							-39(1)	-39(1)		
33	+02(5)																+30(3)	+30(3)	+18(3)	+18(3)		
34																						
35	+07(6)				+24(6)	+32(5)			-08(5)	-10(4)	+07(4)		-13(3)	-20(2)								
36	+14(4)	+14(4)			-08(3)	-08(3)																
37							+19(2)	+19(2)														
38a, c					+18(6)	+20(5)																
38b													-12(4)	-12(4)								
39	-07(9)	-10(8)																				
40	-05(6)						+17(4)	+17(4)					+04(7)									
41											-01(3)	-25(3)										
42	-09(7)		+35(5)	+35(5)					+21(4)	+28(3)									-04(3)			
43	+02(6)						-05(6)										+15(3)	+15(3)	+26(2)	+26(2)	+29(2)	+29(2)
45a																						
46a, b	+17(2)	+17(2)					-12(5)	-15(4)							-18(3)	-18(3)						
47																						
50																						
51	-05(7)		+10(2)	+10(2)			+08(5)										-14(3)	-22(2)			+20(2)	+20(2)
53																						
55									-13(2)	-13(2)												
56																						
57																						
58																						
59																						
61																						
63																						
64													+32(1)	+32(1)								
65	-29(2)	-29(2)																				
66																						
67a, b	+05(6)				+22(7)	+23(6)	-07(6)	-02(4)			-14(6)	-14(6)			-21(3)	-21(3)						
69																						
70																						
71	-12(10)	-18(9)	-14(2)	-14(2)	+02(9)	+14(6)					+15(4)	+27(2)					+03(3)					
72	+16(3)	+16(3)					-23(4)	-31(3)									-49(1)	-49(1)				
73									+36(1)	+36(1)												
74							+58(2)	+58(2)									+20(2)	+20(2)				
75																						
76																						
77	+12(3)	+12(3)																				
78																						
79																						
80	-12(4)	-17(3)					+62(3)	+62(3)													-16(2)	-16(2)

LOADINGS OF SALIENT VARIABLES ON U.I. 16 - U.I. 36 (continued)

Master Index Number	U.I. 16	U.I. 17	U.I. 18	U.I. 19	U.I. 20	U.I. 21	U.I. 22	U.I. 23	U.I. 24	U.I. 25
81			+36(1) +36(1)							
82	+23 (5) +26(4)	+15(3) +29(2)	+18(5) +37(3)	+09(3) +21(2)		-04(4) -04(4)				
83		-01(8)	+21(7) +23(6)				+21(7) +37(5)			
84a, b, c	+38(4) +47(2)	+05(6) +05(6)		+07(5) +08(4)		+41(3) +47(2)		-19(4) -19(4)		
87						+34(1) +34(1)				
89										
91		-39(2) -53(1)								
92				+26(2) +26(2)			+25(2) +25(2)			
93		+23(2) +48(1)				-18(2) -18(2)	-33(2) -33(2)			
94			-04(2)				+25(4) +25(4)			
95						+41(2) +41(2)	+22(2) +22(2)			
96a	+14(5) +14(5)		+26(3) +26(3)						-18(2) -30(1)	
96b										
97										
98a	+16(5) +24(4)									
98b										
99	+16(3) +36(2)			+24(3) +32(2)						
100										
101a, b	+36(1) +36(1)			-02(5) -17(3)	-41(1) -41(1)	-07(6) -16(4)		-08(6)		
101c						-07(6) -16(4)				
102										
104						-18(2) -18(2)				
105		+14(8) +21(7)	-04(7)	+06(10)		-05(9)				
106	+09(5) +22(3)				+11(5) +11(5)	+17(5) +17(5)				
107		+25(2) +25(2)		+33(2) +33(2)						
108		+05(9) +14(6)	+02(8) +02(8)			-15(9) -18(8)	-03(9)		-18(10) -19(9)	
109										
110		-03(4)			+20(2) +20(2)			-18(2) -18(2)		-33(1) -33(1)
111			+06(5) +08(4)	-06(5) -10(4)						
112	+10(6) +17(3)	+16(7) +16(7)						+10(5) +12(4)		
113					-32(4) -46(2)				-43(1) -43(1)	
114								-17(2)		
115			-42(1) -42(1)							
116a	-11(8) -13(6)		+00(8)	+07(11)	+14(7) +33(5)		-07(8) -11(6)		+22(9) +22(9)	
116b										
117	+34(5) +34(5)	+18(4) +21(3)								
118	+29(3) +29(3)	+08(2)								
119										
120a-g	-17(8) -36(5)	+02(9)		-20(2)	-05(6)	+06(9)	-05(11) -05(11)	+31(13) +31(13)	+07(9) +11(7)	+30(3) +30(3)
121										
122					+04(4) +21(3)	+09(4) +11(3)				
123										
124		-21(2) -39(1)	-19(3) -27(2)		+31(2) +68(1)					
125a	+22(3) +35(2)									-30(1) -30(1)
126		-19(2) -19(2)								
133		+11(6) +12(5)		-07(5)					+14(5) +17(4)	
136										
143	+26(8) +31(7)		+25(8) +25(8)	+05(7)		+13(7)	+03(8) +03(8)	+06(5) +06(5)		+04(7)
144	+02(3) +32(2)				+16(3) +18(2)	+08(5) +11(4)			+19(3) +21(2)	
145a, b, c										
146a				+41(5) +41(5)						-16(4) -67(2)
146b			-02(7) -14(5)	+33(9) +33(9)	-01(7)	-29(8) -29(8)		-02(5)		-19(7) -21(6)
147b				+07(4)		-17(3) -17(3)			-39(1) -39(1)	
148			-18(2) -18(2)							
150	-21(2) -21(2)	+22(3) +22(3)								
151							-22(2) -22(2)	+18(3) +29(1)		
152			+02(5)		+52(10) +52(10)	+16(10) +22(9)		-17(4) -17(4)	+24(11) +24(11)	
153	+20(3) +31(2)		+30(5) +30(5)							
155				-21(2) -21(2)			+21(2) +21(2)			
156				-19(2) -19(2)						
157						-24(2) -24(2)				
158										
159a		-33(1) -33(1)		+45(1) +45(1)						
159c		+49(1) +49(1)								
161a, b					+04(4)	+03(4)				
162b								-32(3) -32(3)		-27(2) -27(2)
163					-30(2) -30(2)					
164					-24(2) -24(2)					
165	-18(2) -41(1)				-45(2) -45(2)					
166		-24(2) -24(2)		-21(2) -21(2)	-16(2) -16(2)		-17(2) -35(1)			

Appendix

Master Index Number	U.I. 26		U.I. 27		U.I. 28		U.I. 29		U.I. 30		U.I. 31		U.I. 32		U.I. 33		U.I. 34		U.I. 35		U.I. 36	
81																						
82							-11(3)	-11(3)														
83	-10(8)	-11(7)			-14(2)		-11(6)	-14(5)									-32(3)	-32(3)				
84a, b, c													+04(2)									
87																						
89																						
91			-16(2)	-16(2)																		
92																						
93																						
94									+17(2)	+17(2)												
95																						
96a					-01(3)																	
96b	-71(1)	-71(1)																				
97					+52(4)	+52(4)																
98a							+10(4)	+30(3)														
98b									-12(3)	-45(2)					-30(1)	-30(1)						
99	+15(3)														+19(2)							
100															+25(3)	+25(3)						
101a, b			-25(2)	-25(2)					-11(4)	-11(4)												
101c																						
102	-33(1)	-33(1)					+30(2)	+30(2)														
104	-19(2)	-19(2)																				
105	+12(9)	+17(7)											+01(6)									
106									-01(4)	-17(3)												
107					-25(2)	-25(2)																
108	-07(10)	-07(10)	-07(4)	-13(3)	-03(9)	-25(6)	+15(7)	+20(6)			+00(5)		+12(7)	+13(6)	-25(4)	-25(4)						
109									-45(1)	-45(1)												
110	+17(2)	+17(2)							-33(1)	-33(1)												
111	-02(4)				-03(5)	-08(3)	+16(5)	+23(3)														
112			-24(3)	-33(2)			-11(5)		-04(5)	-04(5)			+05(4)	+14(3)	+28(4)	+43(3)						
113											-11(3)	-27(2)			+05(4)							
114																						
115																						
116a			-06(4)	-14(3)	+18(7)	+26(5)																
116b																	-29(3)	-52(2)				
117																						
118	+18(3)	+18(3)	+16(2)	+16(2)			+18(3)	+18(3)														
119	+15(3)	+15(3)					+13(3)	+13(3)														
120a-g	+07(8)	+07(8)			+14(8)	+17(7)	+03(4)						+05(8)				-31(5)	-31(5)				
121											+62(1)	+62(1)										
122			+35(3)	+35(3)																		
123					+49(6)	+49(6)													-04(2)			
124																						
125a			+17(3)	+17(3)	-07(3)	-15(2)																
126							+08(2)															
133							-27(2)	-27(2)	+07(4)	+10(3)												
136					-14(3)																	
143							+23(5)	+25(4)	-01(4)													
144	+13(3)	+13(3)									-20(2)	-20(2)										
145a, b, c			+34(2)	+34(2)																		
146a	-16(4)	-67(2)									+08(5)		+12(6)	+13(5)								
146b	+11(7)	+14(5)																				
147b	-13(4)	-26(2)					-09(3)															
148							+17(2)	+17(2)														
150											-21(2)	-21(2)										
151																					-35(1)	-35(1)
152	+04(7)	+12(5)			+24(9)	+27(8)							+03(6)	+14(4)							-41(2)	-41(2)
153	+07(4)		+00(3)																			
155					+19(2)	+40(1)			+48(1)	+48(1)												
156																						
157			-18(2)	-18(2)																		
158	-21(2)	-21(2)																				
159a																						
159c													-42(1)	-42(1)								
161a, b	+25(4)	+34(3)																				
162b	-17(3)	-17(3)																				
163																						
164					-12(2)	-31(1)																
165							+25(2)	+53(1)														
166											+20(2)	+20(2)			-23(2)	-23(2)						

LOADINGS OF SALIENT VARIABLES ON FACTORS U.I. 16 - U.I. 36 (continued)

Master Index Number	U.I. 16	U.I. 17	U.I. 18	U.I. 19	U.I. 20	U.I. 21	U.I. 22	U.I. 23	U.I. 24	U.I. 25
167a,b					+11(3) +11(3)	+25(7) +25(7)		+34(1) +34(1)		
168a,b						+28(3) +28(3)				
169					+26(1) +26(1)					
170				+30(2) +30(2)		-47(1) -47(1)				-30(1) -30(1)
171	+23(3) +23(3)					+17(3)		+36(1) +36(1)		
175				+01(10)	+12(4) +18(3)	+26(5) +26(5)	-48(5) -48(5)			
176		+17(5) +23(3)		-18(5) -26(4)	+05(4) +37(2)	+03(5)	-51(13) -51(13)		+10(6) +10(6)	-08(9) -17(7)
177a,b				+06(5) +15(3)		+08(6) +15(4)				
178										
191										
192				+11(5) +22(3)		+20(6) +20(6)				
193a			+13(8) +13(7)		-11(7)	-12(6) -16(4)		+15(2) +15(2)		
194						-19(3) -19(3)		+10(3) +10(3)		+07(3) +07(3)
198				+10(3) +10(3)	+01(3)					-05(3) -05(3)
199	+02(7) +15(4)					+25(8) +26(7)	-02(9) -02(9)	+21(7) +21(7)	-08(8) -12(5)	+30(9) +33(8)
201				+16(2) +16(2)						
202			+06(2)					-34(1) -34(1)		
203				+02(5) +02(5)	+02(5)		-07(5)			
205					+07(4) +15(3)				+24(5) +24(5)	
206	+16(4) +16(4)			+26(8) +26(8)		+05(7) +05(7)				+01(5) +16(3)
211a				-05(9)	+12(8) +12(8)	-03(7)			+52(10) +52(10)	
211b									+50(1) +50(1)	
212	+35(2) +35(2)					-02(3) -02(3)	+13(4) +13(4)			
216		+33(3) +43(2)						-16(2) -16(2)		
218			+46(2) +46(2)					+26(2) +26(2)		
219			-01(9)	-08(12) -10(11)	+27(9) +27(9)	+03(9)	-07(11) -18(8)	-04(7)	+29(14) +31(13)	
227a,b			-14(3)					-25(4) -25(4)		+02(5) +02(5)
231				+35(1) +35(1)			+37(1) +37(1)			
234	+41(3) +41(3)						+17(3)			
237	+46(1) +46(1)									
240										+35(1) +35(1)
242						-31(1) -31(1)				
243						-03(3)			+39(3) +39(3)	
244	+24(2) +24(2)					+60(4) +60(4)				
245									-32(1) -32(1)	
246					-26(5) -26(5)				-09(4) -37(2)	
247a	+21(3) +33(2)									-18(6) -20(5)
247b			+20(4) +29(3)							
249						+28(2) +28(2)				+19(2) +19(2)
260										
261										
263	-05(4)		-12(5) -16(4)			+06(6)	-40(5) -40(5)			-14(5) -21(3)
264	+35(1) +35(1)									
268	+49(3) +49(3)		-12(5) -16(4)			+09(4) +23(3)				
269	+23(5) +23(5)		-01(6)						+03(8) +06(6)	+18(5) +18(5)
270	+27(7) +27(7)				-03(6)				+05(7) +16(4)	+13(7) +19(6)
271		+08(5) +11(4)				+35(8) +35(8)			+07(6) +07(5)	
272	+29(1) +29(1)									+11(5) +13(4)
273	-12(5) -16(3)		-09(8) -21(5)							-10(8) -11(7)
274									+30(2) +30(2)	
275										+30(1) +30(1)
276				+12(2)		-10(2)			+23(3) +23(3)	
277				+12(3) +22(2)						
278,511,516	+57(4) +57(4)					+59(1) +59(1)		+36(2) +36(2)		
280										
282	+27(7) +28(6)	+20(8) +20(8)		+06(6) +08(5)	+00(6)	+20(8) +27(6)	+21(8) +21(8)		+02(11)	-06(8) -09(6)
283	+11(3) +17(2)									
286					+05(2)					
287										
288		+26(3) -32(2)		-10(3) -10(3)		+56(3) +56(3)				+13(2) +13(2)
289						+63(1) +63(1)				
291					-21(2) -21(2)					
300a										
303		-63(1) -63(1)								
304		-56(1) -56(1)								
305								-31(1) -31(1)		
307a,b	+25(4) +28(3)					+42(4) +42(4)				
308	+29(2) +29(2)					+48(3) +48(3)				
309	+52(3) +64(2)		-18(2)			+45(2) +45(2)				
316	+16(4) +16(4)						+04(4) +04(4)			+25(2) +25(2)
320										-21(2) -21(2)

Master Index Number	U.I. 26	U.I. 27	U.I. 28	U.I. 29	U.I. 30	U.I. 31	U.I. 32	U.I. 33	U.I. 34	U.I. 35	U.I. 36
167a,b	+29(5) +29(5)			+23(3) +23(3)			+04(6)			-16(3) -16(3)	
168a,b	-07(2)										
169											
170			+16(3) +23(2)								
171	-04(2)		+34(3) +34(3)								
175											
176				+16(5) +16(5)							
177a,b						-21(4)					
178		-24(1) -24(1)									
191			-27(4) -27(4)								
192	+16(3) +16(3)		-29(6) -29(6)	-12(3)		-38(4) -38(4)		-53(2) -53(2)			
193a	+04(3)		+17(6) +13(4)				-09(4)				
194		+22(3) +22(3)	+21(6) +29(4)								
198											
199	+00(9) +00(9)						-01(8)			-25(3) -25(3)	
201											
202											
203						-45(4) -45(4)					
205	+19(4) +19(4)				-03(4) -12(3)						
206											
211a	+07(7)		+14(5) +14(5)	+00(3)		-08(4)		+34(1) +34(1)		+16(2)	
211b											
212	+05(4) +05(4)		+13(4) +13(4)								
216											
218											
219	+09(9)						-05(9) -08(7)				
227a,b									-12(3) -12(3)		
231											
234											
237											
240											
242	+20(3) +20(3)										
243											
244											
245											
246			-20(4) -20(4)		-20(2)		+12(3) +12(3)				
247a											
247b											
249											
260											
261				+36(1) +36(1)							
263							-04(5) -11(3)				
264											
268				+17(5) +17(5)	-21(3) -31(2)						
269	+04(7) +04(7)				-41(5) -41(5)	+05(3)				-14(2) -14(2)	
270					-35(6) -41(5)						
271	-20(6) -20(6)								+29(2) +29(2)		
272											
273	+33(10) +35(9)						+04(7) +07(6)			+00(3)	
274	+37(1) +37(1)										
275			-34(1) -34(1)				+22(2) +46(1)				
276	+26(3) +26(3)								-31(1) -31(1)		
277											
278,511,516											
280			-21(4) -21(4)			-42(3) -42(3)					
282					-17(4) -17(4)		+18(8) +21(7)		+21(5) +21(5)		
283	-41(3) -50(2)						+18(3) +18(3)				
286	+17(2) +17(2)										
287					+44(1) +44(1)						
288											
289											
291											
300a					-46(1) -46(1)						
303											
304											
305								-16(2) -31(1)			
307a,b				+25(2) +25(2)							
308											
309											
316			+22(3) +32(2)				+28(4) +28(4)				
320											

LOADING OF SALIENT VARIABLES ON FACTORS U.I. 16 - U.I. 36 (continued)

Master Index Number	U.I. 16	U.I. 17	U.I. 18	U.I. 19	U.I. 20	U.I. 21	U.I. 22	U.I. 23	U.I. 24	U.I. 25
321		+44(2) +44(2)				+00(11)				-22(2) -22(2)
325		+27(1)					+44(1) +44(1)			
327a					+31(3) +38(2)				+40(4) +47(2)	
327b		-25(1) -25(1)								
327d										
330									+24(2) +24(2)	
332										
334										
335	-31(1) -31(1)						-26(2) -26(2)			
336		+38(6) +38(6)					+01(6)		-00(6)	+09(5) +18(4)
339										
340	-25(2) -40(1)						+34(2) +34(2)			
341										
343a							+39(1) +39(1)			
346	+46(1) +46(1)									
347						+30(1) +30(1)				
348					+63(1) +63(1)					
349										
350						+32(1) +32(1)				
352a		+31(1) +31(1)						+42(1) +42(1)		
353		-32(1) -32(1)								
354										
355										
356a										+33(2) +33(2)
356b								+14(3) +14(3)		
357										
359									+62(3) +62(3)	-09(3) -12(2)
361										
363										
364										
371										
372										
374		-53(1) -53(1)								
375	+45(1) +45(1)									
378	+44(1) +44(1)									
379	+62(2) +62(2)									
382	+22(2) +46(1)									
383									+33(1) +33(1)	
384										
385			+44(2) +44(2)							
386										-35(1) -35(1)
388								-38(1) -38(1)		
389										+40(1) +40(1)
391										
393					+31(1) +31(1)					
400		-52(1) -52(1)								
401										
407								+38(1) +38(1)		
409								+30(1) +30(1)		
420a										
421										
422					+40(1)					
423										
425						+52(1) +52(1)				
426				-20(2) -20(2)		-21(2)				
427		-50(1) -50(1)								
428b		-40(1) -40(1)	-34(1) -34(1)	-17(3) -17(3)		+25(2) +25(2)				
429		-72(1) -72(1)								
430		-65(1) -65(1)								
437										
439								+35(1) +35(1)		
443				-13(3) -13(3)				-20(3) -20(3)		
444	+14(3) +30(1)					+21(2) +21(2)			+07(4) +20(2)	
445						-22(2) -22(2)				
448										
449										
454				+14(3) +14(3)				-11(3) -18(1)	+53(4) +53(4)	
455a									+01(4)	
456		-03(3)				+18(2) +18(2)				
457										
458						+29(2) +29(2)			-06(5) -16(3)	
459						+22(2)				

Master Index Number	U.I. 26	U.I. 27	U.I. 28	U.I. 29	U.I. 30	U.I. 31	U.I. 32	U.I. 33	U.I. 34	U.I. 35	U.I. 36
321											
325											
327a										+30(1) +30(1)	
327b											
327d								+33(1) +33(1)			
330											
332							+36(1) +36(1)				
334										-43(1) -43(1)	
335			+34(1) +34(1)						-48(1) -48(1)		
336	+08(3) +14(2)								+13(5) +16(4)		
339			+48(3) +59(2)								
340											
341				-43(1) -43(1)							
343a			-32(1) -32(1)								
346	+30(1) +30(1)										
347					-36(1) -36(1)						
348											
349										+31(1) +31(1)	
350											
352a											
353											
354										+36(1) +36(1)	
355	+42(1) +42(1)										
356a											
356b						+63(1) +63(1)					
357			+46(3) +66(2)								
359							+25(2) +25(2)				
361						-36(1) -36(1)					
363						+00(1) +00(1)					
364						+37(2) +37(2)	-23(2) -23(2)				
371						+32(1) +32(1)					
372								-30(1) -30(1)			
374											
375			+33(1) +33(1)								
378											
379			-16(2) -35(1)								
382											
383											
384								-31(1) -31(1)			
385						-20(2) -20(2)					
386											
388											
389											
391								-38(1) -38(1)			
393											
400								-29(1) -29(1)			
401								-32(2) -32(2)			
407											
409											
420a							-42(1) -42(1)				
421							-42(2) -42(2)				
422							-45(3) -45(3)				
423							-46(1) -46(1)				
425											
426											
427											
428b											
429											
430						-20(2) -20(2)					
437								-38(1) -38(1)			
439											
443	-08(3)		-36(2) -36(2)								
444	-14(4) -14(4)						+23(2) +23(2)				
445	+06(3)										
448					+34(1) +34(1)						
449							-33(1) -33(1)				
454									+18(3) +18(3)		
455a									+19(2) +19(2)		+12(2) +12(2)
456	+06(3)										
457											
458	+09(3)									+34(3) +34(3)	
459											

LOADING OF SALIENT VARIABLES ON FACTORS U.I. 16 - U.I. 36 (continued)

Master Index Number	U.I. 16	U.I. 17	U.I. 18	U.I. 19	U.I. 20	U.I. 21	U.I. 22	U.I. 23	U.I. 24	U.I. 25
460		-00(3)								+26(2) +38(1)
461	+11(2)			+18(3) +28(2)						
462										
463				+05(3)						
464		+15(3) +15(3)						-11(3)	-21(3) -21(3)	
465	-10(2) -30(1)		+22(2) +22(2)	-13(3)					+02(3)	
466						+32(2) +32(2)				
467		+10(3) +18(2)		-21(3) -21(3)						
469				+25(3) +25(3)		-20(2) -44(1)	+14(4) +22(3)			
470					-35(1) -35(1)					
471								-02(3)		
472				+19(3) +19(3)					+06(3)	
473									-21(3) -21(3)	
474							+39(1) +39(1)			
475		+30(2) +30(2)					+23(3) +34(2)		+03(2)	
476				-18(3) -18(3)		-22(2) -22(2)		-26(3) -26(3)		-29(2) -29(2)
481									+34(2) +34(2)	
485	+13(3) +29(2)	-17(3) -29(2)								
486	+18(3) +35(2)	-15(3) -25(2)				-26(2) -26(2)				-22(2) -22(2)
487	+36(3) +36(3)	-05(3) -17(2)								-22(2) -22(2)
489										
490		-24(2) -51(1)								
491						-17(2) -17(2)				
492	-24(2) -24(2)									
493				-30(1) -30(1)						
504b								+42(2) +42(2)		
506						-31(1) -31(1)				
509	-20(2) -20(2)	-31(2) -31(2)		+17(2) +37(1)				+42(2) +42(2)		
510				+36(1) +36(1)				+57(1) +57(1)		+19(2) +19(2)
511								+58(1) +58(1)		
513						+41(1) +41(1)				
515		-30(1) -30(1)	+32(1) +32(1)							
516								+36(2) +36(2)		
530										
531										
542								+55(2) +55(2)		
557				+35(1) +35(1)						
560									-31(1) -31(1)	
561										
570										
574										
576		+27(1) +27(1)				-30(1) -30(1)				
583										+23(2) +23(2)
586										
595									+33(2) +33(2)	
596								+45(2) +45(2)		
597								+31(1) +31(1)		
602								+30(1) +30(1)		
604								+55(2) +55(2)		
605a								-24(2) -24(2)		
605b								+44(1) +44(1)		
606								+40(2) +40(2)		
609			+30(1) +30(1)				+34(1) +34(1)	+45(3) +45(3)		
610								+57(2) +57(2)		
613								+30(1) +30(1)		
615								+43(1) +43(1)		
638								+30(3) +53(2)		
641										
645								-16(3) -16(3)		
653										
657									-36(1) -36(1)	
674									-27(2) -27(2)	+26(2) +26(2)
680										+20(2) +20(2)
681										
682									-11(2)	
684									-16(2)	
685										
686										
687										
689										+22(2) +22(2)

Appendix

Master Index Number	U.I. 26	U.I. 27	U.I. 28	U.I. 29	U.I. 30	U.I. 31	U.I. 32	U.I. 33	U.I. 34	U.I. 35	U.I. 36
460				-38(1) -38(1)			+20(3) +20(3)		-21(2) -34(1)	-20(3) -20(3)	
461	+16(3) +16(3)									+22(2) +22(2)	
462			-16(2) -33(1)		-36(1) -36(1)				-25(2) -25(2)		-22(2) -22(2)
463											
464							-11(2) -31(1)			-29(2) -29(2)	
465											
466											
467											+10(2) +10(2)
469											
470											
471	-14(3) -20(2)										
472	+18(3) +29(2)						-02(2)				
473										-34(1) -34(1)	
474	+41(1) +41(1)										
475	+20(2) +20(2)										
476	-11(3)										+16(2) +16(2)
481											
485						+21(2) +21(2)					
486			+34(1) +34(1)								
487											
489			+38(1) +38(1)								
490											
491			+38(1) +38(1)				-20(2) -20(2)				
492											
493											
504b											
506											
509	+35(2) +35(2)										
510	+28(2) +58(1)						-11(2)				
511											
513									+42(1) +42(1)		
515									-50(1) -50(1)		
516											
530									+06(2)	-30(1) -30(1)	
531										+40(1) +40(1)	
542											
557											
560											
561											
570											
574											
576											
583											
586									+19(2) +19(2)		
595											
596											
597											
602											
604											
605a											
605b											
606											
609											
610											
613											
615											
638											
641									+49(1) +49(1)		
645											
653											
657											
674											
680											
681									-18(2) -18(2)		
682											
684							+13(3) +13(3)				
685									+16(2) +16(2)		
686							+03(3) +31(1)				
687									+11(2) +11(2)		
689											

LOADING OF SALIENT VARIABLES ON FACTORS U.I. 16 - U.I. 36 (continued)

Master Index Number	U.I. 16	U.I. 17	U.I. 18	U.I. 19	U.I. 20	U.I. 21	U.I. 22	U.I. 23	U.I. 24	U.I. 25
690										+18(2) +18(2)
691										+37(2) +37(2)
692										+24(2) +24(2)
695										
696										-26(2) -26(2)
698										-22(2) -22(2)
699									-26(2) -26(2)	
703										
704										
705										
706										
707										
711										
712									+41(2) +41(2)	
713										
714										
715										+35(3) +35(3)
716	+36(1) +36(1)									
717										
718									+13(2) +33(1)	
719									-24(2) -24(2)	
731										
732										
733										
736									-05(2)	
737										
738										
740									+17(2) +17(2)	
741									-13(2) -13(2)	
742									-10(2)	
755						-32(1) -32(1)				
758										+25(2) +25(2)
761									-01(2) -30(1)	
763									-22(3) -22(3)	
764									-16(2) -30(1)	
767									-25(2) -25(2)	
808										+31(1) +31(1)
839	-39(1) -39(1)									
847										
853										
865				+39(1) +39(1)						
866										
867										
886										
920				-07(3)			+03(3)			
927a			+16(2)	+21(3) +21(3)			+21(3) +21(3)		+17(3) +17(3)	
927b									+18(3) +18(3)	+05(2)
929b				-13(3) -13(3)			-21(3) -21(3)		-12(3) -12(3)	
929e										
933a				-14(3) -14(3)						
933b	-22(2) -22(2)						-05(3) -05(3)			
963		-31(1) -31(1)								
965								-45(1) -45(1)		
982									+32(1) +32(1)	
1029				-32(1) -32(1)						-41(1) -41(1)
1041				-36(1) -36(1)						
1107										+40(1) +40(1)
1128			+32(1) +32(1)							
1146	+35(1) +35(1)									
1160										
1174										+35(1) +35(1)
1245										
1250										
1336									-31(1) -31(1)	
1351				-34(1) -34(1)						-32(1) -32(1)
1366								-52(1) -52(1)		
1410				+51(1) +51(1)						
1414				+30(1) +30(1)						+41(1) +41(1)
1416										
1418				+30(1) +30(1)						

Master Index Number	U.I. 26	U.I. 27	U.I. 28	U.I. 29	U.I. 30	U.I. 31	U.I. 32	U.I. 33	U.I. 34	U.I. 35	U.I. 36
690											
691											
692									-02(2)		
695							+25(2) +25(2)				
696							+21(2) +21(2)				
698											
699											
703											
704									+19(2) +19(2)		
705									+16(2) +30(1)		
706							+23(2) +23(2)				
707							-25(2) -25(2)				
711									-28(2) -28(2)		
712											
713							-20(2) -20(2)		-06(2)		
714							+23(2) +23(2)				
715											
716											
717							+17(2) +32(1)				
718									+17(2) +17(2)		
719									+13(2) +36(1)		
731									+20(2) +20(2)		
732									+25(2) +25(2)		
733							-17(2) -17(2)				
736											
737							+20(2) +20(2)				
738							+19(2) +19(2)				
740											
741											
742											
755											
758											
761											
763			+30(3) +30(3)				+26(6) +26(4)		+25(3) +35(2)		
764											
767							+17(2) +17(2)				
808		-25(1) -25(1)									
839											
847										+34(1) +34(1)	
853							+33(1) +33(1)				
865		+32(1) +32(1)									
866										-30(1) -30(1)	
867		+30(1) +30(1)					+32(1) +32(1)				
886			-38(1) -38(1)				+33(1) +33(1)				
920										+18(2) +18(2)	
927a		+47(1) +47(1)	-02(2) -02(2)								-19(3) -19(3)
927b		+35(1) +35(1)					+22(2) +22(2)				
929b			-15(2) -32(1)								
929e		-49(1) -49(1)									
933a		+34(1) +34(1)								+13(2)	+24(3) +24(3)
933b											+38(3) +38(3)
963											
965											
982											
1029											
1041											
1107											
1128											
1146											
1160			-39(1) -39(1)								
1174											
1245	+44(1) +44(1)										
1250					-61(1) -61(1)						
1336											
1351											
1366											
1410											
1414					-40(1) -40(1)						
1416					-42(1) -42(1)						
1418											

LOADING OF SALIENT VARIABLES ON FACTORS U.I. 16 - U.I. 36 (continued)

Master Index Number	U.I. 16	U.I. 17	U.I. 18	U.I. 19	U.I. 20	U.I. 21	U.I. 22	U.I. 23	U.I. 24	U.I. 25
1421										-30(1) -30(1)
1426										
1428										
1429										
1434							-40(1) -40(1)			
1439						+47(1) +47(1)	+38(1) +38(1)			
1440				+32(1) +32(1)						
1443										+38(1) +38(1)
1444										+50(1) +50(1)
1445										+33(1) +33(1)
1447									-41(1) -41(1)	
1448										
1450									+31(1) +31(1)	
1452										
1455										
1462										-30(1) -30(1)
1463					+49(1) +49(1)					
1478			-39(1) -39(1)							
1487										
1489								+38(1) +38(1)		
1490								+45(1) +45(1)		
1513										-30(1) -30(1)
1518				-05(5) -13(3)						
1530								+31(1) +31(1)		
1716a			+50(1) +50(1)							
1716b		-33(1) -33(1)								
1717										
1719							+36(1) +36(1)			
1728										
1733										
1734		+30(1) +30(1)								
1735						+69(1) +69(1)				+48(1) +48(1)
1736						+50(1) +50(1)				+32(1) +32(1)

Appendix

Master Index Number	U.I. 26	U.I. 27	U.I. 28	U.I. 29	U.I. 30	U.I. 31	U.I. 32	U.I. 33	U.I. 34	U.I. 35	U.I. 36
1421	+46(1) +46(1)										
1426					-38(1) -38(1)						
1428					-63(1) -63(1)						
1429					-51(1) -51(1)						
1434											
1439											
1440											
1443											
1444											
1445											
1447							+35(1) +35(1)				
1448									-31(1) -31(1)		
1450							+31(1) +31(1)				
1452									-35(1) -35(1)		
1455				+38(1) +38(1)							
1462							+45(1) +45(1)				
1463											
1478								-33(1) -33(1)			
1487											
1489							+36(1) +36(1)				
1490											
1513											
1518											
1530											
1716a										-42(1) -42(1)	
1716b										-38(1) -38(1)	
1717											
1719											
1728									+30(1) +30(1)		
1733									+35(1) +35(1)		
1734											
1735											
1736											

APPENDIX 2

LIST OF TESTS FROM WHICH SALIENT VARIABLES ARE SCORED

T1: Backward Writing: Motor-Perceptual Rigidity G[1]

The test consists of several parts; in each part S has to write numbers or familiar words as fast as he can. In half of the parts S has to write them forwards (normal or control condition), in the other half backwards (novel or impeded condition).

T2: Gestalt Closure G

S is given a series of incomplete line drawings. An open-ended format is used and S has to write down for each drawing the name of the object drawn. The test is moderately speeded.

T3: Alternating Perspective G

The Necker Cube is used. In two successive periods S has to put down a mark each time the perspective reverses.

T4: Cancellation of Letters G

In each of 20 consecutive parts S is given a simple letter cancellation task. The test is highly speeded.

T5: Reading Preferences G

Each item asks for a choice between two fictitious book titles, with the content of each book being indicated in a brief sentence. In each case one book is of questionable content. The test is liberally timed.

T6: Reading Tempo and Memory for Interesting Material G

S has to read an interesting-emotional and a dry-factual passage; reading tempo is measured by having S mark how far he got in each passage in the time allotted. This is followed by a recall test on both passages, using recognition as test format. The procedure is repeated with another passage of the same type.

T7: Riddles: Ideational Rigidity G

S is given a series of riddles (e.g., "What has pains and won't ache?") under moderately timed conditions. An open-ended test design is used.

[1] G indicates that the test is group administered. I that it is individually administered, I(G) that it can be administered on either a group or individual basis, and GA that the test is group administered but involves apparatus (eg. tape play-back machine).

T8: Criticalness of Evaluation G

In each item S has to evaluate a human performance. The given response alternatives express various degrees of criticalness. The test is moderately timed.

T9: Opinion Inventory X G

For practical purposes, this test has been designed to include several otherwise independent tests. S has to answer 100 opinionnaire type items of the multiple choice type. (On most items the response alternatives extend from "strongly agree" to "strongly disagree"). After each set of 20 items S is given a recall test on the previously answered items. In addition S has to give time estimates of the length of these working periods and a series of relaxed periods. The test is liberally timed but for the recall sections.

T10: Opinion Inventory Y G

This test contains the same 100 items as test T9. The first 20 items are repeated unchanged; with each of the second 20 items additional arguments of opinion are given (to measure "immaturity of opinion"). The remaining 60 items contain suggestions in the sense that S is told the opinion of authorities (items 41 - 60), of successful people (items 61 - 80), and of neurotics (items 81-100). Thus several measures of attitude shift can be obtained.

T11: Logical Assumptions G

Each item of this test contains a statement and four assumptions, one of which is the logically correct premise to the statement. S is asked to indicate his choice of the best fitting assumption.

T12: Classification Fluency G

S is given a list of objects (e.g., "books", "cities") and has to suggest three different categories of classification for each. The test is moderately timed.

T13: Criticalness vs. Appreciation of Self and Other Persons G

This test uses ideational fluency as format. S is asked to list positive and negative personal characteristics about himself and other people. Each of the four combinations for self vs. others and positive vs. negative characteristics is represented by two items. The test is highly speeded.

T14: Association to Emotional Words G

S has to write associations to a series of emotional words and a series of emotionally neutral words. The test is highly speeded, fluency of response being the principal measure.

T15: Memory for Emotional Words G

In this test S has to memorize a set of phrases, some of emotional content, others emotionally neutral. Memory is tested afterwards by asking S to complete each beginning of these phrases. For greater reliability this procedure (memorizing-recall) is then repeated twice.

T16: Pessimism About Events G

The items of this test represent a wide variety of optimistic or pessimistic attitudes, primarily as regards human nature. S has to indicate for each whether he agrees or disagrees. The test is liberally timed.

T17: Aspiration Level in Coding G

The task in this test is simple symbol-letter coding. At the end of each of the five parts S determines the number he completed and gives an estimate of how many elements he thinks he will do on the following part. The test is highly speeded.

T18: Aphorism Acceptance G

S has to respond twice to the same series of obvious statements. The first time he indicates all those which he considers trivial; the second time he is to express his agreement or disagreement with each on a four-point scale. Both sections are moderately speeded.

T19: Time Estimates for Everyday Tasks G

Each item describes a certain task; in the first part S has to indicate (by choosing one of five possible answers) how long it would take him to complete it, in the second part how long he thinks it would take the average person. The test is liberally timed.

T20: Unstructured Drawings G

S is shown, one at a time, a series of abstract line drawings; for each he has to write down all objects, etc., he can identify in it. The test is highly speeded.

T21: Risk Taking with Unqualified Statements G

The items of this test cover a wide range of over-generalizations (e.g., children like milk) or simplifications. For each, S has to indicate whether or not he thinks this statement is always true.

T22: Skills-Experience and Confidence G

Some 20 different areas of competence and skill (ice skating, playing the piano, etc.) are listed in this test. A double multiple-choice format is used, and S is to show for each (a) his degree of experience or training in it, and (b) how well he thinks he could manage the particular performance or task. The test is liberally timed.

T23: Pleasant vs. Unpleasant and Past vs. Future Associations G

This test again uses fluency of response as measuring device. Each of the four possible combinations for pleasant vs. unpleasant associations regarding the past vs. the future constitutes one item; in each case S has to write down as many applying ideas as he can think of. The test is highly speeded.

T24: Unusual Events: Consequences G

Twenty possible events are listed. For each, S has to indicate whether or not he thinks it would affect him personally -- and if so, whether it would affect him favorably or unfavorably. Liberal timing is given on this test.

T25: Restrained Book Preferences G

The test is identical to test T5 but for a more specific item content. The items of this contrast either a morally preferable with a sensational, cheap goal or a calm, restrained interest with a readiness to become emotionally embroiled in terror, grief, or vicious action. Liberal timing is given on this test.

T27: Highbrow Tastes G

The subject is presented with a series of items asking for his preference over a range of activities (reading, aesthetics, decorating, etc.), and he selects one of the three alternative answers. Each alternative is weighted for "highbrowness". Timing is liberal.

T28: Values: Individual vs. Conventional G

The subject receives a set of items giving statements concerning behavior which is directed by either individual or conventional (institutional) standards, and expresses his extent of agreement or disagreement. Timing is liberal.

T29: Verbal Ability G

This test has three parts: synonyms, opposites, and sentence usage (grammar and style) of ten items each. The test is designed as a brief but reliable measure of ability factor V. The timing is strict.

T30: Arithmetical Reasoning G

The subject is presented with a series of arithmetical problems involving reasoning and logic rather than computation. The test is speeded and the timing is strict.

T31: Aphorisms G

S is instructed to check a series of aphorisms as either sound and wise or doubtful, weak, and not worth following. The timing for the test is liberal.

T32: Decision Making: According to Principles vs. Particulars G

S is presented with two sets of statements, and rates his extent of agreement with each statement. The first set of statements concerns general principles while the second contains specific examples of the previous principles. Timing is very strict on each part of the test.

T33: Hidden Pictures G

A series of pictures are presented to the subject. Each picture is of some natural scene but contains certain imbedded common objects that are alien to the scene. The imbedded objects form part of the 'ground' and are thus not immediately apparent. The subject has to list these imbedded objects.

T34: Authoritarianism G

The subject expresses his extent of agreement or disagreement to a set of items originally obtained from the Adorno F-scale. The items have since been modified to give higher correlations with U.I. 20 and U.I. 28. Timing is liberal.

T35: Numerical Ability G

This test has eight parts and involves items of simple addition, subtraction, and multiplication. In addition the subject is required to estimate how many errors he made in each part. The test is speeded, with strict timing.

T36: Emotionality of Comment G

The subject is presented with a series of incidents (mainly sensational in character), and is required to endorse one of three possible comments as being the closest to what he himself would like to say. The responses contrast a sober, quiet, but apt comment with two increasingly emotional comments.

T37: Gottschaldt: Perceptual Analysis G

The task set for the subject is to locate simple geometric designs within a series of more complex designs. The test is speeded with strict time limits.

T38: Annoyability G

The subject rates as either "very annoying", "somewhat annoying" or "not annoying" a series of common annoyances. The annoyances concern things and people, both purposeful and nonpurposeful. The test is liberally timed.

T39: Goal Seeking: Long-Term Goals (Questions) G

The subject rates on a three point scale his chances of obtaining certain goals. Attainment of the goals is usually conceivable, but unlikely. The test is liberally timed.

T40: Criticalness in Humor G

There are two parts to this test. Part A concerns the extent to which the subject endorses critical comments concerning the tests and administration. In Part B the subject gives his preference within a set of paired jokes (paired comparison). One member of each pair involves mischievous humor and snide aggression. The timing on both parts of this test is liberal.

T41: Honesty in Admitting Common Frailties G

S is asked to endorse with either agreement or disagreement whether or not he has been 'guilty' of certain common frailties, weaknesses, etc. The frailties are those common to most people. The test is liberally timed.

T42: Mazes (Pencil) G

S is instructed to use a pencil in running a simple paper maze. There are 4 runs in all, the boundaries of the path being 1/4" apart for the first two runs, and 1/8" apart for the last two runs. This test is highly speeded, with strict timing.

T43: Fluency: Verbal, Personal, Dreams G

There are three parts to this test. Part A contains story completion, number of words produced by S beginning with a given letter, and anagrams. Part B is the subject's fluency on writing his own life story. Part C is a description of two dreams that the subject has experienced. Timing is strict.

T44: Letter and Number Comparison G

There are four parts to this test. In Parts A and B the subject compares two columns of letter-combinations (one pair of letters at a time) and checks them as the same or different. In Parts C and D the comparison is between numbers. Parts B and D contain more difficult items than Parts A and C (respectively). This test is speeded and the timing is strict.

T45: Line Length Judgment G

The subject is presented with pairs of lines and has to judge whether they are different or equal. The length of the lines to be compared in length is such that a few can be easily distinguished, but most lie near the threshold of certainty-uncertainty. This is a highly speeded test and the timing is strict.

T47: Ethical Preference in Stories G

There are two parts to this test. In Part A the subject selects one from a pair of conclusions for a short story. The solution should be 'most satisfying' to the reader. In Part B a series of short stories is again presented, but this time the subject has to say which one of the two main characters he would like better. The pairs of items in each part concern a dimension with high cultural standards, social aspiration and self control at one pole, and oafishness, disregard of standards and delinquency at the other.

T48: Cancellation G

The subject has four trials of the simple task of cancelling certain given letters in rows mainly (90%) containing irrelevant letters. The task is highly speeded with strict timing.

T49: Letter Placement: Ideomotor Speed G

There are two parts to this test. In Part A the subject is given a simple alphabetical code (e.g., P = X and Z = A) and codes a series of rows of random letters. In Part B the subject writes the following letter (in the alphabet) under certain designated letters in a series of rows of random letters. This test is highly speeded and requires very exact timing.

T50: Ideomotor Tempo G

The test has two parts. Part A is simply the natural rate or tempo of reading lines of poetry. In Part B the subject is required to copy the figures in a drawing. Instructions to the subject are to work at a normal rate. The test is strictly timed.

T51: Endurance of Difficulty GA

There are two subtests. In the first S has to copy and correct a passage of increasingly jumbled and misspelled words and sentences. In the second S takes dictation (in long hand) from a tape recording in which the passage is read at an increasing speed. This test is highly speeded and strictly timed.

T54: Ideal Self Values G

Ten personality traits have been selected out of the sixteen factors measured in the 16 P.F. Test. Each is represented by two synonymous adjectives describing the desirable trait pole and two synonymous adjectives describing the undesirable trait pole. Thus four lists of ten adjectives are obtained (two containing virtues only, two containing only vices). S is given one list at a time; in each he has to rank the 10 traits. The test is liberally timed.

T55: Decision Speed: Aesthetic-Emotional vs. Synaesthetic-Logical G

The test has three parts of equal length. The first one contains questions on matters of aesthetic taste, the second one on synaesthesia, and the third part is a short test of general reasoning. S is given each part under highly speeded conditions.

T57: Memory: Effects of Emotional Interests GA

This test contains several parts, arranged in a balanced design. In each part S is shown some pictures on the screen and asked to memorize certain details. Afterwards S is asked questions about these details as well as others which he has not been instructed to remember. The test is moderately speeded.

T58: Moral Expediency G

All scorable items of this test describe a difficult situation for which several alternative solutions are given, each however immoral. S has the choice of leaving these items unanswered or choosing what he considers the best solution. This test is moderately speeded.

T60: Private Information G

S is given a questionnaire which contains a high proportion of questions about definitely private and personal matters. He is allowed not to answer an item. This test is liberally timed.

T61: Logical Consistency in Emotional Syllogisms G

Classical syllogisms have been constructed on a wide variety of emotional topics, each consisting of two premises and the conclusion. The three resulting items for each syllogism are not presented in series, but distributed throughout the test. Each item is phrased as an opinionnaire item, with two response alternatives. Part of the syllogisms included in this test are also contained in test T9. The test is given moderately speeded.

T62: Hesitancy G

The test simulates a game situation. Depending on the appropriateness of his answers S can gain or lose points; however, he neither gains nor loses for not answering a question. Both verbal and non-verbal items are used; the test is highly speeded.

T64: Friends and Acquaintances G

In the first part of this test fluency of response is utilized as test format and this part is therefore given under speeded conditions. First S has to write down the names of his friends and thereafter the names of his acquaintances.

In the second part S is asked questions such as "Always talking too much is   " and he is to insert the name of this friend or acquaintance to whom the particular statement would apply best. An equal number of these statements refers to desirable and undesirable personal characteristics. This part is liberally timed.

T65: Memorizing of, and Free Associating to, Words G

There are six parts to this test and a final recall section. In each part S is given five words which he has to memorize; in addition, he has to write down free associations to the same stimulus words. The final recall section (format: free reproduction) is on the original stimulus words only. All parts are moderately speeded.

T66: Novel Situations: Originality G

S is presented with a series of strange situations (e.g., if human beings completely lost their sense of smell) and is asked to list possible consequences. Timing is strict.

T68: Shove Nickel: Risk Taking I

The subject is required to score as many points as possible in a series of trials on a modified shove-nickel board. Highest score is obtained from that area of the board furthest away from S.

T71: Horrifying Pictures GA

The subject is presented with two sets of pictures, the first contains blurred scenes while the second contains horrifying pictures of automobile accidents. A measure is taken of attitudes towards automobile driving before and after each set of pictures. A section on interpretation of blurred pictures is given before and after the horrifying pictures. Timing is strict for all sections.

T76: Time Interval Estimations for Idle vs. Working Periods G

S is asked to estimate the length of certain time intervals. Half of the time intervals are of working time (doing tests of knowledge, memory, etc.) and in half the subject is idle or resting. The length of the idle times should correspond exactly to those of working times, and both should be irregularly spaced throughout the testing session. Timing is strict.

T78: Novel Situations: Adaptability G

S is told to imagine that he is wrecked alone on an island. He is asked to write down in what way he would obtain substitutes for such things as 'fire', 'knife', 'shoes', etc. Timing is strict.

T79: Likes and Dislikes G

There are two parts to this test. In the first the subject chooses between members of pairs of actions, objects, etc., that are approximately equal in being fearful, disgusting, frustrating, etc. In the second he chooses between members of pairs of attractive objects, actions, etc. It is impossible for the subject to finish either set of comparisons, and the timing is strict.

T80: Maturation Norms: Accuracy of Judgment G

The subject is asked to estimate how old a child or teen-ager should be, or is likely to be, before he can accomplish certain skills. Five alternative responses are given in multiple choice form. Timing is liberal.

T82: Memory for Drawings GA

The subject is presented with sixteen drawings on slides. E names the drawing on each occasion. After each slide is switched off S writes down the name of the drawing, and draws the figure from memory. Following the final slide S is again required to draw as many of the figures (and name them) as he can. This procedure is repeated once more. The original drawings are simple but ambiguous representations of the names. Due to the recall parts the timing of the test is strict.

T84: Classification Breadth G

This test has two parts: Figure Classification and Word Classification. The subject's task in both parts is to make as large a group with the stimulus objects (figures or words) as he can. He is given several different sets of stimuli, but can give only one classification for each set. S is informed that he may have to justify his groupings. Timing is strict.

T85: Cautiousness in Statements G

This test has two parts. In Part A, S is required to agree, disagree, or endorse "don't know" on a set of statements including both factual items and matters of opinion. In Part B, S is required to endorse one of a series of consequences that would result from a particular happening (e.g., if the moon were to disappear). The consequences are weighted in terms of their importance or general significance. Timing is liberal.

T88: Aesthetic Judgment: Avoidance of Monotony G

S is required to complete or change a series of pairs of drawings in the way that is most pleasing or aesthetically satisfying for himself. The test is not timed, and all Ss should finish.

T90: Sound Identification and Music Emotionality GA

S is required to identify certain common sounds (distorted) such as voices, boat whistle, etc., first against a background of silence and later against a background of music. Timing is strict.

T93: Name Choosing: Unconventionality G

S is given a series of groups of names. In each case he has to choose the two names that he would prefer for a variety of people and objects, e.g., a boy, an inn. In each case two of five alternatives are keyed as being unorthodox or unconventional. There is no time limit, and all Ss should finish the test.

T94: Compliance with Test Instructions G

This test requires the subject to give agreements for and against certain conservative or mundane statements about everyday life. In addition S has to abide by a set of detailed and potentially frustrating requirements as to the manner in which he records his answer (e.g., block capitals only, drawing a straight line under each answer). Timing is adequate but strict.

T97: Crime and Punishment G

S is given a list of crimes, and for each crime he has to (i) indicate on a five-point scale the degree of severity of the crime, and (ii) the amount of punishment that should be given. Timing is strict and it is not anticipated that S will complete the test.

T98: Pitch Discrimination and Music Emotionality GA

This test has four parts. In Parts A and C the subject has to discriminate between two tones (i.e., record if the second tone was higher vs. lower than the first). In Parts B and D the task is similar but there is an accompanying music background. Timing is strict.

T99: Fidgetometer I

The fidgetometer is a specially designed or modified swivel chair (or foot rest) which enables measurement of body movement to be made. A counter is usually employed to assess the number of such movements (or fidgets). S is seated in the chair to wait for further individual testing and is thus not immediately occupied in any way. It is important that S be unaware that he is being tested. Timing is strict.

T102: Drawing Changes Under Disapproval I

This test consists of four sets of subtests, with three subtests per set. Sets I and IV involve success or praise while sets II and III involve failure and criticism. In set I, S engages in a target game, a memory test, and the drawing of a tree. The target game provides an experience of success. In the latter two subtests S is praised for his performance. Set II involves the same three experimental situations (except that the memory task is more difficult and S has to draw a person), and S is failed and criticized on all. In Set III the procedure is the same as for Set II for the target game and memorizing. The drawing task is similar to that in Set I -- except that it has to be a different kind of tree. In all three subtests S experiences failure and criticism. The target game and memory task for Set IV are made easier, and S is praised. The drawing task is of a different kind of person from that produced in Set II. Praise is given at points on which S was criticized before. S is then given, in turn, his drawings of trees and people, and is asked questions forcing him to compare and contrast his productions under the various experimental treatments. Timing is liberal.

T103: Risk Taking in Mental Tasks I

S is presented with a small booklet. On the first page he is given a score and he may then decide either to 'take a chance' and turn over the page in the hope of improving this score (and also run the risk of diminishing it) or not to turn over and thus retain his score. There are five parts to the test, each containing 10 trials similar to that presented on the first page. S has to record in each trial the result of his decision before turning over and discovering its outcome. S's purpose is to accumulate as many points as he can. The test continues until S has completed all five parts of the test.

T106: Hand Tremor I

S is submitted to any standard objective procedure for obtaining amplitude and frequency of hand tremor. The test is strictly timed.

T108: Pulse Rate Under Shock I

S's heart rate is recorded (EKG) prior to shock and for 90 seconds after shock. Shock is given by either a gunshot or cold pressor. Timing for this test is strict.

T109: Voice Amplitude I

S has a recording made under standard conditions of his normal speaking voice. S reads four stories, the first and last being rated as emotionally exciting while the second and third being rated as emotionally dull. The test is strictly timed.

T110: Goal Seeking: Long Term Goals G

S is asked to write down his principal life goals. Then he has to indicate for each in how many years he expects to achieve this goal.

T111: Familiar vs. Strange Story Preferences G

The test consists of several groups of four story beginnings; in each group two of the stories are about conventional, familiar topics and two are about strange, unusual topics. Within each group S has to rank the four stories on the basis of how interested he is in hearing them continued.

T112: Spatial Judgment: Where Do the Lines Cross? GA

In both parts of this test S is provided with a diagram showing letters and numbers distributed over a page. His task is to find out (without drawing any lines on the diagram) in which number two lines would cross when the position of each line is defined by the position of two letters in the diagram. There are 20 such items to each part; the letters defining the lines are presented visually in the first 10 items and orally (preferably from audio tape) in the second ten items. The test is moderately speeded.

T113: Color-Form Classification in Pictures GA

The items are presented to S on a projection screen. Each consists of three figures, a test figure and two response figures. Of the latter, one resembles the test figure more in color, the other more in form or shape. For each item S has to indicate which of the two response figures is generally more similar to the test figure. The test is given moderately speeded.

T114: Observation GA

Both instructions and test items are presented on a projection screen. Each item consists of a figure of certain shape and color. The instructions specify a set of rules, based on these two attributes, according to which each of the figures should be classified. S has to give his classification while the item is still shown on the screen. The test is moderately speeded.

T115: Color Blending: Aesthetic Choice GA

The test items are projected on a screen. Each item shows two different color patterns, one always being preferable to the other on aesthetic grounds. S is to show which of the two he considers aesthetically more pleasing. The test is liberally timed.

T116: Color-Form Ratio in Picture Preferences GA

This test is similar to test T115 in mode of presentation and in instructions given to S. Each slide shows two pictures, one always being black-and-white, the other one in color. For each item S is asked to indicate which picture he prefers. The test is liberally timed.

T117: Drawing: Expansiveness of Copying GA

A series of line drawings (varying in complexity from a circle to the drawing of a car) is presented on the screen; S's task is simply to copy each drawing. The test is moderately speeded.

T118: Memory for Names and Objects GA

S has to memorize a list of proper names and names of familiar objects, which are shown on the screen. This is followed by a recall section. The same procedure is then repeated three more times.

T119: Classification Under Distraction GA

In a test design balanced for practice effects, S is tested on a classification task (marking that word in a series of words which does not belong with the same class as the others) under both normal conditions and intensive distraction by loud noise. The test is given highly speeded.

T120: Cancellation Under Distraction GA

This test is identical to test T119 above but for the difference in S's task (simple letter cancellation).

T121: Cursive Miniature Situations (C.M.S.) Test G

S is presented with a highly speeded and complex cancellation task, asking for carefulness and fast speed of performance and quick decisions. The test consists of four parts or "runs", each comprising six sections. Each individual section is represented by a pathway inside which small lines are drawn in varying arrangements. S gains points from cancelling vertical or horizontal lines but loses points for erroneously cancelling slanting lines. S can increase his gain by not circling lines singly but encircling a mass of lines as a whole; however, he is only allowed six such circles per run. The test is further complicated as the pathway frequently divides; at such points S has to decide which "path" to choose in order to maximize his score (since the number of lines to be cancelled -- and thus, the number of points to be gained -- is different in the different alternative paths).

The four successive runs increase in difficulty. In addition, less time is allowed per section on runs 3 and 4 than on runs 1 and 2.

Both an individual and group form exist of this test; only the latter has been described here since it has been used more frequently than the former. Special child forms have also been developed of this test.

T122: Reaction Times I

This test consists of the following parts:

1. Simple visual reaction time; auditory warning signal, preceding the actual stimulus at irregular intervals (10 trials).
2. Simple auditory reaction time; visual warning signal, preceding the actual stimulus at irregular intervals (10 trials).
3. Simple visual reaction time; auditory warning signal, preceding the actual stimulus at regular intervals. On some trials the actual stimulus is an auditory stimulus to which S should not respond (14 trials).
4. Simple auditory reaction time; visual warning signal, preceding the actual stimulus at regular intervals. On some trials the actual stimulus is a visual stimulus to which S should not respond (14 trials).
5. Complex reaction time with irregularly spaced warning signals and interspersed irrelevant stimuli (20 trials).

T123: Cancellation Under Disapproval I

Identical to test T120 above in format and task. On some parts S is praised for "good" performance and criticized on others for "poor" performance. The test is highly speeded.

T124: Myokinesis I (G)

S is shown a line of standard length and asked to trace it. Then S is blindfolded and his task is to draw similar lines of same length and same spacing. An adequate group form of this test has been developed recently.

T125: Treadmill Run -- Questionnaire G

S is told E would appreciate his participation in an experiment, part of which will be an exhausting treadmill run. S is given a questionnaire asking if he is willing to participate, for how long, etc.

T126: Two-Hand Coordination I

S is required to tap with his right hand in successive order on four plates numbers 1, 2, 3, and 4. This procedure is followed with the left hand using a different set of plates, and with the numbers being in a different order. Finally S is required to tap with both hands simultaneously. Successful taps for all three trials are recorded on an electronic counter. Timing is strict for this test.

T127: Body Sway Suggestibility I

The subject is blindfolded and his static ataxia is recorded on any of the standard methods of measuring body sway. S then hears a recording suggesting that he is falling forward, and later, falling backward. This test is strictly timed.

T128: Psychogalvanic Reflex I

Any standard apparatus may be used here from which a continuous record is obtainable indicating basal level, and changes of level in skin resistance. Stimuli classed as 'mental' are printed words, pictures, and a voice recording. Stimuli classed as 'physical' are electric shock, whistles, and loud noises. Timing should be kept as standard as possible for all subjects.

T129: Mazes: Blind Stylus I

S has four trials with different blind stylus mazes. On the second and fourth trials S is given a one-second electric shock every eight seconds. S is informed that the shock is a punishment for bad mistakes. Strict timing is important for this test.

T130: After Images I

Standard laboratory equipment for obtaining times of positive and negative after images is used. The test is not terminated until S has completed all trials.

T131: Closure in Spelling G

S has to memorize the misspelled names of familiar objects (e.g., pensil). To make sure he recognizes each name (and in order to increase interference) each is accompanied by a simple drawing of the particular object. Afterwards S is given a recall test (format: free production). The test is only slightly speeded.

T132: Readiness to Imitate Various Sounds I

E asks S to imitate various sounds, such as animal sounds (goat, lion), sounds of an automobile, etc. Time is measured until S imitates a given sound as well as length of time of imitation.

T133: Perceptual Accuracy Under Movement Restraint I

A test design balanced for practice effects is used. S has to perform parallel tasks (counting the number of interweaving geometrical figures on a page) under normal and movement restraint conditions (in which S is tied to the chair). The test is highly speeded.

T134: Flicker Fusion I

Standard laboratory equipment is used. The test is not terminated until S has completed all trials.

T135: Shock Suggestibility I

S is strapped into a shock apparatus and instructed to indicate on a dial when he feels the first signs of shock. No shock is administered. Timing is liberal and sufficient for S to accomplish four trials.

T136: Tapping I

Standard laboratory apparatus for recording number of taps is used. There are four trials, the first two being at natural tempo and the last two at maximum possible speed. Timing is strict for this test.

T137: Leg Circling I

S is instructed to make circling movements with his left, and later, his right foot, from a standing position. The size of the circle described is controlled. S is instructed to work at his most comfortable natural rate. Timing for this test is strict.

T138: Arm Circling I

S is instructed to make circling movements with his arms and shoulders. The size of movement is demonstrated by E. S is instructed to work at his most comfortable natural rate. Timing is strict.

T139: Classification Under Disapproval I

S is instructed to underline the one word in a group of five that does not belong to the same class as the others. There are four parts to the test, each one containing several sets of such five words. During Parts I and IV, S is given praise, while in Parts II and III he is given criticism; in all cases the treatment is applied regardless of the actual level of S's performance. Strict timing is required.

T141: Jokes: Amount of Laughter I

A series of jokes is read out to S, and his expressive behavior (smiling, laughing) is rated for each joke on a four-point scale. There is no time limit for this test.

T142: Color Naming: Ideational Rigidity (Child) G

Both parts of this test are highly speeded. In part I, S is tested for straight color naming (identifying each color item in a series varying between four colors); in part II the series varies between two colors only, and S has to name each item by the word for the other color used in the series.

T143: Picture Inspection: Emotional Disturbance Effects (Child) I

S is shown two pictures at a time, one always emotionally disturbing or unpleasant and one emotionally neutral or pleasant. In addition, the pictures can be classified in terms of internal (or: ego) control, malevolent external intervention, and benevolent internal intervention. S is asked to decide in each case which of the two pictures he prefers. Also the time he spends looking at each is recorded.

Afterwards S is given a recall test (format: free reproduction) on the content of the pictures he was shown.

T144: Drawing in Mirror I

Standard mirror drawing equipment is used. S has to draw three straight lines: a horizontal line, a vertical line, and a diagonal line.

T149: Story Completion (Child) G

Each item consists of an unfinished story in which the central character is exposed to a difficulty. S always has the choice between two story completions; in one the central character masters the situation, in the other external forces control the situation (either to the benefit or to the deteriment of the central character). The test is liberally timed.

T150: Design Evaluation Speed G

S is presented with pairs of abstract designs; in each pair one design is simple and the other complex. S has to choose one design in each pair according to his preference. The test is moderately speeded.

T151: Knowledge (Child) G

S has to answer simple two-choice questions on factual knowledge. The test is given moderately speeded.

T152: Acquiescence G

S is given the same questions twice, once formulated in inverted direction (e.g., Are you ever sick? -- Are you never sick?). S has to answer each question with "yes" or "no". Interpolated between the two questionnaires is a recall test (format: free reproduction) on the first list of questions. The test is liberally timed but for the recall part.

T155: Tidiness: Questions G

S has to answer a series of questions on personal habits regarding bodily hygiene. The test is given moderately speeded.

T156: Elation-Depression Swings (Child) G

S is asked questions about how he felt at various occasions in the past (on each item the choice is between really fine -- o.k. -- not too good). The test is liberally timed.

T158: Paired Associations G

This is a word association test of the two-choice type, i.e., S always has to select one of the two association words given for each stimulus word. The test is highly speeded.

T159: Identification with Main Character in Story (Child) G

S is given a list of familiar fairy tales and asked which part he would like to play in each. For each fairy tale four characters are listed between which

S has to choose. These characters have been selected such that each possible combination of the two scoring categories (main vs. subsidiary character, "good" vs. "bad" character) is represented.

In addition, at the end of the test a short account is given of each fairy tale if S should not know it. In such a case S has to check off each fairy tale he did not know. The test is liberally timed.

T163: Compliance in Unpleasant Tasks (Child) G

Each item in this test refers to an unpleasant duty. S has to answer each one twice, once indicating how much he would like to carry it out, and then whether or not he would actually do it. The test is liberally timed.

T164: "Auditory Hallucinations" GA

From audiotape S is presented a series of words, some actual English words and some nonsense words. By using various techniques (cutting out certain frequency bands, using a different playback than recording speed, etc.) the intelligibility of the recorded words is decreased considerably. S's task is to identify as many words as he can. The test is liberally timed.

T165: Preference for Animate vs. Inanimate Objects (Child) G

In this test S has to answer questions about the degree to which he likes various things and activities, some of which are concerned with human beings or animals and some with inanimate objects. The test is liberally timed.

T167: Preference for Successful vs. Unsuccessful Tasks (Child) G

S is asked to write down activities (in school or out of school) which he likes much. Then S has to rate each activity as to how successful he considers himself in it. The test is liberally timed.

T168: Mimesis: Copying Letters and Words G

In the first part of this test S simply has to copy three-letter words. In the second part his task is, instead of straight copying, to write underneath each given word a different three-letter word. Both parts are highly speeded.

T171: Picture Interpretation and Recall (Child) G

In part 1 each item shows a simple line drawing which constitutes an ambiguous picture. Two interpretative alternatives are given for each drawing (e.g., the children are (a) playing, (b) wrestling) and S has to choose one. In each case the choice is between an aggressive and an unaggressive interpretation. In part 2 is a recall test (format: recognition) of these picture interpretations. The test is liberally timed but for part 2.

T177: Muscle Tension I

S's arm is placed on a rocker arm behind a screen. S is given an arithmetic test to distract him from the actual test purpose. At certain times E releases a spring mechanism which snatches the rocker arm away from S, the angle of maximal displacement being 35°. E measures each time how far the rocker arm moves; since its displacement is a joint function of the motive power of the spring and S's involuntary muscle tension, with the former being constant, the latter can be measured from the angular displacement reached by the rocker arm. (Control experiments showed no significant correlation between this measure and S's body weight.)

T179: Dark Adaptation I

S is asked to look into a light-shielded box. After maximal light adaptation a faintly illuminated letter display is exposed and the time recorded until S recognizes all letters correctly. The procedure is repeated three times.

T180: Bridge Construction with Blocks (Child) I

S is asked to build a simple bridge (two towers with a bar across the top joining the two) with six bricks. This is repeated several times with different groups of bricks. Performance time is recorded and various aspects of S's approach to the task are rated on a rating scheme.

T181: Abnegation: Willingness to Accept Sacrifices G

This test consists of a list of 25 common goals. By using a rating scale S has to indicate how much self-sacrifice he believes would be necessary for its achievement. The test is liberally timed.

T182: Tower Construction with Blocks (Child) I

S is asked to build a tower by using as many as he wants of 20 blocks. He also has to tell E when he thinks it no longer safe to continue because the tower might fall over. The experiment is repeated twice.

T185: Shape Comparison (Child) G

Each item contains one stimulus shape and three comparison shapes. The task is to identify this one of the comparison shapes which is identical to the stimulus shape. The test is highly speeded.

T187: Practical Jokes G

A series of practical jokes is listed and S has to indicate which ones he enjoys. The test is liberally timed.

T188: Dotting: Competitiveness G

The task utilized in this test is simply to connect dots by a continuous line. The test is given in four parts; on parts 1 and 4 S is instructed to go as fast as possible, on parts 2 and 3 to go as slow as possible. In addition, monetary incentive is promised on parts 3 and 4 for those Ss which obey best to the instructions. The test is highly speeded.

T194: Reading Backwards: Perceptual Rigidity G

S's speed of reading is measured by the length of text read in the time allotted. In part 1 normal reading speed is tested, in part 2 speed of reading a text printed backwards (e.g., EMOH EMAC YEHT).

T195: Alphabet Skipping G

S has to write out the alphabet, first by skipping every other letter, then by skipping two letters at a time, and finally by skipping three at a time. The test is given under highly speeded conditions.

T196: Crayoning (Child) G

S is given a booklet containing three pages. Page 1 has 12 familiar and 12 strange objects. Page 2 has 12 large surfaces (easy to color) and 12 small broken-up areas (difficult to color). Page 3 is blank. He is instructed to draw and color in the booklet in any way he wishes. Timing is strict but performance is unhurried.

T197: Social Activity Preference (Child) G

S follows a story both in picture form and as read by E. At certain prescribed points S is given the choice as to what will happen next (in terms of activities and company). Choice points are between (a) the company of the mother vs. the company of a peer group; (b) seeking dangerous activities rather than safe; (c) seeking activities alone vs. adults in company; (d) seeking competitive activities vs. non-competitive activities. Timing is strict but adequate for S's to make relatively unhurried decisions.

T200: Complex Task: Where Do You Land? G

Each of the items in this test consists of a drawing of square figures in the test booklet. These squares are marked in different ways according to a key. Thus if S lands on a square containing an X, then he moves forward two squares, and so on. A blank square indicates a final stopping position. From a prescribed starting square S's task is to work through the items as quickly as he can; his score is the number of correct final positions advanced. This test is highly speeded and timing is strict.

T201: Memorizing G

There are two parts of this test, differing only in content. S is required to read a story. The words are intermingled with irrelevant words. The relevant, story words are underlined. On the left hand side of the page S has to write down the names of people who are described as happy, unhappy, poor, etc. On the following page S is required to recall elements of the story and parts of the interpolated irrelevant material. The test is speeded and requires strict timing.

T203: Complex Task: Line Drawing G

The items of this test consist of patterns of small circles, some of which are blackened in while others are open. S's task is to join the circles together (alternating between black and white) by the longest line possible. The test is speeded and strictly timed.

T207: Memory: Distraction Effects G

S is required to read a passage concerning scientific research. He is then tested for recall of the passage. A more interesting passage is then read, after which recall is again tested on the first passage. Timing is strict.

T209: Metabolic Rate I

Standard laboratory equipment is used for this test. Timing is sufficient for accurate measurement.

T210: Word Closure Under Approval, Disapproval and Shock I

There are four parts to this test. S receives shock in the first part, praise in the second, disapproval in the third, and no treatment in the fourth. The task in each part is to correct lists of defaced and illegible words. This test is speeded and the timing is strict.

T211: Writing Pressure I

Standard laboratory equipment is used for this test. It is essential that S remains unaware that his writing pressure is being measured. Timing is sufficient for accurate measurement.

T212: Design Copying G

S is presented with lines of complex figures and geometric shapes. His task is to copy the figures in the space between the lines. There are two parts of the test, the first using small, compact figures while the second has broader, more diffuse figures. The test is speeded and strictly timed.

T213: Risk Taking in Answering Questions G

S is given a difficult information test with True-False responses. He is informed that a correct answer is worth five points and that for an incorrect answer one point is subtracted from his total. No score attaches to an item left blank. The test is liberally timed and almost all S's should finish.

T217: Drawings in Reverse G

The items in this test are geometric shapes. S's task is to draw them in reverse, as in a mirror reflection of the original drawings. The test is speeded and the timing strict.

T218: Altruism (Child) I

S rolls a marble down an inclined plane. The marble lands in either a black or red area. The landing of the marble is controlled by E, but this is not known by S. Whenever the marble lands in a black area S is rewarded by candy. When the marble lands in a red area no reward is given, but S is asked whether he wishes to give any of the candy to poor boys (or girls) who do not have candy, or whether he will keep it. Timing is liberal to cover all trials.

T224: Psychotic Skidding (Word Association) G

S is presented with a list of words to each one of which he gives an associated word. The test words are chosen for their likelihood in evoking rhyming or alliterative associations. There is no time limit for this test and S should complete all items.

T225: Self-Evaluation G

S is given a list of items of behavior showing either neurotic or stable characteristics. S evaluates himself on a five-point scale as to the extent of which he believes himself to be above or below average. Timing is liberal.

T226: Picture Preference: Unfamiliar vs. Familiar (Child) G

The child is presented with drawings of pairs of objects. One member of each pair is familiar to each child while the second is unusual or exotic. S has to express preference for a member of each pair. Timing is liberal.

T229: Drawings: Expansiveness G

There are three pairs to this test. In the first S copies designs. In the second S makes a drawing of himself. Finally S draws other human beings. Timing is strict but sufficient for most S's to finish their work.

T230: Leg Persistence I

S is required to extend his leg straight out and to hold it there as long as he can. The test continues until S's leg falls below a prescribed mark.

T233: Salivary pH I

Standard physiological testing procedure is utilized. Two samples of 30cc of distilled water are analyzed after S had each for 30 seconds in his mouth.

T234: Eidetic Imagery I

This test consists of 8 colored pictures. After the exposure of each picture S is instructed to look at a grey card; then E questions S about the presence of an eidetic image and asks about various details in the previously exposed picture.

T235: Mirror Tracing I

Six designs of different complexity are used in this test, always two of comparable difficulty. S has to trace one set of these designs under normal conditions, the other in a standard mirror drawing apparatus. This test is untimed.

T238: Personal Prowess G

S has to rate himself on a series of personality and character traits. The purpose of the test is to measure S's self-evaluation on these traits, many of which represent very desirable but rare personal characteristics. The test is liberally timed.

T240: Smell Preferences I

In this test S is presented a series of widely different smells. He has to rate each in two respects: how weak or strong this smell is, and how much he likes or dislikes it. The test is untimed.

T241: Pupil Diameter I

S's head is held in a frame. A photographic picture of his right eye is taken twice under standard conditions, and 10 seconds after S had been startled by a loud noise.

T242: Designs: Simplification G

S has to memorize a series of simple line drawings, each one loosely resembling a familiar object. To stress this resemblance the name of this object is written underneath each drawing. This is followed by a recall test which gives 7 alternatives for each drawing among which S has to select the one which is most similar to the original. Only one out of the 7 alternatives is correct, the remaining ones represent various degrees of simplification, gestaltwise completion, and regression to the intended object. The test is moderately speeded.

T245: Tidiness in Drawings (Child) GA

S is shown 25 pairs of drawings on the screen; for each pair he has to select the drawing he prefers. In 20 of these items one drawing always shows a neat and clean object, the other a dirty and untidy (but otherwise attractive) object. The test is given under moderately speeded conditions.

T246: Neologisms G

S has to find new words for fictitious objects (e.g., something between a tree and a rose). This first part is followed by a recall section in which S is asked to write down the words he has used in part 1. The test is moderately speeded.

T250: Psychotic Skidding: Story Completion G

Each item of this test contains a story beginning with two alternative ways of completion. Of these two alternatives one provides a logical continuation of the story, the other one is of a more superficial reasoning type and branches off into irrelevant topics. In each case S has to choose between the two story continuations. The test is moderately speeded.

T252: Formboard: Ideomotor Speed (Child) I

A standard formboard is used and S has to assemble it several times. Only speed is measured.

T257: Bodily Dimensions I

Standard anthropometric measures are taken of amount of fatty tissues, of shoulder, chest, hips, arms, and legs.

T259: Poetic Appropriateness G

Each item presents a line of original poetry, with one word omitted for which three alternatives are given (including the correct one). S has to select what he considers the most appropriate expression. The test is moderately speeded.

T262: Anagrams G

S has to solve a series of anagrams, giving as many solutions to each as he can think of. The test is given under moderately speeded conditions.

T266: Word Completion G

Each item of this test is a three-letter word with one letter omitted. S's task is to write in the missing letters. The test is highly speeded.

T268: Schneider Index I

Standard procedure is obeyed, with pulse rate and blood pressure being recorded before and after physical exercise. The over-all cardiovascular response is expressed in an index number.

T269: Writing Speed G

The test sheet contains a large number of small squares. S is asked to write an "o" into each square, working as fast as he can for three minutes. The only kind of allowed resting is to change from writing o's to writing v's. S may do such switches as often as he likes.

T271: Achievement Satisfaction G

The same list of goals is used as in test T118. By using a rating scheme, S has to indicate for each how satisfied he is with the progress he has made so far in achieving it. The test is liberally timed.

T272: Embarrassing Situations: Checklist G

S is given a list of potentially embarrassing situations. For each item S has to show the degree of embarrassment he would feel when experiencing this situation. The test is liberally timed.

T274: Independence of Mind (Child) G

This is a child form of the adult test T21.

T275: Number Checking G

S is given a column of figures (one and two-digit). His task is to place a check mark next to each number that contains 7 or else is 7 multiplied by something. This test is highly speeded and strictly timed.

T278: Suspiciousness: Autism (Child) I

S is instructed to indicate with a signal when he thinks that E is pointing at him. E then retires behind a screen. Timing is strict.

T279: Etiquette G

The items for this test pose various social questions of dress, manners, and habits. S selects one or more of five alternative responses, which are keyed for correctness of etiquette. Timing is liberal.

T280: Cancellation of Circles G

S is given a test paper consisting of lines of circles. His task is to cancel through as many of these circles as he can in the time allowed. The test is highly speeded with strict time limits.

T283: Difficult: Improvement G

There are two parts to this test, each being in turn divided into two sections in order to get improvement scores. The first task (Part 1) is reading backward, the second (Part 2) involves complex addition and subtraction operations. The test is speeded and the timing is strict.

T285: Frustration: Tolerance During Computation G

This test contains three parts. In Part A the subject performs a series of simple addition problems. In Part B he performs subtraction. At the end of Part B he is given the choice of either subtraction or addition for the remaining part. He is then instructed to carry out in Part C the operation that he did not choose. The test is strictly timed and speeded.

T288: Color Naming: Faster Speed (Child) I

S is given a set of cards of different colors. His task is to call out the names of the colors as quickly as he can. The test continues until S has called out a name for all colors.

T294: Inhibition of Criticism (Child) G

S is given a series of pictures and asked to mark those that he considers to be poorly done. When this is completed S is given another series of pictures and again the same instructions except that on this occasion he is forewarned that he will have to justify his criticisms in front of the group. Timing is strict but sufficient for S to finish the two parts.

T295: Disturbing Sounds GA

S is given a series of paired comparisons in which he gives his preference for one of two sounds. The recorded sounds are either (1) startling, eerie or suggestive of distress; or (2) neutral. Timing is strict.

T296: Disturbing Pictures (Child) I

S is given a series of paired comparisons in which he gives his preference for one of two pictures. The pictures are either startling, eerie or distressful or (2) neutral.

T298: Deliberateness I

S is required to give quantity estimates in unfamiliar fields (e.g., "How many pins would fit into a match-box?"). The objects are present for S's inspection. Time of decision is recorded.

T299: Reading Speed Under Frustration I

S reads (to himself) the beginning parts of two passages (one being dull and one interesting). He is then given the choice of which one he would like to read aloud. He is then instructed to read the passage that he did not choose.

T301: Electrocardiogram I

Standard laboratory equipment is used.

T302: Dynamometer I

Standard laboratory equipment is used. S is required to maintain a level of grip 2/3 of his strongest record in two test trials. The test continues until S's grip falls below this point.

T304: Blood Pressure I

Standard laboratory equipment is used for obtaining systolic and diastolic blood pressure.

T313: Physical Fitness I

This test is a series of measures for measuring strength of back, legs, and hands, plus performance on such tasks as "chins" and "jumps". Full details appear elsewhere (79).

T314: Heartogram I

This apparatus, described fully elsewhere (79) enables a more objective and complete record to be made of cardiovascular functions (e.g., diastolic and systolic blood pressure) than is obtainable from T304.

T339: Mobilization of Response (Child) I

There are four parts to this test. In the first part S is required to form patterns with colored blocks similar to those on cards. In part II he is given a series of simple information questions (e.g., "What do we cut with?"). The same set of block patterns is presented in part III as in part I but this time S has to select the correct pattern from four alternative displayed answers. In part IV the questions are the same as in part II but the child points to one out of a set of toys representing the answers. S should complete all items.

T340: Everyday Task Performance: Self Reliance (Child) I

S is required to perform certain everyday tasks such as moving a book from a chair and putting it on a table. The test continues until S has completed all items.

T342: Parental Dependence: Pictures (Child) I

S is shown a series of pictures, each one showing a few young children in an everyday life situation; some of the children are shown together with their parents, some alone or together with other children. S has to indicate on each picture that child whom he considers acting most like himself. The test is liberally timed.

T349: Fluency of Association G

This test comprises 10 subtests of verbal fluency (ink-blots, drawings, story completion, etc.), all given under highly speeded conditions.

T350: Fear Situations I

E presents S with a variety of fear arising situations (drinking a horribly colored liquid, etc.); S's behavior (e.g., asking questions about the kind of liquid, etc.) and his willingness to do what he is asked are recorded.

T351: Inhibition from Failure (Getting the Principle) G

The same procedure is followed throughout the several parts of this test: S is presented with a task for which no rules are given as to how a correct answer is to be obtained. Then S learns a principle for solving the problems (E tells S after each item what the correct answer has been). Later in this series E, still announcing the "correct" answer after S has given his own, departs from this principle. S's responses on these "failure" trials are scored, primarily for persistence despite failure. The test is given under moderately speeded conditions.

T352: Difficult Coding G

This test has the same format and purpose as test T4, but S has to perform a coding rather than a cancellation task. The test is highly speeded.

T354: Coordination Test G

This is a group test of honesty in taking tests. S is asked to place a dot in each of the circles scattered over a page, but he is instructed to do this with eyes closed. High scores are interpreted as indicative of cheating.

T355: Memory for Stories G

S is instructed to read two stories. After each story a test of recall is given on the first half of each story. Timing is strict.

T356: Male-Female Person Choices I

S is presented with a series of paired comparisons of pictures of sculpture. He is instructed to show preference on aesthetic and artistic grounds. One member of each pair of sculptures is male, the other female. The test continues until S has responded to all pairs.

T357: Word Judgment G

There are four parts to this test. In Parts A and D the subject is required to select the one word that does not belong out of each member of a series of word groupings. In Part B, S is instructed to read a passage of interesting material at his own pace. Part C is a recall test on Part B, many items of which concern material not encountered by S in his reading. Timing is strict.

T358: Agreement with Majority G

The test consists of a series of Likot scale items covering a wide range of attitude and belief. Below each alternative response is the percentage of S's parent group (e.g., students) that have previously endorsed the alternative.

T360: Speed of Social Judgment (Child) I

The subject is asked a series of questions by E. The time lag in response is recorded for each item. The test is terminated when all items have been answered.

T361: Hard-Headed Realism Decisions G

S is presented with statements about people, events and opinions, permiting either hard-headed and realistic or sentimental, wishful-thinking alternatives. S's extent of agreement to each item is indicated on a seven-point scale. The test is speeded and the timing is strict.

T362: Whole vs. Detail Speed of Decision G

This test consists of several parts; in some S has to give decisions on more general matters, in others on rather specific ones. The test is highly speeded.

T363: Memory for Film Content G

S is shown a film, certain passages of which are frightening. He later is given (a) a recall test (format: free reproduction) on the film content, and (b) a time estimation test in which he is asked to estimate the length of each film passage.

T364: Distraction by Aesthetic Material GA

This test is on slides. Each slide gives certain numerical or verbal problems; half of the slides only show these problems, the remaining show the problems written over an interesting picture. S's task is to solve these problems, not paying attention to the pictures. The test is highly speeded.

T365: Mind Wandering G

S has to solve numerical problems in his head, without writing anything down but the final results. The test is given moderately speeded.

T367: Everyday Situations G

Each item of this test presents an everyday life problem. For some several alternatives are given between which S has to choose; on others S has to invent a solution. The test is highly speeded.

T368: Pleasant vs. Unpleasant Comments on Self vs. Others G

S is given a list of personal attributes, some desirable, some undesirable personal characteristics. His task is to select (a) a given number that would best describe himself, and (b) an equal number of attributes which would best describe other people he knows.

T370: Respect for People (Child) G

There are two parts of this test. In Part 1 the child is required to print the names of people he respects (elders and friends). In Part 2 the child prints the names of people who respect him. Timing is strict.

T371: Perceptual Lability vs. Constancy (Child) I

S is presented with a series of paired comparisons of pictures, and has to choose, in each case, the picture he prefers. The same test is repeated on a second day of testing. Timing is liberal.

T373: Restlessness (Child) I

This test is a modified version of the adult fidgetometer test (T99). The child sits in a modified fidgetometer chair and is told to "sit quietly for a couple of minutes". During the 3-minutes duration of the test E rates S's behavior in terms of (1) gross behavior, and (2) lip-play (talking, etc.). At the termination of the test the counter reading from the fidgetometer is recorded. This test is strictly timed.

T374: Performance Under Interruption (Child) I

S is shown how to play four different games. He is also told that he may have to change from one game to another if he is told to do so by E. After preliminary trial periods, S is switched from one game to another for very short periods. Timing is strict.

T375: Fairytale Solutions I

S is presented, successively, with the ingredients and beginning plot to six stories. He is required to complete the stories. Timing is strict.

T378: Alertness in Following Directions G

This test has two parts. In Part 1, S reads a story, having been previously instructed to note (mentally) (1) all objects falling into certain categories (colors, personal characteristics) and (2) objects falling simultaneously in three such categories. In Part 2, S is required to recall the objects in (1) and (2) above. Adequate time is given for S to read the whole passage. Timing is strict on both parts.

APPENDIX 3

LIST OF SALIENT VARIABLES

MI.	T no.	Variables (MI.'s) In Numerical Order
MI. 1	(T349)	Fluency of Association: higher fluency
MI. 2a-h	(T1)	Backward Writing: higher rigidity
	(T288)	Color Naming: higher rigidity
MI. 4	(T122)	Reaction Times: slower average reaction time (both regular and irregular warning)
MI. 5	(T122)	Reaction Times: higher ratio of regularly to irregularly warned reaction time
MI. 6a	(T49)	Ideomotor Speed: faster speed
MI. 6b	(T142)	Color Naming: faster speed
MI. 7	(T2)	Gestalt Closure: faster speed of closure
MI. 8	(T3)	Alternating Perspective: higher frequency of fluctuation
MI. 9	(T50)	Ideomotor Tempo: faster tempo
MI. 10	(T179)	Dark Adaptation: faster time of adaptation
MI. 11b	----	Thurstone's PMA: higher verbal and numerical score
MI. 13a	(T4)	Cancellation of Letters: greater variability in accuracy (more oscillation of performance)
MI. 13b	(T352)	Coding: greater variability in accuracy (more oscillation of performance)
MI. 14	(T141)	Jokes: more jokes considered funny
MI. 15	(T121)	C.M.S.: more use of circles
MI. 16a	(T121)	C.M.S.: more slanting lines crossed
MI. 16b	(T121)	C.M.S.: more excess use of circles and more slanting lines crossed

MI.	T no.	Variables (MI.'s) In Numerical Order
MI. 16d	(T121)	C.M.S.: more excess use of circles
MI. 17	(T121)	C.M.S.: higher level of aspiration
MI. 20a	(T354)	Coordination Test: more dishonesty
MI. 21	(T5)	Reading Preferences: fewer questionable reading preferences
MI. 22a	(T355)	Memory for Stories: better incidental relative to purposeful observation and memory
MI. 23a	----	Immediate Memory for Words (obsolete; see MI. 167)
MI. 24a	(T1)	Backward Writing: higher ratio of final to initial novel performance
MI. 24c	(T194)	Reading Backwards: higher ratio of final to initial novel performance
MI. 24d	(T121)	C.M.S.: higher ratio of final (fast) to initial (slow) total score
MI. 24e	(T121)	C.M.S.: higher ratio of final to initial performance
MI. 25a	(T15)	Memory for Emotional Words: better recall of emotional relative to non-emotional words
MI. 25b	----	Emotionally Interesting and Emotionally Dry Studies: better recall or words from the emotionally interesting than the emotionally dry stories (obsolete now: see MI. 87)
MI. 26	(T7)	Ideational Rigidity: greater number of riddles solved
MI. 28	(T51)	Endurance of Difficulty: more endurance (higher "dynamic momentum")
MI. 29	(T40)	Criticalness in Humor: more mischievousness
MI. 30	(T13)	Criticalness of Self vs. Others: more criticism of self relative to criticism of others
MI. 31	(T10)	Opinion Inventory Y: more fluctuation of attitudes
MI. 33	(T124)	Myokinesis: large size of myokinetic movement
MI. 34	(T10)	Opinion Inventory Y: more willingness to change attitude after receiving additional information (more immaturity of opinion)

MI.	T no.	Variables (MI.'s) In Numerical Order
MI. 35	(T10)	Opinion Inventory Y: more suggestibility to authority
MI. 36	(T11)	Logical Assumptions: higher logical ability
MI. 37	(T12)	Classification Fluency: greater ability to suggest classifications
MI. 38a	(T9)	Opinion Inventory X: higher ratio of consonant to dissonant recall (corrected for tendency to agree)
MI. 38b	(T9)	Opinion Inventory X: Higher ratio of consonant to dissonant recall (uncorrected for tendency to agree)
MI. 39	(T113)	Color-Form Sorting: higher ratio of color to form in sorting
MI. 40	(T122)	Reaction Times: more reactions to irrelevant signals
MI. 41	(T126)	Two-Hand Coordination: many correct movements
MI. 42	(T127)	Body Sway Suggestibility: more swaying
MI. 43	(T128)	P.G.R.: higher mean percentage deflection to (mental and physical) threatening stimuli
MI. 45a	(T51)	Endurance of Difficulty: higher ratio of final relative to initial performance
MI. 46a	(T129)	Mazes: more impairment of performance (reduction of distance covered) by shock punishment
MI. 47	(T235)	Mirror Tracing: much embarrassment in mirror drawing task
MI. 50	(T378)	Alertness in Following Directions: higher alertness in following directions
MI. 51	(T114)	Observation: more carefulness in following detailed instructions (higher index of carefulness)
MI. 53	(T13)	Criticalness of Self vs. Others: higher ratio criticism of self to appreciation of self
MI. 55	(T14)	Association of Emotional Words: greater fluency fo association on emotional relative to non-emotional stimulus words
MI. 56	(T14)	Association of Emotional Words: more increase in number of emotional associations after fear story
MI. 57	----	Sympathetic Increase in Emotional Recall (obsolete)

MI.	T No.	Variables (MI.'s) In Numerical Order
MI. 58	(T124)	Myokinesis: greater myokinetic drift
MI. 59	(T207)	Memory: less impairment by interpolation of interesting material
MI. 61	(T357)	Word Judgment: greater influence of frustration on judgment
MI. 63	(T271)	(Miles Terman): more masculinity of interests
MI. 64	(X)	Male Sex
MI. 65	(T9)	Opinion Inventory X: more logical consistency of attitudes
MI. 66	----	Picture Understanding: more correct picture titles chosen (obsolete)
MI. 67a	(T9)	Opinion Inventory X: greater extremity of viewpoint
MI. 67b	(T18)	Aphorisms: greater extremity of viewpoint
MI. 69	(T358)	More agreement with majority of sample
MI. 70	(T130)	After-Images: faster arrival of negative after-images
MI. 71	(T122)	Reaction Times: greater number of errors under complex instructions
MI. 72	(T122)	Reaction Times: higher ratio of complex to simple reaction time (more slowing of reaction time under complex instructions)
MI. 73	(T268)	Schneider Index: higher index
MI. 74	(T209)	Metabolic Rate: higher basal metabolic rate
MI. 75	(T209)	Metabolic Rate: more increase in basal metabolic rate after stimulation
MI. 76	(T198)	Voice Pitch: higher pitch
MI. 77	(T233)	Salivary pH: more alkalinity
MI. 78	(T177)	Muscle Tension: more involuntary muscle tension
MI. 79	(T234)	Eidetic Imagery: longer duration of images
MI. 80	(T128)	P.G.R.: more upward drift when relaxed than under shock
MI. 81	(T235)	Mirror Tracing: more carefulness
MI. 82	(T129)	Mazes: greater distance covered

MI.	T no.	Variables (MI.'s) In Numerical Order
MI. 83	(T99)	Fidgeting: higher score
MI. 84a	(T304)	Physiological Measures: greater increase in heart rate after startle
MI. 84b	(T108)	Pulse Rate: greater increase with stress
MI. 84c	(T314)	Heartogram: greater increase in heart rate after startle
MI. 87	(T6)	Reading: better recall of emotionally interesting relative to dry material
MI. 89	----	(obsolete; now MI. 46a, b)
MI. 91	(T278)	Autistic Suspicion: more suspiciousness
MI. 92	(T132)	Animal Sounds: longer time to begin imitation (less readiness to imitate animal sounds)
MI. 93	(T133)	Perceptual Accuracy: more reduction under restraint
MI. 94	(T134)	Flicker Fusion: higher mean critical flicker fusion frequency
MI. 95	(T124)	Myokinesis: more decrease of movements under threat
MI. 96a	(T299)	Reading Speed: less impairment by frustrated preference
MI. 96b	(T285)	Frustration Tolerance: less effect of frustrated preference on computational speed
MI. 97	(T76)	Time Interval Estimates: greater length of passing time estimates
MI. 98a	(T121)	C.M.S.: larger proportion decisions correct
MI. 98b	(T121)	C.M.S.: higher absolute number of correct decisions
MI. 99	(T351)	Thurstone's PMA: higher verbal relative to numerical score
MI. 100	(T16)	Pessimism About Events: more pessimism over doing good
MI. 101a	(T17)	Aspiration Level: little excess of aspiration over performance in coding
MI. 102	(T18)	Aphorisms: tendency to consider remarks "obvious"
MI. 104	(T238)	Personal Prowess: higher self-estimate of personal prowess

MI.	T no.	Variables (MI. 's) In Numerical Order
MI. 105	(T20)	Drawings (Unstructured): greater proportion of threatening objects seen
MI. 106	(T21)	Risk Taking in Unqualified statements: more unreflective acceptance of unqualified statements
MI. 107	(T279)	Etiquette: more knowledge of etiquette
MI. 108	(T22)	Skills: more confident assumption of skill in untried performance
MI. 109	(T23)	Pleasant vs. Unpleasant Associations: more pleasant relative to unpleasant associations
MI. 110	(T23)	Past vs. Future: more future relative to past associations
MI. 111	(T24)	Unusual Events: more self reference
MI. 112	(T24)	Unusual Events: more favorable relative to unfavorable self reference
MI. 113	(T9)	Opinion Inventory X: more acceptance of reality principle
MI. 114	(T19)	Time Estimates for Everyday Tasks: greater underestimation
MI. 115	(T10)	Opinion Inventory Y: more independence through ego strength
MI. 116a	(T9)	Opinion Inventory X: higher severity of judgment
MI. 117	(T27)	Highbrow Tastes: more highbrow tastes
MI. 118	(T259)	Poetic Appropriateness: higher score
MI. 119	(T115)	Color Blending: higher aesthetic score as evaluated by artists
MI. 120c	(T42)	Mazes: greater accuracy relative to speed
MI. 121	(T9)	Opinion Inventory X: greater indecisiveness of viewpoint
MI. 122	(T127)	Body Sway: great static ataxia
MI. 123	(T76)	Time Interval Estimates: longer time estimated for working relative to idle periods
MI. 124	(T16)	Pessimism About Events: more tendency to agree (corrected for optimism-pessimism)
MI. 125a	(T9)	Opinion Inventory X: higher personal relative to institutional values

MI.	T no.	Variables (MI.'s) In Numerical Order
MI. 126	(T356)	Male-Female Person Choices: higher ratio of male to female person choices
MI. 133	(T8)	Criticalness of Evaluation: more criticalness
MI. 136	----	(obsolete; equals MI. 39)
MI. 143	(T121)	Cursive Miniature Situations: higher total score
MI. 144	(T31)	Aphorisms: more acceptance
MI. 145a	(T17)	Aspiration Level:higher responsiveness of aspiration level to performance
MI. 146a	(T2)	Gestalt Closure: greater absolute accuracy
MI. 146b	(T2)	Gestalt Closure: greater percentage correct
MI. 147b	(T22)	Skills: greater breadth of experience and accomplishment
MI. 148	(T17)	Aspiration Level: higher aspiration for improvement in coding
MI. 150	(T18)	Aphorisms: more acceptance of obvious aphorisms
MI. 151	(T32)	Decision Making: faster speed on particulars relative to principles
MI. 152	(T9)	Opinion Inventory X: more tendency to agree
MI. 153	(T121)	C.M.S.: faster speed of decision
MI. 155	(T134)	Flicker Fusion: higher range of successive critical flicker fusion frequencies
MI. 156	(T134)	Flicker Fusion: greater lag
MI. 157	(T141)	Jokes: more overt laughter at jokes
MI. 158	(T124)	Myokinesis: greater increase of tempo of myokinetic movements under threat
MI. 159a	(T19)	Time Estimates for Everyday Tasks: greater variability of other-referent time estimates
MI. 159c	(T19)	Time Estimates for Everyday Tasks: greater inaccuracy of other-referent and self-referent time estimates
MI. 161a	(T123)	Cancellation under Disapproval: higher ratio of performance under approval relative to disapproval
MI. 162b	(T120)	Cancellation: more impairment in correct performance by distraction (noise)

MI.	T no.	Variables (MI.'s) In Numerical Order
MI. 163	(T210)	Word Closure: higher ratio of performance under approval relative to disapproval
MI. 164	(T210)	Word Closure: more impairment by shock
MI. 165	(T139)	Classification: higher ratio of performance under approval relative to disapproval
MI. 166	(T119)	Classification: more impairment by shock
MI. 167a	(T9)	Opinion Inventory X: better immediate memory
MI. 167b	(T118)	Memory: higher total score
MI. 168a	(T360)	Speed of Social Judgment: faster speed of social judgment
MI. 169	(T142)	Color Naming: more awareness of error
MI. 170	(T33)	Hidden Pictures: more hidden objects correctly seen
MI. 171	(T33)	Hidden Pictures: more hidden objects seen (not scored for accuracy)
MI. 175	(T122)	Reaction Time: slower regularly warned reaction time
MI. 176	(T122)	Reaction Time: slower irregularly warned reaction time
MI. 178	(T9)	Opinion Inventory X: more agreement with majority of persons
MI. 191	(T19)	Time Estimates for Everyday Tasks: more considered possible for others in given time
MI. 192	(T19)	Time Estimates for Everyday Tasks: more considered possible for self in given time
MI. 193a	(T10)	Opinion Inventory Y: more shifting of attitudes towards those of successful people
MI. 194	(T10)	Opinion Inventory Y: more shifting of attitudes away from those of neurotics
MI. 198	(T262)	Anagrams: more hidden words found
MI. 199	(T35)	Numerical Ability: higher score
MI. 201	----	Thurstone's PMA: higher numerical score
MI. 202	(T213)	Risk Taking in Answering Questions: more willingness to take a chance
MI. 203	(T35)	Numerical Ability: more confidence

MI.	T no.	Variables (MI.'s) In Numerical Order
MI. 205	(T36)	Emotionality of Comment: more emotionality
MI. 206	(T37)	Gottschaldt Perceptual Analysis: greater accuracy
MI. 211a	(T38)	Annoyability: more susceptibility to annoyances
MI. 211b	(T38)	Annoyances: higher susceptibility to annoyance involving ego-threats
MI. 212	(T39)	Goal Seeking: greater belief in attainability of goals
MI. 218	(T187)	Practical Jokes: more willingness to play practical jokes and tease
MI. 219	(T41)	Honesty in Admitting Frailties: more frailties admitted
MI. 227a	(T116)	Picture Preferences: more color choices relative to form choices
MI. 231	(T42)	Mazes: longer distance travelled
MI. 234	(T42)	Mazes: more accuracy
MI. 237	(T42)	Mazes: higher ratio of speed on difficult relative to easy maze pattern
MI. 240	(T35)	Numerical Ability: faster speed
MI. 242	(T38)	Annoyability: higher ratio of social relative to non-social annoyance
MI. 243	(T38)	Annoyability: higher ratio of purposeful relative to non-purposeful annoyance
MI. 244	(T361)	Hard-Headed Realism Decisions: faster speed of judgment
MI. 245	(T19)	Time-Estimates for Everyday Tasks: more exactness of time estimates
MI. 246	(T34)	Authoritarianism: little submission
MI. 247a	(T117)	Drawing Size: larger size
MI. 247b	(T229)	Drawings: greater expansiveness
MI. 249	(T118)	Memory for Names and Objects: more names recalled correctly
MI. 260	(T123)	Cancellation: less impairment in accuracy under disapproval
MI. 261	(T123)	Cancellation: less impairment in accuracy after shock

MI.	T no.	Variables (MI.'s) In Numerical Order
MI. 263	(T122)	Reaction Times: greater variability in simple reaction times
MI. 264	(T136)	Tapping: faster speed
MI. 268	(T136)	Tapping: faster tempo
MI. 269	(T137)	Leg Circling: faster tempo
MI. 270	(T138)	Arm Circling: faster tempo
MI. 271	(T43)	Fluency: higher total verbal fluency on topics
MI. 272	(T188)	Dotting: faster speed
MI. 273	(T43)	Fluency: higher proportion of fluency on self relative to total verbal fluency
MI. 274	(T29)	Verbal Ability: higher verbal ability
MI. 275	(T30)	Arithmetical Reasoning: higher total correct
MI. 276	(X)	High school or academic grade
MI. 277	(X)	Higher chronological age
MI. 278	(T6)	Reading: faster tempo (equals also MI. 516)
MI. 280	(T76)	Time Interval Estimates: lower accuracy
MI. 282	(T20)	Unstructured Drawings: greater number of objects seen
MI. 283	(T43)	Fluency: higher proportion of fluency on dreams relative to total verbal fluency
MI. 286	(T122)	Reaction Times: higher ratio of reaction time to auditory relative to visual stimuli
MI. 287	(T126)	Two Hand Co-ordination: more awareness of errors (higher proportion of errors corrected)
MI. 288	(T8)	Criticalness of Evaluation: faster speed of judgment
MI. 289	(T97)	Crime and Punishment: faster speed of judgment
MI. 291	(T129)	P.G.R.: larger number of deflections during nonsense readings
MI. 300a	(T230)	Leg Persistence: more persistence
MI. 303	(T362)	Whole/Detail Speed: faster speed on "whole" judgments
MI. 304	(T362)	Whole/Detail Speed: faster speed on "detail" judgments

MI.	T no.	Variables (MI.'s) In Numerical Order
MI. 305	(T128)	P.G.R.: higher ratio of P.G.R. deflection to mental than physical threatening stimuli
MI. 307a	(T44)	Letter Comparison: faster speed
MI. 308	(T44)	Number Comparison: faster speed
MI. 309	(T45)	Line Length Judgment: faster speed
MI. 316	(T13)	Criticalness of Self vs. Others: more fluency concerning own than other people's personal characteristics
MI. 320	(T144)	Drawing in Mirror: longer estimate of time taken working in mirror drawing
MI. 321	(T25)	Book Preferences: more restraint
MI. 325	(T22)	Skills: higher total level of self-estimated experience
MI. 327a	(T9)	Opinion Inventory X: more logical inconsistency in attitude, (on double presentation of same items, once inverted) (obsolete now)
MI. 327b	(T152)	Acquiescence: more logical inconsistency of responses on double presentation of same items, once inverted)
MI. 327d	(T61)	Opinion Inventory X: more logical inconsistency in reasoning about emotional topics ("emotional syllogisms")
MI. 330	(T47)	Ethical Choices: higher score
MI. 332	(T218)	Altruism: more altruism
MI. 334	(T42)	Mazes: great relative accuracy (i.e., ratio of accuracy to speed) in difficult relative to easy mazes
MI. 335	(T122)	Reaction Time: slower reaction times under complex conditions
MI. 336	(T20)	Unstructured Drawings: larger absolute number of threatening objects seen
MI. 339	(T144)	Drawing in Mirror: slower speed
MI. 340	(T252)	Form Board: faster speed
MI. 341	(T123)	Cancellation: greater relative accuracy (i.e., ratio of accuracy to speed) under approval relative to disapproval
MI. 343a	(T252)	Formboard: higher ratio of speed under approval relative to disapproval

MI.	T no.	Variables (MI.'s) In Numerical Order
MI. 346	(T230)	Leg Persistence: little decrease in persistence over time
MI. 347	(T122)	Animal Sounds: more readiness to imitate (higher total number of animal sounds imitated)
MI. 348	(T274)	Independence of Mind: more independence (more readiness to reject loose generalizations)
MI. 349	(T17)	Aspiration Level: greater consistency in aspiration
MI. 350	(T185)	Shape Comparison: more errors
MI. 352a	(T20)	Unstructured Drawings: greater variability in number of objects seen
MI. 353	(T138)	Arm Circling: greater variability of tempo
MI. 354	(T121)	C.M.S. (child form): many errors of omission
MI. 355	(T2)	Gestalt Closure: high cautiousness (many "don't know" responses)
MI. 356a	(T142)	Color Naming: higher total correct
MI. 356b	(T142)	Color Naming: higher total number of errors
MI. 357	(T144)	Drawing in Mirror: more meandering (more venturesomeness)
MI. 359	(T38)	Annoyability: more extremity of response on test of annoyances
MI. 361	(T151)	Knowledge: more confident assumption of knowledge
MI. 363	(T149)	Story Completion: more internal relative to malevolent external control
MI. 364	(T149)	Story Completion: more internal relative to external control
MI. 371	(T143)	Picture interpretation: higher ego control relative to benevolent external intervention.
MI. 372	(T143)	Picture Interpretation: higher ego control relative to malevolent external intervention
MI. 374	(T295)	Disturbing Sounds: greater preference for disturbing sounds
MI. 375	(T280)	Circle Cancellation: greater accuracy
MI. 378	(T62)	Hesitancy: greater accuracy in judgment of size

MI.	T no.	Variables (MI.'s) In Numerical Order
MI. 379	(T42)	Mazes: faster speed and higher accuracy ("goodness" of performance)
MI. 382	(T150)	Designs: faster speed of evaluative judgment
MI. 383	(T294)	Inhibition of Criticism: more inhibition
MI. 384	(T226)	Picture Preferences: more preference for strange rather than familiar pictures
MI. 385	(T185)	Shape Comparison: more accuracy
MI. 386	(T229)	Drawings: greater expansiveness in human figure drawing
MI. 388	(T229)	Drawings: greater expansiveness in drawing others relative to drawing self
MI. 389	(T229)	Drawings: greater tendency to draw whole rather than part human figures
MI. 391	(T196)	Crayoning: more untidiness
MI. 393	(T196)	Crayoning: greater preference for crayoning original (i.e., S's own drawings rather than provided drawings)
MI. 400	(T197)	Social Activity Preference: greater preference for dangerous situations rather than safe situations
MI. 401	(T197)	Social Activity Preference: greater preference for competitive situations rather than non-competitive situations
MI. 407	(T158)	Paired Associations: slower speed of decision
MI. 409	(T158)	Paired Associations: faster speed of decision when many alternative answers supplied relative to when few alternatives supplied
MI. 420a	(T182)	Tower Construction: longer time taken
MI. 421	(T182)	Tower Construction: more cautious anticipation
MI. 422	(T182)	Tower Construction: greater height of single tower construction
MI. 423	(T180)	Bridge Construction: more planfulness
MI. 425	(T20)	Unstructured Drawings: high absolute number of aggressiveness implements perceived
MI. 426	(T143)	Picture Inspection: more distractibility

MI.	T no.	Variables (MI.'s) In Numerical Order
MI. 427	(T143)	Picture Inspection: more attention to aggressive relative to non-aggressive pictures
MI. 428b	(T296)	Disturbing Pictures: more attention to disturbing relative to non-disturbing pictures
MI. 430	(T296)	Disturbing Pictures: greater preference for disturbing pictures relative to non-disturbing pictures
MI. 437	(T221)	Doodling: more doodling (more irrelevant marking)
MI. 439	(X)	More deviant questionnaire responses (obsolete)
MI. 443	(T316)	G.S.R.: greater absolute level of resistance (in ohms)
MI. 444	(T304)	Physiological Measures: higher systolic blood pressure
MI. 445	(T241)	Pupil Diameter: larger pupil diameter at stress
MI. 448	(T299)	Information: greater diversity of interest on an information test
MI. 449	(T181)	Abnegation: more willingness to make sacrifices
MI. 454	(T225)	Self Evaluation: more anxiety-tension symptoms checked
MI. 455a	(T233)	Salivary pH: greater volume of saliva secreted in 30 seconds
MI. 456	(T122)	Reaction Times: greater slowing of reaction time when electric shock is applied
MI. 457	(T269)	Writing Speed: greater decrease in writing size as a function of foresight
MI. 458	(T110)	Goal Seeking: more long term goals (life goals more distant in time)
MI. 459	(T363)	Memory for Film Strip-Material: better recall of frightenging than non-frightening film strip material
MI. 460	(T111)	Stories: greater preference for familiar relative to strange in written material
MI. 461	(T363)	Memory for Film Strip Material: higher ratio of time estimates for frightening vs. non-frightening passages
MI. 462	(T240)	Smell Preferences: greater preference for weaker rather than stronger smells
MI. 463	(T188)	Dotting: greater acceleration under competition

MI.	T no.	Variables (MI.'s) In Numerical Order
MI. 464	(T211)	Writing Pressures: greater hand writing pressure
MI. 465	(T49)	Letter Placement: more decrement in coding performance with anxiety sound distraction
MI. 466	(T106)	Hand Tremor: higher frequency
MI. 467	(T364)	Distraction by Aesthetic Material: more distraction in numerical and verbal tasks by aesthetic material
MI. 469	(T316)	G.S.R.: greater amount of conditioning (higher amplitude of conditioned G.S.R.)
MI. 470	(T316)	G.S.R.: faster rate of conditioning
MI. 471	(T350)	Fear Situations: more reluctance to enter fear situations
MI. 472	(T64)	Friends and Acquaintances: more acquaintances relative to friends recalled
MI. 473	(T64)	Friends and Acquaintances: higher total number of friends recalled
MI. 474	(T64)	Friends and Acquaintances: higher total number of acquaintances recalled
MI. 475	(T351)	Getting the Principle: higher action impetus (more persistence with old response to unrewarding situation)
MI. 476	(T365)	Mind Wandering: more mind wandering vs. ability to do problems in one's head
MI. 481	(T272)	Embarrassing Situations: more susceptibility to embarrassment
MI. 484	(T22)	Skills: higher total level of self-confidence in a range of skills
MI. 485	(T257)	Bodily Dimensions: Larger amount of fatty tissue (more endomorph)
MI. 486	(T257)	Bodily Dimensions: greater length and girth of muscles (more mesomorph)
MI. 487	(T257)	Bodily Dimensions: greater length and girth of bones (more ectomorph)
MI. 489	(T313)	Physical Fitness: greater total physical strength
MI. 490	(T301)	Electrocardiogram: large T wave amplitude

MI.	T no.	Variables (MI.'s) In Numerical Order
MI. 491	(T301)	Electrocardiogram: larger area under curve of pulse wave
MI. 492	(T125)	Treadmill: longer endurance time
MI. 493	(T62)	Hesitance: greater willingness to risk a decision
MI. 504b	(T195)	Alphabet Skipping: higher score on alphabet skilling forwards and backwards
MI. 506	(T257)	Bodily Dimensions: greater weight
MI. 508	(T247)	Bodily Dimensions: greater strength relative to weight
MI. 509	(T299)	Reading Speed: higher articulatory efficiency (normal reading)
MI. 510	(T109)	Voice Amplitude: more articulatory efficiency under delayed feedback conditions
MI. 511	(T299)	Reading Speed: faster rate of reading (normal conditions)
MI. 513b	(T109)	Voice Amplitude: higher amplitude
MI. 515	(T109)	Voice Amplitude: higher amplitude under normal relative to delayed feedback conditions
MI. 516	(T299)	Reading Speed: faster rate of reading to oneself (equals also MI. 278)
MI. 530	(T55)	Decisiveness: faster synaesthetic relative to cognitive-logical decision time
MI. 531	(T55)	Decisiveness: faster aesthetic-emotional relative to logical decision time
MI. 542	(T302)	Multiplication: more persistence (higher number of correct responses)
MI. 557	(T313)	Physical Fitness: greater strengh of back, leg and hand
MI. 560	(T313)	Physical Fitness: higher Larson index (C-VJ-D index: chins, vertical jumps, and dips)
MI. 561	(T108)	Pulse Rate: faster rate after treadmill run
MI. 570	(T314)	Heartogram: higher pulse rate change over short time interval
MI. 574	(T257)	Bodily Dimensions: greater girth of biceps

MI.	T no.	Variables (MI.'s) In Numerical Order
MI. 576	(T257)	Bodily Dimensions: larger shoulder width
MI. 583	(Cattell Humor Test)	Factor 2: more good-nature play vs. dry wit
MI. 586	(Cattell Humor Test)	Factor 5: more hostile derogation vs. urbane pleasantness
MI. 595	(Cattell Humor Test)	Higher total score on form B (many jokes considered funny)
MI. 596	(T266)	Word Completion: faster speed
MI. 597	(T266)	Word Completion: greater perseverations of letters used over a short time interval
MI. 602	(T367)	Everyday Situations: faster speed of inventing responses
MI. 604	(T200)	Complex Task (Where Do You Land?): higher number of correct responses
MI. 605a	(T225)	Self-Evaluation: higher total score on items scored for neuroticism
MI. 605b	(T225)	Self-Evaluation: more in between responses on items scored for neuroticism
MI. 606	(T275)	Number Checking: more items checked correctly
MI. 609	(T112)	Spatial Judgment: greater accuracy
MI. 610	(T217)	Drawings in Reverse: higher number of correct responses in reversed drawings
MI. 613	(T212)	Design Copying: faster speed
MI. 615	(T203)	Line Drawing: more accuracy in finding the longest line
MI. 638	(T17)	Aspiration Level: higher absolute level of aspiration
MI. 641	(T185)	Shape Comparison: faster total speed
MI. 653	(T313)	Physical Fitness: greater strength of hand
MI. 657	(T313)	Physical Fitness: greater number of "dips"
MI. 674	(T275)	Number Checking: higher accuracy

MI.	T no.	Variables (MI.'s) In Numerical Order
MI. 680	(T246)	Neologisms: larger number of newly devised words used only once
MI. 681	(T55)	Decisiveness: more total synaesthetic than total logical items correct
MI. 682	(T55)	Decisiveness: higher total synaesthesia
MI. 684	(T55)	Decisiveness: faster aesthetic decision time
MI. 685	(T55)	Decisiveness: higher ratio of total number synaesthetic and asthetic items completed relative to total reasoning correct
MI. 686	(T55)	Decisiveness: higher ratio of number of aesthetic items done to number of synaesthetic items done
MI. 687	(T55)	Decisiveness: higher ratio of number of aesthetic items done to total number of reasoning items correct
MI. 689	(T242)	Designs-Simplification: better recognition score
MI. 690	(T242)	Designs-Simplification: more simplification
MI. 691	(T242)	Designs-Simplification: more regression
MI. 692	(T242)	Designs-Simplification: more distortion
MI. 695	(T131)	Closure in Spelling: larger proportion of correct letters inserted
MI. 696	(T164)	Auditory Hallucinations: more real words correctly identified
MI. 698	(T164)	Auditory Hallucinations: higher total number of stimuli identified correctly
MI. 699	(T164)	Auditory Hallucinations: more items attempted
MI. 703	(T84)	Classification Breadth: greater breadth
MI. 704	(T84)	Classification Breadth: more drawing items completed
MI. 705	(T84)	Classification Breadth: higher proportion of drawing items completed (relative to total number attempted)
MI. 706	(T84)	Classification Breadth: higher average inclusiveness on word items
MI. 707	(T84)	Classification Breadth: more word items completed

MI.	T no.	Variables (MI.'s) In Numerical Order
MI. 711	(T250)	Story Completion: greater number of logical sequences maintained
MI. 712	(T224)	Psychotic Skidding: higher proportion of rhyming words given
MI. 713	(T224)	Psychotic Skidding: higher proportion alliterative words given
MI. 714	(T224)	Psychotic Skidding: lower proportion of rhyming and alliterative association words given
MI. 715	(T224)	Psychotic Skidding: greater fluency in associations
MI. 716	(T65)	Memory for Free Associations: higher total number of words remembered
MI. 717	(T65)	Memory for Free Associations: higher number of words remembered correctly
MI. 718	(T65)	Memory for Free Associations: higher ratio of number of words remembered correctly to total remembered
MI. 719	(T65)	Memory for Free Associations: higher number of association words intruded in recall of original words
MI.731	(T283)	Difficult Task: more items attempted
MI. 732	(T283)	Difficult Task: more items actually answered
MI. 733	(T283)	Difficult Task: higher proportion of number of items answered (relative to number of items attempted)
MI. 736	(T283)	Difficult Task: higher proportion of items answered on "Which is Larger?"
MI. 737	(T62)	Hesitancy: more figures scanned
MI. 738	(T62)	Hesitancy: more figures checked
MI. 740	(T168)	Mimesis: higher final relative to initial performance
MI. 741	(T168)	Memesis: more obtrusion by immediately adjoining letters
MI. 742	(T168)	Mimesis: greater distance of obtrusion (i.e., from which S inserts a stimulus)
MI. 755	(T340)	Everyday Task Performance: faster speed
MI. 758	(T124)	Myokinesis: larger absolute (vertical) deviation

MI.	T no.	Variables (MI.'s) In Numerical Order
MI. 761	(T22)	Unstructured Drawings: greater proportion of animate objects seen
MI. 763	(T13)	Criticalness of Self vs. Others: more fluency concerning people's characteristics
MI. 764	(T13)	Criticalness of Self vs. Others: more criticism relative to appreciation of people's characteristics
MI. 767	(T38)	Annoyability: greater number of non-social relative to social annoyances
MI. 808	(T66)	Novel Situations: more solutions presented
MI. 839	(T79)	Likes: faster speed in checking things disliked relative to things liked
MI. 847	(T82)	Memory for Drawings: poorer planning of drawing layout
MI. 853	(T88)	Aesthetic Judgment: more concreteness
MI. 865	(T93)	Name Choosing: greater preference for unusual names
MI. 866	(T94)	Compliance: greater preference for negative arguments
MI. 867	(T98)	Suspiciousness: more suspicion towards higher occupational groups
MI. 886	(T102)	Drawings: Larger size of drawings of trees and people
MI. 965	(T54)	Ideal Self Values: more inconsnstency
MI. 1029	(T60)	Private Information: more admission of troubles and conflict
MI. 1041	(T64)	Friends and Acquaintances: more persons arousing hostility
MI. 1107	(T68)	Shove Nickel: faster speed
MI. 1128	(T71)	Horrifying Pictures: smaller proportion of words used to describe people in horrifying than in pleasant pictures
MI. 1146	(T79)	Likes: faster speed checking things disliked
MI. 1160	(T96)	Suspiciousness: more suspicion towards occupations
MI. 1179	(T103)	Risk Taking in Mental Tasks: more cheating in reporting success
MI. 1245	(T156)	Elation-Depression: more elation

MI.	T no.	Variables (MI.'s) In Numerical Order
MI. 1250	(T167)	Tasks: more successful (average rating) on tasks liked
MI. 1351	(T60)	Private Information: more readiness to answer
MI. 1366	(T163)	Compliance: more acceptance of unpleasant duties
MI. 1414	(T4)	Letter Cancellation: higher number of correct cancellations
MI. 1416	(T17)	Aspiration Level in coding: faster total speed
MI. 1418	(T368)	Pleasant vs. Unpleasant Comments on Self and Others: more excess of pleasant over unpleasant comments on self
MI. 1421	(T156)	Elation-Depression Swings: more extreme mood states
MI. 1426	(T155)	Tidiness: higher total number of items completed
MI. 1428	(T167)	Fluency Concerning Successful Tasks: greater fluency
MI. 1429	(T370)	Respect for People: higher total number of persons listed
MI. 1434	(T171)	Picture Interpretation and Recall: greater number of aggressive interpretations
MI. 1439	(T43)	Fluency: Verbal: Personal: Dreams: higher absolute fluency on self
MI. 1440	(T371)	Perceptual Lability vs. Constancy: more lability in perceptual preferences
MI. 1443	(T371)	Lability vs. Constancy: more lateral lability in paths chosen on successive days
MI. 1444	(T371)	Lability vs. Constancy: more approach-avoidance lability in paths chosen on successive days
MI. 1445	(T371)	Lability vs. Constancy: less meticulousness in tracing paths through mazes
MI. 1447	(T339)	Mobilization of Response: higher score for inventive relative to selective questions (more capacity to mobilize response)
MI. 1448	(T373)	Restlessness: more gross behavior during forced quiet period
MI. 1450	(T374)	Performance under Interpretation: more work done during uninterrupted periods relative to interrupted periods

MI.	T no.	Variables (MI.'s) In Numerical Order
MI. 1452	(T342)	Parental Dependence: Pictures: more awareness of own willingness to perform self-helped tasks
MI. 1455	(T245)	Tidiness in Drawings: greater preference for tidiness
MI. 1462	(T375)	Fairytale Solutions: more tendency to apply fairytale solutions to real life problems
MI. 1478	(T80)	Maturation Norms: greater belief in early maturity
MI. 1487	(T71)	Horrifying Pictures: more cautious attitudes to automobile driving after seeing horrifying pictures
MI. 1489	(T71)	Horrifying Pictures: greater accuracy in recalling details of horrifying than pleasant pictures
MI. 1490	(T90)	Sound Identification: higher total accuracy in novel sound identification
MI. 1513	(T54)	Ideal Self Values: higher cultural eccentricity of ideal values
MI. 1518	(T71)	Horrifying Pictures: more nouns and noun-modifiers used to describe blurred pictures after seeing horrifying pictures
MI. 1530	(T98)	Pitch Discrimination: more accuracy

APPENDIX 4

LIST OF NON-SALIENT VARIABLES

MI.	T no.	Variables (MI.'s) In Numerical Order
MI. 3	----	Speed of Judgment (obsolete, separate measures now)
MI. 6c	(T288)	Color Naming: faster speed
MI. 11a	----	A.C.E.: higher total score
MI. 12	(T199)	Honesty About Book Reading: more dishonesty
MI. 13c	(T280)	Circle Cancellation: greater variability in accuracy (more oscillation of performance)
MI. 18	(T277)	Confidence in Own Performance: more confidence
MI. 19	(T353)	General Information Test: higher total information
MI. 22b	(T201)	Memory for Confused Material: better incidental relative to purposeful observation and memory
MI. 22c	(T57)	Memory: more purposeful than incidental memory
MI. 24b	(T253)	Quantity Estimation: higher ratio of final to initial performance
MI. 24f	(T126)	Two-Hand Coordination: higher ratio of final to initial score
MI. 24h	----	Higher Ratio of Final To Initial Reading and Recording Performance (obsolete now)
MI. 27	----	Impairment of Mental Performance by Unpleasant Emotion (obsolete)
MI. 32	(T308)	Fair Mindedness: more fair mindedness
MI. 38c	(T338)	Memory for Pictures: greater number of consonant to dissonant pictures remembered
MI. 44	(T128)	P.G.R.: higher frequency of P.G.R. deflections when unstimulated

MI.	T no.	Variables (MI.'s) In Numerical Order
MI. 46b	(T235)	Mirror Tracing: more impairment of mirror drawing performance by shock punishment
MI. 48	(T289)	Ergograph: greater effort
MI. 49b	(T39)	Goal Seeking: better memory for higher relative to lower mental sets
MI. 52	(T205)	Riddles: better memory for difficult relative to easy examples
MI. 54	(T206)	Planning: poorer planning
MI. 60	(T208)	Memory: less impairment by frustration
MI. 62	(T299)	Reading Speed: faster speed for emotional relative to non-emotional material
MI. 68	(T67)	Criticalness of Tests: higher fluency of personal excuses given for defective performance
MI. 85	(T236)	Timidity Associations: greater increase in timidity associations after fear story effect
MI. 86	(T235)	Mirror Tracing: more improvement (learning) in mirror drawing under stimulation
MI. 88	(T67)	Criticalness of Tests: greater number of extrapunitive criticisms
MI. 90	----	More loss of recall from frustration and humiliation (obsolete)
MI. 101b	(T42)	Mazes: little excess of aspiration over performance
MI. 103	----	(obsolete: is now MI. 192)
MI. 116b	(T28)	Moral Standards: more critical severity
MI. 116c	(T361)	Moral Standards: more hard-headed realism
MI. 120a	(T4)	Cancellation of letters: greater accuracy relative to speed
MI. 120b	(T44)	Letter and Number Comparison: greater accuracy relative to speed
MI. 120e	(T126)	Two Hand Co-ordination: greater accuracy relative to speed
MI. 120g	(T280)	Circle Cancellation: greater accuracy relative to speed

MI.	T no.	Variables (MI.'s) In Numerical Order
MI. 131	----	(obsolete; equals MI. 22a, 22b)
MI. 134	----	(obsolete; equals MI. 30)
MI. 137	----	(obsolete; equals MI. 46a, 46b)
MI. 145b	(T42)	Mazes: higher responsiveness of aspiration level to performance
MI. 147a	(T22)	Skills: more confidence relative to opportunity
MI. 149	(T17)	Aspiration Level: greater reduction in aspiration level by failure
MI. 159b	(T19)	Time Estimates for Everyday Tasks: greater inaccuracy of self-referent time estimates
MI. 161b	(T45)	Line Length Judgment: higher ratio of performance under approval relative to disapproval
MI. 168b	(T58)	Moral Expediency: faster speed of socio-emotional judgment
MI. 177a	(T1)	Backward Writing: faster motor speed (normal forward writing)
MI. 177b	(T126)	Two Hand Coordination: faster motor speed (corrected for manual dexterity)
MI. 186	(T133)	Greater Effect of Restraint on Memory (now obsolete)
MI. 197	(T33)	(obsolete; equals MI. 171)
MI. 207	----	Ratio of human to non-human contents remembered (empathy) (obsolete now)
MI. 208	(T214)	Analogies: more readiness to accept help
MI. 209	(T216)	Credulity: more willingness to believe in unusual events
MI. 210	(T118)	Memory: better memory for proper names relative to objects
MI. 213	(T9)	Trend to Agreement (obsolete now)
MI. 215	(T215)	Sex Bias: more information about other sex
MI. 216	(T135)	Shock Suggestibility: more suggestibility
MI. 223a	(T136)	Tapping: more endurance
MI. 224	(T317)	Pessimism as to correctness in remembering story material

MI.	T no.	Variables (MI.'s) In Numerical Order
MI. 225	----	Artistic Preference: more preference for natural scenes rather than man-made structures (obsolete)
MI. 228	----	High sensitivity to neatness in drawings (obsolete)
MI. 229	(T97)	Crime and Punishment: more severe standards
MI. 232a	(T10)	Opinion Inventory Y: greater tendency to agree (on items presented twice, once in reversed direction)
MI. 233	(T129)	Mazes: higher magnitude of expressive reaction by shock
MI. 235	(T212)	Design Copying: more attention to details
MI. 236	(T44)	Letter and Number Comparison: higher ratio of performance on difficult relative to easy items
MI. 238	(T97)	Crime and Punishment: decrease of laxity with increasing ratio of difficult to easy items
MI. 250	(T99)	Fidgeting: more fidgeting under frustration
MI. 252	(T128)	P.G.R.: more deflection per time during difficult reading
MI. 253	(T128)	P.G.R.: more deflection under physical threat
MI. 254	(T128)	P.G.R.: higher ratio of deflection under threat relative to more values
MI. 255	(T128)	P.G.R.: more deflection to review of social adjustment
MI. 256	(T128)	P.G.R.: more deflection under threat to self regard
MI. 257	(T128)	P.G.R.: more deflection to questioning of self regard
MI. 262	(T122)	Reaction Time: greater number of errors under simple instructions
MI. 266a	(T121)	(obsolete; equals MI. 24e)
MI. 266b	(T121)	(obsolete; equals MI. 24d)
MI. 279	(T140)	Time Estimates of Own Performance: lower accuracy
MI. 284	(T43)	Fluency: higher proportion of fluency on social topics relative to total verbal fluency
MI. 290	(T311)	Time Estimation for Everyday Tasks: higher estimation of time required (inventive items)
MI. 292	(T311)	Time Estimation for Everyday Tasks: longer time estimation for self than for others

MI.	T no.	Variables (MI.'s) In Numerical Order
MI. 295	(T311)	Time Estimation for Everyday Tasks: higher estimation of time required for others (inventive items)
MI. 297	(T128)	P.G.R.: higher lag conductance
MI. 299	(T123)	Cancellation: higher ratio of performance under disapproval relative to control condition
MI. 300b	(T184)	Breath Holding: more endurance
MI. 301	(T362)	Whole/Detail Speed: higher ratio of speed on "whole" relative to "detail" judgment
MI. 302	(T362)	Whole/Detail Speed: higher percentage of errors in "detail" judgments
MI. 310	(T44)	Letter Comparison: greater accuracy
MI. 311	(T44)	Number Comparison: greater accuracy
MI. 312	(T45)	Line Length Judgment: greater accuracy
MI. 313	(T44)	Letter Comparison: greater number of difficult relative to easy comparisons attempted
MI. 314	(T44)	Number Comparison: greater number of difficult relative to easy comparisons attempted
MI. 315	(T45)	Line Length Judgment: greater number of difficult relative to easy comparisons answered correctly
MI. 323	(T10)	Opinion Inventory Y: more suggestibility towards approved attitudes
MI. 333	(T261)	Learning Willingness: more readiness to learn non-sense syllables
MI. 338	(T235)	Shooting: more critical exactness
MI. 342	(T210)	Drawing: faster speed
MI. 344	(T231)	Liking for People: more liking of people
MI. 351	(T185)	Shape Comparison: higher ratio of inaccuracy to speed
MI. 358	(T45)	(obsolete; equals MI. 312)
MI. 428a	(T296)	Disturbing Pictures: more attention to (more time spent looking at) disturbing pictures
MI. 429	(T143)	Picture Inspection: greater preference for aggressive relative to non-aggressive pictures

MI.	T no.	Variables (MI.'s) In Numerical Order
MI. 446	(X)	More preoccupation with task (rating) (obsolete)
MI. 447	(T299)	Information: more spread of reactivity to task detail
MI. 450	(T269)	Writing Size: more increase of writing size when hastened
MI. 451	(T186)	Essay: more self-reference (self-referring personal pronouns in writing and speaking)
MI. 452	(T186)	Essay: total fluency in writing and speaking
MI. 453	----	Higher ratio of performance on difficult vs. easy tasks
MI. 455b	(T233)	Salivary PH: greater volume of saliva secreted in 1 minute
MI. 468	(T269)	Writing Size: higher type-taken ratio
MI. 478	(T298)	Deliberateness: more deliberateness (slowness) in answering
MI. 479	(T269)	Writing Size: more crampedness of writing
MI. 480	(T272)	Embarrassing Situations: more embarrassing circumstances recalled
MI. 482	(T366)	Life Goals: more self sacrifice deemed necessary to achieve goals
MI. 488	(T304)	Physiological Measures: higher diastolic blood pressure after exercise
MI. 507	(T257)	Bodily Dimensions: greater thinness (height divided by weight)
MI. 508	(T257)	Bodily Dimensions: greater strength relative to weight
MI. 520	(T270)	Health Inventory: greater number of anxious responses
MI. 527	(T232)	Rhythm Reproduction: better reproduction
MI. 535	(T56)	Handwriting Identification: more conviction of correctness of own judgment
MI. 538	(T269)	Handedness: faster speed of writing with dominant vs. non-dominant hand
MI. 558	(T313)	Physical Fitness: greater residual vital capacity
MI. 559	(T313)	Physical Fitness: higher total score on Cureton's test
MI. 562	(T304)	Physiological Measures: higher systolic blood pressure after exercise

MI.	T no.	Variables (MI.'s) In Numerical Order
MI. 563	(T314)	Heartogram: higher score for oblique angle
MI. 564	(T314)	Heartogram: higher systolic amplitude
MI. 365	(T314)	Heartogram: higher diastolic amplitude
MI. 566	(T314)	Heartogram: higher sitting pulse rate
MI. 567	(T314)	Heartogram: higher diastolic surge
MI. 568	(T314)	Heartogram: higher diastolic blood pressure (standing)
MI. 569	(T314)	Heartogram: higher pulse rate (standing)
MI. 571	(T314)	Heartogram: higher systolic pressure change over short time interval
MI. 572	(T314)	Heartogram: higher total number of R-waves in EkG
MI. 573	(T314)	Heartogram: higher total number of S-waves in EkG
MI. 575	(T257)	Bodily Dimensions: more fat on cheeks
MI. 587	(Cattell Humor Test)	Factor 6: more resignation vs. impudent defiance of decency
MI. 588	(Cattell Humor Test)	Factor 7: more cold realism vs. theatricalism
MI. 589	(Cattell Humor Test)	Factor 8: more ponderous humor vs. neat, light-hearted wit
MI. 608	(T15)	Memory for Emotional Words: higher ratio of emotional to correct words recalled in immediate memory
MI. 626	(T257)	Bodily Dimensions: higher ponderal index
MI. 654	(T313)	Physical Fitness: greater strength of back
MI. 655	(T313)	Physical Fitness: greater strength of leg
MI. 656	(T313)	Physical Fitness: greater number of 'chins'
MI. 658	(T313)	Physical Fitness: greater number of 'vertical jumps '
MI. 659	(T266)	Word Completion: greater perseveration in letters used over a short time interval divided by total number of items attempted

MI.	T no.	Variables (MI.'s) In Numerical Order
MI. 675	(T275)	(obsolete; equals MI. 120b)
MI. 676	(T249)	Alertness in Word Games: higher accuracy
MI. 677	(T249)	Alertness in Word Games: larger total number of responses
MI. 678	(T249)	Alertness in Word Games: higher ratio of accuracy to accomplishment
MI. 679	(T246)	Neologisms: larger number of newly devised words
MI. 683	(T55)	Decisiveness: higher color synaesthesia
MI. 688	(T55)	Decisiveness: more aesthetic items done relative to reasoning items done
MI. 693	(T131)	Closure in Spelling: higher number of incorrectly spelled words remembered correctly
MI. 694	(T131)	Closure in Spelling: higher proportion of incorrect words correctly remembered
MI. 697	(T164)	Auditory Hallucinations: more nonsense stimuli correctly identified
MI. 700	(T164)	Auditory Hallucinations: greater proportion of stimuli identified correctly
MI. 701	(T164)	Auditory Hallucinations: more real word stimuli guessed
MI. 702	(T164)	Auditory Hallucinations: greater proportion of real word stimuli guessed
MI. 708	(T84)	Classification Breadth: higher proportion of word items completed (relative to total number attempted)
MI. 709	(T248)	Design Changes: greater tendency to perceive changes earlier
MI. 710	(T248)	Design Change: faster speed
MI. 720	(T65)	Memory for Free Associations: higher proportion of association words intruded in recall of original words
MI. 721	(T64)	(obsolete; equals MI. 473)
MI. 722	(T64)	(obsolete; equals MI. 472)
MI. 723	(T64)	Friends and Acquaintances: more persons judged pleasant

MI.	T no.	Variables (MI.'s) In Numerical Order
MI. 724	(T64)	Friends and Acquaintances: more persons judged unpleasant
MI. 725	(T64)	Friends and Acquaintances: higher ratio of pleasant to unpleasant characteristics
MI. 726	(T64)	Friends and Acquaintances: higher number of pleasant characteristics left blank
MI. 727	(T64)	Friends and Acquaintances: higher number of unpleasant characteristics left blank
MI. 728	(T64)	Friends and Acquaintances: greater proportion of friends relative to acquaintances criticized
MI. 729	(T64)	Friends and Acquaintances: more surnames relative to first names of acquaintances given
MI. 730	(T64)	Friends and Acquaintances: higher number of "no one" responses
MI. 734	(T283)	Difficult Task: higher number of decisions attempted on "Which is larger?"
MI. 735	(T283)	Difficult Task: higher number of items answered on "Which is Larger?"
MI. 739	(T62)	Hesitancy: higher ratio of number of items checked to number of items scanned
MI. 743	(Cattell Music Test)	Factor 1: higher adjustment vs. frustrated emotionality
MI. 744	(Cattell Music Test)	Factor 3: higher hypomanic self-centeredness vs. self-distrust and doubt
MI. 745	(Cattell Music Test)	Factor 4: higher tough sociability vs. tender-minded individuality
MI. 746	(Cattell Music Test)	Factor 5: higher introspectiveness vs. social contact
MI. 747	(Cattell Music Test)	Factor 7: higher complex eccentricity vs. stability, normality

MI.	T no.	Variables (MI.'s) In Numerical Order
MI. 748	(Cattell Music Test)	Factor 8: higher resilience vs. withdrawn schizothymia
MI. 751	(T3)	Alternating Perspective: higher final relative to initial frequency
MI. 752	(T22)	Skills: more confidence in untried social skills
MI. 753	(T22)	Skills: more confidence in untried non-social skills
MI. 754	(T22)	Skills: more confidence in social relative to non-social skills
MI. 756	(T30)	Arithmetical Reasoning: greater accuracy relative to speed
MI. 757	(T33)	Hidden Pictures: higher ratio of major to minor hidden figures seen
MI. 762	(T20)	Unstructured Drawings: greater proportion of human objects seen
MI. 765	(T38)	Annoyability: more non-social annoyance
MI. 766	(T38)	Annoyability: more social annoyance
MI. 773	(T257)	Bodily Dimensions: greater standing height
MI. 796	(T52)	Sentence Completion: more bland than emotional words attempt
MI. 807	(T63)	Public Notices: more suggestions for removal of ambiguity
MI. 809	(T67)	Criticalness of Tests: more satisfaction with own test performance
MI. 810	(T67)	Criticalness of Tests: more criticalness of tests and examiner
MI. 819	(T70)	Poker Game: greater reduction in risk taking with higher stakes
MI. 828	(T73)	Moral Behavior: greater fluency on social acts
MI. 829	(T73)	Moral Behavior: greater fluency on anti-social acts
MI. 832	(T104)	Picture Exploration: longer inspection of pictures
MI. 835	(T104)	Picture Exploration: more ideas expressed about pictures containing people relative to pictures without people

MI.	T no.	Variables (MI.'s) In Numerical Order
MI. 838	(T75)	Risk Taking in Routes: higher number of risks taken in mazes
MI. 840	(T77)	Proof Reading: higher quality of work on dull relative to exciting passages
MI. 843	(T80)	Maturation Norms: greater accuracy
MI. 844	(T80)	Maturation Norms: more emphasis on early responsibility than on freedom
MI. 845	(T80)	Maturation Norms: greater belief in more rapid maturation in childhood than in adolescence
MI. 849	(T83)	Self-Concept: greater amplitude of real self description
MI. 850	(T83)	Self-Concept: greater distance of ideal from real self concept
MI. 852	(T87)	Conformity: more social conformity in speech and manners
MI. 858	(T91)	Serial Choice: higher intelligence score
MI. 863	(T92)	Brunswick's Faces: more use of favorable traits
MI. 868	(T95)	Hallstead-Goodfellow Speech Sounds: greater accuracy
MI. 902	(T105)	Drawing Changes: more retracing of edges of drawings
MI. 904	(T105)	Drawing Changes (Requested): more change in associations to drawings for which request has been made for change
MI. 927a	(Cattell Motivation Test)	Higher Sex Erg (Greater desire to satisfy sexual needs)
MI. 927b	(Cattell Motivation Test)	Higher Sex Erg (Greater desire for romantic love)
MI. 928a	(Cattell Motivation Test)	Self-assertive Erg (Greater desire to be smartly dressed)

MI.	T no.	Variables (MI.'s) In Numerical Order
MI. 928b	(Cattell Motivation Test)	Self-assertive Erg (Greater desire to take part in political arguments)
MI. 929a	(Cattell Motivation Test)	Fear Erg (Accident-disease)
MI. 929b	(Cattell Motivation Test)	Fear Erg (Greater desire for protection against atomic terror)
MI. 933a	(Cattell Motivation Test)	Higher Self-Sentiment (Greater desire for good control over mental processes)
MI. 933b	(Cattell Motivation Test)	High Self-Sentiment (Greater reluctance to damage self-respect)
MI. 934	(Cattell Motivation Test)	Higher Super-Ego Strength
MI. 938	(Cattell Motivation Test)	Higher Curiosity Erg
MI. 939	(Cattell Motivation Test)	Higher Gregariousness Erg
MI. 945c	(T338)	Memory for Pictures: better consonant recall
MI. 950	(T344)	Criticalness of Drawing: more criticalness
MI. 967	(T32)	Decision Making: faster speed on particulars
MI. 876	(T345)	Self Acceptance: greater number of perception of self as different from other people

MI.	T no.	Variables (MI.'s) In Numerical Order
MI. 977	(T346)	Clay Modeling: more fragmentation of clay
MI. 981	(T346)	Clay Modeling: more naming of objects
MI. 982	(T346)	Clay Modeling: longer time required
MI. 983	(T346)	Clay Modeling: longer objects made
MI. 984	(T347)	Pasting: greater accuracy
MI. 990	(T56)	Handwriting Identification: more specimens considered alike
MI. 995	(T348)	Parental Preferences: larger number of preferences shared with mother
MI. 997	(T52)	Sentence Completion: more self reference
MI. 1010	(T57)	Memory: more recall of relevant non-emotional material than irrelevant emotional material
MI. 1011a	(T57)	Memory: better memory for material to which attention is directed
MI. 1012a	(T57)	Memory: better incidental memory
MI. 1030	(T60)	Private Information: more recent imigration of family
MI. 1032	(T60)	Private Information: higher socio-economic status of father's occupation
MI. 1033	(T60)	Private Information: higher education of parents
MI. 1035	(T60)	Private Information: higher father orientation relative to mother orientation
MI. 1038	(T63)	Public Notices: higher awareness of ambiguity in public notices
MI. 1040	(T71)	Horrifying Pictures: greater accuracy in recall of details
MI. 1043	(T65)	Friends and Acquaintances: more friends and acquaintances recalled
MI. 1050	(T64)	Memory for Free Associations: more word associations made relative to number remembered
MI. 1071	(T68)	Shove Nickel: more extreme caution (average)
MI. 1101	(T68)	Shove Nickel: large increase in risk taking (average)
MI. 1113	(T67)	Criticalness of Tests: more fluency in criticizing tests relative to one's own performance

MI.	T no.	Variables (MI.'s) In Numerical Order
MI. 1115	(T67)	Criticalness of Tests: more criticism of tester's administration relative to own performance
MI. 1125	(T70)	Poker Game: greater variability in risk taking
MI. 1129	(T71)	Horrifying Pictures: more qualifying phrases used to describe pictures
MI. 1133	(T73)	Moral Behavior: greater fluency on social relative to anti-social sets
MI. 1142	(T77)	Proof Reading: more corrections made
MI. 1144	(T77)	Proof Reading: higher quality of work
MI. 1147	(T79)	Likes: faster speed checking things liked
MI. 1148	(T82)	Memory for Drawings: more perceptual levelling
MI. 1149	(T82)	Memory for Drawings: better distant recall of levelling than sharpened figures
MI. 1150	(T82)	Memory for Drawings: greater increase in levelling with more distant recall of labelled figures
MI. 1154	(T85)	Cautiousness in Statements: greater caution
MI. 1155	(T85)	Cautiousness in Statements: greater variability in caution
MI. 1156	(T88)	Aesthetic Judgment: greater complexity
MI. 1157	(T88)	Aesthetic Judgment: more sinuosity in free drawings
MI. 1158	(T88)	Aesthetic Judgment: more imbalance in simple objects
MI. 1165	(T94)	Compliance: more heedlessness of test instructions
MI. 1167	(T94)	Compliance: greater fluency in producing arguments
MI. 1172	(T100)	Time Interval Memory: more over-estimation (guessing)
MI. 1174	(T100)	Time Interval Memory: greater variability (measuring)
MI. 1176	(T71)	Horrifying Pictures: larger proportion of connective words used to describe blurred pictures after seeing horrifying pictures
MI. 1177	(T71)	Horrifying Pictures: more nouns and noun modifiers used to describe blurred pictures
MI. 1183	(T105)	Drawing Changes (Requested): more details included in drawings of people

MI.	T no.	Variables (MI.'s) In Numerical Order
MI. 1247	(T165)	Preferences: more disapproval in evaluation
MI. 1328	(T159)	Story Identification: more identification with hero
MI. 1339	(T282)	Home Atmosphere: greater number of pleasant pictures chosen as resembling own home
MI. 1344	(T202)	Parental Factors: more approaches to parents of one's own sex
MI. 1352	(T157)	Company Preferences: more self confidence
MI. 1353	(T146)	Dermographia: higher latency and persistence
MI. 1354	(T183)	Finger Temperature: higher temperature
MI. 1355	(T175)	Ambiguous Drawings: more suggestibility to authority
MI. 1363	(T145)	Balloon Blowing: greater capacity
MI. 1364	(T161)	Strategy in Test Performance: longer span of attention
MI. 1365	(T163)	Compliance: more liking for unpleasant duties
MI. 1368	(T165)	Preferences: liking for animate relative to inanimate objects
MI. 1370	(T163)	Compliance: more compliance
MI. 1372	(T202)	Parental Factors: more approaches to parental authority
MI. 1373	(T169)	Honesty in Marking Own Test: more honesty
MI. 1389	(T162)	Story Completion: greater preference for happy endings
MI. 1390	(T170)	Observation: more awareness of being observed
MI. 1391	(T173)	Self-Concept: more validity
MI. 1392	(T173)	Self-Concept: more morality
MI. 1410	(T341)	Frustration During Story: less tolerance
MI. 1411a	(T343)	Neighbor Preferences: greater number of institutional persons chosen
MI. 1411b	(T343)	Neighbor Preference: greater number of adults chosen
MI. 1411c	(T343)	Neighbor Preference: greater number of children chosen
MI. 1411d	(T343)	Neighbor Preference: greater number of exotic persons chosen
MI. 1412	(T226)	Picture Preference: greater preference for movement

MI.	T no.	Variables (MI.'s) In Numerical Order
MI. 1413	(T36)	Artistic Preferences: greater preference for natural scenes relative to man-made structures
MI. 1415	(T4)	Letter Cancellation: higher ratio of errors to number correct
MI. 1417	(T368)	Pleasant vs. Unpleasant Comments on Self and Others: more excess of pleasant over unpleasant comments on others
MI. 1419	(T192)	Shape Shading: more lines used
MI. 1420	(T146)	Dermographia: longer persistence
MI. 1422	(T368)	Paired Words: Exuberance of Choice: more exuberance
MI. 1423	(T159)	Story Identification: more identification with main character
MI. 1424	(T159)	Story Identification: more knowledge of stories
MI. 1425	(T160)	Credulity in Events: more credulity
MI. 1427	(T166)	Beliefs: more confidence in factual than emotional items
MI. 1430	(T370)	Respect for People: more persons listed as respected by S than persons listed as respecting S (more outgoing respect)
MI. 1433	(T239)	Social Problems: more willingness to make decisions without full evidence
MI. 1435	(T171)	Picture Interpretation and Recall: better recall of aggressively interpreted pictures
MI. 1436	(T172)	Mechanical vs. Human Intervention Judgment: more frequent interpretation in terms of human influences relative to physical influences
MI. 1437	(T174)	Shape Formation: more items correct
MI. 1438	(T174)	Shape Formation: later stage of shape decision
MI. 1446	(T371)	Lability vs. Constancy: more inflect on points in paths through maze and open field
MI. 1449	(T373)	Restlessness: more oral activity during forced quiet period
MI. 1451	(T342)	Parental Dependence: Pictures: more awareness of grown-up behavior

MI.	T no.	Variables (MI.'s) In Numerical Order
MI. 1453	(T342)	Parental Dependence: Pictures: more awareness of adult emotional control
MI. 1456	(T348)	Parental Preferences: smaller number of preferences shared with father
MI. 1457	(T348)	Parental Preferences: less similarity of own and like-sexed parent's preferences
MI. 1458	(T348)	Parental Preferences: less similarity of own and unlike-sexed parent's preferences
MI. 1459	(T348)	Parental Preferences: larger number of things liked by self
MI. 1460	(T348)	Parental Preferences: less perceived similarity between parents' preferences
MI. 1461	(T348)	Parental Preferences: more things liked by family as a whole
MI. 1463	(T376)	Memory for Unusual Pictures: more imaginative falsification in memory for pictorial details
MI. 1464	(T377)	Pathemic vs. Practical Choices: more realistic choices of things to take for camping
MI. 1465	(T152)	Acquiescence: higher ratio of tendency to agree to tendency to disagree (on double presentation of items)
MI. 1466	(T152)	Acquiescence: higher total number of "yes" responses on first presentation of items
MI. 1467	(T57)	Memory: better memory for emotional relative to dry material
MI. 1468	(T58)	Moral Expediency: higher percentage of morally unacceptable solutions declined
MI. 1469	(T59)	Perfectionism: more perfectionism
MI. 1470	(T65)	Memory for Free Associations: more stimulus repetitions while associating towards
MI. 1471	(T67)	Criticalness of Tests: higher fluency of criticism of test and examiner
MI. 1472	(T70)	Poker Game: more readiness to make further venture for gain

MI.	T no.	Variables (MI.'s) In Numerical Order
MI. 1480	(T76)	Time Interval Estimates: more over-estimation of idle periods
MI. 1481	(T103)	Risk Taking in Mental Tasks: higher readiness to make fresh venture for gain
MI. 1482	(T91)	Serial Choice: higher total number checked
MI. 1483	(T92)	Brunswick Faces: more agreement with Brunswick's norms following group decision
MI. 1484	(T98)	Pitch Discrimination: more decrement in pitch discrimination with musical background
MI. 1485	(T102)	Drawings: higher ratio of clothing to physical detail in human drawings
MI. 1486	(T65)	Memory for Free Associations: higher number of free associations given
MI. 1488	(T60)	Private Information: higher socio-economic status index
MI. 1491	(T90)	Sound Identification: higher number of errors involving description of non-human sounds as human
MI. 1492	(T60)	Private Information: higher regard for religious values in self and family
MI. 1493	(T67)	Criticism of Test and Examiner: more excuses for defective performance
MI. 1494	(T71)	Horrifying Pictures: greater accuracy in identifying blurred pictures
MI. 1495	(T71)	Horrifying Pictures: fewer words used in remembering horrifying rather than pleasant pictures
MI. 1496	(T71)	Horrifying Pictures: fewer details attributed to horrifying than to pleasant pictures
MI. 1497	(T71)	Horrifying Pictures: more details attributed to photographs in memory test
MI. 1498	(T55)	Decisiveness: faster emotional-aesthetic relative to synasthetic decision time
MI. 1499	(T55)	Decisiveness: faster cognitive logical decision time
MI. 1500	(T83)	Self-Concept: higher firmness of real self-concept

MI.	T no.	Variables (MI.'s) In Numerical Order
MI. 1501	(T83)	Self-Concept: higher ratio of direct change to story relative to "sleeper" effect
MI. 1502	(T83)	Self-Concept: higher percentage of change in traits of self-concept
MI. 1503	(T129)	Mazes: more increase in time required in blind stylus maze by shock
MI. 1504	(T129)	Mazes: longer time taken on blind stylus maze
MI. 1505	(T129)	Mazes: higher number of noise shocks received in blind stylus maze
MI. 1506	(T65)	Memory for Free Associations: more words remembered
MI. 1507	(T106)	Hand Tremor: Greater improvement in hand steadiness with time
MI. 1508	(T106)	Hand Tremor: greater improvement in relative hand steadiness with time
MI. 1509	(T67)	Criticalness of Tests: more criticism of tester's performance
MI. 1510	(T64)	Friends and Acquaintances: higher number of pleasant character items unanswered
MI. 1511	(T64)	Friends and Acquaintances: higher number of unpleasant character items unanswered
MI. 1512	(T64)	Friends and Acquaintances: higher number of pleasant and unpleasant character items unanswered(more modesty of own judgment concerning people)
MI. 1514	(T92)	Brunswick Faces: more increase in certainty in describing Brunswick faces following group decision
MI. 1515	(T92)	Brunswick Faces: less certainty in describing Brunswick faces
MI. 1516	(T92)	Brunswick Faces: more increase in rate of marking schematic faces after group decision
MI. 1517	(T84)	Classification Breadth: faster total speed
MI. 1519	(T71)	Horrifying Pictures: greater proportion of words used to describe blurred pictures

MI.	T no.	Variables (MI.'s) In Numerical Order
MI. 1520	(T52)	Sentence Completion: higher proportion bizarre sentences written from bland stems
MI. 1521	(T59)	Perfectionism: more tendency to perseverate in error
MI. 1522	(T59)	Perfectionism: lower consistency in applying perfectionist standards
MI. 1523	(T92)	Brunswick Faces: higher agreement with Brunswick's norms for schematic faces
MI. 1524	(T92)	Brunswick Faces: more increase in use of favorable traits after group decision on Brunswick's faces
MI. 1525	(T75)	Risk Taking in Routes: greater proportion of easy paths chosen
MI. 1526	(T66)	Novel Situations: greater variability in number of solutions presented
MI. 1527	(T90)	Sound Identification: less accurate identification of novel sounds
MI. 1528	(T71)	Horrifying Pictures: greater increase in number of qualifying phrases used in description of horrifying pictures
MI. 1529	(T82)	Memory for Drawings: greater size of drawings
MI. 1531	(T98)	Pitch Discrimination: more improvement in pitch discrimination with practice
MI. 1532	(T72)	Moral Judgment: greater rapidity of decision on improper relative to proper courses of action
MI. 1533	(T72)	Moral Judgment: more runs in two improper rather than in two proper courses of action
MI. 1534	(T70)	Poker Game: more risk taking
MI. 1535	(T105)	Drawing Changes (Requested): larger size of drawings of trees and people
MI. 1536	(T105)	Drawing Changes (Requested): higher total ratio of clothing to physical details in human drawings
MI. 1537	(T248)	Designs: more discernment of gradual changes
MI. 1538	(T100)	Time Interval Memory: more tendency to over-estimate when measuring five-second intervals

MI.	T no.	Variables (MI.'s) In Numerical Order
MI. 1539	(T100)	Time Interval Memory: more variation in measurement of five-second interval
MI. 1716a	(Cattell Motivation Test)	Higher appeal erg (More desire to serve God)
MI. 1716b	(Cattell Motivation Test)	Higher appeal erg (More desire to heed parent's advice)
MI. 1719	(T382)	Cattell Culture Fair I: Higher Score on Sub-Scale 1 (Substitution)
MI. 1720	(T382)	Cattell Culture Fair I: Higher Score on Sub-Scale 2 (Classification)
MI. 1721	(T382)	Cattell Culture Fair I: Higher Score on Sub-Scale 3 (Mazes)
MI. 1722	(T382)	Cattell Culture Fair I: Higher Score on Sub-Scale 4 (Selecting Named Objects)
MI. 1723	(T382)	Cattell Culture Fair I: Higher Score on Sub-Scale 5 (Following Directions)
MI. 1724	(T382)	Cattell Culture Fair I: Higher Score on Sub-Scale 6 (Wrong Pictures)
MI. 1725	(T382)	Cattell Culture Fair I: Higher Score on Sub-Scale 7 (Riddles)
MI. 1726	(T382)	Cattell Culture Fair I: Higher Score on Sub-Scale 8 (Similarities)
MI. 1727	(T383)	Color Pattern preferences: Greater preference for dark shades rather than middle shades
MI. 1728	(T383)	Color Pattern Preferences: Greater preference for symmetric rather than non-symmetric designs
MI. 1729	(T383)	Color Pattern Preferences: greater preference for warm colors rather than cool colors
MI. 1730	(T384)	Judging Facial Expressions: more faces judged as cheerful rather than depressive

MI.	T no.	Variables (MI.'s) In Numerical Order
MI. 1731	(T384)	Judging Facial Expressions: more faces judged as energentic rather than tired
MI. 1732	(T384)	Judging Facial Expressions: more faces judged as relaxed rather than tense
MI. 1733	(T385)	Remembering Ideas From Film Pictures: higher total imaginative fluency
MI. 1734	(T385)	Remembering Ideas From Film Pictures: higher proportionof sad, fearful, ideas
MI. 1735	(T386)	Letter Exercises: higher total number correct in letter exercise
MI. 1736	(T386)	Letter Exercises: more initial difficulty in re-adaptation
MI. 1737	(T387)	Ratings of Personal Attributes: greater extremity of rating in self-description
MI. 1738	(T387)	Ratings of Personal Attributes: greater vagueness of self description
MI. 1739	(T387)	Ratings of Personal Attributes: greater difference between real and ideal self
MI. 1740	(T387)	Ratings of Personal Attributes: greater vagueness of ideal self
MI. 1741	(T122)	Reaction Time: slower reaction time of (erroneous) reactions to irrelevant signals.
MI. 1743	(T314)	Heartogram: higher systolic blood pressure (standing)

Author Index

Subject Index